# FROM TRAGEDY TO TRIUMPH

*SURREY'S BITTERSWEET CHAMPIONSHIP SUCCESS 2002*

## TREVOR JONES

**SPORTING DECLARATIONS BOOKS**

WWW.SPORTINGDECLARATIONS.CO.UK

PO BOX 882, SUTTON, SURREY, SM2 5AW

First published in 2003 by Sporting Declarations Books

© Trevor Jones 2003

All rights reserved. No part of this publication may be reproduced, stored in a retrieval system, or transmitted, in any form or by any means, electronic, mechanical, photocopying, recording or otherwise, without the prior written permission of the publishers

ISBN 0 9535307 5 2

*Cover Photographs*

*TOP:*
*The players, officials and crowd observe the two-minute silence for Ben Hollioake and the Rashid brothers before the season's opening match against Sussex at The AMP Oval.*
*Photo by Richard Spiller*

*MIDDLE:*
*Happier times at the end of the season as Adam Hollioake admires the County Championship trophy while Jimmy Ormond and Alex Tudor share a joke.*
*Photo by Phil Booker*

*BOTTOM:*
*The Surrey squad line up to celebrate their success during the presentation ceremony at The AMP Oval*
*Photo by Richard Spiller*

Typesetting and design by Trevor Jones

Printed and bound in Great Britain by MPG Books, Bodmin, Cornwall
Colour work by APG, Unit 9, Mitcham Industrial Estate, Mitcham, Surrey CR2 4AP

# Dedications

This book is dedicated to the memory of John Cartland and Ben Hollioake

## John Cartland (1932-2002)

A passionate and dedicated Surrey fan, and a good friend from 1977 when we first met while I was writing for the Supporters' Club's magazine. Encouraged me to continue writing about the team we both loved, and also to play, as well as watch, the great game. I'm glad I heeded his wise advice.

## Ben Hollioake (1977-2002)

A talented cricketer and much-loved young man, who was taken from us far too soon.

# The Ben Hollioake Fund

In March 2002, the world lost a very special person. The Hollioake family lost a cherished son and brother, and the cricketing world lost a great talent. Adam Hollioake and his family have therefore decided to set up The Ben Hollioake Fund in his memory.

CHASE Children's Hospice Service supports life-limited children and their families. In November 2001, CHASE opened Christopher's Hospice - a purpose-built hospice designed to provide a home from home, where families can stay or take a much needed break by allowing the CHASE care team to follow their child's routine. The CHASE community care team members, who are all specialists trained in working with life-limited children, also take their expertise into the home, where they work alongside the children, their parents, siblings and other close family members.

The Ben Hollioake Fund, in association with CHASE Children's Hospice Service, will set out to raise money to build, fund and support a new London-based centre, in the name of Ben Hollioake, for life-limited children and their families. Adam and his family aim to raise over five million pounds in a five-year period to make this a reality.

Adam Hollioake has dedicated the next five years of his life to The Ben Hollioake Fund; he wants something good to come out of something tragic. We can help him to do this.

Thank you for your support.

Loraine Bicknell
Ben Hollioake Fund Co-ordinator
CHASE Children's Hospice Service
Loseley Park
Guildford
GU3 1HS

Tel: 01483 454213
Fax: 01483 454214
E-mail: **loraine@chasecare.org.uk**
Web: **www.benhollioake.maxmoment.co.uk**
CHASE web: **www.chasecareorg.uk**
Registered charity no 1042495

# Contents

**Introduction**   *6*

**1 Tragedy**   *7*

**2 A Difficult Pre-Season**   *13*

**3 The Show Must Go On**   *16*
   County Championship Match One: Sussex at The AMP Oval

**4 Headingley History**   *32*
   County Championship Match Two: Yorkshire at Headingley

**5 Three Out Of Three**   *47*
   Benson & Hedges Cup Qualifying Matches
   County Championship Match Three: Lancashire at The AMP Oval
   National Cricket League Match One: Lancashire Lightning at The AMP Oval
   National Cricket League Match Two: Gloucestershire Gladiators at Bristol

**6 Stalled By Somerset**   *71*
   County Championship Match Four: Somerset at The AMP Oval

**7 Domination And Frustration**   *83*
   C&G Trophy Round Three: Scotland at Edinburgh
   County Championship Match Five: Lancashire at Old Trafford
   National Cricket League Match Three: Northamptonshire Steelbacks at Northampton

**8 Adam Returns**   *103*
   County Championship Match Six: Kent at The AMP Oval
   National Cricket League Match Four: Hampshire Hawks at The Rose Bowl
   C&G Trophy Round Four: Glamorgan at The AMP Oval
   National Cricket League Match Five: Sussex Sharks at The AMP Oval
   National Cricket League Match Six: Lancashire Lightning at Old Trafford

**9 A Record-Breaking Stalemate**   *127*
   County Championship Match Seven: Somerset at Taunton
   National Cricket League Match Seven: Middlesex Crusaders at Southgate

**10 The Bears Bite Back**   *150*
   County Championship Match Eight: Warwickshire at The AMP Oval

**11 A Pause For Thought**   *171*
   C&G Trophy Quarter-Final: Sussex at Hove

**12  The Canterbury Tale    *175***
  County Championship Match Nine: Kent at Canterbury

**13  Reclaiming The Crown?    *202***
  County Championship Match Ten: Yorkshire at Guildford
  National Cricket League Match Eight: Essex Eagles at Guildford
  C&G Trophy Semi-Final: Yorkshire at Headingley
  National Cricket League Match Nine: Northamptonshire Steelbacks at Whitgift School
  National Cricket League Match Ten: Middlesex Crusaders at Whitgift School

**14  A Surprising Setback    *228***
  National Cricket League Match Eleven: Sussex Sharks at Hove
  County Championship Match Eleven: Sussex at Hove

**15  Foxes On The Run    *247***
  County Championship Match Twelve: Leicestershire at Leicester
  National Cricket League Match Twelve: Derbyshire Scorpions at The AMP Oval

**16  The Spinners' Turn    *265***
  National Cricket League Match Thirteen: Hampshire Hawks at The AMP Oval
  County Championship Match Thirteen: Hampshire at The AMP Oval

**17  Almost There    *281***
  County Championship Match Fourteen: Warwickshire at Edgbaston
  National Cricket League Match Fourteen: Derbyshire Scorpions at Derby

**18  Triumph    *300***
  National Cricket League Match Fifteen: Essex Eagles at Chelmsford

**19  Ward's West End Premier Performance    *307***
  County Championship Match Fifteen: Hampshire at The Rose Bowl

**20  Young Guns Fire Champions    *321***
  County Championship Match Sixteen: Leicestershire at The AMP Oval
  National Cricket League Match Sixteen: Gloucestershire Gladiators at The AMP Oval

**21  Summing Up    *339***

**22  Leading Questions, Leading Answers    *342***

**Appendix - Statistical Compendium    *345***

**Acknowledgements/Sponsor-Subscribers    *350***

# Introduction

Following a blank year, brought about by Yorkshire's 2001 Championship success, it's nice to be able to celebrate another Surrey triumph with another celebratory book.

Given the bittersweet nature of the county's 2002 season, I knew I was going to be facing quite a challenge with this new volume, but I was keen to take it on. I had a delayed start, owing to the production of *'268'*, my commemorative booklet about Ali Brown's amazing world record-breaking innings in the C&G Trophy, but gradually, as autumn turned to winter, and winter turned to early spring, all the piles of notes and photos metamorphosed into *'From Tragedy To Triumph'*. The title of this book may sound rather clichéd but it describes Surrey's 2002 campaign pretty well, even though it in no way suggests that the triumph made up for the tragedy. Winning the Championship title merely helped to provide some balance to a sad year, though, like the tragedy, the triumph was one that will never be forgotten. From my point of view, this has been far and away the hardest book I have written so far, for obvious reasons, and I hope that you, the reader, will feel that I have handled the low points in a sensitive manner, as well as bringing out the pleasure and excitement of the many high points.

The performance of the team to win a third Championship crown in four years was certainly outstanding, and supporters were treated to some phenomenal matches and feats throughout the course of the summer. This current Surrey squad is a very special collection of cricketers that gives hope for further successes in both the near and distant future, and I will be doing my best to continue recording their triumphs for posterity. To that end, I owe a debt of gratitude to all my sponsor-subscribers, without whose backing I would be unable to publish these books. It is most humbling to receive support from so many people who, in effect, commission me to write about the team's triumphs, in the absence of any interest - for obvious and understandable financial reasons - from large publishing companies. Many thanks to you all.

Trevor Jones

March 2003

# 1  Tragedy

In common with a great many other people, I won't forget the moment. It was about 10.45pm on March 22nd and I was tuned in to Sky Sports, watching play on the third day of the second Test between England and New Zealand in Wellington, when the phone rang in my flat. I don't tend to get a lot of calls that late in the evening so I was curious as to who it might be as I tore myself away from the action on the television. It was my friend and fellow Surrey fan, Elliott Hurst. 'Hello, Trev,' he said, 'Have you heard the news about Ben Hollioake?' I had to confess that I hadn't but, since it had warranted a late-night phone call, I had an immediate sense of foreboding. 'He's been killed in a car crash in Perth,' said Elliott. An inevitable few seconds of stunned silence followed then, when words did come, they were the stupid, knee-jerk reaction words that people almost always come out with when they can't, or don't want to, believe what they have just heard - 'You're joking?' As if anyone would be less than serious about something so terrible and so tragic. But then I'm sure I wasn't the only person to utter those ridiculous and disbelieving two words that night.

An equally stunned Elliott went on to tell me that he'd been listening to Radio Five when, during one of his regular reports from Wellington, Pat Murphy had informed listeners of the news that had just reached the press box. Then, just as I was wondering why I'd heard nothing about this on Sky, building up hopes that it might be some wicked and cruel hoax that the BBC station had fallen for, Bob Willis began speaking in sombre tones on my television in the background. I broke off from my telephone conversation to listen as Willis repeated the same story that had just been imparted to me by my friend. There seemed little or no room for doubt now... this was for real. It was a most awful case of déjà vu for anyone connected with Surrey County Cricket Club, too, since this shattering announcement brought back memories of the traumas of New Years Day 1997 when the news had broken of wicketkeeper Graham Kersey's death following a road accident in Brisbane a week earlier. It seemed as if lightning had struck the Club for a second time in the most awful way imaginable.

To be perfectly honest, I can't remember another word of my conversation with Elliott - I guess that was the effect of this shocking revelation - but I do recall sitting down in front of the television and checking all the teletext services I could find, in the still very faint hope that I might be imagining this whole scenario. They all told the same story, though.

After returning to Sky and hearing tributes from all and sundry to a young man forever lost to us, I found myself simply staring at the screen in disbelief. There was a Test match being played out on the screen in front of me but it just wasn't registering at all, which was hardly surprising in the circumstances. It seemed impossible to comprehend that I would never again see Ben hitting a glorious straight drive or cling on to an astounding catch in the gully, and my thoughts went back to his marvellous climax to the 2001 season when his maiden first-class century against Yorkshire had followed a pair of classy half-centuries in the previous match at Taunton. So good were those innings that I was convinced he was going to be one of the county's top run-scorers in 2002. Now, the season was going to be starting, in just four weeks time, without him. It seemed impossible.

Breaking away from my own selfish thoughts, I tried to imagine what Adam and the rest of the Hollioake family must be going through - my grief was obviously nothing compared to theirs. It didn't bear thinking about and I knew I could never begin to feel what they would be feeling at this moment in time.

On my television the game of cricket carried on and the England players looked in a state of shock. I can't recall if this was after the lunch break when, it was later revealed, they had been informed of the tragedy in Perth, or before. Clearly, however, word must have spread quickly from spectators with radios in the ground. Nor can I remember precisely when I went to bed. For someone who likes to report things as accurately as possible, it seems rather lame to admit this… but I hope you will appreciate that my excuse for this rather blurred recall is entirely valid. The Test match had obviously lost its appeal in the circumstances and it must have been desperately difficult for the England lads to find the strength and the will to carry on playing. I do recall that I couldn't face continuing to watch the match and went to bed.

When I awoke in the morning the news was full of 'the Ben Hollioake tragedy'… it was the final devastating confirmation that this hadn't just been some awful nightmare - well, not in the true sense of the word anyway. Details had emerged of how the accident had occurred when Hollioake's black Porsche 944 coupe had skidded off the road just after midnight local time while taking a tight left-hand bend on Perth's Mill Point Road freeway ramp, careering into a brick wall with fatal results for the Surrey all-rounder and inflicting life-threatening injuries to his long-term girlfriend, 23-year-old Janaya Scholten. The whole of the Hollioake family had been returning home after a family meal at a city centre restaurant before the brothers flew to London for the forthcoming English season and, quite horrifically, Ben's sister, Eboni, had been travelling in the car behind and witnessed the accident at first hand. The rest of the family, who had taken different turnings off the Kwinana Freeway, were then summoned to the scene by calls from Eboni. It was impossible to imagine a worse scenario for the Hollioakes.

As I had expected, the tragedy was front-page news for almost all of the dailies and I read through them in something of a daze. It was also the first or second item on all the television news bulletins that I watched, and also a major headline when I logged on to my internet service provider, AOL, to check my email. There was no escaping the extremely grim news and I suppose it said everything about Ben's media profile as one of cricket's most talented and marketable young players. Although it seemed almost ghoulish for me to seek out all the coverage of the tragedy that I could find, I felt that I simply had to be as well informed as possible, given that I had been documenting Surrey's recent history for future generations. It certainly wasn't a pleasant task because it was hard to dwell on the subject for very long without feeling extremely emotional. Even though I can't say that I actually knew Ben personally, I still felt as if I'd lost someone close to me.

It was certainly no surprise to see and hear how badly his friends and team-mates had been hit by the tragedy. Ian Salisbury, his eyes hidden from view behind dark glasses, was shown on one television news bulletin speaking about 'the loss of a great mate' on the outfield at The AMP Oval and it was obvious how utterly devastated he was. Paul Sheldon, Surrey's Chief Executive, shouldered a lot of the burden of dealing with the media, and echoed a comment I'd made to Elliott the previous night by stating that the Club must, and indeed would, dedicate the forthcoming season, and any trophies that were won, to Ben's memory. In this, the darkest of hours, that seemed to be the only possible way of extracting any sort of triumph from a truly awful tragedy. Even so, this variation on the old saying that something good can come out of the very worst of situations was hard to believe at this particular moment in time.

Within hours of the news of the accident breaking, messages had begun appearing on Oval World Online, the Surrey Supporters' Club's website on the internet. The site's message board facility enabled fans from all around the country, and even the globe, to come together to share their grief at this terrible time. The County Club had a similar area on its official website and announced that books of condolence would be available at The AMP Oval for people to sign.

Meanwhile, back in Perth, investigators were still unable to discover what had caused the accident, with alcohol and excessive speed having been ruled out, and no significant evidence having been found to support suggestions that road conditions were especially hazardous after a recent rain shower. The exit road off Perth's chief freeway where the accident happened was a well-known accident black spot, however, and John Townsend, a Perth cricket writer, was quoted in the Australian press as saying 'That is a very tight corner. When you take the exit road, you're almost running parallel to the freeway. It would take a split second to lose control, and that touch of rain could have been critical. By the time Ben realised what was happening it would have been too late.' This was just one man's theory, however, and it already seemed that this had been nothing more or less than a terribly tragic and unavoidable freak accident.

Over in New Zealand, the Test match carried on somehow, with a minute's silence being observed before the start of the fourth day's play. It was a pity that the game couldn't have been abandoned for the sake of all those players in the match who knew and loved Ben, but it would appear that this course of action was never seriously mentioned or discussed.

There was one area of serious debate, however, since the England management and players had to decide which members of the party were going to attend the funeral service for their late friend and team-mate in Perth on 27th March, just two days after the final day of the second Test and three days before the start of the third. There were obviously going to be problems in terms of logistics, especially with time being so tight, and this seemingly ruled out any possibility of the whole squad attending. Looking at the situation logically from afar, it appeared that the best option would be to allow the Surrey players to attend, since they were the people closest to Ben, while the rest of the England touring party stayed behind in New Zealand, but, for reasons that never became public, it was eventually decided that Nasser Hussain, as captain, should go on his own. I feel sure that there would have been a lot of disappointment and disagreement over this matter, but everything was, reasonably enough, kept quiet, since it was clearly not a time for anyone to be airing any disputes in public. As a result, the England squad organised their own private service to take place at the same time as the funeral mass in Perth.

Back in England, plans were made for many of the Club's officials and players to fly out to Australia for the service. The AMP Oval had been an understandably sad place ever since the accident took place, with flowers having been brought to the ground by a number of supporters upon hearing the tragic news, and members of staff left deeply shocked and upset by events. Life had to go on, of course, but it certainly can't have been easy for those who knew Ben well.

With the Wellington Test having ended in a draw - an appropriate result, since it had become almost an irrelevance to most people - Nasser Hussain made his way to Perth for the funeral. The service was held in the tiny Our Lady Of Mount Carmel Catholic church in Hilton, Perth and was attended by around three-hundred mourners, including family, friends and many cricketers, including a dozen from Surrey and a number from Western Australia, including Justin Langer and Brendon Julian, the former Surrey all-rounder.

Those gathered in the church witnessed a tearful and highly emotional tribute from Adam Hollioake, who read out a letter of tribute to his younger brother in which he stated that Ben was "too cool to grow old". "We can all imagine one another with grey hair or a bald head, with a walking stick or in a wheelchair, hunched over and bitter," he told the congregation, "but I can't imagine Ben as anything other than youthful, strong, athletic, handsome, energetic, vibrant, powerful and noble. He was a beautiful work of art, a classic sculpture." With dark glasses hiding his tears, the Surrey captain went on to say how he felt their cricket had "got in the way of a most amazing brotherhood" but that he was glad he had told his brother he loved him many times in the past year. "I know we loved each other a million times more than we could ever let on to anyone," he stated. And, in a moving message to his brother, Adam added "It's OK, Benni, I'll get with you again one day, I promise you. I'm always here for you, Ben, I always have been ... I love you, Benni Boy." He also asked that his brother's death shouldn't be seen as a tragedy, stating, "I think he was 100 per cent happy. Once you experience 100 per cent happy, let's face it, 99 per cent seems no good." Finally, Adam told everyone that he and his seven-months pregnant wife, Sherryn, planned to name their baby daughter Bennaya, after Ben and his girlfriend, Janaya. At this time, Janaya was still in a 'critical but stable' condition in the Royal Perth Hospital and prayers were offered for her recovery during the service.

Once the formalities of a very emotional occasion were complete, Nasser Hussain presented John and Daria Hollioake with their son's England team blazer, which Ben had left in New

Zealand after his participation in the one-day international series had been cut short by a knee injury.

While the funeral mass had been taking place in Perth, the England squad had been holding their own private ceremony in the picturesque Michael Joseph Savage Memorial Gardens at Bastion Point, overlooking Auckland's Waitemata harbour. The service was written by the former Worcestershire secretary, the Reverend Mike Vockins, and was conducted by operations manager, Phil Neale, who read a tribute and prayer to Hollioake. Mark Butcher then performed an emotional rendition of Bob Marley's 'Redemption Song' to end the service. England media manager, Andy Walpole, later said that "it was a sombre occasion but very dignified. The weather was wonderful and the setting was lovely. It was very fitting."

Back in England, the funeral in Perth had been featured briefly on all the news bulletins. It was amazing to see how many Surrey players and officials had flown across to the other side of the world to pay their last respects to Ben, and it certainly sent a powerful message to all those people outside of the Club who claimed the Surrey dressing room was 'full of big egos'. Those who were closer to the team knew that wasn't the case and these television pictures hopefully brought the truth home to a few more people. Maybe, in a hugely ironic way, this tragedy would change the way people viewed Surrey? Perhaps the stupid 'most hated team' tag could now become a thing of the past? And you had to believe that if the team reached one of the Lord's finals then surely only the hardest-hearted neutral would not want Surrey to win the trophy for Ben. How crazy it would be if the terrible tragedy of 23rd March turned out to be the thing that changed attitudes, after all previous efforts to improve the Club's image had seemingly failed.

From a personal point of view, I was still finding it hard to come to grips with the fact that I'd seen Ben play for the last time, even though there was a degree of comfort to be taken from the way he had ended the 2001 season - his final three innings were great knocks to remember him by. Having attended just about every Surrey match for the past four seasons, I had at least been fortunate enough to witness the greater part of his career and, though Ben had suffered more than his fair share of low points and criticism, I always told people that he was going to come through in the end, even though there weren't too many supporters who could understand why I held that belief.

Adam's comment at the funeral that his brother was 'too cool to grow old' had also struck a familiar chord with me and it wasn't for a couple of days that I realised why. Suddenly it clicked that, for floodlit National League games, Ben chose to walk out to bat to the strains of The Who's 'My Generation' which, of course, features the line 'Hope I die before I get old'. I don't know whether Adam had remembered that when he was writing the letter that he read out at the funeral, but I am certain that whenever I hear that song on the radio in the future I will think only of Ben.

As I've stated before, I couldn't claim to know Ben personally, since the only time I really spoke to him at any length was for 'The Dream Fulfilled', my book about Surrey's 1999 County Championship triumph. Even then, it was a close-run thing. Although I had managed to speak to a number of players to tape their interviews during the final games of the campaign, I'd just missed out on catching Ben on two or three occasions during the penultimate game at Lord's. I was therefore left hoping that he would call me before he returned to Perth at the end of the season. As the days passed by, my hopes of him calling faded, until it reached the stage where I knew he had returned to Australia. Then, suddenly, quite out of the blue, at 9.30am one morning the phone rang - 'Hi, it's Ben Hollioake here, calling from Perth to answer your questions for the book'. To say I was surprised, albeit pleasantly, would be an understatement. He then went on to tell me that he'd have to keep the interview reasonably short as he was calling from his parents' home and he didn't want to ring up too big a phone bill! That said, he answered every question I asked of him during a twenty-minute call.

Back on the Oval World internet message board, tributes had continued to arrive, with John Hollioake managing to find the strength and courage to post a message thanking everyone for their comments and expressing his feelings in a most incredibly open manner. I doubt that anyone could have read his moving tribute to his son without their eyes filling with tears. In the final two paragraphs he told everyone:-

*"Yes, we are all suffering terribly but rest assured our other beautiful young man will come to grips with it all in time and will come back an even stronger person, if that is possible. I can't wait to see some of the performances Adam will give this season as a mark of respect to Ben. I'm sure Benni boy will be looking down with that permanently beautiful smile, standing guard over us all and ensuring that good things happen.*
*"I love Surrey CCC and thank them so much for giving Ben the opportunity to perform in such a talented team of genuine gentlemen. Ben also loved Surrey deeply and he was such a loyal person that I would give anything to be anywhere near as good as he is. Rest in peace my wonderful Benni boy, you are in our hearts forever."*

Additionally, Martin Bicknell, an occasional visitor to the board, kindly posted a message to let everyone know "what is going through the players' minds at the moment." Describing the previous week as "probably the hardest week in our lives" he went on say:-

*"What makes this all the harder to bear is that this has affected so many people we know. The Hollioake family are obviously very close to us all, as is Ben's girlfriend, Janaya. The courage they have shown during this has been nothing short of unbelievable, and to hear Adam's speech at the Church will live with me for all time, the love for his brother extraordinary.*
*"We have all held Adam in very high regard for many years with his leadership but as a person he has risen to a new level in our eyes, his courage and his love for his family will lead him out of this and give him a new purpose in life.*
*"In many ways that is what we all feel, it would be easy to say that we will dedicate this season to Ben, and win a trophy in his honour, but I believe it goes deeper than this. We all feel bonded by what has happened and have vowed to become better people, to have no regrets in life and live for today. I believe this will all help us at this time.*
*"I am glad we are moving away from 'Ben, the cricketer'. This formed a very small piece of his life. It is as a friend we loved him, cricket was just a thing he did, it's irrelevant to talk about what he might have become and being a sad loss to the game.*
*"On Thursday we go back to The Oval on what will be a very hard day for us all. However, we will pull together and support each other. We will become better people and move on."*

The books of condolence at The AMP Oval were already drawing people to the ground, too, and the Club website's special section dedicated to Ben gave those who couldn't get to London the opportunity to leave messages of sympathy, or simply post their personal memories of the young man who had been taken from us. For some people the written form of communication was the best way for them to express how they were feeling, as Jason Ratcliffe so rightly pointed out in a lengthy tribute that appeared on the front page of the Surrey CCC site. Ratcliffe's eulogy was a very personal piece that told us a lot about his lost colleague and, though it is too long to reprint here and would lose impact if I picked out a few sentences, it is, in my opinion, worth seeking out on www.surreycricket.com if you wish to understand why Ben was so loved.

One thing that reflected credit on everyone, I think, was that no-one had once mentioned the effect Ben's loss would have on the strength and make-up of the Surrey team, even though he was a key member of the one-day side, in particular. Everyone realised and appreciated that the tragedy of a lost life far outweighed the prospects of a cricket team at this moment in time, though the situation would, inevitably, have to be addressed at some point as life began to move on.

An example of how some of Surrey's most dedicated fans had been affected by the events of March 23rd was brought home to me on the following Saturday when I attended the monthly meeting of the away supporters group at The Beehive pub, near The AMP Oval. It was the first time that most of us had spoken, let alone met, since the tragedy and the meeting was, not surprisingly, rather muted. There was plenty of discussion, as usual, but I think most of those in attendance felt unsure about whether or not certain topics were off-limits. For example, normally at the March meeting there would be a lengthy debate about Surrey's best line-up for the first game of the forthcoming season and the prospects of success but, understandably, that kind of chat was a little suppressed.

So many questions needed to be answered, though. Would Adam return? If so, when? Would it be best for him to take the whole season off? The Club had certainly told him that he had to put his family first and could take as much time away from the game as he required, so the decision was in his hands. And how would the players cope, especially those who were going through this trauma for a second time? Given that Saqlain Mushtaq would be absent with Pakistan for the early part of the season, would the Club take the opportunity to sign an overseas batsman or all-rounder to fill the huge void left by the absence of Ben and Adam? How would recent events affect the team's performance? Was it right to even be asking these questions? If not, how long would it be before it was acceptable to be talking cricket again?

I think, when all was said and done, it was felt that life had to go on, despite our sadness, and that maybe everything would feel a little better once the players got out onto the pitch and started playing. From a personal point of view, I was still looking forward to the new season in the belief that we simply had to try and move on. It was not as if we were going to forget Ben, in any case, because there were bound to be many incidents throughout the summer that would bring back fond memories of him. Others confessed that they would rather the season wasn't starting so soon and that the thrill of a new campaign had lost its edge. No-one was right and no-one was wrong, of course. It didn't make me a callous person just because I felt that moving on would be the best way to get over our loss and, equally, I didn't look upon those with the opposite viewpoint as being overly sensitive or excessively emotional. It was simply a case of accepting that we are all different - maybe more markedly so when it comes to death and grieving than anything else - and therefore had a different perspective of things. But one fact was inescapable - the new season was only a couple of weeks away, whether anyone liked it or not.

## 2  A Difficult Pre-Season

With everyone still reeling from the loss of Ben Hollioake, another tragedy struck the county cricket fraternity with the deaths of Sussex's Umer Rashid, 26, and his younger brother, Birhan, 18, on Easter Monday, 1st April, during the county's pre-season tour of Grenada, where they were taking part in a three-way tournament with Yorkshire and Northamptonshire. According to media reports, the younger brother had got into difficulties while swimming in the pool beneath the waterfall at Concord Falls, a notoriously dangerous beauty spot on the island, and Umer had tried to rescue him, only to be dragged under by the current himself. It was another awful loss of life in unexpected circumstances, and utterly horrific for the Rashid family to lose not just one, but two, much-loved young men in one terrible accident.

Quite incredibly, despite the fact that she and her family were going through a terrible time of their own, Daria Hollioake immediately asked Adam to find contact details for the Rashid family and took time out to write to them, offering the condolences and support of the Hollioake family. It was a quite amazing gesture of kindness and selflessness by a bereaved mother, and the Rashids wrote back in a similar vein, also including their phone number. Consequently, Daria rang them, and a close bond, which still thrives to this day, was formed between the two families. When the Hollioakes came over to England later in the summer, the families met up and were entertained, both by Surrey and by Sussex, at games they attended together. As John Hollioake told me, "Both counties have been so very supportive of both families. We feel very close to the Rashids."

By a cruel twist of fate, the two counties so devastated by these pre-season tragedies, were due to meet just nine days later in a three-day friendly match at Hove, and then again in the opening round of County Championship fixtures starting on the 19th April. While the Championship match obviously had to go ahead, the friendly had to be in considerable doubt - cancellation seemed likely, since both counties had far more important things on their minds.

The considerable air of gloom that was now hanging over the pre-season period - normally a time of optimism, whether genuine or faked, for all teams, players and supporters - certainly wasn't lifted by Graeme Wright, the retiring editor of *Wisden Cricketers' Almanack*, who poured scorn on county cricket in the 2002 edition of the 'cricketers bible'. The suggestion that the county game had run its course and that city teams should be introduced seemed to me to be the final act of a man hoping to be remembered as a visionary editor of the almanack in twenty to thirty years time. Naturally enough, his words created plenty of negative publicity for domestic cricket, and it was immensely disappointing that a man in his position should have considered his personal future glory to be more important than the good of the game.

Several journalists also indulged in their familiar springtime cricket-bashing routine with a number of woeful diatribes. Simon Barnes of *The Times* came up with a particularly shameful piece, in opposition to Christopher Martin-Jenkins' article in support of county cricket, in the edition of the paper published on Friday 5th April. Fortunately, Barnes was stupid enough to state '*I don't go to county cricket for work or pleasure: I don't often bother to look at the scores*', instantly rendering his arguments completely worthless and irrelevant - how could he possibly make statements such as '*County cricket should either be providing a conveyor belt of excellent young players to the England cause or providing great entertainment, preferably both. It does neither*' and '*County cricket has a going-through-the-motions atmosphere*' when, by his own admission, he didn't follow it and hadn't been to a game in years? I wrote to *The Times*, pointing this out, with no great hope of a letter attacking their award-winning journalist getting published, but, much to my surprise, it did... along with several others telling Barnes to stick to the sports that he might know something about. The damage these people do to the game with their lazy and spiteful comments is inestimable, and I find it particularly galling that, in some cases, these 'hacks' are attacking the very sport that earns them a living. While there are, of

13

course, some excellent writers working on some of the broadsheets, there are others who either have no interest in cricket in the first place, or appear to have grown bitter and tired of the 'job' of writing about the game. Perhaps it's time for some of them to move aside in favour of people with a genuine passion for the sport, as only then will cricket, and the county game in particular, get the coverage it deserves and needs.

With the start of the new season drawing ever closer, the funeral of the Rashid brothers took place on Saturday 6th April at Southall Mosque, and it was decided that the pre-season friendly at Hove from the 10th to 12th April should go ahead, with the Rashid family telling Peter Moores, the Sussex coach, that the team should continue to play positive cricket in memory of Umer and Burhan.

Surrey had another friendly to fulfil before the Sussex match, however, as they travelled to Chelmsford to take on Essex on Tuesday 9th April. Although it must have been hard to focus on playing cricket, the visitors scored an easy 101-run win in the 50-overs-a-side contest, with Ian Ward making 107 out of Surrey's 253-8, and Alex Tudor taking 3-30 as Essex finished a very distant second on 152-9.

Buoyed by this success - which was quite remarkable considering that the players had been through emotional turmoil and a return trip to the other side of the world, when they would have expected to be preparing for the upcoming season - the team moved on to Hove for a contest that was clearly going to prove very difficult for all the participants. Starting with the players - plus the Rashid family and the Sussex administration staff - lining up on the outfield to pay silent respects to their lost team-mates, the game turned out to be totally dominated by the batsmen on a low, slow pitch with a short boundary on the pavilion side of the ground. After Richard Montgomerie had made 137 as Sussex declared at 427-4, and Nadeem Shahid had replied with 128 in Surrey's 330-6, the game took a slightly strange twist on the final day. Although Sussex scored 206-4, with Tim Ambrose becoming the third centurion of the match, the captains then agreed that the final innings of the game should be played under Benson & Hedges Cup rules, with Surrey chasing an agreed target of 270 from their fifty overs. Thanks to a blistering innings of 112 from just 65 balls by Alistair Brown and an unbeaten ninety-four from Alec Stewart, the visitors coasted home by six wickets, and everyone had got some cricket under their belts as part of the first stage of the healing process.

During the first day of the match, the ECB had announced the names of the eleven players who would be centrally contracted to England for 2002. Although quite a few Surrey players had been in contention at one point during the winter, the final list of names included only two, Mark Butcher and Graham Thorpe. After two largely unproductive Test series, during which lady luck was rarely on his side, it didn't come as a shock to see that Mark Ramprakash hadn't been awarded a contract, while the inclusion of Jamie Foster as the wicketkeeper, ahead of Alec Stewart, had also been expected, despite the Essex youngster's far from convincing glovework in India and New Zealand. From an entirely parochial point of view, these decisions would merely improved Surrey's chances of success in all the domestic competitions, as would the fact that both Alex Tudor and the county's new arrival, Jimmy Ormond, had also been overlooked when the central contracts were being handed out. Ormond's non-selection had been almost inevitable, since he had incurred the wrath of Duncan Fletcher, the England coach, by turning up for the New Zealand leg of the winter tour schedule in a less than perfect physical condition. The former Leicestershire fast bowler had received a great deal of negative press coverage, too, and a number of very unflattering photos had appeared in most of the newspapers, including, predictably enough, those that rarely take an interest in cricket.

England's loss would be Surrey's gain, in any case, and, with the squad seemingly unlikely to be too badly affected by international call-ups, the bookmakers installed Surrey as red-hot favourites to regain the County Championship crown that had been surrendered to Yorkshire in 2001, when no fewer than nine of the county's players - Alec Stewart, Graham Thorpe, Ian

Ward, Saqlain Mushtaq, Mark Butcher, Mark Ramprakash, Alex Tudor, Alistair Brown and Ben Hollioake - had been absent on international duty at some point. With a more settled side, there was every reason to expect that the bookies would be right in their assessment of the county's prospects, so long as there was no serious hangover from the recent tragedy. The signing of Ormond during the close season had certainly strengthened the seam bowling department - Surrey's weakest link, principally in terms of depth, in recent seasons - and it was to be hoped that Saqlain Mushtaq wouldn't be required by Pakistan on too many occasions. Since the off-spinner was certainly going to miss the early weeks of the campaign, while playing for his country against New Zealand, the Club had acted swiftly to engage Azhar Mahmood, the Pakistani all-rounder, for the first five weeks of the season. Being a close friend of Saqlain, and having had treatment at The Oval for injuries in the past, Azhar was well known to most of the Surrey squad, and his talents with both bat and ball would clearly be valuable to the Club, especially in the Benson And Hedges Cup qualifying matches. It was just as well that the regulations had been changed for 2002 to allow counties to replace any overseas player who was injured or called up by his country.

The final event of the pre-season period was the delayed Press Day, which took place on 17th April, just two days before the start of the opening Championship match. There must have been around fifty to sixty media men and photographers at The Oval that day, which was around twice the number that would usually attend. Although I tried hard to convince myself that the increased attendance indicated a greater interest in cricket, I knew that we were really witnessing a kind of 'vulture effect' after the harrowing events of recent weeks. Those people who were there to grab a 'human interest' story, rather than write about cricket, would have been most interested to hear Mark Butcher - who was to captain the Surrey side until the international season began - saying that it had been very therapeutic for the players to get back together as a team and that the squad had developed an even closer bond as a result of the Ben Hollioake tragedy - 'we were a very close-knit group anyway,' he said, 'but now we all appreciate one another's company even more'. On the cricket front, Keith Medlycott suggested that Yorkshire would probably be his team's main rivals in the County Championship - which was now to be sponsored by Frizzell, the insurance and financial services company - and indicated that the squad was starting the season injury-free, with the exception of Jason Ratcliffe, who was still struggling with his long-standing knee injury. It was also revealed that AMP Limited (formerly known as Australian Mutual Provident Society) had secured the sponsorship of both Surrey County Cricket Club and The Oval in a £500,000 deal. The ground should now be referred to as The AMP Oval, with those in attendance urged to use the new name at all times.

# 3  The Show Must Go On

It had been an incredible, almost macabre, act of the fixtures computer to decree that the opening round of Frizzell County Championship matches should include Surrey versus Sussex, but to my eyes this seemed, on the surface, to be no bad thing, since each of these two teams would know exactly what the other had been through in recent weeks. This was still likely to prove a very testing time, though, and we were about to find out how the players would react to their traumatic pre-season period.

| FRIZZELL COUNTY CHAMPIONSHIP - MATCH ONE |
|---|

### SURREY versus SUSSEX
### at The AMP Oval
### First Day - Friday 19th April
### Surrey 461-4

***The Teams And The Toss*** - *Surrey's opening line-up of the season is the strongest available to them, with Pakistani Test star, Azhar Mahmood, making his debut for the club as the stand-in overseas player for Saqlain Mushtaq. Jimmy Ormond also plays his first competitive match for the Club following his close season move from Leicestershire, while Graham Thorpe is rested, at England's request, until the beginning of May.  Like their hosts, Sussex are free of injuries and select what they consider to be their strongest eleven.  Having scored a century against Surrey in the pre-season friendly, Tim Ambrose looks unlucky to have lost out to Michael Yardy in the middle-order.  Paul Hutchison, Sussex's close-season signing from Yorkshire, makes his debut for the visitors.  With the pitch looking a beauty, and better weather forecast for later in the day after an overcast start, Mark Butcher, captaining Surrey in Adam Hollioake's absence, elects to bat upon winning the toss.*

Before the start of play, a two-minute silence is held in memory of Ben Hollioake and Umer Rashid.  The players and umpires file out onto the outfield and line up in front of the Bedser Stand, with Surrey officials and staff also in attendance, standing shoulder to shoulder along the boundary edge.  All around the ground, heads bowed, a period for quiet reflection begins.

As would be expected from the crowd at a cricket match, it is impeccably observed, the silence only broken by the hum of traffic circling The AMP Oval and a helicopter passing over the ground, its noise seemingly magnified by the hush of the solemn gathering beneath its flight path.  Today's attendance is very impressive, too, for an April weekday.  It would appear that the combination of fine weather, the anticipation of the start of a new season, relatively local opposition and a chance to pay their respects to two young cricketers so tragically lost to us in recent weeks has proved to be a powerful attraction to many people.

It can't be easy for the players as the match commences but, as they say in entertainment circles, 'the show must go on' and it duly does.  Perhaps unsurprisingly, the game gets away to a quite subdued start as Mark Butcher and Ian Ward content themselves with the occasional single off the visitors' opening pairing of James Kirtley and Jason Lewry, until Ward registers Surrey's first boundary of the season with an airy clip backward of square leg off Kirtley.  Butcher then follows his partner's lead, picking off two fours, with a steer to third man and an off-drive, in the next over from Lewry to take the hosts' score to 26-0 after seven overs.

It has all been fairly plain sailing up until this point but in the space of thirteen deliveries the picture changes dramatically as both openers fall to Kirtley, Ward being trapped on the crease by a ball of full length with the score still on twenty-six and Butcher, caught in two minds as to whether to play or leave, deflecting the ball down on to his stumps seven runs later.

At 33-2, Mark Ramprakash and Alec Stewart are facing a minor crisis. In typical style, the former plays himself in steadily, while the latter is away to a scintillating start, showing how a batsman can use the pace of the ball to his advantage by steering Kirtley backward of point for three, and then gliding and glancing Lewry for two boundaries behind square on the leg-side.

At this point, left-arm-over replaces left-arm-over as Hutchison takes over from a rather disappointing Lewry and, with both batsmen piercing the cover field with eye-catching strokes, the Surrey fifty arrives in the fifteenth over. The home side's innings now looks to be back on course, though Ramprakash offers just a sniff of a chance, with his score on fourteen and the total at sixty-five, when a diving Murray Goodwin, in a fine gully position, just gets his hand to a thick edge off Hutchison. Unperturbed, the batsman takes two fours from the former Yorkshire bowler's next over, the first with a glorious lofted on-drive just short of the rope, and the second with a deflection to third man that raises the fifty partnership for the third wicket. Meanwhile, at the other end, Stewart has seen off Kirtley and then his replacement, Lewry, whose two-over spell from the Vauxhall end yields three more sumptuous boundaries to the seemingly in-form Peter Pan of cricket, who has recently celebrated his thirty-ninth birthday.

With the Surrey score closing in on three figures, Chris Adams finally turns to Robin Martin-Jenkins for the twenty-second over of the innings, though this move makes little difference for Sussex as the ball rarely manages to beat the bat and the Ramprakash-Stewart partnership continues to prosper. The hundred comes up in Martin-Jenkins' third over, courtesy of a fine on-driven four by Stewart, before a brace of square-cut boundaries off the same bowler take the batsman through to an excellent 63-ball half-century four overs later. Ramprakash is starting to look in top form, too, as he crashes the persevering Hutchison through extra cover for a pair of fours of his own in the tiring bowler's tenth over.

After a spell of bowling too short and too wide, Martin-Jenkins finally settles into a better line and length as lunch approaches, but by this stage Surrey are very much in charge, as Ramprakash demonstrates when he caresses Hutchison's replacement, Mark Davis, through the covers for four to raise the hundred partnership in the penultimate over before the break.

*Lunch:- Surrey 134-2 (Ramprakash 48\*, Stewart 55\*) from 36 overs*

Chris Adams pairs Kirtley and Lewry again after lunch, though the left-armer is surprisingly down to just one slip at this relatively early stage of the innings. The Sussex skipper's judgement is vindicated, however, as his bowlers stray too frequently to leg, allowing easy runs to be picked up through a series of glances to fine leg. Ramprakash also takes the opportunity to complete a 92-ball fifty by clipping one such loose delivery to the rope at midwicket. It has been a fine knock by the former Middlesex man, though he has largely played second fiddle to an outstandingly fluent Stewart.

Since Lewry has rarely located the right line and length during his first three overs of the session, Martin-Jenkins is soon back in the attack, though he has a chastening start as Stewart drives him through extra cover for four to herald the arrival of the Surrey 150. Kirtley has, by now, begun to exercise a little more control, returning four successive maiden overs, but, having been injured and unable to bowl during pre-season, Martin-Jenkins continues to look as rusty as he had during the morning. Kirtley's good work is, therefore, largely nullified as Stewart helps himself to four more boundaries in the course of two loose overs that cost the tall all-rounder twenty-two runs. Despite this, it is Kirtley, after a spell of 6-4-5-0, who is withdrawn from the firing line first, with Hutchison succeeding him at the Vauxhall end. It appears to be a very strange decision by Adams but it turns out that he has made another inspired move as the former Tyke removes Ramprakash with his second delivery. It must be said, however, that there is a lot of luck involved in the dismissal as the batsman glances a leg-side delivery through to the wicketkeeper and, much to his credit, 'walks' after an innings of fifty-six from 120 balls. The manner of Ramprakash's departure doesn't bother the delighted Hutchison, of course, since this is his first wicket for Sussex and it has pegged Surrey back slightly at 176-3.

The new batsman, Alistair Brown, is quickly off the mark in confident style, clipping his third ball backward of square leg for a one-bounce four, and from this moment until tea the pace of the Surrey innings never slackens. While Stewart loses a little momentum after the loss of his partner, Brown tears into Hutchison, clipping another four behind square on the on-side in the left-armer's twelfth over and then plundering four further boundaries in his thirteenth. It's exhilarating stuff as two meaty drives through extra cover bring up Surrey's first bonus point of the 2002 campaign and then the bowler's fortunate dismissal of Ramprakash is evened up by a stroke of bad luck next ball. Brown's score is on twenty when he edges an off-side forcing stroke and emerges with another boundary to his credit as Matt Prior, the Sussex wicketkeeper, fails to hold on to a very catchable chance at a good height as he dives away to his right. Just to rub salt into Hutchison's wounds, Brown then dismisses the final ball of the over to the rope at cover with a glorious drive 'on the up'.

With Surrey's middle-order stalwart looking in such great form, it is no surprise to see him adding another three fours to his collection in the next three overs as the runs continue to flow, forcing Adams to try his hand in the attack in place of Martin-Jenkins. Stewart, meanwhile, is looking set for a century, but having gone to ninety-nine - and taken the fourth wicket stand to fifty at better than a run a ball - with a hooked boundary off Hutchison, he edges a drive at the next delivery to fall one run short of the landmark. He receives a fine ovation as he leaves the field, nevertheless, having played quite immaculately in giving his team, now on 229-4, a fine start to the match. His performance won't have done his prospects of an England recall any harm either.

Any thoughts Sussex might have had about being back in contention at this point are soon dispelled by Nadeem Shahid, who sets off as confidently as his current partner had, opening his account with two spanking off-driven boundaries. Consequently, the tempo of the innings actually increases, with Brown raising the Surrey 250 and reaching his personal half-century shortly afterwards, courtesy of a quite amazing straight-driven six off the former Yorkshire left-arm seamer. His towering hit goes so high that the scorers almost have time to check that Brown's fifty has indeed come from just 45 balls before the ball finally comes to ground beyond the rope at the Vauxhall end.

Having been in the thick of the action for seven overs, this is the final straw for Hutchison, who is replaced by Kirtley after a very mixed spell that has seen him pick up two wickets at a cost of fifty-four runs. Then, having conceded two leg-side boundaries to Shahid, Adams gives way to Lewry at the pavilion end and, for just a few overs, the fury of the Surrey assault subsides slightly. Despite this brief lull, Brown and Shahid go on to complete a half-century partnership inside ten overs, before a sudden rush of six fours - five of them to Shahid with a mixture of perfectly-executed cuts, pulls and drives - sees the home side passing three-hundred in the penultimate over before the tea interval.

Surrey have scored 175 runs in the session from thirty-six overs, providing the excellent crowd with superb entertainment and giving those who decry county cricket food for thought.

*Tea:- Surrey 309-4 (Brown 70\*, Shahid 44\*) from 72 overs*

Despite the hammering handed out to the Sussex bowlers during the middle session, Chris Adams had failed to utilise his off-spinner to provide some variety, so it isn't entirely surprising that this glaring oversight is rectified immediately after the break as Mark Davis appears at the pavilion end. Although Brown soon cuts him for four, the spinner fares a lot better than James Kirtley at the other end as Shahid forces the paceman's opening delivery of the session to the cover boundary and then clips his second behind square leg for another four to take him through to an exhilarating half-century from just 46 balls with eleven fours. It has been a fantastic knock but it nearly ends soon afterwards when Davis lures the batsman down the track and induces a loose drive straight to Michael Yardy at short midwicket. The ball is well struck but at a good height for the fielder and his failure to hang on to a very acceptable chance, with Shahid on fifty-six and the total at 326-4, sees a few Sussex heads dropping.

With Kirtley's two overs after tea having cost fifteen runs, despite the presence of sweepers on both square boundaries, Adams recalls Martin-Jenkins at the Vauxhall end. This move certainly meets with Ali Brown's approval as he pulls the new bowler's opening delivery to the fence at midwicket to complete a high-octane century partnership from just 119 balls and then sends a drive skimming through mid-off later in the over. Despite his skipper's apparent faith in him, Martin-Jenkins looks really out of sorts as he concedes three further boundaries in his next two overs, as a consequence of bowling too short to Shahid and too full to Brown, who is rapidly closing in on a century. The 350 rattles up during this period and the initially economical Davis starts to suffer the same harsh treatment as the seamers. The Surrey batsmen are now using their feet well when facing the off-spinner and, after Shahid sashays down the track to drive through extra cover for four and to long-on for a single, Brown completes an excellent ton in the grand style, advancing down the wicket and launching the ball over long-off for six. Surrey's middle-order maestro immediately looks towards the heavens, embraces his batting partner in mid-pitch and then squats down on his haunches in an obviously emotional state. For a man not known for over-exuberant celebrations his reactions speak volumes. As a tribute to a lost colleague, the innings couldn't have been any better, coming from 110 balls and containing two sixes and eighteen fours. Perhaps surprisingly, it is Brown's first-ever first-class century against Sussex, leaving him with just Lancashire to tick off in order to complete a full set of tons against the other counties.

With Surrey's opening century of the campaign completed and celebrated, the run-rate drops a little as Davis exerts tighter control again and Yardy, replacing the ineffective Martin-Jenkins, manages the impressive feat of getting a number of balls past the outside edge with his left-arm seamers.

For a while, as the fifth-wicket partnership passes the 150 mark, runs come principally in singles, until Shahid eventually breaks the spell by cutting Yardy backward of point for four to move into the nineties. As the former Essex batsman progresses steadily towards three figures, the main threat to him appears to be the new ball, which Kirtley takes in the ninety-second over after taking over from Yardy at the Vauxhall end. It transpires that the new 'cherry' is no obstacle for Shahid, however, as he immediately slashes the ball over backward point for the boundary that takes him to his first County Championship century since June 1998. As well as completing the batsman's hundred, from 109 balls with seventeen fours, this boundary also raises Surrey's four-hundred and prompts further emotional celebrations both out in the middle and around the ground.

Contrastingly, the Sussex side is looking understandably downcast, with only the new ball to offer any hope of salvation. Jason Lewry seems to be out of favour after his erratic bowling earlier in the day so the almost equally inconsistent Hutchison partners Kirtley as the visitors try to salvage something from the day with some late wickets. The batsmen are seeing the ball very well by now, though, and Brown lifts each bowler back down the ground for a boundary, the first of these taking the partnership on to 181, thereby equalling the existing Surrey fifth-wicket record stand against Sussex by Alec Stewart and Ian Greig at The Oval in 1989. A single to third man later in the over erases the old mark from the record book and, before long, the new record is extending past two-hundred as Brown clips Kirtley to the rope at backward square leg.

The Sussex bowlers appear absolutely powerless to contain two well-set in-form batsmen on a very good pitch, and, when Adams recalls the previously economical Yardy to the attack in place of Kirtley, the left-arm seamer finally feels the lash, too, as Shahid drives his first ball to the extra cover boundary and then lofts him over mid-off for a second four. The visitors' day-to-forget is then capped with three overs to go when, following an unnecessary overthrow which raises the 450 earlier in the over, the alert Surrey pair pick up two runs following a half-stopped drive from Shahid which runs only a few yards away from the dispirited fielder.

As the players leave the field both batsmen are rightly lauded for their outstanding innings. It is fitting that they are both unbeaten on 132 as there has been nothing to choose between two fine knocks, though Sussex have paid a very heavy price for missing reasonably straightforward catches when Brown was on twenty and Shahid on fifty-six. In many ways it has been an incredible day - the weather, the batting and the attendance have all been magnificent and each of these things has helped to brighten a day that had started on such a very sad note.

*Close:- Surrey 461-4 (Brown 132\*, Shahid 132\*) from 104 overs*

## VIEWS FROM THE DRESSING ROOM

*It was a freak coincidence that the two counties who had suffered a pre-season bereavement were playing one another in the opening friendly and the opening Championship match. Did that make the situation any easier to cope with, or did it actually make it harder?*

**NADEEM SHAHID** - It was good to have people around who understood what you were going through, but I can honestly say I did not feel like playing cricket. It was the most emotional game I've ever been involved in at The Oval.

**ALI BROWN** - We didn't really know what had hit us in March. There was a kind of bonding - it's very easy to take people for granted, and when they are not there you miss them. That made us take stock of all our fellow players and how much we did perhaps care for each other and work for each other. So when these games came around I think everyone was grieving together. The friendly game was very difficult because Umer Rashid's family turned up unexpectedly, so, suddenly, we were feeling for them even more, seeing their grief - in some ways that made the feeling twice as bad.

*Having had the emotional experience of the two-minute silence before play started, was it better for us to be batting first rather than the whole side having to go out to field?*

**NADEEM SHAHID** - Yes, definitely, because you couldn't see the tears under the helmets of the batsmen. To be honest, I think we were all numb on that day.

*Judging by your reaction, I assume you must have been feeling highly emotional when you became the first man to score a first-class hundred to dedicate to Ben?*

**ALI BROWN** - When I was in the church in Australia, I broke down in the service briefly - I'm sure everyone did at some stage - and all I could say to myself was that I really wanted to score a hundred in the first game, purely for Ben. I have my beliefs and as I was sitting there I was thinking that was the thing I wanted to do most. So when that first game came around I had never wanted to score a hundred more, and it was just a bonus that I had never scored a century against Sussex in the Championship before. I had a little bit of luck, but it was the most satisfying hundred I will ever score and it meant an awful lot to me. I was dropped on twenty but after that I felt I hit the ball pretty much as well as I did in the 268 later in the season. I just felt there was someone else with me - that's probably the best way to describe it, just an amazing feeling. I'd never ever been so emotional after scoring a hundred and I'll probably never feel that emotional ever again.

*It must have been very special for you to end a fairly long spell without a Championship century by scoring one to dedicate to the memory of Ben?*

**NADEEM SHAHID** - It was the most special hundred I'll ever score because I knew that the Hollioake family were following every ball on the internet back in Perth. It wasn't just scoring the hundred, it was the way I scored it that made it so special.

## Second Day - Saturday 20th April

## Surrey 575-8 dec; Sussex 308-9

It looks like another good day for batting as play gets under way on an unseasonably bright and sunny April morning. Although Robin Martin-Jenkins has two unconvincing lbw appeals against Ali Brown turned down at the start of an opening maiden over, the bat is soon dominating the ball again with Nadeem Shahid forcing James Kirtley's second delivery to the cover boundary and then sailing past his previous best first-class score of 139 with a lofted square drive that also goes for four. Brown then joins his partner on the attack, picking up six runs from a couple of leg-side deliveries by Martin-Jenkins to extend the record-breaking fifth-wicket partnership beyond 250.

Milestones are being clocked up with great regularity now, the next one being Shahid's personal 150, from 179 balls, which arrives when he follows a cover-driven four with a simple steer backward of point for a single. The innings that must surely rate as the best of his career, and not just in statistical terms either, ends next ball, however, as Kirtley gains a small measure of relief for his side by having the Surrey man taken at the wicket from a outswinger that takes the edge of a defensive bat. Shahid's fine knock has contained no fewer than twenty-three fours and he is, unsurprisingly, accorded a hearty ovation as he returns to the pavilion with the score at 491-5 after a stunning partnership of 262 runs from a mere 335 balls.

Unaffected by the loss of his partner, Brown continues to prosper, reaching his own 150, from the 194th ball he faces, with a forcing stroke to deep cover for a single that also sees the Surrey total clicking up to 500. He then celebrates reaching the landmark by pulling Kirtley to the midwicket boundary and greeting Paul Hutchison, who has just replaced Martin-Jenkins at the pavilion end, with a lofted drive for four runs wide of mid-on.

At the other end, Azhar Mahmood, whose first innings for Surrey had started rather uncertainly, is now getting into his stride, terminating Kirtley's opening spell with a cover drive for three and a square cut for four in an over costing eight runs. The following over is even more expensive for the visitors as both batsmen tuck into Hutchison, whose tendency to overpitch results in Brown picking up four and three runs, respectively, for drives through cover and mid-on, and Azhar notching a boundary of his own with a one-bounce lofted hit down the ground. This flamboyant stroke turns out to be the Pakistani's last contribution to the Surrey total, however, as Jason Lewry strikes with his fifth delivery after replacing Kirtley, an inswinger that traps the batsman lbw on the crease for sixteen with the total at 533. Alex Tudor's stay at the wicket is then both brief and unconvincing, with just a single coming his way from eight deliveries before he pops up a simple catch to Martin-Jenkins at mid-off from the bowling of Hutchison to make it 538-7.

With lunch about an hour away and plenty of runs already on the board, Martin Bicknell now strides out to play a real cameo of an innings at the expense of Lewry, picking off five fours and a six in the space of just fourteen deliveries. Four boundaries - glanced, edged, driven and pulled - come from the first five deliveries of the left-arm swing bowler's eighteenth over and then, after Brown has driven Hutchison for a towering straight six in the intervening over, Bicknell adds to Lewry's misery with a drive high over wide mid-on for six and a one-bounce drive over extra cover for four. The bowler does manage to regain a little pride, however, by extracting Brown's middle stump with the final ball of the over as the batsman attempts a huge slog over midwicket, prompting an immediate Surrey declaration at 575-8. With forty minutes to go until lunch, Brown makes his way from the field to a fine ovation from another good-sized crowd for a superb 222-ball innings of 177 that has included twenty-eight fours and three sixes.

The Sussex openers then emerge ten minutes later with a tricky period to survive until the break. Although they make an edgy start when Richard Montgomerie snicks Martin Bicknell's opening delivery wide of fourth slip to the third man boundary, the same batsman has no problems locating the middle of his bat in the second over, bowled by Alex Tudor, helping himself to four boundaries in an over costing twenty runs. The first ball, a no-ball, is clipped through midwicket, the third disappears through backward square leg, the fourth is pulled wide of mid-on and the sixth is driven through mid-off, before the over ends on a more sedate note as the seventh, compensatory, delivery is pushed to mid-on for two.

Since Mark Butcher has set a very attacking field, this flood of early runs isn't totally unexpected and his bold six-man close-catching cordon soon brings reward and revenge for Tudor. Having added another on-driven boundary to his personal tally, Montgomerie fences at the third ball of the big paceman's second over and sees Azhar pull off a very good catch low down at third slip as the ball dies on him. It's the wicket Surrey had desperately wanted before the interval and it has split up the opening partnership of Montgomerie and Goodwin, which had proved so prolific in 2001 for the reigning Championship Division Two champions. Although no further breakthrough is forthcoming, Tudor, improving ball by ball, causes Chris Adams several anxious moments in his final over before the break.

*Lunch:- Sussex 49-1 (Goodwin 11\*, Adams 7\*) from 7 overs*

Upon the resumption, Sussex's fifty comes up immediately, courtesy of an Alex Tudor no-ball, during a mixed over which sees Adams driving pleasantly through mid-off for four and then, for the third time in his brief innings, almost playing the ball onto his stumps. The Sussex skipper's luck doesn't hold for much longer, though, as the fourth ball of Tudor's next over sees him flashing at a delivery just outside off stump and edging to Alec Stewart. A very scratchy innings has been ended by a loose stroke and the visitors now find themselves pegged back to 61-2. Nor do things get any better for Sussex as Tudor strikes again with the final ball of his third over of the session, when the diminutive Tony Cottey, unable to cope with a good lifting delivery, merely diverts the ball to Azhar at third slip for a routine catch - it's 67-3 and the Surrey speedster has figures of 6-1-38-3.

At this point, with the batting side in real trouble, Mark Butcher attempts to turn up the heat on the fourth-wicket pairing of Murray Goodwin and Michael Yardy by introducing Jimmy Ormond at the pavilion end in place of Martin Bicknell.

The former Leicestershire fast bowler starts well and almost takes a wicket with his sixteenth delivery for his new team when a straightforward chance to the Surrey skipper at second slip is spurned with Goodwin on twenty-six and the score on 75-3. Up until this point, the former Zimbabwe batsman has looked relatively untroubled, whereas his stocky left-handed partner is encountering early difficulties outside the off stump. The Sussex duo manage to battle through, however, seeing off Tudor after nine pacy overs from the Vauxhall end and raising the hundred without too many further alarms.

For a while, progress is slow against Ormond and Azhar Mahmood, Tudor's replacement, then Yardy suddenly breaks loose by pulling the Pakistani all-rounder through midwicket and clipping him backward of square leg for two boundaries in an over. Sussex's pleasure at breaking free from their shackles is short-lived, though, as they lose their fourth wicket in the next over from Ormond. There is no escape for Goodwin this time as he tries to bail out halfway through a pull stroke and merely succeeds in lobbing a simple catch in the direction of midwicket. Nadeem Shahid moves around from mid-on to complete the dismissal, simultaneously handing Ormond a well-deserved first success for Surrey in his tenth over and reducing Sussex to a precarious 111-4.

The sturdily-built paceman is, unsurprisingly, rewarded with an eleventh over but it turns out to be a bridge too far as the new batsman, Robin Martin-Jenkins, feeds off his opponent's apparent fatigue by striking a pair of off-side boundaries. Ormond promptly retires to the outfield, his impressive figures of 11-3-29-1 having been spoiled slightly by that final over and three earlier wides.

Azhar has, meanwhile, been struggling with a no-ball problem, and his eighth over proves to be a microcosm of his highly promising first spell for Surrey. Despite overstepping the crease three times, he suffers the twin agonies of seeing Martin-Jenkins missed by Mark Ramprakash at fourth slip - a fast-travelling head-high chance which the fielder is unable to cling on to - and Yardy edging, in uncontrolled fashion, to third man for four runs. Azhar thus ends his opening burst wicketless as Martin Bicknell and Ian Salisbury are paired up in the attack.

This double change almost brings results for the home side as Salisbury poses a few early problems, with Yardy edging to the third man boundary again and Martin-Jenkins' bat-pad ricochet just eluding the grasping left hand of Ian Ward at silly point. It is Bicknell who comes closest to gaining another breakthrough, however, as Ali Brown at first slip fails to grasp an edged chance high to his left-hand side offered by Martin-Jenkins with the batsman's score on sixteen and the total 153.

The Surrey faithful are left wondering if this latest dropped catch will prove more costly than the previous two as the reprieved batsman cuts Salisbury for three in the next over and then watches from the other end as Yardy drives through extra cover and square cover for two boundaries. This eleven-run over prompts the return of Alex Tudor, however, and, for the third time in the innings, a spurned catching opportunity proves inexpensive as the new bowler terminates Martin-Jenkins' innings with his third ball. Having square-cut the tall Surrey paceman's opening delivery for four, the batsman has no answer two balls later as his off stump is sent flying out of the ground in spectacular style. Although it appears that Martin-Jenkins has been beaten for pace there is also a strong suspicion that the ball has kept a little low and, as he makes his way back to the pavilion with twenty-four runs to his name and his side back in the mire at 170-5, the lofty Sussex all-rounder may be reflecting that his earlier good fortune has been balanced up by the ball that has brought about his dismissal.

With tea now fast approaching, Sussex clearly need to rebuild again as the 21-year-old Yardy is joined out in the middle by Matt Prior, one year his junior. A big task lies ahead for the two youngsters but they cope well in the last five overs before the break, Prior picking up runs on the off-side with confident strokes, and a more assured Yardy easing the ball through extra cover for three in the last over of the session to move within one run of a battling half-century.

*Tea:- Sussex 187-5 (Yardy 49\*, Prior 10\*) from 48 overs*

Although all his bowlers have stuck to their task well on this good batting pitch, it is no great surprise to see Mark Butcher starting the day's final session with the two who have looked most penetrative thus far in the innings, Alex Tudor and Jimmy Ormond.

Prior appears to be in fine touch with the bat, however, and accepts the challenge of facing the two Surrey pacemen by going on to the attack. Having driven Ormond through mid-on for three runs in the opening over, he takes ten runs from the following over by Tudor, including two elegant strokes to the cover boundary, one off the front foot and the other off the back. The latter stroke brings up the Sussex 200 and this is closely followed by Yardy reaching his half-century, predictably enough with three runs to third man, albeit courtesy of a well-controlled deflection on this occasion. The young man's 127-ball innings may not have been particularly attractive or entirely convincing, but there is no doubt that Sussex would have been in a very much deeper hole without his gutsy effort.

The weight of responsibility resting on Yardy's shoulders then increases still further two overs later when Ormond strikes another blow for the home side during an over that starts well for Sussex but ends in triumph for Surrey. Although Prior takes the early honours by forcing a delivery to the cover fence and then steering the ball backward of point for two runs, Ormond hits back in style, inducing a snick over the slips for a streaky boundary and then finding the edge again as the batsman attempts to cut the final delivery. He might having profited from his previous indiscretion but this time the Sussex keeper is out of luck as Ali Brown, at first slip, flies away to his right to pull off an excellent catch and send Prior packing for an eye-catching run-a-ball thirty-five. With the scoreboard now reading 217-6, it hasn't been an innings ideally suited to the situation, however, and the target of 426 to avoid the follow-on is still a daunting 209 runs away. In the circumstances, Yardy and the new batsman, Mark Davis, do well to play out the remainder of the Surrey pair's post-tea spells with only a couple of edges by the latter off Tudor, both of which fall well short of the slips, offering further encouragement to the home side.

Butcher's decision to change the bowling at this point seems a wise one, with his strike pair having already contributed sixteen overs apiece in the innings. The introduction of Azhar at the Vauxhall end and Ian Salisbury at the pavilion end is clearly to the liking of Yardy, however, as he steps up a gear and expands his range of strokes, driving and cutting boundaries off the seamer and sweeping the leg-spinner for another four before producing a more delicate stroke, a late cut for three. Although there is also a thick edge to third man off Azhar in the midst of these more assured strokes, Yardy's sudden surge pushes the seventh-wicket partnership beyond fifty and takes him through to a career-best score when he reaches ninety-one with a bottom-edged cut that again crosses the rope at third man.

Despite their still-precarious position, Sussex are suddenly enjoying a sustained period of dominance as Davis launches an assault on Salisbury that sees the off-spinner taking four boundaries from the leg-spinner in the space of two overs. Having found the rope at point with a square cut for four, the batsman then peppers the leg-side boundary with a lofted drive and two slog-sweeps, the second of which disappears over the fence for a huge six.

While Davis has been making hay, Azhar has come close to making the breakthrough for Surrey at the other end, seeing Stewart, diving away to his left in front of first slip, put down a chance offered by Yardy on ninety-three from the final ball of his thirteenth over. Unfortunately for Sussex, the young left-hander doesn't learn from his mistake, though, flirting in similar fashion with an identical short-of-a-length delivery the next time he is on strike and merely directing the ball straight to a grateful Ian Salisbury at a fine gully. As Yardy departs to generous applause for a fine, battling knock, Azhar celebrates his first wicket for Surrey, with Sussex's fragile-looking tail now exposed and the follow-on looking inevitable.

This appears to be an even greater certainty as the home side's new overseas import takes just six balls, one of which is a no-ball, to notch his second wicket for the Club, Davis hooking a short ball straight to long leg where Jimmy Ormond takes a good low catch - 296-8.

With Jason Lewry now ambling out to the middle and only Paul Hutchison still in the 'hutch', Sussex are in desperate trouble and, though Kirtley manages to hang on grimly against Salisbury, despite a couple of edgy moments, it doesn't take Azhar long to add a further wicket to his tally, finding Lewry's outside edge as the batsman drives limply. Stewart accepts a straightforward catch and the tail-ender departs for a seven-ball duck to make it 298-9.

Having delivered eight overs off the reel, Azhar is now rested, despite his three-wicket burst, in favour of Martin Bicknell. This allows Sussex a rare moment of joy in a bleak closing period of play as Kirtley immediately produces an off-driven boundary to see his side through to three-hundred and another batting point.

The last six overs of the day then yield just three singles and a Salisbury no-ball as the last-wicket pair live to fight again tomorrow. There is no escaping the fact that it has been a great day for Surrey, however, and, thanks to the superb efforts of their bowlers on a flat track, they now hold all the aces in the match.

*Close:- Sussex 308-9 (Kirtley 10\*, Hutchison 1\*) from 80 overs*

# VIEW FROM THE DRESSING ROOM

*After an expensive first over, you looked to be in great rhythm and top form, so I assume you must have felt that you'd really benefited from your time at the Academy in the winter?*
**ALEX TUDOR** - Yes, things had gone really well - I'd worked on technical things and grooved my action, so coming into the game I was full of confidence and very determined to make a mark at the start of the season. I wanted to send out the message that Alex Tudor had come back fitter and stronger, and was bowling a lot better and wanted to regain his place in the Test side.

### Third Day - Sunday 21st April
### Surrey 575-8 dec and 23-0; Sussex 308 and 379

The last wicket pair's defiance of the previous evening counts for nothing as Ian Salisbury's second ball of the day, a googly, traps James Kirtley on the crease and the lbw appeal that inevitably follows finds favour with umpire Barry Dudleston.

With a lead of 267 and the bowlers fresh, Butcher's decision to enforce the follow-on is entirely predictable and the Surrey team are back out on the pitch ten minutes later with the Sussex openers, Richard Montgomerie and Murray Goodwin.

Montgomerie is only in the middle for a very short time, however, as Alex Tudor nips the second ball of the second over back into the right-hander, hitting him on the back pad and winning a second lbw verdict from umpire Dudleston in the space of three balls at his end. It's 0-1 and Surrey are cock-a-hoop.

Although he had started poorly in the first innings and never settled, Chris Adams is away confidently second time around, immediately glancing Tudor to the fine leg boundary and, three overs later, taking fours off Bicknell through square leg and extra cover. Not to be outdone by his skipper, Goodwin cuts Tudor for three boundaries in two overs as the tall paceman allows a little too much width to a batsman who is renowned for his back-foot strokeplay.

After this positive riposte from the Sussex second-wicket pair, Bicknell manages to offer his captain a little more control with successive maiden overs, though he doesn't look especially threatening in these batsman-friendly conditions. Neither does Tudor, for that matter, and when Adams hooks him for six in his sixth over and follows up by driving the ball to the rope at long-on and cover in his seventh to bring up the fifty, it is time for a double bowling change.

Having clearly put his first innings failure behind him, this is a very different Chris Adams we are seeing second time around, even though he is initially becalmed by the new bowling combination of Azhar Mahmood and Jimmy Ormond, both of whom start with a maiden over. Although Goodwin keeps the scoreboard ticking with a brace of boundaries off the Pakistani all-rounder, Adams adds just two runs to his tally in seven overs before finally breaking free to race to fifty in Ormond's fourth over. His half-century arrives in 62 balls as he follows a cut to the rope backward of point and a clip for four through midwicket with a drive into the gap at extra cover for two runs. Despite his quiet spell, he has dominated the second-wicket partnership and reminded everyone just what he is capable of after his unimpressive first innings effort. He also makes it clear that he intends to maintain a positive approach in an action-packed over from Azhar where three sumptuously-driven off-side boundaries are split by a no-ball off which the Sussex skipper is 'caught' at point by Ian Ward. It is the Surrey debutant's eleventh overstepping offence of the match and this time it has cost him more than just two runs.

With his moment of good fortune quickly forgotten, Adams continues on his merry way, clipping Ormond through square leg for four just a couple of balls after Goodwin has raised the Sussex hundred and the century partnership with a leg-side single.

Although lunch is now just four overs away, Mark Butcher decides that it is time for another double bowling change, with Bicknell recalled at the Vauxhall end and Salisbury introduced at the pavilion end. It looks like a good move to confront the batsmen with something different just before the interval and it soon pays dividends as Goodwin, having swept the leg-spinner to the boundary earlier in the over, pushes forward to the fourth delivery, a googly, and is well snapped up by Nadeem Shahid off bat and pad at silly point. It's a major blow for the visitors to lose their overseas opener for a diligently compiled thirty-four with lunch so close and, even though Adams comes safely through the final over of the session from Bicknell, they are in dire straits, still trailing by 154 runs, as the players leave the field.

*Lunch:- Sussex 113-2 (Adams 71\*, Cottey 0\*) from 30 overs*

As the afternoon session begins, with Bicknell and Salisbury continuing in the attack, another good crowd settles back in gloriously warm sunshine. They are witnessing a fine contest, too, as Adams restarts in blistering style, driving the leg-spinner through wide mid-on for three fours in two overs and then reeling off two more superlative drives, through mid-on and then straight, in Bicknell's second over of the session. The latter stroke takes him quickly into the nineties, and a back-foot forcing shot to the cover fence in Salisbury's next over takes him on to ninety-five.

At the other end, Tony Cottey is starting to establish himself, too, steering Bicknell to the rope at third man and then pushing a single to midwicket to raise the Sussex 150, before Adams clips to the midwicket boundary to move his score on to ninety-nine. Another on-drive off Salisbury in the next over, this time for just a single, takes him through to a very well-played 112-ball century, including no fewer than twenty fours and a six, and his celebrations are fully justified as a typically appreciative Oval crowd offers up generous applause.

With the batsmen looking in complete control at this stage, Butcher replaces Bicknell with Tudor in the hope that a pace and leg-spin combination might produce the wicket his side needs. The early signs are not good, however, as Tudor's opening over costs seven, including a leg-glanced boundary by Adams which completes a fifty partnership for the third wicket inside nine overs, and then Salisbury is twice cut for four by Cottey in the following over.

With two further boundaries, one to each batsman, coming in the next three overs and the score racing towards two-hundred, Ian Ward, fielding at cover, suddenly appears to decide that enough is enough, clapping loudly and imploring his team-mates to produce a greater effort with an impassioned outburst which lasts for around ten seconds. It is easily the most extended exhortation I have ever witnessed on a cricket field, yet it seems to do the trick as Azhar enters the fray in place of Salisbury, the bowling gets spicier and things start to happen. Although Cottey seems to be more affected than his captain - miscuing a pull off Tudor just short of wide mid-on before gloving a hook at the same bowler and seeing a leaping Alec Stewart just manage to get fingertips to the ball - it is Adams who falls victim to Surrey's sudden surge of aggression and a fine piece of bowling by the tall England fast bowler. Having sown seeds of doubt in the batsman's mind with a couple of quick, short-pitched deliveries, Tudor exploits Adams' subsequently tentative footwork with a delivery of fuller length that cannons into leg stump via the inside edge of the bat. With Sussex still sixty-nine runs short of making Surrey bat again this is a very big wicket indeed and it is celebrated as such by the home team as Adams departs to a well-deserved ovation for a high-quality innings.

The visitors now need to dig in again and, while Cottey retreats into his shell somewhat, the new batsman, Michael Yardy, attempts to emulate his skipper's positive approach. His only real successes are a cut off Tudor, which sees the end of the paceman's sparky seven-over spell, and a deflection off Azhar, both of which find the boundary backward of point, before the new bowler, Jimmy Ormond, ousts him with the fifth ball of his new spell. It's possible that the ball which traps him lbw keeps a little low but there is no doubting the fact that the batsman is back on his stumps nor that umpire Dudleston's third such verdict of the day is the correct one. Yardy is out for ten, Sussex are 214-4 and the visitors know that another major partnership is needed if they are to have any hope of avoiding defeat.

Robin Martin-Jenkins now enters the fray at number six but he doesn't last very long as Azhar finally gets his just deserts for some very good bowling. His first wicket of the innings arrives in the eighth over of his second spell when he lures the Sussex all-rounder into hooking a short ball straight down the throat of Mark Ramprakash, who has been posted at deep backward square leg specifically for that reason. Cottey, who has meanwhile battled through to a worthy 76-ball half-century at the other end, is surely unimpressed by his team-mate's careless stroke, which has reduced the visitors to 231-5, leaving them still thirty-six runs in arrears.

What the little Welshman is thinking two overs later, as the next batsman, Matt Prior, perishes in identical fashion to the same bowler and fielder, is almost certainly unprintable. If Martin-Jenkins' dismissal was foolish, then Prior's has to represent the peak of stupidity and as he trudges back to the pavilion, doubtless wondering why he has played such a reckless shot, his team is sinking fast at 237-6. Credit must go to Azhar, nevertheless, for leading the batsmen into temptation during a stint from the pavilion end that has been decidedly lively, as well as lengthy.

The Pakistani international carries on for another two overs, in fact, taking his spell to eleven overs in duration, before giving way to Ian Salisbury, with Bicknell having, in the meantime, replaced Ormond at the Vauxhall end.

On a day when the Surrey skipper's bowling changes have worked a treat, these moves soon bear fruit for the leg-spinner after a near miss for the swing maestro. Bicknell is out of luck in his second over when Mark Davis edges to third man for four and then survives a very acceptable chance to Azhar at third slip, with his score on ten at 255-6, the ball flying away via the fielder's hands to the third man boundary to add insult to injury for the unlucky bowler. The batsman fails dismally to capitalise on his good fortune, however, for as soon as he is put back on strike by a Cottey late-cut for three at the start of the opening over of Salisbury's new spell, he is very well snapped up by Shahid at silly point as the ball flies out on the off-side, at speed, from a mixture of bat and pad. The leg-spinner's third-ball success leaves Sussex still five runs behind with seven wickets down and, even though they move ahead with a sweetly swept boundary by James Kirtley and a couple of leg-byes, the writing is now surely on the wall. An on-driven four by Cottey off Bicknell and a second sweep off Salisbury to the rope at deep backward square leg by Kirtley extend the visitors' advantage to twelve as tea arrives but the capture of five wickets in the session has represented a great effort by the Surrey bowlers and it has almost certainly secured an opening-match victory for their team.

*Tea:- Sussex 279-7 (Cottey 71\*, Kirtley 10\*) from 69 overs*

Mark Butcher returns to his pace and leg-spin combination after tea as Alex Tudor is recalled to the attack in place of the rather unfortunate Bicknell.

Hopes of finishing off the Sussex innings rapidly are thwarted, however, by the eighth-wicket pair who take their side past three-hundred with surprisingly few alarms as Cottey picks off singles to a deep-set field, while Kirtley sweeps two further fours off Salisbury and on-drives Tudor handsomely for another boundary. It could be that the pitch has got even slower as the game has progressed, but a more likely explanation is that the bowlers are tiring after a hard day under a surprisingly warm April sun.

Whatever the reason, Salisbury is replaced by Azhar after being cut to the cover boundary by the increasingly competent Kirtley, who then adds two further fours to his tally, one off each Surrey seamer, in completing a fifty partnership with Cottey. Fortunately for the home side, the Cottey-Kirtley alliance has added just three more runs when Tudor collects his third wicket of the innings by removing the Sussex pace bowler's middle stump with a superlative yorker. It is testimony to the excellence of Kirtley's batting effort that it has taken such a fine delivery to dismiss him for a well constructed thirty-four, all but two of which have come in boundaries.

As Jason Lewry takes guard, Surrey must feel confident about converting Sussex's 317-8 to an all-out total in the region of 330 to 340, but their hopes are soon dispelled as the left-arm swing bowler promptly strikes Azhar for three fours with authentic strokes - a cover drive, a square cut and a square drive - in his second over at the crease. Cottey then hooks the Pakistani international for another four to move his score on to eighty-eight, before marking the return of Salisbury at the Vauxhall end with a further boundary, driven wide of mid-on, to progress into the nineties. The Welshman's fighting effort is making life tough for the Surrey bowlers, and their increasing tiredness is maybe in evidence again as Salisbury offers up a full-toss which Cottey gleefully strikes to the midwicket boundary to complete a very fine century from 140 deliveries with ten fours. For the fourth time in the match, a batsman has a ton to dedicate to a lost friend, giving added poignancy to both the Sussex man's celebrations and the crowd's generous applause.

Although Azhar continues to bowl aggressively - at one point striking Lewry on the helmet with a bouncer and conceding four leg-byes in the process - and Salisbury tries all his variations, Surrey are still struggling to find a breakthrough and a second successive fifty partnership comes up in the eighty-ninth over when Cottey drives Azhar to the extra cover boundary, taking the home side's victory target beyond a hundred. It is even starting to look as if the new ball might have to be the hosts' salvation when Salisbury finally strikes to end the Swansea-born batsman's brave innings. At 372, with Cottey having matched his skipper's score of 114, courtesy of a swept boundary from the first ball of the over, the former Glamorgan man top-edges a cut at a sharply lifting googly and is very well taken behind the stumps by Stewart, much to the relief of everyone with Surrey at heart.

As Cottey returns to the dressing room to a well-deserved ovation, no one really expects Sussex's last-wicket pair to resist for very long... and so it proves. Despite Salisbury's success, Butcher immediately claims the new ball that is now due and hands it to Martin Bicknell and Jimmy Ormond. Within five overs, at a cost of just six runs, the innings is over, Bicknell polishing things off with his first wicket of the season when Hutchison edges a drive to Salisbury at fourth slip to leave Surrey needing just 113 runs to win the match.

As the players leave the field, the home fans show their appreciation for a display of bowling which, though not perhaps as outstanding as in the first innings, has been extremely praiseworthy, given the quality of the pitch. Indeed, had Surrey's close catching behind the wicket been of the same high standard as the bowling then the game might be ending at this moment in time. As it is, Mark Butcher and Ian Ward are hurrying off to pad up, since four overs remain for them to face tonight.

This final short period of batting seems to hold no fears for the Surrey openers as they cope admirably with everything that is thrown at them by Lewry and Kirtley, picking off four boundaries on their way to stumps, including two - forced through the covers and hooked - by Butcher in the last over from Kirtley. With their target reduced to ninety, it's fair to say that Surrey look set to coast home sometime tomorrow morning.

*Close:- Surrey 23-0 (Butcher 14\*, Ward 9\*) from 4 overs*

## VIEWS FROM THE DRESSING ROOM

*About 30-40 minutes after lunch, Adams and Cottey were going well and were close to wiping off Sussex's arrears when, suddenly, Ian Ward burst into life, giving a real 'gee-up' call, clapping and shouting for about fifteen seconds. Do you recall that, and what he was saying?*

**ALEX TUDOR** - Wardy obviously sensed that we were little bit flat in the field, so it was his way of trying to pick things up. It can happen that everyone can be flat when things aren't quite going according to plan, so Wardy assessed the situation really well, thought the guys needed picking up, and I think we sprung into life after that.

*Not long after this, you were paired with Azhar and things really started to happen. Mark Butcher's instructions were to bowl very aggressively, I believe?*
**ALEX TUDOR** - Yes, I remember Butch telling me to really run in and hit the middle of the pitch for a couple of overs to make things a little bit uncomfortable for Chris Adams. Then, because I'd pinned him back, once I pitched one up his feet didn't move as well and he played on. It worked out perfectly, so it was very satisfying for Butch and for me.

### Fourth Day - Monday 22nd April
### Surrey 575-8 dec and 116-0; Sussex 308 and 379
#### Surrey won by ten wickets
#### Surrey 19.75pts, Sussex 5

It's another beautiful morning as the players emerge from the dressing rooms to complete the formalities of the match in front of an understandably fairly small crowd.

On such an excellent batting pitch, there really can be no result other than a Surrey victory, and the openers set about their task with due confidence as Butcher drives Kirtley through mid-off for three in the second over and follows up with a brace of even better off-drives for four in the next over bowled by Hutchison, preferred to Lewry at the pavilion end. Ward then unfurls a glorious straight drive in the left-armer's following over and clips Kirtley through square leg for three shortly afterwards to take the opening partnership to fifty in the tenth over. There can be no doubt that the game will finish well before lunch as Ward continues his personal surge with a boundary in each of the next two overs, before Butcher gets back into the act with three fours, two driven and one pulled, in a particularly wayward fifth over from Hutchison.

Knowing that his side's fate is well and truly sealed, Adams makes no attempt to change the bowling despite the punishing pace being set by the Surrey openers, and a clip through midwicket for three takes Butcher to an immaculate fifty, from just 43 balls, with nine fours, in the sixteenth over, with the total already advanced to eighty-eight.

As the game reaches its 'last rites' stage, Adams finally rests his opening bowlers, allowing both Lewry and Davis a chance to turn their arm over. Although they each bowl a tidy first over, Butcher then drives the left-arm seamer wide of mid-on for three to raise the hundred before Surrey clinch the game in fine style with four successive fours - Butcher drives and cuts the fifth and sixth balls of Davis' second over to the fence before Ward cuts and glances the opening two balls of Lewry's next over for further boundaries to put the seal on an emphatic ten-wicket win at 12.05pm.

As the home team and their supporters celebrate the Club's first opening-match County Championship victory since they beat Gloucestershire in a memorable game at The Oval in 1995, the only minor disappointment is the deduction of a quarter of a point as a penalty for the side's slightly below-par over rate in the match.

### Surrey 575-8 dec and 116-0; Sussex 308 and 379
### Surrey won by ten wickets. Surrey 19.75pts*, Sussex 5
### * deducted 0.25pt for slow over-rate

## VIEW FROM THE DRESSING ROOM

*In recent years we hadn't started our Championship campaign too brilliantly, so I'm sure we must have been delighted to start this season with a win. Was the dry weather a factor, possibly?*
**NADEEM SHAHID** - The dry weather helped as far as preparing a very good wicket was concerned, but I honestly believe it was the Ben factor that helped us to get off to a flying start at the beginning of the Championship campaign - it gave us such a sense of togetherness.

## SURREY v SUSSEX at The AMP Oval. Played from 19th to 22nd April

Surrey won the toss and elected to bat   Umpires:- Nigel Cowley and Barry Dudleston

### SURREY - First Innings

| Fall Of Wkt | Batsman | How | Out | Score | Balls | 4s | 6s |
|---|---|---|---|---|---|---|---|
| 2-33 | M.A. Butcher * | | b Kirtley | 15 | 30 | 3 | 0 |
| 1-26 | I.J. Ward | lbw | b Kirtley | 12 | 23 | 1 | 0 |
| 3-176 | M.R. Ramprakash | c Prior | b Hutchison | 56 | 120 | 10 | 0 |
| 4-229 | A.J. Stewart + | c Prior | b Hutchison | 99 | 139 | 18 | 0 |
| 8-575 | A.D. Brown | | b Lewry | 177 | 222 | 28 | 3 |
| 5-491 | N. Shahid | c Prior | b Kirtley | 150 | 180 | 23 | 0 |
| 6-533 | Azhar Mahmood | lbw | b Lewry | 16 | 21 | 2 | 0 |
| 7-538 | A.J. Tudor | c Martin-Jenkins | b Hutchison | 1 | 8 | 0 | 0 |
| | M.P. Bicknell | Not | Out | 28 | 14 | 5 | 1 |
| | I.D.K. Salisbury | Did not bat | | | | | |
| | J. Ormond | Did not bat | | | | | |
| | Extras | (1b, 14lb, 4w, 2nb) | | 21 | | | |
| | **TOTAL** | (126 overs) | (for 8 dec) | **575** | | | |

| Bowler | O | M | R | W | NB | Wd |
|---|---|---|---|---|---|---|
| Lewry | 19 | 4 | 89 | 2 | - | 1 |
| Kirtley | 32 | 8 | 122 | 3 | - | - |
| Hutchison | 28 | 0 | 146 | 3 | 1 | - |
| Martin-Jenkins | 24 | 4 | 112 | 0 | - | 1 |
| Davis | 12 | 2 | 44 | 0 | - | - |
| Adams | 4 | 0 | 19 | 0 | - | - |
| Yardy | 7 | 0 | 28 | 0 | - | - |

### SUSSEX - First Innings (Needing 426 to avoid the follow-on)

| Fall Of Wkt | Batsman | How | Out | Score | Balls | 4s | 6s |
|---|---|---|---|---|---|---|---|
| 1-33 | R.R. Montgomerie | c Azhar | b Tudor | 27 | 13 | 6 | 0 |
| 4-111 | M.W. Goodwin | c Shahid | b Ormond | 36 | 80 | 6 | 0 |
| 2-61 | C.J. Adams * | c Stewart | b Tudor | 11 | 25 | 2 | 0 |
| 3-67 | P.A. Cottey | c Azhar | b Tudor | 2 | 8 | 0 | 0 |
| 7-293 | M.H. Yardy | c Salisbury | b Azhar | 93 | 169 | 14 | 0 |
| 5-170 | R.S.C. Martin-Jenkins | | b Tudor | 24 | 39 | 4 | 0 |
| 6-217 | M.J. Prior + | c Brown | b Ormond | 35 | 35 | 5 | 0 |
| 8-296 | M.J.G. Davis | c Ormond | b Azhar | 28 | 48 | 3 | 1 |
| 10-308 | R.J. Kirtley | lbw | b Salisbury | 10 | 41 | 1 | 0 |
| 9-298 | J.D. Lewry | c Stewart | b Azhar | 0 | 7 | 0 | 0 |
| | P.M. Hutchinson | Not | Out | 1 | 31 | 0 | 0 |
| | Extras | (1b, 4lb, 8w, 28nb) | | 41 | | | |
| | **TOTAL** | (80.2 overs) | | **308** | | | |

| Bowler | O | M | R | W | NB | Wd |
|---|---|---|---|---|---|---|
| Bicknell | 17 | 3 | 48 | 0 | - | - |
| Tudor | 16 | 1 | 84 | 4 | 4 | - |
| Ormond | 16 | 4 | 52 | 2 | - | 4 |
| Azhar | 16 | 5 | 59 | 3 | 9 | - |
| Salisbury | 15.2 | 2 | 60 | 1 | 1 | - |

### SUSSEX - Second Innings (Following on, 267 runs in arrears)

| Fall Of Wkt | Batsman | How | Out | Score | Balls | 4s | 6s |
|---|---|---|---|---|---|---|---|
| 2-110 | M.W. Goodwin | c Shahid | b Salisbury | 34 | 87 | 6 | 0 |
| 1-0 | R.R. Montgomerie | lbw | b Tudor | 0 | 2 | 0 | 0 |
| 3-198 | C.J. Adams * | | b Tudor | 114 | 133 | 22 | 1 |
| 9-372 | P.A. Cottey | c Stewart | b Salisbury | 114 | 155 | 12 | 0 |
| 4-214 | M.H. Yardy | lbw | b Ormond | 10 | 26 | 2 | 0 |
| 5-231 | R.S.C. Martin-Jenkins | c Ramprakash | b Azhar | 8 | 19 | 1 | 0 |
| 6-237 | M.J. Prior + | c Ramprakash | b Azhar | 2 | 6 | 0 | 0 |
| 7-262 | M.J.G. Davis | c Shahid | b Salisbury | 14 | 19 | 2 | 0 |
| 8-317 | R.J. Kirtley | | b Tudor | 34 | 62 | 8 | 0 |
| | J.D. Lewry | Not | Out | 21 | 47 | 4 | 0 |
| 10-379 | P.M. Hutchinson | c Salisbury | b Bicknell | 1 | 19 | 0 | 0 |
| | Extras | (4b, 13lb, 10nb) | | 27 | | | |
| | **TOTAL** | (95 overs) | | **379** | | | |

| Bowler | O | M | R | W | NB | Wd |
|---|---|---|---|---|---|---|
| Bicknell | 19 | 8 | 60 | 1 | - | - |
| Tudor | 21 | 2 | 81 | 3 | 1 | - |
| Azhar | 23 | 3 | 95 | 2 | 4 | - |
| Ormond | 13 | 6 | 33 | 1 | - | - |
| Salisbury | 19 | 0 | 93 | 3 | - | - |

| SURREY - Second Innings (Requiring 113 runs to win) |||||||||
|---|---|---|---|---|---|---|---|---|
| Fall Of Wkt | Batsman | How | Out | | Score | Balls | 4s | 6s |
| | M.A. Butcher * | Not | Out | | 68 | 64 | 12 | 0 |
| | I.J. Ward | Not | Out | | 43 | 65 | 7 | 0 |
| | Extras | (1b, 2w, 2nb) | | | 5 | | | |
| | TOTAL | (21.2 overs) | (for 0 wkts) | | 116 | | | |

| Bowler | O | M | R | W | NB | Wd |
|---|---|---|---|---|---|---|
| Lewry | 4.2 | 1 | 20 | 0 | - | - |
| Kirtley | 8 | 0 | 43 | 0 | - | 1 |
| Hutchison | 7 | 0 | 43 | 0 | 1 | - |
| Davis | 12 | 2 | 44 | 0 | - | - |

## Other Division One Results

There were two wildly contrasting finishes to the other matches in this round. While Lancashire pipped Leicestershire by one wicket in an enthralling climax at Old Trafford, Kent and Hampshire played out the most turgid of draws on a very flat deck at Canterbury.

April 19-22
*Old Trafford:-* **Lancashire beat Leicestershire by one wicket.** Leicestershire 385 (Wells 74, Stevens 74, Bevan 66, Burns 51, DeFreitas 51) and 277 (Maddy 66, Burns 62, Hogg 5-48); Lancashire 275 (Swann 80, Lloyd 51, DeFreitas 6-101) and 388-9 (Lloyd 73, Law 69, Chilton 53). **Lancashire 17pts, Leics 7**

*Canterbury:-* **Kent drew with Hampshire.** Kent 577-7dec (Key 160, Fulton 98, Symonds 89, Smith 52, Patel 50*, Tremlett 4-129) and 163-4dec; Hampshire 671 (Crawley 272, Johnson 117). **Kent 10pts, Hampshire 11**

# 4 Headingley History

Comprehensive and impressive though the triumph over Sussex had been, the team now faced a much tougher task with a visit to Leeds to play the reigning champions, Yorkshire. With games at Headingley having proved historically very testing for Surrey - no win there in the Championship since 1973 - this certainly looked like being the toughest assignment of the campaign. It was perhaps a little disappointing, therefore, that such a mouth-watering encounter should have been scheduled so early in the season, yet it seemed to me that this could work in our favour. We had, after all, just produced a fine performance in a hard-fought contest on a very good pitch, whereas Yorkshire's only action to date had been a far from competitive fixture against the Bradford and Leeds University Centre of Cricketing Excellence - impressive name, not so impressive cricket. Nor had the champions played especially well in that match, with the bowlers conceding no fewer than forty wides, many of them delivered by Gavin Hamilton, whose dramatic loss of confidence was causing great concern. Additionally, Surrey's problems in recent contests at Headingley had largely stemmed from having a seam attack that was inferior, in terms of depth, to Yorkshire's. With the four-prong pace and swing battery of Bicknell, Tudor, Ormond and Azhar at our disposal on this occasion I was confident that we were truly competitive in this crucial area - in fact, I felt we were superior, given the expected absence from the home attack of Messrs Gough, Hoggard and White.

As I prepared to leave for Leeds, I felt sufficiently bullish about our prospects to conclude my weekly round-up for the official Surrey CCC website with the following two sentences:- *'This would therefore appear to be Surrey's best chance of recording a victory at Headingley for many years, weather permitting. If the lads are able to take advantage of these factors in their favour then the bookies will be slashing our title odds... and all the other counties in the first division will be quaking in their boots.'* A bold statement, maybe, and there was a possibility that in four days time I'd be looking extremely foolish... but I was prepared to put my neck on the block.

By the time I got to Leeds it was clear that things weren't going well for Yorkshire *off* the field of play either. Every time we play there it seems that there is some kind of controversy raging as the white rose county attempts to shoot itself in the foot. After the previous fiascos concerning the pitch at Scarborough and the new gates at Headingley, this time you could take your pick from a whole range of problems. The most publicised news was the calling in of the police to investigate the goings on at the Club Shop, where retail profits dipped from around £32,000 to just £460. Quite unbelievably, it seemed that no-one had suspected foul play until the matter was raised at the Club's AGM - it was crazy that the Club and the auditors hadn't launched an immediate investigation.

The newspapers then reported that the Club owed Darren Gough £16,000 for sales of merchandise during his benefit year. And there was I thinking that Yorkshire folk were supposed to be very careful with money! Given the financial mess they appeared to be in, I wasn't too shocked to discover that their adult ground admission charge for a day of Championship cricket was £12. Compare that with the £5 charge at The AMP Oval.

Additionally, as I wandered around the ground before the start of play, I witnessed an incredible degree of mayhem and disorganisation at the Club offices, and discovered that there had been numerous mix-ups with membership passes. Then, to cap it all, I also learned that there was a problem with the players' new sweaters - some locals told me that it was to do with the advertising logo, while others said that the garments had been made from the wrong material! Whatever the truth was, it seemed that the county champions were in a state of utter turmoil. But could Surrey exploit this where it counted most... out in the middle.

| FRIZZELL COUNTY CHAMPIONSHIP - MATCH TWO |
|---|

## YORKSHIRE versus SURREY
### at Headingley
### First Day - Wednesday 24th April

### Yorkshire 140; Surrey 115-0

*The Teams And The Toss* - While Surrey, predictably, name the same eleven that beat Sussex in their opening match, the reigning county champions have a number of problems, with Darren Gough still recovering from a knee operation and both Craig White and Anthony McGrath missing with groin strains. Additionally, Michael Vaughan and Matthew Hoggard are rested by England, though, on a more positive note, Darren Lehmann is available to lead the side. The gaps in the Yorkshire batting line-up - brought about by the absence of White, McGrath and Vaughan - are filled by Scott Richardson, Chris Taylor and Gary Fellows. The hosts go into the game without a specialist spinner in their line-up yet include Gavin Hamilton, despite his well-publicised struggle for form and confidence in pre-season. As the captains toss up in the middle, overhead conditions are fine on a bright and sunny, yet chilly, morning. There is a tinge of green to the pitch, however, so when Mark Butcher calls correctly he elects to field first.

With their captain having inserted the opposition for the first time in a Championship match since May 2000, when Durham went on to win by 231 runs at the Riverside, there is real pressure on Surrey's seamers to perform as Martin Bicknell, from the rugby ground end, and Alex Tudor, from the Kirkstall Lane end, bowl the opening overs of the game to Matthew Wood and Scott Richardson. Despite this, they make an encouraging start, giving absolutely nothing away before teaming up to snare the valuable early wicket of Wood with the first ball of the sixth over, bowled by Tudor. Although the batsman's attempted off-drive is undeniably loose, he probably has some cause to feel aggrieved as Bicknell, at fourth slip, hangs on to a brilliant instinctive catch, low and one-handed to his right, sparking off excited, and wholly justified, Surrey celebrations. It's just the start that the visitors would have wanted - Wood gone without scoring and Yorkshire 5-1.

Things don't get any easier for the hosts either as Bicknell finds plenty of swing, and the Surrey opening pair probe away on or just outside off stump to a very aggressive field-setting of four slips and two gullies. The bowling is so unstintingly accurate, in fact, that there are only eighteen runs on the board at the end of the fourteenth over and it comes as something of a shock when Michael Lumb drives the first ball of the fifteenth back past Bicknell for the first boundary of the innings as the bowlers reach the end of their spells. Although they have both beaten the bat on a number of occasions, neither bowler has been properly rewarded for his efforts and their figures as they take a rest (Bicknell 8-3-12-0; Tudor 7-3-11-1) certainly don't do them justice.

If the Yorkshire batsmen are tempted to think that they have now weathered the Surrey storm then they soon have second thoughts as Jimmy Ormond, at the Kirkstall Lane end, and Azhar Mahmood, at the rugby ground end, both make the ball swing extravagantly in their opening overs. The spectators are witnessing a real war of attrition out in the middle as disciplined batting meets disciplined bowling head on, with Richardson, an old-fashioned opening batsman whose range of strokes appears to be extremely limited, very much in his element.

Confronted by Surrey's fine bowling, even the more naturally gifted Lumb finds the going tough, though he does eventually conjure up Yorkshire's second four in the twenty-first over of the day when he drives Azhar through mid-on. To everyone's surprise, Richardson then almost follows suit in the following over when a clip backward of square leg off Ormond is pulled up just short of the unmanned long leg boundary. The three runs that the Yorkshire opener adds to his score prove to be his final contribution to the innings, however, as Azhar puts both batsman and spectators out of their misery with a good outswinger that Richardson can only steer tamely to Mark Butcher at second slip. Although he has done a fair job for his side by seeing off the early overs of the new ball, it has to be said that the departing batsman's innings of sixteen from seventy balls hasn't contained a single memorable stroke as Yorkshire have struggled to 41-2 from 24.1 overs.

It is now 'game on', however, as Darren Lehmann strides purposefully out to the middle. No one can envisage him being content to poke and prod around aimlessly and he signals his intentions immediately by driving his fourth ball through extra cover for three. Then, just to underline the fact that Surrey might now have a different game on their hands, Lumb forces the next delivery to the rope at cover to end the most eventful over of the day to date.

Any thoughts that the champions might now start to take the initiative are quickly put on ice, though, as the runs dry up again and Tudor, replacing Ormond after six good overs from the former Leicestershire man, almost unseats both left-handers in the first over of his new spell. Having beaten Lumb comprehensively outside the off stump with his first delivery, he sees Lehmann edge just short of third slip later in the over and then almost has Lumb taken in the gully by Ian Salisbury from the last delivery. It's difficult to tell whether or not the ball carries to the Surrey fielder but damage has clearly been inflicted to the leg-spinner's hand since he leaves the field immediately to get some treatment.

Although Tudor has been desperately unlucky in this over, it isn't long before he has another wicket to his name as the final ball of his second over since returning to the attack sees Lumb, on thirty, attempting to hook and skying the ball almost vertically off the top edge. Alec Stewart dashes in from behind the stumps to complete the catch in a position close to backward short leg and the visiting team celebrates their third success of the morning with the Yorkshire score on fifty-seven. It is now very much Surrey's morning and they come close to adding a fourth wicket to their collection during the final five overs of the session as Tudor and the recalled Bicknell get deliveries past the outside edge of the bat on a number of occasions.

*Lunch:- Yorkshire 63-3 (Lehmann 10\*, Taylor 2\*) from 35 overs*

Following the fantastic pre-lunch efforts of Bicknell and Tudor, Mark Butcher opts for status quo upon the resumption and there is no let-up in the quality of the bowling as just two runs come from the first four overs of the new session. It is perhaps no surprise to see the inexperienced Chris Taylor struggling to score against two high-quality bowlers, but it's most unusual to see the ultra aggressive Lehmann being kept on such a tight rein.

The chunky Australian does eventually break the Surrey stranglehold by cutting Tudor to the backward point boundary, while Taylor follows his captain's lead by clipping Bicknell through midwicket for three, but these prove to be the home crowd's last moments of pleasure for some while as Yorkshire plunge headlong towards disaster in the space of thirty-one deliveries.

The rot sets in when Lehmann flicks the second ball of Bicknell's next over straight to Mark Ramprakash, lurking at square leg, and becomes the 900th victim of the Surrey swing bowler's seventeen-year career. As the Yorkshire skipper drags himself back to the pavilion this impressive statistic is announced over the public address system and draws warm applause from the usually begrudging Headingley crowd. Bicknell acknowledges the ovation by raising the water bottle that has just been thrust into his hand by the visitors' twelfth man and maybe reflects on the statistical coincidence that this dismissal has brought about - Lehmann had, rather bizarrely, also been his 800th first-class victim at The Oval in July 2000.

Just minutes later, with their premier batsman and talisman now departed, Yorkshire lurch rapidly from 74-4 to 80-6 as Tudor strikes with two wickets in seven balls, first removing Taylor, courtesy of a catch by Bicknell at fourth slip, and then trapping Gavin Hamilton back on his stumps to win a straightforward lbw decision from umpire Burgess. The magnificent bowling of Surrey's opening pair is finally reaping its due rewards, though Tudor is rested shortly after his double strike, having delivered twelve successive overs from the Kirkstall Lane end either since of lunch. His figures of 19-8-31-4 paint an accurate picture of his sterling performance.

A flurry of runs follows Tudor's removal from the attack as Richard Blakey slices Bicknell over gully for a boundary, and the first four balls of Jimmy Ormond's new spell yield four, two, one and four runs respectively to finally raise the Yorkshire hundred in the fifty-second over. This landmark is followed, five balls later, by the loss of a seventh wicket, however, as Fellows edges a fine delivery from Bicknell through to Stewart behind the stumps and departs for fifteen. It's turning out to be a truly sensational day for the Surrey team and the few supporters who have made the trip up north, while the impressively large home crowd is finding little to savour except for the gloriously sunny weather that has been another feature of the day.

Chris Silverwood is not able to supply any cheer for the home fans either, his miserable half-an-hour at the crease producing a lofted on-drive for three runs and numerous air shots before he is cleaned up by Azhar, thanks to a fine catch in the slips by Butcher from an edged drive, soon after the Pakistani replaces Bicknell in the attack. Surrey's senior bowler is certainly deserving of his rest, having contributed a quite outstanding spell of 11-3-19-2 since lunch.

Having produced an immaculate bowling and fielding performance so far to reduce their hosts to 109-8, the quality drops a little for the first time with the job almost complete - while Jimmy Ormond struggles with his line, Ryan Sidebottom is given a life before he has scored when Butcher fails to cling on to a catch off Azhar at second slip. It doesn't look likely to be an expensive mistake, however, as the Yorkshire seamer's flamboyant strokes repeatedly fail to make contact with the ball - it's almost comical, in fact, as Azhar beats him five times in one particular over. Against all odds, Sidebottom does, however, manage to outlast his partner, Richard Blakey. The smart money for 'next man out' goes down the drain as Ormond finally pitches his outswinger perfectly, inducing a defensive outside edge that flies straight to Ali Brown at first slip, pushing the champions deeper into the mire at 119-9.

With just one wicket to fall, the tea interval is delayed, though it's hard to believe that a last-wicket partnership between Sidebottom and Steve Kirby, two genuine tail-enders, will keep the players out on the field for long.

The Yorkshire seam bowlers obviously haven't read the script, however, as a frustrating period of playing-and-missing, punctuated by two well-struck boundaries, one to each batsman, follows. Initially, it's possible for those of a Surrey persuasion to see the funny side of things as, in a moment of high farce, Kirby, the non-striker, runs through for a bye to a fumbling Stewart despite having called 'no' very loudly, but the joke soon wears thin as Azhar sees Bicknell, at third slip, drop an awkward catch offered by Sidebottom and then Kirby pokes back a simple caught-and-bowled from a no-ball later in the same over. Bicknell is eventually returned to the attack in an attempt to end all the frivolity but Azhar finishes things off in the next over when his short delivery tempts Kirby into a pull shot that results in a skied catch to Stewart.

The last-wicket pair have added twenty-one, the third-highest stand of the innings, and have demonstrated that there is little wrong with the pitch, save for an occasional ball keeping a touch low. Yorkshire's total of 140 looks to be well below par and is largely the result of a top-class bowling and fielding display, late blemishes apart, from the county champions of 1999 and 2000. As the Surrey players take tea they know that a good first innings reply will put them well on the way to justifying their current status as red-hot favourites to claim the 2002 crown.

*Tea:- Between innings*

As a result of the tea interval being delayed, the players return to the field at 5pm with just twenty-eight overs to play in the final session. It looks likely to be an important period of action, too, since a clutch of wickets would put Yorkshire back in the match, while a steady effort with the bat would greatly increase Surrey's advantage.

Everyone knows that the opening overs are vital, therefore, as a bleached-blond Chris Silverwood sprints in to bowl the first over from the Kirkstall Lane end. Mark Butcher is on strike and he quickly gets off the mark with two easy-looking strokes, through backward square leg and mid-on, for two runs apiece.

At the other end, Ian Ward looks no less confident as he opens his account with an extra cover drive for three off Yorkshire's other opening bowler, the flame-haired Steven Kirby. With three balls remaining in the over, Butcher instantly looks to fight fire with fire, flashing boldly outside the off stump and profiting by four runs as the ball flies away over the slips, much to the anger of the typically pumped-up former Leicestershire quickie. It would appear that the visitors have already signalled their intent to bat positively.

It is also immediately noticeable that Yorkshire's field-settings are less aggressive than Surrey's, something they are soon left to rue as Butcher snicks the opening delivery of Silverwood's second over through the fourth slip position that Surrey had kept manned throughout the home side's innings. Instead of a wicket to the home side, it's four runs to the visitors and, though the horse has just bolted, Lehmann immediately closes the stable door by installing the extra close catcher. To the bowler's obvious and understandable frustration, Butcher then plays and misses at the second delivery and upper-cuts the third over the close catching cordon for another boundary. Yorkshire are already rattled and Surrey, with a little luck on their side, are off to a flyer.

Nor does the situation get any better for the reigning county champions in the next over as the snarling Kirby delivers two no-balls and then watches despairingly as Ward's sliced drive squirts away wide of a diving gully fieldsman to add four more to the Surrey score. Two thousand-plus Yorkshire folk in the ground groan audibly. They have no reason to feel hard done by in the next two overs, however, as a sequence of classy drives, plus a needless gift of four overthrows, takes the total past fifty after just five-and-a-half overs.

In the wake of Surrey's storming start, an unhappy Kirby is rested with gruesome figures of 3-0-28-0, and his replacement, Ryan Sidebottom, immediately brings some order to proceedings with an opening maiden. Silverwood, too, regains a semblance of control before he is surprising pulled from the attack, in favour of Kirby, after just five overs. The change of ends doesn't help the red-haired paceman, though, as Ward drives him to the extra-cover boundary during another highly erratic over.

With runs flowing so freely off Kirby, who is glanced for four and driven for two by Butcher in the second over of his return, the good work being done by Sidebottom in contributing four successive maidens from the rugby ground end is instantly being undone. After just thirteen largely frenetic overs the score stands at an incredible 70-0 and, at this point, a voice on the public address system announces that today's play is being streamed live on the Internet. Apparently this is a 'first' for Championship cricket, though I would have thought that Yorkshire might, by now, be wishing that they had chosen a different day to make history in this way!

With Surrey already halfway to their opponents' feeble-looking total, Sidebottom finally gets a degree of support from the other end as Kirby settles into a better rhythm, yielding just six runs from his next two overs before being replaced, in another surprising move, by Gavin Hamilton. The Scottish all-rounder, who had destroyed Surrey with match figures of 11 for 72 on this ground in 1998, is said to be suffering from a crisis of confidence at the moment and, consequently, the home crowd seems to be holding its collective breath as he starts his spell. To their delight, he starts with a maiden, which offers no real indication of any problems, yet he starts to lose his line during a second over in which Ward drives him through extra cover for four and then miscues a drive just over midwicket's head for a single. You would think that this apparent momentary lapse in concentration from the Surrey opener might give Hamilton encouragement but, conversely, the beleaguered bowler sprays the ball around most erratically in his next over. Only one wide is called, since the majority of the deliveries pass harmlessly down the leg side, and when he does produce a ball that is within reach Ward clips it away through backward square leg for three. Even though it hasn't been a disastrously bad three-over spell - certainly no worse than Kirby's - a rather distressed Hamilton looks quite relieved when the Yorkshire skipper signals that he won't be required to bowl again today. Add another problem to Lehmann's list.

With Ryan Sidebottom now resting after his tight, though not especially threatening, spell of 7-4-7-0, Silverwood joins Gary Fellows in the attack and soon concedes a cover-driven boundary to Ward that raises the Surrey hundred from exactly twenty-five overs. The openers' personal fifties then follow shortly before the close, in the space of three balls, as Ward drives Fellows through mid-off for four and then Butcher crashes Silverwood over point for a boundary of his own. Ward's half-century has come from 90 balls with six fours, while Butcher's has taken 71 balls and included seven fours. On a day when Surrey's cricket has been out of the very top drawer, their partnership has put the icing on an exceedingly good cake!

*Close:- Surrey 115-0 (Butcher 53\*, Ward 51\*) from 28 overs*

## VIEWS FROM THE DRESSING ROOM

*Was it an easy decision to insert Yorkshire when you won the toss?*
**MARK BUTCHER** - Yes, definitely. There wasn't too much to think about - it looked like a typical Headingley pitch and it was the middle of winter, of course!

*It looked as if you might have been working to a plan with Darren Lehmann's dismissal. Was that the case or not?*
**MARTIN BICKNELL** - No, I can't claim any credit for his dismissal in either innings, really. The idea was to cramp him for room throughout the game in order to stop him hitting boundaries, so we were bowling a very tight line at him and I think that maybe frustration got the better of him in both innings.

*That was an incredibly disciplined effort with the ball in the first innings, wasn't it?*
**MARK BUTCHER** - It was fantastic - it was so controlled that I was able to keep lots of close catchers in for the whole innings and, as a result, every time the batsman made a mistake he was out because someone was there, waiting to take the catch. It was just perfect cricket really.

*I guess Azhar Mahmood would rate as the best fourth seamer Surrey have had for years?*
**MARK BUTCHER** - Yes, he's a very handy bowler indeed. Having him in our attack meant that they had no respite. When we've played at Headingley before, under the same circumstances on the same kind of wicket, they've definitely outgunned us by having four front-line seam bowlers, while we were perhaps only able to field three, or maybe even just two. This time, the roles were reversed and we had all the armoury as far as seam bowling was concerned, so we were able to exploit the conditions all the way through their innings.

*We made a very aggressive start to our reply. Was it a deliberate ploy to go out and attack?*
**MARK BUTCHER** - On a pitch that is doing as much as this one was, you feel that once you get in front then the opposition can start to panic. Because of that, we decided that the best approach was to put the bowlers under pressure and not let them bowl at us. So that's what we did - we flung the bat at a few early on, played a couple of good shots and got away with a few, and that put them on the back foot. They didn't have many runs on the board, which meant that they couldn't afford to keep their close catchers in like we did, so if we edged a ball then it often went for four... and if we hit a good shot that went for four as well! So it was a perfect plan.

## Second Day - Thursday 25th April

## Yorkshire 140 and 0-2; Surrey 510

Under a predominantly blue sky, with conditions set fair for batting, the Surrey openers resume their innings against Silverwood and Sidebottom, Yorkshire's two best bowlers on the evidence of the previous evening.

The going is certainly pretty tough for both batsmen in the early overs as Butcher receives a wicked lifting delivery from Silverwood which he fends off just short of gully, while Ward is beaten several times outside the off stump by Sidebottom. Significantly, however, each of these overs also contains a delivery which the batsman dispatches to the boundary, thus relieving some of the pressure and taking Surrey ever closer to Yorkshire's inadequate 140.

There are still some anxious moments, though, as Butcher survives an appeal for a catch at the wicket off the left-armer and two perilously tight singles in the following over from Silverwood see the batsmen only just making their ground. Even in the Sidebottom over during which Surrey take the lead through Butcher's rasping square-cut boundary there are alarms for Ward as he plays and misses twice and is then forced to dig out a top-class yorker.

As Yorkshire continue to strive desperately for a way back into the game, you just can't take your eyes off the fascinating duel going on out in the middle, and the events of the eleventh over of the morning sum up everything that has gone before it. With the Surrey score just past 150, Silverwood's erratic over includes two boundaries - one via Ward's inside edge and the other off the meat of the blade through the covers - his third no-ball of the morning, and, finally, the first wicket of the innings as the batsman chops the final delivery on to his stumps. Joy at last for Yorkshire, though it has come with the opposition already twenty-one runs in front and very much in the box seats. The home team's pleasure will also have been tempered by the strong suspicion that the delivery which has dismissed Ward for a well-played seventy has kept a little low. This is not the first ball to misbehave so far today… nor does it turn out to be the last.

The new batsman, Mark Ramprakash, soon receives a delivery from Sidebottom that zips through low outside his off stump, and then Butcher receives retribution for lovely square-cut and glanced boundaries off Silverwood when a ball leaps up to rap him on the gloves later in the same over. Although he plays it brilliantly, managing to drop the ball down dead in front of him, he requires on-field treatment for the damage inflicted to his hand.

It's impossible to tell whether or not this injury disturbs his concentration but the very next ball he faces, from Steve Kirby, Silverwood's replacement at the Kirkstall Lane end, brings about his demise. Having compiled an excellent eighty-three and given his side a great start, Butcher's innings ends when he drives at a wide half-volley and edges to second slip, where Matthew Wood takes a comfortable catch. It's now 172-2 and it seems rather unjust that the erratic Silverwood (14-1-76-1) and Kirby have made the breakthroughs while the steady and testing Sidebottom is still wicketless.

If the former England left-arm swing bowler is frustrated by this injustice then the feeling is doubtless magnified in his very next over when Alec Stewart, having got off the mark with a forcing stroke into the covers for two, edges at a good height to the right of third slip and sees Chris Taylor spill a very acceptable chance.

The opportunity to turn a Surrey score of 161-0 into 175-3 has been spurned and it is soon looking like being a costly error as Stewart unfurls two cover-driven boundaries off Gary Fellows, Sidebottom's replacement at the rugby ground end, and then takes ten runs from the next over by Kirby. His score has raced on to twenty-seven within six overs of his arrival at the wicket and, as a result, Surrey have crashed through the two-hundred barrier at speed. Ramprakash is clearly keen to get into the act, too, driving Fellows majestically over wide long-off for six, thereby forcing Lehmann to bring Gavin Hamilton into the attack.

The Yorkshire all-rounder's fragile confidence can't have been helped by his captain's decision to use him as the fifth seamer, after Fellows, but as he starts his new spell it seems that he can't fare much worse than Kirby, whose unimpressive effort has left him with innings figures to date of 12-1-69-1.

Although his first over is a maiden and his second yields just a wide, the fact of the matter is that his radar is still way off target, since the batsmen have nothing much to play at and a number of balls are fired way down the leg-side.

With Fellows looking steady but pretty innocuous at the other end and the third-wicket partnership passing fifty with no recent alarms, the Yorkshire attack is now looking threadbare... and Hamilton's third over merely exacerbates their problems. An over that starts with a wide and an off-driven boundary for Ramprakash concludes with a leg-bye, a no-ball and an extra cover-driven four by Stewart. It all adds up to eleven runs, a bowler further drained of confidence and a worrying situation for Darren Lehmann and Yorkshire.

Although the skipper, replacing Hamilton, and Fellows concede just four further runs in the remaining four overs to lunch, they are played with consummate ease. Things are looking very gloomy for the reigning county champions as Surrey lead by 100 runs at the break.

*Lunch:- Surrey 240-2 (Ramprakash 26\*, Stewart 34\*) from 61 overs*

Somewhat surprisingly, Lehmann retains himself in the attack after the break, a move that seems to be appreciated by Ramprakash as he pulls a full-toss wide of mid-on for four in the opening over. The same batsman then takes five from the Australian's next over before picking off two further boundaries, through extra cover and square leg, at the end of the fourth over of the session, bowled by Silverwood. This sudden spurt of runs enables Ramprakash to overtake Stewart, though the latter quickly regains some of the lost ground when he drives Lehmann for a one-bounce four over mid-off, forcing the Yorkshire skipper to admit defeat and remove himself from the firing line.

He is immediately joined on the sidelines by Silverwood, whose next, truly wretched, over sees the hundred partnership completed and both batsmen through to their fifties. Ramprakash reaches his personal landmark first, from 93 deliveries, by pulling a boundary to square leg and steering the next ball backward of point for two, before Stewart, put back on strike when his partner forces a no-ball through the covers for three, crashes two fours from the last three deliveries of the over. The second of these, a cover drive, completes a 77-ball half-century and sends Silverwood off to the outfield to contemplate an over that has cost him nineteen runs.

Lehmann's enforced double bowling change sees Sidebottom returning at the rugby ground end and Kirby recalled at the Kirkstall Lane end. Apart from the fact that Ramprakash has become the principal aggressor, little has changed since the morning session as the left-armer proves both more accurate and more threatening than his colleague - while Sidebottom gets a couple of balls past the bat and appeals for lbw against Stewart, Kirby is driven to the rope at cover by Ramprakash and then pulled to the square leg fence by Stewart as the Surrey total passes three-hundred. But who gets the wicket when it finally arrives three overs later... yes, Kirby! To add to the injustice of it all, it's another poor ball that makes the breakthrough, too, as Ramprakash, for the second time in two Championship innings, tickles a leg-side delivery through to Blakey and, to his credit, 'walks' with the umpire looking unlikely to raise his finger. It's an unfortunate end to a very well compiled and attractive innings of sixty-five with the score at 309-3 and it hands Yorkshire their first point of the season after 151 overs of play.

Perhaps inspired by his second wicket, Kirby does now begin to produce a few more testing deliveries as Ali Brown makes a slightly uncertain start to his innings and Stewart becomes rather becalmed. Sidebottom meanwhile experiences the familiar feeling of ending a good spell without a wicket, while his replacement, Gary Fellows, starts well by reeling off three successive maiden overs. Only twenty-five runs have accrued from eleven overs since Ramprakash's dismissal, in fact, when Lehmann eventually takes a deep breath and returns Hamilton to the attack in place of a tiring Kirby. It's clear that this could turn out to be an expensive move for Yorkshire but, having selected the former England player as an all-rounder, the skipper simply has to give him some bowling.

Ironically enough, the change actually brings a wicket almost immediately as Brown, having never really settled, clubs a short-of-a-length delivery straight to Silverwood at deepish mid-off and departs for a disappointing ten with the score advanced to 335-4. A happy and relieved Hamilton celebrates with his team-mates in the hope that this wicket might change his fortunes.

Alas, it doesn't. With the Surrey lead having stretched beyond two-hundred in the over following the wicket, Hamilton finds the in-form Nadeem Shahid reminding him of the value of confidence by blasting two fours through the covers in the second over of this new spell.

In the meantime, Stewart is starting to get to grips with the nagging medium-pace of Fellows, moving ever closer to a century with glanced and on-driven fours in successive overs. Richard Blakey, standing up to the stumps, is not enjoying the bowling anywhere near as much as his Surrey counterpart, though, being struck on the ankle by the first ball of one particular Fellows over as the ball shoots through low and then finding the fourth delivery hitting him in the throat as it lifts most unnaturally. Yorkshire's prospects of avoiding defeat in the match are clearly not looking good. In fact, they appear to be about as bright as Hamilton's hopes of a quick return to form, since the beleaguered all-rounder follows up a couple of encouraging overs with another loose one in which he concedes ten runs, including two superbly-timed boundaries, through cover and midwicket, to Shahid. When Stewart then drives the opening delivery of the next over from Fellows for four runs wide of mid-on, the Surrey batsmen have notched three boundaries from consecutive deliveries and the senior partner has moved his score on to ninety-six. Unfortunately for Stewart, Fellows takes revenge for his recent rough handling before the over is out, having his tormentor well caught at head height by Wood at backward point from a well struck, but slightly loose, square drive. It's a great pity that the former England captain has again fallen just short of three figures but as he leaves the field to a generous ovation he will take comfort from the fact that he has put his team in a position from which victory seems assured.

The fall of Stewart's wicket with the total at 381 prompts the belated taking of the new ball after ninety-six overs, giving Silverwood and Sidebottom the chance to make another breakthrough in the final four overs before tea. It would appear that the newly-arrived Azhar Mahmood is very much at risk in the circumstances, yet he reels off five lovely strokes, including a hooked four off Silverwood and a cover-driven boundary off Sidebottom, to reach fourteen by the interval.

*Tea:- Surrey 395-5 (Shahid 24\*, Azhar 14\*) from 100 overs*

Although the Surrey four-hundred arrives within a few balls of the restart, courtesy of two pulls by Shahid off Silverwood that yield two and three runs respectively, the batsmen are pretty well contained during the first five overs of the session.

It's not long before the pace of the action picks up again, though, as the next over, delivered by the persevering Sidebottom, brings six runs for Shahid and further despair for the bowler. Having driven to the cover boundary and then steered backward of point for two runs, the former Essex batsman edges the final ball of the over low to the right-hand side of second slip but survives as Wood fails to cling on to the chance. The luckless Sidebottom instantly drops to his hands and knees in mid-pitch in disbelief, while Shahid, on forty-one at the time, lives to fight on... though not for long.

Having added just four to his personal tally, he perishes three overs later to make the score 431-6, though, inevitably, it isn't Sidebottom who unseats him but Kirby, who has replaced Silverwood at the Kirkstall Lane end. Having cut the previous ball to the rope at point to complete a fifty partnership with Azhar, Shahid's demise comes about when he edges a drive to

Scott Richardson at first slip. It's been another good, positive knock by Karachi-born batsman and it confirms that he is probably in the best form of his career at this moment in time.

With Sidebottom having clearly indicated to his captain that he has had enough - and who can blame him! - at the end of his last over, Fellows returns to the attack to join Kirby as Surrey suddenly stutter. Although Azhar, having largely failed to locate the middle of his bat since tea, suddenly does so with a pull for three off Kirby that puts his side three-hundred runs ahead, he loses two further partners in the same over. First, Alex Tudor, after a brief and uncomfortable stay at the crease, is trapped lbw for two by a well concealed slower off-cutter, then Martin Bicknell departs in the same manner to his second ball, the delivery again cutting back but this time keeping low. As a result of this quick one-two, Kirby now has a five-wicket haul to his credit and, while he has undoubtedly improved with each spell, even his mother would probably be forced to concede that his figures flatter him. And one can only hazard a guess at what Ryan Sidebottom is thinking about it all.

Given their position of immense strength and a far from promising weather forecast for the rest of the week, it now makes sense for Surrey to press on rapidly or declare, and it appears that the former option is favoured as Ian Salisbury makes a whirlwind start to his innings. Having taken five runs from his first few balls when facing Fellows, he immediately pulls Kirby over wide mid-on for four to bring up the 450 and follows up by lofting a drive over extra cover for a second boundary. Azhar then makes it three fours from the over when he pulls a slower ball over midwicket and, shortly afterwards, collects the single that takes Surrey to 466, the highest score ever recorded by the county on Yorkshire soil, beating the 465 that the county had knocked up at Bradford in 1934.

After seven overs, Kirby rests and, with his fast bowlers all looking to be either demoralised or a spent force, Lehmann returns to the attack to partner the ever-willing Fellows. Azhar is back in full flow now, though, and relishes this bowling, lifting the medium-pacer over square leg for six, smashing a Lehmann full-toss over midwicket for four and then completing an 89-ball fifty with a lofted straight drive off Fellows for four.

At the other end, Salisbury strikes another boundary to see the ninth-wicket partnership past fifty before skying a drive off Fellows high behind the bowler, where Sidebottom completes the catch after moving around from mid-on. The Surrey leg-spinner has done a fine job by scoring twenty-seven at almost a run a ball but now, with the score 496-9 and six overs left to play, a declaration looks as if it could be the best option for the visitors. The possibility of capturing a Yorkshire wicket tonight is apparently not sufficiently appealing to the Surrey skipper, however, as Jimmy Ormond emerges from the pavilion in a clear attempt to bat through to the close.

Although Azhar soon takes the total past five-hundred with an on-driven boundary off Lehmann, his partner survives for just four overs before he has his bails trimmed by a good delivery from Fellows. The visitors are, therefore, required to come out and bowl two overs... and I suspect that Ormond is not especially popular with his team-mates on his return to the dressing room!

Before the day is out the former Leicestershire man's popularity rating is quickly restored to its previous level, however, as neither Yorkshire opener manages to survive to the close of play.

With the fourth ball of the innings Martin Bicknell's outswinger induces an outside edge from Matthew Wood, which Alec Stewart takes well as he dives away in front of first slip, thus completing a pair for the hapless batsman, then the second ball of Alex Tudor's over shoots along the ground to 'castle' Richardson before he can bring his bat down.

As the Surrey players celebrate joyfully, the defeated batsman and the nightwatchman, Sidebottom, troop off disconsolately, while Ormond probably contemplates the drink that his team-mates surely owe him!

*Close:- Yorkshire 0-2 (Sidebottom 0\*) from 1.2 overs*

| VIEWS FROM THE DRESSING ROOM |
|---|

*It looked like we didn't want to come out and bowl at the end of the day, until Jimmy Ormond got out, leaving us two overs to bowl. Did he get some stick for that? And then congratulations when we picked up those two late wickets?!*

**MARK BUTCHER** - If we hadn't been bowled out then we certainly would have carried on batting the next day because we only wanted to bat once in the match. It wasn't a big deal that Jimmy got knocked over because the conditions were such that we always had a chance of getting a wicket. They were never going to gain anything in two overs whereas we could... but 0-2 was certainly better we could have expected.

### Third Day - Friday 26th April

### Yorkshire 140 and 202; Surrey 510

### Surrey won by an innings and 168 runs
### Surrey 20pts, Yorkshire 3

With the rain that had been forecast having materialised in large quantities overnight, there is never any prospect of play starting on time, especially as there is also drizzle in the air throughout the early part of the morning. Conditions do gradually improve, though, and the umpires eventually decide upon a 1.25pm start after an early lunch, taken at 12.45pm.

Since twenty-eight overs have been lost, there are seventy-six to be bowled in the rest of the day as Alex Tudor runs in to complete the over that had started so successfully the previous evening with the second-ball wicket of the unfortunate Richardson.

It's a windy and overcast afternoon as Michael Lumb plays out the rest of the over, immediately exposing the nightwatchman to Martin Bicknell at the rugby ground end. The left-handed Sidebottom's idiosyncratic inside-out style of play certainly gives him the look of an authentic tail-ender as he miscues a drive back over the bowler's head for the first run of the day, and it seems only a matter of time before Surrey will dislodge him and get Darren Lehmann in to face the new ball. Surprisingly, however, he manages to survive until the final ball of the seventh over, lofting three drives into the wide open spaces at long-off and deep extra cover along the way, before being comprehensively beaten through the gate and bowled by Bicknell's inswinger, while attempting another shot of similar ilk.

Yorkshire are, therefore, perilously placed at 20-3 as their main man takes guard. Since they are clearly the best of the remaining batsmen, Lumb and Lehmann carry a huge burden on their shoulders at this stage of proceedings, though the former initially makes light of the situation, driving Tudor through midwicket for three and then glancing him to the rope at fine leg later in the over, once Lehmann's first-ball single to cover puts him back on strike.

Disaster is just around the corner for Yorkshire, however, as their skipper departs to the second delivery of the next over from Bicknell, pushing back the tamest of caught-and-bowled chances, which the bowler accepts gleefully before being swallowed up by his ecstatic Surrey colleagues. The third-ball loss of Lehmann for one is clearly a crippling blow for the reigning champions and, following his score of sixteen in the first knock, represents his first double 'failure' in a Championship match since July 2000 when he recorded scores of thirty-eight and two against Lancashire at Old Trafford. I later read that his match aggregate of seventeen runs is his second-worst since he joined Yorkshire in 1997.

With the demise of their captain, the prospect of defeat today looms large for the Tykes, and it appears even more likely when Lumb follows Lehmann back to the pavilion in the very next over. Having just edged Tudor over the slips for four very fortunate runs, the 22-year-old left-hander fails to heed the warning, flashes outside his off stump again and turns to see Bicknell take a fine catch at throat height at fourth slip. It's the third time in the match that Surrey have earned a wicket with a catch in this position and it reduces Yorkshire to 32-5, leaving them still a mammoth 338 runs in arrears.

At this stage the Surrey opening bowlers are again performing admirably and they probably deserve even greater praise this afternoon, since the prevailing wind is making life more difficult for them. Some of the gusts at this stage of the afternoon are so strong that they actually blow the large push-on covers onto the outfield at the Kirkstall Lane end of the ground. It's certainly a bizarre sight to see them rolling down the hill unaided towards the square, forcing the ground staff to dash onto the field in order to haul them back behind the boundary rope.

Once order is restored, the game resumes with Chris Taylor and Gary Fellows battling grimly to restore some Yorkshire pride. To be fair, they cope reasonably well, with Fellows, the more positive of the duo, cutting Bicknell for four and then slicing the next delivery over the slips to bring up the home side's fifty in the fifteenth over. He then turns his attention to Tudor, picking up a brace of twos with pleasant drives through cover and mid-on before rocking on to the back foot and pulling wide of mid-on for three.

This spirited display of counter-attacking strokeplay soon forces a double bowling change which, to the batsman's chagrin, brings about his dismissal almost immediately. It's Jimmy Ormond, Bicknell's replacement at the rugby ground end, who does the trick for his skipper, nipping his third ball back into Fellows' pads to win an lbw verdict, umpire Burgess' decision having been made considerably easier by the fact that the ball has kept rather low. The score is now 67-6 and there remains a possibility of Surrey completing victory before tea, which is still some twenty-six overs away.

These hopes are quickly raised by the early struggles of Gavin Hamilton, who soon edges Ormond over the slips for four and then survives a concerted appeal for a catch at first slip, via Alec Stewart's gloves, as a delivery later in the same over lifts alarmingly at the batsman. Perhaps a little ruffled by these escapes, the left-handed all-rounder doesn't last much longer, being trapped on the crease and adjudged leg-before in the middle of superb over from Azhar Mahmood, who is looking very impressive from the Kirkstall Lane end. With Hamilton gone for seven, Yorkshire are now 80-7.

While three partners have come and gone at the other end, Taylor has been applying himself sensibly and doggedly, venturing few attacking strokes against the high-quality Surrey bowling and only recording his first boundary after seventeen overs at the crease when a leg-glance off Azhar finds the rope at fine leg. With Richard Blakey as company, he takes his team to within four runs of three figures before a squally shower drives the players off the field at 3.20pm and forces the umpires to call an early tea at 3.40pm. This burst of rain had seemingly been predicted by the covers, which had blown onto the field of play for a second time just moments earlier.

*Tea:- Yorkshire 96-7 (Taylor 16\*, Blakey 8\*) from 29.3 overs*

Fortunately, the rain clouds pass over the ground rapidly, enabling play to restart at 4pm with six further overs having been lost from the day's allocation. This still leaves plenty of time for Surrey to force victory, assuming that no further showers interrupt proceedings.

The visitors resume their quest for a three-day triumph by pairing Martin Bicknell with Azhar Mahmood, and Richard Blakey soon brings up the home side's hundred, albeit with another edge over the slips, before Taylor posts a new career-best of twenty, in his fourth Championship match, with an extra cover drive to the boundary off Azhar.

While the youngster continues to play sensibly within his limitations, Yorkshire's veteran wicketkeeper drives fluently through the covers on several occasions, advancing his score to thirty-one before the return of Ormond for Bicknell brings about his downfall. It takes just five balls for Mark Butcher's bowling change to bear fruit as Blakey edges an outswinger low to first slip, where Ali Brown takes a fine catch to leave Yorkshire down and almost out at 129-8.

Given his team's hopeless situation, Chris Silverwood's response is not unreasonable as he launches into the bowling right from the start of his innings, driving Ormond to the fence at extra cover and slashing Tudor, who has returned in place of Azhar, backward of point for a second boundary. Taylor also expands his range of strokes, driving confidently down the ground when Tudor overpitches, and the total goes racing past 150 when Silverwood lofts Ormond back over his head for four and then slices him away over gully later in the same over.

This bold display of defiance, with the game decided and the pressure off, forces Butcher into another of his double bowling changes as Azhar is again recalled, while the skipper introduces himself into the attack at the rugby ground end.

Butcher's medium-pace bowling immediately disappears to the boundary twice as Silverwood completes Yorkshire's first fifty partnership of the match with a pull over square leg, and Taylor forces the ball away through wide mid-on later in an expensive opening over. At least the champions are going down with a little more fight now - and in entertaining style - though Silverwood's bold innings of thirty-eight runs from 35 balls comes to an end in the next over from Azhar when he misses a pull at a delivery on off stump that keeps lower than expected.

With the game almost done and dusted, Yorkshire supporters do at least have one moment of cheer when young Taylor, 21, pulls Butcher behind square on the leg-side to register his maiden first-class fifty. Although it has taken him 123 balls and included just five fours, it has been a very good effort in a losing cause and hints at what might have been if other batsmen had applied themselves as diligently. As it is, his innings is but a small crumb of comfort for a side whose defeat is confirmed three overs later, at 5.45pm, when Azhar pins Kirby back on his stumps with another low-bouncing off-cutter and has his lbw appeal upheld by umpire Gould.

In bright early evening sunlight the Surrey team and their handful of supporters celebrate a richly deserved victory - by the crushing margin of an innings and 168 runs - over the reigning county champions, who have been completely outplayed from first to last. It is especially pleasing to beat Yorkshire at their own game, with top-class seam bowling in their own back yard, and to end a long 29-year run without a Championship victory at Headingley. This win also brings to an end another barren run, albeit a much shorter one, as it is, surprisingly, Surrey's first triumph away from home in the County Championship since they beat Leicestershire at Oakham School in July 2000 - the following ten away fixtures, two in that campaign and eight in 2001, had all ended in draws.

As I linger in the stand at the rugby ground end, basking in the glow of a memorable and historic victory, an elderly Yorkshire supporter turns to offer his congratulations on the Surrey team's performance and then, much to my surprise, informs me that Yorkshire have only ever lost by an innings and 150-plus runs on eleven occasions in their history… 'and five of those defeats were against Surrey,' he adds. Big defeats clearly make a big impression on followers of the white rose county!

Yorkshire 140 and 202; Surrey 510<br>
Surrey won by an innings and 168 runs. Surrey 20pts, Yorkshire 3

## VIEWS FROM THE DRESSING ROOM

*Would this rank as one of the best personal performances of your career?*
**ALEX TUDOR** - It was very pleasing, yes. Geoff Miller was there, so it was nice to bowl well in front of him - it's always good to impress, with the team winning at the same time… especially as they were the champions and we were determined to show that we had just lent them our Championship trophy for one year!

*Would this rate as one of the best and most satisfying Surrey performances that you have ever been involved in?*
**MARTIN BICKNELL** - Without a doubt. When we were driving back that night we were saying that it couldn't get any better than this. At that stage of the season, even though we'd only played two games, the writing was almost on the wall. We'd given them such a hammering that we didn't expect them to bounce back too well from it... and they didn't.
**MARK BUTCHER** - Yes, I remember thinking that at the time, and when I got back home I was talking to some people about the game and I remember saying that it was almost perfect. The bowling and catching on day one was fantastic, the batting was fantastic on days one and two, and then we went out and knocked them over again. We hardly put a foot wrong in the whole game.

*I guess the beauty of this performance was that we had beaten them at their own game, with superior seam bowling at Headingley?*
**MARTIN BICKNELL** - Exactly. We went up there and tried to be very positive - we looked at their side and thought they might be struggling with a couple of injuries, and that this would be a good time to play them, while they were still rusty. I thought it was important that we'd had a good hard game against Sussex under our belt - we'd all had a good bowl and a good bat and so we went up to Headingley with everybody in reasonable form.

### YORKSHIRE v SURREY at Headingley. Played from 24th to 26th April
Surrey won the toss and elected to field    Umpires:- Graham Burgess and Ian Gould

**YORKSHIRE - First Innings**

| Fall Of Wkt | Batsman | How | Out | Score | Balls | 4s | 6s |
|---|---|---|---|---|---|---|---|
| 1-5 | M.J. Wood | c Bicknell | b Tudor | 0 | 15 | 0 | 0 |
| 2-41 | S.A. Richardson | c Butcher | b Azhar | 16 | 70 | 0 | 0 |
| 3-57 | M.J. Lumb | c Stewart | b Tudor | 30 | 80 | 3 | 0 |
| 4-74 | D.S. Lehmann * | c Ramprakash | b Bicknell | 16 | 50 | 1 | 0 |
| 5-80 | C.R. Taylor | c Bicknell | b Tudor | 8 | 50 | 0 | 0 |
| 7-102 | G.M. Fellows | c Stewart | b Bicknell | 15 | 30 | 2 | 0 |
| 6-80 | G.M. Hamilton | lbw | b Tudor | 0 | 6 | 0 | 0 |
| 9-119 | R.J. Blakey + | c Brown | b Ormond | 16 | 62 | 2 | 0 |
| 8-109 | C.E.W. Silverwood | c Butcher | b Azhar | 3 | 21 | 0 | 0 |
|  | R.J. Sidebottom | Not | Out | 15 | 47 | 2 | 0 |
| 10-140 | S.P. Kirby | c Stewart | b Azhar | 7 | 27 | 1 | 0 |
|  | Extras | (1b, 5lb, 2w, 6nb) |  | 14 |  |  |  |
|  | **TOTAL** | **(75.5 overs)** |  | **140** |  |  |  |

| Bowler | O | M | R | W | NB | Wd |
|---|---|---|---|---|---|---|
| Bicknell | 22 | 7 | 39 | 2 | - | - |
| Tudor | 19 | 8 | 31 | 4 | 2 | 1 |
| Ormond | 17 | 6 | 31 | 1 | - | - |
| Azhar | 17.5 | 7 | 33 | 3 | 1 | - |

**SURREY - First Innings**

| Fall Of Wkt | Batsman | How | Out | Score | Balls | 4s | 6s |
|---|---|---|---|---|---|---|---|
| 2-172 | M.A. Butcher * | c Wood | b Kirby | 83 | 120 | 12 | 0 |
| 1-161 | I.J. Ward |  | b Silverwood | 70 | 131 | 10 | 0 |
| 3-309 | M.R. Ramprakash | c Blakey | b Kirby | 65 | 108 | 7 | 1 |
| 5-381 | A.J. Stewart + | c Wood | b Fellows | 96 | 159 | 15 | 0 |
| 4-335 | A.D. Brown | c Silverwood | b Hamilton | 10 | 42 | 1 | 0 |
| 6-431 | N. Shahid | c Richardson | b Kirby | 45 | 55 | 7 | 0 |
|  | Azhar Mahmood | Not | Out | 64 | 111 | 7 | 1 |
| 7-443 | A.J. Tudor | lbw | b Kirby | 2 | 12 | 0 | 0 |
| 8-443 | M.P. Bicknell | lbw | b Kirby | 0 | 2 | 0 | 0 |
| 9-496 | I.D.K. Salisbury | c Sidebottom | b Fellows | 27 | 28 | 3 | 0 |
| 10-510 | J. Ormond |  | b Fellows | 3 | 10 | 0 | 0 |
|  | Extras | (8b, 5lb, 10w, 22nb) |  | 45 |  |  |  |
|  | **TOTAL** | **(127.5 overs)** |  | **510** |  |  |  |

| Bowler | O | M | R | W | NB | Wd |
|---|---|---|---|---|---|---|
| Silverwood | 23 | 2 | 124 | 1 | 5 | - |
| Kirby | 27 | 2 | 129 | 5 | 5 | - |
| Sidebottom | 28 | 6 | 71 | 0 | - | 2 |
| Hamilton | 11 | 2 | 48 | 1 | 1 | 3 |
| Fellows | 27.5 | 5 | 90 | 3 | - | - |
| Lehmann | 11 | 1 | 35 | 0 | - | - |

**YORKSHIRE - Second Innings** (Needing 370 to avoid an innings defeat)

| Fall Of Wkt | Batsman | How | Out | Score | Balls | 4s | 6s |
|---|---|---|---|---|---|---|---|
| 1-0 | M.J. Wood | c Stewart | b Bicknell | 0 | 4 | 0 | 0 |
| 2-0 | S.A. Richardson |  | b Tudor | 0 | 2 | 0 | 0 |
| 3-20 | R.J. Sidebottom |  | b Bicknell | 14 | 25 | 2 | 0 |
| 5-32 | M.J. Lumb | c Bicknell | b Tudor | 15 | 20 | 2 | 0 |
| 4-28 | D.S. Lehmann * | c & | b Bicknell | 1 | 3 | 0 | 0 |
|  | C.R. Taylor | Not | Out | 52 | 126 | 5 | 0 |
| 6-67 | G.M. Fellows | lbw | b Ormond | 24 | 29 | 3 | 0 |
| 7-80 | G.M. Hamilton | lbw | b Azhar | 7 | 16 | 1 | 0 |
| 8-129 | R.J. Blakey + | c Brown | b Ormond | 31 | 68 | 5 | 0 |
| 9-188 | C.E.W. Silverwood |  | b Azhar | 38 | 35 | 8 | 0 |
| 10-202 | S.P. Kirby | lbw | b Azhar | 2 | 21 | 0 | 0 |
|  | Extras | (1b, 7lb, 2w, 8nb) |  | 18 |  |  |  |
|  | **TOTAL** | **(57.3 overs)** |  | **202** |  |  |  |

| Bowler | O | M | R | W | NB | Wd |
|---|---|---|---|---|---|---|
| Bicknell | 14 | 4 | 43 | 3 | - | - |
| Tudor | 15 | 3 | 72 | 2 | 4 | 1 |
| Ormond | 11 | 2 | 40 | 2 | - | - |
| Azhar | 13.3 | 5 | 18 | 3 | - | - |
| Butcher | 4 | 0 | 21 | 0 | - | - |

## Other Division One Results

Lancashire joined Surrey on two wins out of two after coming from behind to record a comfortable win over Warwickshire, thanks to an unbeaten eighty-three from former Yorkshire skipper, David Byas.

April 24-26
*Edgbaston:-* **Lancashire beat Warwickshire by six wickets.** Warwickshire 297 (Smith 96, Betts 56, Martin 4-77) and 150 (Martin 4-41); Lancashire 251 (Lloyd 80, Richardson 5-59, Brown 4-78) and 197-4 (Byas 83*). **Lancashire 17pts, Warwickshire 5**

April 24-27
*The Rose Bowl:-* **Leicestershire beat Hampshire by an innings and 9 runs.** Leicestershire 428 (Wells 150, Stevens 82, DeFreitas 51); Hampshire 273 (Crawley 80, Maddy 4-37) and 146 (Kendall 53*, Maddy 5-37). **Leicestershire 20pts, Hampshire 5**

*Hove:-* **Sussex drew with Somerset.** Sussex 337 (Goodwin 162, Bulbeck 4-104) and 396-7dec (Adams 101, Martin-Jenkins 86, Yardy 73); Somerset 401 (Bowler 94, Cox 65, Wood 54, Kirtley 5-90) and 94-2. **Somerset 12pts, Sussex 10**

## COUNTY CHAMPIONSHIP DIVISION ONE AT 27TH APRIL

| Pos | Prv |  | P | Points | W | D | L | Bat | Bwl | Ded |
|---|---|---|---|---|---|---|---|---|---|---|
| 1 | n/a | Surrey | 2 | 39.75 | 2 | 0 | 0 | 10 | 6 | 0.25 |
| 2 | n/a | Lancashire | 2 | 34.00 | 2 | 0 | 0 | 4 | 6 | 0.00 |
| 3 | n/a | Leicestershire | 2 | 27.00 | 1 | 0 | 1 | 9 | 6 | 0.00 |
| 4 | n/a | Hampshire | 2 | 16.00 | 0 | 1 | 1 | 7 | 5 | 0.00 |
| 5 | n/a | Sussex | 2 | 15.00 | 0 | 1 | 1 | 6 | 5 | 0.00 |
| 6 | n/a | Somerset | 1 | 12.00 | 0 | 1 | 0 | 5 | 3 | 0.00 |
| 7 | n/a | Kent | 1 | 11.00 | 0 | 1 | 0 | 5 | 1 | 0.00 |
| 8 | n/a | Warwickshire | 1 | 5.00 | 0 | 0 | 1 | 2 | 3 | 0.00 |
| 9 | n/a | Yorkshire | 1 | 3.00 | 0 | 0 | 1 | 0 | 3 | 0.00 |

# 5  Three Out Of Three

Rather frustratingly, the County Championship campaign now had to be put on hold for almost two weeks while the Benson And Hedges Cup qualifiers took centre stage. It was an irritating interruption with Surrey having made such an impressive start to their Championship campaign and it was to be hoped that the momentum which had been built up would not be lost during the next fortnight as the players participated in a different form of the game.

## B&H CUP - Surrey Fail Final Bensons Test

Having beaten Yorkshire with a day to spare, the players at least had a day off before they began their B&H qualifying campaign with a trip to Lord's to play Middlesex. Unfortunately, the important opening encounter turned into a disaster for the cup holders as they were bowled out for 123 on a damp, seaming pitch after losing what appeared to be a crucial toss. Only Mark Butcher, with a battling fifty-one, put up much resistance as Chad Keegan creamed off the top-order and the Australian quickie, Ashley Noffke, ensured there would be no recovery by removing Butcher and the lower order. Difficult though conditions were, Surrey didn't help themselves by losing two wickets to run outs and falling short of batting out their innings allocation by a truly criminal twelve overs.

Middlesex never looked likely to fail in their quest for 124, even when they lost wickets in the thirteenth and seventeenth overs of their reply. The second wicket, in fact, merely hastened the champions' demise as Owais Shah came in to stroke his way to an impressive 46-ball fifty that took Middlesex through to victory with almost twenty overs to spare.

The loss of the first match in the series, especially by such a wide margin, put extra pressure on the Surrey side as they took on Hampshire at The AMP Oval three days later.

In a game that swung one way and then the other, the visitors stormed away to reach three figures in the fourteenth over as Neil Johnson (46 from 35 balls) and Derek Kenway (40 from 45) took advantage of some loose Surrey seam bowling, before Azhar Mahmood (2-29) and Ian Salisbury (2-48) struck back to reduce Hampshire to 140-6. Robin Smith, well supported by Giles White (24) and Shaun Udal (17 not out), ensured that the collapse wasn't fatal, however, seeing his team through to a total of 243 all out, which looked far from unattainable on a good Oval pitch.

Despite the early loss of Mark Butcher, Surrey seemed to be well placed at 75-1 in the nineteenth over but the departure of Mark Ramprakash (39) to the first ball he faced from Shaun Udal proved crucial. The home side's run flow quickly dried up against the wily off-spinner and, most disappointingly, against Will Kendall's occasional medium-pace seamers as Alec Stewart and Nadeem Shahid, in particular, failed to impose themselves on the bowling. With the required run rate exceeding seven an over, Udal then struck three times in five overs before Chris Tremlett returned to dispose of Ian Ward and leave Surrey in deep trouble at 157-6 with only ten overs remaining. A scintillating innings of fifty from 32 balls by Azhar Mahmood, in partnership with Alex Tudor, seemed set to win the day for the hosts, however, until the Pakistani ran himself out in the forty-eighth over with eighteen runs still needed from thirteen balls. A seven-run penultimate over from Alan Mullally (10-2-39-1) kept Hampshire in control and by the time the final ball of the match arrived Tudor needed to score two runs to seal victory for Surrey by virtue of losing fewer wickets. Unfortunately for the big fast bowler, and his team, he was only able to manage a single as his well-struck drive went straight to the fielder at deep mid-on, leaving Hampshire victorious by one run and Surrey in grave danger of not qualifying for the quarter-finals for the first time since 1996.

The third game, against Essex at Chelmsford, was very much a must-win affair, therefore, and all went well in the early stages as Mark Butcher scored a sparkling 60-ball sixty-two to put his side in pole position at 107-2 after 21 overs at the point of his dismissal. A large total looked likely but the loss of Brown and Shahid to Ronnie Irani in the space of three balls in the twenty-fourth over necessitated a rebuild which proved rather laborious against a restrictive spell from the accurate Paul Grayson (10-0-30-1). Mark Ramprakash batted well to reach fifty from 64 balls but he couldn't find anyone to stay with him for long enough as wickets fell at regular intervals at the other end. Crucially, his partners also starved him of the strike, allowing him just eighteen balls in the last eleven overs of an innings that tailed off to a disappointing 223 all out.

In good batting conditions, this didn't look to be enough runs, though Martin Bicknell's inspired opening spell of 8-3-21-2 saw off both openers to put Essex in trouble at 8-2. Graham Napier struck out boldly during an innings of forty-one to keep his side up with the required run rate, however, and, after his dismissal, Andy Flower ensured Essex stayed on track during decisive partnerships of forty-six with Ronnie Irani (30) and sixty-two with Aftab Habib (27). The Zimbabwean accelerated rapidly towards the end as Surrey realised that their fate was sealed and only just missed out on a well-deserved century, skying Alex Tudor to extra cover with just four runs required for victory. An Essex victory with twenty-eight balls to spare left their opponents facing almost certain elimination from the competition.

With just an outside chance of scraping through to the quarter-finals as one of the two best third-placed sides in the three groups, Surrey took on Kent at The AMP Oval two days later and finally registered a victory, by the margin of 44 runs. The home side's impressive total of 257-9 was built around an explosive 58-ball innings of seventy-three by Ali Brown, restored to the role of opener, and a typically sensible knock of sixty-one from 76 balls by Graham Thorpe, which ensured that Brown's early efforts were not wasted.

Conversely, Robert Key's fifty-nine received only limited support when Kent replied, and his dismissal at 113-5 seemed to spell the end of the visitors' hopes until David Fulton (42), batting at six, and Matthew Walker (41 not out), at seven, added fifty-nine for the sixth wicket in ten overs. Fears that Surrey might suddenly be facing a fourth consecutive defeat in the competition were quickly dispelled, however, by the return of Alex Tudor, who was excellent throughout, and Jimmy Ormond. This pair swept away the lower order with a minimum of fuss to complete three-wicket hauls that saw their side home with plenty to spare. It was encouraging from a Surrey point of view that Philip Sampson had also captured three wickets earlier in the innings with a good display of fast-medium bowling on his cup debut.

During the Kent match, there had been some significant news from Chelmsford. Jamie Foster had been hit on the arm by medium-pacer Andy Clarke while batting in the nets at Chelmsford and an x-ray had revealed a fracture that would put him out of the game for at least a month. Since the Essex keeper had been certain to be included in the squad for the first Sri Lanka Test to be announced a week later, it suddenly appeared that Alec Stewart's Test career might not be over after all, and the possibility of him playing almost a full season with Surrey was now looking much less likely. It all depended on whether England chose another of the young wicketkeepers around the country or decided to turn back to the dependable Stewart. All would be revealed in seven days time.

Back on the field of play, the path to the knockout stages of the Benson & Hedges competition was, incredibly enough, still not entirely blocked as the side travelled to Hove for their final qualifying match - though it did require something like five other results around the country to go Surrey's way, and some of those by a sizeable margin.

After early rain reduced the contest to 46 overs per side, Ali Brown was again in great form, scoring ninety-seven and, in partnership with Ian Ward (46), putting his side into a position of strength at 145-2. The middle-order succumbed cheaply to Davis (2-47) and Kirtley (2-36), however, before Billy Taylor swept away Ormond, Sampson and Giddins with a hat-trick that left Surrey all out with eight balls of their innings unused.

In reply, Sussex overcame the early loss of Ambrose and Adams, thanks to a 65-run stand for the fourth-wicket by Montgomerie and Cottey, and then managed to survive a spirited Surrey fightback when 133-3 became 163-6, two of those wickets falling to the very occasional medium-pace of captain Ian Ward, pressed into action as a bowler following an injury to Jimmy Ormond. Despite the best efforts of the excellent Azhar, useful contributions down the order from House (20), Yardy (19 not out) and Davis (15) saw the scores levelled with a ball to spare, making the Surrey all-rounder's last-ball dismissal of Kirtley irrelevant, since Sussex had only lost nine wickets to the visitors' ten. Chris Adams' team therefore won by virtue of losing fewer wickets, though it mattered little in the final analysis since Surrey's fate had already been sealed by results elsewhere in the country.

## BENSON AND HEDGES CUP QUALIFYING MATCHES - SOUTH ZONE

April 28
*Lord's:-* **Middlesex beat Surrey by eight wickets.** Surrey 123 (38 ov; Butcher 51, Noffke 4-34, Keegan 3-24); Middlesex 124-2 (30.2 ov; Shah 50*).

May 1
*The AMP Oval:-* **Hampshire beat Surrey by 1 run.** Hampshire 243 (Smith 64, Ormond 3-52); Surrey 242-7 (Stewart 52, Azhar 50, Udal 4-36)

May 2
*Chelmsford:-* **Essex beat Surrey by four wickets.** Surrey 223 (49.2 ov; Ramprakash 70*, Butcher 62, Irani 4-38); Essex 224-6 (45.2 ov; Flower 98, Bicknell 3-24)

May 4
*The AMP Oval:-* **Surrey beat Kent 44 runs.** Surrey 257-9 (Brown 73, Thorpe 61, Symonds 3-47); Kent 213 (45.3 ov; Key 59, Tudor 3-28, Sampson 3-42, Ormond 3-65)

May 6
*Hove:-* **Sussex beat Surrey by losing fewer wickets.** Surrey 220 (44.4 ov; Brown 97, Taylor 4-23); Sussex 220-9 (46 ov; Montgomerie 66, Azhar 4-34)

### FINAL BENSON & HEDGES CUP TABLE - SOUTH ZONE

| Pos |           | P | Pts | W | T | L | N/R | NRR   |
|-----|-----------|---|-----|---|---|---|-----|-------|
| 1   | Essex     | 5 | 9   | 4 | 0 | 0 | 1   | 0.48  |
| 2   | Sussex    | 5 | 8   | 4 | 0 | 1 | 0   | 0.61  |
| 3   | Kent      | 5 | 4   | 2 | 0 | 3 | 0   | -0.48 |
| 4   | Hampshire | 5 | 4   | 2 | 0 | 3 | 0   | -0.42 |
| 5   | Middlesex | 5 | 3   | 1 | 0 | 3 | 1   | 0.37  |
| 6   | Surrey    | 5 | 2   | 1 | 0 | 4 | 0   | -0.29 |

The Benson And Hedges Cup failure was a major disappointment, especially to the players, since it was said to be the competition that they most wanted to win for Ben Hollioake, Surrey's Gold Award-winning hero in the finals of 1997 and 2001.

It was perhaps fortunate, therefore, that the fixture schedule left little time to dwell on this setback and allowed the team to return to the four-day form of the game, where such an impressive start had been made. The next County Championship match, starting just two days after the Hove defeat, saw Lancashire, who had started the campaign almost as well as Surrey, visiting The AMP Oval. Having followed up a one-wicket triumph over Leicestershire at Old Trafford with a six-wicket victory against Warwickshire at Edgbaston, the red rose county were the only other side to boast a two-out-of-two start to the season in Division One, so the upcoming contest qualified as the first top-of-the-table clash of the 2002 campaign. With both sides permitted to select their England-contracted players, a heavyweight contest was to be expected.

| FRIZZELL COUNTY CHAMPIONSHIP - MATCH THREE |

## SURREY versus LANCASHIRE
at The AMP Oval

### First Day - Wednesday 8th May

### Lancashire 320; Surrey 106-7

***The Teams And The Toss*** - *Surrey make one change to the side that won so convincingly at Headingley as the desperately unfortunate Nadeem Shahid makes way for Graham Thorpe, who has been freed to play by England and has shaken off a groin problem which had been troubling him. With Andrew Flintoff similarly cleared to play for Lancashire, the visitors are also able to select what they consider to be their strongest possible eleven. Having elected to play four seam bowlers, their only selection decision rests on whether to play Gary Keedy or Chris Schofield as their spinner and it is the former who gets the nod. Since Paul Brind and his staff look to have prepared another very good pitch, Warren Hegg decides that Lancashire will take first use of it upon calling correctly at the toss, despite the overcast weather conditions that suggest there might be some early encouragement for the bowlers.*

As the Lancashire openers, Mark Chilton and Alec Swann, face the opening overs from Martin Bicknell and Alex Tudor it is clear there will indeed be considerable help for the seamers this morning as Surrey's senior bowler gets the ball to swing quite dramatically at times.

Apart from a drive wide of mid-on by Chilton in the first over from Bicknell, the batsman are understandably cautious in their approach and there are very few strokes of aggressive intent until Swann takes eight runs from Tudor's third over, including the first boundary of the innings, a back-foot force through the covers. The duel between these two is an interesting one as the Surrey paceman troubles the Lancashire opener on a few occasions in his next over, only for Swann to reply with an on-driven boundary when the combatants go head-to-head again two overs later. On what appears to be a very flat track, Tudor looks the more threatening of the opening bowlers, yet he is removed from the attack after five overs and replaced by Azhar Mahmood, who instantly obtains prodigious swing to fully justify Mark Butcher's bowling change.

Given the nature of the pitch, wicket-taking looks likely to be hard work, however, so it is something of a bonus when Surrey are gifted the initial breakthrough of the innings in the thirteenth over with the score on thirty-one. Having eschewed all risks and batted very sensibly up until this point, it is rather surprising to see Swann push the ball into the covers and set off for a risky run. Sensing his opportunity, Ian Ward swoops in and underarms the ball at the non-striker's stumps, with the batsman looking well short of his ground as the wicket is broken. For some unknown reason, umpire Vanburn Holder takes several seconds to raise his finger, but he has certainly come up with the correct verdict as Surrey celebrate the former Northamptonshire batsman's departure for eighteen.

Swann's replacement at the wicket is David Byas, the former Yorkshire skipper, who had retired following his team's 2001 Championship triumph but then shocked everyone by signing for the county from the other side of the Pennines shortly afterwards. Although he gets off the mark with a totally miscued stroke over midwicket as Bicknell's accurate opening spell comes to a close, he follows up with a couple of much more convincing leg-side strokes, for four and two, in the next over, bowled by Azhar. Chilton then raises the Lancashire fifty during an erratic opening over from Jimmy Ormond that sees the batsman edging past leg stump and just short of gully on the one hand, then pulling to the midwicket boundary and driving through mid-on for two on the other.

Although Surrey's Pakistani all-rounder is causing occasional problems for both batsmen at this stage, Byas is looking in ominously good touch, striking the ball cleanly as he scores exclusively on the leg-side and adding two further boundaries to his tally with a hook followed by a clip off his toes. He has moved his score on to twenty-three, in fact, before he registers a run on the off-side, but, having broken this particular duck with a drive into the covers, he is soon forcing the ball away through mid-off for three to conclude a rather disappointing first spell of four overs from Ormond. At the other end, Azhar's more impressive opening burst goes unrewarded as Byas glances him for another four, before Butcher surprises everyone by turning to spin for the twenty-fifth over of the innings.

The stand-in skipper's instincts prove to be absolutely spot-on, however, as Ian Salisbury removes Chilton for twenty-six with his very first ball - though the mode of dismissal is unusual, and not what Butcher would have expected at all when he called on his leg-spinner. The delivery that brings the breakthrough with the total at 79-1 is a slow, thigh-high full-toss that the batsman top-edges high into the air, in attempting to smash the ball to the midwicket boundary. Much to the embarrassment of the Lancashire opener and the amusement of the crowd, the bowler hardly has to move from his position in his follow-through to take a straightforward catch. A red-faced Chilton departs while the Surrey team enjoy the moment and congratulate Salisbury on his fine wicket-taking delivery.

Having achieved his objective of breaking the second-wicket partnership, and with the dangerous Stuart Law now at the crease, Butcher immediately restores Bicknell and Tudor to the attack. Clearly unfazed by this move, the prolific Australian gets away to a flying start by driving Tudor for a boundary through square cover in the big fast bowler's first over back and then greeting Bicknell's return with cover-driven and steered fours.

The Surrey opening bowlers quickly regain control, however, and, as lunch approaches, Tudor strikes another blow for the home side, defeating Byas' defensive push with a fine delivery that flicks off the off-bail as it seams away from the left-hander. The former Yorkshire skipper goes for thirty-one and the score is 99-3.

Andrew Flintoff, the new batsman, then promptly drives his first ball from Tudor powerfully through mid-off for four to remind everyone of the potential threat that he and Law pose to Surrey after the break.

*Lunch:- Lancashire 108-3 (Law 19\*, Flintoff 4\*) from 32 overs*

The dangerous nature of the Law-Flintoff partnership is underlined as twenty-five runs, including five boundaries, come from the first three overs of the afternoon session.

The Law versus Tudor contest has been close fought so far, with the Queenslander having struck four boundaries, and the Surrey paceman having responded with a decent lbw shout just before the break, and several deliveries that have passed the outside edge of the bat.

Despite shading the early stages of the battle, Law loses the war to Tudor in the fourth over of the session, however, when he slices a drive low to gully, where Salisbury makes no mistake with the catch. There is much relief in the Surrey camp to see the back of the Australian for twenty-seven at 134-4, and they are further encouraged when the new batsman, Graham Lloyd, spars loosely at his first ball, and then almost plays his second down onto his stumps.

Meanwhile, Flintoff, having seen off Bicknell with three boundaries straight after the restart, blasts Ormond through the covers for four before enjoying a reprieve on twenty-four, when Ward is unable to hang on to a low, fast-travelling chance at deepish point. Almost inevitably, the unlucky bowler disappears to the rope at cover for a second time before the over is out. Lloyd meanwhile puts his nervy start behind him by pulling, flicking and driving Tudor for eight runs in an over which sees 150 up on the board for the visitors, and then forcing Ormond backward of point for four.

Despite the fact that runs are flowing freely, Butcher stays with his attacking fields and almost gains his reward in the next, highly eventful, over from his tall strike bowler. With Flintoff having picked off boundaries from the first two balls of the over, courtesy of a clip to midwicket and a savage square cut, Lloyd, back on strike for ball four, snicks to the Surrey captain at first slip. Unfortunately, the catch arrives at an awkward height above Butcher's head and he is unable to grasp the opportunity as the ball cannons away off his hands for two runs. The reprieved batsman then takes three runs from the final two deliveries to move his score on to fifteen at the end of an over that has cost the unfortunate Tudor fourteen runs, yet should have brought another breakthrough for his side.

By now it's crystal clear that a wicket is badly needed, too, as five fours flow from the next two overs, during which time a Tudor no-ball completes a fifty partnership for the fourth-wicket pair inside six overs. In total, eighty-five runs, including fifteen boundary hits, have haemorrhaged from ten overs since lunch as Lancashire have rushed on to 193-4 and Flintoff has increased his personal tally to forty-six.

Fortunately for the home side, Lloyd seems to get rather carried away by the prevailing frenzied tempo of the innings and, much to the relief of the Surrey faithful, a rush of blood to the head costs him his wicket in the forty-third over. Having cut Ormond to the fence at point earlier in the over, he flirts fatally with a wide outswinger that he really has no need to play at and edges to Stewart behind the stumps. With the partnership broken at 197 and the son of the former England coach gone for twenty-nine, the situation has improved slightly for Surrey, though everyone is very much aware of the threat that Flintoff poses.

The strapping all-rounder makes this abundantly clear in the very next over, in fact, when Azhar Mahmood, replacing Tudor at the Vauxhall end, is immediately forced to the fence at cover and whipped through midwicket for another four. The first boundary in the over completes a very muscular and impressive half-century, including eleven fours, from just forty-three balls, as well as taking Lancashire past two-hundred.

In bright afternoon sunshine, the field now spreads far and wide for Flintoff as Surrey try to break through again at the other end, where Warren Hegg has made an uncertain start with an edged three and a miscued pull for two. The visiting captain looks to have found his feet a couple of overs later when he hooks Ormond resoundingly for four, but it proves to be a false dawn as Azhar's fine outswinger results in another catch for Stewart in the next over. Hegg is out for nine, and Lancashire are 220-6.

Glen Chapple now joins Flintoff in the middle and, while his partner is kept fairly quiet by the defensive fields, the new batsman, like his skipper before him, starts scratchily, picking up boundaries from an airy drive just wide of the fielder at cover and an edge just short of gully.

Since Ormond has completed eight overs in this spell, Butcher elects to rest him at this point and introduces Ian Salisbury in his place at the pavilion end. This is an interesting move, given that Flintoff is in such commanding form, and, sure enough, the England all-rounder is soon off the leash again. It isn't the Surrey leg-spinner who is on the receiving end of some rough treatment, however - it's Azhar, who comes off very much second-best in an over, costing nineteen runs, that takes the visitors' total fizzing past 250. The over reads 4-2-4-2-6-1 as Flintoff reels off two classical lofted drives for four, and then hooks the penultimate delivery a foot or so over the head of Bicknell at long leg.

Encouraged by this, Azhar attempts to bounce the England man out at the start of his next over but without success as the first ball flies to the boundary, despite the valiant efforts of a diving fine-leg fielder, and the second ends up in the crowd backward of square leg to take Flintoff through to an awesome century from just 75 deliveries. His tremendously powerful knock has included two sixes and seventeen fours and has taken his team into a good position at 274-6.

With the seventh-wicket partnership propelled past fifty by Flintoff's brutal assault on Azhar, the Surrey skipper needs to take action again and he therefore recalls the experienced Bicknell to join forces with Salisbury, who, one lofted straight drive apart, has both contained and troubled the strongly-built all-rounder as well as anyone. The leg-spinner is also proving something of a mystery to Chapple and, having seen the Lancashire opening bowler survive a very difficult chance to Azhar at slip two balls earlier, he finally gets his man when Stewart takes a top-edged cut to make the score 283-7 in the sixty-first over.

Surrey now look to be right back in the game, though Flintoff reminds everyone that anything is still possible while he is at the crease by glancing the otherwise steady Bicknell for four and then launching the same bowler back over his head with a towering drive that just fails to clear the rope. The Surrey swing king gets reward for his persistence with the last ball of the over, though, as the Lancashire number nine, Kyle Hogg, edges low to the finer of two gullies and sees Azhar pull off a good catch as he plunges forward - Hogg out for one, Lancashire 296-8.

By chipping away at the other end, Surrey are putting added pressure on Flintoff, and a degree of anxiety begins to show as the Preston-born all-rounder almost presents long-off with a catch off Bicknell in raising the three-hundred. He then settles down again as he appears to get the measure of Salisbury with a slog-sweep for four and a mighty lofted straight drive into the pavilion for six, but, as it happens, this proves to be the final fling for Lancashire as the last two wickets are swept away in the space of five deliveries with the total at 320. John Wood is the first to go as he edges a drive at an outswinger to fall 'caught Stewart, bowled Bicknell', then Flintoff's magnificent innings of 137 is terminated, quite justly, by Salisbury, who draws the big man down the pitch and defeats him with a googly to present the Surrey wicket-keeper with a simple stumping. Although he has clearly been struggling with a leg injury of some kind, the leg-spinner has bowled really well and richly deserves his third wicket, though all the bowlers have made a contribution in difficult circumstances against Flintoff in top form.

As he leaves the field, the England all-rounder sees the crowd in the pavilion rise as one to deliver a warm and sporting ovation for a truly outstanding innings. All the Surrey players applaud and offer their congratulations, too, as they trail off in Flintoff's wake at the end of a pulsating session of cricket that has seen 212 runs scored for the loss of seven wickets in 38.1 overs. It's been hugely entertaining fare, with an exciting, attacking batsman and a leg-spinner to the fore, and the tea interval hardly seems long enough for everyone to savour the feast of cricket that they have just witnessed. I suspect that even Simon Barnes, Graeme Wright and company might have enjoyed this session of play had they bothered to turn up.

*Tea:- Between innings*

With the pitch having posed no problems, as demonstrated by Flintoff, it's a fair guess that Surrey are not unhappy with their opponents' final total of 320 as they commence their reply.

The ball has swung around consistently, however, and it continues to do so as the opening batsmen make an unconvincing start - Mark Butcher endures a torrid over against Glen Chapple when he edges over the slips for four, survives a confident lbw appeal and twice plays and misses, while Ian Ward almost plays on to Flintoff in the following over.

Putting these early struggles behind them, both men eventually start to locate the middle of the bat, however, the best example of this coming when Ward produces a pleasing extra cover drive off Flintoff in the sixth over to register his first boundary. Ironically, just as the batsmen appear to have settled, so the first wicket falls, with Butcher getting an outside edge to a good ball from Chapple which is angled across him and leaves the bat. The catcher is, almost inevitably, the giant Flintoff, whose big hands simply swallow up the ball as it flies away to his left-hand side. Butcher is out for twelve and Surrey are 24-1.

Having delivered just three overs, the Lancashire all-rounder is immediately replaced in the attack by John Wood, whose opening delivery is forced through extra cover for three by the increasingly assured Ward. Although another flowing off-side drive, this time for four, in the next over from Chapple confirms that the left-handed opener is now really into his stride, Ward's team-mates fare less well as an excellent response from the bowler suddenly puts Surrey on the ropes. Striking with the fifth ball of his sixth over, when Ramprakash edges to Warren Hegg, and the first delivery of his seventh, when Graham Thorpe falls lbw for a second-ball duck to a ball nipping back at him, the former England 'A' opening bowler reduces the home side to 40-3.

Fortunately for Surrey, the experienced Ali Brown is no stranger to a crisis. Starting confidently with a square-cut boundary in the last over of an inspired spell of 8-1-30-3 by Chapple before he gives way to Kyle Hogg, Brown takes Surrey past fifty and then watches from the other end as Ward takes four boundaries from the sixth and seventh overs delivered by John Wood from the pavilion end.

After his positive start, the Surrey beneficiary is successfully contained by Hogg, a tall slim 18-year-old with a nice easy action, who completes four successive maiden overs at the start of his spell and only concedes his first runs when Ward edges him through the vacant third slip position for four. Having survived this rather anxious moment, thanks to Warren Hegg's surprisingly defensive field placings, the Surrey opener moves his score on to forty-eight with a clip to midwicket in the next over from the recently introduced left-arm spinner, Gary Keedy, but is unable to capitalise any further as a tit-for-tat run out brings his departure with the score at eighty-eight. When Ward pushes the ball into the covers and finds his call for a quick single refused by his partner, it is Alec Swann, his victim from the Lancashire innings, who provides the throw to the striker's end that sees him stranded short of his ground.

After battling back with a 48-run partnership, this needless loss of a wicket is very frustrating and leads to the sort of collapse that so often, it seems, follows a silly run out. Surrey do it in style, though, plunging headlong into a tailspin as three more wickets fall in the space of seven deliveries to the returning Flintoff and the deserving Hogg. Alec Stewart is the first to fall, for a second-ball duck, when he gropes defensively at Flintoff's first delivery and edges to Hegg, then, three balls later, Brown cuts straight to Chilton at point, before Azhar snicks the first delivery of the next over from Hogg to first slip, where Byas takes a good low catch. As a result of this sudden Lancashire surge, the Surrey score stands at a sickly 92-7, still seventy-nine runs short of avoiding the follow-on.

Luckily, they manage to get through to the close without further loss as a positive Tudor and a passive Salisbury negotiate the final four overs from Flintoff and the sensibly recalled Chapple. Some excellent bowling, notably from the accurate and probing Hogg, and some undistinguished batting has left the home side with plenty to do if they are to get back into the game but, as I leave my seat, I remind myself that if any team can then Surrey can.

*Close:- Surrey 106-7 (Salisbury 1\*, Tudor 14\*) from 33 overs*

## VIEWS FROM THE DRESSING ROOM

*That was quite some innings by Andy Flintoff. How highly would you rate that performance?*
**ALEC STEWART** - He certainly took away any early advantage we had, and, while I wouldn't say that it was impossible to bowl at him, it was far from easy. It was easily one of the better innings I've seen him play and, but for his innings, they could quite easily have been 180 all out.
**MARK RAMPRAKASH** - It was definitely one of the best innings I've seen in recent times because it completely shifted the initiative of the game and the whole momentum of innings, and put us on the back foot.

*The pitch looked pretty good, so how did we view Lancashire's total of 320?*
**ALEC STEWART** - At The Oval, if a side wins the toss and bats and gets around the 300 mark you can accept that, but with the high standards we set ourselves we've bowled plenty of sides out for 250 or less. A bloke is entitled to play well against us, though, and this was Freddie's day.
**MARK RAMPRAKASH** - It looked a pretty good pitch, yes, but the thing that stood out for me in this match was how much the ball swung throughout the game. Because of that, I thought the fast bowlers were certainly always in the game.

*This was my first sighting of Kyle Hogg and I thought he looked to be a very impressive young bowler. What did you think of him?*
**ALEC STEWART** - He bowled some tidy overs, and I know Lancashire rate him highly, but, yes, for a first sighting he looked good. I think he's got every chance of maturing and developing into a fine cricketer.
**MARK RAMPRAKASH** - I thought he looked steady and he certainly got a lot of rave reports early season. I suppose it's not often that you see a young bowler with a very good temperament and pretty good line and length so, whilst I'm not going to get too excited about him yet, I think he's got nice potential. I think his temperament was what stood out for me - he looked comfortable and relaxed.

### Second Day - Thursday 9th May

### Lancashire 320 and 124-5; Surrey 216

Surrey's starting position is as gloomy as the skies overhead as play gets under way on day two with Hogg and Chapple forming the Lancashire attack. Hegg is again very conservative with his field placings - a third man being preferred to a third slip or a gully - and is left rueing his cautious approach when Hogg's first delivery of the day sees Salisbury snicking through the third slip area. Although it's not certain that the ball would have carried to a fielder in that position, the Lancashire skipper's apparent lack of ambition is amazing considering that Surrey are in such a parlous position.

While young Hogg - the son of former Lancashire and Warwickshire bowler, Willie, and the grandson of Sonny Ramadhin - again impresses with his accuracy, runs flow freely from the bat of Tudor when he faces Chapple. Two boundaries, struck sweetly through point and midwicket, come from the Lancashire paceman's second over of the day, before a square-driven four in his third prompts the placement of a sweeper on the cover boundary.

Any thoughts that Chapple might not represent a serious threat today are soon extinguished, however, as the red-haired bowler from the red rose county suddenly produces a devastating delivery to claim his fourth wicket of the innings and plunge Surrey into deeper trouble at 129-8. His victim is Salisbury, who, seeing the last ball of Chapple's fourth over of the day pitch a long way outside off stump, not unreasonably shoulders arms. Much to everyone's surprise, though, the ball jags back sharply to pluck the batsman's off stump clean out of the ground - a quite incredible delivery which would have done for almost any batsman you care to name.

With the deficit still close to two-hundred, the ninth-wicket pair of Tudor and Bicknell now have a mountain to climb, though they are possibly helped by the removal from the attack of Chapple and Hogg after one further over apiece. Andrew Flintoff, at the Vauxhall end, is still a real danger but John Wood starts poorly, being milked easily for four singles backward of square on the off-side and also sending down a long-hop which Bicknell pulls gratefully to the midwicket boundary.

By the simple process of gathering singles, the 150 arrives safely enough in the forty-seventh over, though there is a minor scare for Tudor shortly afterwards when Graham Lloyd, at backward point, almost pulls off a brilliant one-handed catch diving away to his left as the batsman drives a little uppishly at Flintoff. The sturdy all-rounder certainly looks Lancashire's most likely wicket-taker and it is no surprise when the ineffective Wood is replaced by Gary Keedy after a spell of just four overs.

This proves to be a good move by Warren Hegg as his left-arm spinner terminates the ninth-wicket partnership at thirty-five with his second delivery, Bicknell driving a catch to David Byas at short extra cover and departing for eighteen with Surrey still seven runs short of avoiding the follow-on. It is debatable as to whether or not the visitors will enforce it, given the chance, as Ormond sees out the rest of the over and his now well-established partner plays out a maiden from Flintoff, but it becomes an irrelevant point of discussion in Keedy's next over anyway when Tudor unleashes a powerful slog-sweep for six over midwicket. With this bold stroke the big paceman has not only saved the follow-on, he has also completed an impressive 79-ball half-century, the value of his innings magnified by the desperate situation in which it has been compiled. Surrey's deficit is still of a magnitude that makes defeat a strong possibility, however, so it is clearly vital that the last-wicket pair extend the innings for as long as possible.

As Flintoff completes a hostile but wicketless spell and is replaced by Chapple, both batsmen continue to play with good sense and Ormond demonstrates his not inconsiderable batting ability with a withering assault on Keedy. Although the left-arm spinner is obtaining turn, his accuracy leaves something to be desired as the Surrey paceman follows up a beautifully-struck off-drive for four with a sequence of 4-4-3 in Keedy's next over. The runs are, of course, extremely valuable but the range of strokes is impressive, too, as a lofted extra-cover drive is followed by a sweep and a cut. Thanks to a single by Tudor at the end of the spinner's over, Surrey are then able to secure an unexpected, but very welcome, batting point by reaching two-hundred.

Rather surprisingly, Keedy is then retained in the attack for another over, and Ormond immediately takes advantage of Hegg's questionable decision by blasting a six over midwicket, courtesy of a slog-sweep, though the visiting skipper almost has the last laugh when the Surrey man edges a drive between wicketkeeper and slip for three shortly afterwards.

The gap between the sides is now closing at quite a rate but, with lunch approaching and the fifty partnership having been raised by Ormond's square-cut boundary off Hogg, who has replaced the battered Keedy, Chapple claims his fifth wicket to end the innings. Beaten on the front foot by a well-disguised slower delivery, Tudor finds his fighting 103-ball effort terminated by umpire Lloyds' finger, leaving the home side 104 runs in arrears at the halfway stage of the game. It's a considerable deficit for Mark Butcher's team to contemplate over lunch as the man who has been largely responsible for their first innings demise, Glen Chapple, leads his team off to well-deserved applause with final figures of 5-65.

*Lunch:- Between innings*

It doesn't take a genius to realise that Surrey need to strike some early blows as Lancashire set out on their second innings after the break. Bicknell and Tudor certainly strive hard to conjure up a breakthrough but they come up against a pair of determined opening batsmen, who add steadily to their side's lead without any real alarms until Swann edges Tudor to the third man boundary in the eighth over. The fact that this is the first four of the innings speaks volumes for the accuracy of the bowling, though containment clearly isn't going to be enough for a struggling Surrey at this stage of the game. The match is going Lancashire's way, without question, and when Chilton notches the second and third boundaries of the innings, with well-timed strokes through square leg and extra cover in Bicknell's eighth over, Butcher knows that it is time for a change of bowling.

In a double change, Ormond replaces Tudor at the Vauxhall end while Azhar relieves Bicknell at the pavilion end, and both new bowlers look dangerous from the start. It doesn't take long, in fact, for Azhar to split the openers, as a fine piece of cricket brings the dismissal of

Swann for eleven with the score at forty-one in the nineteenth over. The former Northamptonshire batsman is unseated by an excellent delivery that leaves the bat, takes the edge and brings a very good catch out of Stewart, diving away low to his right in front of first slip. In claiming his sixth victim of the match, the Surrey wicketkeeper has given the home side renewed hope, though Lancashire are, effectively, 145-1 at this point.

Azhar's ability to swing the ball consistently also offers encouragement, though Surrey's position in the match doesn't allow Butcher to be as aggressive with his field placings as he might like to be. As a result, Chilton escapes with an edge through the vacant third slip position which brings two runs and the Lancashire fifty in the twenty-first over.

Although he has missed out on Chilton's wicket on this occasion, the Pakistani international does get his man two overs later, however, when the batsman is pinned in front of his stumps by a superb delivery that nips back sharply to win an lbw verdict from umpire Lloyds. As the Lancashire opener departs for thirty-five, at 60-2, it would seem that the match is very much alive again, and that impression is soon strengthened when David Byas follows his colleague back to the pavilion in Azhar's next over. It's three out of three for Surrey's livewire all-rounder as the former Yorkshire skipper wafts lazily at a wide delivery angled across his bows and sees the resulting edge very well taken by the airborne Stewart in front of first slip. With Byas gone for twelve, Lancashire are now 65-3.

As in the first innings, the fall of Byas brings Law and Flintoff together, though their alliance is almost ended before it has begun when the England all-rounder very nearly plays his first delivery from Azhar onto his stumps. Presumably brimming with confidence after his first innings century, Flintoff recovers his composure to cut Ormond to the backward point boundary. Is this to be the start of another dazzling knock, we wonder?

The answer comes quickly and it's an emphatic 'no'. Azhar ensures that there is to be no repeat of Flintoff's first day pyrotechnics by producing a gem of a delivery, a late inswinging yorker which uproots the batsman's middle stump in spectacular style. Surrey delight is obvious both on the pitch and in the stands as the big all-rounder makes his way from the field with the visitors now, in effect, 179-4. With the pitch still playing well, a fourth innings target of anything up to three-hundred would appear to be attainable, though there are still six wickets to take, including the highly significant one of Stuart Law.

As in the first innings, Lancashire's number six, Graham Lloyd, instantly offers the home side hope, betraying early nerves by getting a thick edge to an Ormond delivery and seeing the ball drop just short of Ward as the fielder dives in from point. This incident accurately sums up the former Leicestershire fast bowler's nine-over spell from the Vauxhall end, since he has been impressive but lacking in both good fortune and wickets.

Opting to give Ormond a well-deserved rest at this point, Butcher recalls Tudor in a bid to gain another breakthrough in the last half-an-hour before tea, though his plan fails to yield results initially as the ominously assured Law strikes both the new bowler and Azhar through the covers for four. Lloyd then hooks a Tudor no-ball for six to raise the Lancashire hundred and forces through the covers for four later in the same over to extend the visitors' lead to 208. A quick-fire partnership of sixty or seventy at this stage could be ruinous for Surrey's prospects but, fortunately, that man Azhar rides to the rescue in the penultimate over before the break, grabbing his fifth wicket when Lloyd's inside-edged drive is well picked up, low down, by the ever agile Stewart behind the stumps.

Hope springs eternal for the home side as the visitors reach tea leading by 216 runs with half their side out. It looks increasingly likely that much is going to depend on how quickly Surrey can rid themselves of the threat of Law.

*Tea:- Lancashire 112-5 (Law 16\*, Hegg 0\*) from 40 overs*

As Martin Bicknell and Alex Tudor take up the attack after tea we appear unlikely to get through the whole session, since the skies are greyer than ever and the light is already gloomy. Law seems to be seeing the ball well enough when he drives Tudor through mid-off for three in the fourth over after the resumption, however, and Hegg has no difficulty in pulling Bicknell to the boundary in the next over. It is, therefore, rather surprising when the umpires discuss the quality of the light after just two balls of the following over, especially since the light meter on the scoreboard has only one bulb aglow. They decide that there is a problem, though, and the Lancashire batsmen appear to agree by accepting the offer to retire to the pavilion at 5.15pm, with more than twenty-six overs of the day's allocation remaining. It seems a slightly strange decision for the batsmen to leave the field with their side still on top in the match, and I can't help but wonder whether they will regret it when they come up against fresh Surrey bowlers tomorrow morning.

*Close:- Lancashire 124-5 (Law 21\*, Hegg 7\*) from 45.2 overs*

## VIEWS FROM THE DRESSING ROOM

*Considering our position at the end of the first day, I expected Lancashire to really attack us at the start of the day two, yet Warren Hegg's tactics seemed surprisingly negative. Was their approach maybe indicative of how much our opponents fear us?*

**ALEC STEWART** - I think sides are frightened of us to an extent because of our strength in depth with the batting - they are always trying to stay in the game against us, in my opinion, as opposed to trying to dominate us. Having said that, we are a difficult side to dominate, largely because of the way we bat as a team, but also because we have match-winning bowlers. As a result, sides will, more often than not, be cautious against us, and when that happens the quality of our side comes through. That's why we end up winning more games and more Championships than most.

### Third Day - Friday 10th May

### Lancashire 320 and 200; Surrey 216 and 200-4

After Alex Tudor completes his unfinished over from the previous evening, Mark Butcher hands the ball to Martin Bicknell and Azhar Mahmood as Surrey look to continue their fightback on another cool, grey morning.

Apart from one classical cover drive for four by Law off Bicknell, the bowlers hold sway in the early stages, with the ball regularly finding its way down to the fielder on the third man boundary, either via the edge or the full face of the bat. The Lancashire pair show great application and skill, however, resisting any temptation to flirt unnecessarily with deliveries wide of the off stump and, consequently, the score rises at only two runs per over until Law breaks free with an on-driven three off Bicknell, and Hegg follows suit with a hooked boundary in the next over from Azhar. A series of singles subsequently takes the visitors' score up to 150, then the lead extends to 258 when Law unfurls another of his trademark cover drives off the Pakistani all-rounder.

At this stage the home side is in dire need of a wicket, and they get a lucky break just in the nick of time with the dismissal of Lancashire's Australian danger man for thirty-nine, adjudged lbw to Azhar by umpire Jeremy Lloyds. From my position, right behind the bowler's arm, the decision appears to be incorrect - even though Law has shuffled across his stumps in aiming through midwicket, the bowler's booming inswinger looks, even to a Surrey eye, to be heading well down the leg side. This doesn't stop the home county's supporters from celebrating a crucial wicket at a vital time, however, and they do so in the knowledge that they have probably just witnessed a key moment - if not *the* key moment - in the match.

Amidst the excitement of Law's demise, it has almost been forgotten that Azhar Mahmood now has all six wickets to fall in the innings, though it's debatable as to whether he can sustain this one-man assault on Lancashire, having already got through six overs this morning.

Bicknell is continuing to do his best to assist from the Vauxhall end but it clearly isn't to be his day as he beats Glen Chapple, the new batsman, several times without finding the edge of the bat. This particular knack doesn't present any problems for Azhar, however, as he soon ends Chapple's brief but unhappy stay at the crease with a delivery that shapes away from the blade and induces a snick into the safe gloves of Stewart. The Pakistani has seven out of seven, the Surrey keeper has nine victims in the match and Lancashire, now 166-7, are leading by 270 runs. It would seem that the visitors still hold the advantage, largely because they have the runs on the board, but Surrey are pushing them hard, thanks to the efforts of their stand-in overseas player.

With Bicknell out of luck in his eight overs, Butcher now has to make a change, and he chooses Ormond over Tudor, while Azhar, no doubt spurred on by the possibility of a clean sweep of the Lancashire wickets, continues at the pavilion end.

Despite the high quality of the bowling, Hegg still looks to attack wherever possible, one such opportunity being seized upon when Surrey's new hero overpitches and is driven to the cover fence in the tenth over of his spell. Undeterred by this, Azhar charges in again for an eleventh over and gets an eighth wicket when Kyle Hogg's thick-edged drive is brilliantly taken low and left-handed in front of first slip by the flying Stewart. This stunning effort by the 39-year-old wicketkeeper-batsman completes a ten-victim haul and it gives his side further hope with Lancashire now, in effect, 284-8.

All eyes are soon firmly focused on Azhar again, though, as he strives to become the first Surrey bowler for forty-six years to take 'all ten'. Having dismissed Hogg with the fifth ball of his over, he has one ball at the new batsman, John Wood, and brings a gasp from the crowd as the tail-ender plays and misses.

Unfortunately for Azhar, but luckily for his team in the wider context of the match, Wood also fails to make contact with the next ball he receives, in the following over from Ormond, and this time it proves fatal. Beaten on the crease by a ball that darts back at him, Wood departs lbw as umpire Holder's upraised finger ends the individual's dream but keeps the team's hopes very much alive.

Lancashire's lead is still below the psychological three-hundred mark as their last man, Gary Keedy, takes guard, though it is immediately boosted by six further runs as Ormond's first ball to the new batsman turns out to be a no-ball that is clipped away to the midwicket boundary. Surrey's subsequent plan, to allow Hegg to take singles in order to get Keedy on strike, then goes slightly awry as each batsman picks up a leg-side four to push the Lancashire total up to two-hundred and the home side's target beyond three-hundred. Thankfully, though, Ormond brings the innings to a close before frustration can set in, knocking out Hegg's off stump with a beautifully concealed slower yorker to leave Surrey chasing 305 to win the match.

While the Lancashire captain's gritty innings of forty-three is rightly applauded as he leaves the field, the bulk of the crowd's adulation is obviously reserved for the highly skilled and hard-working Azhar Mahmood, who has returned career-best figures of 25-5-61-8. Surrey's bowling and fielding has been outstanding this morning and their Pakistani all-rounder's performance throughout the Lancashire second innings has been of the highest class. Consequently, we now have a potentially fascinating contest on our hands.

With lunch still some twenty minutes away, the Surrey openers have to face three overs before the break, but they come through unscathed against Chapple and Flintoff, reducing their side's 305-run target by eleven in the process.

*Lunch:- Surrey 11-0 (Butcher 4\*, Ward 5\*) from 3 overs*

Butcher and Ward take the early honours after lunch, with a series of fluent and attractive off-side strokes pushing the total into the thirties. Although neither Chapple nor Flintoff bowls poorly, the former can't quite recapture his first innings form, while the latter is unable to trouble the batsmen consistently enough and donates further runs to the Surrey cause by overstepping the crease on a couple of occasions. Things are looking good for the home side, with the batsmen finding little to trouble them until Ward edges, on the bounce, through Stuart Law at third slip for four runs in Flintoff's fifth over to take the total up to forty-two without loss.

The score hasn't advanced any further, however, when the introduction of Hogg for Chapple finally brings success for Lancashire. The final ball of the youngster's opening over strikes Butcher on the front pad as he plays well forward and, to the surprise of many, not least the batsman, umpire Holder responds positively to the visiting team's appeal. As the disappointed Surrey opener makes his way from the field it's hard for the home supporters to feel too aggrieved, though, bearing in mind the decision that had 'cut off' Law during the morning session. Holder's verdict has, nevertheless, ended a very promising start and the loss of Butcher for sixteen represents a serious setback to Surrey hopes.

Another important umpiring decision, which this time goes in the home county's favour, then follows just three overs later when a Flintoff no-ball thuds into Mark Ramprakash's pads as the batsman shoulders arms to a delivery cutting back into him. But for the bowler's overstepping offence, umpire Lloyds would certainly have been faced with an interesting decision and, from my seat behind the arm, it looks as though he might have been sending the Surrey number three on his way with a duck to his name. The obvious disappointment and frustration shown by the England all-rounder and by his team-mates behind the wicket suggests that they agree with my viewpoint. Could this be another potential turning point in the match?

Quickly putting this anxious moment behind him, Ramprakash deflects a ball to third man later in the same excellent Flintoff over to raise Surrey's fifty, and it comes as something of a shock when this turns out to have been the last over in the big all-rounder's spell.

Chapple returns in his place and, while the former Middlesex batsman survives another lbw shout from the new bowler, Ward tucks in to Hogg, picking up an off-side boundary in each of three successive overs.

At this stage Ward is dominating the scoring while his partner is settling in after his shaky start, but, as everyone knows, fortunes can change rapidly in cricket and, just as Ramprakash breaks loose in the twenty-first over, his colleague stumbles and then falls in the twenty-second. Chapple's switch back to the Vauxhall end, in place of Hogg, first brings two glorious cover-driven boundaries by Ramprakash and a lucky moment for Ward - when Keedy, at mid-off, spills an awkward low catch as he dives to his left - before John Wood ensures that the reprieved batsman fails to profit from his let-off in his second over after joining the attack. Since Ward has looked to be in good touch throughout his innings of thirty-seven, the manner of his dismissal, a sliced drive that picks out Alec Swann at backward point, is disappointing, and his departure appears to put Lancashire back on top, since their hosts are now two wickets down and 227 runs short of their objective.

Surrey's worries soon recede a little, however, as Graham Thorpe starts his innings positively, driving his fourth ball from Wood to the boundary at backward point and then finding the rope at cover twice more with fine strokes in successive overs. As a result, the hundred clicks up in the twenty-eighth over, giving Surrey's confidence an undoubted lift, before Wood chops down Thorpe to prevent him from doing any further damage to the red rose's cause. Sadly, it's another soft dismissal for the home side, too, as the England left-hander's top-edged hook is very well held low down at deep backward square leg by Kyle Hogg. With Thorpe gone for twenty and the score now standing at 104-3, it looks to be 'advantage Lancashire' again, especially if they can conjure up another wicket before tea.

Given their rather precarious position, the counter-attack that follows from Ramprakash is a little unexpected. Having lofted Chapple over cover for four in the last over of the bowler's fourth spell of the innings and then cut Wood to the point boundary, the former England batsman greets the returning Flintoff with a leg-glanced four and a drive through midwicket for two from a no-ball. With a couple of singles thrown in for good measure, Ramprakash has raised his score by seventeen in just three overs and, perhaps inspired by his partner's strokeplay, Ali Brown drives Wood into the pavilion at long-off for six.

Shaken by this assault, Hegg rapidly goes on to the defensive, leaving just one slip in place for both batsmen. That proves to be enough for Brown, however, as he edges tamely to Byas in that position three overs later, to reward a hostile burst by Flintoff.

The loss of a fourth wicket before tea is exactly what Surrey had been trying to avoid, though the loss of Brown for ten is tempered very slightly by the fact that the total has at least moved on quickly to 139. A larger partnership is badly needed, however, if Surrey are to achieve their objective, and Alec Stewart makes a start towards this goal by sweeping the recently introduced left-arm spin of Gary Keedy for a boundary to fine leg.

Given the tight nature of a contest which is really holding the crowd's attention, much of the play in the last six overs up until tea is tense and very hard-fought, though Ramprakash does break out three overs from the interval, driving Keedy through point for four to simultaneously raise the Surrey 150 and his personal half-century from 84 balls.

As the players adjourn for tea, Surrey need 146 runs with six wickets remaining and the last session of the day looks like it will be pivotal to the outcome of the match.

*Tea:- Surrey 159-4 (Ramprakash 52\*, Stewart 9\*) from 44 overs*

As it happens, the final session is curtailed by bad light that halts play shortly before 6pm, though the fourteen overs of play that are possible see Surrey making significant progress towards their victory target, as they add forty-one precious runs without further loss.

Chapple and Hogg share the first ten overs after the break but rarely cause any problems as each batsman boosts his score with a couple of cover-driven boundaries. These runs push the fifth-wicket partnership past the half-century mark and drive the Lancashire skipper increasingly on to the defensive as the light closes in.

It is only when Hegg pulls a rabbit out of the hat by introducing the medium pace of Mark Chilton that Surrey suffer a serious scare when a yorker-length delivery defeats Ramprakash, the wicketkeeper and, fortunately for the batsman and the home team, the leg stump, too. Another well pitched-up leg-side delivery, which evades Hegg in the gloom and runs away for four byes, convinces the umpires that the final act of this drama should be played out on the final day.

As the batsmen leave the field, it has clearly been Surrey's day, with Azhar and Ramprakash to the fore, though Stewart also has something to celebrate as it has been discovered that he has become the first Surrey wicketkeeper to claim ten victims in a match at The Oval since Edward Pooley in 1878.

*Close:- Surrey 200-4 (Ramprakash 71\*, Stewart 25\*) from 58 overs*

## VIEWS FROM THE DRESSING ROOM

Lancashire started the third day 228 runs ahead with five wickets in hand. What sort of total were we expecting to chase at that stage?

**MARK RAMPRAKASH** - Surrey are capable of getting anything in the fourth innings, as we found out later in the season. Whatever they got, we were mentally getting attuned to knocking

61

the runs off, and we knew we would bat a lot better in the second innings than in the first. But first things first, we had to keep the pressure on them and bowl them out.

*Having gone eleven overs without a breakthrough on the third morning, did we perhaps get a lucky break when Stuart Law was adjudged to be lbw?*
**ALEC STEWART** - It probably wasn't out, and Hawkeye would probably have shown that it wasn't hitting the stumps, but these things even themselves out over the course of a season. It was a big wicket to get, though, with him being their dominant player. Getting him out opened up both ends, really, and Azhar cleaned up.

*How did you view Azhar's amazing second-innings bowling effort?*
**MARK RAMPRAKASH** - Magnificent, wasn't it? It was a true match-winning effort - he beat the bat many times, he really rolled his sleeves up and ran in hard and bowled a long spell. A terrific effort.
**ALEC STEWART** - He was outstanding, that was fantastic bowling. You sign an overseas player to win you games, and that's why I believe the overseas player must be of the right quality. He showed why we signed him, so credit to him, and credit to Surrey for signing the right type of player, as opposed to having an overseas player just for the sake of it. As with our first innings in this game, the majority of the dismissals in Lancashire's second innings were legitimate dismissals, brought about by good deliveries. I thought there was a lot of quality bowling right throughout this game, though.

*I assume you remember that moment, before you had got off the mark, when you padded up to what turned out to be an Andy Flintoff no-ball - a worrying moment for you?*
**MARK RAMPRAKASH** - Yes, I do, and it certainly would have been a very close call, I would imagine. But I suppose over the course of a season you get your bits of luck - sometimes things don't go your way, but I can look back at that as maybe a time when it did.

### Fourth Day - Saturday 11th May

### Lancashire 320 and 200; Surrey 216 and 309-7

### Surrey won by three wickets
### Surrey 16pts, Lancashire 6

Needing 105 runs to win, against Lancashire's requirement of six wickets, Surrey look to be favourites on the final morning of the match as Mark Ramprakash and Alec Stewart take guard.

The opening overs of the day, delivered by Chapple and Flintoff, are understandably tense, with just four singles, all of them from deflections to third man, being gathered in by the experienced Surrey pair. The first truly aggressive stroke isn't seen until the fifth over, in fact, when Ramprakash drives Chapple to the boundary backward of point, and Stewart takes two further overs before he picks up some momentum with a back-foot forcing stroke to the rope at extra cover.

Although Lancashire's first innings bowling hero offers his team moments of hope, appealing confidently for lbw as Stewart pads up, and then inducing an edge from Ramprakash which flies low through an untenanted second slip position, he is rather scuppered by his own inconsistency and Hegg's typically cautious field settings. The batting is undeniably classy, however, as both men break out from watchful defence to capitalise fully on any loose balls that come along and, as a result, with the score having risen to 232-4, Flintoff's opening burst is brought to a close and the Lancashire skipper, surprisingly, opts to bring Mark Chilton into the attack.

The decision to utilise the medium-pace swing bowler ahead of Hogg and Keedy looks flawed, especially when Stewart cuts his first delivery to the point boundary, and the visitors are starting to look down and out when the hundred partnership for the fifth wicket comes up in the next over, following some woeful backing-up which allows two overthrows. With Ramprakash moving serenely into the nineties and Stewart greeting John Wood's introduction, in place of Chapple, with a brace of pulls for two runs apiece, it looks to be plain sailing for Surrey as they reduce their requirement to fifty-seven runs.

At this point, however, Chilton justifies Hegg's faith in him by luring Stewart into a drive that finds the safe hands of David Byas at short extra cover to give the Lancastrians a possible late lifeline. As the former Surrey captain departs for a well-constructed forty-six, Hegg instantly recalls Chapple, at short notice, for another blast from the Vauxhall end.

Seven runs come from the red-haired paceman's return over, though, as the new batsman, Azhar Mahmood, clips the ball confidently over square leg for four, and Ramprakash continues his single-by-single march towards three figures. Two further singles in the following over from Chilton, and another one in the next by Chapple, take the former Middlesex man through to ninety-nine and when he extends his run of singles to six by steering another Chilton delivery to fine third man he completes an excellent hundred, the fifty-sixth of his first-class career. His 197-ball knock might not have been full of blazing strokes but it has been a superb example of how to keep a cool head under pressure in the final innings of a match.

Most importantly, it looks to have sealed victory for Surrey, a fact seemingly acknowledged by Hegg's replacement of Chapple with Wood for a second time, and underlined when Ramprakash unfurls a square-driven boundary in the new bowler's first over. The former Durham seamer does gain a degree of consolation in his next over, however, as Azhar's extra-cover drive to the boundary is immediately followed by a loose swish outside off stump which results in an edge that is well pouched by Hegg as he dives away in front of first slip - the Pakistani international's dismissal for fifteen leaves Surrey at 281-6.

With Ramprakash still in residence, this appears to be nothing more than a minor blip in Surrey's progress towards 305, though the loss of Alex Tudor three balls later, following a bizarre innings - having thrashed his first two balls from the recently introduced Keedy to the cover boundary, he misses a slog-sweep and falls lbw - causes one or two flutters in the crowd and, no doubt, in the home dressing room, too.

The appearance of the experienced and nerveless Martin Bicknell quickly reassures everyone, however, and he instantly demonstrates how the slog-sweep should be played, by locating the midwicket boundary. The score passes three-hundred shortly afterwards and, apart from one testing over from Wood, during which he passes Bicknell's outside edge three times, there are no further alarms before Ramprakash ends the match in fine style by advancing on Keedy and driving the ball majestically into the Bedser Stand for six.

Broad grins adorn the faces of both Surrey batsmen as they make their way from the field and Ramprakash receives a rapturous reception for his masterful innings, which, along with Azhar's inspired bowling, has been the major factor in the home side's completion of an astonishing comeback from the dire position in which they had found themselves at the end of day one. This was like a football team coming back from 0-3 down to win 5-3.

At the end of a hard-fought contest, Surrey have emerged victorious in the battle of the two sides at the top of the nascent Championship table and have, therefore, started their campaign with three straight wins. Quick checks of the record books reveal that this is the first time the men from The Oval have achieved this feat since 1958, the season that saw them claim the last of their seven successive 1950's titles. Could this year's three-out-of-three start lead to the 2002 title, perhaps?

**Lancashire 320 and 200; Surrey 216 and 309-7**
**Surrey won by three wickets. Surrey 16pts, Lancashire 6**

# VIEWS FROM THE DRESSING ROOM

*How highly do you rate this century amongst all those you have scored in your career?*
**MARK RAMPRAKASH** - Without doubt it's in the top five because of the quality of the attack and the situation. We all knew it was a big game and we knew that if we beat Lancashire and Yorkshire at the start of the season then that would be a big step towards getting to the top of the table. I felt very satisfied after that knock because of the pressure of the situation.

*Three wins out of three represented an amazing start for a team that has, traditionally, in recent times, started poorly. What do you think were the principal reasons for this?*
**MARK RAMPRAKASH** - There certainly was a Ben Hollioake factor - it focused everybody. But I also think the balance of the side was important. Instead of having two spinners, Surrey's great strength in recent times, we had four top-quality seam bowlers, with the signing of Azhar, which is important in the early stages of the season when ball is moving around a lot. They bowled brilliantly at Yorkshire and again in this game, so I think that had something to do with it - that early season firepower.
**ALEC STEWART** - Because of the dry early-season weather we were able to have practice wickets on the edge of the square and the surfaces were excellent, so that got both batters and bowlers into good nick. I'm always harping on about how you've got to have good practice surfaces to develop good players, so Paul Brind and his ground staff should take credit for that. Then, because you're playing well, you become confident as an individual, and when everyone's playing well you become a confident team. I think that showed in the Championship form. Also, I don't think we did ourselves justice in 2001, and that gave us a little reminder that we had to show everybody we were the best side by winning the Championship again.

*Your keeping and batting both looked in great order, even at this early stage of the season. Were you benefiting from the winter break you'd had, and driven on by the need to make a point to the people who had written off your England career?*
**ALEC STEWART** - I always knew I was still good enough to play at the top level, given an opportunity, so maybe I had a point to prove to those people who said my international career was finished, yes. With my elbows back to 100 per cent, I had no injury worries, so I worked hard in pre-season in an effort to play well for Surrey and get back into the England side.

*What had it been like to do a pre-season with Surrey for the first time in 14 years?*
**ALEC STEWART** - I enjoyed it. I got my head around what I had to do, whether it was playing for Surrey, or the added goal of playing for England. Whatever I do, I want to do it well, so I put in a big pre-season training-wise and practice-wise, indoors in March, and continued that in the first part of the season with Surrey.

| SURREY v LANCASHIRE at The AMP Oval. Played 8th to 11th May ||||||||
| Lancashire won the toss and elected to bat ||| Umpires:- Vanburn Holder and Jeremy Lloyds ||||
| LANCASHIRE - First Innings ||||||||
| Fall Of Wkt | Batsman | How | Out | Score | Balls | 4s | 6s |
| 2-79 | M.J. Chilton | c & | b Salisbury | 26 | 69 | 1 | 0 |
| 1-31 | A.J. Swann | run | out | 18 | 39 | 2 | 0 |
| 3-99 | D. Byas | | b Tudor | 31 | 49 | 5 | 0 |
| 4-134 | S.G. Law | c Salisbury | b Tudor | 27 | 38 | 6 | 0 |
| 10-320 | A. Flintoff | st Stewart | b Salisbury | 137 | 106 | 20 | 3 |
| 5-197 | G.D. Lloyd | c Stewart | b Ormond | 29 | 28 | 5 | 0 |
| 6-220 | W.K. Hegg *+ | c Stewart | b Azhar | 9 | 12 | 1 | 0 |
| 7-283 | G. Chapple | c Stewart | b Salisbury | 16 | 26 | 3 | 0 |
| 8-296 | K.W. Hogg | c Azhar | b Bicknell | 1 | 12 | 0 | 0 |
| 9-320 | J. Wood | c Stewart | b Bicknell | 4 | 22 | 0 | 0 |
| | G. Keedy | Not | Out | 0 | 4 | 0 | 0 |
| | Extras | (4b, 4lb, 6w, 8nb) || 22 | | | |
| | TOTAL | (70.1 overs) || 320 | | | |

| Bowler | O | M | R | W | NB | Wd |
|---|---|---|---|---|---|---|
| Bicknell | 20 | 4 | 68 | 2 | 1 | - |
| Tudor | 14 | 3 | 79 | 2 | 3 | 1 |
| Azhar | 14 | 2 | 79 | 1 | - | 1 |
| Ormond | 12 | 0 | 56 | 1 | - | - |
| Salisbury | 10.1 | 3 | 30 | 3 | - | - |

## SURREY - First Innings (Needing 171 to avoid the follow-on)

| Fall Of Wkt | Batsman | How | Out | Score | Balls | 4s | 6s |
|---|---|---|---|---|---|---|---|
| 1-24 | M.A. Butcher * | c Flintoff | b Chapple | 12 | 24 | 1 | 0 |
| 4-88 | I.J. Ward | run | out | 48 | 77 | 7 | 0 |
| 2-40 | M.R. Ramprakash | c Hegg | b Chapple | 5 | 16 | 1 | 0 |
| 3-40 | G.P. Thorpe | lbw | b Chapple | 0 | 2 | 0 | 0 |
| 6-89 | A.D. Brown | c Chilton | b Flintoff | 16 | 45 | 2 | 0 |
| 5-88 | A.J. Stewart + | c Hegg | b Flintoff | 0 | 2 | 0 | 0 |
| 8-129 | I.D.K. Salisbury | | b Chapple | 7 | 38 | 0 | 0 |
| 7-92 | Azhar Mahmood | c Byas | b Hogg | 1 | 3 | 0 | 0 |
| 10-216 | A.J. Tudor | lbw | b Chapple | 61 | 103 | 6 | 1 |
| 9-164 | M.P. Bicknell | c Byas | b Keedy | 18 | 43 | 1 | 0 |
| | J. Ormond | Not | Out | 35 | 37 | 4 | 1 |
| | Extras | (1lb, 6w, 6nb) | | 13 | | | |
| | **TOTAL** | **(64.3 overs)** | | **216** | | | |

| Bowler | O | M | R | W | NB | Wd |
|---|---|---|---|---|---|---|
| Chapple | 18.3 | 1 | 65 | 5 | - | 1 |
| Flintoff | 13 | 4 | 32 | 2 | 3 | 1 |
| Wood | 11 | 2 | 41 | 0 | - | - |
| Hogg | 14 | 7 | 26 | 1 | - | 1 |
| Keedy | 8 | 0 | 51 | 1 | - | - |

## LANCASHIRE - Second Innings (Leading by 104 on first innings)

| Fall Of Wkt | Batsman | How | Out | Score | Balls | 4s | 6s |
|---|---|---|---|---|---|---|---|
| 2-60 | M.J. Chilton | lbw | b Azhar | 35 | 70 | 3 | 0 |
| 1-41 | A.J. Swann | c Stewart | b Azhar | 11 | 61 | 1 | 0 |
| 3-65 | D. Byas | c Stewart | b Azhar | 12 | 22 | 1 | 0 |
| 6-154 | S.G. Law | lbw | b Azhar | 39 | 98 | 4 | 0 |
| 4-75 | A. Flintoff | | b Azhar | 6 | 13 | 1 | 0 |
| 5-109 | G.D. Lloyd | c Stewart | b Azhar | 15 | 27 | 1 | 1 |
| 10-200 | W.K. Hegg *+ | | b Ormond | 43 | 96 | 6 | 0 |
| 7-166 | G. Chapple | c Stewart | b Azhar | 1 | 15 | 0 | 0 |
| 8-180 | K.W. Hogg | c Stewart | b Azhar | 4 | 19 | 0 | 0 |
| 9-181 | J. Wood | lbw | b Ormond | 0 | 2 | 0 | 0 |
| | G. Keedy | Not | Out | 10 | 14 | 2 | 0 |
| | Extras | (2b, 6lb, 2w, 14nb) | | 24 | | | |
| | **TOTAL** | **(71.4 overs)** | | **200** | | | |

| Bowler | O | M | R | W | NB | Wd |
|---|---|---|---|---|---|---|
| Bicknell | 19 | 4 | 41 | 0 | - | - |
| Tudor | 14 | 2 | 48 | 0 | 5 | - |
| Ormond | 13.4 | 1 | 42 | 2 | 1 | 1 |
| Azhar | 25 | 5 | 61 | 8 | 1 | - |

## SURREY - Second Innings (Needing 305 to win)

| Fall Of Wkt | Batsman | How | Out | Score | Balls | 4s | 6s |
|---|---|---|---|---|---|---|---|
| 1-42 | M.A. Butcher * | lbw | b Hogg | 16 | 36 | 1 | 0 |
| 2-78 | I.J. Ward | c Swann | b Wood | 37 | 71 | 7 | 0 |
| | M.R. Ramprakash | Not | Out | 119 | 219 | 13 | 1 |
| 3-104 | G.P. Thorpe | c Hogg | b Wood | 20 | 33 | 3 | 0 |
| 4-139 | A.D. Brown | c Byas | b Flintoff | 10 | 24 | 0 | 1 |
| 5-248 | A.J. Stewart + | c Byas | b Chilton | 46 | 86 | 5 | 0 |
| 6-281 | Azhar Mahmood | c Hegg | bWood | 15 | 25 | 2 | 0 |
| 7-290 | A.J. Tudor | lbw | b Keedy | 8 | 3 | 2 | 0 |
| | M.P. Bicknell | Not | Out | 7 | 24 | 1 | 0 |
| | Extras | (10b, 5lb, 2w, 14nb) | | 31 | | | |
| | **TOTAL** | **(85.4 overs)** | **(for 7 wkts)** | **309** | | | |

| Bowler | O | M | R | W | NB | Wd |
|---|---|---|---|---|---|---|
| Chapple | 26 | 4 | 91 | 0 | - | - |
| Flintoff | 19 | 4 | 67 | 1 | 7 | 1 |
| Hogg | 10 | 2 | 32 | 1 | - | - |
| Wood | 14 | 0 | 52 | 3 | - | - |
| Keedy | 9.4 | 0 | 42 | 1 | - | - |
| Chilton | 7 | 3 | 10 | 1 | - | - |

| Other Division One Results |
|---|

Leicestershire continued their surprisingly good start to the season by moving into second place in the table, following a convincing win over promoted Warwickshire, while the champions, Yorkshire, slumped to their second successive defeat at the hands of a Trescothick-inspired Somerset.

May 8-10
*The Rose Bowl:-* **Hampshire beat Kent by eight wickets.** Hampshire 345 (Smith 104, Udal 88, Hamblin 50, Saggers 5-74) and 111-2 (Crawley 50*); Kent 118 (Mascarenhas 4-49) and 337 (Nixon 77*, Smith 77, Patel 58, Mascarenhas 4-73). **Hampshire 18pts, Kent 3**

*Taunton:-* **Somerset beat Yorkshire by seven wickets.** Yorkshire 213 (Lumb 66, Caddick 5-72) and 280 (White 69, Lumb 62); Somerset 232 (Blackwell 114, Silverwood 4-28) and 263-3 (Trescothick 134, Bowler 79*). **Somerset 16pts, Yorkshire 4**

May 8-11
*Leicester:-* **Leicestershire beat Warwickshire by seven wickets.** Leicestershire 523 (Bevan 146, Stevens 125, Sutcliffe 71, Giles 5-126) and 94-3; Warwickshire 177 (Pollock 59) and 439 (Knight 130, Powell 67, Troughton 66, Pollock 66). **Leicestershire 19pts*, Warwickshire 1**
\* deducted 1pt for slow over rate

| COUNTY CHAMPIONSHIP DIVISION ONE AT 11TH MAY |||||||||||
|---|---|---|---|---|---|---|---|---|---|---|
| Pos | Prv | | P | Points | W | D | L | Bat | Bwl | Ded |
| 1 | 1 | Surrey | 3 | 55.75 | 3 | 0 | 0 | 11 | 9 | 0.25 |
| 2 | 3 | Leicestershire | 3 | 45.00 | 2 | 0 | 1 | 13 | 9 | 1.00 |
| 3 | 2 | Lancashire | 3 | 40.00 | 2 | 0 | 1 | 7 | 9 | 0.00 |
| 4 | 4 | Hampshire | 3 | 34.00 | 1 | 1 | 1 | 10 | 8 | 0.00 |
| 5 | 6 | Somerset | 2 | 28.00 | 1 | 1 | 0 | 6 | 6 | 0.00 |
| 6 | 5 | Sussex | 2 | 15.00 | 0 | 1 | 1 | 6 | 5 | 0.00 |
| 7 | 7 | Kent | 2 | 13.00 | 0 | 1 | 1 | 5 | 4 | 0.00 |
| 8 | 9 | Yorkshire | 2 | 7.00 | 0 | 0 | 2 | 1 | 6 | 0.00 |
| 9 | 8 | Warwickshire | 2 | 6.00 | 0 | 0 | 2 | 2 | 4 | 0.00 |

| NUL2 - Lightning Struck Down By Bicknell And Co |
|---|

Surrey's bid for promotion from the second division of the National League got off to a flying start when the Lancashire batting was demolished in double-quick time by the home county's seamers at The AMP Oval.

After Lancashire decided to bat in hazy conditions that encouraged swing bowling, the excellent Martin Bicknell ripped out the middle order to claim 5-26, though Ed Giddins was equally impressive in his opening burst of six overs as Lightning collapsed from a high point of 31-1 to 49-8. A brief rally, led by Warren Hegg, was then ended with the score at sixty-five when Philip Sampson held a brilliant catch off his own bowling to terminate the Lancashire skipper's top-scoring innings on nineteen, allowing Azhar Mahmood, playing the last game of his short spell as Saqlain's stand-in, to dispose of Peter Martin and complete the rout of Lightning for 68, a dismal total that equalled their lowest-ever score in the competition. Although the Lions' high-quality bowling was backed up by some superb fielding, with Michael Carberry and Alec Stewart also holding very fine catches, some of the visiting batsmen were certainly guilty of gifting their wicket to the bowlers in far from impossible conditions.

When the Lions replied, Lancashire did manage to pick up four wickets, but the game ended at 4.18pm as Surrey rushed to victory inside twelve overs, making this one of the shortest matches in Sunday/National League history.

There was one statistical oddity worth noting during the Lancashire innings, when Martin Bicknell managed the very rare feat of bowling at no fewer than *five* different batsmen during his eighth over! This bizarre situation, which doesn't often occur, even in an over containing a hat-trick, came about as follows:-
1st ball - **Stuart Law** - OUT; 2nd ball (following a wide) - **Tim Roberts** - no run; 3rd ball - **Tim Roberts** - OUT; 4th ball - **Warren Hegg** - one run to square leg; 5th ball - **Graham Lloyd** - OUT; 6th ball - **Chris Schofield** - no run.

### SURREY LIONS v LANCASHIRE LIGHTNING at The AMP Oval
**Played on Sunday 12th May** — **Surrey Lions won by six wickets**
Lancashire Lightning won the toss and elected to bat — Umpires:- Vanburn Holder & Trevor Jesty

**LANCASHIRE LIGHTNING**

| Fall Of Wkt | Batsman | How | Out | Score | Balls | 4s | 6s |
|---|---|---|---|---|---|---|---|
| 2-31 | M.J. Chilton | lbw | b Bicknell | 10 | 16 | 1 | 0 |
| 1-4 | G. Chapple | c Stewart | b Giddins | 0 | 10 | 0 | 0 |
| 3-33 | D. Byas | c Stewart | b Giddins | 13 | 28 | 2 | 0 |
| 5-39 | S.G. Law | c Carberry | b Bicknell | 3 | 14 | 0 | 0 |
| 4-36 | A. Flintoff | c Stewart | b Bicknell | 3 | 12 | 0 | 0 |
| 7-41 | G.D. Lloyd | c Stewart | b Bicknell | 1 | 6 | 0 | 0 |
| 6-40 | T.W. Roberts | c Carberry | b Bicknell | 0 | 2 | 0 | 0 |
| 9-65 | W.K. Hegg *+ | c & | b Sampson | 17 | 21 | 3 | 0 |
| 8-49 | C.P. Schofield | c Shahid | b Sampson | 5 | 10 | 1 | 0 |
|  | K.W. Hogg | Not | Out | 3 | 3 | 0 | 0 |
| 10-68 | P.J. Martin | c Stewart | b Azhar | 0 | 3 | 0 | 0 |
|  | Extras | (6lb, 5w, 2nb) |  | 13 |  |  |  |
|  | **TOTAL** | **(20.4 overs)** |  | **68** |  |  |  |

| Bowler | O | M | R | W | NB | Wd |
|---|---|---|---|---|---|---|
| Bicknell | 9 | 2 | 26 | 5 | - | 3 |
| Giddins | 6 | 2 | 8 | 2 | - | 1 |
| Sampson | 4 | 0 | 18 | 2 | - | 1 |
| Azhar Mahmood | 1.4 | 0 | 10 | 1 | 1 | - |

**SURREY LIONS**

| Fall Of Wkt | Batsman | How | Out | Score | Balls | 4s | 6s |
|---|---|---|---|---|---|---|---|
| 2-19 | I.J. Ward * | lbw | b Martin | 6 | 13 | 1 | 0 |
| 1-11 | A.D. Brown | c Chilton | b Martin | 8 | 6 | 0 | 1 |
|  | M.R. Ramprakash | Not | Out | 18 | 22 | 3 | 0 |
| 3-50 | A.J. Stewart + | run | out | 11 | 18 | 2 | 0 |
| 4-61 | N. Shahid | c Byas | b Hogg | 9 | 8 | 2 | 0 |
|  | M.A. Carberry | Not | Out | 4 | 5 | 1 | 0 |
|  | Azhar Mahmood | did not bat |  |  |  |  |  |
|  | A.J. Tudor | did not bat |  |  |  |  |  |
|  | M.P. Bicknell | did not bat |  |  |  |  |  |
|  | P.J. Sampson | did not bat |  |  |  |  |  |
|  | E.S.H. Giddins | did not bat |  |  |  |  |  |
|  | Extras | (4lb, 7w, 2nb) |  | 13 |  |  |  |
|  | **TOTAL** | **(11.5 overs)** | **(for 4 wkts)** | **69** |  |  |  |

| Bowler | O | M | R | W | NB | Wd |
|---|---|---|---|---|---|---|
| Chapple | 5 | 0 | 23 | 0 | - | 2 |
| Martin | 4 | 0 | 24 | 2 | 1 | 3 |
| Hogg | 1.5 | 0 | 14 | 1 | - | 2 |
| Flintoff | 1 | 0 | 4 | 0 | - | - |

## Other NUL Division Two Results

Gloucestershire Gladiators were brought to earth by the Hampshire Hawks to provide a surprise result in the first round of matches. Derbyshire Scorpions' defeat of the Sussex Sharks was also a little unexpected as the NUL division two season got off to an interesting start.

May 12
*Derby:-* **Derbyshire Scorpions beat Sussex Sharks by eight wickets.** Sussex 166-8 (Welch 3-45); Derbyshire 168-4 (42ov; DiVenuto 84, Kirtley 3-49). **Derbyshire Scorpions 4pts**

*The Rose Bowl:-* **Hampshire Hawks beat Gloucestershire Gladiators by 46 runs.** Hampshire 219-5 (Pothas 53*, Kenway 50); Gloucestershire 173 (38.3ov; Spearman 82, Mascarenhas 5-27, Prittipaul 3-33). **Hampshire Hawks 4pts**

| First-Class Friendly - Clarke's Debut Ton Provides Cheer In Fenner's Draw |
|---|

Surrey's trip to Fenner's to play Cambridge UCCE unfortunately clashed with a 2nd XI fixture at The AMP Oval. With a number of first-teamers rested, the eleven that took the field at Cambridge included a large number of second team players, even though it was felt that the Hampshire 2nd XI might well provide a better test than the UCCE team. As a result of this decision, Rikki Clarke, the 20-year-old all-rounder from Guildford, was given his first-class debut and took his chance admirably, completing a maiden first-class century from 160 balls and sharing in a 192-run partnership for the fourth wicket with Mark Ramprakash. Clarke thus became only the eighth Surrey player to achieve the feat of scoring a century on his first-class debut and the first since Adam Hollioake in 1993.

In Surrey's second innings, Michael Carberry followed Clarke's achievement by completing a maiden first-class century of his own, while Phil Sampson - another who was making his first-class debut - and Ian Ward had both previously picked up their maiden first-class wicket during the students' first innings. These statistics aside, the match had little to commend it, and Surrey's final afternoon declaration, which set the UCCE side 507 in under three hours, demonstrated that the county saw the game as little more than a practice exercise.

*Scores:- Surrey 402-4dec (Ramprakash 121, Clarke 107*, Shahid 65) and 322-6dec (Carberry 153*) drew with Cambridge UCCE 218 (Murtagh 3-37) and 96-5 (Giddins 3-7)*

| FCC1 - CHAMPIONSHIP RESULTS SUIT SURREY |
|---|

While the team had been engaged in their match at Fenner's, a full round of Frizzell County Championship matches had been taking place around the country, with the results proving highly satisfactory from a Surrey point of view - Yorkshire had lost again, this time to Kent, while the other three games had ended in draws. Consequently, the white rose county were already an incredible 46.75 points behind Surrey, who remained top of the table, even though the sides in second, third and fourth places had played an extra game.

| Division One Results |
|---|

May 15-18
*Canterbury:-* **Kent beat Yorkshire by four wickets.** Yorkshire 239 (White 104, Khan 6-52) and 346 (Blakey 90, Dawson 87, Lehmann 72, Saggers 5-82, Patel 4-82); Kent 418 (Key 114, Fulton 71, Silverwood 4-82) and 169-6. **Kent 20pts, Yorkshire 4**

*Old Trafford:-* **Lancashire drew with Sussex.** Sussex 423 (Adams 217) and 221-7 (Montgomerie 80, Martin 4-53); Lancashire 366 (Law 218, Swann 51, Lewry 5-88). **Lancashire 11pts, Sussex 12**

*Taunton:-* **Somerset drew with Leicestershire.** Somerset 565 (Cox 176, Wood 79, Dutch 70, Bowler 60, Burns 52, Crowe 4-63); Leicestershire 288-8 (Sutcliffe 73, Stevens 73). **Somerset 11pts, Leicestershire 8**

*Edgbaston:-* **Warwickshire drew with Hampshire.** Warwickshire 472 (Knight 255*, Richardson 91); Hampshire 302 (Johnson 79, Pothas 59) and 306-5dec (Johnson 74*, Pothas 71*, Kenway 54). **Warwickshire 10pts, Hampshire 10**

## COUNTY CHAMPIONSHIP DIVISION ONE AT 18TH MAY

| Pos | Prv |  | P | Points | W | D | L | Bat | Bwl | Ded |
|---|---|---|---|---|---|---|---|---|---|---|
| 1 | 1 | Surrey | 3 | 55.75 | 3 | 0 | 0 | 11 | 9 | 0.25 |
| 2 | 2 | Leicestershire | 4 | 53.00 | 2 | 1 | 1 | 15 | 11 | 1.00 |
| 3 | 3 | Lancashire | 4 | 51.00 | 2 | 1 | 1 | 11 | 12 | 0.00 |
| 4 | 4 | Hampshire | 4 | 44.00 | 1 | 2 | 1 | 13 | 11 | 0.00 |
| 5 | 5 | Somerset | 3 | 39.00 | 1 | 2 | 0 | 11 | 8 | 0.00 |
| 6 | 7 | Kent | 3 | 33.00 | 1 | 1 | 1 | 10 | 7 | 0.00 |
| 7 | 6 | Sussex | 3 | 27.00 | 0 | 2 | 1 | 11 | 8 | 0.00 |
| 8 | 9 | Warwickshire | 3 | 16.00 | 0 | 1 | 2 | 5 | 7 | 0.00 |
| 9 | 8 | Yorkshire | 3 | 11.00 | 0 | 0 | 3 | 2 | 9 | 0.00 |

## NUL2 - Lions Slip Up At The Last In See-Saw Battle

The Surrey Lions slipped to a disappointing defeat at Bristol in their second NUL game of the season as Gloucestershire Gladiators snatched a dramatic one-wicket victory in a match that continually swung one way and then the other.

In bowler-friendly conditions, Surrey were given a stunning start by the excellent Ali Brown and Ian Ward as they raced to 86-0 in the fourteenth over, despite the fact that the ball was doing enough to beat the bat on numerous occasions. The loss of the openers to successive deliveries precipitated a ruinous collapse, however, to 103-7, and then to 131-9 with twelve overs of the innings remaining, as the impressive Jonathan Lewis took advantage of some unintelligent and inexperienced batting to tear out the middle order. A brave last-wicket partnership of thirty-two, which saw Ed Giddins equal his previous best limited-overs score of thirteen, eventually took the Lions through to a total of 163-9, which offered a realistic chance of victory in the prevailing conditions.

This feeling was confirmed as skilful use of the white ball by Bicknell and Giddins reduced the home side to 64-5, before Rikki Clarke entered the fray to remove the dangerous Jack Russell and deepen Gloucestershire's gloom. When Bicknell snared Taylor to make it 98-7 and Saqlain followed up by removing Averis at 115 it looked all over, but the battling Martyn Ball found a reliable ally in Lewis to take the Gladiators to within eighteen runs of their objective before Ball had his stumps rearranged by Clarke, making Surrey red-hot favourites again. Thanks to a pulled six by Lewis off the Lions' young all-rounder and numerous scampered singles, the last pair managed to push the total up to 160, at which point Lewis edged Clarke through a vacant slip area to pick up two lucky runs and leave his side within touching distance of victory. Ian Ward then immediately moved himself to slip, but was unable to hold on to a sharp catch, high to his right-hand side, from the very next ball, and the resulting run levelled the scores. A nervous push to midwicket by Mike Smith finally produced the winning single as Mark Ramprakash was unable to gather the ball cleanly in a potential run-out situation.

Gloucestershire's celebrations at snatching victory from the jaws of defeat after a fascinating battle merely added to Surrey's feelings of despair at losing out yet again in a tight finish in a one-day match. It was clearly an important scalp for the Gladiators to claim in the game between the bookies' two pre-season favourites to win the division two title.

## GLOUCESTERSHIRE GLADIATORS v SURREY LIONS at Bristol
### Played on Sunday 19th May    Gloucestershire Gladiators won by one wicket

Gloucestershire Gladiators won the toss and elected to field    Umpires:- Allan Jones & Neil Mallender

### SURREY LIONS

| Fall Of Wkt | Batsman | How | Out | Score | Balls | 4s | 6s |
|---|---|---|---|---|---|---|---|
| 1-86 | I.J. Ward * | | b Hardinges | 27 | 44 | 3 | 0 |
| 2-86 | A.D. Brown | | b Lewis | 54 | 41 | 8 | 1 |
| 4-97 | M.R. Ramprakash | c Russell | b Lewis | 3 | 11 | 0 | 0 |
| 3-86 | N. Shahid | c Ball | b Lewis | 0 | 5 | 0 | 0 |
| 5-103 | M.A. Carberry | run | out | 5 | 13 | 0 | 0 |
| 7-103 | A.J. Tudor | c Russell | b Lewis | 6 | 17 | 1 | 0 |
| 6-103 | R. Clarke | c Russell | b Hardinges | 0 | 3 | 0 | 0 |
| 8-122 | M.P. Bicknell | | b Smith | 15 | 34 | 0 | 0 |
| | J.N. Batty + | Not | Out | 28 | 61 | 0 | 0 |
| 9-131 | Saqlain Mushtaq | c Smith | b Ball | 3 | 7 | 0 | 0 |
| | E.S.H. Giddins | Not | Out | 13 | 34 | 1 | 0 |
| | Extras | (3lb, 6w) | | 9 | | | |
| | TOTAL | (45 overs) | (for 9 wkts) | 163 | | | |

| Bowler | O | M | R | W | NB | Wd |
|---|---|---|---|---|---|---|
| Smith | 9 | 0 | 35 | 1 | - | - |
| Averis | 9 | 1 | 32 | 0 | - | 1 |
| Lewis | 9 | 3 | 22 | 4 | - | 1 |
| Hardinges | 9 | 1 | 46 | 2 | - | 4 |
| Ball | 9 | 0 | 25 | 1 | - | - |

### GLOUCESTERSHIRE GLADIATORS

| Fall Of Wkt | Batsman | How | Out | Score | Balls | 4s | 6s |
|---|---|---|---|---|---|---|---|
| 1-2 | C.M. Spearman | c Ramprakash | b Bicknell | 2 | 5 | 0 | 0 |
| 2-7 | K.J. Barnett * | lbw | b Giddins | 3 | 11 | 0 | 0 |
| 3-32 | M.G.N. Windows | c Batty | b Bicknell | 9 | 22 | 1 | 0 |
| 4-63 | J.N. Snape | c Batty | b Giddins | 36 | 43 | 6 | 0 |
| 5-64 | M.A. Hardinges | c Batty | b Giddins | 2 | 19 | 0 | 0 |
| 6-77 | R.C. Russell + | c Batty | b Clarke | 2 | 6 | 0 | 0 |
| 9-146 | M.C.J. Ball | | b Clarke | 45 | 64 | 5 | 0 |
| 7-98 | C.G. Taylor | lbw | b Bicknell | 6 | 16 | 1 | 0 |
| 8-115 | J.M.M. Averis | c Giddins | b Saqlain | 7 | 27 | 1 | 0 |
| | J. Lewis | Not | Out | 27 | 32 | 0 | 1 |
| | A.M. Smith | Not | Out | 4 | 16 | 0 | 0 |
| | Extras | (9lb, 12w) | | 21 | | | |
| | TOTAL | (43.3 overs) | (for 9 wkts) | 164 | | | |

| Bowler | O | M | R | W | NB | Wd |
|---|---|---|---|---|---|---|
| Bicknell | 9 | 2 | 24 | 3 | - | 5 |
| Giddins | 9 | 0 | 31 | 3 | - | 1 |
| Tudor | 8 | 0 | 48 | 0 | - | - |
| Clarke | 8.3 | 1 | 32 | 2 | - | 2 |
| Saqlain Mushtaq | 9 | 2 | 20 | 1 | - | 4 |

## Other NUL Division Two Results

There were no real surprises in the second round of games as Essex, Lancashire and Northamptonshire completed comfortable victories over Derbyshire, Sussex and Middlesex respectively.

May 19

*Chelmsford:-* **Essex Eagles beat Derbyshire Scorpions by seven wickets.** Derbyshire 155 (44.2ov; Cowan 3-21, Clarke 3-29); Essex 159-3 (37ov). **Essex Eagles 4pts**

*Old Trafford:-* **Lancashire Lightning beat Sussex Sharks by four wickets.** Sussex 160 (41.4ov; Wood 3-21); Lancashire 161-6 (40.5ov; Law 71*, Yardy 3-36). **Lancashire Lightning 4pts**

*Northampton:-* **Northamptonshire Steelbacks beat Middlesex Crusaders by six wickets.** Middlesex 146 (40.2ov; Cousins 4-13); Northamptonshire 149-4 (31.3ov; Sales 66, Hussey 56). **Northamptonshire Steelbacks 4pts**

# 6 Stalled By Somerset

After such a traumatic pre-season the players had responded magnificently to play some outstanding cricket in the Championship and the county's dominant position at the head of the table was thoroughly deserved. Everyone was all too well aware that there was still a very long way to go, however, though it was nice to have started a campaign so positively for a change. There would be no need to play 'catch-up' this season and, with nine wins usually enough to secure the title, it appeared that our flying start had left us with the target of winning six of the thirteen games that remained. The fixture list suggested that most of the toughest games were to be played in the first half of the season with the final run-in offering two games against both Hampshire, a team with a woeful recent record against Surrey, and an ageing Leicestershire outfit, who might be feeling the effects of a long hard season by that stage.

The only real cloud on the horizon was the realisation that there weren't going to be too many more occasions this season when Keith Medlycott would have a full squad to select from, since the international programme had got under way the previous week, with Alec Stewart having gained his widely predicted recall and Graham Thorpe and Mark Butcher having also played in the first Test against Sri Lanka. These three, plus Alex Tudor, who was also in line for an England recall, were therefore unlikely to play too many more matches.

The old cliché about taking one match at a time was as relevant now as ever, though, and the next fixture, a home encounter with Somerset, certainly promised to be another hard-fought battle. The 'cidermen' had made a very solid start to their campaign, including an impressive victory of their own over the reigning champions, and would clearly be boosted by the fact that Marcus Trescothick and Andy Caddick were permitted to play for them. It promised to be quite a scrap, especially since the combatants were, even at this early stage of the season, the only teams remaining unbeaten in the division.

---

**FRIZZELL COUNTY CHAMPIONSHIP - MATCH FOUR**

### SURREY versus SOMERSET
### at The AMP Oval

### First Day - Friday 24th May

### Surrey 220; Somerset 10-0

***The Teams And The Toss*** - *Surrey go into the match with, arguably, their full-strength side, and the only change to the team that beat Lancashire being the return of Saqlain Mushtaq in place of Azhar Mahmood, who had proved so successful as a temporary replacement. Somerset, whose recent record at The Oval is poor, appear to be just one player short of their best eleven, with Richard Johnson missing out because of a knee injury. This blow is, however, softened by the recovery of Steffan Jones from a damaged hamstring. The match starts forty-five minutes late as a result of heavy overnight, and early morning, rain, with the loss of twelve overs from the day's allocation. Undeterred by the damp conditions, Mark Butcher elects to bat when Marcus Trescothick, the Somerset skipper, calls incorrectly at the toss.*

In fast-improving weather conditions, the loss of a dozen overs hardly seems to matter as the match gets off to an eventful start, with Somerset capturing the first two Surrey wickets in just eight deliveries. Having got off the mark with an airy square drive for four from the second delivery of Caddick's opening over, Mark Butcher has his off stump flattened by a fine yorker next up, then Mark Ramprakash falls to Matt Bulbeck's second ball when a booming inswinger finds bat and pad on its way into the hands of Michael Burns at short leg. Surrey are 7-2 and the innings is already in need of some serious repair work.

Ian Ward and Graham Thorpe are the men entrusted with relaying the foundations and they cope well in their different ways. While Thorpe beds himself in carefully, Ward is responsible for most of the early scoring, playing especially well on the leg-side as he drives Caddick and clips Bulbeck for threes in successive overs. The England paceman is clearly the greater threat at this stage, inducing thick-edged boundaries from both batsmen, while his left-arm partner soon loses his line badly after a promising start, and concedes two wides in the sixth, and final, over of his first spell.

Having successfully stabilised the innings after its woeful beginnings, Surrey continue to progress nicely as Thorpe drives Caddick to the extra cover boundary and Ward greets Steffan Jones, Bulbeck's replacement at the pavilion end, with two boundaries, a drive wide of mid-on which brings up the fifty, and a superbly timed off-drive.

Alas, the recovery is brought to a shuddering halt in the following over when Caddick claims the scalp of Thorpe through a tame clip off the toes straight to Burns at backward square leg. Although there is no power in the shot, the fielder almost spills the catch, juggling the ball twice before eventually holding on at the third attempt to complete a very disappointing dismissal for both the batsman and his team. As Thorpe departs for nineteen, with his side 56-3, Somerset are clearly on top again.

Perhaps unsettled by the loss of his partner, Ward momentarily loses his fluency, miscuing an on-drive and then picking up two runs from a thick edge backward of point, whereas Ali Brown makes an explosive start to his innings by pulling his first delivery, from Jones, high over midwicket for six and piercing the off-side field for two further boundaries later in the same over. He then welcomes Keith Parsons' entry into the attack for the penultimate over before lunch with a straight-driven four before forcing a short-of-a-length delivery from Jones to the rope at backward point to take his score to twenty-five not out from just sixteen balls at the end of the truncated first session of the game.

*Lunch:- Surrey 90-3 (Ward 36\*, Brown 25\*) from 22 overs*

Things are rather different after the break, however, as Ward starts with pleasing strokes through mid-off and midwicket off Caddick, while Brown is becalmed and beaten outside the off stump on several occasions by the reunited Somerset opening bowlers. It seems only a matter of time before a good delivery finds the outside edge and so it proves as Caddick produces an absolute snorter to unseat Brown, shortly after Ward has raised the fifty partnership with an extra-cover drive for four off Bulbeck. As he makes his way from the field, with the game in the balance at 106-4, Surrey's middle-order linchpin might actually feel that he has done well to get a touch to a wicked delivery that has lifted and left the bat on its way through to Rob Turner behind the stumps.

Fortunately for the hosts, Ward is looking in good form, reaching a skilfully-composed 85-ball half-century in the thirty-second over with a straight-driven boundary off Bulbeck, while Stewart starts in the same confident mode as Brown before him, twice picking up three runs with leg-side strokes off Caddick. The tall paceman is quick to gain revenge on his England colleague, however, as another fine delivery takes the outside edge of a defensive bat and comes to rest safely in the hands of Peter Bowler at first slip. Caddick is on fire, Somerset are cock-a-hoop and Surrey are in some trouble at 120-5 as Stewart exits with just seven runs to his name.

And it's not long before the home county is plunged into deeper trouble. With the total advanced by just eight runs, courtesy of two well-timed fours by Ward off Bulbeck, the visitors capture a sixth Surrey wicket. Taking a leaf out of his new ball partner's book, the left-arm seamer wreaks vengeance on his tormentor with a well-directed outswinger which Ward's defensive bat can only direct to second slip, where Keith Dutch takes a good low catch. The left-hander opener has played extremely well for his sixty-two but, in the end, he has been forced to bow to the dangerous pairing of Caddick and Bulbeck who have, between them, reduced Surrey to a distinctly rocky 128-6.

A degree of relief is at hand for the home side, however, as the two opening bowlers, having delivered thirty of the thirty-six overs so far bowled, are rested shortly after Ward's departure. Steffan Jones takes over from Bulbeck (13-1-37-2) at the pavilion end and is instantly forced to the cover boundary by Alex Tudor, while Keith Parsons replaces Caddick (19-7-53-4) at the Vauxhall end.

Given their team's predicament, the Surrey seventh-wicket pair are understandably cautious initially, though Tudor does produce two further classy strokes, a hook off Jones and an extra-cover drive off Parsons, to increase his boundary tally to three as grey clouds gather around the ground. Rain looks inevitable and, shortly after Bicknell takes his side past 150 with a square-cut four at the expense of Parsons, a shower drives the players and umpires from the field. Further bursts of rain follow, one or two of them being quite heavy, though fortunately not prolonged, and as a result the umpires sensibly decide to take an early tea.

*Tea:- Surrey 153-6 (Tudor 16\*, Bicknell 9\*) from 45.3 overs*

Eighty minutes after the players had left the field they return, with a further sixteen overs having been lost from the day's standard 104-over requirement. The break has done Surrey no favours, since a rested Caddick is straight back into the attack and immediately back among the wickets as his first delivery, an excellent yorker, rips out Bicknell's leg stump - it's 153-7 and the delighted bowler has another five-for to add to his career collection.

It very nearly becomes a six-for seconds later, too, when he produces an almost identical delivery for Ian Salisbury's first ball. Luckily for Surrey, their leg-spinner is alert to the danger and manages to squeeze the ball out into the midwicket gap for two runs.

Despite their side's current predicament, both batsmen keep the scoreboard ticking over nicely, with Salisbury cleverly deflecting a Caddick delivery to the third man boundary, and Tudor picking up two fours in the following over from Jones, even though one is a top-edged cut over the slip cordon. For the third time in the innings, however, the aggrieved bowler quickly gets even with the batsman, as the strongly-built Somerset fast bowler nips a ball back into Tudor's pads in his next over and wins an lbw verdict from umpire John Holder. The decline of Surrey's innings therefore continues as Tudor goes for twenty-four with the score now 169-8.

Faced with the prospect of their side failing to collect a batting bonus point, the Surrey spin twins, now united in batting, set about the task of restoring some order to proceedings in their contrasting styles. While Salisbury is steadiness personified, Saqlain is soon bristling with aggressive intent, driving Jones to the rope at extra cover and then repeating the stroke two overs later against Bulbeck, the bustling paceman's replacement at the pavilion end. With Caddick losing a little of his menace after a long stint at the Vauxhall end, there appears to be just a glimmer of light at the end of the tunnel for Surrey, and successive clips backward of square leg by Saqlain off Bulbeck, for four and one respectively, confirm this by taking the hosts through to the relatively prosperous position of 200-8.

Any prospects of a second batting point are quickly dimmed nine runs later, however, as Bulbeck produces another of his big inswingers to defeat Saqlain's hit to leg and earn a highly questionable lbw verdict from umpire Holder.

With just one wicket now to fall, Caddick is rested, though Surrey's hopes that this might enable a significant last-wicket stand to develop are crushed six overs later when Salisbury is dislodged by an outstanding Bulbeck delivery that swings into the right-hander before seaming away to take the outside edge. Turner completes the catch to leave the home team all out for a rather disappointing 220, though, in their defence, it should be pointed out that only one batsman has fallen to a poor stroke, while nine have been dismissed by good deliveries. This reflects much credit on Caddick and Bulbeck, therefore, and they receive a well-deserved round of applause as they lead their team from the field.

Surrey now need similar performances from their own highly dangerous combination of Bicknell and Tudor, though they are unable to part the Somerset openers during the four overs that complete an interesting and highly competitive day's cricket.

Close:- Somerset 10-0 (Cox 8*, Trescothick 1*) from 4 overs

## VIEW FROM THE DRESSING ROOM

*We had Saqi back for this match, but Azhar had done a brilliant job as his stand-in. Were you surprised at how well he had bowled, and would you say bowling is his strongest suit, or is there not much to choose between his batting and bowling?*
**MARTIN BICKNELL** - Yes, he bowled brilliantly - he's quicker than he looks and he's got a lot going for him. He's a good fielder, he can bat and he's great to have in the side. I think most people realised he'd be an excellent bowler in English conditions, and I would say that in this country he'll be more effective as a bowler than a batsman, though he's undeniably a good all-rounder.

### Second Day - Saturday 25th May

### Surrey 220 and 87-3; Somerset 253

After an erratic opening over from Martin Bicknell, which costs five runs, and a really woeful one from Alex Tudor, during which three half-volleys are dispatched to the boundary, the Surrey opening bowlers dominate the early exchanges on day two. Tudor, in particular, comes back magnificently from his first-over mauling and strikes a major blow for his side by removing Marcus Trescothick with the final ball of his second over, a nasty lifting delivery angled across the left-hander that the batsman edges high to Alec Stewart's left-hand side. The England opener departs for seven and the score is 28-1.

Inspired by his success, Tudor looks sharp in pace and causes numerous problems for the batsmen, even though Michael Burns does manage to clip him twice through square leg for four. Bicknell is meanwhile probing away remorselessly at the other end, but his luck is out as Jamie Cox slices a drive at catchable height between gully and backward point and Burns edges a drive over the slip cordon, both of these false strokes costing the bowler four runs and taking the Somerset total close to fifty.

This milestone is passed shortly afterwards, courtesy of a square drive for three by Cox off Tudor, but the score hasn't moved on any further two overs later when the big Surrey paceman induces a loose drive from Burns which results in an edge to Ali Brown at first slip. Somerset are 52-2 and this is developing into a close and interesting contest.

Before too long, the balance swings in favour of the home side, however, as Cox goes with the score at 61, and Keith Parsons follows his team-mate back to the pavilion eight runs later. Somerset's Tasmanian import becomes Tudor's third victim in the twenty-fourth over when his middle stump is sent flying in spectacular fashion by a perfect yorker, while the Taunton-born all-rounder falls prey to Bicknell four overs later, in the bowler's first over of a new spell as replacement for Tudor at the pavilion end. Parsons' dismissal is far less conclusive than Cox's, though, as umpire Holder decides that the batsman's significant forward stride is insufficient reason for him to reject Bicknell's appeal for lbw.

Somerset are now really on the ropes, even though they manage to regain a degree of control through the fifth-wicket pairing of Peter Bowler and Ian Blackwell. They safely negotiate the final stages of a luckless spell by Jimmy Ormond from the Vauxhall end, before Blackwell takes successive fours off Bicknell with beautifully timed strokes through, and then over, extra cover.

With lunch approaching, Saqlain Mushtaq is chosen to replace Ormond, receiving welcoming applause on his return to the side, while Ian Salisbury makes it an all-spin attack when he relieves Bicknell for the final over of the session from the pavilion end.

Although the spinners are immediately into their stride they can't prevent Bowler from nudging his side up to the three-figure mark before the break, and honours appear to be fairly even again as the players troop off the field, despite the magnificent efforts of all the Surrey bowlers, led by Alex Tudor, who boasts figures of 13-7-30-3.

*Lunch:- Somerset 100-4 (Bowler 14\*, Blackwell 19\*) from 37 overs*

It's no surprise to see Tudor back into the attack immediately after the break, though he doesn't start too well again as Blackwell cuts his first ball wide of a diving gully for four in an over that costs eight runs. At the other end, the Surrey captain opts to continue with Saqlain, and it proves to be a wise move as Bowler advances down the pitch to the off-spinner's fourth ball, only to offer a defensive bat and edge to Thorpe at slip.

At 111-5 it's 'even-stevens' again, though Tudor comes desperately close to giving his side a clear advantage on three occasions in his next two overs - Blackwell slices a drive inches over the head of backward point and follows up by edging just short of slip, then Rob Turner looks on anxiously as a short-pitched delivery rebounds off his upper body and drops down perilously close to his leg stump.

While Turner continues to look ill-at-ease, Blackwell quickly recovers from his moments of good fortune by cutting and pulling Saqlain for two fours in quick succession, before moving through to a very fine 44-ball fifty with off-driven, cover-driven and pulled boundaries in an expensive over from Tudor. It is already clear that a well-established Blackwell is a real danger to the home county's prospects, and a glorious back-foot forcing stroke to the fence at cover in the Surrey fast bowler's next over confirms a growing feeling that the tide is turning in Somerset's favour again. Consequently, Butcher sensibly decides to rest Tudor, switching Saqlain to the pavilion end and recalling Ormond at the Vauxhall end. Although Turner struggles on, being beaten three times in one Ormond over, the bowling changes fail to have the desired effect as the visitors cruise past 150, with the partnership reaching fifty when Blackwell again takes two fours from a Saqlain over.

Finally, with the score at 165-5, an opportunity to part the sixth-wicket pair comes Surrey's way when Turner, having moved uncertainly on to ten, edges Ormond at a comfortable height to Bicknell at second slip. It looks to be a routine chance but, to the dismay of the bowler and the home supporters, the catch goes down, and Turner promptly rubs salt into the wound by cutting uppishly through backward point for four. A wicket at this stage could have restored parity to the game but, instead, Somerset assume control as Blackwell drives and cuts the unfortunate Ormond for two further boundaries in the strapping paceman's next over. Then, to add further to the former Leicestershire man's frustration, even Turner gets in on the act, pulling successive balls to the rope at midwicket with the most convincing strokes of his innings by far.

With the pressure growing on his side in the afternoon sunshine, Butcher clearly has to ring the changes again, and recalls Bicknell and Salisbury, both of whom have an initial restraining effect. The much-needed sixth wicket is not forthcoming, however, as the Somerset two-hundred arrives in the sixty-third over, bringing the visitors in clear view of their hosts' inadequate total. A Salisbury full-toss then enables Turner to find the boundary at deep backward square leg and, in the process, complete a priceless century partnership, before

Blackwell moves into the nineties with a well-timed forcing stroke through mid-off in the next over from Bicknell. At this point, Surrey appear to be heading for a very sizeable first innings deficit but, just in the nick of time, their senior bowler comes to the rescue with a burst of three wickets in nine balls.

The initial breakthrough comes with Somerset just three runs shy of Surrey's total, when Turner's thoroughly unimpressive, yet valuable, innings of thirty-four ends with a tame chip into the hands of Tudor at mid-on, then Bicknell storms through the breach he has made for himself, capturing two further hard-earned wickets in his next over.

After taking his side into the lead with two runs from a thick edge to third man, Keith Dutch edges an outswinger to Ramprakash at third slip two balls later, then Matt Bulbeck, having clipped his first ball to the square leg boundary, is summarily cleaned up by the third ball he faces, another of those deadly inswinging yorkers that have been a feature of the game thus far.

Suddenly, with Somerset 225-8, the game is back in the balance, though the dangerous Blackwell still offers his team the chance of gaining a substantial lead as he is fed singles in order to get Andy Caddick on strike. The England seamer looks more than capable, however, as he blasts Bicknell over mid-off for four, and it turns out that the front-line batsman is the one to depart first.

Having made his way steadily through the nineties, and as far as ninety-eight, by taking the singles offered to him, Blackwell is undone by a skilful piece of bowling by Salisbury, whose perfectly-pitched googly, delivered from round the wicket to the left-hander, wins an lbw verdict as the ball straightens to hit the batsman's front pad. Having barely got half-forward, the immensely powerful and promising 23-year-old can have no complaints about umpire Holder's decision as he departs the scene two runs short of what would have been a well-deserved century and receives an appropriate reception from the Oval crowd.

With nine wickets having now fallen, the tea interval is delayed as Somerset's last-wicket pair try to extend their side's current seventeen-run advantage. Caddick does his best, smiting Salisbury for a six over midwicket, but Steffan Jones finds the leg-spinner a total mystery, surviving dropped catches in successive overs - a very sharp one, low and to the left of Ward at silly point, and a simple one to Thorpe at slip - one each side of the arrival of the visitors' 250. The Surrey 'leggie' deserves better, but at least the partnership adds only two more runs before his spin twin, brought on to replace Bicknell at the Vauxhall end, defeats the charging Caddick with embarrassing ease to give Stewart a very straightforward stumping.

Somerset therefore end up with a lead of thirty-three runs and owe a huge debt of gratitude to Blackwell, who has looked far and away the best of their batsmen. All five members of the Surrey attack have performed well to keep their team in contention, and it is again worth noting that the vast majority of the wickets have been gained with good deliveries, as opposed to being gifted to the fielding side by the batsmen.

*Tea:- Between Innings*

Somerset, and Caddick, again have the advantage of a short session as the game recommences after tea with twenty-seven overs remaining to be bowled. Perhaps conscious of the threat posed by the visitors' opening bowlers, Butcher and Ward get away to a slow start before the latter explodes confidently out of his blocks with a well-struck boundary in each of three successive overs. Butcher, on the other hand, fails to fully settle and, with Surrey still seven runs short of clearing their first innings deficit, he is trapped on the crease by a Caddick inswinger, allowing umpire Holder's index finger to make its third appearance of the day in response to a confident lbw appeal.

This is clearly a serious blow for Surrey, though they find comfort in the fact that Mark Ramprakash is instantly into his stride with two neat deflections behind square on the off-side. Since neither opening bowler is looking quite as threatening as in the first innings there are high hopes of a rapid recovery from the loss of Butcher, but these are quickly dashed by a terrible mix-up which results in the run out of Ramprakash for seven, with Surrey just one run in credit. A surprisingly heated debate on the pavilion balcony about who is to blame continues long after Ramprakash's return to the dressing room, though everyone agrees that a serious breakdown in communication has been the principal stumbling block - the Surrey number three's firm drive to mid-on and instant sprint down the wicket has met with no response from the motionless Ward and left Ramprakash to attempt an inevitably doomed return to the crease from whence he came.

What's done is done, however, and Surrey now have to hope that the left-handed pairing of Ward and Thorpe can dig them out of the hole in which they now find themselves. The partnership is almost over before it has begun, however, as Thorpe is forced to dig out a testing Caddick yorker first ball and then, immediately afterwards, edges Bulbeck high to the right of Keith Parsons at third slip and breathes a sigh of relief as the pace of the ball forces it through the fielder's outstretched hands and on to the third man boundary.

Apparently unruffled by this escape, the England left-hander takes Surrey beyond the fifty mark with successive cover-driven fours off Caddick and follows up by clipping Steffan Jones to the rope at midwicket as soon as the muscular seamer joins the attack in place of Bulbeck. With Ward unfurling an attractive cover drive of his own at Caddick's expense and Thorpe continuing his run of fine strokes with two further boundaries, one off each bowler, Surrey are suddenly surging onwards and upwards. The fifty partnership arrives shortly afterwards, in exactly ten overs, when Ward runs the newly introduced Blackwell to third man for three runs, but the Somerset left-arm spinner then strikes back with his very next ball as Thorpe appears to top-edge a sweep and sees Michael Burns, at backward short leg, hang on to a fine reflex catch at chest height. Suddenly, with Thorpe's departure for twenty-nine at 84-3, the visitors look to be back on top and it is left to the two Ians, Ward and Salisbury, to ensure that no further loss is sustained in the last four overs of the day.

*Close:- Surrey 87-3 (Ward 34\*, Salisbury 0\*) from 27 overs*

## VIEWS FROM THE DRESSING ROOM

*Tudes started the season really well and bowled a great first spell here. Do you think he had benefited from his time at the Academy in the winter?*
**MARTIN BICKNELL** - Yes, he bowled really well against Sussex, and at Headingley, and we thought he had more control this year. He really hit his straps and bowled a magic spell on the second morning when he bowled three of them out and looked a class bowler. It was good to see him firing on all cylinders.

*Many of the first Academy intake suffered a very poor 2002 season. Do you have any ideas as to why this might have been?*
**MARTIN BICKNELL** - No, it was quite bizarre really. They are all young cricketers, of course, and you do tend to have more swings in your form when you're younger, but for nearly all of them to suffer that fate was strange. They are all good cricketers, though, and I'm sure they will all bounce back.

*Ian Blackwell played another very impressive innings against us in this match and, in some ways, he reminds me of Ali Brown. How highly do you rate him, and do you feel that, internationally, there is a danger that he could, like Browny, get labelled as a one-day specialist?*
**MARTIN BICKNELL** - Yes, I rate him highly. Time will tell how he goes on against genuine Test bowling, but at county level he is certainly already very destructive - when it's his day and he's feeling confident he can take sides apart. We are always aware of what he can do and we

do try to bowl a certain way at him - it doesn't always work, but some days he's going to come off, and on good pitches he's going to have more good days than bad. And, yes, I do think there is a danger that he may get labelled as a one-day batsman. His game is perfectly adapted to one-day cricket and that's where his initial opportunities have come at international level, so there is a chance that he's going to get pigeon-holed.

### Third Day - Sunday 26th May

### Surrey 220 and 87-3; Somerset 253 (No Play - Rain)

With the game nicely poised, it is a great shame that the third day's play is completely washed out by heavy overnight rain and further showers at regular intervals during the morning and early afternoon. Play is finally, and inevitably, abandoned for the day at 2.45pm and, with just one day left in the match, the prospect of a positive result has been drastically reduced.

### Fourth Day - Monday 27th May

### Surrey 220 and 332; Somerset 253 and 45-1

### Match Drawn
### Surrey 8pts, Somerset 9

With the weather having relented on what is forecast to be a sunshine-and-showers type of day, play starts on time, and in explosive fashion, with Salisbury driving Bulbeck's opening delivery through the covers for four and then being adjudged caught at short leg from the second. The batsman looks extremely disappointed with umpire Burgess' decision, and understandably so, since it is obvious, even from the distance of the pavilion, that the bowler's big inswinger has missed the inside edge of the bat by a considerable distance and ballooned up solely off the batsman's pad.

The new pairing of Ward and Ali Brown soon make this nightmare start a distant memory, however, as they batter Bulbeck for five fours, and a total of twenty-three runs, in his next two overs, sending the score racing into three figures and taking Ward close to a second impressive half-century in the match. That milestone is duly reached in the next over from Caddick when the left-handed opener drives his 91st delivery through mid-off for two.

The Somerset opening bowlers are getting into their stride now, though, and the pace of scoring rather slackens as Bulbeck repays the faith shown in him by his captain by putting the long-hops and full-tosses of his opening overs behind him during an improving spell. He even has Ward, becalmed since reaching his fifty, dropped by Dutch at second slip when a very difficult low chance squirms from the fielder's right hand as he dives across in front of first slip.

The reprieved Ward finally moves his score on from fifty-two in the next over from the left-arm seamer, before Brown brings up the fifty partnership and the Surrey 150 in successive overs. With the home side leading by almost 120, balance has again been restored to the game, though Somerset's hopes of bowling Surrey out receive a setback with the loss of Ian Blackwell, who injures a finger in his opening over of the day when trying to stop a straight-driven boundary by Brown.

As a consequence of Blackwell's departure from the field, Caddick, the man originally replaced by the left-arm spinner, makes an immediate return to the attack at the pavilion end to partner Steffan Jones in a double bowling change. Fortunately for the home team, Jones again starts poorly, with Ward twice driving him to the rope at cover in his opening overs, while Caddick is quickly seen off by Brown, who cuts him for four and then blasts successive boundaries, through mid-on and over cover, later in the same over.

The pendulum is now swinging towards Surrey as the visitors start to look bereft of confidence and ideas, so Trescothick finally turns to his off-spinner, Keith Dutch, for the first time in the match. The former Middlesex man has been criminally ignored until now, and appears to have been given this opportunity only because of the continued absence of Blackwell, yet he soon provides his skipper with a much needed breakthrough by removing Ward with his fifth delivery, an off-break that turns sufficiently to find the edge of a defensive bat on its way to Peter Bowler at slip. Although the Surrey opener's carefully constructed sixty-seven gives him an aggregate of 139 runs for the match, he must be disappointed at having failed to reach a century in either knock as he leaves the field to well-deserved applause. His dismissal also puts this fascinating match back into the melting pot again, with Surrey's score of 174-5 leaving them 141 runs in front.

The home county clearly won't want to lose another wicket before lunch, since that would give Somerset the edge going in to the afternoon session, but that is exactly what happens as Dutch strikes again in his fourth over, with the score advanced by seventeen runs. Having swept a full-toss to the midwicket fence earlier in the over to move within two runs of his fifty, Brown becomes another contentious victim for umpire Burgess when he sweeps again and misses a delivery which appears to be heading down the leg-side. The most worrying thing about the former Somerset all-rounder's resulting lbw decision, for both the batsman and spectators, is the fact that his finger is raised before focus can be switched from the batsman to the umpire. It's not impossible that his verdict is correct, but it certainly needs greater consideration than it has been given.

Alec Stewart and Alex Tudor take their side safely through the last two overs of the session and Surrey are, effectively, 163-6 at the break, with a minimum of 67 overs remaining for play.

*Lunch:- Surrey 196-6 (Stewart 11\*, Tudor 4\*) from 56 overs*

Having returned to the field for the last half-a-dozen overs before the break, suggesting that his finger injury isn't too serious after all, Blackwell comes back into the attack for the opening over of the afternoon session. He is partnered, predictably enough, by a weary-looking Caddick, who is immediately driven and clipped for two boundaries in his first over by Stewart as Surrey pass two-hundred. Blackwell then disappears from the attack after a solitary maiden to be replaced by Dutch, and the off-spinner proves much more to Tudor's liking as the batsman hammers the first ball through the covers for four.

Disappointingly, Trescothick's captaincy continues to be bereft of any imagination, a point amply demonstrated by the way he continues to bowl Caddick into the ground, and, though the scoring rate dips for a few overs before Tudor cuts Dutch for two further boundaries, the home team seems to be sailing clear of any potential choppy waters. The only moment of real alarm, in fact, comes when the Surrey paceman survives a confident shout for a catch at the wicket off the persevering Caddick, with his score on eleven and Somerset still very much harbouring hopes of victory. Umpire Burgess' rejection of the appeal at least proves that his debatable decisions earlier in the day were not indicative of any bias towards his former county, while Tudor remains unfazed by the incident and immediately smites Dutch over the square leg boundary to extend the home county's advantage to almost two-hundred.

With time running out for his side as the seventh-wicket partnership becomes worth fifty runs, the Somerset skipper keeps his England colleague going at the pavilion end, even though Caddick's performance is becoming increasingly erratic, with the occasional good lifting delivery being balanced by a tendency to overstep the crease once in almost every over. In an echo of the previous match, against Lancashire, there is no doubt that the visiting side's bowling is not of the same standard this time around as it had been in the first innings, and thoughts begin to turn to the possibility of a Surrey declaration, even if only to set Somerset a theoretical target.

This idea grows more appealing as Stewart slog-sweeps Dutch for six and Tudor follows up with a similar stroke for four as the total passes 250 and then 260.

In an effort to stem the flow, Bulbeck and Jones are introduced into the attack and before too long the left-armer finally breaks the Stewart-Tudor alliance for his captain when Stewart is adjudged lbw to another big inswinger, shortly after completing an important half-century from 88 balls. Having started his innings with his team still in a position of some danger, Surrey's honorary club captain receives a warm ovation as he returns to the dressing room with the game looking increasingly likely to end in a draw. Certainly, with only forty-five overs remaining for play and the lead standing at 245, it appears to be a case of now or never if Butcher wishes to declare and let his bowlers loose on the Somerset batsmen.

The eighth-wicket pair, Tudor and Bicknell, give a clear indication that we are heading for a turgid final session, however, as they gather runs at no great pace, the only boundaries coming from two edges by the latter, and Trescothick, realising that his side's chance of victory has now gone, falls into line by turning to a defensive bowling partnership of Parsons and Blackwell.

With tea almost upon us, the game finally dies on its feet as Surrey pass three-hundred mark before losing Tudor for forty-four when he makes room to cut and is bowled by Blackwell's arm ball.

*Tea:- Surrey 310-8 (Bicknell 23\*, Saqlain 1\*) from 89 overs*

Had it not been for the loss of the third day's play to rain there seems little doubt that we would have witnessed a positive result in this match but, instead, the final session sees us being 'treated' to the sight of the Surrey lower-order having a net against Parsons and Blackwell. The left-arm spinner eventually turns a delivery enough to have Saqlain taken by Bowler at slip for ten, before the innings ends in the next over from Parsons when Ormond edges a drive at his third ball to be caught at second slip by Dutch. The home side therefore finishes 299 runs ahead with eighteen overs left to play.

Naturally, the contest is aborted at the earliest possible opportunity, with eight of the last hour's sixteen overs remaining to be bowled, though there is still enough time for Tudor to claim the wicket of Trescothick for the second time in the match, in exactly the same manner as in the first innings.

Apart from a volley of fours from the Somerset openers, the most entertaining moment of the final session is provided by one of the many Oval pigeons. Having got its feet tangled up in a white plastic carrier bag while wandering around near the wicket, it provides those in the ground with a humorous spectacle as it tries desperately to fly off but finds it cannot make any headway because of the effect of the plastic 'parachute' that is trailing behind it. After Ian Ward fails with a couple of attempts to catch the bird, it is eventually caught and untangled by Michael Burns.

**Surrey 220 and 332; Somerset 253 and 45-1**
**Match Drawn. Surrey 8pts, Somerset 9**

## VIEWS FROM THE DRESSING ROOM

*The loss of day three to rain rather spoiled an interesting contest. I assume we felt that we didn't have enough time to declare and bowl Somerset out on the final afternoon? Or were we just happy to maintain our lead at the top of the table after three wins from the first three games?*

**MARTIN BICKNELL** - It would have been an excellent game of cricket had it run its natural course. We didn't feel we could set them any sort of target because we would only have had about fifty overs to bowl them out. As the bowling side, you just don't win those sort of games because there's not enough time, and you just give the opposition a chance to pick up a win they have not deserved. And at that stage of the season I had them down as a team that was going to be up there challenging for the title at the end of the season.

**IAN WARD** - Yes, it petered out into a bit of a tame one in the end. You have to decide whether you're going to gamble and go for the win, or just admit that the weather has beaten you. Unfortunately, on this occasion, Butch decided that too much time had gone out of the game. I remember talking with him and I agreed that we didn't need to try and contrive a result.

### SURREY v SOMERSET at The AMP Oval.  Played from 24th to 27th May
Surrey won the toss and elected to bat  Umpires:- John Holder and Graham Burgess

#### SURREY - First Innings

| Fall Of Wkt | Batsman | How | Out | Score | Balls | 4s | 6s |
|---|---|---|---|---|---|---|---|
| 1-4 | M.A. Butcher * |  | b Caddick | 4 | 3 | 1 | 0 |
| 6-128 | I.J. Ward | c Dutch | b Bulbeck | 62 | 101 | 7 | 0 |
| 2-7 | M.R. Ramprakash | c Burns | b Bulbeck | 1 | 3 | 0 | 0 |
| 3-56 | G.P. Thorpe | c Burns | b Caddick | 19 | 44 | 3 | 0 |
| 4-106 | A.D. Brown | c Turner | b Caddick | 30 | 38 | 5 | 1 |
| 5-120 | A.J. Stewart + | c Bowler | b Caddick | 7 | 15 | 0 | 0 |
| 8-169 | A.J. Tudor |  | b Jones | 24 | 57 | 5 | 0 |
| 7-153 | M.P. Bicknell |  | b Caddick | 9 | 24 | 1 | 0 |
| 10-220 | I.D.K. Salisbury | c Turner | b Bulbeck | 26 | 80 | 3 | 0 |
| 9-209 | Saqlain Mushtaq | lbw | b Bulbeck | 21 | 38 | 3 | 0 |
|  | J. Ormond | Not | Out | 7 | 12 | 1 | 0 |
|  | Extras | (6lb, 4w) |  | 10 |  |  |  |
|  | **TOTAL** | **(69.1 overs)** |  | **220** |  |  |  |

| Bowler | O | M | R | W | NB | Wd |
|---|---|---|---|---|---|---|
| Caddick | 28 | 10 | 66 | 5 | - | - |
| Bulbeck | 20.1 | 2 | 60 | 4 | - | 2 |
| Jones | 17 | 3 | 69 | 1 | - | - |
| Parsons | 4 | 0 | 19 | 0 | - | - |

#### SOMERSET - First Innings

| Fall Of Wkt | Batsman | How | Out | Score | Balls | 4s | 6s |
|---|---|---|---|---|---|---|---|
| 3-61 | J. Cox |  | b Tudor | 34 | 67 | 5 | 0 |
| 1-28 | M.E. Trescothick * | c Stewart | b Tudor | 7 | 28 | 1 | 0 |
| 2-52 | M. Burns | c Brown | b Tudor | 13 | 27 | 3 | 0 |
| 5-111 | P.D. Bowler | c Thorpe | b Saqlain | 21 | 66 | 3 | 0 |
| 4-69 | K.A. Parsons | lbw | b Bicknell | 5 | 19 | 1 | 0 |
| 9-237 | I.D. Blackwell | lbw | b Salisbury | 98 | 112 | 15 | 0 |
| 6-217 | R.J. Turner + | c Tudor | b Bicknell | 34 | 96 | 5 | 0 |
| 7-221 | K.P. Dutch | c Ramprakash | b Bicknell | 3 | 6 | 0 | 0 |
| 8-225 | M.P.L. Bulbeck |  | b Bicknell | 4 | 3 | 1 | 0 |
| 10-253 | A.R. Caddick | st Stewart | b Saqlain | 15 | 31 | 1 | 1 |
|  | P.S. Jones | Not | Out | 4 | 28 | 0 | 0 |
|  | Extras | (1b, 10lb, 2w, 2nb) |  | 15 |  |  |  |
|  | **TOTAL** | **(80.2 overs)** |  | **253** |  |  |  |

| Bowler | O | M | R | W | NB | Wd |
|---|---|---|---|---|---|---|
| Bicknell | 22 | 4 | 72 | 4 | - | - |
| Tudor | 19 | 7 | 64 | 3 | - | - |
| Ormond | 13 | 2 | 53 | 0 | 1 | 1 |
| Saqlain Mushtaq | 13.2 | 3 | 31 | 2 | - | - |
| Salisbury | 13 | 3 | 22 | 1 | - | - |

#### SURREY - Second Innings (Trailing by 33 on first innings)

| Fall Of Wkt | Batsman | How | Out | Score | Balls | 4s | 6s |
|---|---|---|---|---|---|---|---|
| 1-26 | M.A. Butcher * | lbw | b Caddick | 9 | 37 | 0 | 0 |
| 5-174 | I.J. Ward | c Bowler | b Dutch | 67 | 143 | 11 | 0 |
| 2-34 | M.R. Ramprakash | run | out | 7 | 8 | 0 | 0 |
| 3-84 | G.P. Thorpe | c Burns | b Blackwell | 29 | 36 | 6 | 0 |
| 4-91 | I.D.K. Salisbury | c Burns | b Bulbeck | 4 | 11 | 1 | 0 |
| 6-191 | A.D. Brown | lbw | b Dutch | 48 | 72 | 8 | 0 |
| 7-278 | A.J. Stewart + | lbw | b Bulbeck | 53 | 97 | 6 | 1 |
| 8-307 | A.J. Tudor |  | b Blackwell | 44 | 88 | 4 | 1 |
|  | M.P. Bicknell | Not | Out | 35 | 87 | 7 | 0 |
| 9-331 | Saqlain Mushtaq | c Bowler | b Blackwell | 10 | 32 | 1 | 0 |
| 10-332 | J. Ormond | c Dutch | b Parsons | 0 | 3 | 0 | 0 |
|  | Extras | (10lb, 16nb) |  | 26 |  |  |  |
|  | **TOTAL** | **(101 overs)** |  | **332** |  |  |  |

| Bowler | O | M | R | W | NB | Wd |
|---|---|---|---|---|---|---|
| Caddick | 27 | 6 | 94 | 1 | 8 | - |
| Bulbeck | 20 | 3 | 80 | 2 | - | - |
| Jones | 15 | 2 | 40 | 0 | - | - |
| Blackwell | 15 | 8 | 19 | 3 | - | - |
| Dutch | 13 | 1 | 52 | 2 | - | - |
| Parsons | 11 | 1 | 37 | 1 | - | - |

| SOMERSET - Second Innings | | | | | | |
|---|---|---|---|---|---|---|
| Fall Of Wkt | Batsman | | How | Out | Score | Balls | 4s | 6s |
| | J. Cox | | Not | Out | 14 | 28 | 3 | 0 |
| 1-28 | M.E. Trescothick * | c Stewart | b Tudor | 12 | 12 | 3 | 0 |
| | M. Burns | | Not | Out | 10 | 22 | 2 | 0 |
| | Extras | | (5lb, 4nb) | | 9 | | | |
| | TOTAL | | (10 overs) | (for 1 wkt) | 45 | | | |

| Bowler | O | M | R | W | NB | Wd |
|---|---|---|---|---|---|---|
| Ormond | 5 | 1 | 17 | 0 | 1 | - |
| Tudor | 4 | 1 | 22 | 1 | 1 | - |
| Ramprakash | 1 | 0 | 1 | 0 | - | - |

## Other Division One Results

With all three games ending in stalemate, largely due to rain around the country, there was little movement in the table following this round of matches. Yorkshire had to fight a major rearguard action against Hampshire in order to avoid the follow-on and another potential defeat, while Leicestershire closed the gap on Surrey by one point following a close-fought draw at a rain-swept Horsham.

May 24-27
*Horsham:-* **Sussex drew with Leicestershire.** Leicestershire 264 (Wells 86*, Stevens 50, Martin-Jenkins 7-51) and 94-2; Sussex 247 (Montgomerie 122*, Malcolm 7-76). **Leicestershire 9pts, Sussex 8**

*Headingley:-* **Yorkshire drew with Hampshire.** Hampshire 354 (Crawley 79, Kendall 67, Hoggard 4-93) and 62-1; Yorkshire 423 (Blakey 83, White 67, Kirby 57, Vaughan 54, Mascarenhas 5-87). **Yorkshire 12pts, Hampshire 11**

## COUNTY CHAMPIONSHIP DIVISION ONE AT 27TH MAY

| Pos | Prv | | P | Points | W | D | L | Bat | Bwl | Ded |
|---|---|---|---|---|---|---|---|---|---|---|
| 1 | 1 | Surrey | 4 | 63.75 | 3 | 1 | 0 | 12 | 12 | 0.25 |
| 2 | 2 | Leicestershire | 5 | 62.00 | 2 | 2 | 1 | 17 | 14 | 1.00 |
| 3 | 4 | Hampshire | 5 | 55.00 | 1 | 3 | 1 | 17 | 14 | 0.00 |
| 4 | 3 | Lancashire | 4 | 51.00 | 2 | 1 | 1 | 11 | 12 | 0.00 |
| 5 | 5 | Somerset | 4 | 48.00 | 1 | 3 | 0 | 13 | 11 | 0.00 |
| 6 | 7 | Sussex | 4 | 35.00 | 0 | 3 | 1 | 12 | 11 | 0.00 |
| 7 | 6 | Kent | 3 | 33.00 | 1 | 1 | 1 | 10 | 7 | 0.00 |
| 8 | 9 | Yorkshire | 4 | 23.00 | 0 | 1 | 3 | 7 | 12 | 0.00 |
| 9 | 8 | Warwickshire | 3 | 16.00 | 0 | 1 | 2 | 5 | 7 | 0.00 |

# 7 Domination And Frustration

The news that Sherryn Hollioake had given birth to Bennaya on Saturday 25th May had come as a welcome boost to everyone at the Club, as had the revelation that Adam would be returning to England with his wife and baby within a week or two. It would certainly be good to see the captain back, since it would at least scotch some of the rumours that had been flying around about Adam's future in the game. Some whispers had suggested that he would not return during the 2002 season, which seemed entirely reasonable, but others intimated that he was about to retire completely from cricket. Thankfully, a man with so much still to offer to the game, to Surrey and, potentially, to England, was going to come back and continue his cricketing career.

As Adam and his family prepared to travel across the globe, so his Surrey team-mates and supporters readied themselves for a week of travelling of their own. The fixture planners had decided that the team should play a Cheltenham & Gloucester Trophy third round match in Edinburgh, then make their way down to Manchester for a four-day Championship fixture and, finally, take part in a Norwich Union League match at Northampton the following day. It was an inconvenient schedule, even if all went well, but it represented a potential minefield if there was any rain around, particularly in Scotland.

The Championship campaign was still going well, though the possible loss of Alec Stewart and Alex Tudor to England for most of the rest of the season was certainly going to upset the balance of a side that had been flush with all-rounders in the early weeks of the summer. Their replacements, Jon Batty and Ed Giddins, were clearly not going to be able to provide the team with the same weight of runs, so life was likely to become considerably more difficult.

The only other real worry was the slip catching, a facet of Surrey's game that had been well below par in 2001 and extremely variable, to say the least, in the current campaign to date. In the games before England call-ups and Saqlain's return, we had been able to field Mark Butcher, Graham Thorpe and Azhar Mahmood in the cordon, but now we were left with Ali Brown as the only real slips specialist in the likely line-up for Old Trafford, unless someone like Rikki Clarke was to be granted a debut in place of one of the missing England players. Although this appeared, on the surface, to be only a relatively minor concern, there was no doubting the fact that the old adage 'catches win matches' still held true.

## C&G Trophy 3rd Round - Perfect Weather For Ducks And Duckworth-Lewis

### Scotland v Surrey at Grange CC, Edinburgh. Played on Thursday 30th May. Surrey won by 55 runs (Duckworth-Lewis method)

It was impossible not to feel sorry for everyone connected with Grange Cricket Club and Scottish cricket as their showpiece game of the season was ruined by the rain that completely washed out play on the designated day of the match. Having worked desperately hard to get the ground fit for play after days of rain leading up to the game, an absolutely torrential five-minute downpour fifteen minutes before the start of play left the outfield saturated and covered in puddles. A decent sized crowd remained hopeful as the umpires inspected at 12noon, 1pm and 2.30pm but another heavy deluge shortly after the final inspection led to the abandonment of play and left everyone facing potential problems on the reserve day.

Although the sunny but breezy conditions that prevailed on the second morning allowed a prompt start, there were few spectators present to witness the contest, with the schoolchildren who had been allowed to attend on day one back in their classrooms and all the corporate hospitality tents gone. It made for an atmosphere more akin to a club cricket match, though Surrey made light of both this and being put in to bat in seamer-friendly conditions to build a decent total after Ali Brown had slapped the first delivery he received straight to cover point.

With the sodden outfield making boundary hits that much harder to achieve, Ian Ward and Mark Ramprakash gradually accelerated the scoring rate throughout a 111-run partnership until Ward ran himself out in attempting an ambitious single in the thirtieth over. From there on in it was all Ramprakash and Shahid as the Scottish bowling was put to the sword, culminating in a brutal assault that brought forty-nine runs from the last five overs. The penultimate over of the innings saw Shahid completing a 61-ball fifty and Ramprakash reaching his century from 133 deliveries, while a fifteen-run final over took the Surrey total up to 246-2, a fine total in the circumstances.

With grey clouds banking up around the ground, and the forecasters' prediction of an afternoon shower looking accurate, it was important that Scotland faced ten overs of their reply in order for us to get a proper result and avoid the need for a trek across the city to an indoor school for a bowl-out. Luckily, this proved possible and the capture of three wickets for twenty-six runs in the first twelve overs from Jimmy Ormond and Martin Bicknell put Surrey well ahead under the Duckworth-Lewis system. The visitors were still in a hurry to finish the game, however, since they had a flight booked to take everyone to Old Trafford for the Championship match that was starting the next day. Similarly, I had a train to catch.

The last thing we all needed, therefore, was a hefty twenty-minute shower at 4.15pm, with Scotland floundering fairly aimlessly at 63-4 in the twenty-fifth over. Consequently, with the finishing time of the game now unknown, it was impossible for the Surrey entourage to make their flight, leaving poor Keith Medlycott wandering around, mobile phone almost constantly at his ear, attempting to arrange alternative transport to get the team to Manchester overnight. Eventually, Medders and his staff back at The AMP Oval managed to arrange for the players to travel in a fleet of hire cars, which was far from satisfactory but the only possible option at such short notice. The whole situation, brought about by the stupidity of a tightly packed fixture list, was ludicrous and I couldn't help but wonder how things would have turned out had the next day's fixture been in Taunton rather than Manchester.

My own situation wasn't too clever either and, as the rain ceased and the sun broke through, I realised that I would have to leave before the end of the game if the players got back out onto the field. Normally, the possibility of a resumption of play would have been good news but, on this occasion, the Surrey team and their supporters were quite happy for the game to be abandoned so that we could all start making our way to Manchester. It was fortunate, therefore, that the rain had left some very damp patches on the square and, after what seemed like an eternity, the umpires decided to abandon the match at 6pm, leaving Surrey deservedly victorious, albeit in unsatisfactory circumstances, by 55 runs under the Duckworth-Lewis system. I was out of the ground like a shot in order to catch my pre-booked train and as I made my way south I found myself hoping that the tiring drive down to Manchester wouldn't affect the Surrey performance on day one of a very important Championship match.

*Scores:- Surrey 246-2 (50 overs; Ramprakash 101\*, Shahid 65\*, Ward 58); Scotland 63-4 (24.1 overs; Ormond 2-9). Surrey won by 55 runs (Duckworth-Lewis method)*

| FRIZZELL COUNTY CHAMPIONSHIP - MATCH FIVE |
|---|

<u>LANCASHIRE</u> versus <u>SURREY</u>
at Old Trafford

First Day - Friday 31st May

Surrey 292-7

**The Teams And The Toss** - *Surrey are forced to make four changes to the team that drew with Somerset, with Butcher, Thorpe, Stewart and Tudor all away on England duty. Their replacements are Michael Carberry, Nadeem Shahid, Jon Batty and Rikki Clarke, who makes* his County Championship debut. Lancashire also field a debutant in Jimmy Anderson, a former England Under-19 fast bowler from Burnley. He comes in for England's Andrew Flintoff, while Neil Fairbrother makes his first appearance of the season in place of broken hand victim, David Byas. Ian Ward, captaining Surrey for the first time in a County Championship match, wins the toss and predictably decides to take first use of what looks to be a very good pitch on a warm and sunny morning. The added bonus of batting first is that his team now has further recovery time after the previous night's motorway trip from Edinburgh.

It's hard to believe we are watching Surrey batting as the Lancashire opening bowlers, Peter Martin and Glen Chapple, keep a very tight stranglehold on Ian Ward and Michael Carberry to reel off five successive maiden overs at the start of the match.

The first runs finally come in Chapple's third over, via a thick edge from Carberry which evades third slip on the bounce and runs away to the boundary, but the run tally doesn't manage to overtake the overs count until the same batsman deflects the flame-haired paceman for a more convincing boundary two overs later.

The ninth over of the innings then brings a trio of 'firsts' - Martin concedes his first runs, Ward finally gets off the mark and runs are recorded in front of the wicket for the first time in the innings as the Surrey skipper forces through extra cover off the back foot for three runs. When he then drives Chapple through square cover for four it is beginning to look as if Surrey's slow but steady start against testing bowling is beginning to pay off, but Kyle Hogg, replacing Chapple at the Warwick Road end, makes a nonsense of that theory by dismissing Carberry with his fifth delivery. The young left-hander receives a good lifting delivery and is eventually caught by Stuart Law at second slip after third slip parries the initial chance high to his right-hand side - Carberry is out for ten and Surrey are 18-1.

On a very lively looking pitch, Hogg and Martin manage to pass the outside edge on a number of occasions and only one run comes from the next four overs as Ward and the new batsman, Mark Ramprakash, opt for a further period of entrenchment. It is only when the experienced former England swing bowler finishes his opening spell of 8-7-3-0 with the scoreboard reading 19-1 after sixteen overs, that the floodgates open with the introduction of the debutant Anderson.

Starting his first-class career with a bouncer, the 19-year-old speedster then overpitches for most of the remainder of his opening over, allowing Ramprakash to drive for two, four and three runs through mid-off, point and wide mid-on respectively. Suddenly, the former Middlesex batsman is away and, though he miscues a pull off Hogg for two in the next over, he is soon driving Anderson for another boundary and a three before steering him backward of point for four in the twenty-first over, during which Surrey reach fifty. Despite his lapses in length, Anderson looks distinctly pacy and the two overs that bring his opening spell to a conclusion require close attention from Ward, with the only runs coming via thick edges to third man.

Sensibly opting not to over-bowl his two teenage seamers, Warren Hegg eventually decides to pair Gary Keedy with Glen Chapple, though the move only succeeds in increasing the scoring rate initially as Ward drives the returning paceman's first ball to the rope at long-off and Ramprakash follows up by driving and cutting successive deliveries from Keedy for four to bring up the fifty partnership.

On a morning where Surrey's runs have come in fits and spurts it is no real surprise that the bowlers gradually regain a little control, bringing about another fairly quiet period as the batsman play every delivery on its merits. Ward looks extremely determined, clearly hoping to make a mark in his first match as Surrey captain, while Ramprakash occasionally uses his feet beautifully in order to drive Keedy, doing so twice in the penultimate over before lunch. On the first occasion he sends the ball fizzing to the extra-cover boundary and on the second he picks up the two runs he requires to complete a classy half-century from 78 balls, and also to put three figures on the board for his team.

As the batsmen leave the field at the end of a final-over maiden from Chapple to Ward, they will no doubt feel very happy with their efforts as their watchful batting has laid solid foundations for the visitors.

*Lunch:- Surrey 100-1 (Ward 38\*, Ramprakash 50\*) from 37 overs*

Warren Hegg's post-lunch pairing of Martin, from the Stretford end, and Keedy, from the Warwick Road end, proves highly restrictive as Surrey add just seventeen runs to their lunch total in the first twelve overs of the afternoon session. The cricket is, nevertheless, competitive and absorbing, before the bowlers' spell is finally broken by a square-cut boundary from Ward off Keedy that completes both the century partnership and the Surrey skipper's personal half-century from 150 balls in 176 minutes. Perhaps losing concentration slightly after reaching this landmark, the left-handed opener is, however, dropped by Law at slip later in the same over when he offers a routine top-edged chance from another cut.

At the other end, Ramprakash, having added just five runs since lunch and remained scoreless for seven overs, finally sparks into action, driving Martin to the rope at cover in the last over of the Accrington-born seamer's post-lunch spell and then dispatching his replacement, Kyle Hogg, to the same area of the ground with a cut and another drive. Although this flurry of boundaries is again followed by a quieter phase of single gathering, the batsmen are looking in complete control under a warm sun and in front of a decent-sized crowd until an inspired piece of fielding brings about a sudden change in fortunes. As Ramprakash clips Keedy towards the deep midwicket boundary and calls his partner back for a second run there appears to be no danger, but the Surrey number three hasn't reckoned on Hogg's outstanding pick-up on the run and finds that he is unable to beat the youngster's bullet-like throw which arrives over the top of the stumps at the striker's end. While the Lancashire fielders rush, as one, to congratulate their young talent on his brilliant work, a dejected Ramprakash picks himself up and departs for the pavilion with his beautifully crafted innings of seventy-one at an end and Surrey now 143-2.

One ball later, the visitors are 143-3. Nadeem Shahid misses a sweep at a low full-toss and finds umpire Cowley's finger instantly shooting skywards in response to the inevitable Lancashire appeal. Has a run out once again changed the course of a match? It looks like it might do as Ali Brown plays and misses before the over is out, though he soon recovers to cut Hogg through point for four runs and then blasts Keedy for six over long-off to raise the 150. As Lancashire rattle through their overs, the Brown versus Keedy contest develops in to a classic confrontation, with the left-arm spinner causing a few anxious moments before the Surrey middle-order maestro rocks back and cuts to the rope at cover.

Just as this duel is taking centre stage, though, Anderson returns to the attack and, in his second over, steals the limelight by taking his maiden first-class wicket with a good lifting delivery that finds the outside edge of Ward's defensive bat on its way through to wicketkeeper Hegg. After facing 198 deliveries the Surrey captain's patient innings is therefore terminated at sixty-one, with the score now 167-4 and Lancashire sensing the possibility of a comeback.

The applause for Ward's innings has barely died away when the resumption of the battle between Brown and Keedy brings despair, but then further joy, for the home side. Having taken ten runs from two balls, with a top-edged cut for four and a towering drive for six into the back row of seating beyond long-on, Brown is comprehensively beaten and bowled by the next delivery, a quicker arm-ball.

At 177-5, with Brown gone for twenty-eight, we now seem to have a real contest on our hands as Jon Batty joins Rikki Clarke at the crease. With tea looming, Clarke concentrates on keeping out his fellow debutant, Anderson, whose tidy second spell has allowed far fewer front-foot opportunities for the batsmen, while Batty takes advantage of a loose Keedy over by sweeping fine for four and then smashing a full-toss high over wide long-on for six. The Surrey two-hundred then arrives shortly before the break, with Batty on fifteen and Clarke on five, the Guildford youngster having opened his County Championship runs account with a leg-glanced single and a steer to the backward point boundary off Anderson.

Tea:- Surrey 202-5 (Clarke 5*, Batty 15*) from 76 overs

Mindful of the fact that the new ball will be available in fourteen overs time, the Lancashire skipper keeps Keedy going from the Warwick Road end after the interval, while Chapple, strangely ignored during the middle session, is allowed a short burst from the Stretford end, where steeper bounce has been evident throughout the day.

With lost ground still needing to be recovered, Surrey make a quiet start to the post-tea session before Batty advances down the pitch to smite Keedy to the long-off boundary in the fourth over after the resumption, and then watches in admiration as Clarke shows the first real glimpses of his potential with a series of classical drives. Having struck Chapple sweetly through mid-off for four and then repeated the boundary dose with a lovely on-drive off Keedy, the tall 20-year-old caresses another Chapple half-volley through straight mid-on to pick up three further runs and take the sixth-wicket partnership past fifty.

These strokes prompt a double bowling change, with Keedy's thirty-one over spell, broken only by lunch and tea, finally coming to an end as Kyle Hogg returns to the fray and Mark Chilton takes the ball for the first time in the innings. With eighty-four overs now bowled, the idea is clearly for these two to fill in until the new ball is due, though Hogg causes one or two flutters by inducing an edge from each batsman in the third, and final, over of his spell. Batty's top-edged cut falls short of the fielder at third man, however, while Clarke's more controlled snick runs away finer to provide him with his fifth boundary.

Despite the fact that Hogg has looked quite dangerous, Hegg sticks to his original plan of retiring the 18-year-old to the outfield as soon as the new 'cherry' becomes available and, as at the start of the day, Martin and Chapple share five straight maidens. Although the bowling is still unerringly accurate, it doesn't initially pose as many problems as it had this morning, allowing Batty and Clarke to continue rebuilding the Surrey innings, albeit at a sedate pace.

The Surrey wicketkeeper eventually gets the score moving again in the following over with a cover drive for four off Chapple, thereby hoisting the visitors' total beyond 250, before Martin suddenly begins to locate a testing line again and immediately comes close to breaking the partnership. Having edged along the ground to fine third man for two runs, Batty is beaten three times in the flaxen-haired swing bowler's next over and then, two overs later, with his score on thirty-six at 266-5, offers a hard overhead chance to Neil Fairbrother at first slip when edging an attempted cut. The luckless Martin can only hold his head in his hands as the ball flies away to the boundary, adding insult to injury in the process. Finally, to confirm that it isn't his day, the 33-year-old seamer then sees Batty miscue a drive just over the head of the fielder at point in the final over of his spell. This stroke brings the Surrey keeper another boundary and takes the Clarke-Batty stand into three figures. It's been a superb effort by the sixth-wicket pair, though the extremely unfortunate Martin might not be entirely appreciative as he ends his day's honest toil with figures that read 22-13-28-0.

Any feelings that Lancashire's senior bowler might harbour about being hard done by today are then probably multiplied when his replacement, young Anderson, picks up the all-important partnership-breaking wicket in his first over back, courtesy of Clarke's edge to Law at second slip. With the day's minimum allocation of 104 overs having already been completed, it is galling that the Surrey debutant should fall in 'overtime', but he can certainly be proud of his performance as he returns to the pavilion with forty-one runs to his name after an impressive 100-ball innings at a crucial stage of the game.

At 279-6, the day is still Surrey's, however, and the point is emphasised by Batty later in the over of Clarke's exit when he cuts high over backward point for four to complete a very good half-century from 147 balls after 129 minutes of determined batting. He then repeats the dose when Anderson pitches short and wide again in his next over, before a highly satisfactory day for the visitors ends on a disappointing note when the recalled Keedy manages to find a way through Martin Bicknell's less than watertight defensive stroke in the last over.

*Close:- Surrey 292-7 (Batty 55\*) from 107.2 overs*

## VIEWS FROM THE DRESSING ROOM

*When were you told that you were going to be making your Championship debut in this match?*
**RIKKI CLARKE** - I found out for definite on the morning of the game, though I had a rough idea I might be playing because I'd had a few hints from the senior players while we were in Scotland for the C&G game.

*They've got a good hand of seamers, and in this game Peter Martin was very accurate and beat the bat regularly, while young Jimmy Anderson looked to be a real handful with his pace. Who did you find the most testing?*
**RIKKI CLARKE** - I thought Jimmy was the most difficult of the bunch - he was very quick and got good carry to the wicketkeeper on what was the fastest wicket I've played on in a long time. Peter Martin was also very tough to play because he was on the spot constantly, with the ball leaving the bat.
**JON BATTY** - The two you have mentioned were both very good. Jimmy Anderson was probably the quickest bowler we saw all year in Division One. He gave a few more opportunities to score than Martin did, but he was impressive for a young lad, he bowled well. I remember Peter Martin bowled a magnificent spell and I didn't feel I was ever going to score a run off him - I was just hanging on, trying to survive and see him off.

### Second Day - Saturday 1st June

### Surrey 382; Lancashire 163-7

With another fair-sized crowd in the ground and a hot sun beating down from a blue sky, Surrey make an ideal start to day two as Ian Salisbury cuts the first ball of Gary Keedy's incomplete over to the cover boundary.

Progress thereafter is slow, however, as the metronomic Martin starts with three further maidens, during which he passes the outside edge on a number of occasions, and Chapple, after a four-run opening over which sees the Surrey total passing three-hundred, is equally unyielding. The typically defensive fields set by Warren Hegg - just one slip is posted for Salisbury - certainly don't allow free scoring and, consequently, the only boundary in the first hour comes when the Surrey leg-spinner receives a rare loose delivery from Martin and drives it to the rope at cover. The visitors are clearly unconcerned about their rate of progress, however, sensibly opting to build the biggest possible total on a pitch that will take an increasing degree of spin as it bakes under the sun, rather than chasing a fourth batting point.

They actually end up ten runs short of the 350 required to gain this reward by the time the cut-off point of 130 overs arrives, though plenty happens in the lead-up overs - on reaching sixty-one Jon Batty records his highest score for Surrey since registering his maiden first-class century in June 2000; Hogg and Anderson replace Martin and Chapple, a move much appreciated by the Surrey keeper, who drives each of the new bowlers for four; and Salisbury departs for nineteen after edging a drive at Keedy to slip, the left-arm spinner having taken over at the Warwick Road end after just two overs from Hogg.

While Anderson continues to steam in from the Stretford end and beats the bat without reward, Saqlain plays himself in sedately and Batty enjoys himself at the expense of Keedy, first advancing to drive to the extra cover boundary, then moving his score into the nineties with two further fours from a drive over mid-on and an edged cut that bisects the wicketkeeper and slip. This second boundary finally takes Surrey past the 350 mark in the 134th over, though they don't have to wait long to reach the next ten-run milestone as the following over sees Saqlain clipping Anderson through square leg for two and then picking up the first two fours of his innings, courtesy of a top-edged pull over the slips and an authentic leg glance.

Typically for this Surrey innings, another period of calm then follows the storm as Keedy stifles the scoring rate by switching to a negative over-the-wicket style and Batty contents himself with singles to edge ever closer to a century. Eventually, however, he is offered some width by Chapple, Anderson's replacement at the Stretford end, and he gratefully crashes a cover drive to the boundary to complete an excellent ton from 211 balls after 263 minutes of impressive concentration and careful shot selection.

The applause from the Old Trafford crowd as the genial Surrey wicketkeeper celebrates his second first-class hundred in mid-pitch with Saqlain is then repeated a few minutes later when his innings comes to an end in the penultimate over before lunch. Having swept Keedy fine for the fourteenth four of his innings, Batty is bowled behind his legs in attempting an instant replay of the stroke with his score advanced to 104 and the total at 377.

During the latter stages of the morning's play, news has filtered through of the untimely death of the former South African captain, Hansie Cronje, in a plane crash in South Africa. Inevitably, it brings back bad memories for everyone with Surrey connections in what is turning out to be a tragedy-filled year for the game of cricket.

*Lunch:- Surrey 380-9 (Saqlain 19\*, Ormond 0\*) from 145 overs*

Surrey's first innings is soon brought to a close after lunch as Martin gets a very well-deserved wicket when Jimmy Ormond's flashing drive results in an edge to Fairbrother at first slip with the total advanced by just two runs to 382. The visitors look to have compiled a very satisfactory score on a good pacy pitch that seems to offer something to everyone, and it is now up to their bowlers to make some inroads into a Lancashire batting line-up that appears to be just a little lacking in both quality and depth.

Apart from an early warning to Bicknell from umpire Constant for following through onto the danger area of the pitch, the bowlers start encouragingly, getting a number of deliveries past the outside edge of the openers' bats and inducing a couple of false strokes to third man. The closest the visitors come to a wicket, however, is when a mix-up in the running between the wickets sees both batsmen stranded in mid-pitch in the eighth over, though, luckily for Lancashire, Michael Carberry's throw from point misses the untenanted stumps at the non-striker's end.

Having survived this scare, the home side's opening pair settle down again, with Alec Swann driving Bicknell for two boundaries in an over, through mid-on and then straight back down the ground, and it is beginning to look as though wickets might be elusive when both men fall in the space of nine deliveries.

With Bicknell's opening seven-over salvo having passed unrewarded, Ian Ward introduces Saqlain for the fifteenth over, and within four balls the first wicket falls, though not to the new bowler. For the second time in his three recent Championship innings against Surrey, Swann is run out as a brilliant piece of fielding by a young player again brings a breakthrough. It is Rikki

Clarke who emulates Kyle Hogg's effort in Surrey's innings by pulling off an excellent diving stop on the midwicket boundary and then fizzing in an accurate return to the non-striker's end. Swann, having hesitated about taking a second run, is unable to regain his ground as Saqlain gathers Clarke's return and Surrey have their first wicket with the total standing at thirty-three.

Then, as so often happens, one breakthrough brings a second in the very next over as Ormond gains his just deserts for a wholehearted and pacy spell when Chilton gloves a lifting delivery angled into his body and watches helplessly as Jon Batty flies away to his left to hold a magnificent catch. As Chilton makes his way back to the pavilion the scoreboard reads 36-2 and the Surrey players gather to congratulate their agile wicketkeeper on a top-class catch.

With two new batsmen now at the crease, Ward elects to introduce Clarke into the attack at the Stretford end after a solitary over from Saqlain, though the Guildford lad's opening over in Championship cricket doesn't turn out to be a happy one as Fairbrother seizes upon three leg-side deliveries to glance twice to the fine leg boundary and clip once to the rope at backward square leg. The former England left-hander then takes advantage of two short and wide deliveries from a tiring Ormond to speed his score to twenty after just five overs at the crease, just moments after Stuart Law has upper-cut Clarke to the third man boundary to raise the Lancashire fifty.

With the home side suddenly on the attack, Surrey's stand-in skipper promptly recalls Saqlain, though this time at the Warwick Road end. Almost inevitably, the Pakistani off-spinner soon proves a calming influence, though Clarke is unable to contain Law at the other end and is driven to the fence at cover on three occasions in two overs before giving way to Bicknell.

This change certainly looks to be a sensible one and so it proves as the visitors' senior bowler takes just eleven deliveries to break a partnership that has just passed fifty. Crucially, the man dismissed is Law, though his dismissal owes more to a brilliant catch than a great delivery as Batty again flies several yards to his left to pouch a legitimate leg-glance from the Australian batsman. With their key batsman gone for eighteen, Lancashire are clearly in trouble, since they are still 295 runs adrift of Surrey's total.

Although the visitors are unable to add another wicket to their tally in the final two overs before the break, they are most definitely the happier of the two sides at tea, thanks to the efforts of their inspired wicketkeeper.

*Tea:- Lancashire 94-3 (Fairbrother 29\*, Lloyd 3\*) from 31 overs*

Having been very subdued in the latter stages of the middle session and then made an unconvincing start to the post-tea period by edging Bicknell over the slips to take his side past the hundred mark, it is not greatly surprising to see Neil Fairbrother dismissed for thirty-five shortly afterwards when he attempts to cut Saqlain and bottom-edges the ball onto his stumps.

With Graham Lloyd looking far from secure at the other end and the new batsman, Warren Hegg, failing to pick the off-spinner's 'wrong un' on a couple of occasions early in his innings, the flow of the game is very much towards Surrey. Lloyd's discomfort is clear for all to see as Bicknell, encouraged by the pace and bounce in the pitch to utilise his bouncer much more than he would normally do, tests the Lancashire man out on the hook before slipping a couple of deliveries past the outside edge.

Although the Surrey swing king's four overs since tea have been impressive, he is rested by Ward at this point, presumably because the visiting captain wishes to test Lloyd against the greater pace of Jimmy Ormond. If this is indeed his thinking then it is spot-on, since the former Leicestershire paceman needs just two deliveries to nail his man with a well pitched-up outswinger that takes the outside edge of Lloyd's flailing bat and ends in the safe hands of Batty.

As the former England coach's son departs for nine, the home side are in some disarray at 107-5, and their plight worsens in the next over from Saqlain as good captaincy and umpiring combine to bring about the dismissal of Hegg. Having had a discussion with his bowler and moved in a second, squarer silly-point fielder just a couple of overs beforehand, Ward gets his reward for an attacking move when his opposite number squeezes the ball out, at pace, to that very position and sees Nadeem Shahid pick up an excellent low catch. Although the Surrey fielders immediately celebrate the capture of another wicket, Hegg suggests he is uncertain about the validity of the catch by standing his ground, forcing umpire Nigel Cowley to take the sensible option of consulting with David Constant, his colleague at square leg. Constant, clearly happy that the ball has carried to Shahid, quickly confirms that the Lancashire captain is out for one, leaving the red rose county in a parlous state at 109-6.

With two new batsmen now at the crease, Surrey sense the possibility of further breakthroughs, but Kyle Hogg gets his head down, contenting himself with the occasional single, while Glen Chapple adopts a more aggressive approach, cutting and pulling fours off Ormond before adding two further leg-side boundaries to his collection in a ten-run over from the previously parsimonious Saqlain.

Consequently, Ian Salisbury replaces Ormond to form an all-spin attack and the scoring rate drops dramatically, with the batsmen restricted to a diet of singles for eight overs. Despite this, the dogged seventh-wicket partnership manages to carry the total beyond 150 in the fifty-eighth over and, as tea approaches, Chapple finally breaks free again to drive Salisbury to the boundary wide of mid-on. Hogg then follows suit by forcing Saqlain to the extra cover fence in the next over, completing a very valuable fifty-run stand in the process, though this stroke turns out to be his last contribution to the Lancashire cause as the Surrey off-spinner takes revenge two balls later by having the teenager taken at silly point by Ward - Hogg out for 16, Lancashire 161-7.

At the close of play, two overs later, the visitors are therefore in complete control of the match, though Chapple, who has played as well as any of the top-order batsmen, is still there on thirty-five and will be keen to see his side past the follow-on target of 233 if he can get support from the tail in the morning.

*Close:- Lancashire 163-7 (Chapple 35\*, Martin 0\*) from 64 overs*

## VIEWS FROM THE DRESSING ROOM

*Given the conditions, and the state of the game, would you regard this as your best innings of the season, ahead of your 153 at Taunton and your 99 at Guildford?*
**JON BATTY** - I would actually say that the 99 at Guildford is the best innings of my whole career, so far, closely followed by this innings at Old Trafford. At that stage of the season, this would have been the best of my career by a mile, though, especially bearing in mind the way those Lancashire guys bowled.

*What aspect of your innings pleased you most? Concentration? Shot selection?*
**JON BATTY** - I think the whole package, really, and the fact that it was chanceless. I concentrated very well and I can't remember too many false shots during my entire innings. It was very pleasing for me because I'd worked so hard during the winter with Alan Butcher on a lot of technical aspects, and also with a sports psychologist on the mental side of the game. This was really the first time that both parts of the game really clicked together for me.

*Our first innings was one of the slowest and steadiest Surrey efforts of recent times - 382 in 147 overs. I assume we were just determined to get a really big total on the board with a view to the pitch offering increasing turn as the match wore on?*
**IAN WARD** - To be fair, I think Lancashire bowled particularly well - Peter Martin bowled a series of miserly spells, and I think we did really well to get through the first session of the game losing just one wicket. They are a fine side and it was tough cricket - that's where two divisions

is working, because Surrey versus Lancashire is a hard-fought contest, a bit like Test cricket. When you win the toss and bat against such a good side, you get in there and you put as many runs on the board as you can - if it takes 150 overs then so be it.

*You took two great leg-side catches at the start of their first innings - when Chilton gloved one off Jimmy Ormond and when Law glanced Martin Bicknell. I'm sure you must have been very proud of both catches but which one gave you the greatest pleasure? And would the catch to dismiss Ian Bell at Edgbaston later in the season rank as even better than these two?*

**JON BATTY** - It was obviously very important to get rid of Stuart Law with what was a bit of a 'burgle' down the leg side, but the Chilton catch was the more difficult one because I had to go a bit further to get to the ball. The Ian Bell catch was probably my best of the season, along with the one I took to get rid of Rob Key at The Oval. Those were very similar in that they were both big nicks, so I had to make quite a late decision to go for the ball when I realised it wasn't going to carry to the slips. I think I ended up somewhere near first slip's right foot for both of them, so they were probably two of the best catches of my career.

### Third Day - Sunday 2nd June

### Surrey 382 and 246-6dec; Lancashire 194

It's a major day for sport as England take on Sweden in the football World Cup, while the second Test Match against Sri Lanka continues at Edgbaston. Those of us who are staying in the marvellous Old Trafford Lodge are well placed to keep in touch with everything, however, as we move our seats into position on our balcony. In front of us we have a perfect view of Surrey's attempt to ram home their advantage against Lancashire, while behind us the television has been turned around so that we can keep in touch with developments in the football match. A radio tuned in to *Test Match Special* alerts us of any events at Edgbaston that might require us to flip television channels quickly! Perfect.

The day had started early for Keith Medlycott and Ian Ward, as I had spied them out in the middle, taking a good hard look at the pitch for some considerable time long before the start of play. I had assumed that they were discussing whether or not to enforce the follow-on, should Lancashire fail in their attempt to make the 233 runs they require to avoid it.

Although the weather is quite bright, if a little hazy, as 11am approaches, the forecasts that most Surrey supporters have seen and heard are not promising, with heavy showers predicted for later today and further spells of rain possible tomorrow. I wonder if this may dissuade us from following our preferred option of not enforcing the follow-on? Time alone will tell.

As play gets under way we have already heard the first major cheer of the day from within the ground, though it has nothing to do with this cricket match - it is for Sol Campbell's early goal for England at 10.53am precisely!

Attention soon turns to the action out in the middle, however, as Chapple starts well for Lancashire, taking ten runs from Bicknell's second over of the morning with a forcing stroke backward of point for four, a hook for two and a sweetly-driven boundary through mid-off. Largely as a result of this flurry of runs, Chapple rapidly completes an impressive half-century, from exactly 100 balls, and Bicknell is succeeded by Salisbury at the Stretford end.

With the Surrey spinners operating in tandem, both Chapple and his partner, Peter Martin, look much less comfortable, and a breakthrough that has looked increasingly likely finally comes in the ninth over of the morning when Salisbury's viciously lifting leg-break takes the outside edge of Chapple's defensive bat and finds its way into the hands of Ali Brown at slip via the gloves of Jon Batty. Now that the flame-haired seamer has gone for fifty-one, at 189-8, Lancashire appear to be struggling to reach their 233 target, especially as Martin seems to be all at sea when facing Saqlain.

As it happens, the end of the innings comes even sooner than anyone had anticipated, with the last two wickets falling in the space of three deliveries three overs later. Gary Keedy goes first, edging a tentative drive at Saqlain to Batty, then Martin simultaneously presents the Surrey keeper with his fifth victim of the innings and Salisbury with the 700th wicket of his first-class career when getting an outside edge to a leg-break. Lancashire are all out for 194 at 11.45am and everyone waits to see whether or not the follow-on will be enforced. With the bowlers still fresh, a lead of 188 runs secured, and a dodgy weather forecast to consider, it seems odds-on that we will see the Surrey side coming back out onto the field again... but, no, to everyone's surprise, it is the Lancashire team that emerges from the pavilion at 11.55am.

The debate as to the merits of this decision then continues throughout the rest of the morning session as Surrey make another slow start against further spells of testing bowling from Martin and Chapple, both of whom operate with reasonably attacking fields, initially. The pitch appears to have got a little quicker as it has baked under the sun on the first two days, necessitating a steady approach by Ward and Carberry, the Surrey openers, as the ball continually carries through to Hegg at a good pace and height. They do a decent job for their side in seeing off the opening overs of the new ball, even though the only boundaries in the first fifteen overs come when Carberry gloves a Chapple lifter just wide of a diving third slip and Ward drives the same bowler through extra cover ten overs later.

Once the opening bowlers take a breather in the last twenty minutes before lunch, everything changes, though. Hegg suddenly spreads his field, leaving just one slip in place and employing a third man and a cover sweeper, and Ward goes on to the attack against Gary Keedy when the left-arm spinner is introduced three overs ahead of the break. Having taken late-cut and swept boundaries from the former Yorkshire bowler's opening over, the Surrey captain reels off two further fours, from a slog-sweep and a drive wide of mid-on, as he brings up his side's fifty from the last ball of the session.

*Lunch:- Surrey 53-0 (Ward 38\*, Carberry 11\*) from 20 overs*

The England football match eventually ends in a draw, a fate that looks unlikely to befall this game unless the weather intervenes. That doesn't appear to be a likely scenario as play resumes after lunch, however, though it is certainly cooler and cloudier than at any other time in the contest to date.

Martin and Keedy, who have both switched from the end they appeared to favour when bowling in the Surrey first innings, open the bowling at the start of the post-lunch session and keep things quiet for four overs as Ward and Carberry attempt to re-establish themselves. Keedy's retention has required an act of faith from Warren Hegg following the spinner's pre-lunch battering by Ward, and he is soon under fire again, this time from Carberry, who suddenly sweeps him over backward square leg for six. The Surrey scoring rate is then boosted further as their stand-in captain welcomes Chapple's return to the attack, after just three overs from Martin, by driving and forcing the ball to the cover boundary twice in quick succession, completing his fourth successive County Championship half-century, from 83 balls, in the process. It has been another top-class innings, and he immediately celebrates by adding to his boundary count with another cover drive, this time off the suffering Keedy.

Despite this rush of runs, the Surrey openers aren't having everything their own way, and Carberry is certainly extremely fortunate to survive Chapple's eighth over when he is dropped twice in the space of three deliveries by Law at second slip, with his score on eighteen and the total on seventy-seven. Both chances are pretty much regulation, as slip catches go, though the first is the more glaring miss, with the ball reaching the Australian at an ideal catching height.

Although Surrey somehow have all their wickets still intact, the Lancashire opening bowler's excellent over sparks something of a revival by the home side - the run rate slows, Carberry survives a confident appeal for a catch at the wicket as soon as Anderson replaces Keedy at the

Stretford end, and Ward, on sixty-eight, has a stroke of luck when Fairbrother, at first slip, grasses another routine chance off the desperately unlucky Chapple.

Lancashire, to their credit, are still getting through their overs at a good rate and, since they are also managing to beat the bat with some regularity, they always look capable of making the breakthrough that eventually comes their way in the thirty-eighth over when the openers are parted with their partnership two short of the century mark. Having seemingly never totally recovered from his earlier moments of good fortune and insecurity, Carberry is the man to go when he fences at Anderson again and is adjudged caught at the wicket, though he looks less than happy about the decision. To be honest, the previous appeal had looked more convincing than this one, but he can hardly claim to have been unlucky since he has led something of a charmed life in struggling to twenty-four from 113 balls.

With this breakthrough finally secured for his side, Anderson then strikes again with his next delivery, a rapid yorker which seemingly beats Mark Ramprakash for pace and earns an lbw verdict from umpire Cowley to make the score 98-2. The impressive young paceman is denied a hat-trick, however, when Ward keeps out the first delivery of the bowler's next over and then finally sees his side through to three figures with an off-side single a few balls later.

It isn't long before Lancashire's mini revival brings another wicket, though, as the Surrey opener loses his third partner in the space of fifteen deliveries when Chapple finally gains reward for his earlier efforts by claiming the scalp of Nadeem Shahid in his fourteenth over. The former Essex batsman completes a miserable match by gloving an attempted pull stroke, allowing Hegg to demonstrate his athleticism with a fine sprawling catch down the leg side that pegs the visitors back to 101-3. This gets some of the home fans very excited, though it's hard to understand why with the opposition already leading by the small matter of 289 runs!

Their hopes of a complete collapse by Surrey are soon dashed in any case as Ali Brown cuts and hooks boundaries within three overs of his arrival at the crease and Ward takes three off-side fours from Hogg when Chapple rests after an excellent nine-over spell. The young Lancastrian seamer consequently finds his second spell, like his first, restricted to just two overs, and gives way to Mark Chilton, while Anderson is replaced by Gary Keedy after a seven-over blast that has again underlined his promise.

The new bowlers quickly find that it is no easy task to contain the Surrey batsmen, however, as a late-cut four from Brown off Keedy completes a rapid fifty partnership, scored at almost exactly a run a ball. Despite having been on the receiving end of a lot of rough treatment, the left-arm spinner continues to persevere, though, and he finally takes revenge when Brown's lofted straight hit in his next over is caught just inside the boundary behind the bowler by Chapple running round from long-off to end an unselfish knock of thirty from 29 balls by Surrey's master blaster.

Tea is just six overs away at this point, with the visitors' lead standing at 343, and the crowd's attention is now focused on Ward, who is progressing through the nineties by means of a steady flow of singles. The Surrey captain watches in admiration from the other end as Rikki Clarke twice drives beautifully to the leg-side boundary when confronted by Keedy bowling over the wicket into the rough outside leg stump, then he takes a single from the next over by Chilton to move his score on to ninety-eight and secure the strike for the session's final over.

Five balls pass without a run scored before Keedy drops the last ball short outside the off stump, allowing the Surrey left-hander to cut to the boundary and thus mark his first game as skipper with a superbly constructed century, scored from 167 balls in 221 minutes and including fifteen fours. It's a perfect way for Ward to end the session and he leaves the field to a well-deserved ovation with his side leading by 365 runs.

*Tea:- Surrey 177-4 (Ward 102\*, Clarke 9\*) from 57 overs*

Warren Hegg surprises everyone by giving Stuart Law's leg-breaks a run out immediately after tea, though it's a fair bet that he is soon regretting the move as the Australian starts with a delivery that brings four wides and is then thumped through extra cover for four by Ward in an over that ends up costing eleven runs.

The employment of the under-used Hogg at the other end represents a much better decision, however, since it brings the almost immediate dismissal of the Surrey captain, whose lofted extra-cover drive is very well held low down by Mark Chilton as he runs in from the boundary and plunges forward. It's a fitting end to a fine innings and one suspects this won't be the last wicket to fall in this period of play, since the visitors' need to press on quickly and declare is made increasingly urgent by ever-darkening skies and the sound and sight of thunder and lightning in the distance.

With the weather forecasters' prediction for once looking accurate, Rikki Clarke does indeed depart in Hogg's next over, skying a pull to Alec Swann at cover the ball after a drive for four runs wide of mid-on has taken his score to twenty-four and the Surrey total close to four-hundred.

It is therefore left to Jon Batty and Martin Bicknell to extend Surrey's advantage, and the veteran swing bowler provides the major impetus with a pulled four off Hogg and a pair of cleanly driven sixes in the following over from Keedy, the first sailing high over the rope at long-on and the second clearing it at long-off. As Hegg understandably spreads his fielders far and wide, Bicknell adds to Keedy's misery by reverse-sweeping him to the third man boundary and then profits by two further runs as Hogg narrowly fails to hang on to a low chance at deep mid-off after a sprint in from the long-off boundary.

At the end of the next over from Hogg, Ward finally decides that enough is enough, calling his batsmen in and thereby leaving Lancashire a theoretical target of 435 runs to win the match in a minimum of 116 overs.

That, of course, is based on the assumption that the rain will stay away... but it doesn't. Within minutes of the declaration a shower hits the ground, though, fortunately, it is a brief cloudburst and it doesn't do too much damage. The light is certainly not good enough for Lancashire to start their innings, however, and play is eventually abandoned for the day with the vast majority of the large number of Surrey fans in the ground again questioning the decision not to enforce the follow-on. If the forecasters are as accurate about tomorrow's weather as they have been today then the home side may yet wriggle off the hook after looking dead in the water earlier in the day.

*Close:- Between Innings*

## VIEW FROM THE DRESSING ROOM

*From my room in the Old Trafford Lodge, I spotted you out in the middle with Medders for some while before the start of the third day's play, looking closely at the pitch. I assume the conversation was mainly concerned with whether or not to enforce the follow-on? How difficult was it to make that decision? Was there much debate about it or was it your decision alone?*

**IAN WARD** - No, it was discussed with Medders and the bowlers. You have to know how they are feeling and whether they need a break - they had bowled really well during long spells in Lancashire's first innings, so they would obviously benefit from recharging their batteries for a while. And, with two spinners in the side, we were relying on the pitch to take more spin once we'd batted again. Also, if Lancashire were going to be major rivals in the Championship, then we weren't going to give them anything, especially as we had completely outplayed them throughout the game. Everything pointed to us not enforcing the follow-on and it was a collective decision, certainly not just made by myself.

## Fourth Day - Monday 3rd June

## Surrey 382 and 246-6dec; Lancashire 194 and 112-3

### Match Drawn
### Surrey 10pts, Lancashire 6

The overnight downpour that had been promised doesn't materialise, though light rain, which starts to fall at about 8.30am, persists, almost without a break, until 11.45am. Since the rainfall is never heavy, the only damage done is to Surrey's victory hopes as the number of overs remaining for play ticks down minute by minute.

To give credit to the umpires they inspect the outfield as soon as the rain stops and then decree that an early lunch will be taken, with play to start at 1pm, assuming that there is no further rain and that the light is satisfactory.

Luckily, this turns out to be the case and the match resumes with twenty-one overs lost this morning, to add to the twenty lost last night. This therefore leaves Surrey with 75 overs in which to dismiss their hosts, weather permitting, having taken 76.1 overs to achieve the same feat in the first innings. It could be interesting if the weather stays fine, though a good start looks absolutely vital.

The dismissal of Alec Swann in only the third over, to a magnificent piece of bowling from Martin Bicknell, is therefore manna from heaven for the visitors. The former Northamptonshire batsman is undone by the final ball of the over as Surrey's senior seamer follows a series of outswingers with a delivery that nips back at Swann as he pads up. The bowler and all of his close fielders appeal as one, umpire Cowley agrees that the batsman is plumb lbw, and Lancashire are instantly on the back foot at 9-1.

Bicknell then almost follows up with another wicket in his second over, as another well-planned piece of bowling fails to produce the desired result only because of a dropped catch. Having stationed himself at leg slip and watched Neil Fairbrother's first-ball glance fly just out of reach to his left-hand side, Ian Ward immediately moves finer and then fails to hang on to an awkward, but catchable, low chance as the batsman obligingly repeats the shot to the next delivery.

Despite this scare, Fairbrother is clearly determined to stay positive, and it's all-action cricket as the former England left-hander mixes edges and drives through the square cover region in almost equal measure. Nor is Chilton slow to take advantage of understandably very aggressive field placings and he also profits handsomely through thick edges, leg glances and cover drives until a further burst of rain sends the players scurrying for cover once again at 1.40pm.

Fine bowling from Bicknell and Ormond has brought just one wicket, though there has been plenty of encouragement for a slip cordon that has been very much kept on its toes throughout the nine overs that have been bowled. With the skies far less encouraging from a Surrey point of view, however, the chances of the visitors adding further wickets to their haul already look to be receding rapidly.

Although the rain is, again, never very heavy it falls steadily and persistently from leaden skies as the minutes tick away and a draw looks increasingly inevitable. The forecast certainly hadn't suggested that we would suffer such a sustained period of rainfall but there is simply nothing anyone can do about it as the umpires finally decide to call an early tea.

*Tea:- Lancashire 44-1 (Chilton 23\*, Fairbrother17\*) from 9.2 overs*

Much to everyone's surprise, the weather relents rapidly, the sun makes an appearance, and play is able to resume at 4.35pm. It's clear that something dramatic would have to occur in order for Surrey to pull off a sensational victory, though, since only 24.4 overs now remain to be bowled.

# TUDOR'S FLYING START

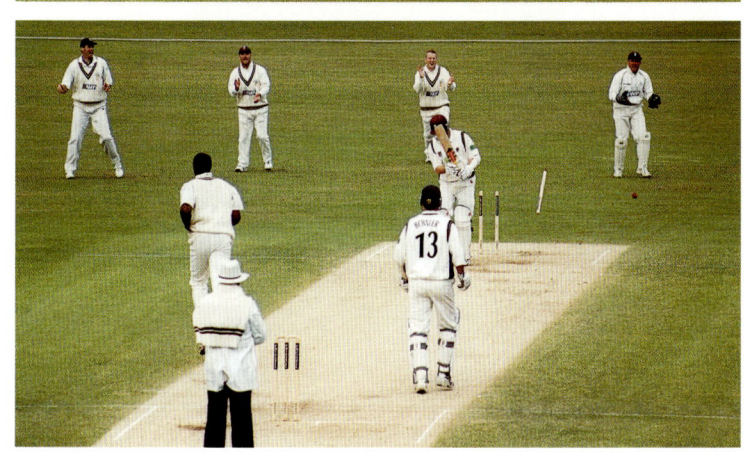

TOP - Robin Martin-Jenkins is comprehensively defeated in the game against Sussex at The AMP Oval
MIDDLE - Tony Cottey is well taken at third slip by Azhar Mahmood in the same match
BOTTOM - Somerset's Jamie Cox has his middle stump extracted in spectacular style by a yorker
*(All photos by Reg Elliott)*

# A HISTORIC VICTORY AT HEADINGLEY

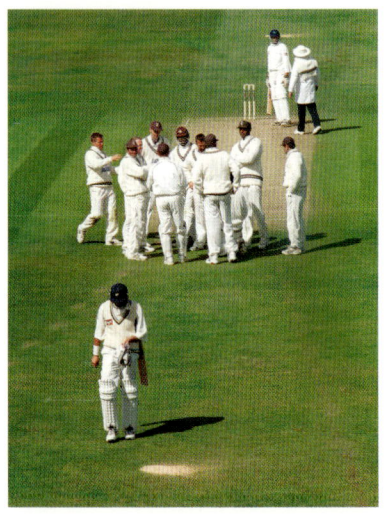

TOP - Azhar Mahmood traps Gavin Hamilton lbw…
MIDDLE - … and the Surrey players celebrate as the crestfallen batsman heads back to the pavilion
BOTTOM - Jimmy Ormond captures the wicket of Gary Fellows, courtesy of another lbw decision
*(All photos courtesy of Surrey CCC)*

# TRIUMPH OVER LANCASHIRE

TOP - A delighted Ian Ward runs out Alec Swann
MIDDLE - Andy Flintoff hooks for six during his powerful innings of 137
BOTTOM - Flintoff's magnificent knock ends with a stumping by Alec Stewart off Ian Salisbury
*(All photos courtesy of Surrey CCC)*

# AZHAR ROUTS THE RED ROSE

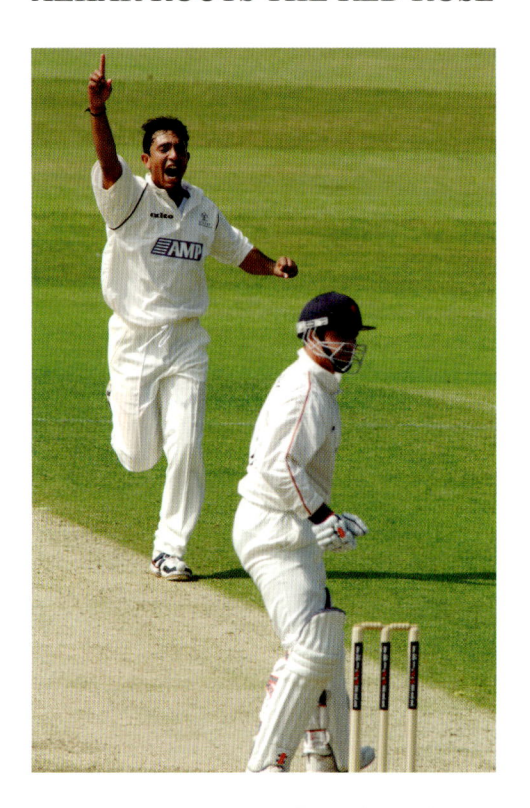

TOP - Azhar celebrates the capture of another Lancashire wicket
*(Photo courtesy of Surrey CCC)*
BOTTOM - Azhar leads the Surrey team off the field after his outstanding 8-61 performance
*(Photo by John Banfield)*

# BATTY STARS AT OLD TRAFFORD

TOP - A flying legside catch off Martin Bicknell sees off Stuart Law
MIDDLE - Mark Chilton brilliantly taken off Jimmy Ormond
BOTTOM - A flashing square cut off Jimmy Anderson takes Batty closer to his century
*(All photos by Reg Elliott)*

# KENT SUCCUMB AT THE OVAL

TOP - Jon Batty takes a great catch off Martin Bicknell to remove Robert Key in Kent's first innings
MIDDLE - Ali Brown cuts Matthew Fleming backward of point during his epic innings of 188
BOTTOM - Jimmy Ormond drives Min Patel through the covers
*(All photos by Reg Elliott)*

# BROWN'S STUNNING 268 STARTS RECORDS AVALANCHE

TOP - Brown acknowledges the crowd's applause for his double-century
while the bowler, Andrew Davies, looks ready to wave the white flag
MIDDLE - Having rewritten the record books, Brown leaves the field to a well-deserved standing ovation
*(Photos courtesy of Surrey CCC)*
BOTTOM - The historic scoreboard at the end of Surrey's record-breaking innings
*(Photo by John Banfield)*

# HAPPIER DAYS

TOP - Adam Hollioake presents Mark Ramprakash with his Surrey cap
*(Photo by Richard Spiller)*
BOTTOM - The Surrey captain enjoys a joke with his team-mates during the National League match at Guildford
*(Photo by Peter Frost)*

The wicket of Chilton, from the final ball of Ormond's incomplete over, does, however, give the Surrey supporters remaining in the ground some hope of such a miracle occurring. At 49-2, with the opener exiting to an lbw decision for twenty-three, Lancashire still have a little work to do if they are to claim the draw that their performance in the match hardly warrants.

They are bolstered by the appearance of Stuart Law, though, and runs flow at quite a rate from both batsmen as an eager posse of slips and other close catchers leave yawning gaps to invite run-scoring. While Fairbrother survives a couple of anxious moments, with inside-edges that whistle past his leg stump, the Australian strokes the ball around confidently, cutting and driving boundaries during an expensive seventh over by Ormond that costs thirteen.

With the home side seemingly heading for a comfortable draw at this stage, Bicknell then wins the third lbw verdict of the innings by trapping Fairbrother in front of his stumps in the following over, with the left-hander's score on thirty-eight, the total standing at eighty-five, and twenty overs left to play. Is there to be a final twist? Graham Lloyd's early insecurity certainly suggests that there could be, but time is very much against the visitors and Law is looking calm and assured.

Surrey eventually opt to give a single to the Queenslander wherever possible, in order to get the still shaky Lloyd on strike, but it proves to no avail and, with eight overs remaining to be bowled, Ward admits defeat in his quest to conjure up a last-gasp win on a frustrating final day.

**Surrey 382 and 246-6dec; Lancashire 194 and 112-3**
**Match Drawn. Surrey 10pts, Lancashire 6**

## VIEWS FROM THE DRESSING ROOM

*The weather forecasts I saw and heard suggested that rain was a strong possibility for the last two days of the match, but I later read an article where Medders stated that the decision to bat again was based on a good forecast from the local weather centre - is that correct? I assume we might have decided to enforce the follow-on had you heard a different forecast?!*
**IAN WARD** - We had to make a tricky declaration and we trusted the weather forecast from Manchester United's computer and, unfortunately, it let us down on the last day. Without the rain, we would have had 116 overs in which to bowl them out, which I'm sure would have been more than enough - with Saqlain and Salisbury in the side, we were always going to come out on top. If we had been able to be certain about the weather then we would have gone a different way, of course, but you can't base declarations on weather forecasts. The advice we got about the weather was just incorrect, unfortunately. Mind you, that was only a small part of the decision not to enforce the follow-on, and to declare when I did.

*Although the rain denied us the chance of claiming victory, I guess we would have settled for a 10-point draw at Old Trafford before the match started?*
**IAN WARD** - We go into any contest believing we can win until it's proved otherwise, so this game was no different from any other in that respect. When you go away to play a side as talented as Lancashire you've got to be at your best, but we go into every game trying to come away with the maximum twenty points. On this occasion we had to accept that the weather beat us and we had to walk away with a draw.

*Do you have any special memories of your Championship debut match?*
**RIKKI CLARKE** - Just that I was pleased to have done quite well. Obviously I didn't bowl a lot of overs, and those I did bowl went for quite a few runs, but I took that as part of my learning curve, especially bowling to Stuart Law. I felt that scoring forty-one and twenty-four wasn't a bad way to start, plus I got a run-out as well.

## LANCASHIRE v SURREY at Old Trafford.    Played 31st May to 3rd June

Surrey won the toss and elected to bat       Umpires:- David Constant and Nigel Cowley

### SURREY - First Innings

| Fall Of Wkt | Batsman | How | Out | Score | Balls | 4s | 6s |
|---|---|---|---|---|---|---|---|
| 4-167 | I.J. Ward * | c Hegg | b Anderson | 61 | 198 | 6 | 0 |
| 1-18 | M.A. Carberry | c Law | b Hogg | 10 | 37 | 2 | 0 |
| 2-143 | M.R. Ramprakash | run | out | 71 | 137 | 9 | 0 |
| 3-143 | N. Shahid | lbw | b Keedy | 0 | 2 | 0 | 0 |
| 5-177 | A.D. Brown | | b Keedy | 28 | 45 | 3 | 2 |
| 6-279 | R. Clarke | c Law | b Anderson | 41 | 100 | 7 | 0 |
| 9-377 | J.N. Batty + | | b Keedy | 104 | 220 | 14 | 1 |
| 7-292 | M.P. Bicknell | | b Keedy | 5 | 11 | 0 | 0 |
| 8-332 | I.D.K. Salisbury | c Law | b Keedy | 19 | 67 | 2 | 0 |
| | Saqlain Mushtaq | Not | Out | 19 | 59 | 2 | 0 |
| 10-382 | J. Ormond | c Fairbrother | b Martin | 2 | 7 | 0 | 0 |
| | Extras | (4b, 16lb, 2nb) | | 22 | | | |
| | **TOTAL** | **(147 overs)** | | **382** | | | |

| Bowler | O | M | R | W | NB | Wd |
|---|---|---|---|---|---|---|
| Martin | 30 | 17 | 36 | 1 | - | - |
| Chapple | 28 | 6 | 72 | 0 | - | - |
| Hogg | 20 | 4 | 54 | 1 | 1 | - |
| Anderson | 19 | 4 | 65 | 2 | - | - |
| Keedy | 45 | 13 | 122 | 5 | - | - |
| Chilton | 3 | 0 | 10 | 0 | - | - |
| Swann | 2 | 1 | 3 | 0 | - | - |

### LANCASHIRE - First Innings (Needing 233 to avoid the follow-on)

| Fall Of Wkt | Batsman | How | Out | Score | Balls | 4s | 6s |
|---|---|---|---|---|---|---|---|
| 2-36 | M.J. Chilton | c Batty | b Ormond | 13 | 51 | 2 | 0 |
| 1-33 | A.J. Swann | run | out | 18 | 47 | 3 | 0 |
| 4-103 | N.H. Fairbrother | | b Saqlain | 35 | 63 | 7 | 0 |
| 3-87 | S.G. Law | c Batty | b Bicknell | 18 | 35 | 4 | 0 |
| 5-107 | G.D. Lloyd | c Batty | b Ormond | 9 | 37 | 0 | 0 |
| 6-109 | W.K. Hegg *+ | c Shahid | b Saqlain | 1 | 16 | 0 | 0 |
| 8-189 | G. Chapple | c Brown | b Salisbury | 51 | 113 | 7 | 0 |
| 7-161 | K.W. Hogg | c Ward | b Saqlain | 16 | 52 | 1 | 0 |
| 10-194 | P.J. Martin | c Batty | b Salisbury | 7 | 41 | 1 | 0 |
| 9-194 | G. Keedy | c Batty | b Saqlain | 3 | 6 | 0 | 0 |
| | J.M. Anderson | Not | Out | 0 | 1 | 0 | 0 |
| | Extras | (11lb, 2w, 10nb) | | 23 | | | |
| | **TOTAL** | **(76.1 overs)** | | **194** | | | |

| Bowler | O | M | R | W | NB | Wd |
|---|---|---|---|---|---|---|
| Bicknell | 17 | 6 | 43 | 1 | - | - |
| Ormond | 15 | 3 | 47 | 2 | 2 | - |
| Saqlain Mushtaq | 29 | 10 | 43 | 4 | 2 | - |
| Clarke | 5 | 0 | 34 | 0 | 1 | 1 |
| Salisbury | 10.1 | 2 | 16 | 2 | - | - |

### SURREY - Second Innings (Leading by 188 on first innings)

| Fall Of Wkt | Batsman | How | Out | Score | Balls | 4s | 6s |
|---|---|---|---|---|---|---|---|
| 5-193 | I.J. Ward * | c Chilton | b Hogg | 106 | 169 | 16 | 0 |
| 1-98 | M.A. Carberry | c Hegg | b Anderson | 24 | 113 | 1 | 1 |
| 2-98 | M.R. Ramprakash | lbw | b Anderson | 0 | 1 | 0 | 0 |
| 3-101 | N. Shahid | c Hegg | b Chapple | 1 | 7 | 0 | 0 |
| 4-155 | A.D. Brown | c Chapple | b Keedy | 30 | 29 | 4 | 0 |
| 6-205 | R. Clarke | c Swann | b Hogg | 24 | 38 | 4 | 0 |
| | J.N. Batty + | Not | Out | 12 | 25 | 0 | 0 |
| | M.P. Bicknell | Not | Out | 29 | 20 | 2 | 2 |
| | Extras | (10b, 6lb, 4w) | | 20 | | | |
| | **TOTAL** | **(67 overs)** | **(for 6 dec)** | **246** | | | |

| Bowler | O | M | R | W | NB | Wd |
|---|---|---|---|---|---|---|
| Martin | 11 | 4 | 17 | 0 | - | - |
| Chapple | 15 | 5 | 36 | 1 | - | - |
| Hogg | 9 | 0 | 46 | 2 | - | - |
| Anderson | 9 | 1 | 22 | 2 | - | - |
| Keedy | 17 | 0 | 84 | 1 | - | - |
| Chilton | 5 | 0 | 14 | 0 | - | - |
| Law | 1 | 0 | 11 | 0 | - | - |

| LANCASHIRE - Second Innings | | (Needing 434 to win) | | | | | |
|---|---|---|---|---|---|---|---|
| Fall Of Wkt | Batsman | How | Out | Score | Balls | 4s | 6s |
| 2-49 | M.J. Chilton | lbw | b Ormond | 23 | 35 | 4 | 0 |
| 1-9 | A.J. Swann | lbw | b Bicknell | 3 | 7 | 0 | 0 |
| 3-85 | N.H. Fairbrother | lbw | b Bicknell | 38 | 34 | 6 | 0 |
| | S.G. Law | Not | Out | 33 | 45 | 5 | 0 |
| | G.D. Lloyd | Not | Out | 6 | 38 | 0 | 0 |
| | Extras | (1lb, 2w, 6nb) | | 9 | | | |
| | TOTAL | (26 overs) | (for 3 wkts) | 112 | | | |

| Bowler | O | M | R | W | NB | Wd |
|---|---|---|---|---|---|---|
| Bicknell | 11 | 2 | 52 | 2 | - | - |
| Ormond | 12 | 2 | 58 | 1 | 3 | 1 |
| Saqlain Mushtaq | 3 | 2 | 1 | 0 | - | - |

## Other Division One Results

At the start of the campaign, Yorkshire had been tipped to challenge for the title again, while Leicestershire had been heavily backed for relegation. These views were already in need of reassessment, however, following the Foxes five-wicket win over the champions at Grace Road. Yorkshire's crown was already slipping badly after six weeks of the season, while Vince Wells' team moved past Surrey to the top of the table, though they had played one more game. Kent advanced to fifth places, with games in hand over all of the teams above them, after their four-wicket victory over struggling Sussex.

May 31-June 3
*The Rose Bowl:-* **Hampshire drew with Warwickshire.** Warwickshire 250 (Powell 92, Troughton 63, Mullally 6-56) and 329-8dec (Troughton 131*); Hampshire 277 (Crawley 60, Pollock 4-37) and 142-7. **Hampshire 9pts, Warwickshire 9**

*Tunbridge Wells:-* **Kent beat Sussex by four wickets.** Sussex 180 (Saggers 6-39) and 354 (Montgomerie 79, Goodwin 76, Prior 67, Symonds 6-105); Kent 343 (Symonds 89, Ealham 83*, Kirtley 4-88) and 195-6 (Smith 82). **Kent 18pts, Sussex 3**

*Leicester:-* **Leicestershire beat Yorkshire by five wickets.** Yorkshire 310 (White 62, Lehmann 51, Malcolm 6-72) and 239 (Lehmann 119*, DeFreitas 5-38, Malcolm 4-76); Leicestershire 346 (Bevan 142, Maddy 61) and 207-5 (Bevan 76*, Maddy 58). **Leicestershire 18pts, Yorkshire 5.5***
* deducted 0.5pt for slow over rate

### COUNTY CHAMPIONSHIP DIVISION ONE AT 3RD JUNE

| Pos | Prv | | P | Points | W | D | L | Bat | Bwl | Ded |
|---|---|---|---|---|---|---|---|---|---|---|
| 1 | 2 | Leicestershire | 6 | 80.00 | 3 | 2 | 1 | 20 | 17 | 1.00 |
| 2 | 1 | Surrey | 5 | 73.75 | 3 | 2 | 0 | 15 | 15 | 0.25 |
| 3 | 3 | Hampshire | 6 | 64.00 | 1 | 4 | 1 | 19 | 17 | 0.00 |
| 4 | 4 | Lancashire | 5 | 57.00 | 2 | 2 | 1 | 11 | 14 | 0.00 |
| 5 | 7 | Kent | 4 | 51.00 | 2 | 1 | 1 | 13 | 10 | 0.00 |
| 6 | 5 | Somerset | 4 | 48.00 | 1 | 3 | 0 | 13 | 11 | 0.00 |
| 7 | 6 | Sussex | 5 | 38.00 | 0 | 3 | 2 | 12 | 14 | 0.00 |
| 8 | 8 | Yorkshire | 5 | 28.50 | 0 | 1 | 4 | 10 | 15 | 0.50 |
| 9 | 9 | Warwickshire | 4 | 25.00 | 0 | 2 | 2 | 7 | 10 | 0.00 |

### NUL2 - Greenidge Has Last Laugh As Lions Snatch Defeat From Jaws Of Victory

On the Bank Holiday Tuesday that marked the Queen's Golden Jubilee, Surrey made a right royal mess of their Norwich Union League match against the Northamptonshire Steelbacks at Northampton. Overcoming early adversity when Mike Hussey and Mal Loye put on 127 for the first wicket in twenty-seven overs, the Lions put themselves in a strong match-winning position before losing their way with some brainless batting and then surrendering to Surrey old boy, Carl Greenidge, who wiped out the tail.

The Steelbacks' solid start, during which Hussey was missed by Stewart off the excellent Giddins on three, should have produced a bigger total, but the loss of the Australian left-hander and David Sales to consecutive balls in Giddins' second spell, coupled with their inability to deal effectively with the spin of Saqlain and Salisbury, left them grateful for a late Tony Penberthy-inspired surge that produced sixty-two runs from the last nine overs of the innings.

On a typically flat Wantage Road pitch, Surrey's target of 230 looked far from testing, especially once Ali Brown, with a stunning 29-ball fifty, and Ian Ward had powered the score up to 82-1 after just nine overs. Carl Greenidge had been quickly removed from the attack after conceding seven fours in two overs, while another former Surrey man, Darren Cousins, conceded forty-seven runs in his opening burst of five overs as Brown rapidly reduced the Lions' requirement for the rest of the innings to four runs an over.

The loss of the Surrey beneficiary for fifty-five in the eleventh over came just in the nick of time for the home side, however, as first Penberthy and then Jason Brown exercised tight control for the Steelbacks. Unfortunately for Surrey, only Mark Ramprakash seemed to appreciate that there was no need to take risks after such a wonderful start, and dismal strokes by his experienced middle-order partners gave the home side renewed hope.

When the former England batsman finally found a sensible ally in Rikki Clarke, it seemed that the visitors would recover from their self-induced mini crisis, especially as Greenidge proved only marginally more effective during a second spell of 2-0-16-0, and Ricky Anderson chalked up nine wides in an otherwise decent spell.

A brilliant leaping overhead catch by Cousins at mid-off to dismiss Ramprakash in the thirty-fourth over with just fifty runs required then brought the Steelbacks back into contention, however, before two more poorly conceived strokes, this time by Tudor and Bicknell against Jeff Cook and a much improved Cousins, put the game right back in the balance.

Clarke continued to bat bravely and sensibly in reaching his maiden limited-overs fifty from 67 balls, but Hussey's brave decision to recall Greenidge turned the tide decisively as the former Surrey seamer took the wickets of Clarke and Saqlain with his first two deliveries and then shattered Salisbury's stumps in his next over to pull off an astonishing win.

While it was impossible to begrudge the likeable Greenidge his moment of glory as he led his new team-mates from the field with a broad grin spread wide across his face, it was immensely disappointing that yet another one-day game had been lost by a small margin, in this case from a position where it had looked harder to lose the match than to win it.

## NORTHAMPTONSHIRE STEELBACKS v SURREY LIONS at Northampton
### Played on Tuesday 4th June    Northamptonshire Steelbacks won by 5 runs
Northamptonshire Steelbacks won the toss and elected to bat    Umpires:- Nigel Llong & George Sharp

**NORTHAMPTONSHIRE STEELBACKS**

| Fall Of Wkt | Batsman | How | Out | Score | Balls | 4s | 6s |
|---|---|---|---|---|---|---|---|
| 1-127 | M.E.K. Hussey * | | b Giddins | 69 | 84 | 5 | 1 |
| 5-208 | M.B. Loye | | b Bicknell | 86 | 115 | 7 | 3 |
| 2-127 | D.J.G. Sales | lbw | b Giddins | 0 | 1 | 0 | 0 |
| 3-158 | R.J. Warren | c & | b Salisbury | 17 | 19 | 3 | 0 |
| 4-160 | J.W. Cook | | b Salisbury | 1 | 7 | 0 | 0 |
| 6-224 | A.L. Penberthy | run | out | 38 | 37 | 3 | 0 |
| | T.M.B. Bailey + | Not | Out | 8 | 6 | 1 | 0 |
| | R.S.G. Anderson | Not | Out | 1 | 2 | 0 | 0 |
| | C.G. Greenidge | did not bat | | | | | |
| | D.M. Cousins | did not bat | | | | | |
| | J.F. Brown | did not bat | | | | | |
| | Extras | (4lb, 3w, 2nb) | | 9 | | | |
| | **TOTAL** | **(45 overs)** | **(for 6 wkts)** | **229** | | | |

| Bowler | O | M | R | W | NB | Wd |
|---|---|---|---|---|---|---|
| Bicknell | 9 | 0 | 47 | 1 | - | - |
| Giddins | 9 | 1 | 35 | 2 | - | - |
| Clarke | 3 | 0 | 29 | 0 | 1 | 2 |
| Tudor | 9 | 0 | 46 | 0 | - | - |
| Saqlain Mushtaq | 8 | 0 | 33 | 0 | - | - |
| Salisbury | 7 | 0 | 35 | 2 | - | 1 |

### SURREY LIONS

| Fall Of Wkt | Batsman | How | Out | Score | Balls | 4s | 6s |
|---|---|---|---|---|---|---|---|
| 1-68 | I.J. Ward * | c Hussey | b Penberthy | 25 | 23 | 6 | 0 |
| 2-84 | A.D. Brown | c Hussey | b Anderson | 55 | 36 | 10 | 1 |
| 5-180 | M.R. Ramprakash | c Cousins | b Anderson | 44 | 68 | 3 | 0 |
| 3-112 | A.J. Stewart + | c Penberthy | b Anderson | 5 | 13 | 0 | 0 |
| 4-117 | N. Shahid | st Bailey | b Brown | 2 | 11 | 0 | 0 |
| 8-215 | R. Clarke | c Cook | b Greenidge | 52 | 71 | 4 | 0 |
| 6-188 | A.J. Tudor | c Bailey | b Cook | 4 | 9 | 0 | 0 |
| 7-203 | M.P. Bicknell | c Hussey | b Cousins | 8 | 17 | 0 | 0 |
| 10-224 | I.D.K. Salisbury | | b Greenidge | 6 | 12 | 0 | 0 |
| 9-215 | Saqlain Mushtaq | lbw | b Greenidge | 0 | 1 | 0 | 0 |
| | E.S.H. Giddins | Not | Out | 5 | 5 | 1 | 0 |
| | Extras | (4lb, 14w) | | 18 | | | |
| | TOTAL | (44.2 overs) | | 224 | | | |

| Bowler | O | M | R | W | NB | Wd |
|---|---|---|---|---|---|---|
| Cousins | 9 | 0 | 54 | 1 | - | 1 |
| Greenidge | 5.2 | 0 | 49 | 3 | - | 1 |
| Penberthy | 9 | 0 | 27 | 1 | - | 1 |
| Anderson | 7 | 0 | 30 | 3 | - | 9 |
| Brown | 9 | 0 | 35 | 1 | - | 1 |
| Cook | 5 | 0 | 25 | 1 | - | 1 |

## Other NUL Division Two Results

Even at this early stage of the season, only the Hawks and the Steelbacks remained unbeaten. Gloucestershire followed up their victory over Surrey by beating Lancashire convincingly at Old Trafford.

May 26
*Old Trafford:-* **Lancashire Lightning v Middlesex Crusaders - Match abandoned without a ball bowled. Lancashire Lightning 2pts, Middlesex Crusaders 2**

June 4
*Old Trafford:-* **Gloucestershire Gladiators beat Lancashire Lightning by 79 runs.** Gloucestershire 269-8 (Barnett 66, Wood 5-49); Lancashire 190 (41ov). **Gloucestershire Gladiators 4pts**

*Lord's:-* **Hampshire Hawks beat Middlesex Crusaders by 2 runs.** Hampshire 183-8 (Abdul Razzaq 3-25); Middlesex 181-9 (Udal 3-35). **Hampshire Hawks 4pts**

*Horsham:-* **Sussex Sharks beat Essex Eagles by 32 runs.** Sussex 240 (45ov; Prior 73, Irani 3-45); Essex 208 (40.2ov; Irani 51, Napier 50, Davis 3-40). **Sussex Sharks 4pts**

### NATIONAL LEAGUE DIVISION TWO AT 4TH JUNE

| Pos | Prv | | P | Pts | W | T | L | A |
|---|---|---|---|---|---|---|---|---|
| 1 | n/a | Hampshire Hawks | 2 | 8 | 2 | 0 | 0 | 0 |
| = | n/a | Northamptonshire Steelbacks | 2 | 8 | 2 | 0 | 0 | 0 |
| 3 | n/a | Gloucestershire Gladiators | 3 | 8 | 2 | 0 | 1 | 0 |
| 4 | n/a | Lancashire Lightning | 4 | 6 | 1 | 0 | 2 | 1 |
| 5 | n/a | Derbyshire Scorpions | 2 | 4 | 1 | 0 | 1 | 0 |
| = | n/a | Essex Eagles | 2 | 4 | 1 | 0 | 1 | 0 |
| 7 | n/a | Surrey Lions | 3 | 4 | 1 | 0 | 2 | 0 |
| = | n/a | Sussex Sharks | 3 | 4 | 1 | 0 | 2 | 0 |
| 9 | n/a | Middlesex Crusaders | 3 | 2 | 0 | 0 | 2 | 1 |

## NUL Division Two Results

A very wet Sunday saw all three scheduled matches abandoned, with only 32 deliveries bowled in total.

June 9

*The Rose Bowl:-* **Hampshire Hawks v Derbyshire Scorpions - Match abandoned without a ball bowled. Hampshire Hawks 2pts, Derbyshire Scorpions 2**

*Lord's:-* **Middlesex Crusaders v Sussex Sharks - No Result.** Sussex 25-1 (5.2ov). **Middlesex Crusaders 2pts, Sussex Sharks 2**

*Northampton:-* **Northamptonshire Steelbacks v Gloucestershire Gladiators - Match abandoned without a ball bowled. Northamptonshire Steelbacks 2pts, Gloucestershire Gladiators 2**

### NATIONAL LEAGUE DIVISION TWO AT 9TH JUNE

| Pos | Prv | | P | Pts | W | T | L | A |
|---|---|---|---|---|---|---|---|---|
| 1 | 1 | Hampshire Hawks | 3 | 10 | 2 | 0 | 0 | 1 |
| = | 1 | Northamptonshire Steelbacks | 3 | 10 | 2 | 0 | 0 | 1 |
| 3 | 3 | Gloucestershire Gladiators | 4 | 10 | 2 | 0 | 1 | 1 |
| 4 | 5 | Derbyshire Scorpions | 3 | 6 | 1 | 0 | 1 | 1 |
| 5 | 4 | Lancashire Lightning | 4 | 6 | 1 | 0 | 2 | 1 |
| = | 7 | Sussex Sharks | 4 | 6 | 1 | 0 | 2 | 1 |
| 7 | 5 | Essex Eagles | 2 | 4 | 1 | 0 | 1 | 0 |
| 8 | 7 | Surrey Lions | 3 | 4 | 1 | 0 | 2 | 0 |
| 9 | 9 | Middlesex Crusaders | 4 | 4 | 0 | 0 | 2 | 2 |

# 8 Adam Returns

The Surrey team now had a seven-day break to recover from the eight days on the road in Edinburgh, Manchester and Northampton that had followed hard on the heels of the match against Somerset in the Championship.

Much to everyone's delight, Adam Hollioake was now back in the country, with his family due to join him a few weeks later. Although cricket had rather paled into insignificance for him after the loss of his brother and the birth of his daughter, he would doubtless have been pleased with Surrey's position in the Frizzell County Championship, though he might not have been so impressed by the team's disappointingly inconsistent start to their NUL Division Two campaign and their early exit from the Benson And Hedges Cup. It was because the semi-finals of the latter competition were taking place at this point in the calendar that Surrey were now having a break. Although everyone would have wanted to be involved in the semis, attempting to get to another Lord's final and retain the trophy that Ben had done so much to win in 2001, it was no bad thing to have this opportunity to take stock after a hectic period.

The Championship campaign was going incredibly well and, but for the rain that had badly affected the last two matches, it was not inconceivable that Surrey could have been boasting a record of five wins out of five. There were a number of possible reasons why a team who traditionally started the season very slowly had hit the ground running on this occasion but, quite apart from the overwhelming desire to 'do it for Ben', the two I favoured were the increased strength-in-depth of the seam attack and the unseasonably fine weather.

The close season capture of Jimmy Ormond and the short-term employment of Azhar Mahmood, had given the county their most impressive battery of seam and swing bowlers for many seasons - in fact it became a point of interest to ask older supporters if they could think of a better Surrey quartet. One of the strengths of this foursome was that each bowler offered something different, though the presence of a left-armer would have given even greater variety, of course. Alex Tudor, deservedly back in the England fold, and the now-departed Azhar had certainly been tremendous in the early weeks of the campaign, while Martin Bicknell had been his usual consistent self, though not seemingly at the peak of his form yet. Ormond was the one man who had looked short of his best to date, though it had to be taken into account that he had suffered more than anyone from dropped catches, and also probably needed a bit longer to settle in at his new county. It had been immediately obvious, however, that the Club had signed a very skilful bowler with plenty of weapons in his armoury in terms of pace, swing, seam, yorkers, slower balls and bouncers.

In previous seasons Surrey had been vulnerable in the early weeks of a campaign because of their lack of depth in the seam department, a weakness that was always exacerbated by the damp green pitches often encountered in April and May. Unusually, in the opening stages of the 2002 season we had been lucky enough to enjoy a great deal of fine warm weather, which was certainly of assistance to a side like Surrey with exceptional talent in batting and spin bowling. The batsmen were able to get into their stride straight away and find their form, while, on the occasions that spin was needed in the attack, the bowlers were not handicapped by a wet or greasy ball. It was quite possible to believe that someone 'upstairs' was smiling upon Surrey.

There was a lot of cricket still to be played, however, as we turned our attention to the next match, with Kent the visitors to The AMP Oval. David Fulton's team had started the season reasonably well, having won two games out of four, and sat twenty-three points behind Surrey with a game in hand. An interesting contest appeared to be in the offing, though it had come too soon for Adam Hollioake, who had decided to play in the second eleven's match at Canterbury in order to try and find some form ahead of his return to first team action.

| FRIZZELL COUNTY CHAMPIONSHIP - MATCH SIX |
|---|

## SURREY versus KENT
## at The AMP Oval

### First Day - Wednesday 12th June

### Kent 153; Surrey 111-5

***The Teams And The Toss*** - *Kent are able to select what would appear to be their strongest possible side for this match after restoring Matthew Fleming to their team, having dropped him for the first time in eleven seasons to accommodate Ben Trott in the eleven that defeated Sussex at Tunbridge Wells in their previous outing. Surrey meanwhile make one change of their own after the draw at Old Trafford, electing to play an extra specialist seam bowler, Ed Giddins, in place of Michael Carberry, with Jon Batty moving up the order to open the batting. The inclusion of Giddins, making his first County Championship appearance of the season, seems to be a sensible one, given that conditions are very damp and overcast - several rainy days have preceded the match and a heavy overnight downpour delays the start of play until 1.40pm, following an early lunch. In the circumstances it is no great surprise when Ian Ward invites Kent to bat upon winning the toss.*

The late start to the match has at least given everyone time to come down from the high of England's qualification for the second stage of the World Cup, following a 0-0 draw with Nigeria earlier in the morning, though everyone is now fully focused on the cricket - which is just as well since the game gets off to an explosive start.

Martin Bicknell's opening over starts disappointingly with a wide and an off-driven two for the Kent skipper, David Fulton, but ends on a high, with the fifth ball beating the outside edge and the final delivery nipping back the other way to trap the batsman plumb in front of his stumps. Umpire John Steele has no hesitation in raising his finger and Kent are 4-1.

Like Bicknell, Jimmy Ormond, operating from the pavilion end, has a shaky start as Robert Key drives his first delivery to the rope at long-on, though the Surrey paceman soon bounces back, finding the edge of the Kent opener's bat once in his first over, bringing two runs to third man, and twice in his second, with the ball not quite carrying to the slips on either occasion. Key retaliates with another on-driven four off the former Leicestershire paceman and then forces Bicknell to the boundary backward of point in the sixth over but, from here on, it's pretty much downhill all the way for the visitors. Although they reach a high point of 27-1 when Ed Smith pulls the slightly wayward Ormond over wide mid-on for the fourth boundary of the morning, four wickets then tumble in the space of seven highly eventful overs as Kent subside to 48-5.

Bicknell starts the Kent slide, removing Key with a brilliant piece of Surrey cricket as the batsman's defensive edge to a superb outswinger is magnificently picked up very low in front of first slip by the airborne Batty, before Ormond takes wickets in consecutive overs to put the home side firmly in the driving seat. A score of 27-2 becomes 38-4 as Andrew Symonds' square cut picks out Ian Salisbury in the gully, then Matthew Walker edges a fine, lifting delivery straight to Rikki Clarke at second slip in just the tenth over of the innings.

Despite the loss of three partners since his arrival at the crease at the end of the first over, Ed Smith has maintained a positive approach throughout, even though he has enjoyed a few slices of good fortune along the way. He finally comes unstuck in Bicknell's seventh over, however, when he drives loosely at a markedly slower outswinger and holes out to Ian Ward at backward point, the relieved fielder holding the head-high chance at the second attempt to send the batsman on his way for twenty.

Despite this clatter of wickets there appears to be nothing wrong with the pitch, a point that is underlined by Paul Nixon as he drives his first ball wide of mid-on for three to raise the Kent fifty, before following up with two more drives, both for four, in the ninth, and final, over of Bicknell's top-quality spell. Having almost secured his third wicket when Mark Ealham edges a delivery just past his leg stump for four, Ormond then joins his colleague in taking a break, with the bowling baton passing to Ed Giddins and Rikki Clarke.

Although the new bowlers allow few liberties, the sixth-wicket pair continue to bat purposefully, with Nixon, by far the more assured of the duo, once again proving to be a serious irritation to Surrey. Ealham never looks likely to make a significant score, however, and, though he brings up the fifty partnership with the best shot of his innings, a square-driven boundary off Giddins, and raises the Kent hundred from the following delivery, he departs later in the same over when he hits across the line of a ball seaming back into him and falls lbw. Giddins' first Championship wicket of the season puts the opposition back in the mire at 100-6 and brings together two gutsy competitors as Matthew Fleming, joins the nuggety Nixon at the crease.

Although the seventh-wicket pair initially seem content to batten down the hatches, Fleming does eventually open his account in typical style by launching a leg-side drive to the boundary off Giddins. Consequently, sensing the veteran all-rounder's desire to attack, Ward shrewdly turns to Saqlain Mushtaq in place of Clarke and almost immediately gets the result he is seeking when the impetuous former Kent skipper dances down the pitch and edges a drive just wide of slip, adding two rather fortunate runs to his score as a result. The visitors' nerves are then further frayed by a mix-up in the running that almost costs Nixon his wicket, before Kentish composure is briefly restored when each batsman drives Giddins to the cover boundary.

With tea now just five overs away, Ward abandons his three-over flirtation with Saqlain and brings Giddins' inconsistent nine-over stint to a halt in order to reintroduce his opening bowlers. This turns out to be a masterstroke as the final ball of Ormond's opening over tempts Fleming into a rash drive, without footwork, at a delivery wide of off stump, leaving Batty to pouch the resulting outside edge and thereby complete the seventh dismissal of the Kent innings with the total at 129.

Much to the home side's delight, Bicknell's return at the other end is then also justified when Min Patel falls three overs later for a second-ball duck, his equally reckless drive at an outswinger presenting Nadeem Shahid with a low chance at third slip. The Surrey fielder makes an awkward catch look easy and the loss of this eighth wicket in the penultimate over of what has been a long session leaves Kent floundering badly at the interval.

*Tea:- Kent 140-8 (Nixon 46\*, Khan 0\*) from 40 overs*

Kent's woes multiply after the break as Surrey require a mere eighteen deliveries to capture the visitors' last two wickets.

It takes just two of these to produce the ninth wicket of the day, and it comes in stunning fashion as Amjad Khan's fierce sliced drive at a Bicknell outswinger is plucked out of the air, high to his left-hand side, by Ian Salisbury in the gully. This truly breathtaking catch brings a standing ovation from many spectators and also prompts inevitable memories of Surrey's lost son. Since Ben Hollioake was one of the finest gully fielders you could ever wish to see, it is no surprise that supporters around me are echoing my own feeling that Ben would have been proud to call this catch his own. The wicket of Khan also takes Bicknell through to a highly significant career milestone, since it completes his set of five-wicket hauls against every other county team. This statistic, which bears testimony to his enduring quality and consistency, is announced over the public address system, prompting another sustained and appreciative ovation before play resumes.

When it does, Nixon soon completes a determined 82-ball half-century by driving Ormond to the boundary at backward point, before Bicknell finishes off the innings in his next over with the score at 153. After conceding fours from a thick-edge by Saggers and a miscued drive over square cover by Nixon, Surrey's senior bowler has the last laugh as he ends the Kent wicketkeeper's doughty knock with the assistance of Saqlain, who runs around from mid-off to hold a good catch behind the bowler after another mishit stroke has spiralled skywards.

As a happy and contented Bicknell leads his colleagues from the field to well-deserved applause with figures of 13-5-42-6 to his name, it would seem that Surrey are already in a position of strength in the match, since Kent's total looks well below par. Although the ball has moved around, especially in the air, it hasn't done so to an outrageous degree, and the visitors' dismal showing appears largely down to their own frenetic batting performance, coupled with some very good bowling and outstanding catching by their hosts.

With his decision to insert the opposition fully vindicated, Ian Ward has a chance to further enhance his side's position as he comes out to open the Surrey innings with Jon Batty.

Unfortunately, however, the stand-in skipper is soon back in the pavilion as umpire Barry Dudleston adjudges him caught behind off Khan from the fifth ball of the second over, the ball having jagged back between bat and pad. Ward clearly feels that he hasn't got a touch as he departs with the score at 3-1, and it isn't long before he is joined back in the dressing room by Mark Ramprakash, who falls to the same combination of bowler and umpire in Khan's next over, the verdict this time being lbw as another ball cuts back sharply. It's very much 'game on' at 5-2, with Surrey in danger of losing their hard-earned advantage.

Nadeem Shahid attempts to tackle the situation head on, however, picking up three early fours off Khan, an extra-cover drive and a square cut which are very much middled, plus a thick inside edge that fairly rockets through square leg. Batty, meanwhile, looks the more secure of the Surrey pair, handling Kent's Danish import with care, while still managing to force Saggers to the rope at cover on two occasions when the former Durham man pitches a little too short.

The home team's recovery is nipped in the bud all too soon, however, as the introduction of Matthew Fleming, after just four overs from Khan, brings another breakthrough for the visitors. Shahid has already snicked the former Kent skipper through the vacant fourth slip position to register the fourth boundary of his innings when he is adjudged caught down the leg side by Nixon from the first ball of Fleming's third over. Judging by the batsman's reaction, umpire Dudleston is now going to be short of another greetings card come December 25th as the former Essex man exits slowly at 39-3.

With Mark Ealham now linking up with Fleming in the attack, and Alistair Brown arriving at the crease to join Batty, the game enters quite a tense phase, and a lack of courage by the Kent captain at this stage costs his side dearly. Although each batsman strikes Ealham for a boundary with a legitimate stroke, they both follow up with an edge that flies through an untenanted slip position on its way to the rope at third man, making Fulton's extreme reluctance to place more than two slips look all the more foolish.

As luck would have it, two slips are sufficient a couple of overs later, when Batty's drive at a Fleming leg-cutter results in an edge that Andrew Symonds picks up low down at second slip to put Surrey back in deep trouble at 58-4, yet the feeling persists that Kent could have been better placed had their skipper been more aggressive.

Lack of aggression is certainly not a criticism that could ever be levelled at Brown, though, and he responds to the loss of Batty with a brief but sustained assault on Ealham that forces the withdrawal of the former England man from the attack. After clipping the medium-pacer to the square-leg boundary in the nineteenth over of Surrey's reply, Brown crashes three further fours from the second, third and fifth balls of Ealham's next over to take his side beyond the halfway point of their initial objective of gaining a first innings lead.

Unfortunately for the home team, they lose Rikki Clarke immediately after this blitz by Brown, the youngster getting a leading edge to Amjad Khan at mid-off in aiming to work a delivery from Fleming to leg and departing with just five runs to his name. The bowler certainly deserves his third wicket of the innings, having clearly been the pick of the visitors' attack, and he almost adds another victim to his haul in bizarre circumstances when Martin Bicknell manages to toe-end an attempted pull stroke in the direction of third man, shortly after the dismissal of Clarke. Luckily for Bicknell the ball falls safely into space, earning him three runs in the process, and he has no further problems in making it through to the close of play, by which time Brown has taken his side past the hundred mark and raced on to forty-nine with two off-driven fours at the expense of the returning Saggers and a square-cut boundary off Min Patel when the left-arm spinner is introduced to bowl the penultimate over of the day.

*Close:- Surrey 111-5 (Brown 49\*, Bicknell 8\*) from 27 overs*

## VIEWS FROM THE DRESSING ROOM

*It's very rare for us to win the toss at The Oval and elect to field. I assume that the damp conditions leading up to the match - and on the first morning - prompted that decision?*
**MARTIN BICKNELL** - Yes, because it was damp, it was touch-and-go, we weren't sure what to do and we weren't certain what side to select. I was quite keen for us to have Giddo in the side, simply to give us another seam bowling option if we were going to win the toss and bowl. More often than not if you win the toss and put the other side in at The Oval you don't normally get much out of the pitch, so it was nice to see the ball swing. It didn't do much else, though, and I think they contributed to their own downfall by playing some rash shots here and there. We stuck to our task and bowled them out cheaply as a result.

*During their first innings you completed a full set of five-wicket hauls against all the other counties. It seems to me that this bowling feat receives far less attention than a batsman completing a set of centuries against all the other counties. Would you agree?*
**MARTIN BICKNELL** - Certainly, I think you are definitely right, but it was very satisfying for me because it was something I'd had in my mind for about four years that I very much wanted to do. There are some landmarks in the game that mean quite a lot to me and that was one of them.

*Knowing the friendly rivalry that exists between you and Bickers, I guess he might have made a comment or two to you about completing his full set of five-wicket hauls before you completed your full set of centuries against all other counties?!*
**ALI BROWN** - No, he didn't say anything, actually... he must have forgotten! We do have a fun rivalry and we do get on very well, though. When he scored his maiden hundred at Canterbury, I couldn't have been more delighted for him, because I know how the first time you achieve something is often the most special, though I must say that I don't recall him being particularly chuffed for me when I got my first wicket at Old Trafford in 2000! I'll be looking forward to the Lancashire match next year - it's a nice early opportunity in April and I hope I'll have a couple of innings in which to complete my full set.

*On a day when the first fifteen wickets had fallen for 233 runs you raced, seemingly without too much difficulty, to 49 not out by the close of play. Did you feel as comfortable as you looked?*
**ALI BROWN** - There were days last year when I felt very good, and I also had a couple of times when I felt a bit out of sorts, but this was a day when I did feel very comfortable. I think the wicket was very slow when the match started, but Kent came out and played like it was a wicket that was much quicker. By playing fast-wicket shots that weren't suited to the surface,

they got themselves into trouble and ended up being dismissed quite cheaply. I think perhaps the surface had quickened up a bit by the time we batted, though I think we'd also learnt a bit from the way they'd played.

## Second Day - Thursday 13th June

## Kent 153 and 79-1; Surrey 361

There is a bizarre start, or rather non-start, to the second day of the match as most of the Kent players fail to make it to the ground by the time play is due to commence. While spectators are filing into The AMP Oval, news filters through that nine members of the visiting eleven are trapped in a traffic jam somewhere between their Bayswater Road hotel and Vauxhall Bridge Road following chaos caused by a burst water main in Buckingham Palace Road. The umpires therefore decide that play will commence half-an-hour after the Kent team manage to make it to the ground, with the lost time being made up at the end of the third and fourth days of the match.

Over the course of the next hour the opposition players gradually turn up in dribs and drabs, with the relatively short journey from their hotel having taken something like three hours. By midday all are at the ground except Min Patel, whose BMW has overheated. Consequently the umpires announce revised playing hours for the day, as follows:-

*'Morning' session - 12.30pm-2.15pm; Afternoon session - 2.55pm-5.10pm (or when 26 overs remain, whichever is the later); Close of play at 7pm (or after 88 overs have been bowled, whichever is the later).*

It's the strangest schedule for a day's cricket that I can recall, and the sixteen overs that have been lost from today's play will be made up in two batches of eight overs on days three and four. One can only wonder how this morning's nightmare journey will affect Kent's performance, especially in the early stages of the day, though the short first session would appear to favour them, since it will allow David Fulton to utilise his strike pair of Saggers and Khan for a good part of that period of play and then bring them back fully rested after 'lunch', should he so wish.

Predictably enough, it is the Saggers-Khan pairing that we see in action first, though the Dane's opening spell lasts only three overs before he is blasted out of the attack by Ali Brown. Surrey's middle-order marvel carries on exactly as he left off the previous evening, driving the first ball of the day wide of mid-on for two to complete a superbly belligerent 43-ball fifty before cutting and driving two off-side boundaries during the remainder of Khan's opening over. Two further boundaries, the first lofted back over the bowler's head to complete a run-a-ball fifty partnership for the sixth wicket, and the second an on-drive, make Fulton's decision to remove his Copenhagen-born paceman from the firing line quite a straightforward one.

At the other end, meanwhile, Bicknell has also started confidently, striking Saggers back down the ground for three in the former Durham bowler's opening over and driving him through square cover for four in his second, adding to the Kent captain's problems in the process. It's hard to say whether their troubled trip to the ground is having an effect on the visitors' performance but there is no doubt that the Brown-Bicknell alliance is putting Surrey in complete command of the match as they take the total past 150 in the eighth over of the session and overtake Kent's inadequate score in the following over.

Despite being under the cosh, there are a couple of encouraging features for Fulton and his team - the ground fielding remains excellent, with Walker particularly outstanding in the gully/cover/point region this morning, and Matthew Fleming manages to beat Brown on three occasions in an over during a fine start to his first spell of the day. The former skipper again looks by far the best of the Kent bowlers, so it is no surprise when he provides his team with a much needed breakthrough in the thirteenth over of the day by removing Bicknell for twenty-seven with the score at 166. Ironically, it is one of his poorest deliveries, a short ball wide of the off stump, which brings him success, courtesy of a top-edged cut to wicketkeeper Nixon.

With Bicknell's scalp having further improved his overnight figures to 11.1-5-15-4, Fleming then almost completes a five-wicket haul next ball when Ian Salisbury miscues a pull just over wide mid-on, though runs come from every other ball of the over as the leg-spinner recovers instantly from his first-ball aberration and Brown continues on his merry way. The power of Brown's strokeplay is magnificent to behold, in fact, as he hooks Saggers to the boundary and then storms into the nineties with a drive wide of mid-on for four and a lofted off-drive for two in Fleming's next over. The twenty-ninth first-class century of his career is not long in coming, either, as he slashes the ball high over gully to the rope at backward point when he next faces the former Kent captain, and immediately turns to the dressing room and the pavilion to acknowledge the applause for a superb, potentially match-changing century that has come from exactly 100 balls and included eighteen fours.

With the total only 187 at this point, there is still much to do if Surrey are to build a match-winning first innings lead, however, though it seems that nothing can bother Brown as he celebrates his ton with two further boundaries off the previously economical and potent Fleming, thereby forcing Fulton into a double bowling change.

Amjad Khan, at the Vauxhall end, and Mark Ealham, at the pavilion end, duly take over bowling duties from Saggers and Fleming but find the going just as tough when bowling to Brown, both being driven for consecutive fours in the second over of their comeback spells as another fifty partnership is completed to further strengthen Surrey's position. Khan is immediately removed from the attack again and, with the 2.15pm break entitled 'lunch' just four overs away, Min Patel comes on to replace him.

Having only arrived at ground at 1.30pm, not much is expected of the left-arm spinner but he confounds everyone by bowling two successive maidens to Brown, while, at the other end, Ealham emulates his colleague's feat when bowling to Salisbury. Although the last four overs of the session are therefore scoreless, Surrey are doubtless delighted with their position in the match as play is adjourned with Brown very much the hero on 128, out of a total of 225-6.

*Lunch:- Surrey 225-6 (Brown 128\*, Salisbury 9\*) from 53 overs*

Kent's hopes of restricting Surrey's lead receive a boost immediately after lunch with the capture of Salisbury's wicket in the second over with the score at 231. Having just boosted his share of the 65-run seventh-wicket partnership to thirteen with a classy cover drive to the boundary, the leg-spinner falls later in the same over from Khan when his edged forcing stroke is well taken high to his right at second slip by Symonds.

While Brown remains at the crease anything is possible for Surrey, though, and after a quiet start to the session he finally makes some headway against Patel, driving him to the long-off boundary and then finding the rope again later in the same over with a deft late cut to third man. Ominously for Kent, Saqlain Mushtaq looks in the mood to stick around with Brown, resisting the temptation to attempt anything too daring, though he inadvertently provides the four runs that take his team past 250 when a short-pitched Khan delivery ricochets away to the fine leg boundary via his helmet. Far from unsettling the Surrey off-spinner, this appears to strengthen his resolve, and the Dane is soon leaking boundaries again as Saqlain drives to the rope at long-on and long-off and then increases his score by four more runs with a thick edge to third man. When Brown follows up with a cover-driven boundary in Khan's next over, the 21-year-old paceman's fate is again sealed, and Fulton asks Saggers to return to the attack opposite Fleming, who has made an economical start to a new spell from the pavilion end after replacing Patel.

This change proves to be a good one, since Saggers soon ends a partnership that has passed fifty in the over before his reintroduction, thanks to a confident square drive for four by Saqlain. The Pakistani's score has swollen by a further single to twenty-five when the Kent paceman produces a good delivery that swings away to take the outside edge of a defensive bat on its way through to Nixon.

Although Saqlain looks disappointed as he makes his way from the field, he has played a valuable role, like Bicknell and Salisbury before him, in helping boost Surrey's total to a point where victory looks increasingly likely. The hosts' lead is now up to 134, in fact, and could yet extend further, since Brown, having just reached 150 from 161 balls, is not one to give anything away once he is established and in sight of a double century.

In an attempt to slow the Beckenham-born batsman's progress and attack the newly arrived Jimmy Ormond, Kent allow Brown to take singles by spreading the field, but the strongly-built Surrey fast bowler soon makes a mockery of the tactic by reeling off five superb drives for four in as many overs, all of them in the arc between cover and mid-on, and four coming off the surprisingly ineffective Saggers. The second of these Ormond boundaries takes the hosts to a third batting point, which had been unimaginable at 80-5; the third, brilliantly struck on the up and probably the shot of the day, takes the home side's lead past 150; while the fourth and fifth, from consecutive deliveries, bring Saggers' expensive four-over spell to a close.

With Ealham and Patel now restored to the attack, Kent are clearly starting to suffer, since their previously immaculate fielding starts to slip, the nadir coming when a simple run out opportunity is missed in almost comical circumstances. As Ormond lies prostrate in mid pitch, having slipped over when sent back by Brown, Patel fails to gather a simple return from Fleming at mid-off and, unaware that the Surrey man is in no position to easily regain his ground, stands at the stumps cursing his error, instead of retrieving the ball, which has ended up little more than a yard away from him. Ormond is consequently able to pick himself up and make it back to his crease before punishing Patel further with a slog-sweep to the midwicket fence.

Having now taken his score to thirty-three, the big paceman's luck runs out in the next over, however, when Ealham spears a quicker delivery through his defences to disturb the off stump, ending an attractive and impressive innings, while also striking a blow for those who believe in the wicket-taking power of a 'Nelson' total… it's 333-9.

With Ed Giddins making his way to the crease, Kent are now hopeful of finally finishing the innings off, while the Surrey faithful try to remain optimistic about the possibility of their team gaining a fourth batting point. It is clear, though, that Brown has to take charge if this is to happen and, having stolen the strike with a run off the returning Fleming, he immediately breaks a run of seventeen largely spoon-fed singles by twice manoeuvring the ball skilfully into gaps for two runs and then blasting Ealham through the covers for the twenty-eighth four of his innings. Since Giddins is now on strike against Fleming, Kentish hopes rise again, but the Surrey number eleven quickly gets his partner back down to the striker's end in the best possible way with three runs to third man, leaving Brown to clinch the fourth point with a clip to the square leg boundary and a single pushed to extra cover.

Although any further runs can now be considered a bonus, the Surrey centurion manages to extend his team's lead beyond two-hundred with an extra-cover drive for six off Ealham before he perishes to Patel as soon as the spinner returns at the pavilion end in place of Fleming, a lofted drive down the ground finding the safe hands of Robert Key at long-on.

While the Kent fielders breathe an almost audible sigh of relief, the crowd rises to acclaim Brown as he returns to the dressing room, having scored 188 out of a final total of 361. It has been an absolutely epic innings, similar in style to Andrew Flintoff's explosive 137 for Lancashire just a month ago, and also reminiscent of Brown's own incredible match-winning knock of 295 not out at Oakham School in 2000. Here, as then, the lower-order batsman have supported him and turned a position of adversity into one of clear superiority. With no other batsman having scored more than fifty-four in the match so far, Brown's amazing 208-ball innings certainly deserves to prove decisive, and the final session of the day will go some way to determining whether or not it will.

*Tea:- Between Innings*

Facing a 208-run first innings deficit, Kent's second knock gets away to a dreadful start. After David Fulton plays out a maiden from Martin Bicknell, Rob Key immediately forces Jimmy Ormond to the cover boundary before falling lbw later in the over when the bowler nips a delivery back into his pads. There appears to have been a suspicion of an inside edge, however, and the stocky Kent opener's irritated reaction tends to confirm that umpire Steele has missed this rather important factor in assessing the merits of the bowler's appeal. The damage is done, though, and life doesn't get any easier for the new pairing of Fulton and Ed Smith over the next few overs, with both men edging boundaries and finding few opportunities to play attacking strokes.

Smith does eventually cut loose, however, initially picking up runs through clips and pushes to leg before twice locating the cover boundary, once off each bowler, with well timed strokes. Fulton, meanwhile, has only four runs to his name after nine overs, though he, too, gradually expands his repertoire with a cover drive off Ormond and a pull off Bicknell, both of which race away to the rope.

This acceleration of the scoring rate prompts a double bowling change by Ian Ward as Saqlain Mushtaq appears at the pavilion end and Ed Giddins at the Vauxhall end, though it does nothing to slow the run flow as Fulton immediately forces Giddins away to the backward point boundary to raise the Kent fifty, while Smith whips a short delivery from Saqlain to the midwicket fence to complete a fighting half-century partnership.

No sooner has this landmark been reached than Giddins comes up with a magnificent second over, during which Fulton edges for four, survives a confident appeal for lbw, is beaten outside the off stump and, most frustratingly of all for the bowler, is dropped at second slip by Rikki Clarke. The Surrey youngster's error, with Fulton on twenty-nine at 60-1, appears to result from him not picking the ball up in increasingly gloomy light and, though the batsmen don't seem to be struggling to see the ball as they notch three further boundaries in the next five overs, it comes as no great surprise when play is suspended four overs early, with three lights aglow on the scoreboard.

*Close:- Kent 79-1 (Fulton 41\*, Smith 32\*) from 22.1 overs*

## VIEW FROM THE DRESSING ROOM

*I described your 188 as being like a 'mini Oakham'. Would that be a fair assessment of it, in the way that it turned the match around?*
**ALI BROWN** - It was almost certainly my most important innings of the summer, as it gave us a good springboard to get a good lead over them, and once we got that far ahead of them we knew that if we bowled well we would win the game. I did play quite aggressively but we didn't have a tail, apart from Ed, so I always had a lot of faith in the guys down the bottom to support me, which was similar to Oakham.

*How much - if at all - do you think Kent's performance was affected by the problems they had experienced in getting to the ground?*
**MARTIN BICKNELL** - It's difficult to know, really. Sometimes it works in your favour, because you've had the morning off, so you almost enjoy it more, just turning up and going straight out on to the field - but the way Browny played, I don't think it was ever going to be a great day for them.
**ALI BROWN** - I don't think it made a massive amount of difference, to be honest... it just made the game a bit disjointed. I was raring to go, I kept looking around and their players just weren't there. So, while we were waiting, I ended up in one of the boxes having a chat with a few friends.

# ALISTAIR BROWN'S 188 AGAINST KENT
Original run chart as compiled by Keith Seward

SURREY V KENT,      THE OVAL,      12/13-6-02

A. BROWN      CT KEY BLD PATEL   188
RHB

6.06 - 5.06     291 mins      50 in 55 mins. 45 balls
                208 balls      100 in 124 mins. 100 balls
                              150 in 216 mins. 161 balls

||4·4·|·4·4·4·4·4·|·2·4·|·4·4·|·4·|·2·4·4·4·||·4·|·2·|·4·|||·2·||·4·|·4·2·4·4·4·3·4·4·4·4·||||·4·4·2·|||·4·||||||||
||||||||·2·2·4·4·|·2·6·||

Start delayed until
12.30 on 13-6-02 due
to Kent team being unable to get to the ground because of London traffic problems.

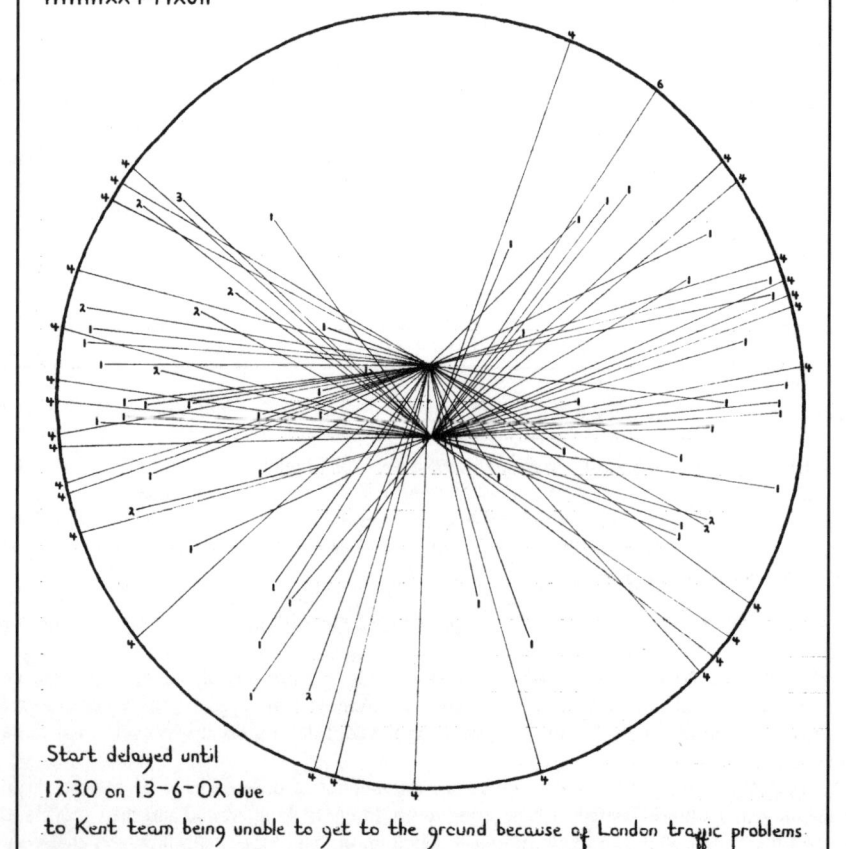

## Third Day - Friday 14th June

## Kent 153 and 268; Surrey 361 and 61-1

### Surrey won by nine wickets
### Surrey 19pts, Kent 3

Conditions are dramatically different as day three starts with a potential 112 overs available for play. The Kent players are all present and correct as the action gets under way on a bright, warm morning with Ed Giddins allowed to continue at the Vauxhall end after completing his unfinished over from last night and Martin Bicknell taking up the attack from the pavilion end.

Although the ball swings readily in the prevailing sultry conditions, the overnight batsmen begin this potentially decisive day in confident style, with Smith forcing and cutting off-side boundaries in consecutive overs from Bicknell, and Fulton producing two cover drives, worth two and four runs respectively, off Giddins. Having thereby increased his overnight score to forty-eight, the Kent skipper is then denied a half-century by Ian Salisbury's second stunning gully catch of the match - and this one is even better than the first. While there might have been an element of luck about his one-handed plucking of the ball out of thin air in the first innings, there's not a trace of good fortune about this one as he intercepts a well-timed forcing stroke low and right-handed as he dives away full-length towards point. The Ben comparisons are, again, both undeniable and inevitable as the home team and their supporters celebrate Fulton's demise, which leaves the scoreboard reading 94-2.

There is still a buzz of excitement around the ground, in fact, with all-time great catches doubtless the topic of conversation, when Giddins strikes again in his next over. Surrey are cock-a-hoop and the visitors plunged into even deeper trouble at 99-3 when Smith is comprehensively beaten by an excellent outswinger that moves late from around leg stump, striking the batsman plumb in front of his stumps and winning a leg-before verdict from umpire Dudleston.

Giddins is obviously delighted to have made these two breakthroughs in the space of eleven deliveries, and he continues to bowl impressively, twice finding the edge of Matthew Walker's bat, only for the ball to fly away safely to the rope at third man on each occasion. In contrast to his team-mate, the other new batsman, Andrew Symonds, looks composed and controlled, despite the quality of the Surrey swing bowling, regaining the initiative from Giddins with pulled and cover-driven boundaries in consecutive overs. He loses his struggling partner almost immediately afterwards, however, as Bicknell follows a series of inswingers with a ball that swerves away late from the left-hander and takes the leading edge of the bat as Walker aims to leg, providing Jimmy Ormond at mid-off with a comfortable catch at head height. As the disconsolate batsman makes his way back to the changing room at the end of an unequal struggle that has seen him score twelve of his eighteen runs in edges, Kent are 130-4, still seventy-eight runs in arrears.

While Walker's departure had been entirely predictable, the loss of Symonds five balls later comes as more of a surprise, though it owes nothing to the introduction of Ormond in place of Giddins or, for that matter, any significant act of skill from a Surrey player. The wound is entirely self-inflicted as the newly arrived Paul Nixon pushes towards midwicket and looks on in horror as his Australian team-mate, seeking an extremely unlikely single to Ian Ward, loses his footing in mid-pitch and ends up on his backside, much as Ormond had on day two. The fielders make no mistake on this occasion, however, as Ward lobs the ball back to the bowler, who trots back to the non-striker's stumps to remove the bails and complete the dismissal of the opposition's potentially most dangerous batsman. Half the Kent side are now out with the score at 133, and a Surrey win is looking increasingly certain... probably with a day to spare, too, unless Kent can put together a couple of decent partnerships.

Having already done their fair share of fire-fighting in the Kent first innings, Nixon and Mark Ealham are left with a sense of déjà vu as they join forces again with their team in disarray. Given the seriousness of the predicament they now face, their initial caution is understandable, with the next six overs yielding just five runs and the day's first sighting of Saqlain Mushtaq as Bicknell takes a hard-earned break.

This change brings a fairly swift response from Ealham as he dances down the track to the Surrey off-spinner and drives him over mid-on for the first boundary in nine overs and then, having seemingly got the taste for the lofted drive, he repeats the dose with strokes over point and extra cover in the following over from Ormond, taking his side past 150 in the process. This flurry of strokes proves to be nothing more than a minor inconvenience to Surrey, however, as the Kent all-rounder is brought to book by Saqlain in the very next over, his attempt to hit the off-spinner over the top for a second time resulting in a steepling skier to Ormond at deepish mid-off as the spin wizard's "wrong 'un" finds the leading edge.

The prospects of everyone being able to watch England's World Cup football match against Denmark tomorrow lunchtime from the comfort of their own armchair have improved markedly with Ealham's exit for twenty-one at 159-6, and they take an even more decisive turn for the better as Matthew Fleming's stay in the middle turns out to be extremely brief. Having faced fourteen deliveries and scored just two runs, the former Kent captain pushes forward to Saqlain and becomes the Pakistani's second victim of the innings as the ball rebounds, at speed, to Ward at silly point via bat and pad. A very sharp catch is required since the ball has cannoned away on a very low downward trajectory and, consequently, Fleming awaits confirmation from the square-leg umpire that all is well with the Surrey captain's handiwork before leaving the crease with Kent's hopes in tatters at 162-7.

With lunch not too far away, Ed Giddins returns to the attack in place of Ormond, and Min Patel gives an early indication of how he intends to play in this most dire of situations for his team by smashing five fours in the final three overs of the session. Four of these come from sweeps off Saqlain, though the final one, which takes the Kent total to two-hundred, is rather fortunate, since it flies over the head of short fine leg on its way to the boundary.

*Lunch:- Kent 200-7 (Nixon 9\*, Patel 35\*) from 56 overs*

Patel's cool and calculated pre-lunch burst has put his side within eight runs of making Surrey bat again, though he fails to complete the job, as he falls to Giddins in the second over after the break when he fences fatally at an outswinger and is caught at the wicket. His 33-ball innings of thirty-seven has at least provided some entertainment for the crowd and taken the contest further than had seemed likely at one stage. Defeat inside three days now looms large for Kent, however, as Giddins and Bicknell look to finish the job off for the home side.

This proves to be slightly harder than anyone had imagined, though, as Nixon gradually perks up with boundaries driven through extra cover and glanced to fine leg, while Amjad Khan attempts to emulate Patel with a few bold strokes. Although the Dane edges Bicknell over the slips at one point he also reels off genuine strokes of quality through the covers and back down the ground, both of which bring him four runs. Thirty-two runs are added in this style before Surrey finally capture the wicket of Nixon, giving Bicknell his second wicket of the innings in his twenty-first over. It's all the bowler's own work, too, since he dives away to his right-hand side to complete a fine one-handed catch when the Kent keeper's leading edge lobs unexpectedly back down the wicket.

Fully aware that the game is up for his team, since they still only lead by twenty-six runs, Khan lashes out immediately at Giddins, advancing his score by twelve with a sliced drive over backward point, a miscued drive to square leg and then a nicely middled pull over wide mid-on. This last stroke takes Khan to a career-best score of twenty-seven and also convinces the Surrey captain that the young Kent paceman has some ability with the bat, since we suddenly witness the spreading of the field to allow the number ten batsman to take singles. It seems a rather unnecessary move, especially when Martin Saggers promptly unfurls a classic cover drive to advance his score by four runs at Bicknell's expense, though everyone knows that the game is already won and lost, whatever tactics are adopted.

Showing that he can maybe play spin as well as seam, Khan then greets Saqlain's return at Giddins' expense with a lofted on-drive for four and a sweep for three, but the recall of Jimmy Ormond, with his extra pace, finally concludes the innings three overs later when Saggers edges a drive at an outswinger and sees Nadeem Shahid take a good catch low down at third slip. Khan is left unbeaten with forty-two runs to his name, Kent are all out for 268 and Surrey need to score just sixty-one to win, with as many overs left for play on this the third day of the match.

Despite there being no pressure whatsoever in terms of the scoring rate, Surrey's opening pair make a bright start, with Ward initially to the fore as he drives the second ball of the innings from Saggers to the long-off boundary and then pulls and on-drives further fours in the fourth over, bowled by Khan. With Batty subsequently joining the party by taking two boundaries of his own off Saggers, Surrey seem to be racing to victory until the introduction of Ealham and Patel first brings a chance, when Walker, at gully, just fails to hold a tough catch offered by Batty, on sixteen, off Ealham, then a wicket, when a ball from Patel spins sharply out of the rough and defeats Ward as he backs away to attempt a cut.

Just a couple of overs later, at 4.15pm, with Surrey just twenty-two runs from victory, increasingly heavy drizzle forces the umpires to take the players off and call an early tea.

*Tea:- Surrey 39-1 (Batty 22\*, Ramprakash 1\*) from 15.3 overs*

Play resumes at 4.55pm and once Patel has completed his unfinished over, Fulton waves the white flag of surrender by handing the ball to Walker, bowling medium-pace seamers, and Khan, bowling a species of leg-break at a pace not much slower than Walker. Although the bowling is not especially testing, it is respectable enough to take play into the seventh over of the post-tea period, at which point Batty cuts successive deliveries from Walker to the third man boundary to complete a resounding victory for Surrey at 5.13pm.

Another top-quality display by Keith Medlycott's team has brought them their fourth win of the Championship campaign, with the first innings' efforts of Martin Bicknell and Ali Brown pivotal to Surrey's first win over Kent in the competition since their 1999 victory at Tunbridge Wells, most of the games since then having been badly affected by rain.

**Kent 153 and 268; Surrey 361 and 61-1**
**Surrey won by nine wickets. Surrey 19pts, Kent 3**

| VIEW FROM THE DRESSING ROOM |
|---|

*The Surrey catching in this game was excellent, but pride of place must go to Ian Salisbury's two fine efforts in the gully, I guess?*
**ALI BROWN** - Yes, those catches do stick out in my mind, and you could tell by the look on his face that he was stunned to have caught them. They were probably better than anything he thought he could do... and anything we thought he could do, too! Gully is a very important position, and Ben took some fantastic catches there - you almost expected him to take the very difficult ones, but with Sals the expectation isn't quite so high.

**SURREY v KENT at The AMP Oval.    Played from 12th to 14th June**

Surrey won the toss and elected to field    Umpires:- Barry Dudleston and John Steele

### KENT - First Innings

| Fall Of Wkt | Batsman | How | Out | Score | Balls | 4s | 6s |
|---|---|---|---|---|---|---|---|
| 1-4 | D.P. Fulton * | lbw | b Bicknell | 2 | 6 | 0 | 0 |
| 2-27 | R.W.T. Key | c Batty | b Bicknell | 15 | 18 | 3 | 0 |
| 5-48 | E.T. Smith | c Ward | b Bicknell | 20 | 40 | 3 | 0 |
| 3-32 | A. Symonds | c Salisbury | b Ormond | 1 | 5 | 0 | 0 |
| 4-38 | M.J. Walker | c Clarke | b Ormond | 6 | 8 | 1 | 0 |
| 10-153 | P.A. Nixon + | c Saqlain | b Bicknell | 54 | 87 | 7 | 0 |
| 6-100 | M.A. Ealham | lbw | b Giddins | 25 | 46 | 4 | 0 |
| 7-129 | M.V. Fleming | c Batty | b Ormond | 12 | 33 | 2 | 0 |
| 8-138 | M.M. Patel | c Shahid | b Bicknell | 0 | 2 | 0 | 0 |
| 9-140 | A. Khan | c Salisbury | b Bicknell | 0 | 6 | 0 | 0 |
|  | M.J. Saggers |  | Not Out | 5 | 8 | 1 | 0 |
|  | Extras | (4b, 1lb, 6w, 2nb) |  | 13 |  |  |  |
|  | TOTAL | (43 overs) |  | 153 |  |  |  |

| Bowler | O | M | R | W | NB | Wd |
|---|---|---|---|---|---|---|
| Bicknell | 13 | 5 | 42 | 6 | - | 1 |
| Ormond | 14 | 2 | 56 | 3 | - | 2 |
| Giddins | 9 | 2 | 37 | 1 | 1 | - |
| Clarke | 4 | 2 | 6 | 0 | - | - |
| Saqlain Mushtaq | 3 | 0 | 7 | 0 | - | - |

### SURREY - First Innings

| Fall Of Wkt | Batsman | How | Out | Score | Balls | 4s | 6s |
|---|---|---|---|---|---|---|---|
| 1-3 | I.J. Ward * | c Nixon | b Khan | 0 | 7 | 0 | 0 |
| 4-58 | J.N. Batty + | c Symonds | b Fleming | 24 | 48 | 5 | 0 |
| 2-5 | M.R. Ramprakash | lbw | b Khan | 1 | 5 | 0 | 0 |
| 3-39 | N. Shahid | c Nixon | b Fleming | 20 | 30 | 4 | 0 |
| 10-361 | A.D. Brown | c Key | b Patel | 188 | 208 | 29 | 1 |
| 5-80 | R. Clarke | c Khan | b Fleming | 5 | 17 | 1 | 0 |
| 6-166 | M.P. Bicknell | c Nixon | b Fleming | 27 | 42 | 4 | 0 |
| 7-231 | I.D.K. Salisbury | c Symonds | b Khan | 13 | 44 | 2 | 0 |
| 8-287 | Saqlain Mushtaq | c Nixon | b Saggers | 25 | 60 | 5 | 0 |
| 9-333 | J. Ormond |  | b Ealham | 33 | 51 | 7 | 0 |
|  | E.S.H. Giddins |  | Not Out | 4 | 12 | 0 | 0 |
|  | Extras | (4b, 13lb, 2w, 2nb) |  | 21 |  |  |  |
|  | TOTAL | (87.1 overs) |  | 361 |  |  |  |

| Bowler | O | M | R | W | NB | Wd |
|---|---|---|---|---|---|---|
| Saggers | 22 | 2 | 96 | 1 | - | - |
| Khan | 16 | 2 | 81 | 3 | 1 | 1 |
| Fleming | 23 | 5 | 68 | 4 | - | - |
| Ealham | 15 | 4 | 68 | 1 | - | - |
| Patel | 11.1 | 3 | 31 | 1 | - | - |

### KENT - Second Innings (Trailing by 208 runs on first innings)

| Fall Of Wkt | Batsman | How | Out | Score | Balls | 4s | 6s |
|---|---|---|---|---|---|---|---|
| 2-94 | D.P. Fulton * | c Salisbury | b Giddins | 48 | 79 | 9 | 0 |
| 1-6 | R.W.T. Key | lbw | b Ormond | 4 | 6 | 1 | 0 |
| 3-99 | E.T. Smith | lbw | b Giddins | 44 | 85 | 8 | 0 |
| 5-133 | A. Symonds | run | out | 14 | 26 | 2 | 0 |
| 4-130 | M.J. Walker | c Ormond | b Bicknell | 18 | 20 | 4 | 0 |
| 9-234 | P.A. Nixon + | c & | b Bicknell | 23 | 67 | 2 | 0 |
| 6-159 | M.A. Ealham | c Ormond | b Saqlain | 21 | 37 | 3 | 0 |
| 7-162 | M.V. Fleming | c Ward | b Saqlain | 2 | 14 | 0 | 0 |
| 8-202 | M.M. Patel | c Batty | b Giddins | 37 | 33 | 6 | 0 |
|  | A. Khan | Not | Out | 42 | 47 | 7 | 0 |
| 10-268 | M.J. Saggers | c Shahid | b Ormond | 7 | 12 | 1 | 0 |
|  | Extras | (2b, 2lb, 4nb) |  | 8 |  |  |  |
|  | TOTAL | (70.4 overs) |  | 268 |  |  |  |

| Bowler | O | M | R | W | NB | Wd |
|---|---|---|---|---|---|---|
| Bicknell | 23 | 7 | 78 | 2 | - | - |
| Ormond | 14.4 | 4 | 44 | 2 | 1 | - |
| Saqlain Mushtaq | 15 | 0 | 62 | 2 | - | - |
| Giddins | 18 | 3 | 80 | 3 | 1 | - |

| SURREY - Second Innings (Needing 61 to win) | | | | | | | |
|---|---|---|---|---|---|---|---|
| Fall Of Wkt | Batsman | How | Out | Score | Balls | 4s | 6s |
| 1-35 | I.J. Ward * | | b Patel | 15 | 41 | 3 | 0 |
| | J.N. Batty + | Not | Out | 32 | 64 | 6 | 0 |
| | M.R. Ramprakash | Not | Out | 11 | 30 | 1 | 0 |
| | Extras | (1lb, 2w) | | 3 | | | |
| | TOTAL | (22.3 overs) | (for 1 wkt) | 61 | | | |

| Bowler | O | M | R | W | NB | Wd |
|---|---|---|---|---|---|---|
| Saggers | 4 | 0 | 15 | 0 | - | - |
| Khan | 6 | 2 | 15 | 0 | - | 1 |
| Patel | 5 | 2 | 8 | 1 | - | - |
| Ealham | 4 | 1 | 7 | 0 | - | - |
| Walker | 3.3 | 1 | 15 | 0 | - | - |

## Other Division One Results

Surrey moved back to the top of the table following Leicestershire's defeat at Edgbaston, while Yorkshire's fifth loss of the season, a drubbing at the hands of Sussex, left them with no realistic chance of retaining their title. Somerset, the other county who had been fancied to challenge Surrey for the Championship crown, were also struggling for form, though they did come close to beating Hampshire in an extraordinary rain-affected game at Bath.

June 12-15
*Bath:-* **Somerset drew with Hampshire.** Hampshire 252 (Kendall 88) and 98 (Johnson 7-43); Somerset 161-9dec (Mullally 4-64) and 173-8. **Somerset 7pts, Hampshire 9**

*Edgbaston:-* **Warwickshire beat Leicestershire by 144 runs.** Warwickshire 462 (Troughton 130, Ostler 81, Bell 72, Flower 4-66) and 206-7dec (Pollock 65); Leicestershire 370 (Ward 89, Flower 75, Burns 64) and 154 (Smith 5-42). **Warwickshire 20pts, Leicestershire 6**

*Headingley:-* **Sussex beat Yorkshire by an innings and 94 runs.** Sussex 435 (Ambrose 149, Prior 83); Yorkshire 216 (McGrath 71, Blakey 52, Kirtley 5-49) and 125 (Kirtley 5-41). **Sussex 20pts, Yorkshire 4**

## COUNTY CHAMPIONSHIP DIVISION ONE AT 15TH JUNE

| Pos | Prv | | P | Points | W | D | L | Bat | Bwl | Ded |
|---|---|---|---|---|---|---|---|---|---|---|
| 1 | 2 | Surrey | 6 | 92.75 | 4 | 2 | 0 | 19 | 18 | 0.25 |
| 2 | 1 | Leicestershire | 7 | 86.00 | 3 | 2 | 2 | 24 | 19 | 1.00 |
| 3 | 3 | Hampshire | 7 | 73.00 | 1 | 5 | 1 | 21 | 20 | 0.00 |
| 4 | 7 | Sussex | 6 | 58.00 | 1 | 3 | 2 | 17 | 17 | 0.00 |
| 5 | 4 | Lancashire | 5 | 57.00 | 2 | 2 | 1 | 11 | 14 | 0.00 |
| 6 | 6 | Somerset | 5 | 55.00 | 1 | 4 | 0 | 13 | 14 | 0.00 |
| 7 | 5 | Kent | 5 | 54.00 | 2 | 1 | 2 | 13 | 13 | 0.00 |
| 8 | 9 | Warwickshire | 5 | 45.00 | 1 | 2 | 2 | 12 | 13 | 0.00 |
| 9 | 8 | Yorkshire | 6 | 32.50 | 0 | 1 | 5 | 11 | 18 | 0.50 |

## NUL2 - Adam Enjoys A Warm And Winning Return

Although he'd had an unproductive match for the second eleven at Canterbury, scoring just thirteen runs and taking 1-33 in an eight-wicket defeat, it was decided that Adam Hollioake should return to first-team action against the Hampshire Hawks at The Rose Bowl on Sunday 16th June, not quite three months since the tragedy that had delayed his return to England. Since most supporters hadn't really expected to see Adam playing in 2002, it was fantastic to see him back in Surrey colours again and making an immediate impact with the ball as the Lions emerged victorious by three wickets after a close-fought battle.

What made the day extra special, however, was the heart-warming reception that the people of Hampshire afforded to Adam. Each and every time the Surrey captain entered or exited from the field of play - even for the pre-match warm-ups - or had his name announced, the crowd would burst into spontaneous applause. Although it was yet another painful reminder of the events of March 23rd, those feelings of sadness were more than balanced by the unbelievable support that the cricket fans of Hampshire offered Adam throughout the afternoon. Much credit was due to them, and while I couldn't say how the bereaved Surrey skipper coped, I know that I, personally, found myself with a lump in my throat every time the West End crowd served up one of its ovations.

As far as the cricket was concerned, it seemed significant that Hollioake's return coincided with Surrey winning a close match, rather than losing it, for the first time in the season.

Having put the opposition in on a slow and slightly damp pitch upon winning the toss, the visitors were very much in control at the start as the outstanding Martin Bicknell (7-1-13-1) and Ed Giddins (7-1-14-1) took full advantage of the conditions to leave the Hawks hopelessly bogged down on 29-2 after fourteen overs. After Rikki Clarke followed up by removing the out-of-touch Derek Kenway with the total at thirty-nine, Hampshire launched a minor recovery through John Crawley and Lawrence Prittipaul before Hollioake struck with his third ball, having the England batsman caught at the wicket for thirty-four at 75-4. The home side's innings then stalled again as Hollioake and the returning Bicknell picked up further wickets, until Nick Pothas and Will Kendall eventually provided some much needed impetus with a stand of forty-four in nine overs, before Dimitri Mascarenhas' fifteen-run penultimate-over assault on Giddins took the total to a respectable 178-8.

In awkward batting conditions, the Lions' target looked a tricky one and, though they were well anchored by the watchful Ian Ward, wickets fell at regular intervals at the other end as Surrey reached 99-4 in the twenty-fourth over. The loss of Mark Ramprakash in the thirteenth over, following another run out mix-up with Ward, had been entirely avoidable, though Clarke and Shahid could both consider themselves a little unfortunate to fall to brilliant catches behind the wicket by Johnson and Pothas. Clarke's exit, with eighty runs needed from 21.2 overs, brought Hollioake to the crease, but the returning Surrey skipper proved unable to work any magic with the bat, scoring fifteen before departing at 128-6, four overs after Ward's praiseworthy vigil had been ended by the impressive Chris Tremlett. As the overs began to ebb away with little progress being made, the Hawks became marginal favourites to win the match until a nine-run over from Neil Johnson, which had started with Bicknell being dropped at backward point, put the Lions back in the box seat, needing just thirteen from four overs. Three good, tight overs raised the tension level again, however, and it was still anyone's game as the inexperienced Prittipaul was assigned to bowl the last over with five runs required. Bad memories of the one-run Benson & Hedges Cup defeat against Hampshire earlier in the season came flooding back, but Ian Salisbury ensured that there would be no repeat of that disappointing loss by heaving the first delivery high over deep midwicket for a match-clinching six. A memorable afternoon had ended with Surrey smiles and a win for their returning captain.

## HAMPSHIRE HAWKS v SURREY LIONS at The Rose Bowl
**Played on Sunday 16th June**     **Surrey Lions won by three wickets**
Surrey Lions won the toss and elected to field     Umpires:- Barrie Leadbeater & Roy Palmer

### HAMPSHIRE HAWKS

| Fall Of Wkt | Batsman | How | Out | Score | Balls | 4s | 6s |
|---|---|---|---|---|---|---|---|
| 1-5 | J.R.C. Hamblin | c Ormond | b Giddins | 5 | 12 | 0 | 0 |
| 2-7 | N.C. Johnson | c Clarke | b Bicknell | 0 | 4 | 0 | 0 |
| 3-39 | D.A. Kenway | | b Clarke | 9 | 42 | 1 | 0 |
| 4-75 | J.P. Crawley | c Batty | b Hollioake | 34 | 67 | 3 | 0 |
| 5-90 | L.R. Prittipaul | c Batty | b Hollioake | 20 | 41 | 2 | 0 |
| 6-102 | G.W. White | c Ward | b Bicknell | 14 | 21 | 2 | 0 |
| 8-153 | N. Pothas + | c & | b Hollioake | 27 | 34 | 1 | 0 |
| 7-146 | W.S. Kendall * | c Shahid | b Giddins | 21 | 30 | 2 | 0 |
| | A.D. Mascarenhas | Not | Out | 25 | 14 | 2 | 1 |
| | S.D. Udal | Not | Out | 4 | 5 | 0 | 0 |
| | C.T. Tremlett | did not bat | | | | | |
| | Extras | (7lb, 12w) | | 19 | | | |
| | TOTAL | (45 overs) | (for 8 wkts) | 178 | | | |

| Bowler | O | M | R | W | NB | Wd |
|---|---|---|---|---|---|---|
| Bicknell | 9 | 1 | 15 | 2 | - | 3 |
| Giddins | 9 | 1 | 34 | 2 | - | 1 |
| Ormond | 9 | 0 | 25 | 0 | - | 7 |
| Clarke | 8 | 1 | 44 | 1 | - | 1 |
| Hollioake | 9 | 0 | 45 | 3 | - | - |
| Ward | 1 | 0 | 8 | 0 | - | - |

### SURREY LIONS

| Fall Of Wkt | Batsman | How | Out | Score | Balls | 4s | 6s |
|---|---|---|---|---|---|---|---|
| 5-121 | I.J. Ward | | b Tremlett | 51 | 90 | 4 | 1 |
| 1-27 | A.D. Brown | c & | b Tremlett | 14 | 17 | 2 | 0 |
| 2-57 | M.R. Ramprakash | run | out | 12 | 16 | 1 | 0 |
| 3-62 | R. Clarke | c Johnson | b Hamblin | 1 | 4 | 0 | 0 |
| 4-99 | N. Shahid | c Pothas | b Prittipaul | 19 | 25 | 0 | 0 |
| 6-128 | A.J. Hollioake * | c Pothas | b Macarenhas | 15 | 27 | 2 | 0 |
| 7-155 | J.N. Batty + | lbw | b Tremlett | 15 | 35 | 0 | 0 |
| | M.P. Bicknell | Not | Out | 19 | 41 | 0 | 0 |
| | I.D.K. Salisbury | Not | Out | 15 | 11 | 1 | 1 |
| | J.Ormond | did not bat | | | | | |
| | E.S.H. Giddins | did not bat | | | | | |
| | Extras | (2b, 3lb, 12w, 2nb) | | 19 | | | |
| | TOTAL | (44.1 overs) | (for 7 wkts) | 180 | | | |

| Bowler | O | M | R | W | NB | Wd |
|---|---|---|---|---|---|---|
| Mascarenhas | 9 | 1 | 36 | 1 | - | 2 |
| Tremlett | 9 | 0 | 25 | 3 | - | 4 |
| Johnson | 9 | 0 | 41 | 0 | 1 | 1 |
| Hamblin | 3 | 0 | 13 | 1 | - | 2 |
| Udal | 9 | 1 | 27 | 0 | - | 1 |
| Prittipaul | 5.1 | 0 | 33 | 1 | - | 2 |

## Other NUL Division Two Results

Gloucestershire took over top spot after an easy win over Middlesex, while the last two unbeaten records in the division tumbled as Derbyshire and Surrey beat Northamptonshire and Hampshire, respectively.

June 16
*Derby:-* **Derbyshire Scorpions beat Northamptonshire Steelbacks by three wickets.** Northamptonshire 180-8 (Penberthy 55*, Dean 3-29); Derbyshire 182-7 (43.4 ov; Kerr 65*, Greenidge 3-25). **Derbyshire Scorpions 4pts**

*Old Trafford:-* **Essex Eagles beat Lancashire Lightning by seven wickets.** Lancashire 203 (44.2ov; Chilton 84, Irani 3-29, Grayson 3-45); Essex 204-3 (39ov; Robinson 76, Flower 56*, Irani 51*). **Essex Eagles 4pts**

*Bristol:-* **Gloucestershire Gladiators beat Middlesex Crusaders by five wickets.** Middlesex 142 (37.3ov; Strauss 65, Ball 3-13, Alleyne 3-30); Gloucestershire 144-5 (24.2ov; Harvey 60). **Gloucestershire Gladiators 4pts**

## NATIONAL LEAGUE DIVISION TWO AT 16TH JUNE

| Pos | Prv | | P | Pts | W | T | L | A |
|---|---|---|---|---|---|---|---|---|
| 1 | 3 | Gloucestershire Gladiators | 5 | 14 | 3 | 0 | 1 | 1 |
| 2 | 4 | Derbyshire Scorpions | 4 | 10 | 2 | 0 | 1 | 1 |
| = | 1 | Hampshire Hawks | 4 | 10 | 2 | 0 | 1 | 1 |
| = | 1 | Northamptonshire Steelbacks | 4 | 10 | 2 | 0 | 1 | 1 |
| 5 | 7 | Essex Eagles | 3 | 8 | 2 | 0 | 1 | 0 |
| 6 | 8 | Surrey Lions | 4 | 8 | 2 | 0 | 2 | 0 |
| 7 | 5 | Sussex Sharks | 4 | 6 | 1 | 0 | 2 | 1 |
| 8 | 5 | Lancashire Lightning | 5 | 6 | 1 | 0 | 3 | 1 |
| 9 | 9 | Middlesex Crusaders | 5 | 4 | 0 | 0 | 3 | 2 |

## C&G Trophy 4th Round - Brown's Amazing 268 Sets The Records Tumbling

### Surrey v Glamorgan at The AMP Oval.  Played on Wednesday 19th June.
### Surrey won by nine runs

This was probably the most incredible limited-overs match ever played at first-class level, with no fewer than seven world records being smashed, and countless UK, competition, club and personal records also perishing in an incredible blaze of strokeplay on a magnificent Oval pitch. Ali Brown was the catalyst with an awesome, record-shattering innings of 268, leading Surrey to a seemingly insurmountable score of 438-5 that plucky Glamorgan challenged with centuries from Robert Croft and David Hemp, falling only ten runs short of what would have been a breathtaking victory at the end of an unbelievable day's entertainment.

After a relatively sedate start, with his personal tally being nineteen out of a total of 35-0 at the end of the seventh over, Brown's innings really took off with three fours in the following over, bowled by Andrew Davies.  Thereafter, he was simply unstoppable, offering just one awkward chance, to wicketkeeper Mark Wallace with his score on forty-seven, as he marched into the history books, trampling all over a host of records along the way.

Brown's fellow opener, Ian Ward, also batted quite superbly, even though his innings of ninety-seven was understandably overshadowed by his partner's phenomenal knock, and a magnificent opening partnership, which grew to 286 in 35 overs before Robert Croft sneaked a ball through Ward's defences, broke a number of records all on its own.  By this stage of the Surrey innings, Brown had already surpassed his previous best score in the UK's premier limited-overs cup competition (72 v Holland at The Oval in 1996) by the small matter of ninety-nine runs, and there was no time to pause for breath as he went on to convert an 80-ball century into a sensational 134-ball double-ton, thereby becoming the first man to record two first-class limited-overs scores in excess of two-hundred.   Although there was a short boundary down towards the gasholders, many of the Surrey beneficiary's fours came from booming extra-cover drives to the longer boundary, and any six that crossed the rope on the shorter side usually ended up disappearing out of the ground in any case.

Once he had sailed past Alvin Kallicharran's 206 v Oxfordshire at Edgbaston in 1984 to claim the record for the highest individual one-day score ever registered in the UK, Brown's next goal - though there were few people in the ground who knew it - was Graeme Pollock's 27-year-old world-record individual tally of 222 not out, scored for Eastern Province against Border at East London. This mark was duly achieved in the forty-sixth over, with the score at this stage already an incredible 381-3, and by the time Brown fell to the first ball of the final over, departing to a hero's reception from the fairly small crowd, he had stormed on to his new world-best score of 268 from 160 balls, with twelve sixes and thirty fours.  This stunning innings pushed the Surrey total up to a world record-breaking 438-5 and, though all the bowlers suffered grievously at Brown's hand, none was more harshly treated than Darren Thomas, who set an unwanted new world mark for the most expensive bowling figures in returning 9-1-108-3.

Facing the 'mission impossible' task of scoring 439 to win, Glamorgan made a rapid start through Croft as he smashed Martin Bicknell's first five deliveries of the innings for four on his way to a 22-ball fifty that saw the visitors' score racing up to 76-0 after just six overs. With nothing to lose, Croft continued to take advantage of some indifferent Surrey seam bowling to convert his half-century into Glamorgan's fastest-ever limited-overs hundred as he reached the landmark from just 56 deliveries.

It appeared that the home side might just have a game on their hands after all as the score rushed along to 145-1 by the time the fielding restrictions were lifted after fifteen overs and, though the visitors' stand-in skipper departed shortly afterwards for a glorious 69-ball 119, the pace barely slackened at all.

A quick-fire innings of forty-nine by Adrian Dale kept Glamorgan very much in contention during a stand of ninety-eight for the fourth wicket with David Hemp, but even when Adam Hollioake struck twice in three balls to remove Dale and the dangerous Mike Powell, the Welsh dragon kept on breathing fire. With Hemp picking up steam after a relatively slow start and even the normally reliable Saqlain appearing to be cannon-fodder in the prevailing conditions, Surrey's concerns grew, and with ten overs to go the gutsy visitors needed 103 with five wickets remaining, and another world record had fallen - the highest match aggregate for any first-class limited-overs encounter. Luckily for Surrey, Hemp fell to Bicknell almost immediately after completing his excellent 85-ball century, and when the home side's senior bowler then also disposed of Wallace in his next over it looked like the Glamorgan storm might just be blowing out at 352-7.

Not a bit of it. Desperate to atone for his nightmare with the ball, Darren Thomas blazed away, finding a reliable ally in Michael Kasprowicz and racing to a defiant half-century from just 30 balls to put the game back in the balance. With forty-four needed from the last four overs, Ed Giddins then came up with a tight seven-run over, and when Kasprowicz was run out two overs later, leaving twenty-two to be scored from nine balls, it finally looked like curtains for the Welshmen.

Since only five runs had accrued from the penultimate over of the match, bowled by Giddins, Glamorgan were therefore left needing nineteen runs from the last over, which proved to be a bridge too far against the experienced Hollioake, who was playing his first game at The AMP Oval since his return to England. Cleaning up Andrew Davies, courtesy of a catch at wide mid-on, and Dean Cosker, with an off stump yorker, the Surrey captain ended with figures of 5-77 to see his side safely into the quarter-finals by the astonishingly slender margin of nine runs.

Summing up Hollioake's crucial contribution to Surrey's cause as the pressure grew in the final overs of this truly memorable scrap, Rob Steen certainly hit the nail on the head in the following morning's *Guardian* when he wrote "after all the sadness of his past few months, he was probably the only one capable of coolness."

*The seven world records broken in this exceptional match were as follows:-*
**Highest Team Total In Any Limited-Overs Match**
Surrey 438-5 *beating 413-4 by Somerset v Devon at Torquay in 1990*
**Highest Team Total By A Side Batting Second In Any Limited-Overs Match**
Glamorgan 429 *beating 362 by India B v India at Chennai in 2000/01*
**Highest Individual Score In Any Limited-Overs Match**
268 by Alistair Brown *beating 222 not out by Graeme Pollock for Eastern Province v Border at East London in 1974/75*

**Most Boundaries In An Innings By An Individual In Any Limited-Overs Match**
42 (12 sixes and 30 fours) by Alistair Brown  *beating 32(6 sixes and 26 fours)\*\* by Graeme Pollock for Eastern Province v Border at East London in 1974/75  (\*\* previous best mark unconfirmed)*
**Most Double-Centuries Scored By An Individual In First-Class Limited-Overs Cricket**
2 by Alistair Brown
**Highest Run Aggregate In Any Limited-Overs Match**
867 runs (for 15 wkts)  *beating 754 (for 16 wkts), India (392-6) v India B (362) at Chennai in 2000/01*
**Most Expensive Bowling Analysis In Any Limited-Overs Match**
9-0-108-3 by Darren Thomas  *beating 12-0-107-2 by Chris Lovell for Cornwall v Warwickshire at St. Austell in 1996*

### SURREY v GLAMORGAN at The AMP Oval
Played on Wednesday 19th June      Surrey won by 9 runs
Surrey won the toss and elected to bat     Umpires:- Peter Willey & Ian Gould

**SURREY**

| Fall of wkt | Batsman | How | Out | Score | Balls | 4s | 6s |
|---|---|---|---|---|---|---|---|
| 1-286 | I.J. Ward | | b Croft | 97 | 95 | 8 | 4 |
| 5-431 | A.D. Brown | | b Kasprowicz | 268 | 160 | 30 | 12 |
| 2-354 | M.R. Ramprakash | c & | b S.D. Thomas | 26 | 27 | 2 | 0 |
| 3-376 | R. Clarke | c Wallace | b S.D. Thomas | 5 | 6 | 0 | 0 |
| 4-424 | A.J. Hollioake * | c I.J. Thomas | b S.D. Thomas | 4 | 6 | 0 | 0 |
| | A.J. Stewart | Not | Out | 2 | 4 | 0 | 0 |
| | J.N. Batty + | Not | Out | 6 | 3 | 1 | 0 |
| | M.P. Bicknell | Did not bat | | | | | |
| | Saqlain Mushtaq | Did not bat | | | | | |
| | J. Ormond | Did not bat | | | | | |
| | E.S.H. Giddins | Did not bat | | | | | |
| | Extras | (8lb, 20w, 2nb) | | 30 | | | |
| | TOTAL | (50 overs) | (for 5 wkts) | 438 | | | |

| Bowler | O | M | R | W | NB | Wd |
|---|---|---|---|---|---|---|
| Kasprowicz | 10 | 0 | 53 | 1 | - | 2 |
| Davies | 8 | 0 | 88 | 0 | - | 1 |
| S.D. Thomas | 9 | 0 | 108 | 3 | 1 | 7 |
| Croft | 8 | 0 | 62 | 1 | - | - |
| Dale | 8 | 0 | 68 | 0 | - | - |
| Cosker | 7 | 0 | 51 | 0 | - | 4 |

**GLAMORGAN**

| Fall of wkt | Batsman | How | Out | Score | Balls | 4s | 6s |
|---|---|---|---|---|---|---|---|
| 2-163 | R.D.B. Croft * | c Ward | b Hollioake | 119 | 69 | 18 | 3 |
| 1-113 | I.J. Thomas | run | out | 23 | 19 | 2 | 1 |
| 6-336 | D.L. Hemp | c Ormond | b Bicknell | 102 | 88 | 10 | 3 |
| 3-197 | M.P. Maynard | c Ramprakash | b Giddins | 21 | 19 | 3 | 0 |
| 4-295 | A.Dale | c Clarke | b Hollioake | 49 | 33 | 6 | 1 |
| 5-295 | M.J. Powell | c Giddins | b Hollioake | 0 | 2 | 0 | 0 |
| | S.D. Thomas | Not | Out | 71 | 41 | 5 | 3 |
| 7-352 | M.A. Wallace + | c Ramprakash | b Bicknell | 5 | 7 | 0 | 0 |
| 8-417 | M.S. Kasprowicz | run | out | 25 | 18 | 2 | 1 |
| 9-421 | A.P. Davies | c Ormond | b Hollioake | 1 | 2 | 0 | 0 |
| 10-429 | D.A. Cosker | | b Hollioake | 0 | 1 | 0 | 0 |
| | Extras | (7lb, 6w) | | 13 | | | |
| | TOTAL | (49.5 overs) | | 429 | | | |

| Bowler | O | M | R | W | NB | Wd |
|---|---|---|---|---|---|---|
| Bicknell | 10 | 0 | 84 | 2 | - | - |
| Giddins | 8 | 0 | 77 | 1 | - | - |
| Ormond | 9 | 0 | 72 | 0 | - | 2 |
| Saqlain Mushtaq | 10 | 0 | 82 | 0 | - | 2 |
| Hollioake | 8.5 | 0 | 77 | 5 | - | 2 |
| Clarke | 4 | 0 | 30 | 0 | - | - |

*For the full over-by-over story of an amazing day's cricket I would, naturally, recommend that you read the commemorative booklet '268 - The Blow-By-Blow Account Of Ali's Amazing Onslaught'. Details of how you can obtain a copy of this publication can be found at the back of this book, on the page entitled 'Other Books By Trevor Jones'*

## NUL2 - Giddins' Career Best Sinks Sharks

The difference between red-ball and white-ball cricket was demonstrated in emphatic style as the pitch that had been used for the record-breaking C&G Trophy match against Glamorgan was in service again just four days later and yielded barely more than a third of the 867 runs that were scored on that historic day earlier in the week. Using the bowler-friendly white ball to great effect, Ed Giddins continued his outstanding start to the season in the Norwich Union League by returning his best figures in limited-overs cricket to set up an easy six-wicket victory over one of his previous counties, Sussex, at The AMP Oval.

Having won the toss and elected to bat, the visitors, missing the injured Chris Adams, struggled from the off as Giddins claimed the important wickets of Montgomerie and Goodwin in the space of three deliveries in only the fourth over. The visitors weren't alone in having problems, however, since the next serious blow of the match befell Surrey when Martin Bicknell lost his footing in his follow-through, crashed to the deck and was forced to retire from the fray with what was later diagnosed as a broken wrist.

While Surrey fans worried about the long-term implications of this serious injury, Giddins provided a little short-term comfort with the wickets of House, Yardy and Zuiderent in the space of seven balls to reduce the Sharks to a pitiful 40-5, with thirty-one overs of their innings still to be bowled. Rikki Clarke then went on to remove Matt Prior to make it 53-6 just before the former England bowler completed his nine-over stint with 5-20, edging out his previous limited-overs best of 5-21 for Warwickshire against Leicestershire in the 1999 Benson & Hedges Cup.

With Giddins out of the way, Kevin Innes subsequently helped Robin Martin-Jenkins to double the score, though the damage had already been done. To give Sussex credit, they did manage to take their innings into the penultimate over, with Martin-Jenkins compiling a worthy fifty from 75 balls before becoming the last man to fall when he holed out to deep midwicket from the first ball of the forty-fourth over with the Sussex total at 150.

Although the Lions' victory task looked pretty straightforward, some spirited bowling and fielding, with fine catches claiming the wickets of Brown and Ramprakash, gave notice that the Sharks weren't going to go down without a fight. Indeed, at 46-3 after nineteen overs, with Clarke being well contained by Mark Davis and Mark Robinson, it looked almost even-stevens.

The loss of Clarke to an alert piece of wicketkeeping by Prior changed the game, though, as it brought together Adam Hollioake and Nadeem Shahid, who combined to launch a decisive assault on Robinson when he returned to the attack for the thirty-sixth over with the score at 109-4. First, Hollioake blasted the medium-pacer for massive consecutive sixes, then, in the following over, Shahid added a six and three fours in the space of five balls to put the result beyond doubt. The former Essex batsman reached his first limited-overs half-century against county opposition since September 2000 in the final over of the match as Surrey ultimately cruised home with plenty to spare.

*Although he had only scored ten when Surrey batted, there had been some good news earlier in the day for Mark Ramprakash - he was deservedly awarded his county cap during the tea interval.*

## Other NUL Division Two Result

Surrey's win saw them advance to third place in the table, while Derbyshire Scorpions become surprise leaders of the division following an easy home victory over Lancashire Lightning.

June 23
*Derby:-* **Derbyshire Scorpions beat Lancashire Lightning by seven wickets.** Lancashire 174-7; Derbyshire 179-3 (41.1ov; Stubbings 98*). **Derbyshire Scorpions 4pts**

## SURREY LIONS v SUSSEX SHARKS at The AMP Oval
**Played on Sunday 23rd June** — Surrey Lions won by six wickets
Sussex Sharks won the toss and elected to bat
Umpires:- Vanburn Holder & Alan Whitehead

### SUSSEX SHARKS

| Fall Of Wkt | Batsman | How | Out | Score | Balls | 4s | 6s |
|---|---|---|---|---|---|---|---|
| 4-40 | M.H. Yardy | c Batty | b Giddins | 21 | 39 | 2 | 0 |
| 1-12 | R.R. Montgomerie * | c Batty | b Giddins | 2 | 11 | 0 | 0 |
| 2-12 | M.W. Goodwin | lbw | b Giddins | 0 | 2 | 0 | 0 |
| 3-27 | W.J. House | c Salisbury | b Giddins | 7 | 21 | 1 | 0 |
| 10-150 | R.S.C. Martin-Jenkins | c Clarke | b Hollioake | 50 | 76 | 5 | 0 |
| 5-40 | B. Zuiderent | | b Giddins | 0 | 2 | 0 | 0 |
| 6-53 | M.J. Prior + | c & | b Clarke | 10 | 14 | 1 | 0 |
| 7-106 | K.J. Innes | lbw | b Hollioake | 22 | 35 | 1 | 0 |
| 8-115 | M.J.G. Davis | | b Saqlain | 6 | 15 | 1 | 0 |
| 9-137 | B.V. Taylor | c sub (Newman) | b Clarke | 16 | 26 | 1 | 1 |
| | M.A. Robinson | Not | Out | 7 | 20 | 0 | 0 |
| | Extras | (5lb, 2w, 2nb) | | 9 | | | |
| | **TOTAL** | **(43.1 overs)** | | **150** | | | |

| Bowler | O | M | R | W | NB | Wd |
|---|---|---|---|---|---|---|
| Bicknell | 5.1 | 1 | 16 | 0 | - | - |
| Giddins | 9 | 1 | 20 | 5 | - | - |
| Clarke | 8.5 | 0 | 38 | 2 | 1 | 1 |
| Salisbury | 5 | 0 | 24 | 0 | - | - |
| Saqlain Mushtaq | 9 | 1 | 32 | 1 | - | 1 |
| Hollioake | 6.1 | 0 | 15 | 2 | - | - |

### SURREY LIONS

| Fall Of Wkt | Batsman | How | Out | Score | Balls | 4s | 6s |
|---|---|---|---|---|---|---|---|
| 2-45 | I.J. Ward | | b Davis | 23 | 51 | 2 | 0 |
| 1-19 | A.D. Brown | c & | b Taylor | 11 | 18 | 2 | 0 |
| 3-45 | M.R. Ramprakash | c Montgomerie | b Robinson | 10 | 24 | 1 | 0 |
| 4-77 | R. Clarke | st Prior | b Innes | 13 | 39 | 2 | 0 |
| | N. Shahid | Not | Out | 50 | 67 | 5 | 1 |
| | A.J. Hollioake * | Not | Out | 42 | 34 | 4 | 2 |
| | J.N. Batty + | did not bat | | | | | |
| | M.P. Bicknell | did not bat | | | | | |
| | I.D.K. Salisbury | did not bat | | | | | |
| | Saqlain Mushtaq | did not bat | | | | | |
| | E.S.H. Giddins | did not bat | | | | | |
| | Extras | (1b, 1lb, 1w) | | 3 | | | |
| | **TOTAL** | **(38.5 overs)** | **(for 4 wkts)** | **152** | | | |

| Bowler | O | M | R | W | NB | Wd |
|---|---|---|---|---|---|---|
| Martin-Jenkins | 8.5 | 0 | 25 | 0 | - | 1 |
| Taylor | 7 | 0 | 23 | 1 | - | - |
| Robinson | 8 | 2 | 55 | 1 | - | - |
| Davis | 9 | 1 | 19 | 1 | - | - |
| Innes | 6 | 1 | 28 | 1 | - | - |

## NATIONAL LEAGUE DIVISION TWO AT 23RD JUNE

| Pos | Prv | | P | Pts | W | T | L | A |
|---|---|---|---|---|---|---|---|---|
| 1 | 2 | Derbyshire Scorpions | 5 | 14 | 3 | 0 | 1 | 1 |
| = | 1 | Gloucestershire Gladiators | 5 | 14 | 3 | 0 | 1 | 1 |
| 3 | 6 | Surrey Lions | 5 | 12 | 3 | 0 | 2 | 0 |
| 4 | 2 | Hampshire Hawks | 4 | 10 | 2 | 0 | 1 | 1 |
| = | 2 | Northamptonshire Steelbacks | 4 | 10 | 2 | 0 | 1 | 1 |
| 6 | 5 | Essex Eagles | 3 | 8 | 2 | 0 | 1 | 0 |
| 7 | 7 | Sussex Sharks | 5 | 6 | 1 | 0 | 3 | 1 |
| 8 | 8 | Lancashire Lightning | 6 | 6 | 1 | 0 | 4 | 1 |
| 9 | 9 | Middlesex Crusaders | 5 | 4 | 0 | 0 | 3 | 2 |

## FCC1 - PRE-SEASON FANCIES CONTINUE TO MAKE NO IMPRESSION

While Surrey enjoyed a break from Championship action, their lead at the top of the table remained intact, since Leicestershire were also resting. Somerset's first defeat of the season, at the hands of Warwickshire, dropped them to eighth in the table, thus leaving the bookies' and fans' anticipated two main challengers to Surrey some considerable distance behind the leaders as we moved towards the halfway point of the season. Kent bounced back from their defeat at The AMP Oval to record an impressive win over Lancashire at Liverpool and, as a result, they moved up into fourth place.

### Division One Results

June 26-29
*Liverpool:-* **Kent beat Lancashire by six wickets.** Lancashire 226 (Law 75, Driver 56, Khan 5-74) and 347 (Swann 85, Martin 80*, Chilton 60, Chapple 55); Kent 214 (Martin 5-54) and 360-4 (Symonds 116*, Fulton 116, Key 78). **Kent 15.5pts\*, Lancashire 4**
*Deducted 0.5pt for slow over-rate

*Arundel:-* **Sussex drew with Yorkshire.** Yorkshire 255 (Lehmann 71) and 458-8dec (Lehmann 216, Lumb 92); Sussex 392 (Prior 85, Montgomerie 78, Davis 70*, White 4-49) and 216-9 (Prior 70*). **Sussex 11pts, Yorkshire 9**

*Edgbaston:-* **Warwickshire beat Somerset by 88 runs.** Warwickshire 230 (Jones 4-46) and 423 (Ostler 175, Troughton 52, Wagg 51, Jones 6-110); Somerset 208 (Bowler 57, Burns 54, Wagg 4-43) and 357 (Turner 83*, Blackwell 64, Burns 54). **Warwickshire 16pts, Somerset 4**

### COUNTY CHAMPIONSHIP DIVISION ONE AT 29TH JUNE

| Pos | Prv |  | P | Points | W | D | L | Bat | Bwl | Ded |
|---|---|---|---|---|---|---|---|---|---|---|
| 1 | 1 | Surrey | 6 | 92.75 | 4 | 2 | 0 | 19 | 18 | 0.25 |
| 2 | 2 | Leicestershire | 7 | 86.00 | 3 | 2 | 2 | 24 | 19 | 1.00 |
| 3 | 3 | Hampshire | 7 | 73.00 | 1 | 5 | 1 | 21 | 20 | 0.00 |
| 4 | 7 | Kent | 6 | 69.50 | 3 | 1 | 2 | 14 | 16 | 0.50 |
| 5 | 4 | Sussex | 7 | 69.00 | 1 | 4 | 2 | 21 | 20 | 0.00 |
| 6 | 5 | Lancashire | 6 | 61.00 | 2 | 2 | 2 | 12 | 17 | 0.00 |
| = | 8 | Warwickshire | 6 | 61.00 | 2 | 2 | 2 | 13 | 16 | 0.00 |
| 8 | 6 | Somerset | 6 | 59.00 | 1 | 4 | 1 | 14 | 17 | 0.00 |
| 9 | 9 | Yorkshire | 7 | 41.50 | 0 | 2 | 5 | 13 | 21 | 0.50 |

### NUL2 - Surrey Suffer More Manchester Misery

Four weeks after being denied a highly likely victory in the County Championship, Surrey were foiled by the Manchester weather again on World Cup Final day as they were heading for an imposing total when persistent rain finally forced the umpires to suspend play after 31 overs of the visitors' innings. Launched in fine style by Ali Brown, who blasted his way to a 38-ball fifty, the Lions' promising position had been enhanced by the efforts of Mark Ramprakash and Rikki Clarke, clearing the way for potential fireworks in the last fourteen overs.

The rain did relent briefly at 5.30pm, raising the possibility of Lightning chasing an unlikely looking ninety-three from ten overs under the Duckworth-Lewis system at some stage after 6pm, but as soon as the ground staff began removing the covers another shower swept across the ground. This cloudburst soon forced the umpires to announce the abandonment of the match, leaving Surrey cursing the possible loss of two points against a struggling Lancashire side

## LANCASHIRE LIGHTNING v SURREY LIONS at Old Trafford
### Played on Sunday 30th June — No result - match abandoned

Surrey Lions won the toss and elected to bat    Umpires:- David Constant & Mike Dixon

### SURREY LIONS

| Fall Of Wkt | Batsman | How | Out | Score | Balls | 4s | 6s |
|---|---|---|---|---|---|---|---|
| 1-36 | I.J. Ward | c Lloyd | b Martin | 5 | 21 | 0 | 0 |
| 2-79 | A.D. Brown | | b Chapple | 56 | 42 | 7 | 1 |
| | M.R. Ramprakash | Not | Out | 39 | 70 | 3 | 0 |
| 3-131 | R. Clarke | st Hegg | b Chilton | 28 | 43 | 3 | 0 |
| | N. Shahid | Not | Out | 11 | 11 | 1 | 0 |
| | A.J. Hollioake * | did not bat | | | | | |
| | J.N. Batty + | did not bat | | | | | |
| | I.D.K. Salisbury | did not bat | | | | | |
| | Saqlain Mushtaq | did not bat | | | | | |
| | J. Ormond | did not bat | | | | | |
| | E.S.H. Giddins | did not bat | | | | | |
| | Extras | (7lb, 4w, 2nb) | | 13 | | | |
| | TOTAL | (31 overs) | (for 3 wkts) | 152 | | | |

| Bowler | O | M | R | W | NB | Wd |
|---|---|---|---|---|---|---|
| Martin | 6 | 0 | 26 | 1 | - | 1 |
| Chapple | 6 | 0 | 43 | 1 | - | 1 |
| Wood | 4 | 0 | 16 | 0 | 1 | - |
| Driver | 8 | 0 | 21 | 0 | - | 1 |
| Schofield | 5 | 0 | 26 | 0 | - | - |
| Chilton | 2 | 0 | 13 | 1 | - | 1 |

**LANCASHIRE LIGHTNING did not bat**
M.J. Chilton, D. Byas, G. Chapple, A.J. Swann, N.H. Fairbrother, G.D. Lloyd, W.K. Hegg *+, R.C. Driver, C..P. Schofield, J. Wood, P.J. Martin

## Other NUL Division Two Results

While the basement clubs, Sussex Sharks and Middlesex Crusaders, were able to play out a full, if uninspiring, match at Arundel, Gloucestershire Gladiators were hit by both rain and the Essex Eagles as they lost out in a Duckworth-Lewis adjusted run chase at Gloucester. Things were becoming very congested towards the top of the table, with the bottom three sides already losing touch with the top six.

June 30
*Gloucester:-* **Essex Eagles beat Gloucestershire Gladiators by 12 runs (D/L method).** Essex 215-9 (42.3ov; Flower 80, Pettini 75, Gidman 3-46); Gloucestershire 187-9 (35ov; Alleyne 76, Clarke 4-30). **Essex Eagles 4pts**

*Arundel:-* **Middlesex Crusaders beat Sussex Sharks by eight wickets.** Sussex 125 (41.4ov; Weekes 3-17, Abdul Razzaq 3-19); Middlesex 126-2 (38.5ov). **Middlesex Crusaders 4pts**

## NATIONAL LEAGUE DIVISION TWO AT 30TH JUNE

| Pos | Prv | | P | Pts | W | T | L | A |
|---|---|---|---|---|---|---|---|---|
| 1 | 1 | Derbyshire Scorpions | 5 | 14 | 3 | 0 | 1 | 1 |
| 2 | 1 | Gloucestershire Gladiators | 6 | 14 | 3 | 0 | 2 | 1 |
| = | 3 | Surrey Lions | 6 | 14 | 3 | 0 | 2 | 1 |
| 4 | 6 | Essex Eagles | 4 | 12 | 3 | 0 | 1 | 0 |
| 5 | 4 | Hampshire Hawks | 4 | 10 | 2 | 0 | 1 | 1 |
| = | 4 | Northamptonshire Steelbacks | 4 | 10 | 2 | 0 | 1 | 1 |
| 7 | 9 | Middlesex Crusaders | 6 | 8 | 1 | 0 | 3 | 2 |
| 8 | 8 | Lancashire Lightning | 7 | 8 | 1 | 0 | 4 | 2 |
| 9 | 7 | Sussex Sharks | 6 | 6 | 1 | 0 | 4 | 1 |

# 9 A Record-Breaking Stalemate

As we moved into July, Surrey's position at the top of the Frizzell County Championship Division One was looking increasingly promising, with the expected challengers yet to run into form, and no other county, with the possible exception of Kent, currently looking likely to pose a serious threat to the champions of 1999 and 2000. There were still a great many points to be won and lost, however, so there was no room for complacency, especially since Martin Bicknell's broken right wrist was almost certain to keep him out of action for a minimum of six weeks. The loss of the man who had been the country's leading all-rounder for the past two seasons was an undoubted setback for the county, though the blow had been softened by the return of Adam Hollioake, whose presence had already appeared to lift everyone at the Club. It was great to see him playing again, though no-one could yet be certain to what degree the traumas of the past few months might affect his game, if at all. He would get all the support he needed from his team-mates, that was for sure, and if the pressure of captaincy proved an unwelcome burden there was always the option of letting someone else take charge, since both Mark Butcher and Ian Ward had led the team well in his absence, demonstrating that Surrey had impressive reserves in this area, as well as in batting, bowling and wicketkeeping.

This strength in depth was underlined by the fact that Bicknell's replacement would be Ed Giddins, who had played for England as recently as June 2000, even though he had been relegated to the sidelines by Jimmy Ormond's arrival in the close season. Giddins' first year with the county had been rather a disappointment, especially in the County Championship, where he managed only thirty wickets at 36.73, though he had been a key performer in the triumphant Benson And Hedges Cup campaign. This year, following thirty-four wicketless overs in four Benson And Hedges qualifying matches, he had been showing great form with the white ball in the Norwich Union League, while his performance in the Championship victory over Kent had been encouraging. 'Giddo' now had the tough task of filling the void left by Bicknell's injury as the team entered an important phase in the season. With the next four Championship games including visits to Taunton and Canterbury, and a home game against Yorkshire, there were some awkward encounters ahead, though everyone was aware that if Surrey could come through these fixtures with their lead at the top of the table still intact, or even increased, then the team would be red-hot favourites to win the title.

| FRIZZELL COUNTY CHAMPIONSHIP - MATCH SEVEN |
|---|

### SOMERSET versus SURREY
### at The County Ground, Taunton

### First Day - Wednesday 3rd July

### Surrey 448-5

***The Teams And The Toss*** - *With the Nat West Series claiming four players - Stewart, Thorpe, Tudor and Trescothick - and injuries ruling out five more - Butcher (knee), Bicknell (wrist), Cox (thumb), Caddick (side) and Johnson (hamstring) - both sides are well below full strength. Adam Hollioake for Bicknell is Surrey's only change after their victory over Kent, while Somerset call up Simon Francis, the former Hampshire seamer, to replace Johnson following their defeat at Edgbaston. With a huge volume of rain having fallen in Taunton on the eve of match - from the moment of my arrival at 4.30pm until gone midnight - I'm not expecting any play before lunch as I make my way to the County Ground but, much to my surprise, the combination of a fast-drying outfield and a sterling effort by ground staff allows us to get away*

127

to a prompt start. Perhaps swayed by the possibility of moisture in the pitch and a fairly cloudy sky, Michael Burns, Somerset's stand-in skipper, invites Surrey to bat when he wins the toss.

Burns' decision to field first brings an early strike for his team when Steffan Jones claims Jon Batty lbw with the tenth ball of the match, the stand-in opener shuffling across his stumps and barely managing to get half-forward as the ball thuds into his pads. It's 0-1 and Surrey have made a nightmare start at a venue that hasn't been a happy hunting ground for them in recent years.

With the ball darting around a fair bit in these early stages, it's understandable that runs prove hard to come by, except when the rather wayward Matt Bulbeck is clipped through midwicket and glanced to fine leg for fours in his third over from the old pavilion end. While the young left-armer wastes the new ball by spraying it around, Jones continually attacks the stumps and, consequently, proves much the more threatening bowler during a fine opening spell of 7-4-8-1. Luckily for Surrey, Ian Ward and Mark Ramprakash manage to keep the scoreboard ticking over during these tricky opening overs with some good running between the wickets, which is comforting to see after all the recent problems they have had when running together.

It's not a run out that separates them today, though - it's the introduction of Simon Francis in place of the erratic Bulbeck. The first ball of the lively right-arm paceman's second over is angled across the left-handed Ward and tempts him into a fatal flirtation that results in an edge to Peter Bowler at first slip... Ward is out for thirteen and Surrey are 32-2.

The rest of Francis' over sees Nadeem Shahid beaten on a couple of occasions, adding further fuel to the fears of the Surrey fans in the ground, but the reappearance of Bulbeck in place of Jones at the river end eases everyone's nerves, especially when he starts with a really poor over that sees Ramprakash driving a full-toss through mid-on for three, and Shahid getting off the mark with a square-cut boundary.

The new batsman continues to look rather ill at ease, though, and in Francis' fourth over he edges low to Bowler at first slip and survives when the ball appears to slip from the fielder's fingertips after initially looking to be safely caught. Having only scored five at the time, this represents a real reprieve for Shahid, and he celebrates his good fortune two overs later by pulling the unlucky bowler for the four that brings up Surrey's fifty.

While Ramprakash continues to look in almost complete control, following an earlier on-drive off Francis with an off-driven boundary at Bulbeck's expense, Shahid continues to frustrate the former Hampshire bowler, edging him through the vacant third/fourth slip region in the final over of an impressive opening burst of 7-2-12-1.

Full credit should go to the Karachi-born batsman for sticking to his task in testing conditions, however, and he gradually begins to look in better touch as lunch approaches, driving Jones to the rope at square cover when the strongly-built paceman appears at the old pavilion end for a brief and unimpressive spell, then cutting Ian Blackwell, the replacement bowler, through point for another four. The simultaneous introduction of Parsons also meets with Shahid's approval, as the batsman pulls the last two balls of the Somerset medium-pacer's second over to the midwicket fence to take Surrey into lunch at a very acceptable 94-2.

While Shahid has undoubtedly ridden his luck during an extended sketchy start to his innings, Ramprakash has batted beautifully, rarely looking in any difficulty, despite the excellent opening spells of Jones and Francis. From a Somerset point of view, it's strange that Bulbeck, the least impressive bowler by a distance, has delivered four more overs than anyone else - his figures of 13-4-42-0 are pretty shocking, considering that the conditions have offered him some assistance.

*Lunch:- Surrey 94-2 (Ramprakash 40\*, Shahid 30\*) from 33 overs*

Taking the morning's performances as a guide, the smart money is on Jones and Francis to resume for Somerset after the break but, surprisingly, Mike Burns chooses the inconsistent

Bulbeck to partner Jones. The 22-year-old left-armer doesn't reward his captain for his act of faith, though, since his second over of the session is a truly wretched one, costing fifteen runs. It starts with a no-ball, which Shahid steers to third man for the single that takes the Surrey total into three figures, then Ramprakash punishes three successive half-volleys with sublime drives that skate away to the boundary at long-on, extra cover and straight long-off, the second of these strokes completing an excellent half-century from 111 balls.

With Jones looking much less impressive than he had at the start of the day, despite being back at his favoured river end, the third-wicket partnership passes the century mark in the following over when Shahid picks off two off-side boundaries, and the tally of runs since lunch then grows to fifty-one from ten overs as Bulbeck, who is surprisingly allowed to continue at the old pavilion end, concedes a dozen more runs to Ramprakash in the over after that. When Shahid then pulls Jones fine for four to reach a battling fifty, from 78 balls with ten fours, the penny finally drops for the Somerset skipper, and he makes a double bowling change, turning to Ian Blackwell at the old pavilion end and Simon Francis at the river end.

By now, the pitch and overhead conditions are favouring the batsmen, as Francis soon discovers when Ramprakash plunders two boundaries from his first over back. Blackwell's introduction is far more rewarding for the home side, though, as the left-arm spinner snares Shahid with the fifth ball of his second over. Seemingly deceived by a shorter, quicker delivery, the batsman goes right back onto his stumps to play a pull stroke and misses, giving umpire Gould little option but to raise his index finger. It is 162-3 as Shahid departs for a hard-fought fifty-one, with the innings now on a firm footing after the early loss of the openers.

This breakthrough has come just in the nick of time for Michael Burns, since his decision to put Surrey in to bat had been starting to look rather foolish, even allowing for the fact that Bulbeck (18-4-74-0) has been a major disappointment and Jones has not impressed since his opening blast, as figures of 8-1-38-0, from his second and third spells combined, testify. The Somerset captain is therefore further cheered by the capture of a fourth Surrey wicket just five overs after Shahid's exit, when Alistair Brown, after a brief and pretty unconvincing stay at the crease, flashes at a Francis delivery wide of his off-stump and nicks the ball through to Rob Turner, who takes a good catch away to his right-hand side. At 179-4, with the dangerous Brown gone for ten, the home team has almost levelled the game up as Adam Hollioake walks to the crease, accompanied by a warmer than average welcome from the crowd.

While the Surrey skipper looks a little insecure as he starts out, miscuing a hook off Francis backward of square leg for two to get off the mark, Ramprakash moves serenely into the nineties with a cut for four off Blackwell and seems certain to make a century, so assured has he looked throughout his innings. It comes as a major shock, therefore, when, on ninety-six, he pushes forward to the persevering Francis and snicks low to Keith Parsons at first slip. Maybe on another day the catch would stick, but not today, as the ball bursts through the hapless fielder's fingers and runs away to the rope at third man, thereby taking Ramprakash through to a very classy century, expertly compiled from 170 balls. Since his innings has been absolutely flawless until this point, there can be no doubting the fact that he has deserved his moment of good fortune, though one has to feel sorry for Francis, who is continuing to look easily the best of the Somerset bunch. Almost inevitably, the reprieved batsman celebrates his achievement by taking another boundary off the unlucky bowler later in the same over, a square drive simultaneously bringing Ramprakash his thirteenth four and elevating the total to exactly two-hundred.

Having come so close to removing the Surrey centurion, it is surprising to see Francis immediately pulled from the attack, even though he has only bowled six overs in his current spell. His replacement, Steffan Jones, is only employed for three overs, however, as both batsmen drive the thickset paceman back down the ground for boundaries and, with Blackwell looking anything but threatening from the old pavilion end, Somerset quickly lose their way again. The return of Parsons at the river end is certainly welcomed by the Surrey duo, and a fusillade of five powerfully driven fours in the course of the sixty-sixth and sixty-seventh overs of the innings, four of them to Hollioake, sees both the fifty partnership and the visitors' 250 arriving in quick succession. The Surrey skipper's increasing belligerence then brings him the first six of the innings as he advances on Blackwell and smites him cleanly over long-on, before an on-driven four in the next over from Parsons completes a quick-fire fifty from just 60 balls. The visitors are now firmly in control and Ramprakash confirms this by pulling the medium-pacer to the midwicket fence in the last over before tea.

*Tea:- Surrey 276-4 (Ramprakash 129\*, Hollioake 56\*) from 72 overs*

Somerset fans are doubtless hoping for better things from their team as the players appear for the final session. In addition to looking an increasingly directionless outfit as the afternoon had worn on, there had been clear signs of on-field unrest, with a very sulky Bulbeck responding badly to exhortations from Keith Dutch and Peter Bowler to look lively and refrain from leaning against the boundary fence at fine leg. From a captaincy point of view, Burns' utilisation of his resources again had to be questioned, with Blackwell being easily 'milked' and overbowled, while Francis had been given only thirteen overs, and off-spinner Dutch had yet to see active service. By way of contrast, things were looking good for Surrey, and the events of the first few overs after the break merely strengthen their position and darken Bulbeck's mood still further.

Having returned to the attack for the first over of the session, the left-arm swing bowler is immediately lofted to the extra-cover boundary, making the fifth-wicket partnership worth 101, and then hooked for a huge six over backward square leg, both strokes coming from the bat of Hollioake. Ramprakash then follows up with a rasping square-cut for four off Francis, before the visiting skipper gives Bulbeck further reason to scowl, taking fours from the first, third, fourth and fifth deliveries of his second post-tea over, with a cut, two pulls and an off-drive, blasting the Surrey score past three-hundred in the process. After a truly rank over, full of long-hops and half-volleys, the Somerset youngster can have no complaints about being banished to the outfield again and replaced by Dutch, who is granted a belated opportunity with the score standing at 312-4.

With the weather bright and sunny, and Burns' decision to insert Surrey looking to have backfired completely, the breakthrough that Somerset now desperately need comes in the over after Dutch's introduction, when Hollioake falls thirteen runs short of three figures, mistiming a hook off the deserving Francis to be well caught by Parsons running in from deep backward square leg. After an uncertain start, Hollioake's first Championship innings of the season has been richly entertaining, his eighty-seven runs coming from just 83 balls and including eleven fours and two sixes, and he receives a very well deserved ovation as he returns to the pavilion.

If Somerset are hoping for a little respite now they have removed the Surrey captain they are soon disappointed, since Rikki Clarke immediately indicates that he intends to keep the pressure on the bowlers by advancing on Dutch in his third over at the crease and blasting him for a mighty six over long-on - the ball carrying way over the stand and out of the ground - before clipping Francis confidently through square leg for four.

As the score mounts and the carnage continues, it's not hugely surprising that errors start to creep into the home side's previously good ground fielding, with one of a number of misfields allowing Ramprakash to pass his previous best score for Surrey, the 146 he made against Kent on debut in 2001, shortly before he completes an excellent 150 from 246 balls.

With Francis now taking a well-deserved rest, Dutch being easily worked around for singles, and Jones starting his fourth spell of the day with a ten-run over in which Clarke twice pulls him for four, another substantial partnership looks to be developing. Disappointingly, from Somerset's point of view, Jones once again proves unable to recapture the consistency of his opening spell of the day - after being savagely cut to the fence at point and driven to the rope wide of mid-on by Ramprakash in successive overs, as the sixth-wicket stand becomes worth fifty inside a dozen overs, he is then hooked to the boundary by Clarke.

Surrey are now rapidly closing in on 400, and Burns faces a tough decision, since a new ball is available to him. With Ramprakash well set and Clarke already looking in good touch, there seems a fair chance that taking it could bring a further acceleration in the scoring rate, but, as he is desperate for a wicket or two before the close, the Somerset skipper opts to take it anyway.

The initial signs aren't good for Burns, as Ramprakash clips and forces boundaries off the recalled Bulbeck, and Clarke on-drives a four of his own off Jones, but the run flow dries up a little thereafter as the Surrey all-rounder passes his previous best Championship score of forty-one and then survives a run-out scare in bizarre circumstances while taking the run that brings up the visitors' 400. Having driven a Bulbeck delivery towards mid-on and sprinted down the pitch for the run, Clarke collides with the bowler in mid-pitch and is still in a crumpled heap short of the non-striker's crease, apparently injured, as the return comes in from the fielder. It seems as if the young all-rounder must be run out until umpire Gould intervenes to suggest that the dismissal should not be completed, given Clarke's condition following the accidental collision. Sportingly, Somerset accede to the umpire's request and, after a short delay while the batsman recovers, he is allowed to resume his innings. Luckily, Clarke appears to suffer no ill effects from this incident, as he demonstrates a few overs later when he drives Jones through mid-on for two to complete a maiden Championship fifty, from 75 balls, and then hooks for four later in the same over to celebrate reaching this special milestone. Somerset's misery then continues, as Ramprakash pulls Bulbeck for the twenty-second boundary of his innings in the next over, raising the hundred partnership in the process and also forcing a double bowling change with just five overs left for play.

These changes see Blackwell, operating negatively from over the wicket and getting called for a leg-side wide first ball, and Francis return to the attack. Having taken three wickets and also had two catches dropped off his bowling, the latter has been consistently impressive, though his day ends on an unsatisfactory note when Ramprakash savages him for four successive fours in the third-to-last over. The Bushey-born batsman takes his boundary count to twenty-six and his score to 196 with gloriously executed strokes - a force backward of point, a pull to midwicket, a straight drive and a back foot forcing stroke that fairly rockets through extra cover - and has a chance to complete his double-century before the close when he comes to face the last over from Dutch, recalled at the river end in place of the weary Francis. A late cut for two from the first ball improves his prospects before he turns down easy singles to long-on from balls two and three, and then blocks the fourth delivery with a forward defensive stroke. Finally admitting defeat, he drives the fifth ball to long-on and this time takes the single to end the day unbeaten on 199, taking the crowd's applause for a masterful knock as he leaves the field moments later.

Ramprakash's innings has been faultless but for one or two nervy moments, including the dropped catch, either side of reaching his century, while Clarke has been scarcely any less impressive and Hollioake has played a truly stunning knock on his return to Championship action. It's been a terrific day for Surrey, especially as we have also discovered that Taunton has been the only ground to see a full day's play. The other three Division One matches have seen a total of just 10.3 overs of action, all of these at Hove, as rain has swept across the country.

*Close:- Surrey 448-5 (Ramprakash 199\*, Clarke 60\*) from 104 overs*

## VIEWS FROM THE DRESSING ROOM

*I assume we were put in to bat because of the overnight rain and the overhead conditions at the start of play. Would you have inserted Somerset if you had won the toss?*
**ADAM HOLLIOAKE** - No, in a word, and I was actually surprised they put us in because there's a history at Taunton of the pitch looking green but still playing very well. If there is any

movement at all for the bowlers then it's usually when the wicket is green, so I toyed with the idea briefly before deciding that we would bat if we won the toss.

*This was the first Championship match you had played in since your return to England. I guess you must have been quite moved by the reception you got from the crowd here, and even more so at The Rose Bowl when you made your first return appearance in the NUL match?*
**ADAM HOLLIOAKE** - Yes, it was a fantastic response. I couldn't have imagined it because I haven't been a favourite with the crowds around the country over the years. I wasn't quite sure how to handle it really - it was a new thing for me - but I was very touched by it and it's something I'll remember for a long time.

*At about this stage of the season it seemed that every time there was a Ramprakash-Clarke partnership it added a minimum of a hundred runs. Do you have any idea why the two of you were so successful together?*
**MARK RAMPRAKASH** - I've no real idea. The first time I batted with him, I thought I should go down and have a chat with him as he might be nervous, but he just took it all in his stride and proceeded to play very solidly and hit some fantastic shots. So, after that, I thought there was no need to try and coax him along because he'd obviously got a very good temperament - that shone out straight away. He's got shots all round the wicket and can play off both feet - that's probably the key to his success.
**RIKKI CLARKE** - I don't know why, but we just seem to bat really well together. If I was going through a bad patch, he'd have some advice for me, and he always seemed to know what to say in terms of calming me down. When I first started out, I was a bit worried about the one-day game if I felt I wasn't scoring quickly enough, and he'd tell me that I perhaps didn't need to blaze it around at this stage, or whatever. He was always very good at the times when I was feeling a bit vulnerable.

*There was an interesting incident just before you reached fifty when you collided with Matt Bulbeck in mid-pitch and you were left in a heap well short of your crease as the ball was returned to the bowler's stumps. No attempt was made to complete a simple run-out - am I right in thinking that umpire Ian Gould had intervened or was it just a sporting gesture by Somerset not to take advantage of the situation?*
**RIKKI CLARKE** - I went to run around him, but he went in the same direction in order to back up the throw as it came in, so we collided and both went down on the deck. I realised that if I got up to try and complete the run then there was a good chance I would be run out, so I stayed down and, as a result, Ian Gould called 'dead-ball' straight away. I'm surprised I thought that quickly, actually, because I wouldn't say that's my greatest strength!

### Second Day - Thursday 4th July

### Surrey 608-6dec; Somerset 304-3

It takes Mark Ramprakash just four balls to complete his double-century on the second morning, an extra-cover drive for two off Steffan Jones taking him through to the landmark from his 301st delivery. Generous applause rings out around the ground as the batsman celebrates the sixth double-ton of his first-class career, three of the previous five having been scored against his current team while he was playing for Middlesex.

In now excellent batting conditions, with the pitch as flat as a pancake, Somerset know that further toil is ahead of them, though they are maybe surprised to find that it is Rikki Clarke who dominates the scoring in the early stages, the twenty-year-old unfurling five beautifully-timed drives to various parts of the ground against a single four, forced away backward of point, by his vastly experienced colleague that heralds the arrival of the 150 partnership.

Having opened the bowling with Francis and Jones today, Burns turns back to Bulbeck for the ninth over of the morning when Jones rests after another unexceptional spell of four overs, and the left-armer's first delivery is cut away over point for four runs by Clarke, taking the young all-rounder's score into the nineties.

He has advanced his score to ninety-seven, and taken Surrey through the five-hundred barrier, with a firm clip to the midwicket boundary in the next over from Francis when a well-timed straight drive from the fifth delivery is stopped by the bowler in his follow-through at the expense of what appears to be a broken finger. The luckless ex-Hampshire seamer departs to the pavilion immediately, leaving Jones to reappear and complete the over with a short, wide ball which Clarke cuts to the cover sweeper for a single that takes him on to ninety-eight.

Back on strike and facing Bulbeck, the Surrey youngster doesn't have to wait long to reach three figures as the left-armer immediately serves up a leg stump half-volley, allowing Clarke to clip the ball away through midwicket for the two runs he requires to complete an excellent maiden County Championship century from just 123 balls, with sixteen fours and one six in the mix. It has been an excellent innings and it represents quite an achievement for the Guildford lad to have notched a hundred in only his third match in the UK's premier domestic competition. He celebrates joyously with Ramprakash, soaking up the Taunton crowd's applause, before continuing on his merry way with an on-driven boundary off Jones and two further fours in an over from Bulbeck that sees the arrival of the two-hundred partnership. With his partner still surprisingly subdued, Clarke then cracks a Jones half-volley to the extra-cover fence to push the Surrey score beyond 523, thereby wiping out ninety-one years of history in setting a new record for the county's highest total ever made at Taunton.

Since this stroke has also taken the sixth-wicket partnership to 209, the county's 103-year-old record for this wicket against Somerset - 211 by Abel and Crawford in 1899 - also looks set to fall but, with just one run added, Jones finally separates the Surrey pair, switching his line of attack to round the wicket and almost immediately inducing Ramprakash to play on in attempting to hook. Despite having 218 runs to his name, the Surrey number three is furious with himself, and, though we have seen a very well contained Ramprakash add only nineteen runs during almost sixteen overs at the crease today, his innings still rates very highly indeed, since it has been the bedrock of a formidable Surrey total. As he returns to the pavilion to a fine reception, Ian Salisbury strides out to bat with the scoreboard reading 527-6 and, one assumes, given the situation, licence to thrill.

If this is indeed the case then he certainly doesn't disappoint as he takes fours off both the remaining balls of Jones' over, first with a hook and then with a perfect pick-up just backward of square leg. The brawny Somerset paceman then switches back to an over-the-wicket approach for his next over, though he continues to come off second best as Salisbury again picks off two boundaries, the first driven over the head of mid-off and the second clipped through midwicket. Consequently, Jones is pulled from the attack and replaced by Dutch, who fares no better as he concedes three sixes in his first two overs, the first a massive straight hit by Salisbury which clears the Ian Botham Stand by some considerable distance, and the next two by Clarke over wide long-on, courtesy of a drive and a slog-sweep.

Meanwhile, at the old pavilion end, Blackwell has taken over from Bulbeck, and his left-arm spin, having proved hard to get away, almost brings him a wicket when Clarke, on 141, charges and misses. Rob Turner fluffs the routine stumping, however, allowing the seventh-wicket stand to progress further and reach fifty when Salisbury drives the disappointed bowler back over his head for four later in the same over.

With lunch now around forty-five minutes away, the battering of Dutch continues apace, as Clarke launches the former Middlesex man high over wide long-on and into the car park beyond the stands to complete his 150 from 178 balls, with twenty fours and four sixes to his credit. The off-spinner's over ends up costing fourteen, and when Blackwell finally starts to receive similar treatment in the following over, with Salisbury twice advancing and driving fours to send the total thundering beyond six-hundred, Adam Hollioake decides that enough is enough, declaring the innings closed at 608-6 after the addition of 160 runs in just under twenty-seven overs this morning. With his captain having thereby shown mercy on the suffering Somerset bowlers, Rikki Clarke leads the players from the field with a magnificent unbeaten 153 to his name, further underlining his talent and marking him out to the England selectors as one to watch for the future. Credit is due to Salisbury, too, for his entertaining and unselfish unbeaten forty-six, compiled from just thirty balls with seven fours and that huge six.

Facing the daunting task of scoring 459 to avoid the follow-on, the Somerset openers, Matt Wood and Piran Holloway, come out to bat at 12.55pm for what looks likely to be a tricky twenty minutes. As it happens, however, they are gifted some easy runs in the opening two overs as Ed Giddins concedes twelve, including two fours, from the first four balls of the opening over and Jimmy Ormond also yields a boundary in a second over that costs seven. Although four much-improved overs follow, the Surrey opening pair never look very likely to secure the wicket that Hollioake would have hoped for when he declared.

*Lunch:- Somerset 23-0 (Holloway 12\*, Wood 7\*) from 6 overs*

Although Giddins and Ormond bowl with slightly better control and discipline upon the resumption, the Somerset openers continue to look pretty comfortable, with Wood doing the bulk of the scoring as he drives Ormond for boundaries on both sides of the wicket and pulls him wide of mid-on for another four. Although the former Leicestershire paceman also finds the edge of the bat a couple of times, it is the less threatening but more consistent Giddins who comes closest to a breakthrough in the eleventh over when Nadeem Shahid claims a low catch, possibly via bat and boot, at short leg. The umpires confer but they decide that there is insufficient evidence for them to give Holloway out, allowing him to continue and the opening partnership to reach fifty in the next over.

Some of Surrey's cricket is undeniably shabby during this period of the game, with no-balls, the occasional wide, and byes, some of which verge on being called wide, abounding to such an extent that extras account for exactly a third of the total by the time it reaches sixty-six. The sundries count has already overtaken Holloway's score, which has only advanced by four singles in seventeen overs since he took twelve from Giddins' opening over. He is doing a good job for his side, however, and part of his mission is accomplished when the opening bowlers are replaced, after ten rather erratic overs apiece, by Rikki Clarke and Ian Salisbury. The left-handed Holloway instantly finds Clarke more to his liking, finally freeing himself from his shackles with a pulled boundary in each of the young all-rounder's first two overs, though he very nearly falls for the old three-card trick when he mishits another short-pitched delivery out to the deliberately positioned Shahid at deep backward square. Unfortunately for the bowler and his team, the fielder fails to hang on to an awkward chance away to his left-hand side, giving Holloway a life with his score on twenty-four and the total on eighty-eight.

On such a good surface, it's clear that every chance needs to be taken, and this point is hammered home as the batsmen continue to dominate, with a series of square cuts and on-drives by Wood, at Salisbury's expense, taking him through to, and beyond, a well-played 84-ball fifty, containing ten fours. The opening partnership has already exceeded 100 by this point, and things look to be going from bad to worse for Surrey when Holloway finally moves up a gear, sweeping Salisbury for a one-bounce four, seeing off Clarke with three off-side boundaries, and then greeting the all-rounder's replacement, Saqlain Mushtaq, with a late-cut to the rope at third man that sees him suddenly surging to a half-century from 101 balls.

The Surrey bowlers are now suffering in much the same way as their Somerset counterparts had earlier. Even the celebrated Saqlain and Salisbury spin partnership is repelled with surprising ease on this superb batting track, with Wood plundering further boundaries through extra cover and square leg off the leg-spinner, and Holloway driving a full-toss through mid-on for four as Surrey's ground fielding rarely rises above the average, and frequently qualifies for the tag of 'poor'. The visitors already look to be facing a long hard struggle for the next day or so, though, with tea imminent, Salisbury offers his side a ray of hope with a well-pitched leg-break that Wood edges between wicketkeeper and slip at catchable height.

*Tea:- Somerset 178-0 (Holloway 62\*, Wood 90\*) from 43 overs*

With the first two sessions of the second day's play having yielded just one rather fortunate wicket, it is crystal clear that both sides are missing their absent bowlers far more than their absent batsmen on this pitch. Adam Hollioake therefore opts to pair his fastest bowler, Jimmy Ormond, with his most potent spinner, Saqlain Mushtaq, at the start of the final session in an attempt to make some belated inroads into the Somerset batting line-up.

Hopes that this might prove to be a winning combination are soon dimmed, however, when Holloway's late cut to the rope at third man off Ormond takes the opening partnership to 183, making it the highest for Somerset against Surrey at Taunton, and then Wood races to the second County Championship century of his career with three excellent leg-side strokes for four, two and four off Saqlain. His fine innings, spanning 139 balls and including eighteen fours, is enthusiastically acknowledged by the home fans, who are then further delighted when he drives the Surrey off-spinner wide of mid-on for another boundary to end an expensive fourteen-run over and take his side to within one run of two-hundred.

Although this mark is reached when Holloway pushes Ormond to square leg at the start of the next over, the opening stand has advanced by only two further runs when the Surrey paceman finally brings it to a close with a rapid yorker that extracts Wood's off stump. The sense of relief in the visitors' camp is almost tangible as the 21-year-old opener, who had first played against Surrey for Devon in the 2000 Nat West Trophy, makes his way back to the pavilion to a standing ovation with 106 runs to his name.

Surrey's principal concern now is to build on this opening success and they achieve this six overs later, again through Ormond, when the sturdy seamer coaxes a little extra bounce out of the pitch to surprise Holloway and induce an outside edge to Hollioake at second slip.

With the left-handed opener gone for seventy-seven at 217-2, and two new batsmen, Mike Burns and Peter Bowler, at the crease there is now a chink of light at the end of the tunnel, since 242 runs are still required to avoid the follow-on. Ormond looks in good rhythm, too, and, while Saqlain ties up an end with his probing off-spin, the big paceman continues his hostile and skilful spell from the old pavilion end, mixing bouncers and slower balls in with his occasional yorkers. Hard though he tries, he is unable to gain any further success, though, and when Burns cuts and drives him for boundaries in the eighth over of his spell, Hollioake wisely opts to rest his main strike bowler and replace him with Giddins.

Having previously only bowled at the river end, the new bowler seems to take a while to settle, conceding a cover-driven boundary to each batsman in the meantime, before the final delivery of his second over brings further joy for Surrey when Bowler plants his front foot, hits across his pad and misses a straight delivery to fall lbw for nineteen with the total on 261.

Although this wicket brings further hope for the visitors, the fourth-wicket pair encounter very few problems on this fine pitch and gradually consolidate their team's position in their own different styles. While Burns attacks wherever possible, at one point launching Saqlain over long-off for a splendid six on his way to completing an 85-ball half-century in the third-from-last over of the day, Parsons happily plays second fiddle, producing only one memorable stroke, a square cut for four off Clarke when the all-rounder replaces Saqlain at the river end.

On a day when Surrey's display has been largely below par, it is perhaps appropriate that Somerset's three-hundred arrives, in the last over of play, courtesy of a wide from Clarke that escapes Batty's grasping gloves, gifting the home side three runs.

*Close:- Somerset 304-3 (Burns 51\*, Parsons 13\*) from 75 overs*

## RIKKI CLARKE'S MAIDEN COUNTY CHAMPIONSHIP CENTURY
### Original run chart as compiled by Keith Seward

SOMERSET V SURREY,   TAUNTON,   3/4-7-02

R. CLARKE                         NOT OUT    153
RHB

5·07 – (12·40)      203 mins         50 in 79 mins   75 balls
                    180 balls        100 in 147 mins  123 balls
                                     150 in 199 mins  178 balls

1·6 4 11 4 4 111 4 4 4 4 11 2 111 22 4 4 111 4 11 4 4 1 4 4 4 1 2 4 1 2 4 1 4 4 2 4 1111 6 6 2 1111 6 11

Career best score

Shared 6th wicket stand of 210 in 167 mins with M. RAMPRAKASH.

# VIEW FROM THE DRESSING ROOM

*I suppose it was nicely set up for your maiden Championship century, starting the second day with sixty runs already to your name?*
**RIKKI CLARKE** - Yes, it certainly helped. You can't really say you're 'in' when you start again the next day, but you perhaps play more freely and can get on with your game a little bit earlier without having to play yourself in quite as much. Before I went out, Adam told me to keep going, to make a name for myself, and that advice stuck with me for the rest of my innings.

## Third Day - Friday 5th July

### Surrey 608-6dec and 96-0; Somerset 554

With the match at the halfway point, and Somerset exactly halfway to Surrey's 608-6, it is already looking likely that the contest will end in a draw unless the home side fails to reach their follow-on target of 459. As we prepare to start the third day there are factors that offer encouragement to the visitors, however - a grey and overcast morning should encourage swing bowling; a new ball is due in fifteen overs time; and Somerset are likely to be batting a man short, as a result of the fractured finger suffered by Simon Francis on day two. Surrey will have an absentee of their own, however, since Ali Brown has gone down with a dose of food poisoning, leaving Tim Murtagh to act as the substitute fielder.

When play gets under way, Adam Hollioake again turns to Ormond and Saqlain, and his selected paceman starts well, but without luck, as Burns edges through the vacant third/fourth slip area for four in the third over and is then dropped two overs later, on fifty-seven, by Jon Batty as the Surrey keeper dives away in front of first slip. It's a low chance but, having got both hands to the ball, Batty will feel that he should have held it to make Somerset 316-4.

As if he hasn't been unfortunate enough already during a fine opening burst, Ormond then suffers again in his next over when the other overnight batsman, Parsons, also enjoys a reprieve as Mark Ramprakash, at first slip, fails to hang on to a fast-travelling overhead chance, the ball bursting through his hands and running away to the boundary. Although far from an easy chance, with the batsman on nineteen and the total having advanced to 319, it is undoubtedly the kind of opportunity that cannot be spurned if Somerset are to be bowled out before reaching the magic figure of 459.

While all this is going on at the old pavilion end, Saqlain, at the river end, is giving nothing away, though he is not troubling the batsmen anywhere near as much as Ormond, who again rues his luck when Parsons almost pops back a return catch and then edges just short of first slip in the strongly-built fast bowler's sixth over of the day.

Having survived their early scares, both batsmen subsequently profit at their tormentor's expense, however, when Ormond, perhaps tiring slightly at the end of his excellent opening spell, is pulled for four by Parsons and then glanced to the boundary by Burns. Figures this morning of 8-1-31-0 simply don't do justice to Surrey's newest recruit, who has given his all on an unresponsive surface.

It is actually rather surprising that Hollioake has kept Ormond going for so long, since the new ball becomes due at the precise moment the former Leicestershire man is rested and replaced at the old pavilion end by Ed Giddins. With the inexperienced Rikki Clarke the only other realistic option to use the new 'cherry', it would seem that Surrey plan to continue with the old one, and so it proves as Burns pulls Giddins to the fence at long-on to raise the Somerset 350 and then breaks Saqlain's spell by sweeping the off-spinner over square leg for six to bring up the hundred partnership with Parsons. After Ormond's early efforts, it's the home side that is assuming control, as both batsmen advance their score with a straight-driven boundary, Parsons off the largely ineffective Giddins, and Burns at the expense of the newly introduced Clarke.

Given the way the game is going, Surrey are probably grateful that a sudden shower hits the ground at this point, causing a half-hour break, and the loss of seven overs, with the score at 377-3 in the ninety-seventh over.

Any thoughts that the new ball might be taken immediately upon the resumption and given to Ormond are quickly dispelled, however, as Hollioake, rather surprisingly, joins Clarke in the attack as soon as play gets under way again with half-an-hour to go until lunch.

This short session turns out to be a fruitful one for Surrey and Clarke, though, with both partners in the fourth-wicket stand falling in quick succession as the visitors' young all-rounder suddenly makes things happen for his team. Parsons is his first victim, adjudged lbw for forty-seven to an inswinging yorker with the score at 378, then Burns, having progressed to ninety-nine with two boundaries in Hollioake's second over, falls without addition at the end of a very eventful next over from Surrey's rising star. The over in question contains a wide; a thick-edged drive just short of gully and an off-driven three by Blackwell; a no-ball resulting from a very high bouncer to raise the home side's four-hundred; and, finally, another inswinger of full length that traps the Somerset skipper in front of his stumps. Having driven the previous delivery straight to the fielder at cover, Burns has every right to feel particularly disappointed at falling one short of a hundred as he makes his way off the park to a well deserved ovation, passing a scoreboard that reads 401-5.

With the home team now well on the way to saving the follow-on, and Surrey suddenly in with a chance of claiming at least one further bowling point, the rest of the players join the Somerset captain back in the pavilion a few minutes later when rain returns just four balls before lunch is due to be taken.

*Lunch:- Somerset 410-5 (Blackwell 12\*, Turner 4\*) from 102.2 overs*

Blackwell is quickly out of his blocks after lunch, taking three boundaries off Clarke in the space of ten balls, courtesy of a square drive, a pull and a cover drive, before a light sprinkling of rain prompts the umpires to ask the batsmen if they wish to leave the field. Surprisingly, they do, whereas the Surrey fielders demonstrate a more positive attitude by showing great reluctance to return to their dressing room. With the score having advanced by seventeen runs in sixteen balls since lunch, and the follow-on almost avoided, Somerset's actions perhaps betray a degree of fear, which hardly appears to be warranted at this moment in time.

As luck would have it, however, the rain clouds soon pass over the ground, permitting everyone to return to the middle after fifteen minutes, with the loss of just four overs, and also allowing Clarke to get even with Blackwell. Although the chunky left-hander soon adds another two fours to his collection, with a booming drive over mid-off and a less impressive thick edge to third man, Surrey's new talent snaps back with a bouncer that Blackwell hooks straight down the throat of Tim Murtagh at long leg with the total at 440 and his personal tally thirty-four.

The visitors have certainly seemed to be fired up since the rain break, and Ormond fans the flames of Surrey's fightback with a well-deserved wicket in the next over as Somerset's decline from a high point of 378-3 continues. When Keith Dutch's outside edge is excellently taken low down to his right at first slip by Ian Salisbury, the home side are still sixteen runs short of their primary objective at 443-7 and, with some tension creeping into the game at last, things nearly become worse for them three balls later when Rob Turner, on eleven at the time, snicks a Clarke delivery to Hollioake at second slip. Luckily for Somerset, the Surrey skipper is unable to hang on to a reasonably straightforward catch at a good height to his right-hand side and a possible scoreline of 445-8 becomes 446-7 as the ball runs away for a single.

This proves to be the visitors' last chance of a wicket before their hosts pass the follow-on mark five overs later with a boundary whipped through midwicket by Matt Bulbeck. With the match now seemingly condemned to end as a draw, the pursuit of their final bowling point would appear to be the limit of Surrey's ambitions, so, with two wickets required from fourteen overs, Hollioake replaces the tiring Clarke and Ormond with Giddins and Salisbury.

Although the previous bowlers have done a fine job, the introduction of the most sparingly used, and therefore freshest, members of his attack makes sense and almost brings an instant breakthrough as the left-handed Bulbeck edges Giddins first over, and then just wide of, the slips. Thereafter, the eighth-wicket pair look rather more comfortable, however, with each man driving the former England bowler to the fence at extra cover to complete a fifty partnership and raise the five-hundred, forcing the Surrey skipper to recall Saqlain in the hope that an all-spin attack might bring the breakthrough his team requires.

And so it does, as the Pakistani off-spinner strikes with his second delivery, courtesy of Bulbeck's outside edge and Batty's catch. Somerset are now eight down as the batsman departs for twenty-seven with the score at 506, and forty-six deliveries remain for Surrey to capture the all-important ninth wicket.

Fortunately for the spinners, Steffan Jones looks likely to offer them a fair chance of success, though maybe at a cost, as he lofts Saqlain away for three leg-side boundaries in an over and then hits Salisbury over the top of mid-on for another four. Although it seems inevitable that he will eventually hole out somewhere, he manages to restrain himself for the next few overs and it is only when the 130-over cut-off for bonus points is upon us that he finally edges an ambitious drive at Salisbury. With just four balls to spare, Surrey have at least maintained their record of capturing every bowling point this season, even if a twelve-point draw already appears to be the best they can hope for from the match.

At this point, everyone thinks the Somerset innings is complete, given that Francis is nursing a broken finger, but, much to everyone's surprise, the 23-year-old fast bowler suddenly appears from the pavilion. It seems pointless, really, though it again indicates that the hosts feel the match is not yet a certain draw, as well as demonstrating a lack of self-belief that offers Surrey some encouragement.

As a consequence of the number eleven batsman's appearance, the innings meanders on for another five overs, during which time Turner completes a solid 81-ball half-century and Somerset pass 550, before Saqlain completes a hard-earned five-wicket haul by snaring Francis with a leading-edge catch to the substitute, Murtagh, at backward point.

*Tea:- Between Innings*

In the best weather of the day, Ian Ward and Jon Batty set out to add to Surrey's pretty insignificant first innings advantage of fifty-four runs against Jones and Bulbeck. Batty is soon off his pair with a nicely timed forcing stroke to the rope backward of point, and adds further pleasing drives through cover and mid-on as he makes a confident start. Scarcely a ball beats the bat as the Surrey keeper continues to dominate the scoring, though it is Ward who brings up the fifty in the sixteenth over with a flowing off-drive for four off Bulbeck.

With the opening bowlers into their ninth overs, Ward does offer a low caught-and-bowled chance to Jones, with his score on twenty-three, and Batty picks up a less than convincing boundary with a thick edge to third man off Bulbeck, but, these incidents aside, it's plain sailing for the Surrey openers as the visitors' lead steadily grows.

Despite these minor moral victories, the Somerset pacemen immediately give way to Dutch and Parsons, and the flow of runs dries to a mere trickle for almost half an hour until Batty makes a sudden surge to his fifty with a drive to the cover boundary off Parsons, followed by an imperious straight six and another cover drive for four at Dutch's expense. The Surrey gloveman has certainly put his first innings duck behind him with his 77-ball half-century and he continues in fluent style, sweeping and driving the off-spinner for further boundaries in the closing overs as Surrey's advantage extends to 150.

The day's entertainment ends in glorious sunshine, and it would appear that we have once again been blessed, since the other three Division Ones games have again suffered a blank day, due to rain. With twelve points now surely guaranteed from this match, Surrey's lead at the top of the Championship table looks likely to have grown by this time tomorrow.

*Close:- Surrey 96-0 (Ward 31\*, Batty 63\*) from 33 overs*

## VIEWS FROM THE DRESSING ROOM

*We didn't take the new ball in Somerset's first innings, using the same ball for 135 overs. What was the thinking behind that?*
**ADAM HOLLIOAKE** - I can't remember exactly why it was on this occasion, but there is usually a good reason if we keep the same ball. It happened quite a lot this season that we stayed with the old ball if it was swinging or reversing - if you take the new ball you run the risk of getting one that doesn't swing. Also, you can keep control of one end with a spinner, whereas if you take the new ball then it means you've got to have two seamers bowling, which sometimes can just open the floodgates.

*I thought Jimmy Ormond was probably the pick of our bowlers and deserved more than the three expensive wickets he ended up with. How did you see it from behind the stumps?*
**JON BATTY** - Definitely. We went through a phase during that part of the season where we would miss a chance off Jimmy at the start of his spell when he was bowling well, so he ended up with only one or two wickets. Maybe if we had taken the early catch then he might have gone on to get four or five wickets in those innings.

**Fourth Day - Saturday 6th July**

**Surrey 608-6dec and 324-5dec; Somerset 554 and 329-7**

**Match Drawn**
**Somerset 11pts, Surrey 12**

The final day's play starts in warm sunshine, which is some consolation for the fact that the game appears likely to end in a fairly sterile draw at around 5.20pm.

When the action gets under way, we see roles reversed from the previous evening as Jon Batty plays second fiddle to a very fluent Ian Ward, who takes advantage of some loose bowling and poor ground fielding to find the off-side boundary on four occasions in the early overs on his way to a 126-ball half-century. It's clear that the pitch remains a 'belter' as Ward continues to time his drives beautifully, stretching his side's lead past two-hundred by striking Jones through extra cover for his seventh four of the morning, before adding an eighth boundary with an on-drive in the next over from Bulbeck. Although this stroke takes his score to seventy-five - level with Batty's tally, despite the Surrey keeper having had a thirty-two run advantage overnight - it turns out to be his last contribution to the innings, since the Somerset left-armer picks up a belated first wicket of the match later in the same over with a far from deserving leg-side delivery that Ward touches as it flies through to Rob Turner. The Surrey lead is 207 as their disappointed opener departs for the pavilion.

Having ended Ward's participation in the game, Bulbeck's own involvement ends shortly afterwards, too, when he pulls up with some kind of foot injury four balls into his next over and immediately leaves the field, thus ending a particularly unhappy match for the young seamer. Since his side is now two bowlers short, and Jones is at the end of an eight-over spell, Mike

Burns' options are suddenly rather limited, so it's no surprise that he turns to Keith Parsons and Ian Blackwell, his two most defensive bowlers.

In the prevailing conditions, with the batsmen under no pressure, it will be no easy task to restrict the scoring, though, as Batty demonstrates by immediately advancing on Blackwell and driving him high over long-off into the neighbouring graveyard for six. When he then follows up with a similar stroke for four in the left-arm spinner's third over he moves within range of his second century of the season and, shortly after Mark Ramprakash has raised the two-hundred with successive drives for four and three off Parsons, it duly arrives with a hooked single to deep backward square leg off the same bowler. The Surrey wicketkeeper's third first-class ton has come from 168 deliveries and included fifteen fours and two sixes.

With Batty reverse-sweeping Blackwell for four soon afterwards to pass the 104 he made at Old Trafford, thereby registering a new career-best score, and Ramprakash looking in predictably dominant form, the score rattles along at a rate of knots, exposing Somerset's unathletic fielding, though, to be fair to them, their situation isn't helped by the use of the veteran Graham Rose and the county coach, Kevin Shine, as substitutes for their injured fast bowlers. Although the game still looks to be dead in the water, the crowd is at least able to enjoy the strokeplay of the Surrey batsmen, though Blackwell understandably fails to appreciate either Ramprakash's slog-sweep for six at his expense or Batty's ability to reverse-sweep to the fine third man boundary almost at will. Parsons is also suffering, of course, and, with lunch fast approaching, concedes the square-cut four that simultaneously takes Ramprakash to an excellent 40-ball fifty and the visitors' lead to three-hundred.

Both Somerset bowlers get some reward for their efforts in their final over before the break, however, as the Surrey number three loses his leg stump to Blackwell when he advances and misses an on-drive, while Ian Salisbury, promoted up the order to have a blast, soon top-edges a cut at Parsons and is well taken by Rob Turner standing up to the stumps.

Surrey's lunchtime lead of 315 looks fairly insignificant, given the ideal batting conditions, and, with only around sixty-five overs left to play, any sort of declaration and run chase still looks out of the question.

*Lunch:- Surrey 261-3 (Batty 122\*) from 63.3 overs*

Upon the resumption, the visitors add to their advantage in busy fashion, with Batty and the newly arrived Rikki Clarke each plundering two boundaries in the opening ten deliveries of the session. The batting is certainly more purposeful than would be expected if Surrey were planning to bat out the match, and the total has motored on to three-hundred within twenty-one balls of the restart when Batty sweeps Blackwell fine for two in the sixty-seventh over.

Although Clarke perishes for a quick-fire twenty-two in the next over, his firm lofted drive off Parsons being safely clutched by Burns at wide mid-on, the pace doesn't slacken as Batty completes his 150 from exactly 200 balls following further sweeps, for four and then one, at the expense of the returning Dutch. Healthy applause around the ground acknowledges the Surrey wicketkeeper's fine achievement, and is then repeated five balls later when he pulls a catch to Wood at deep midwicket, giving Parsons his third wicket and prompting an instant, and rather unexpected, declaration from the visiting captain.

The gauntlet has, therefore, been thrown down, with the home side challenged to chase a very testing 379 off fifty-seven overs. Will Somerset be tempted to have a dart at this target or will they feel that a required run rate of 6.65 per over is beyond the realms of possibility, even with a flat track, a fairly fast outfield and a couple of reasonably short boundaries in their favour? From a Surrey point of view, the capture of ten wickets looks close to impossible... unless the opposition get involved in a run chase and have to take outrageous chances, of course. At least we might yet see some entertaining and positive cricket, thanks to Hollioake's bold closure.

Somerset's openers certainly start purposefully after the ten-minute break between innings, with Wood glancing and square-driving Ormond for two early boundaries, and Holloway keeping the Surrey fielders busy by picking up threes to long-on, midwicket and cover.

It's the fifth over of the innings that really gives the total a major boost, however, as Wood finds the rope on three occasions, courtesy of two on-drives and a thick edge off Giddins, while Holloway, quite bizarrely, extends his run of threes to five with a couple of nice strokes through extra cover at the expense of Ormond.

Much to the relief of the batsman and the perspiring fielders, Somerset's left-handed opener finally times a stroke well enough to save a lot of unnecessary running when he pulls Ormond to the midwicket fence in the eighth over, bringing up the home team's fifty in the process. Although their task is daunting, this represents a fine base for Somerset, at an almost ideal pace, and when Giddins is again edged to the third man boundary by Wood, the Surrey skipper decides to take some pace off the ball by replacing his rather unlucky opening bowler with Saqlain Mushtaq.

This move is soon looking a good one, as the off-spinner, well supported by three tight overs from Ormond, drags the scoring rate back below five an over, to the relief of everyone in the Surrey camp. An opening wicket would be even more welcome, however, and it takes another change of bowling to achieve this, when Salisbury takes over from Ormond at the old pavilion end. Although the leg-spinner is quickly cut and driven for fours by Wood, the fourth ball of his second over earns him the scalp of Holloway for thirty-three, with the score at seventy-five, when the left-hander is brilliantly caught by Shahid diving away low to his left at short leg.

The loss of this wicket and the close proximity of tea now combine to squeeze the scoring rate a little further, though Mike Burns clearly suggests that his team hasn't yet thrown in the towel by striking a leg-side boundary in each of the final three overs of the session. With just thirty-four overs left for play it looks as if Hollioake's declaration will come to nothing, however, since Somerset still need the small matter of 276 runs and Surrey require an equally improbable nine wickets.

*Tea:- Somerset 103-1 (Wood 43\*, Burns 20\*) from 23 overs*

Although they need more than eight runs per over, Somerset, to their credit, still look up for the chase as play resumes after tea with Ormond operating from the old pavilion end and Saqlain from the river end.

After a late-cut boundary by Burns off Saqlain, Wood is the principal aggressor in the early overs, completing a 74-ball half-century in the third over of the session, before cover-driving Ormond for the ninth four of his innings and then increasing his boundary tally to eleven with a pull and an on-drive in the next over bowled by Saqlain.

Although both batsmen are now well set, with the second-wicket partnership exceeding fifty, they are unable to keep up with the required run-rate as the next four overs yield just a single four, glanced to fine leg by Wood at the expense of the off-spinner. Appreciating that loss of momentum at this stage could snuff out their flickering hopes, the batsmen start to take a few chances and Wood almost comes unstuck as a result, top-edging a hook off Ormond over Batty's head and then surviving a very difficult chance to Hollioake at leg slip off Saqlain with his score on eighty-two and the total at 173. With 1,659 runs scored in the contest to this point, the record for the highest match aggregate in a game involving Surrey has already been broken, the tedious 1,650-run batting display involving Lancashire at The Oval in 1990 having been pushed down to second place in the list, and, with a possible twenty-two overs left for play, it would appear that both the Somerset record of 1,795 and the all-time British record of 1,808 could yet be under threat.

At this point in the match, Ormond is rested after six overs of hard graft, during which he has conceded runs at an acceptable five-and-a-half an over, and his replacement, Ian Salisbury, immediately induces an outside edge from Wood that flies safely to the third man fence for four.

Even though they still have nine wickets intact, the asking rate for Somerset is now pushing 9.4, an unlikely figure that prompts their skipper to move up a gear - having brought his long run of singles and twos to a halt by lofting Saqlain over mid-on for the four that takes him to a 61-ball fifty, he follows up by sweeping Salisbury for a second boundary in the following over. It would appear that the batsmen's roles have now reversed, in fact, with Wood taking over as single-scorer in making his way through the nineties, and Burns continuing his sudden boundary spurt by advancing on Saqlain and driving him over wide long-on for six to keep his side in with an outside chance of pulling off a stunning victory. By way of contrast, Surrey's hopes already look to be at an end, though they do at least break the second-wicket partnership later in the same over when Burns attempts to repeat his six-hit and is very well caught by the ice-cool Clarke running in from the boundary to pouch a towering skier at deep mid-on.

As the home skipper returns to the pavilion with sixty-eight runs to his name at 216-2, so the Somerset danger man, Ian Blackwell, strides forth, with 163 runs needed to win the match from exactly sixteen overs. This would appear to be the key phase of the run chase, since everyone knows that it is not 'mission impossible' for the home side if the powerful 24-year-old can get away to a good start and stay around for eight to ten overs. When the fourth delivery he faces, bowled by Salisbury, promptly disappears over the deep midwicket boundary for six, it looks like this appraisal is spot-on.

Before Blackwell can do any further damage, Wood creates a little bit of history, clipping Saqlain to the midwicket fence to complete his second century of the match, thereby becoming the first man to achieve this feat against Surrey since Neil Taylor scored 204 and 142 for Kent at Canterbury in 1990. The 21-year-old Devonian's 127-ball innings has been another fine effort, containing sixteen fours, and it continues to anchor his team's determined assault on a cricketing Everest as Blackwell explodes into life again at the end of the next over from Salisbury. Despite the fact that the leg-spinner has seven men out on the fence, the Somerset left-hander manages to find the boundary from consecutive deliveries, as a very streaky Chinese cut to fine leg for four is followed by a meaty drive off the middle of the blade over long-on for six. With twelve runs having come from this over, the alarm bells are ringing for the visitors, though, much to their relief, they are muted temporarily by the capture of the prize wicket of Blackwell in Saqlain's next over. Charging down the track recklessly, the sturdy all-rounder is comprehensively beaten on the outside edge by a quicker, shorter delivery that allows Batty to complete a routine stumping to end the batsman's 16-ball innings on twenty-two and peg Somerset back to 247-3.

Surrey's joy is short-lived, however, as Wood launches a fierce attack on Salisbury to keep his team in contention, taking eighteen runs from an over that ends with three consecutive lofted straight drives for four, six and four. As the ball disappears for the second time, Hollioake, fielding just below my viewing position, and seemingly calm despite Wood's ferocious assault, responds to some friendly banter from the crowd with a smile and the comment 'we're just having a bit of fun out here'. I don't suppose his leg-spinner would agree with him at this precise moment in time.

With 112 runs now needed from eleven overs, the draw is still the favoured result, especially after an excellent over from the wily Saqlain, during which the off-spinner almost forces the new batsman, Parsons, to play on, and then sees Wood survive a regulation stumping chance with his score on 119 at 268-3. Much to the chagrin of Surrey's Pakistani magician, the Somerset opener then promptly under-edges a pull to the fine-leg boundary to register a new career-best score, surpassing the 122 he had made against Northamptonshire on this ground in 2001.

Predictably enough, Hollioake, an expert at bowling in these end-of-innings situations, now brings himself into the attack to replace the battered Salisbury and immediately comes up with a three-run over to increase the difficulty of Somerset's challenge. Then, to make matters worse for the hosts, they suffer a further setback when a rather panicky Wood loses his wicket in trying to make up the ground lost in the previous over. Having just got away with a skier into space behind the bowler, the young opener again dances down the wicket to Saqlain and, in identical fashion to Blackwell before him, is left high and dry as a quicker delivery fizzes past the outside edge, allowing Batty to atone for his earlier error.

As Wood departs for 131 to a standing ovation, Somerset promote Keith Dutch to number six in the order, demonstrating that they intend to carry on pursuing the target, even though they now face a required run rate in excess of eleven an over. With six wickets still in hand this seems to make sense... as does Dutch's elevation, since he immediately drives Hollioake over wide mid-on for four. The Surrey captain bowls well to his very defensive field for the rest of the over, however, yielding only singles and leaving the home side needing eighty-four runs from the last seven overs, a tough task with fielders posted all around the boundary edge.

Nor is their victory attempt made any easier by the continued excellence of the shrewd Saqlain. His priceless ability to remain cool when under fire is again underlined by another tight over that brings just five runs from the first five balls and leaves Dutch desperate for a boundary from the final delivery to keep his team in contention. Though the batsman hits the ball hard and flat towards long-on he is unable to clear Clarke, who again makes a very tricky catch under pressure look simple. The young all-rounder has been mightily impressive in the field while the visitors have been under the hammer, though an improved second innings fielding effort by Surrey has also seen Ward and Ramprakash excelling in the outfield.

Despite the loss of Dutch with the score at exactly three-hundred, Somerset keep coming at Surrey, with Parsons' drives for four and three off successive Hollioake deliveries at the heart of a twelve-run fifty-second over of the innings. The aforementioned Somerset match aggregate record, set in the game versus Northamptonshire on another flat Taunton track in 2001, tumbles during the over, at the end of which the home side require sixty-seven runs from five overs. It remains a very distant target and by the end of the next superb over from the inestimable Saqlain, which yields just a two and two singles, it is almost off the radar.

When Rob Turner is then deceived and bowled by the slower leg stump yorker with which Hollioake starts his next over, the Surrey captain at last senses a chance to attack, rather than defend, pulling in the field and posting two slips. The new batsman, Peter Bowler, prompts an immediate rethink, however, by running down the wicket to drive his first ball over mid-on for four. This sign of continued aggressive intent from Somerset brings a wave of the hands from Hollioake that sends all the fielders scampering back to their positions on the boundary. Consequently, the batsmen are, again, restricted to singles and, in attempting to take two from the final delivery of the over, the hosts lose their seventh wicket when Bowler fails to beat Giddins' fine direct-hit throw at the non-strikers' stumps from deep mid-on.

With fifty-five runs now needed from just three overs, Somerset finally wave the white flag, and Surrey fielders cluster around the bat in great numbers for the last three overs from Saqlain and the recalled Salisbury. To no-one's great surprise, Parsons and Bulbeck survive comfortably to the close on an excellent batting pitch that had seen the British match aggregate record of 1,808 runs (Sussex v Essex at Hove in 1993) fall when Somerset reached 323 in the over of Bowler's dismissal.

Although the game has reached its almost inevitable drawn conclusion, Hollioake's bold declaration, coupled with a positive approach to a daunting target by Somerset, has at least brought about an entertaining and interesting finale to confound those of us who had felt that the Taunton pitch would be the only winner on a drab day.

**Surrey 608-6dec and 324-5dec; Somerset 554 and 329-7**
**Match Drawn. Somerset 11pts, Surrey 12**

# VIEWS FROM THE DRESSING ROOM

*Had you set yourself any batting targets at the start of the season? If so, I guess that 700-plus runs, including two hundreds and a ninety-nine, would have exceeded your expectations?*
**JON BATTY** - To be perfectly honest, with the prospect of Alec being around an awful lot, I went into the season feeling that I probably wouldn't play many games at all and, as a result, I didn't feel it was appropriate to set any targets, in terms of runs. I just decided that if I got a chance to play in the first team I would really enjoy it, and if I didn't get to play I would try not to get upset, and get through the season enjoying my cricket as much as possible, whether I was playing in the first team or the second team.

*Many people were surprised that you declared and set Somerset any sort of target at all, since it looked nigh on impossible to bowl a side out on that track. Was your view that we might have a chance to win if we could tempt them into a run chase? And were you ever seriously concerned that Somerset were going to reach the very stiff target you had set them?*
**ADAM HOLLIOAKE** - Definitely, yes, that was the thinking behind my declaration. The game wasn't going too well for us at one point in that final innings but we knew we wouldn't lose because we've got so many tricks up our sleeve. For example, we always had the option of putting everybody back on the boundary or bowling a couple bouncers over the batsman's head, just to make life very difficult for them. We were never ever going to lose that game, especially with someone like Saqlain in our attack. But we gave it a fair crack, and at the end we were just three good balls away from winning the match.

*Rikki Clarke had a couple of testing catches to take during that run chase and he made them look so easy. How does he rate in the 'safe hands' stakes, in your opinion?*
**JON BATTY** - He is as good as they come at the Club, either in the slips or in the outfield. He's got huge bucket-like hands and he is a class fielder whether the ball is in the air or on the ground.

*I recorded a total of twelve missed catches/stumpings, of varying difficulties, in this match, quite a few of them in the close-catching cordon, and you certainly seemed to have a tough time behind the stumps. In the fielders' defence, however, it did seem that the ball often moved quite a lot after passing the bat - was that how you saw it and have you any explanation as to why that might have been?*
**JON BATTY** - Yes, we wicketkeepers call it turbulence and, unless you have ever kept wicket or fielded in the slips, you probably don't believe it can happen, that a ball can actually wobble. Obviously it can actually swing once it's gone past the bat, as people will have seen, but it can also wobble up and down. Getting technical, when the bowler lets go of the ball it is obviously rotating backwards with the seam generally in an upright position, but when the ball pitches on the wicket the ball then normally gets forward rotations on it. If it has got forward rotations on it - and occasionally even when it's got backwards rotations on it - it travels through the air perfectly, but if the ball hasn't got any rotation on it after pitching then it messes up the aerodynamics of the ball, making it wobble. I've now kept wicket in about a hundred first-class matches and I'd never seen wobble like we got during this game - it seemed to happen for the whole match, and it even happened with slip catches, which is very unusual because when a ball is nicked that normally puts rotations on the ball. You can do as much practice as you want but if a ball is coming towards you at seventy or eighty miles an hour and all of a sudden it moves a foot up and then a foot down as it gets halfway to you it can be quite disconcerting and very difficult to catch. This was probably the worst game of my career in terms of 'gloving'. I can only think of about four or five balls that I missed, but they all went for four, so it probably looked a lot worse than it was.

## SOMERSET v SURREY at Taunton.     Played from 3rd to 6th July

Somerset won the toss and elected to field     Umpires:- Ian Gould and Alan Whitehead

### SURREY - First Innings

| Fall Of Wkt | Batsman | How | Out | Score | Balls | 4s | 6s |
|---|---|---|---|---|---|---|---|
| 2-32 | I.J. Ward | c Bowler | b Francis | 13 | 51 | 2 | 0 |
| 1-0 | J.N. Batty + | lbw | b Jones | 0 | 4 | 0 | 0 |
| 6-527 | M.R. Ramprakash | | b Jones | 218 | 339 | 28 | 0 |
| 3-162 | N. Shahid | lbw | b Blackwell | 51 | 87 | 10 | 0 |
| 4-179 | A.D. Brown | c Turner | b Francis | 10 | 15 | 2 | 0 |
| 5-317 | A.J. Hollioake * | c Parsons | b Francis | 87 | 83 | 11 | 2 |
| | R. Clarke | Not | Out | 153 | 180 | 20 | 4 |
| | I.D.K. Salisbury | Not | Out | 46 | 30 | 7 | 1 |
| | Saqlain Mushtaq | did not bat | | | | | |
| | J. Ormond | did not bat | | | | | |
| | E.S.H. Giddins | did not bat | | | | | |
| | Extras | (10lb, 12w, 8nb) | | 30 | | | |
| | TOTAL | (130.5 overs) | (for 6 dec) | 608 | | | |

| Bowler | O | M | R | W | NB | Wd |
|---|---|---|---|---|---|---|
| Bulbeck | 28 | 4 | 141 | 0 | 3 | 3 |
| Jones | 33.1 | 6 | 157 | 2 | - | - |
| Francis | 25.5 | 2 | 104 | 3 | 1 | - |
| Parsons | 7 | 0 | 37 | 0 | - | - |
| Blackwell | 24.5 | 3 | 89 | 1 | - | 1 |
| Dutch | 12 | 1 | 70 | 0 | - | - |

### SOMERSET - First Innings   (Needing 459 to avoid the follow-on)

| Fall Of Wkt | Batsman | How | Out | Score | Balls | 4s | 6s |
|---|---|---|---|---|---|---|---|
| 2-217 | P.C.L. Holloway | c Hollioake | b Ormond | 77 | 153 | 14 | 0 |
| 1-202 | M.J. Wood | | b Ormond | 106 | 144 | 19 | 0 |
| 5-401 | M. Burns * | lbw | b Clarke | 99 | 155 | 14 | 2 |
| 3-261 | P.D. Bowler | lbw | b Giddins | 19 | 27 | 3 | 0 |
| 4-378 | K.A. Parsons | lbw | b Clarke | 47 | 129 | 6 | 0 |
| 6-440 | I.D. Blackwell | c sub (Murtagh) | b Clarke | 34 | 27 | 6 | 0 |
| | R.J. Turner + | Not | Out | 56 | 88 | 5 | 0 |
| 7-443 | K.P. Dutch | c Salisbury | b Ormond | 2 | 7 | 0 | 0 |
| 8-506 | M.P.L. Bulbeck | c Batty | b Saqlain | 27 | 42 | 5 | 0 |
| 9-537 | P.S. Jones | c Batty | b Salisbury | 23 | 29 | 4 | 0 |
| 10-554 | S.R.G. Francis | c sub (Murtagh) | b Saqlain | 8 | 19 | 1 | 0 |
| | Extras | (1lb, 8lb, 9w, 28nb) | | 56 | | | |
| | TOTAL | (134.2 overs) | | 554 | | | |

| Bowler | O | M | R | W | NB | Wd |
|---|---|---|---|---|---|---|
| Giddins | 21 | 5 | 83 | 1 | 5 | - |
| Ormond | 33 | 3 | 137 | 3 | 2 | 2 |
| Clarke | 20 | 2 | 104 | 3 | 6 | 2 |
| Salisbury | 22 | 4 | 85 | 1 | - | - |
| Saqlain Mushtaq | 35.2 | 8 | 110 | 2 | 1 | - |
| Hollioake | 3 | 0 | 16 | 0 | - | - |

### SURREY - Second Innings   (Leading by 54 on first innings)

| Fall Of Wkt | Batsman | How | Out | Score | Balls | 4s | 6s |
|---|---|---|---|---|---|---|---|
| 1-153 | I.J. Ward | c Turner | b Bulbeck | 75 | 151 | 11 | 0 |
| 5-324 | J.N. Batty + | c Wood | b Parsons | 151 | 203 | 22 | 2 |
| 2-258 | M.R. Ramprakash | | b Blackwell | 53 | 43 | 8 | 1 |
| 3-261 | I.D.K. Salisbury | c Turner | b Parsons | 2 | 4 | 0 | 0 |
| 4-309 | R. Clarke | c Burns | b Parsons | 22 | 14 | 3 | 0 |
| | N. Shahid | Not | Out | 8 | 6 | 0 | 0 |
| | Extras | (1b, 6lb, 2w, 4nb) | | 13 | | | |
| | TOTAL | (69.5 overs) | (for 5 dec) | 324 | | | |

| Bowler | O | M | R | W | NB | Wd |
|---|---|---|---|---|---|---|
| Jones | 17 | 4 | 59 | 0 | - | - |
| Bulbeck | 17.4 | 3 | 63 | 1 | 1 | - |
| Dutch | 9 | 3 | 35 | 0 | - | - |
| Parsons | 17.1 | 4 | 91 | 3 | 1 | 1 |
| Blackwell | 9 | 0 | 69 | 1 | - | - |

**SOMERSET - Second Innings** (Needing 379 to win)

| Fall Of Wkt | Batsman | How | Out | Score | Balls | 4s | 6s |
|---|---|---|---|---|---|---|---|
| 1-75 | P.C.L. Holloway | c Shahid | b Salisbury | 33 | 49 | 2 | 0 |
| 4-286 | M.J. Wood | st Batty | b Saqlain | 131 | 148 | 19 | 1 |
| 2-216 | M. Burns * | c Clarke | b Saqlain | 68 | 76 | 6 | 1 |
| 3-247 | I.D. Blackwell | st Batty | b Saqlain | 22 | 16 | 1 | 2 |
|  | K.A. Parsons | Not | Out | 33 | 29 | 3 | 0 |
| 5-300 | K.P. Dutch | c Clarke | b Saqlain | 6 | 7 | 1 | 0 |
| 6-316 | R.J. Turner + |  | b Hollioake | 5 | 5 | 0 | 0 |
| 7-324 | P.D. Bowler | run | out | 6 | 3 | 1 | 0 |
|  | M.P.L. Bulbeck | Not | Out | 1 | 10 | 0 | 0 |
|  | Extras | (4b, 8lb, 6w, 6nb) |  | 24 |  |  |  |
|  | **TOTAL** | (56.4 overs) | (for 7 wkts) | 329 |  |  |  |

| Bowler | O | M | R | W | NB | Wd |
|---|---|---|---|---|---|---|
| Giddins | 5 | 0 | 29 | 0 | - | - |
| Ormond | 13 | 1 | 65 | 0 | - | 2 |
| Saqlain Mushtaq | 23.4 | 3 | 111 | 4 | 3 | - |
| Salisbury | 11 | 0 | 79 | 1 | - | 1 |
| Hollioake | 4 | 0 | 33 | 1 | - | - |

## Other Division One Results

Twelve points proved to be a very good return for Surrey, since no other team was able to gather in more than ten points because of the very wet weather that had dogged the country. Kent, who could well have forced a victory over Warwickshire at Maidstone had more play been possible, were emerging as potential title challengers, even though they were still 25.25 points behind the leaders, while Leicestershire continued to confound everyone who felt that their good start to the season was a fluke and that they would soon be dragged into the relegation dogfight.

July 3-6
*The Rose Bowl:-* **Hampshire drew with Sussex.** Sussex 246 (Martin-Jenkins 80*, Udal 5-56) and 111-4dec; Hampshire 163 (Martin-Jenkins 5-37) and 56-0. **Hampshire 7pts, Sussex 8**

*Maidstone:-* **Kent drew with Warwickshire.** Kent 306 (Fulton 101, Key 62) and 118-5dec; Warwickshire 172 (Patel 5-56). **Kent 10pts, Warwickshire 7**

*Leicester:-* **Leicestershire drew with Lancashire.** Leicestershire 219 (Maddy 59) and 206-4dec (Maddy 79*, Wells 50); Lancashire 180 (Chilton 57, Malcolm 5-52). **Leicestershire 8pts, Lancashire 7**

### COUNTY CHAMPIONSHIP DIVISION ONE AT 6TH JULY

| Pos | Prv |  | P | Points | W | D | L | Bat | Bwl | Ded |
|---|---|---|---|---|---|---|---|---|---|---|
| 1 | 1 | Surrey | 7 | 104.75 | 4 | 3 | 0 | 24 | 21 | 0.25 |
| 2 | 2 | Leicestershire | 8 | 94.00 | 3 | 3 | 2 | 25 | 22 | 1.00 |
| 3 | 3 | Hampshire | 8 | 80.00 | 1 | 6 | 1 | 21 | 23 | 0.00 |
| 4 | 4 | Kent | 7 | 79.50 | 3 | 2 | 2 | 17 | 19 | 0.50 |
| 5 | 5 | Sussex | 8 | 77.00 | 1 | 5 | 2 | 22 | 23 | 0.00 |
| 6 | 8 | Somerset | 7 | 70.00 | 1 | 5 | 1 | 19 | 19 | 0.00 |
| 7 | 6 | Lancashire | 7 | 68.00 | 2 | 3 | 2 | 12 | 20 | 0.00 |
| = | 6 | Warwickshire | 7 | 68.00 | 2 | 3 | 2 | 13 | 19 | 0.00 |
| 9 | 9 | Yorkshire | 7 | 41.50 | 0 | 2 | 5 | 13 | 21 | 0.50 |

### NUL2 - Ramprakash Revels In Putting Crusaders To The Sword

Another excellent three-figure partnership by Mark Ramprakash and Rikki Clarke enabled the Surrey Lions to continue their recent good form in the Norwich Union League second division with a crushing eight-wicket win over Middlesex Crusaders at a very damp Walker ground in Southgate. Middlesex's dreadful run against Surrey in the Sunday/National League extended to fourteen matches without a win as the dynamic Lions duo joined forces at 76-2 and saw their team home in magnificent style with almost two overs to spare. Ramprakash, returning to face his old county on a ground where he averaged 123 in first-class cricket, gave just one chance, on forty-two, when he was badly missed at backward point by Paul Weekes off Simon Cook, and, once this had gone begging, the visitors' victory was never in any doubt. The Surrey pair's century partnership took just 103 balls as the fast-maturing Clarke notched a 52-ball half-century, while Ramprakash compiled his fifty from 65 deliveries.

In a match which started on time but was reduced to forty-two overs per side by a twenty-minute shower at 2pm, Middlesex had been hit hard by a highly impressive opening burst by Tim Murtagh, who claimed the wickets of Alleyne, Strauss and Koenig to reduce the home side to 34-3. Although Owais Shah played a fine innings to aid the Crusaders' recovery, tight mid-innings bowling by Saqlain Mushtaq and Jason Ratcliffe, finally returning to the side after injury, ensured that Surrey's target was never likely to be too demanding on a ground where the bat almost always dominates.

### MIDDLESEX CRUSADERS v SURREY LIONS at Southgate
**Played on Sunday 7th July — Surrey Lions won by eight wickets**
Surrey Lions won the toss and elected to field — Umpires:- Barry Dudleston & Tony Clarkson
Match reduced to 42 overs per side

#### MIDDLESEX CRUSADERS

| Fall Of Wkt | Batsman | How | Out | Score | Balls | 4s | 6s |
|---|---|---|---|---|---|---|---|
| 2-22 | A.J. Strauss * | c Batty | b Murtagh | 9 | 15 | 1 | 0 |
| 1-6 | D. Alleyne + | lbw | b Murtagh | 0 | 8 | 0 | 0 |
| 3-34 | S.G. Koenig | c Hollioake | b Murtagh | 16 | 26 | 1 | 0 |
| 4-89 | E.C. Joyce | c Clarke | b Ratcliffe | 31 | 57 | 3 | 0 |
| 7-178 | O.A. Shah | | b Clarke | 74 | 92 | 4 | 1 |
| 5-95 | Abdul Razzaq | c Batty | b Saqlain | 3 | 7 | 0 | 0 |
| 6-130 | J.W.M. Dalrymple | c Murtagh | b Ratcliffe | 16 | 20 | 2 | 0 |
| 8-190 | S.J. Cook | | b Giddins | 21 | 21 | 1 | 0 |
| | A.W. Laraman | Not | Out | 8 | 4 | 0 | 1 |
| | P.N. Weekes | Not | Out | 4 | 2 | 0 | 0 |
| | I. Jones | did not bat | | | | | |
| | Extras | (5lb, 7w) | | 12 | | | |
| | TOTAL | (42 overs) | (for 8 wkts) | 194 | | | |

| Bowler | O | M | R | W | NB | Wd |
|---|---|---|---|---|---|---|
| Giddins | 8 | 1 | 22 | 1 | - | 3 |
| Murtagh | 9 | 0 | 38 | 3 | - | 3 |
| Clarke | 5 | 0 | 30 | 1 | - | 1 |
| Saqlain Mushtaq | 8 | 0 | 33 | 1 | - | - |
| Ratcliffe | 9 | 0 | 41 | 2 | - | - |
| Hollioake | 3 | 0 | 25 | 0 | - | - |

#### SURREY LIONS

| Fall Of Wkt | Batsman | How | Out | Score | Balls | 4s | 6s |
|---|---|---|---|---|---|---|---|
| 2-76 | I.J. Ward | c Abdul Razzaq | b Cook | 30 | 62 | 3 | 0 |
| 1-21 | A.D. Brown | c Strauss | b Jones | 6 | 12 | 0 | 0 |
| | M.R. Ramprakash | Not | Out | 87 | 111 | 5 | 2 |
| | R. Clarke | Not | Out | 62 | 59 | 6 | 0 |
| | N. Shahid | did not bat | | | | | |
| | A.J. Hollioake * | did not bat | | | | | |
| | J.N. Batty + | did not bat | | | | | |
| | J.D. Ratcliffe | did not bat | | | | | |
| | Saqlain Mushtaq | did not bat | | | | | |
| | T.J. Murtagh | did not bat | | | | | |
| | E.S.H. Giddins | did not bat | | | | | |
| | Extras | (6lb, 2w, 4nb) | | 12 | | | |
| | TOTAL | (40.2 overs) | (for 2 wkts) | 197 | | | |

| Bowler | O | M | R | W | NB | Wd |
|---|---|---|---|---|---|---|
| Jones | 8 | 0 | 37 | 1 | - | 1 |
| Laraman | 8 | 0 | 30 | 0 | 1 | - |
| Cook | 9 | 0 | 48 | 1 | - | - |
| Abdul Razzaq | 8.2 | 1 | 47 | 0 | 1 | - |
| Weekes | 7 | 0 | 29 | 0 | - | 1 |

## Other NUL Division Two Results

With Gloucestershire Gladiators also winning, though by a surprisingly small margin over Derbyshire Scorpions, the two pre-season favourites now shared top spot in the table, though the weekend's other winners, the Steelbacks and the Hawks, sat just four points behind with two games in hand. It was looking increasingly likely that there would be a maximum of six teams involved in the promotion shake-up, since Middlesex Crusaders, Lancashire Lightning and Sussex Sharks were already hopelessly adrift at the bottom.

July 7
*Derby:-* **Gloucestershire Gladiators beat Derbyshire Scorpions by 7 runs.** Gloucestershire 161 (40.3ov; Welch 5-18); Derbyshire 154-9 (45ov; Averis 3-44). **Gloucestershire Gladiators 4pts**

*The Rose Bowl:-* **Hampshire Hawks beat Sussex Sharks by 93 runs.** Hampshire 203 (45ov; Johnson 92, Taylor 4-22); Sussex 110 (34.2ov; Udal 4-31). **Hampshire Hawks 4pts**

*Northampton:-* **Northamptonshire Steelbacks beat Lancashire Lightning by 62 runs.** Northamptonshire 261-8 (Cook 102, Sales 64, Wood 3-40); Lancashire 199 (41.2ov; A. Swann 61, Cook 3-16, G. Swann 3-43). **Northamptonshire Steelbacks 4pts**

### NATIONAL LEAGUE DIVISION TWO AT 7TH JULY

| Pos | Prv | | P | Pts | W | T | L | A |
|---|---|---|---|---|---|---|---|---|
| 1 | 2 | Gloucestershire Gladiators | 7 | 18 | 4 | 0 | 2 | 1 |
| = | 2 | Surrey Lions | 7 | 18 | 4 | 0 | 2 | 1 |
| 3 | 5 | Hampshire Hawks | 5 | 14 | 3 | 0 | 1 | 1 |
| = | 5 | Northamptonshire Steelbacks | 5 | 14 | 3 | 0 | 1 | 1 |
| 5 | 1 | Derbyshire Scorpions | 6 | 14 | 3 | 0 | 2 | 1 |
| 6 | 4 | Essex Eagles | 4 | 12 | 3 | 0 | 1 | 0 |
| 7 | 7 | Middlesex Crusaders | 7 | 8 | 1 | 0 | 4 | 2 |
| 8 | 8 | Lancashire Lightning | 8 | 8 | 1 | 0 | 5 | 2 |
| 9 | 9 | Sussex Sharks | 7 | 6 | 1 | 0 | 5 | 1 |

# 10  The Bears Bite Back

Given the nature of the pitch at Taunton, a return of twelve points was about as good as could have been expected and it had strengthened Surrey's grip at the head of the Championship table. We had been incredibly fortunate to see so much play down in the west country, since the nation was going through a very wet spell that had ruined most of the fixtures in the last round of matches... not that Surrey were complaining. Besides, everyone was aware that these things tend to even out over the course of a season, so there was a good chance that we would get rained off at some stage when everyone else was playing.

The Somerset match had also produced a number of plus points for the Championship leaders. Apart from the outstanding batting of Mark Ramprakash and the fine performance of the captain on his return to the side, the centuries scored by Rikki Clarke and Jon Batty were most encouraging. Clarke had played like an experienced first-team regular, rather than a young lad in his fourth first-class match, and, in addition to delivering a stunning maiden Championship century, he had picked up three wickets on a flat track and also confirmed all the reports I'd heard from regular second-team followers that he had a fantastic pair of hands in the field. Batty, meanwhile, was clearly in the best form of his career to date, showing greater batting ability than anyone had realised he possessed... possibly even himself. The Surrey keeper had struggled with the bat throughout the 2001 season, averaging 15.93 from sixteen innings, and by the end of that campaign it was hard to find a single person who felt he should continue to bat at number seven, especially given the weight of runs coming from those below him in the order. One or two even thought he should drop as low as number ten, which seemed a little harsh, though it was understandable, since confidence seemed to have deserted him completely. Now, less than one year on, he had two centuries to his name, both fine knocks, played in different styles, from very different positions in the order, and everyone was delighted for him. The transformation was truly amazing, and fears that losing Alec Stewart to England for most of the summer would upset the balance of the side had been assuaged. In fact, by showing that he could score runs from either number seven or as an opener, the team's options had actually increased. It was typical of this Surrey side that when the team needed something there always seemed to be someone coming to the fore to provide it.

The next match, which completed the first half of the County Championship campaign, was against an improving Warwickshire side who had seemingly taken a while to find their feet in Division One. They certainly looked a decent side on paper, with several promising young players in their ranks. The most talked-about of these, Ian Bell, had struggled for form thus far, whereas the left-handed Jamie Troughton, grandson of the former Doctor Who star, Patrick, had been scoring heavily and impressing plenty of people after getting an unexpected run in the team earlier in the season when both Mark Wagh and Dominic Ostler were out injured. I was looking forward to seeing both of these lads bat... though, hopefully, not for *too* long!

| FRIZZELL COUNTY CHAMPIONSHIP - MATCH EIGHT |
|---|

<u>SURREY versus WARWICKSHIRE</u>
at The AMP Oval

First Day - Wednesday 10th July

Surrey 191-5

*The Teams And The Toss* - Following the draw at Taunton, Surrey name an unchanged side, while Warwickshire - like their hosts, missing players involved with England in the Nat West Series (Nick Knight and Ashley Giles) - show three changes from the side that played Kent at Maidstone. With three experienced players - Dougie Brown, Mark Wagh and Keith Piper -

*recalled or returning from injury, it's the youngsters Graham Wagg, Jamie Spires and Ian Clifford who make way. Owing to the Championship splitting into two divisions at the end of the 1999 season, this is the first meeting between the sides in the competition since July of that year. There are two points of statistical interest ahead of the match - the first is that there hasn't been a drawn game in this fixture since 1992, and the second is that Warwickshire haven't recorded a win at The Oval in the Championship since 1975. Although rain delays the start of play, Adam Hollioake has no hesitation in electing to bat first upon winning the toss.*

It's a frustrating morning for everyone as a series of short showers at 10.30am, 11.45am and 12.10pm keeps pushing back the starting time. Much credit is due to umpires John Hampshire and Tony Clarkson, however, since they are clearly keen to get play underway and finally do so at 12.27pm, with twenty-three overs of the day's allocation lost.

A short opening session of around forty-five minutes looks to be of ideal length for the Warwickshire opening bowlers, Shaun Pollock and Neil Carter, but we only manage twenty minutes of action, in fact, before another burst of rain brings about an early lunch at 1pm. During the 5.1 overs that are completed, Jon Batty almost plays on to Pollock in the third over, while Ward edges between the slips and gully for four in the next over from Carter. On the other side of the coin, Ward picks up two pleasing boundaries off the left-armer, courtesy of a forcing stroke backward of point and a clip through midwicket.

*Lunch:- Surrey 19-0 (Ward 14\*, Batty 2\*) from 5.1 overs*

With the rain having abated during the interval, we are able to restart on time at 1.40pm, with Carter and Pollock resuming from the Vauxhall end and pavilion end, respectively.

While the South African captain is, as ever, a model of accuracy, his bowling partner is extremely wayward, and Batty takes full advantage, driving and cutting three boundaries in successive overs. Carter, with the unflattering figures of 6-0-31-0, consequently gives way to Dougie Brown, though this move initially accelerates the scoring rate, as seven runs accrue from the next over by Pollock, and the new bowler's opening over costs twelve as he strays frequently to leg. Having conceded four leg-byes from his first delivery, Brown fails to correct his line, allowing Ward to clip and glance boundaries that take the total past fifty and the left-handed opener's personal tally to thirty-four.

With everything going so well for the home side, the events of the next four overs come as something of a shock, since four wickets fall in the space of twenty-three deliveries, transforming a prosperous 57-0 into a decidedly rocky 59-4.

The rot starts with a bad error of judgement by Batty, who inexplicably pads up to a straight delivery from Pollock and falls lbw for sixteen, and continues when Ward edges a forcing stroke into the midriff of Dominic Ostler at second slip in the following over from Brown.

Having lost both openers at fifty-seven, the score is finally moved on, in unconvincing fashion, by a miscued stroke backward of square leg for two by Nadeem Shahid off Brown, before the former England one-day international all-rounder strikes twice in three balls during his next over. First, Shahid edges a loose drive, providing Ostler with another catch at second slip, then Alistair Brown is left to rue a rather strange umpiring decision by Tony Clarkson. After Brown scampers through for a leg-bye from his first delivery, the umpire signals 'dead ball' and sends him back down to the striker's end, ruling, highly contentiously, that the Surrey batsman has played no stroke at the leg-side delivery. Perhaps still perplexed by the official's decision, Brown then emulates Batty, shouldering arms to the next delivery from his namesake and becoming another leg-before victim, as Clarkson's previous decision suddenly becomes a very significant and costly one for both the batsman and his team.

Having rocked the opposition back on their heels, Michael Powell, the Warwickshire captain, now makes a shocking decision by pulling Pollock from the attack. Since the flame-haired all-rounder has bowled just six overs since lunch, one can only assume that the move is not made on cricketing grounds but as the result of an agreement between the county and the South African cricket authorities to limit the length of Pollock's spells. In any case, the outcome is wholly predictable as the pressure on the batsmen, Mark Ramprakash and Adam Hollioake, is eased considerably.

Having seen three of his colleagues depart in next to no time since his arrival at the wicket, Ramprakash has started steadily, but the introduction of Melvyn Betts in place of Pollock allows him to move swiftly on to the attack. After a reasonable first over, the former Durham seamer serves up a very poor second, during which the Surrey number three advances his score by thirteen, with square-cut and cover-driven boundaries being the pick of five nicely executed run-scoring strokes. Almost inevitably, Betts is removed from the attack forthwith, forcing Powell to recall Carter, since he has no other viable seam bowling option in his line-up.

Although the left-armer has now switched ends, he continues to struggle with his line, repeatedly firing the ball down the leg-side, though, ironically, only conceding a boundary when Hollioake blasts a rare off-side delivery to the extra cover boundary. Meanwhile, Dougie Brown, his confidence inevitably boosted by his burst of three wickets in nine balls, has settled into a good spell and is causing a few problems with the movement he is able to extract from the pitch. The support for his Scottish all-rounder is so patchy, however, that Powell is probably not too disappointed when another heavy shower hits the ground at 3.15pm, sending the players scurrying for cover once again with Surrey on the road to recovery at 99-4.

Unfortunately, the shower lasts long enough for the umpires to call for an early tea at 3.40pm, with the loss of further overs already a certainty.

*Tea:- Surrey 99-4 (Ramprakash 25\*, Hollioake 9\*) from 27.3 overs*

Play is eventually able to resume at 5.15pm, though another twenty-seven overs have been lost, leaving twenty-two-and-a-half to be played out this evening.

The break certainly hasn't done Adam Hollioake any favours, that's for sure, as he endures a torrid few overs at the hands of Dougie Brown, inside-edging the second delivery of the session to fine leg for four to raise the Surrey hundred, offering an extremely difficult low caught-and-bowled chance with his score still on thirteen, and then profiting by four runs again when another Chinese cut just eludes the diving Piper. Although this boundary raises the fifty partnership, the fifth-wicket stand looks unlikely to progress much further at this moment in time, especially since Pollock's predictable return at the pavilion end is providing Ramprakash with a stern test of both temperament and technique.

In fact, as play continues, there are almost two different games going on out in the middle. While Ramprakash shows great skill and determination to block out the dangerous South African skipper, playing out four maidens on the bounce, Hollioake starts to take control, hooking successive Brown bouncers for six and then launching an assault on Carter when the left-armer surprisingly returns to the fray in place of Pollock. Having cut and driven consecutive Carter deliveries to the boundary, Hollioake does offer another chance, however, when Neil Smith, in the gully, fails to accept a low offering off Betts almost as soon as the ex-Durham man replaces Brown. On forty-three at the time, the Surrey captain rushes to a 61-ball fifty in the next over from Carter, with a miscued drive through backward point and a deliberate deflection high over the slip cordon earning four runs apiece. This is high-octane stuff from Hollioake, while the patient Ramprakash is yet to add to his teatime score in the dozen overs that have been bowled since the restart. The former Middlesex batsman is still on twenty-five, in fact, when he loses his fifth-wicket partner in the next over, Hollioake's rather limp defensive stroke proving no match for a ball from Betts that nips back to pluck out the off stump. As the Surrey skipper departs for fifty-six, the score looks a little more healthy for the home county at 147-5, though there is still hard work ahead for the rock-like Ramprakash and the new batsman, Rikki Clarke.

Given this pair's recent run of century partnerships, hopes of the recovery being sustained are bright, and Clarke certainly starts well, pulling his second ball from Betts for four and following up with a repeat stroke next ball, though this time only for two. Then, with fifty-four runs added since the break in fifty-five minutes, Ramprakash finally gets his score moving again, assisted by a poorly directed over from Carter that includes a full-toss which the batsman drives to the long-on boundary and a leg-stump half-volley that is clipped to the rope at midwicket.

This loose over immediately signals the end of Carter's spell and heralds the introduction of spin for the first time in the innings, with Neil Smith's appearance at the Vauxhall end swiftly followed by the introduction of the occasional off-spin of Mark Wagh at the pavilion end in place of Betts. Encouragingly for Surrey, there are signs of turn, though this doesn't worry Ramprakash in the slightest as he takes three fours from Smith's fourth over, with a chipped drive over mid-on and a pair of sweeps, to complete a polished personal fifty from 108 balls.

Ominously for Warwickshire, Surrey's in-form batsmen are still together at the close, leaving honours fairly even at the end of a rain-shortened but fascinating day's cricket.

*Close:- Surrey 191-5 (Ramprakash 57\*, Clarke 9\*) from 50 overs*

## Second Day - Thursday 11th July

## Surrey 475; Warwickshire 120-5

After the fearful battering suffered by Neil Carter and Melvyn Betts on the first day, Michael Powell predictably chooses to pair Shaun Pollock and Dougie Brown at the start of day two.

In greatly improved conditions for batting, Ramprakash beds himself in studiously, adding just two runs to his overnight score in the day's first nine overs, while Clarke collects three boundaries off Brown in successive overs - a drive through midwicket to raise the fifty partnership, a pull to deep backward square to bring up his side's two-hundred, and a superbly-timed clip through square leg.

Having been punished so heavily while straying frequently to leg, Brown then surprises everyone with a quite exceptional fourth over, during which Clarke almost plays on and is then beaten outside the off stump by four consecutive deliveries. It shows what can be done when the bowler puts the ball in the right place, though that lesson is still to be learnt by Betts, who concedes three fours in his opening over after replacing Pollock at the Vauxhall end, the South African having again been rested after just four overs, all of them tight and fairly testing. Ramprakash certainly approves of this bowling change, since he is the man to profit from Betts' waywardness, glancing, forcing and pulling the boundaries that increase his personal tally dramatically after his almost scoreless start. The former Durham man continues to bowl poorly, too, conceding a pulled four to Clarke and two cover-driven boundaries to Ramprakash as the score races up to 250 and the Surrey pair register yet another century partnership. It is just as well for the home county that Betts is so loose, because Brown is now really in the groove, beating the outside edge on a number of occasions during an increasingly impressive spell.

The former England one-day international has to take a well-deserved break after ten excellent overs, however, leaving captain Powell's options looking extremely limited. Having already given up on the profligate Betts, whose four overs have cost twenty-eight runs, and turned to the off-spin of Neil Smith, the similarly erratic Neil Carter is pretty much the last card he has left in his deck. He must therefore be an extremely worried skipper when the left-arm seamer's second delivery is driven wide of mid-on by Ramprakash for an all-run four, and his third is pulled to the fence at deep midwicket to take the batsman on to ninety-six. Nor do things get any better for Warwickshire, as Clarke advances on Smith and drives him for a towering six over wide long-on in the next over, before Ramprakash completes an excellent century when a firm push through midwicket for two is followed by a rasping square-cut four, the eighteenth

153

boundary of his innings, off Carter. The Surrey number three is clearly delighted with his 174-ball knock, celebrating in an untypically animated style as the Surrey faithful acclaim his tremendous effort.

This applause has barely faded away before the crowd are acknowledging another milestone, as Clarke again dances down the track to Smith and launches the ball straight back over the bowler's head for the four that takes him through to another very impressive fifty, compiled from 107 balls, and including seven fours and a six.

Surrey are now utterly dominant, and Powell, in a move that smacks of desperation but which, in truth, has been forced upon him by Carter's dismal concession of seventeen runs in two overs, introduces Ian Bell into the attack to bowl gentle medium-pace seamers. The youngster proves no more effective than the front-line Warwickshire bowlers, however, yielding four flowing drives to the boundary, one to Ramprakash and three to Clarke, during four bland overs, as the sixth-wicket stand passes 150 and the total motors beyond three-hundred.

With Smith having proved slightly more economical, if rarely a threat to the batsmen's dominance, the visiting captain opts for a double change as lunch approaches, trying Jamie Troughton's occasional left-arm spin at the Vauxhall end and turning back to Brown at the pavilion end. Although Troughton's opening over offers little encouragement, Brown's return brings an almost instant reward for Powell and his team, as Clarke, on seventy-nine, shuffles across his stumps and misses a hit to leg, giving umpire Hampshire the opportunity to raise his index finger above his head and thereby end the partnership at 175.

The young all-rounder's departure momentarily lifts Warwickshire spirits, though they are reminded that they still have plenty to do after lunch as Salisbury, with a cut off Troughton, and Ramprakash, with a glance off Brown, quickly add further boundaries to the home side's total.

The return of Betts, in place of the ineffective part-time left-arm spinner, for the last over of the session then has entirely predictable results as Ramprakash drives through wide mid-on for four in the course of another expensive over from the out-of-sorts seamer.

*Lunch:- Surrey 339-6 (Ramprakash 128\*, Salisbury 4\*) from 86 overs*

Since the poor length and, in particular, line of the Warwickshire bowling had been an obvious feature of the Surrey innings to date, I had spent some time checking my notes during the lunch interval and had been astonished to discover that no fewer than 136 of the first 219 runs scored off the bat had come in the arc between mid-on and backward square leg, with only one drive in the 'V' between mid-off and mid-on so far recorded. These were shocking stats for the visitors and their coach, since they showed how many deliveries had been short and/or directed down the leg-side. They would clearly be hoping to bowl a lot better as play resumed.

With the new ball just four overs away, Powell opts to fill in with Brown and Wagh until it is available and, as a result, the Surrey total moves on smoothly past 350, with Salisbury's forcing stroke off Brown to the rope at backward point and Ramprakash's delicate late cut for three off Wagh the most eye-catching strokes.

While it comes as something of a surprise that the hard-working Brown is overlooked in favour of Carter when the new ball is taken, it is much less of a shock that the left-armer again fails to use it well, both batsmen driving him to the cover boundary in his first three overs, with the second of these strokes making the seventh-wicket partnership worth fifty. Worryingly for Warwickshire, even Pollock, operating at the Vauxhall end, is less effective in this spell as Salisbury deals with him competently and Ramprakash, really at the peak of his game now, caresses him through extra cover for four to underline Surrey's current superiority. The former England batsman looks unstoppable in this form and reaches his 150, from 270 balls, shortly afterwards with an off-driven boundary at the expense of Carter, before piercing Pollock's ring of off-side fielders again in the next over to secure his team's final batting point at four-hundred.

With the South African again rested after a short spell - five overs on this occasion - it is hard to see where Warwickshire's next wicket is coming from until Carter finally claims his first victim in his twentieth over when Salisbury, having scored a valuable thirty, fails to middle a pull at the left-arm paceman and is well held overhead by Smith at midwicket.

Having taken eighteen overs to secure their seventh scalp, it takes the visitors a mere seven balls to snare the eighth Surrey wicket as Saqlain falls to the fifth ball of Brown's first over back in place of Pollock. The Pakistani departs for a duck with the score at 405 when his attempt to turn a short-of-a-length delivery to leg results in a leading edge that loops back to the grateful bowler, thereby completing a very hard-earned five-wicket haul for the highly competitive Warwickshire all-rounder.

These two quick wickets have suddenly reduced Ramprakash's chances of being able to achieve the very rare feat of recording double centuries in successive matches, since he needs a further thirty-eight runs at this point. He manages to move eight runs closer to his target in the very next over, however, by taking boundaries off Carter either side of point with a cut and a square drive, and his hopes are further boosted by the confident manner in which his new partner, Jimmy Ormond, immediately forces Brown to the extra-cover fence for four. The instant replacement of Carter with Betts certainly doesn't slow the Surrey scoring rate either, and, as Ramprakash twice drives the former England 'A' bowler through wide mid-on for three and Ormond repeats his boundary stroke off Brown, the Warwickshire skipper again appears short of bowling options. Luckily for Powell, his Stirling-born bowler comes to the rescue once again, though, securing his sixth wicket in his thirtieth over when Ormond drives low to mid-on, where the captain himself hangs on to an awkward catch.

Ramprakash, on 179, now has only Ed Giddins to see him through to his personal landmark, and the confirmed number eleven batsman hits a problem immediately when a mistimed first-ball drive to cover results in a worried inspection of the toe end of the bat and an immediate call for a replacement! Inevitably, the field is now spread far and wide for Ramprakash, yet he still manages to find the boundary three times with a variety of cuts as Betts continues to struggle with his line and length. Giddins meanwhile survives more comfortably than expected, and even succeeds in pulling one delivery from Brown over midwicket for the two runs that take the Surrey total past 450.

Back on strike, Ramprakash then moves to 198 with a drive through wide mid-on for two and a lofted drive over extra cover for four, both off Betts, before Giddins' first-ball single to square leg in the next over from Brown gives the former Middlesex man five deliveries in which to secure a piece of history. As it happens, however, he is only able to pick up a single from the fifth ball, leaving everyone on the edge of their seats as Giddins faces the last delivery with his partner on 199. Fortunately for Ramprakash, his partner comes through this test with flying colours, allowing him the chance of a whole over against the erratic Betts, and when the inevitable long-hop comes along after three scoreless deliveries the Surrey number three dispatches it high over the midwicket boundary to reach his double-century in the grand style. The crowd rises to offer congratulatory applause for a truly majestic and virtually flawless innings that has spanned 305 deliveries and contained thirty-one fours and a six, while Ramprakash celebrates with his team-mate. Although he surely doesn't know it at the time, he has become the first man to achieve the feat of scoring double-centuries in successive Championship matches since Aravinda de Silva for Kent in 1995, and the first England-qualified batsman to do so since Graeme Hick in 1986. Furthermore, he joins Walter Read (v Lancashire and then Cambridge University in 1887) and Thomas Shepherd (v Lancashire and then Kent in 1921) in becoming only the third Surrey batsman to accomplish this very rare feat.

Once the applause dies away, Ramprakash celebrates further by cutting Betts' next ball for four and, having succeeded in his goal of seeing his partner through to his magical milestone, Giddins also loosens up by stepping back to leg and lifting the first delivery of Brown's next over, a slower ball, to the extra-cover boundary. Although an attempt to find the leg-side fence four balls later merely results in a skier that the deserving bowler races across to take at short midwicket, Surrey are unconcerned, since their final total of 475 looks to be a very good one. Ramprakash ends unbeaten on 210, to add to the 218 and 53 he had made at Taunton, and receives a rapturous welcome upon his return to the pavilion for a hard-earned break of twenty-minutes, since tea is now to be taken.

*Tea:- Between Innings*

With Warwickshire requiring 326 to avoid the follow-on, Mark Wagh starts confidently against Ed Giddins and Jimmy Ormond, twice clipping the latter through the leg-side, for four and three, before on-driving Giddins for two. He has scored fifteen of the visitors' seventeen runs, in fact, when he loses his skipper in the eighth over as Ormond strikes an early blow for his team. Having mustered just two runs from twenty balls, Powell drives loosely in the direction of mid-on and is comprehensively 'castled' by the delighted Surrey paceman.

A couple of uncertain moments then follow for Wagh and the new batsman, the much-vaunted Ian Bell, before Ormond claims his second wicket in twelve balls when Wagh fences meekly at a decent delivery just outside off stump and edges to Jon Batty behind the stumps. Warwickshire are 26-2 and already on the back foot.

Fortunately for the Bears, Giddins is not looking anything like as threatening as his new-ball partner and also leaks boundaries to both batsmen as the score races along to fifty at almost four runs an over, the landmark being reached when Dominic Ostler forces Ormond backward of point for four.

Once Giddins has completed seven overs and Ormond eight, Adam Hollioake opts for a double bowling change, introducing Saqlain Mushtaq at the pavilion end and Rikki Clarke at the Vauxhall end. Although this immediately stems the flow of boundaries, the third-wicket pair manage to maintain Warwickshire's recovery by pushing the ball into gaps and scampering singles, even though one or two of these prove to be very tight runs indeed. The score is kept moving, nevertheless, and an inside edge by Bell to long leg off Clarke completes a very welcome half-century partnership inside a dozen overs.

Having taken a tumble in his delivery stride - a la Bicknell - during his second over, there is bad news for Surrey when their young all-rounder has to leave the field at the end of his next over, though consolation comes six balls later when Ostler takes a similar walk back to the dressing rooms after falling to Saqlain with his score on twenty-two and the total on seventy-nine. Rarely an impressive player of quality spin bowling, the experienced middle-order batsman is guilty of poor shot selection when his attempt to run an off-break to third man results in him being bowled.

The departure of Clarke, presumably for treatment from the Surrey physio, brings the introduction of Ian Salisbury for the twenty-fourth over, though the leg-spinner isn't initially allowed to settle by Bell, who takes boundaries from the new bowler's second and third deliveries, with a dab to third man and a drive wide of mid-on. The young Warwickshire batsman then follows up with a square-cut four in Salisbury's next over and appears to be well in control when Saqlain brings him to book with an off-break that produces an excellent bat-pad catch by Nadeem Shahid diving away high to his right from short leg. With Bell's nicely constructed innings ended at thirty-nine, the visitors are again in serious trouble at 98-4.

Warwickshire certainly can't afford to lose another wicket before the close, but the pressure exerted by the Surrey spin twins as they settle into a controlling rhythm eventually produces another breakthrough in the day's penultimate over. To be fair to Jamie Troughton, the man who fails to make it through to the close, it is a special piece of bowling by Saqlain that brings about his dismissal. Having fizzed a big side-spinning off-break past the outside edge of the young left-hander's bat, the Pakistani magician follows up with his trademark delivery that turns back the other way, trapping Troughton lbw as he pads up.

*Close:- Warwickshire 120-5 (Pollock 13\*, Brown 0\*) from 38 overs*

| MARK RAMPRAKASH'S 210 NOT OUT AGAINST WARWICKSHIRE |
|---|
| Original run chart as compiled by Keith Seward |

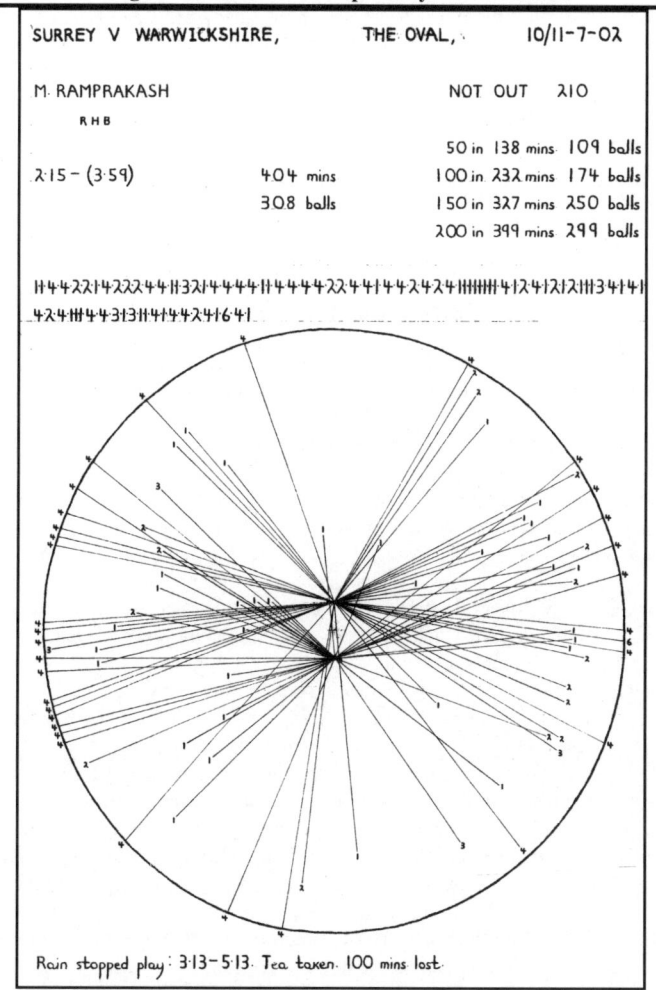

SURREY V WARWICKSHIRE,    THE OVAL,    10/11-7-02

M. RAMPRAKASH                           NOT OUT    210
    RHB
                                        50 in 138 mins  109 balls
2.15 - (3.59)         404 mins         100 in 232 mins  174 balls
                      308 balls         150 in 327 mins  250 balls
                                        200 in 399 mins  299 balls

1144221422244113214444114444224411442424HHHH4124121211134141
_424111443131141444241641_

Rain stopped play: 3.13-5.13. Tea taken. 100 mins lost.

## VIEWS FROM THE DRESSING ROOM

*You clearly relished your battle with Shaun Pollock in this match and faced a very high proportion of the balls he bowled in the first innings. Was that purely coincidence or was it part of a team plan that you should try to blunt him?*

**MARK RAMPRAKASH** - It's always very tough against Shaun Pollock - the guy is just so accurate, he doesn't seem to bowl any bad balls, and everything is in that area where you're not sure whether to go forward or back. He's a very mean bowler and rightly ranked in the top five in the world. I knew that if I could survive his spells then I could look to score off the other guys, and that's how it panned out.

*Upon completing your hundred, your celebrations were, by your normal standards, very animated - was there any reason why this particular century meant so much to you?*
**MARK RAMPRAKASH** - I was very happy because I felt I'd had to work very hard for it. When we collapsed to 59-4, there was a period where Adam and I had to really battle against Dougie Brown. It's very satisfying to reach a hundred when you know you've really earned it.

*Mark Ramprakash recorded a second successive double-century here - what do you think he has added to the team since his arrival from Middlesex?*
**ADAM HOLLIOAKE** - I think he has given added stability to the side. Number three is a crucial position, even though we've got a lot of good players, and he is very consistent. With England not selecting him we've been lucky to have him around all year, and he and Wardy have been our cornerstones really.

### Third Day - Friday 12th July
### Surrey 475; Warwickshire 293 and 165-3

After a rainy start to the morning, full marks are once again due to umpires Clarkson and Hampshire as they decide play can start at 11.08am, even though it is still drizzling.

Despite the damp conditions, Adam Hollioake throws Saqlain Mushtaq the ball for the first over of the day, pairing him with Jimmy Ormond, whose opening over is a very mixed bag indeed. Although Shaun Pollock glances his first delivery to the fine-leg boundary and drives to the rope at extra cover later in the over, Ormond also beats the bat a couple of times, as well as inducing an edge which flies over the head of gully for another four. Twelve runs have come off the over, though honours have been considerably more even than the stat suggests.

Following this early flurry of runs, Pollock settles down to play a very steady innings, while Dougie Brown, after five overs of reconnaissance, suddenly increases his score from one to sixteen in the space of two overs, taking seven runs from Ormond's eleventh over and then picking off two fours in Saqlain's sixteenth, courtesy of a sweep and a force to the fence at extra cover. Although the first of these boundaries has taken Warwickshire past 150 as the drizzle continues to fall, there is only one further significant stroke, a Pollock cover drive for four off Saqlain, before Brown becomes Ormond's third victim of the innings when a lovely delivery nips back at the batsman, penetrating his defensive stroke and trimming the off bail. This wicket strengthens Surrey's position in the match, though they are unable to make any further inroads before a heavier burst of rain brings a suspension of play for twenty-five minutes at midday, with the loss of seven overs to add to the two that had been deducted following the late start.

Upon the resumption, Neil Smith immediately sweeps Saqlain for four, and then launches a blistering attack on Ormond that brings him six successive boundaries off the Surrey opening bowler. Having upper-cut the final delivery of Ormond's fifteenth over to the rope at backward point and then taken a six off Saqlain with a slog-sweep, Smith dispatches the first five balls of the Coventry-born paceman's next over to the boundary, rushing the total past two-hundred, the seventh-wicket partnership to fifty inside eight overs, and his personal tally to forty in the process. Although the second four is squeezed to third man, and the fifth comes via a rustic slog to long-on, the other strokes in this thrilling counter-attack - a square drive over point and two on-drives, one along the ground and the other lofted over mid-on - are perfectly legitimate and well executed strokes.

Unfortunately, the Smith versus Ormond battle is then interrupted by another shower, which lops off a further six overs, before the umpires again swiftly return the players to the middle for a ten-minute session before lunch. Although Ormond soon manages to inconvenience his tormentor with a short delivery that the batsman fends away uncomfortably towards third man, Smith has already won another victory by cutting through extra cover for four, and he goes on to complete an extremely valuable fifty for his side, from just 45 balls, when he picks up a single backward of point from the last ball of the session delivered by Saqlain. The former captain's feisty effort, which has contained nine fours and a six, allows Warwickshire to breathe a little more easily as they lunch at 228-6 and, though the visitors are still 247 runs adrift of Surrey's total, they will feel that they are still in the game while Pollock and Smith remain at the crease.

*Lunch:- Warwickshire 228-6 (Pollock 49\*, Smith 50\*) from 59 overs*

After their forty-minute break for lunch, Ormond and Saqlain are back in business again immediately after the break, with Ormond instantly gifting the opposition six runs when his opening delivery, a no-ball, beats the despairing dive of Jon Batty and races away to the boundary. The temptation to think of this as a sign of tiredness is quickly forgotten, however, when the big fast bowler removes Pollock in his next over, shortly after the South African captain has completed a very composed 78-ball half-century with a single to square leg off Saqlain. It's another well-worked dismissal by the bowler, too, as Ormond follows a lifting delivery on off stump with a ball of fuller length that nips back and catches Pollock almost immobile on the crease to win a straightforward leg-before verdict from umpire Clarkson.

This would appear to be a significant breakthrough for the home side in their attempt to enforce the follow-on, though it prompts another violent counter-surge from Smith, this time at Saqlain's expense. During an action-packed over that sees the total streak up from 237 to 253, a no-ball is followed by a lofted straight drive for four; a lofted on-drive for six; a surprise bouncer to demonstrate the bowler's irritation; a square cut for two; two leg-byes; and, finally, the sanity of a scoreless delivery.

It is obvious that Smith's bold approach is giving the bowlers something to think about at this stage of proceedings, though the feeling that he needs to continue in the same vein if his side are to get out of trouble is amplified when he loses another partner, the newly arrived Keith Piper, in the next over from Ormond. Surrey's close-season signing secures his first five-wicket haul for his new county when the Warwickshire keeper, having got off the mark with a straight drive for three earlier in the over, gropes at a delivery outside off stump and edges to Brown at first slip.

The visitors' response to the loss of their eighth wicket at 261 is again aggressive, however, with Smith's uncontrolled cut at Saqlain earning him three runs, and the new batsman, Melvyn Betts, introducing himself to the off-spinner with a mighty drive over wide long-on for six. The former Durham man appears to be lucky later in the same eventful over, though, when a very confident appeal for a catch at the wicket is turned down by umpire Hampshire, and he goes on to enjoy two further strokes of luck shortly afterwards - first, Hollioake's poor throw allows the former England 'A' seamer to regain his ground after a terrible mix-up looks sure to result in him being run out, then a Chinese cut off Ormond narrowly misses his leg stump. Undeterred by these near misses, Betts hits back straight away with a rasping square-cut boundary as the Warwickshire duo continue to chance their arms.

Smith's luck runs out a couple of overs later, though, when Shahid claims a catch low to his right at short leg off Saqlain, and umpire Hampshire this time gives the Warwickshire batsman out. Judging by Smith's reaction, there must be a suspicion that the decision is incorrect, but the former Bears skipper has to go for a belligerent and defiant seventy-four, leaving the visitors nine down and still forty-five runs short of avoiding the follow-on.

Although neither Betts nor the new man, Neil Carter, are mugs with the bat, the task confronting them looks to be a tough one, and, after a boundary apiece at the expense of Giddins, recalled in place of a weary Ormond, it eventually proves to be beyond them when Betts edges a drive at an outswinger from the new bowler to Batty behind the wicket.

With fifty-four overs left for play today and a further ninety-six tomorrow, the first innings lead of 182 that Surrey have gained largely through the efforts of Ormond (5-116) and Saqlain (4-97) looks insufficient for the hosts to follow their frequently preferred option of batting again. Consequently, Adam Hollioake enforces the follow-on, leaving Warwickshire a tricky period to negotiate before tea.

If the Surrey captain is reckoning on picking up a couple of cheap early wickets he is to be disappointed, however, as Wagh and Powell are quickly out of the traps. No fewer than twenty-seven runs come from the first four overs of the innings as the visiting skipper punishes some leg-side looseness from Ormond to take ten runs from the third over, while his team-mate follows up by glancing Giddins to the fine-leg boundary and forcing him through mid-off for three. Having already bowled fifteen overs today, Ormond's rather lacklustre start is perhaps to be expected, whereas the inconsistent line bowled by his new-ball partner is distinctly disappointing as the total reaches forty-two after eight overs.

Rather than allow his opening bowlers to continue to leak precious runs, Hollioake turns to Rikki Clarke, for the ninth over, and Saqlain Mushtaq, for the tenth, in an attempt to gain a little more control.

While his off-spinner immediately does the trick by starting with three successive maidens, Clarke fares no better than the opening pair, unfortunately, as an initial tendency to stray to leg is heavily punished by both batsmen. Although the youngster manages to correct his line in his fourth over, Wagh is still able to pick on errors in length to force through the covers off the back foot for two and then drive through square cover for four, forcing the home skipper to pair his spinners by introducing Ian Salisbury at the Vauxhall end. Although the flow of runs dries up instantly as a result of this move, with just six runs coming from the final six overs of the session, the visitors reach the safe haven of tea with all their second innings wickets still intact.

*Tea:- Warwickshire 73-0 (Powell 28\*, Wagh 36\*) from 22 overs*

While Saqlain maintains a tight grip after tea, most of the early action takes place at the other end where Salisbury concedes a boundary to each batsman before landing Surrey's first blow of the second innings in his third over. His victim is Wagh, who misses a sweep at a delivery straightening from around leg stump and falls lbw for forty-three with the total standing at eighty-five. This is just the start to the day's final session that the home side needed and, with the spinners operating in tandem to close-set fields, there is considerable promise of further wickets before the close.

As the spin twins hunt for further prey, so the pattern of the early overs is repeated - Saqlain is accurate without looking especially dangerous, while Salisbury produces the occasional poor delivery, yet also beats the outside edge and sends down a number of undetected googlies.

A prime example of this exciting mix, which is so typical of all leg-spinners bar the freakishly talented Shane Warne, comes shortly after the Warwickshire total passes the hundred mark, when Salisbury elects to attack from round the wicket at the start of his tenth over. The experiment looks doomed to fail, initially, as Powell cuts consecutive deliveries to the boundary and then glances for the single that takes him through to a determined, if not always convincing, half-century from 107 balls. Nor does Ian Bell seem to have a problem as he deflects the final ball of the over, a leg-break, to third man and gathers two runs. This turns out to be part of the Surrey leg-spinner's master plan, however, as a delivery of almost identical line and length in his following over turns out to be a googly which comprehensively defeats the England Academy batsman as he shapes to play a similar stroke and traps him plumb lbw. Much credit goes to a Surrey bowler once again as Salisbury and his team mates celebrate his success, while Bell departs for eight, with the total on 113 and the visitors still sixty-nine runs in arrears.

Since the spinners are now firmly in control as Dominic Ostler arrives at the crease, expectations of a further wicket grow, though it is Powell who comes close to dismissal in the next over from Saqlain when an inside edge takes the ball perilously close to leg stump on its way down to fine leg for three. This is the closest the Pakistani has come to a wicket in the second innings, despite the fact that, by this stage, he is producing just about every ball in his repertoire in an attempt to secure wicket number for three for his side.

Rather surprisingly, even the normally nervy Ostler seems to cope reasonably well, eventually forcing a short ball from the off-spinner past mid-off for Warwickshire's first boundary in almost ten overs to take his personal score into double figures. Saqlain's next delivery is a faster, flatter off-break, however, and when the ball flies into the hands of Shahid at short leg the ensuing Surrey appeal for a bat-pad catch finds favour with umpire Clarkson.

With an irate Ostler on his way, probably erroneously, for thirteen, and the Bears still fifty behind, things are looking good for Surrey as Jamie Troughton enters the fray. The young left-hander appears to be completely unfazed by the situation, though, since he instantly sweeps Saqlain for four and then, two overs later, drives him high over long-on for six to raise the Warwickshire 150. Troughton even proves the truth of the saying that luck favours the brave as an inside edge off Saqlain results in the ball rattling into the crash helmet behind wicketkeeper Batty to earn his side five penalty runs, though there is nothing lucky about the glorious extra-cover drive in the off-spinner's following over that sends the ball fizzing to the fence.

With the light closing in fast, on a day when grey clouds have been a constant feature, this turns out to be the third day's last moment of note, as the umpires soon rule that conditions are too gloomy to continue and play is suspended four overs early at 6.15pm. Since Surrey are in a very strong position, they will be pleased to know that the weather forecast for the final day suggests that we will finally see some warmth and sunshine.

Close:- *Warwickshire 165-3 (Powell 66\*, Troughton 15\*) from 50 overs*

| VIEW FROM THE DRESSING ROOM |
|---|

*Would I be correct in assuming that you enforced the follow-on because there appeared to be insufficient time left in the match to follow your preferred course of batting again?*
**ADAM HOLLIOAKE** - To be honest, I'm not a big fan of enforcing the follow-on, because you can get caught in exactly the situation we got into here. I figure that the follow-on is something you only really enforce when there's rain predicted or when you're running out of time. There was supposed to be some rain coming on this occasion, though we didn't end up getting any at all, and I firmly believe that if we had batted again we would have won the game.

### Fourth Day - Saturday 13th July

### Surrey 475 and 137; Warwickshire 293 and 350

### Warwickshire won by 31 runs
### Warwickshire 17pts, Surrey 8

The forecasters have got it right, as play commences in bright sunshine. If Warwickshire are to get out of the game with a draw they will, therefore, have to do it without any help from the weather and, consequently, they begin their task in cautious style, with just two runs coming from the first three overs delivered by Adam Hollioake's chosen bowlers, Jimmy Ormond and Saqlain Mushtaq.

Mike Powell, in fact, goes scoreless for eight overs after a gloved single off Ormond in the first over of the day, whereas Jamie Troughton adopts a more positive approach, taking his side into the lead, and the fourth-wicket partnership past fifty, with glanced and cut boundaries off Saqlain and an off-drive that adds four to Ormond's 'runs conceded' column.

This boundary apart, the big fast bowler's opening burst is impressive, though it is no great surprise to see him removed from the attack after the morning's tenth over in order to allow Surrey's spin twins to bowl in tandem.

Ian Salisbury's appearance at the Vauxhall end receives an aggressive response from Troughton, however, as the 23-year-old left-hander slog-sweeps the leg-spinner's first delivery over midwicket and pulls his fourth to backward square leg, both shots earning four runs. While Saqlain appears unlucky to be denied the wicket of Powell in the next over, umpire Clarkson rejecting an appeal for a catch at silly point despite there being two clear sounds as the batsman pushes forward, Salisbury's sticky start continues with the concession of three further boundaries in his second over as the total fairly races past two-hundred. Two of these fours are scored by Powell, who, having added just two runs to his overnight score in the day's first dozen overs, suddenly opens up with a square cut and a drive just over the head of mid-off, following his apparent reprieve in the previous over.

With both batsmen showing the required degree of application for the situation in which they find themselves, and the pitch looking to have become rather slow and low in the bounce, it is apparent that Surrey face a much tougher task if they are to force victory than had seemed to be the case. Although Powell confirms this by rocking back to cut Salisbury for a four and a two in successive overs, the overall scoring rate slows appreciably as the spinners settle into a consistent rhythm and Troughton throttles back to pick up a series of singles on his way to an excellent fifty, which he completes from the eighty-fifth ball that he receives.

With this milestone reached, the young left-hander adds to his boundary count of eight fours and a six by driving Salisbury over deep mid-on and Saqlain through extra cover to complete the century partnership for the fourth wicket, taking Warwickshire further down the road to safety. Their lead is now fifty and, with lunch fast approaching, Hollioake changes the bowling in an attempt to snatch a wicket before the break. While Salisbury switches to the pavilion end, the almost forgotten Giddins is introduced at the Vauxhall end and immediately gets a couple of outswingers past the edge of Powell's bat, before inducing a snick to third man for a single.

Although Salisbury fails to settle after his change of end, yielding a couple of boundaries to the Warwickshire captain in a two-over spell before giving way to Hollioake, the return of Giddins proves to be a master stroke, since it brings the much sought-after breakthrough three overs before the interval. Having moved his score on to ninety-five with a single off his opposite number, Powell finds a lack of footwork exposed by a good delivery from Giddins that nips back off the pitch and traps him lbw with the total at 245 and the Warwickshire lead advanced to sixty-three.

Although Shaun Pollock helps Troughton increase the visitors' advantage by seven runs in the final two overs of the session, Giddins' impressive pre-lunch spell of five overs has revived the home county's hopes of pushing for victory after the break. It certainly won't be easy, but, with the new ball just seven overs away, there could yet be an interesting finish to the game.

*Lunch:- Warwickshire 252-4 (Troughton 65\*, Pollock 3\*) from 83 overs*

Saqlain and Giddins continue their spells after the break, and Surrey are soon offered some encouragement by the batsmen, even though no wicket is forthcoming. First, Pollock edges Giddins through the vacant third slip position, then Troughton has a very lucky escape on sixty-nine, with the score at 269, when a miscued drive off Saqlain sends the ball looping away towards deep backward point. The nearest fielder, Ian Ward, runs back in an attempt to take the catch over his shoulder but, at the crucial moment, he loses the ball in the sun and the chance goes begging.

Warwickshire's survival hopes are boosted by these moments of good fortune and they appear to be further enhanced when Hollioake elects not to take the new ball, despite the fact that Giddins is still managing to beat the bat every now and again. This decision then looks all the more bizarre when Saqlain is replaced by Ormond, shortly after Pollock has taken his side's lead into three figures with a firm clip to the square leg boundary and a forcing stroke through the covers for two, both off Giddins. The returning Ormond shows that the extra hardness of a new ball isn't a prerequisite for success, however, as his fourth delivery brings the wicket of the South African captain, ironically with a bouncer, to once again rekindle Surrey's victory hopes. Having scored twenty-four, Pollock's attempted pull results in the ball spiralling high into the air behind the slips off the top edge, and Ali Brown races back towards the boundary to take a very good over-the-shoulder catch.

Undeterred by the loss of his partner, the combative Troughton immediately hooks another Ormond bouncer for four, but the new batsman, Dougie Brown, soon finds the former Leicestershire bowler too hot to handle, ending a torrid over by edging a perfect outswinger low to second slip where the Surrey captain accepts the chance with great aplomb.

With around fifty overs left for play, Warwickshire are now effectively 111-6 and things are looking very interesting again as Ormond and Giddins strive for further breakthroughs. While the latter seems to have slightly lost his edge, being driven through the covers for four in the seventh over of his post-lunch spell by the newly arrived Neil Smith, Ormond, despite being similarly punished by Troughton, is looking lively as he strikes for a third time in the fourth over of his spell. His eighth victim of the match is the dangerous Smith, who has his middle stump extracted in thrilling and spectacular fashion by a magnificent inswinging yorker to reduce the visitors to 309-7.

With their latest recruit in such devastating form, Surrey are looking likely winners again, though they still need to remove Troughton, who is desperately seeking a colleague to stay with him as he nears a well-deserved century. His latest partner, Keith Piper, starts shakily with an edge and a miscued drive, though the Warwickshire wicketkeeper does manage to locate the middle of his bat in driving Giddins through mid-off for three in the final over of the former Bear's ten-over spell.

Holloake's decision to revert to his favoured combination of Ormond and Saqlain at this point, with his premier strike bowler switching to the Vauxhall end in the process, brings instant frustration - when Piper, on twelve, offers a high and hard caught-and-bowled chance which Saqlain cannot hang on to - and then success, when Troughton's sliced drive at a wide delivery from Ormond is well held above his head by the Surrey off-spinner right on the boundary edge in front of the Bedser Stand. Having fallen short of what would have been an excellent hundred by just six runs, and probably about as many inches, the young left-hander departs, crestfallen, to a justifiably warm ovation, while the home side celebrate their continued surge towards a possible victory.

Since the visitors are now 145 ahead, with some forty overs remaining, the hosts need to capture the last two wickets pretty quickly, however, and Piper immediately offers hope by attempting a series of risky reverse sweeps in the next over from Saqlain. Although he manages to pull the stroke off on one occasion, earning four runs for himself and his team, it also nearly brings about his downfall when Brown, at slip, intercepts another attempt and almost manages to throw down the stumps with the batsman out of his ground.

Surrey only have to wait a few more balls to pick up the ninth wicket, though, as Ormond produces another rip-snorting yorker which results in both the off stump and the batsman, Melvyn Betts, taking a walk in the direction of the pavilion. In taking four wickets for fifteen runs in the space of twenty-seven deliveries, Ormond has recorded another five-wicket haul, captured his first-ever bag of ten wickets in a match, and put his new team firmly on course for another Championship victory.

There is still one wicket to fall, however, and, though Piper continues to take risks, three precious overs pass by without any major incident as both sides show signs of anxiety. Warwickshire's concern is evidenced by the appearance of some of their players and the coach,

Bob Woolmer, on their changing room balcony to signal to the umpires that they believe, mistakenly, that tea should be taken, despite the fact that they are nine wickets down. They clearly believe that the loss of two overs for the change of innings when they are finally bowled out will give them a greater chance of escaping with a draw, but the umpires are right, under the Championship regulations, to keep going, even though the usual last-day teatime of 3.40pm has passed.

Ignoring the ongoing furore, Piper eases his colleagues' nerves slightly with a hooked four and an on-driven two in the next over from Ormond to take the total up to 350, though the innings ends, without addition, just a few balls later when Saqlain lures Neil Carter into popping up the most simple of bat-pad catches to Shahid at short leg. As Jimmy Ormond leads his team from the field to great acclaim from the home crowd for his career-best match figures of 10-178, Surrey have a target of 169 to chase after tea in a minimum of thirty-four overs.

*Tea:- Between Innings*

The consensus of opinion during the break is that Surrey's target is well within reach, since a required run-rate of five an over is not especially daunting. Additionally, it is felt that the only real threat in Warwickshire's bowling line-up is Pollock, whose contribution might well be limited, even though Powell would probably like to keep him involved for most of the innings. The visitors will, therefore, need all their expertise and skill as a one-day unit - underlined by their success against Essex in the Benson & Hedges Cup final exactly three weeks ago, and the fact that they currently lead the NUL Division One table - if they are to defend this sort of target.

After the first over of Surrey's chase, the whole situation is in need of reassessment. Although Ian Ward gets his team off on the right foot by forcing Pollock's first delivery through the covers for three, the South African hits back in style by claiming two wickets in the final three balls of an over extended to seven deliveries by a no-ball. Jon Batty is the first to go, adjudged lbw by umpire Hampshire when pulling at a delivery that doesn't appear short enough for the stroke, then Pollock claims the vital wicket of the in-form Ramprakash, who does well to get a thin outside edge to a classic delivery that lifts and leaves the bat. Surrey are therefore up with the run-rate at the end of the opening over... but two wickets down.

Hopes that these losses might prove insignificant rise when Ward hooks Neil Carter over midwicket for four and Nadeem Shahid bags a brace of boundaries in Pollock's second over, which surprisingly costs twelve runs, but then fall as Ward goes for seven in the fourth over, with the total on twenty-one. The left-handed opener's departure represents another serious blow for the home county and is brought about by an edged drive that Piper picks up brilliantly, low and left-handed, as he dives away in front of first slip. Now we have a game on our hands.

Despite these setbacks, Surrey remain positive, with both Shahid and the new batsman, Alistair Brown, taking an off-side boundary off Pollock, before Carter, surprisingly economical and suddenly a real threat, claims his second wicket of the innings in the eighth over when Shahid edges a drive to the South African skipper at first slip. The Championship leaders' condition is now critical at 32-4, and a real area of concern for them is the amount of seam movement that the Warwickshire opening bowlers have so far been able to extract from a pitch that had appeared to be getting slower and less responsive.

Even though the visitors suddenly appear to hold the upper hand, it seems highly unlikely that Brown and Adam Hollioake, the new pair out in the middle for Surrey, will suppress their aggressive instincts, and so it proves as Brown drives Carter over mid-off's head for four and Hollioake smashes Pollock high over square cover for a stunning six. Although both batsmen subsequently enjoy a little luck with strokes that fall just a couple of yards short of fielders, the fifty comes up in the thirteenth over and the field starts to spread. With four or five men already back on the boundary, Powell appears to be playing a dangerous game, since there are plenty of ones and twos now on offer, and, as a result, the score builds steadily without the batsmen needing to take any undue risks.

The pendulum that had already been swinging slightly back towards Surrey then takes a serious lurch in their favour when Pollock takes a breather after eight overs and the previously dependable Carter suddenly haemorrhages twenty-one runs from his eighth and ninth overs. Although the left-armer is slightly unlucky when Piper can only get fingertips to Brown's gloved hook, there is nothing fortunate about the same batsman's forcing stroke to the backward point boundary, nor Hollioake's two rocket-like off-drives which add a total of ten runs to the Surrey total and take the recovery partnership beyond fifty.

With eleven runs coming from Dougie Brown's first two overs as Pollock's replacement, and Powell understandably reluctant to employ the out-of-form Melvyn Betts, the Warwickshire skipper makes a surprising move with the score at 93-4 after nineteen overs by introducing the very occasional left-arm spin of Jamie Troughton at the pavilion end. Since he is so new to the first-class game, nobody knows what to expect, apart from a deep-set field and an over-the-wicket line of 'attack'. Five men, in fact, line up around the boundary edge, though it doesn't stop Hollioake from pulling the part-time bowler high over wide long-on for six in a ten-run over that sees the home side moving within sight of victory.

With sixty-six runs needed from fourteen overs, Surrey certainly seem to be red-hot favourites again, though the visitors hit back straight away by making a vital breakthrough in the next over. If truth be told, the loss of the wicket owes more to flawed running between the wickets than any Warwickshire brilliance as Brown's mid-pitch hesitation, following Hollioake's push to backward point, costs him dearly. Unable to make his ground at the striker's end, the home team's middle-order linchpin departs for thirty-three, bringing the visitors back into the contest, even if only as outsiders at this moment in time.

Although the damage done during an over that yields just one run after the loss of Brown is quickly repaired when Troughton's next over sees the addition of seven to the total, Dougie Brown is now rising to the challenge that faces him. Having produced two successive tight and testing overs, the first delivery of his fourth over brings him a well-deserved wicket when Rikki Clarke shuffles across his stumps and is rapped on the pads by something akin to a shooter. Umpire Hampshire is left with a straightforward decision, and the Surrey all-rounder exits with the home side now 111-6 and the game pretty much back in the balance.

With the visitors' former England one-day international proving so difficult to get away, it seems strange that Troughton is allowed to continue at the pavilion end, not that Hollioake is complaining as he completes an excellent 52-ball half-century with an enormous straight six that smashes a glass panel in the Media Centre on the fourth floor of the Bedser Stand, just a few yards away from the hospitality box where his family are sitting. The Surrey skipper's knock, which has so far contained the unusual mix of four sixes and one four, looks to be keeping his team just about on course, and when Ian Salisbury spoils a potential Dougie Brown maiden by cutting the final delivery to the rope at backward point the Championship leaders are 125-6 with nine overs remaining.

Everyone knows that the acid test is imminent, however, as Pollock inevitably returns in place of Troughton at the pavilion end. With the required run rate just below five an over, the Surrey batsmen are aware that all they really need to do now is gather ones and twos but, in trying to follow this simple plan by running the ball down to third man, Salisbury gets an outside edge to Pollock's third delivery and sees Piper pouch a regulation catch to his right-hand side. As the visitors celebrate this seventh wicket they doubtless appreciate that, with just fifty-one deliveries of the match remaining, they are, for the first time since Surrey were 59-4 on day one, on top and in with a realistic chance of emerging victorious.

With Saqlain Mushtaq coming out to bat, and just Jimmy Ormond and Ed Giddins back in the pavilion, Surrey clearly need to reassess their position. Maybe it is now time to shut up shop and accept the four points for a draw, rather than risk defeat in chasing runs against a top-quality bowler, Pollock, and an inspired competitor, Brown? What will the home captain, still out in the middle, decide?

As he plays out the first five deliveries of Brown's over it appears that he has settled for the draw, but then the fiery Scotsman digs in a bouncer which Hollioake, perhaps recalling his six-hitting hooking successes of the first innings, is unable to resist. Maybe because he plays the shot almost as an afterthought, or maybe because Brown has put a bit extra into the delivery, the ball flies high into the air off the top edge backward of square leg. The players and the crowd hold their breath as Carter sprints in from the boundary at deep backward square and the ball plummets towards the ground. It is just inches from the turf, in fact, when the Warwickshire paceman plunges forward to hold a very good low catch and, almost before he knows it, he is rapidly engulfed by his team mates offering their congratulations.

By way of contrast, Hollioake is a picture of disappointment as he makes his way from the field with the scoreboard reading 126-8 and Warwickshire, quite incredibly, now the clear favourites to win the match. A maximum of forty-two nerve-wracking deliveries remain at the fall of this wicket and, as Surrey's final abandonment of the run chase becomes obvious over the course of the next two overs, the close fielders gradually crowd in like vultures.

The ninth-wicket pair of Saqlain and Ormond have survived only fifteen of the forty-two balls, however, when disaster strikes for the home side, with the Surrey off-spinner falling lbw to Pollock, despite having got forward to a ball nipping back at him. The Warwickshire players go wild again at the realisation that they are suddenly on the brink of an amazing and historic victory, with a possible twenty-six deliveries to bowl at Ormond and Ed Giddins. Suddenly, it seems, the visitors are delighted that the umpires ignored their complaints about the timing of the tea break!

After Giddins survives the last two deliveries of Pollock's over, amidst almost unbearable tension, Ormond surprises everyone by pulling and driving boundaries off Brown, though, crucially, he is unable to find a single in the later stages of the over, leaving his partner on strike for the next over from the Proteas skipper.

Much to everyone's surprise, however, Pollock is unable to produce a decent delivery until the last ball, a well-directed yorker that Surrey's confirmed 'rabbit' does brilliantly to keep out. Had the visitors won their case in the minor dispute over tea, this would have been the last delivery of the match but, as it is, we still have two overs to go and, having seen the ease with which Ormond played Brown's last over, Powell makes the bold decision to throw the ball to Neil Smith, his experienced off-spinner, for the penultimate over.

And what a good move it turns out to be. Ormond fails to make contact with the new bowler's first delivery and is adjudged lbw by umpire Hampshire, though, from my vantage point, the ball looks to be sliding down the leg-side. Maybe Ormond feels the same way, since he disturbs the stumps behind him with his bat, but, when all is said and done, it would be churlish to deny Warwickshire their moment of glory as their excited players celebrate an incredible comeback that has seen them snatch victory in true 'smash and grab' style. Having dominated the game, Surrey's bold approach to the eventual run chase has cost them dearly, though we have witnessed a truly memorable match and no team should ever be criticised for looking to be positive. One must also admire the tenacious way in which the visitors have fought back to claim their first County Championship victory at The Oval since 1975 and, as the statisticians later reveal, become the first-ever Warwickshire side to win a match after being forced to follow-on.

From a Surrey point of view, this is only the second occasion since 1893 that the team has been defeated after enforcing the follow-on, the previous instance being when Kent triumphed by 72 runs at Guildford in 1992. Finally, another proud, though often overlooked, run has come to an end, as this is the first defeat suffered by a Surrey side weakened by England call-ups since the loss to Gloucestershire at Cheltenham in July 1998. All five of the defeats in the intervening four years had come when Surrey were fielding a side selected from a full-strength squad.

**Surrey 475 and 137; Warwickshire 293 and 350**
**Warwickshire won by 31 runs. Warwickshire 17pts, Surrey 8**

## VIEWS FROM THE DRESSING ROOM

*I assume we felt pretty confident about chasing 169 in 34 overs to win the match?*
**MARK RAMPRAKASH** - Yes, possibly we were over-confident about it - the Surrey attitude is that whatever they've got we will go and knock them off. We knew that Pollock was there, of course, and I did wonder whether we should try to see off his first three or four overs but, as it was, we were two wickets down at the end of the first over.

*I suppose the crucial moment in the run chase was the run out of Ali Brown?*
**ADAM HOLLIOAKE** - Yes, without a doubt. If he hadn't been run out then we would have won the game, simple as that.

*You had an interesting contest with Dougie Brown in this match. In the first innings you certainly won the battle when he kept on trying to bounce you but he took the honours in the second innings when he had you caught hooking. Was that stroke in the second innings almost an afterthought, since you had dead-batted the first five balls of the over?*
**ADAM HOLLIOAKE** - We'd just lost a wicket, but I said we'd still go for the runs - I decided that if they bowled badly, I was still going to try and hit the ball, whereas at the beginning I was trying to hit almost everything. But I think you are exactly right, it was an afterthought. I think if I'd carried on batting the way I had been earlier then I'm pretty confident I would have hit that ball for six, but, as it was, it ended up being a half-hearted shot. I think I learnt a lot from that for the rest of the season, as there weren't many occasions after that when I was half-hearted.

*At the fall of which wicket did you actually decide that we should put up the shutters?*
**ADAM HOLLIOAKE** - That point was probably as I walked off the field!

*To be honest, we didn't chase the target very well, did we? And I guess the limited-overs nature of the final innings suited Warwickshire since they are a good one-day side?*
**MARK RAMPRAKASH** - We felt robbed there really - we had outplayed them for three-and-a-half days, so it was very demoralising to get bowled out in that way. Taking two wickets in the first over gave them a terrific boost and suddenly Pollock had his tail up. Then once we got to 30-4 they knew they had a very good chance of defending the total and, as a result, they really lifted themselves, and their one-day skills came into it, yes.

*At the end of the game, did you have any regrets about the run chase? That maybe we had pursued it for too long, or that we might perhaps have changed the batting order in some way?*
**ADAM HOLLIOAKE** - No, not at all, there were no regrets apart from the fact that we'd lost. They bowled well and maybe we could have done one or two things differently in the run chase, but we'd had nearly two days in the field, which might have had an effect in terms of tiredness. This was probably one of the best games of cricket I have ever played in, though, and it was just disappointing to be on the wrong side of the result at the end.

*I felt the umpires deserved a lot of credit in this game for the way they wanted to play, even when there was drizzle falling. Are you in favour of umpires who are keen to keep the game moving and play even when there is a little bit of rain around?*
**ADAM HOLLIOAKE** - I think we go off far too easily for both bad light and drizzle, although, speaking to the umpires, I think it's more because of directives they get from above - legally, they have to go off because of bad light, which is crazy, especially if you've got two spinners

bowling. But, because people don't know about these directives, it's unfortunately the umpires - and sometimes the players - who have to take the abuse of the crowd.

*You must have been very disappointed to score successive double-centuries without ending up on the winning side on either occasion?*
**MARK RAMPRAKASH** - Yes, I was, because you always want to make a contribution to the side and win - that's why I rate my century against Lancashire as my most important knock of the season, with the Warwickshire innings, without a doubt, the better of my two double-centuries, because it was made against better bowlers in more testing conditions.

*I thought Jimmy Ormond had been rather short of luck up until this match. He appears to have all the skills a fast bowler needs and lots of variations in his bowling.*
**MARK RAMPRAKASH** - If you look at certain bowlers, for example Angus Fraser, they can be very one-dimensional, bowling line and length no matter what, not many yorkers, not many bouncers. On the other hand, Jimmy is a very versatile fast bowler because he can swing the ball in orthodox style, or if the pitch gets dry he can come back and reverse the ball. He's also got slower balls, yorkers and bouncers - he's a good all-round bowler, and that's why he was selected for England. He's certainly a very good addition to the Surrey squad and, although he got fifty wickets this year, I think he's been very unlucky and I think he'll do a lot better in 2003.

### SURREY v WARWICKSHIRE at the AMP Oval    Played 10th to 13th July
Surrey won the toss and elected to bat    Umpires:- Tony Clarkson and John Hampshire

**SURREY - First Innings**

| Fall Of Wkt | Batsman | How | Out | Score | Balls | 4s | 6s |
|---|---|---|---|---|---|---|---|
| 2-57 | I.J. Ward | c Ostler | b Brown | 34 | 52 | 7 | 0 |
| 1-57 | J.N. Batty + | lbw | b Pollock | 16 | 36 | 3 | 0 |
|  | M.R. Ramprakash | Not | Out | 210 | 308 | 32 | 1 |
| 3-59 | N. Shahid | c Ostler | b Brown | 2 | 6 | 0 | 0 |
| 4-59 | A.D. Brown | lbw | b Brown | 0 | 2 | 0 | 0 |
| 5-147 | A.J. Hollioake * |  | b Betts | 56 | 65 | 10 | 2 |
| 6-322 | R. Clarke | lbw | b Brown | 79 | 139 | 12 | 1 |
| 7-404 | I.D.K. Salisbury | c Smith | b Carter | 30 | 46 | 4 | 0 |
| 8-405 | Saqlain Mushtaq | c & | b Brown | 0 | 6 | 0 | 0 |
| 9-435 | J. Ormond | c Powell | b Brown | 13 | 19 | 3 | 0 |
| 10-475 | E.S.H. Giddins | c & | b Brown | 9 | 18 | 1 | 0 |
|  | Extras | (3b, 17lb, 2w, 4nb) |  | 26 |  |  |  |
|  | **TOTAL** | **(115.5 overs)** |  | **475** |  |  |  |

| Bowler | O | M | R | W | NB | Wd |
|---|---|---|---|---|---|---|
| Pollock | 22 | 11 | 37 | 1 | - | - |
| Carter | 21 | 1 | 114 | 1 | - | 1 |
| Brown | 33.5 | 7 | 110 | 7 | - | - |
| Betts | 17 | 0 | 106 | 1 | 2 | - |
| Smith | 12 | 1 | 49 | 0 | - | - |
| Wagh | 4 | 1 | 9 | 0 | - | - |
| Bell | 4 | 0 | 23 | 0 | - | - |
| Troughton | 2 | 0 | 7 | 0 | - | - |

**WARWICKSHIRE - First Innings** (Needing 326 to avoid the follow-on)

| Fall Of Wkt | Batsman | How | Out | Score | Balls | 4s | 6s |
|---|---|---|---|---|---|---|---|
| 1-17 | M.J. Powell * |  | b Ormond | 2 | 20 | 0 | 0 |
| 2-26 | M.A. Wagh | c Batty | b Ormond | 17 | 34 | 2 | 0 |
| 4-98 | I.R. Bell | c Shahid | b Saqlain | 39 | 57 | 6 | 0 |
| 3-79 | D.P. Ostler |  | b Saqlain | 22 | 47 | 3 | 0 |
| 5-119 | J.O. Troughton | lbw | b Saqlain | 12 | 47 | 1 | 0 |
| 7-237 | S.M. Pollock | lbw | b Ormond | 50 | 80 | 8 | 0 |
| 6-162 | D.R. Brown |  | b Ormond | 16 | 38 | 3 | 0 |
| 9-281 | N.M.K. Smith | c Shahid | b Saqlain | 74 | 70 | 11 | 2 |
| 8-261 | K.J. Piper + | c Brown | b Ormond | 3 | 8 | 0 | 0 |
| 10-293 | M.M. Betts | c Batty | b Giddins | 18 | 26 | 2 | 1 |
|  | N.M. Carter | Not | Out | 7 | 11 | 1 | 0 |
|  | Extras | (4b, 11lb, 18nb) |  | 33 |  |  |  |
|  | **TOTAL** | **(71.5 overs)** |  | **293** |  |  |  |

| Bowler | O | M | R | W | NB | Wd |
|---|---|---|---|---|---|---|
| Giddins | 8.5 | 2 | 32 | 1 | 1 | - |
| Ormond | 23 | 5 | 116 | 5 | 4 | - |
| Saqlain Mushtaq | 29 | 3 | 97 | 4 | 1 | - |
| Clarke | 3 | 0 | 8 | 0 | - | - |
| Salisbury | 8 | 0 | 25 | 0 | - | - |

**WARWICKSHIRE - Second Innings** (Following on, 182 runs in arrears)

| Fall Of Wkt | Batsman | How | Out | Score | Balls | 4s | 6s |
|---|---|---|---|---|---|---|---|
| 4-245 | M.J. Powell * | lbw | b Giddins | 95 | 242 | 13 | 0 |
| 1-85 | M.A. Wagh | lbw | b Salisbury | 43 | 80 | 6 | 0 |
| 2-113 | I.R. Bell | lbw | b Salisbury | 8 | 34 | 0 | 0 |
| 3-132 | D.P. Ostler | c Shahid | b Saqlain | 13 | 23 | 1 | 0 |
| 8-327 | J.O. Troughton | c Saqlain | b Ormond | 94 | 164 | 13 | 1 |
| 5-284 | S.M. Pollock | c Brown | b Ormond | 24 | 45 | 3 | 0 |
| 6-293 | D.R. Brown | c Holliokae | b Ormond | 5 | 9 | 1 | 0 |
| 7-309 | N.M.K. Smith | | b Ormond | 6 | 12 | 1 | 0 |
| | K.J. Piper + | Not | Out | 25 | 40 | 3 | 0 |
| 9-337 | M.M. Betts | | b Ormond | 4 | 7 | 0 | 0 |
| 10-350 | N.M. Carter | c Shahid | b Saqlain | 2 | 15 | 0 | 0 |
| | Extras | (2b, 8lb, 10w, 6nb) | (+ 5 pens) | 31 | | | |
| | **TOTAL** | **(111.2 overs)** | | **350** | | | |

| Bowler | O | M | R | W | NB | Wd |
|---|---|---|---|---|---|---|
| Ormond | 18 | 2 | 62 | 5 | 1 | 2 |
| Giddins | 19 | 1 | 63 | 1 | - | - |
| Clarke | 4 | 0 | 24 | 0 | 2 | - |
| Saqlain Mushtaq | 43.2 | 14 | 90 | 2 | - | - |
| Salisbury | 26 | 4 | 95 | 2 | - | 3 |
| Holliokae | 1 | 0 | 1 | 0 | - | - |

**SURREY - Second Innings** (Needing 169 to win in a minimum of 34 overs)

| Fall Of Wkt | Batsman | How | Out | Score | Balls | 4s | 6s |
|---|---|---|---|---|---|---|---|
| 3-21 | I.J. Ward | c Piper | b Carter | 7 | 9 | 1 | 0 |
| 1-5 | J.N. Batty + | lbw | b Pollock | 0 | 4 | 0 | 0 |
| 2-5 | M.R. Ramprakash | c Piper | b Pollock | 0 | 2 | 0 | 0 |
| 4-32 | N. Shahid | c Pollock | b Carter | 15 | 20 | 3 | 0 |
| 5-103 | A.D. Brown | run | out | 33 | 41 | 4 | 0 |
| 8-126 | A.J. Holliokae * | c Carter | b Brown | 52 | 62 | 6 | 1 |
| 6-111 | R. Clarke | lbw | b Brown | 5 | 10 | 0 | 0 |
| 7-126 | I.D.K. Salisbury | lbw | b Pollock | 1 | 12 | 0 | 0 |
| 9-129 | Saqlain Mushtaq | c Piper | b Pollock | 6 | 13 | 1 | 0 |
| 10-137 | J. Ormond | lbw | b Smith | 9 | 14 | 2 | 0 |
| | E.S.H. Giddins | Not | Out | 0 | 8 | 0 | 0 |
| | Extras | (1b, 4lb, 4nb) | | 9 | | | |
| | **TOTAL** | **(32.1 overs)** | | **137** | | | |

| Bowler | O | M | R | W | NB | Wd |
|---|---|---|---|---|---|---|
| Pollock | 12 | 2 | 44 | 4 | 2 | - |
| Carter | 9 | 1 | 37 | 2 | - | - |
| Brown | 8 | 1 | 26 | 2 | - | - |
| Troughton | 3 | 0 | 25 | 0 | - | - |
| Smith | 0.1 | 0 | 0 | 1 | - | - |

## Other Division One Results

Fortunately for Surrey, their defeat had little effect on their strong position at the head of the table, since the other three matches all ended in draws. Consequently, no side picked up more than three points on the leaders, save for their conquerors, who moved nine points closer. At the approximate halfway stage of the season, Leicestershire, Kent and Warwickshire appeared to be the sides most likely to mount a challenge, with the reigning champions, Yorkshire, now only concerned with the relegation battle that faced them.

July 10-13
*Leicester:-* **Leicestershire drew with Hampshire.** Hampshire 311 (Pothas 63, Crawley 60) and 283 (Smith 104, Francis 82, Maddy 4-37); Leicestershire 300-9dec (Burns 101, Bevan 62) and 72-4. **Leicestershire 10pts, Hampshire 10**

*Hove:-* **Sussex drew with Kent.** Sussex 145 (Khan 6-56) and 450 (Goodwin 135, Ambrose 124, Innes 56, Prior 53); Kent 349 (Smith 141*, Khan 58) and 85-5. **Sussex 7pts, Kent 10**

*Scarborough:-* **Yorkshire drew with Somerset.** Somerset 498-9dec (Bowler 84, Dutch 74, Holloway 65, Turner 63, Parsons 59, Dawson 4-154); Yorkshire 323 (Lehmann 64, Lumb 57, Craven 51, Blackwell 4-49, Bulbeck 4-94). **Yorkshire 9pts, Somerset 11**

## COUNTY CHAMPIONSHIP DIVISION ONE AT 13TH JULY

| Pos | Prv |  | P | Points | W | D | L | Bat | Bwl | Ded |
|---|---|---|---|---|---|---|---|---|---|---|
| 1 | 1 | Surrey | 8 | 112.75 | 4 | 3 | 1 | 29 | 24 | 0.25 |
| 2 | 2 | Leicestershire | 9 | 104.00 | 3 | 4 | 2 | 28 | 25 | 1.00 |
| 3 | 3 | Hampshire | 9 | 90.00 | 1 | 7 | 1 | 24 | 26 | 0.00 |
| 4 | 4 | Kent | 8 | 89.50 | 3 | 3 | 2 | 20 | 22 | 0.50 |
| 5 | 7 | Warwickshire | 8 | 85.00 | 3 | 3 | 2 | 15 | 22 | 0.00 |
| 6 | 5 | Sussex | 9 | 84.00 | 1 | 6 | 2 | 22 | 26 | 0.00 |
| 7 | 6 | Somerset | 8 | 81.00 | 1 | 6 | 1 | 23 | 22 | 0.00 |
| 8 | 7 | Lancashire | 7 | 68.00 | 2 | 3 | 2 | 12 | 20 | 0.00 |
| 9 | 9 | Yorkshire | 8 | 50.50 | 0 | 3 | 5 | 16 | 23 | 0.50 |

### NUL Division Two Results

While the Lions had a Sunday off, the Gladiators moved clear at the top of the table with an easy win over the Crusaders. Meanwhile, there were defeats for both Northamptonshire and Hampshire, the latter snatching defeat from the jaws of victory in an incredible finish at Southend as Essex surged up to third in the table, with games in hand over both of the top two teams.

July 14

*Southend:-* **Essex Eagles beat Hampshire Hawks by 5 runs.** Essex 200-9 (Habib 50, Tremlett 4-25); Hampshire 195-8 (Johnson 83, Middlebrook 4-33). **Essex Eagles 4pts**

*Blackpool:-* **Lancashire Lightning beat Derbyshire Scorpions by one wicket.** Derbyshire 169 (44.5ov; Selwood 52, Hogg 3-20, Wood 3-36); Lancashire 170-9 (40.4ov; Byas 78). **Lancashire Lightning 4pts**

*Southgate:-* **Gloucestershire Gladiators beat Middlesex Crusaders by 78 runs.** Gloucestershire 272-7 (Alleyne 93, Spearman 78); Middlesex 194-8 (Weekes 53*, Averis 3-45). **Gloucestershire Gladiators 4pts**

*Hove:-* **Sussex Sharks beat Northamptonshire Steelbacks by 38 runs.** Sussex 185-6; Northamptonshire 147 (38.3ov). **Sussex Sharks 4pts**

## NATIONAL LEAGUE DIVISION TWO AT 14TH JULY

| Pos | Prv |  | P | Pts | W | T | L | A |
|---|---|---|---|---|---|---|---|---|
| 1 | 1 | Gloucestershire Gladiators | 8 | 22 | 5 | 0 | 2 | 1 |
| 2 | 1 | Surrey Lions | 7 | 18 | 4 | 0 | 2 | 1 |
| 3 | 6 | Essex Eagles | 5 | 16 | 4 | 0 | 1 | 0 |
| 4 | 3 | Hampshire Hawks | 6 | 14 | 3 | 0 | 2 | 1 |
| = | 3 | Northamptonshire Steelbacks | 6 | 14 | 3 | 0 | 2 | 1 |
| 6 | 5 | Derbyshire Scorpions | 7 | 14 | 3 | 0 | 3 | 1 |
| 7 | 8 | Lancashire Lightning | 9 | 12 | 2 | 0 | 5 | 2 |
| 8 | 9 | Sussex Sharks | 8 | 10 | 2 | 0 | 5 | 1 |
| 9 | 7 | Middlesex Crusaders | 8 | 8 | 1 | 0 | 5 | 2 |

# 11  A Pause For Thought

Although defeat at the hands of Warwickshire had been an undoubted setback, the halfway point of the season had arrived with Surrey still on course to win the trophy that they had pledged to dedicate to Ben Hollioake's memory, having earned themselves a decent lead in the County Championship, a challenging second position in the National League and a place in the quarter-finals of the Cheltenham & Gloucester Trophy.

The next date in the diaries of players and supporters was the 'Service Of Thanksgiving For The Life Of Ben Hollioake' at Southwark Cathedral, close to London Bridge, on Monday 15th July.  At the time the date was announced I'd been uncertain about the wisdom of holding it at this stage of the summer - though, if truth be told, there were probably few, if any, other options - but as the day arrived it seemed perfect... a good time to remember Ben, and what the players were trying to achieve in his memory.

Since tickets had been available from the Club since 1st May, with no restrictions on who was able to attend, it was always likely to be a major event.  I wasn't hugely surprised, therefore, to find Keith Booth, the Surrey scorer, and his wife, Jennifer, at Sutton railway station, nor to bump into Nicola Randall - a long-standing friend and supporter of the Club - almost as soon as we alighted at London Bridge.   As we were early for the service, Nicola and I took the opportunity to stop in the station for a coffee and a few reminiscences about Ben, before crossing the busy Borough High Street in glorious sunshine to get to the cathedral, passing Ben Smith, the Worcestershire and former Leicestershire batsman, on the way.  Since I couldn't instantly recall Smith having been a team-mate at any stage or level of Ben's career, I was suddenly forced to reassess both how big this event was going to be and how popular 'Pelly' must have been with players throughout the game.

Then, as we reached the cathedral, I was faced by a sea of familiar faces - county and international cricketers, officials and staff from The AMP Oval, figures from the cricketing media, and many of my fellow Surrey fans.  Everywhere I turned there was someone I knew or recognised, all of us drawn together to celebrate Ben's life and career.  The Rashid family, having formed a special bond with the Hollioakes out of shared tragedy, were also in attendance to offer their support.  I later discovered that over eight-hundred people had attended the service, including more than 140 professional cricketers from just about every county side in the country.

The hour-long service was led by the Dean of Southwark, the Very Reverend Colin Slee, and began with readings by Alec Stewart and Paul Sheldon, before Mark Butcher sat down at the front of the cathedral with his acoustic guitar to give a flawless and courageous performance of a song, entitled *'You're Never Gone'*, which he had composed as a tribute to his late friend.  The lyrics are reproduced here, with Mark's kind permission:-

*You're never gone, I know you're not alone,*
*'cause people loved to be with you,*
*I know you're far from home*
*But home was anywhere with you;*

*You're never gone, you're always there,*
*The perfect smile, you're everywhere,*
*Although you're gone an age too soon*
*You'll always be the bright side of the moon*

*You left us to get old,*
*I guess we knew it wouldn't have suited you,*
*There's a story left untold,*
*I hope you'll make it up between the two of you;*

*You're never gone, you're always there,*
*The perfect smile, you're everywhere,*
*Although you're gone an age too soon*
*You'll always be the bright side of the moon*

*So they welcomed you up to the sky,*
*To the place where our heroes have gone,*
*Did you know just how far you could fly?*
*Did you know that our love was so strong?*

© Mark Butcher 2002

When Butcher finished the song there was a brief, uncertain silence before the congregation burst into applause, though silence soon returned as Adam Hollioake took to the lectern to pay his tribute. Those of us who had only read about the Surrey's captain's outpourings of grief at the funeral service in Australia, soon began to appreciate what it was like to witness it at first hand as Adam's voice cracked up with emotion almost as soon as he started speaking. With every one of us present in the cathedral clearly feeling his pain, it was one of the most moving experiences imaginable to listen to his occasionally faltering words. As in Australia, he had chosen to read from a letter to Ben that he had prepared in advance, saying, "Ben, you know I've always been a shallow person. I only worry about things in this world. I am sorry I nagged you about not doing your training. Though I am glad that I told you several times in the last year that I love you, I wish I had told you the thousands of times I felt it." He went on to reveal the despair that his family had felt since Ben's passing, telling the congregation: "Life has changed for my family. Before, there were good days, bad days, hard-working days and relaxing days. Now, all these times have gone and been replaced with before and after Ben." Then, in a highly-charged and most distressing passage that must have brought tears to just about everybody's eyes, he stated: "That's how my life will be from now on. I'm a prisoner on earth. I'll live my life to the best of my ability, but I can't wait to be with you again." After this rather disturbing line, it was comforting to hear Adam end on a more forward-looking note by saying, "This is my last goodbye, Ben. I can't keep holding on to you forever. I know you have important work to do, so I have to let you go."

With one or two members of the congregation audibly sobbing, and tears filling eyes all around the cathedral, Adam left the lectern and handed over to John Major, the former Prime Minister and Surrey C.C.C. President, who described Ben as "an unforgettable young man who had left a legacy of love both on and off the pitch." Remaining every bit as composed and measured in his address as one would expect from a former PM, Mr Major told everyone: "Ben had that most indefinable of gifts: he had charisma, and, partly for that reason, he has left his friends and admirers many memories. He had talent, languid grace and the physique of an athlete, humour, bearing, intellect and a gift for cricket and love for life. He gave the impression that no single moment of his playing day was to be wasted. Almost as if he knew that time was not to be unending. He left an imperishable mark. As with Archie Jackson and Collie Smith, we will always wonder what might have been."

After the service had ended with an address from the Reverend Andrew Wingfield-Digby - the former official chaplain to the England team - and further hymns, we all filed out slowly, stopping briefly at the rear of the cathedral, where the Hollioake family - Adam, his parents John and Daria, his sister Eboni, and his wife Sherryn, with baby daughter Bennaya - had formed a receiving line to thank people for their attendance. The sun was still shining brightly outside and, as everyone drifted away through the grounds of the cathedral, the bells pealed out joyously. It had been a very fitting tribute in so many ways and, though it was highly unlikely that any Surrey player or supporter had forgotten who and what this season was about, as an exercise in refocusing minds this emotionally-charged service could not have been surpassed.

## THE BEN HOLLIOAKE MEMORIAL SCHOLARSHIP

On the day of the service, it was announced that the *London Evening Standard* would be sponsoring a new scheme, called The Ben Hollioake Memorial Scholarship, which would benefit one promising young cricketer every season. Under the terms of the scholarship, the newspaper had agreed to finance the first professional contract of a top young player tipped by Surrey for future stardom, with James Benning later revealed as the first to benefit from the scheme. Chief Executive, Paul Sheldon, welcomed the setting up of the memorial scholarship, saying: "We think it is a fantastic idea and Ben's family have been especially moved by this initiative. They are thrilled and delighted that something so positive is being planned in Ben's memory." Adam Hollioake indeed gave the scheme a warm welcome in the newspaper by stating: "It's clearly a good idea, a really positive way to remember Ben. Every time anyone makes a kind gesture like this I really appreciate it. There have been hundreds of gestures, all as important as each other because they come from the heart. Anything that people want to do for Ben, or in Ben's name, is great. You don't expect people to be as kind as they have been. My faith in mankind has been restored to how it was when I was a child."

### C&G Trophy Quarter-Final - Hollioake's Powerful Tribute Sees Surrey Through

**Sussex v Surrey at Hove. Played on Wednesday 17th July.**
**Surrey won by 14 runs**

Just two days after paying an emotional tribute to his late brother in Southwark Cathedral, Adam Hollioake produced an almost superhuman performance on the field of play in the Cheltenham & Gloucester Trophy quarter-final at Hove. The Surrey captain's amazing unbeaten 117, containing eleven fours and five sixes, came from just 59 balls and propelled his team to an almost unassailable score of 337-3 as 142 runs flowed from the last thirteen overs of the innings.

Hollioake had arrived at the wicket with the total standing at 189 in the thirty-sixth over, and proceeded to play an innings that managed to overshadow a sublime knock of 107 from 103 balls by Mark Ramprakash that would have stolen the headlines on almost any other day. As the Sussex bowlers were splattered around the ground with increasing violence, a fairly average start, which saw Surrey reach 49-2 after ten overs as Robin Martin-Jenkins claimed both openers in the space of three overs, seemed light years away. With help from Rikki Clarke, who contributed a composed fifty-five, Ramprakash had then re-established control for Surrey while completing an excellent fifty from just 53 deliveries but, once Hollioake arrived at the crease and started creating havoc on his way to a 30-ball half-century, the former Middlesex batsman sensibly fed his skipper the strike with a series of singles. Having had a 76-run start on his partner, Ramprakash just managed to beat his partner to three figures, reaching the landmark from 98 deliveries in the forty-seventh over, while Hollioake blasted away to make the mark two overs later from his fifty-second ball. By the time the innings closed on 337-3, the unbroken fourth wicket partnership had realised a staggering 148 runs from a mere 87 balls.

After the events of the Glamorgan match in the previous round, there was no room for complacency as Surrey set out to defend their score on a good pitch, and this was especially true once Jimmy Ormond had been battered for six fours in his first two overs. With Richard Montgomerie firing his way to a 44-ball fifty, the home side got away to a racing start, before first Clarke and then Saqlain Mushtaq contributed good restraining spells to level up the contest. The loss of Chris Adams to Clarke before he could hit top gear was a major blow for Sussex and, though Montgomerie decelerated before being well taken by Alec Stewart standing up to Jason Ratcliffe, Murray Goodwin kept his team in the hunt through skilful placement of the ball on his way to a 43-ball half-century that contained just one six and two fours. When Matt Prior was run out for a busy thirty-four by a brilliant piece of fielding by Clarke, and Tony Cottey was cleaned up by a fine delivery from Hollioake later in the same over, it looked like Surrey were back in control, but Goodwin ensured that they could never relax as he upped the tempo to complete the third fine century of the match from 78 deliveries in the forty-eighth over. Despite the former Zimbabwe international's presence at the wicket, targets of 44 from four overs, 35 from three and 26 from two always looked just beyond Sussex, and the game was over as a contest once Saqlain had restricted the batsmen to just five runs from the penultimate over. Crucially, the Pakistani off-spinner didn't concede a single boundary in his ten-over spell, quite an achievement in a high-scoring match... though there was no question that Adam Hollioake was the deserved recipient of the Man Of The Match award.

### SUSSEX v SURREY at Hove
**Played on Wednesday 17th July**     **Surrey won by 14 runs**

Surrey won the toss and elected to bat     Umpires: - Barrie Leadbeater & John Steele

**SURREY**

| Fall of wkt | Batsman | How | Out | Score | Balls | 4s | 6s |
|---|---|---|---|---|---|---|---|
| 1-39 | I.J. Ward | c Prior | b Martin-Jenkins | 12 | 22 | 1 | 0 |
| 2-48 | A.D. Brown | c Adams | b Martin-Jenkins | 36 | 31 | 6 | 0 |
|  | M.R. Ramprakash | Not | Out | 107 | 103 | 8 | 1 |
| 3-189 | R. Clarke | c Montgomerie | b Yardy | 55 | 85 | 4 | 0 |
|  | A.J. Hollioake * | Not | Out | 117 | 59 | 11 | 5 |
|  | A.J. Stewart + | Did not bat |  |  |  |  |  |
|  | J.D. Ratcliffe | Did not bat |  |  |  |  |  |
|  | I.D.K. Salisbury | Did not bat |  |  |  |  |  |
|  | Saqlain Mushtaq | Did not bat |  |  |  |  |  |
|  | J. Ormond | Did not bat |  |  |  |  |  |
|  | E.S.H. Giddins | Did not bat |  |  |  |  |  |
|  | Extras | (5lb, 5w) |  | 10 |  |  |  |
|  | **TOTAL** | **(50 overs)** | **(for 3 wkts)** | **337** |  |  |  |

| Bowler | O | M | R | W | NB | Wd |
|---|---|---|---|---|---|---|
| Taylor | 10 | 1 | 59 | 0 | - | - |
| Martin-Jenkins | 10 | 1 | 65 | 2 | - | 3 |
| Yardy | 8 | 0 | 56 | 1 | - | 1 |
| Innes | 7 | 0 | 45 | 0 | - | 1 |
| Davis | 10 | 0 | 56 | 0 | - | - |
| Cottey | 3 | 0 | 23 | 0 | - | - |
| Goodwin | 2 | 0 | 28 | 0 | - | - |

**SUSSEX**

| Fall of wkt | Batsman | How | Out | Score | Balls | 4s | 6s |
|---|---|---|---|---|---|---|---|
| 3-174 | R.R. Montgomerie | c Stewart | b Ratcliffe | 88 | 93 | 12 | 0 |
| 1-55 | T.R. Ambrose | c Brown | b Clarke | 12 | 19 | 1 | 0 |
| 2-127 | C.J. Adams * | c Stewart | b Clarke | 33 | 39 | 4 | 0 |
| 4-238 | M.W. Goodwin | Not | Out | 110 | 86 | 8 | 1 |
|  | M.J. Prior + |  | run out | 34 | 31 | 3 | 0 |
| 5-240 | P.A. Cottey |  | b Hollioake | 1 | 2 | 0 | 0 |
| 6-275 | R.S.C. Martin-Jenkins |  | b Giddins | 15 | 17 | 1 | 0 |
| 7-311 | M.H. Yardy |  | b Hollioake | 10 | 12 | 0 | 0 |
| 8-316 | K.J. Innes | c Stewart | b Saqlain | 1 | 3 | 0 | 0 |
|  | M.J.G. Davis | Not | Out | 1 | 1 | 0 | 0 |
|  | B.V. Taylor | Did not bat |  |  |  |  |  |
|  | Extras | (1b, 1lb, 10w, 6nb) |  | 18 |  |  |  |
|  | **TOTAL** | **(50 overs)** | **(for 8 wkts)** | **323** |  |  |  |

| Bowler | O | M | R | W | NB | Wd |
|---|---|---|---|---|---|---|
| Giddins | 10 | 0 | 58 | 1 | - | 1 |
| Ormond | 7 | 0 | 61 | 0 | 1 | 2 |
| Clarke | 10 | 0 | 56 | 2 | 1 | 0 |
| Saqlain Mushtaq | 10 | 0 | 49 | 1 | 1 | - |
| Ratcliffe | 4 | 0 | 33 | 1 | - | 2 |
| Salisbury | 2 | 0 | 14 | 0 | - | - |
| Hollioake | 7 | 0 | 50 | 2 | - | - |

# 12 The Canterbury Tale

Only five days had passed since the Warwickshire defeat as Surrey prepared to take the field in their next Championship fixture against Kent at Canterbury, yet it felt longer because so much had happened in between. Apart from the Ben Hollioake Memorial Service and then the C&G Trophy victory at Hove, Graham Thorpe had been in the news, following his announcement that he was retiring from one-day international cricket with immediate effect. This decision certainly took everyone by surprise and, given that the turbulence of Thorpe's private life was reported to be affecting his concentration and thinking on the field of play, it was only natural to wonder whether or not it had been given sufficient consideration. It was to be hoped that this wasn't a knee-jerk reaction that the England stalwart would end up regretting.

At the same time, a Thorpe injury left Surrey facing a tricky decision. Since he had missed the last four games of the Nat West Series with a slight calf strain, the England hierarchy wanted Thorpe to play at Canterbury in order to get some match practice, thereby causing a selection problem for the Championship leaders. Although Alec Stewart (rested) and Alex Tudor (shin splints) were to miss the Kent match at England's behest, Mark Butcher had been promised a run-out ahead of the forthcoming first Test against India in order to test out the knee that had undergone surgery at the end of the Sri Lanka series. With Ian Ward, Mark Ramprakash, Alistair Brown and Adam Hollioake filling four of the other top five places in the order, the other spot simply had to go to Rikki Clarke - quite apart from being in excellent form, he was needed to balance the side, since Surrey were, understandably, not keen to go into the Kent game with just four frontline bowlers, including two spinners. Additionally, although nothing was confirmed, it was rumoured that Thorpe had requested to be rested from the C&G match at Hove, a fact that, if it were true, wouldn't have counted in his favour when it came to selection for Canterbury. With Surrey possessing such a strong squad it was always likely that this situation would arise one day, and now it had finally happened - England had been rebuffed and there was no place in the Surrey team for the man many people rated as the nation's best batsman. Although Keith Medlycott explained the reasoning behind the Club's entirely logical decision to the media, I don't suppose it went down well in England circles.

With so much going on, it couldn't have been easy for everyone to focus fully on the forthcoming match, though I suspected that the Warwickshire defeat wouldn't be preying on anyone's mind. It wouldn't be taking anything away from Michael Powell's team to say that the overall Surrey performance had been very good until they were mugged on the final afternoon, having been forced to chase a small total against the clock by the loss of more than seventy overs to numerous rain breaks earlier in the match.

A good result at Canterbury against one of the other Championship hopefuls would go a long way towards getting Surrey back on track, though history wasn't in their favour - they hadn't won at the St. Lawrence ground since 1989.

| FRIZZELL COUNTY CHAMPIONSHIP - MATCH NINE |
|---|

### KENT versus SURREY
at The St. Lawrence Ground, Canterbury

First Day - Friday 19th July

Kent 374; Surrey 20-1

***The Teams And The Toss*** - *Kent are able to select from a full-strength squad and make two changes from their previous match - a disappointing draw with Sussex at Hove in a match they really should have won - with James Hockley and James Golding replacing Matthew Walker and David Masters. There is no place in the Championship side for Matthew Fleming, despite* *the Kent one-day skipper's heroics in the C&G Trophy quarter-final against Gloucestershire earlier in the week. As expected, Surrey's only change from the Warwickshire match sees Mark Butcher returning to the side in place of Nadeem Shahid. On a glorious, sunny morning, with a crowd in excess of 2,000 inside the ground, Adam Hollioake calls incorrectly at the toss, allowing David Fulton to claim first use of what looks to be an excellent pitch for his Kent side.*

The match that a local newspaper has billed as 'Kent versus the old enemy' gets off to an action-packed start as David Fulton and Robert Key ride their luck to put early runs on the board. Surrey's opening bowlers enjoy contrasting fortunes, with Ed Giddins, much the steadier of the two, moving the ball both ways and causing the Kent captain several anxious moments, while Jimmy Ormond is rather wild and erratic, conceding runs freely, off both the middle and the outside edge of the bat. In his first three overs the big paceman yields an off-driven three and a square-driven four to Key, as well as an upper-cut boundary to Fulton, yet he also suffers great frustration as three edged strokes cost him a total of nine runs. His fourth over has little to commend it, however, as Fulton picks off two boundaries through backward point to force his Surrey counterpart's hand - Ormond is removed from the attack with figures of 4-0-34-0.

Rikki Clarke, Adam Hollioake's only viable alternative at this early stage of proceedings, therefore steps into the breach for the tenth over of the innings and very nearly makes the opening breakthrough straight away when Key, on fifteen at the time, badly mistimes a square cut, offering a low catch to gully which Ian Salisbury grasses. Since the vast majority of the forty-four runs scored to date have come behind square on the off-side it's no surprise that the chance has come in this region, though it is unexpected that Key, hitherto the more secure of the two batsmen, and Salisbury, a reliable catcher at gully all season, have been the men involved.

At the other end, Fulton, after a rather hit-and-miss start, is now beginning to bristle with confidence, pulling Clarke to the rope at midwicket to bring up the Kent fifty, while Key, suddenly the more vulnerable of the Kent openers, has a second lucky escape in Clarke's third over. Incredibly, it is again Salisbury at gully who puts down the catch, as another cut, admittedly well struck on this occasion, arrives at a good height but fails to stick in the hapless fielder's hands. The reprieved batsmen promptly rubs salt into Surrey's wounds by driving the next ball from the twice-unlucky bowler through extra cover for three to take his score up to twenty-one and the total to fifty-seven.

At this point, having contributed eight largely excellent overs in a top-class spell, Giddins gives way to Ormond at the Nackington Road end as the visitors desperately seek their first wicket. It is not through lack of trying on Clarke's part that they haven't already broken the opening partnership, of course, and an unlucky morning for the 20-year-old all-rounder soon becomes worse when Ali Brown, at first slip, grants Key his third life in the space of five Clarke overs by allowing a head-high chance to burst through his hands with the batsman on twenty-four and the total on sixty-two.

This is rapidly becoming Surrey's worst session of the summer so far, and matters don't improve in the course of the next few overs as the score lurches forward by nineteen runs, with Fulton's clip to the square leg boundary off Clarke taking him through to a 65-ball fifty and Key's push through midwicket off Ormond yielding an all-run four as Butcher, looking some way short of full fitness, chases very gingerly after the ball.

In an effort to get some sort of grip on the game, Hollioake subsequently introduces Saqlain Mushtaq in place of the desperately unlucky Clarke, though this has no immediate effect as Key, finally emerging from his sticky patch, advances down the pitch to drive straight for four in the off-spinner's second over, before whipping him through midwicket for another boundary in his third. The second stroke takes the opening partnership into three figures and, with Ormond at the end of a much-improved second spell of five overs, the Surrey skipper's options are now rather limited. The obvious move is to call up Ian Salisbury, especially since Saqlain has found

176

some early signs of turn, but Hollioake decides instead to bowl himself from the Nackington Road end. This doesn't prove to be a successful change, however, as Key, following up an on-driven boundary off Saqlain that completes his personal half-century from 90 balls, takes six runs from the Surrey captain's second over, including a neat deflection to the rope at third man.

Since lunch is now only twenty minutes away, the visitors look set to go through the session wicketless until careless errors by both opening batsmen bring sudden success for Saqlain and succour for Surrey as two wickets fall in the space of twelve balls.

Having made sixty-two in an opening stand of 121, the Kent captain is the first to depart when he dances down the track to the off-spinner and drives loosely to mid-on, where Clarke shows his team-mates how to take a catch, then Key's poor shot selection brings about his downfall in the bowler's next over. Despite the fact that Saqlain has six fielders on the leg-side and only two men in front of square on the off, he elects to shuffle across his stumps in order to work a straight delivery in the direction of midwicket and, consequently, gives umpire David Constant an easy decision to make when he fails to make contact. With the England Academy batsman gone for fifty-seven, and the total advanced by just one run since the loss of Fulton, Kent's advantage has been slightly eroded, though they still hold the whip hand as lunch arrives, thanks to Surrey's lacklustre display in the opening session of the match.

*Lunch:- Kent 123-2 (Smith 2\*, Symonds 0\*) from 34 overs*

Kent's third-wicket pairing of Ed Smith and Andrew Symonds make a positive start against Giddins and Saqlain after lunch, scoring fourteen from the first three overs, though Symonds' lofted on-drive off the spinner flies perilously close to the fielder at deepish mid-on, and Smith's aerial clip through square leg off Giddins briefly offers hope of a catch to the fieldsman in that position. Unfortunately for Surrey, both strokes are struck firmly enough to be safe for the batsman concerned, and Kent continue to turn up the heat on their visitors with a flurry of four boundaries from eight deliveries that sends the score racing past 150 in the fortieth over. Saqlain is not his normal accurate self as Smith whips him through midwicket for consecutive fours, while Giddins, looking much less impressive than he had done during the morning session, concedes square-cut and cover-driven boundaries to Symonds.

With the home side so clearly on top at this stage, Surrey are extremely grateful to be gifted another wicket with the run-out of Smith, for nineteen, just a few balls later. Although there is no denying the quality of Rikki Clarke's pick-up and direct-hit throw at the stumps at the striker's end, both batsmen are guilty of poor cricket, Symonds for seeking an unlikely run for his push into the covers, and Smith for a belated reaction to his partner's questionable call.

On this fine-looking pitch, which appears to have sufficient pace and bounce to offer something to everybody, Kent's 155-3 now looks to be little better than par for the course. As a result, Symonds, another square-cut boundary off Giddins excepted, reins himself in a little, while the new batsman, James Hockley, plays out a couple of maidens.

Hopes that Surrey have now got things under control are soon dashed, however, when Ormond returns at the Nackington Road end in place of his new-ball partner and is promptly driven high over cover for six by Symonds. This first-ball greeting is then followed by an extra-cover drive for four two balls later, and only a brilliant stop by Salisbury at backward point prevents the big paceman's comeback over from costing fourteen. Kent's Australian import then does further damage to the Surrey cause in the next over from Saqlain, not only by cutting the off-spinner twice for four but also by striking Hollioake a fearful blow at short leg with a full-blooded sweep. Nursing what appears to be a hand injury, the Surrey skipper leaves the field immediately, with the captaincy of the side passing to Mark Butcher.

The visitors' twelfth man, Nadeem Shahid, is then into the action straight away, almost in dramatic style, when Hockley slightly miscues a hook off Ormond and breathes a sigh of relief as the ball only narrowly evades the substitute fielder at long leg. This near miss seemingly triggers a short period of dominance for the ball over the bat, however, as Brown, at slip, correctly anticipates a late dab by Hockley off Saqlain and almost pulls off a great catch low to his right-hand side, while Ormond goes past Symonds' outside edge three times in an over.

Unfortunately for the visitors, their time on top is soon over, as a drive to deep cover for two by the Australian takes Kent to two-hundred, and a late cut for three by Hockley completes a fifty partnership for the fourth wicket. Then, just to underline the fact that the hosts are back in control, the erratic Ormond comes up with a truly woeful over, during which he loses his line completely. Having conceded four off-side byes with a wide, swinging delivery and then fired two balls way down the leg-side to gift Kent six wides and two further byes, the over ends with Symonds cutting another wide off-side delivery thunderously through the covers to complete a sparkling 58-ball half-century containing nine fours and a six.

Unsurprisingly, Ormond, rumoured to be carrying a knee injury, is immediately pulled from the attack and replaced by Salisbury, whose introduction, for the fifty-ninth over of the innings, seems to be long overdue. With Symonds in full flow and Hockley now established, it's not a great time for the leg-spinner to be starting his first spell and, consequently, indiscretions in length during his first two overs are fully punished by both batsmen, as the big Aussie cuts and drives to the rope at extra cover and then watches his partner pull a long-hop over wide long-on for six to take the score beyond 250.

The problems that are seemingly mounting up for Surrey's stand-in skipper are then exacerbated by his decision to replace Saqlain with Clarke at the pavilion end. Unable to reproduce the consistent line and length of his morning spell, the young all-rounder is mercilessly hammered for twenty-nine runs in two overs, conceding three sixes and a four in the process. Having started his first over with a long-hop that Symonds dispatches over deep midwicket for six to take the fourth-wicket partnership past a hundred, things go from bad to worse in his second over when Hockley twice pulls for six and then cover-drives for four, much to the delight of the typically partisan Canterbury crowd. This rash of boundaries rushes the Beckenham-born youngster's score on to forty-six, making it the highest of his Championship career, though he fails to complete a maiden half-century as he departs in the next over from Salisbury. Perhaps carried away by his success against Clarke, and the resulting surge of adrenaline, he charges recklessly at a nicely flighted leg-break and is comprehensively beaten on the outside edge and stumped, much to Surrey's relief and delight. Kent are very much on top in the game, however, at 285-4, though another wicket before tea would clearly give the visitors renewed hope for the final session of the day.

Inevitably, Saqlain makes a rapid return to the fray in place of poor Clarke, who has received some fearful stick from the more unpleasant elements in the crowd and must now be feeling even more disappointed about the catches that were missed off his bowling in the morning session. What's done is done, however, and Surrey now need to ensure that they don't allow the dangerous Symonds any extra lives as he moves close to a century with a variety of cuts and sweeps, two of which find the boundary off Saqlain to push the Kent total past three-hundred.

With the Australian scoring almost at will with his two favourite shots against the spinners, it is almost inevitable that he goes to three figures with a sequence of sweep-cut-sweep that garners three twos in Salisbury's sixth over. As the crowd rises to acknowledge an outstanding 94-ball innings containing thirteen fours and two sixes, it's obvious that Surrey desperately need to remove the Aussie before he can do any more damage. Hopes that he might 'give it away' now that he has completed his ton are quickly dashed, though, as Saqlain's next over yields a late-cut four and then a brace of sweeps to fine leg, for two and four runs respectively.

A welcome boost is just around the corner for the struggling visitors, however, as Paul Nixon, having looked rather uncomfortable against Salisbury right from the outset of his innings, finally receives a long-hop from the leg-spinner in the penultimate over before tea and obligingly hits it straight to Giddins at mid-on. All donations are gratefully received by Surrey, however, especially when they come at the end of a hard session that has seen Kent add 199 runs to their total, 112 of them coming from the bat of the flamboyant Symonds.

*Tea:- Kent 322-5 (Symonds 112\*, Ealham 0\*) from 72 overs*

Although Symonds starts the final session by sweeping Salisbury fine for two and then pulling him wide of mid-on for three, he is heading back to the pavilion three overs later, much to Surrey's relief, when he misses an ugly slog-sweep at Saqlain and has his off stump knocked back. While the Pakistani off-spinner and his colleagues celebrate the capture of this vital wicket, the big Aussie gets a well-deserved ovation as he leaves the field with 118 runs to his name out of a Kent total of 329-6.

Having made this breakthrough, the visitors now have a real opportunity to get back into the game, since the Kent lower-order has a rather frail and slightly inexperienced look about it. Mark Ealham, though not a great player of quality spin bowling, is clearly the most dangerous of the remaining batsmen, so when he edges a Salisbury leg-break to Batty in the next over the Surrey team are cock-a-hoop. There is a problem, however - the batsman doesn't walk and umpire Trevor Jesty doesn't raise his finger. Salisbury is clearly disappointed that Jesty hasn't detected a snick that has been obvious even from the top of the Woolley Stand, and Ealham lives to fight another day, adding insult to injury by cutting Saqlain to the boundary in the following over. If truth be told, neither the former England international nor his partner, James Golding, look especially comfortable against the Surrey spin twins, though they do dig in determinedly, with Golding twice breaking free, by pulling Saqlain for six and Salisbury for four, to take the total beyond 350. His confidence clearly boosted by these strokes, the young all-rounder then follows up by sweeping successive balls from the off-spinner to the boundary and this, in turn, seems to encourage Ealham to emerge from his shell in the next over. The first really aggressive gestures of an uncomfortable struggle for the former England man come when he, too, reels off consecutive fours - one with a top-edged cut to third man and the other with a sweep to backward square leg - though he is unable to sustain the assault and falls to the final ball of the over. With twelve, possibly crucial, overs having passed since Ealham survived the previous confident appeal for a catch behind the wicket, Salisbury again finds the outside edge of the bat with a leg-break and this time the decision goes in the bowler's favour as umpire Jesty sends the batsman on his way for eighteen at 371-7.

Having looked the more likely wicket-taker of the two spinners, Salisbury then gains further reward in his next over with another lovely piece of bowling, deceiving Min Patel through the air and defeating the batsman's drive with a googly that turns through the gate to pluck out the leg stump. With 285-3 having now become 373-8, the visitors' fightback continues apace, and the Surrey leg-spinner almost strikes again with his next ball as Amjad Khan pads up to a googly, provoking an impassioned appeal from the bowler and close fielders. Although umpire Jesty rules in favour of the batsman it matters little, except to the bowler, as Saqlain promptly mops up the home side's tail in the space of four balls in his next over - Khan walks across his stumps and is trapped on the crease by an off-break, then Martin Saggers is bowled three balls later when the ball dribbles back onto the stumps via his pads.

Kent's collapse is therefore complete, the last four wickets having fallen for three runs in eighteen deliveries, and the last seven wickets having added a meagre eighty-nine runs. With six of the home batsmen guilty of gifting their wicket to the opposition, Kent have to settle for a first innings total of 374, when something in excess of five-hundred had looked likely, and the Surrey spinners have emerged with a clean-sweep of the wickets, with the exception of the Ed Smith run out. Salisbury, the pick of the bowlers despite being inexplicably ignored for so long, finishes with 4-59, and Surrey are right back in the match as their openers emerge to face ten overs at the end of the day.

Once play gets under way, Ian Ward and Mark Butcher are both quickly off the mark with a well-struck boundary apiece, prompting David Fulton to confirm the view that there is already turn for the spinners by introducing Min Patel, in place of Martin Saggers, for the fifth over. Although the left-arm spinner reels off three straight maidens, it is Amjad Khan, building up a fair head of steam from the Nackington Road end, who provides Kent with a breakthrough three overs from the close when Ward, on seven, edges a good delivery leaving the bat and is taken behind the wicket by Paul Nixon. The visitors are 16-1.

As Salisbury enters the fray in his role as nightwatchman, the Surrey faithful, though disappointed by the loss of Ward, reflect that their team is still in a better position than they had been in mid-afternoon. That said, there is still much to be done with the bat in the morning.

*Close:- Surrey 20-1 (Butcher 5\*, Salisbury 2\*) from 10 overs*

## VIEWS FROM THE DRESSING ROOM

*It looked a good pitch, so I guess you therefore saw it as a bad toss to lose?*
**ADAM HOLLIOAKE** - Yes, I did - but then as soon as we started bowling we actually realised there was a bit more in the wicket than we had first thought. But I think we bowled very poorly at the beginning and almost put ourselves in a losing position in that first session.

*I thought Kent batted recklessly in their first innings and that they had the chance to bat us out of the game. Did we feel that we had rather got out of jail at the end of the first day?*
**ADAM HOLLIOAKE** - Pretty much so, yes, though I think our bowlers deserve credit for pressurising the batsman into playing like that. When you've got people around the bat and the batsman tries to take the aggressive option he can sometimes be made to look reckless.

*You seemed to enjoy bowling on this pitch. Did it offer you a little more help than previous pitches you had bowled on up until this stage of the season?*
**IAN SALISBURY** - This was an excellent cricket wicket, one of the best we played on all year because it had pace and bounce, and it turned enough for me and for Saqi - you could still play your shots on it, so it was a good batting deck, as we proved later on, but it offered something to the bowlers too. Quite a few of the wickets we played on during the season were really slow and low, and horrible to bowl on, whereas this one was good if you got the ball in the right areas.

### Second Day - Saturday 20th July

### Kent 374 and 174-6; Surrey 225

In contrast to the opening day, when glorious sunshine created almost perfect conditions for batting, rather more humid and overcast conditions prevail at the start of day two, suggesting that the seamers, rather than the batsmen and spinners, will be in a better position to hold sway. The overall weather situation is far better than the forecasters had predicted, however, so we are grateful that we have at least managed to avoid the rain that had been promised. There is still one dark cloud on Surrey's horizon, though, since it has been revealed that Adam Hollioake suffered a chipped index finger on his left hand when hit at short leg yesterday. Fortunately, it is said that the injury will not prevent him from batting.

This is just as well, since Surrey collapse disastrously after Mark Butcher takes six from Khan's second over of the day, dipping from 29-1 to 34-4 in the space of two overs. Although there's a degree of bad luck about the first two dismissals - Salisbury plays on to Saggers, while Ramprakash flicks fatally at the next ball down the legside and is adjudged caught behind - it is a fine delivery by Khan, lifting and leaving the bat, that sees off Rikki Clarke at the end of the following over. As Nixon celebrates his second catch in eleven balls Surrey are in real trouble, since they require 225 to avoid the follow-on, a mark which is still some 191 runs away.

Butcher, who has been watching the carnage from the other end, is joined by Ali Brown at the start of the fifth over of the morning, and the fifth-wicket pair launch a counter-attack, with the left-handed opener very much to the fore. Having driven Saggers to the rope backward of point, he twice forces Khan through mid-off, for three and then two, before cutting violently for four as the total rises rapidly towards fifty. Brown then takes Surrey to that milestone with an off-drive at Saggers' expense before Butcher continues his assault on Khan with successive boundaries, upper-cut over the slips and then driven straight down the ground. Alas, Butcher's aggressive approach then brings about his downfall when a loose drive at the fifth ball of the over results in a fast-flying edge, which Fulton does well to hang on to at first slip.

Although the Surrey captain is, as expected, able to bat despite his injured finger he is doubtless unhappy that he is having to make his appearance inside the first hour of the day with his side in real strife at 59-5, following Butcher's exit for thirty-four. It isn't an easy situation in which to start an innings, either, since Kent are buzzing, with both Saggers and Khan looking lively and producing some unplayable balls. Fortunately, there are also some loose deliveries on offer and, with the field settings predictably aggressive, Surrey continue to take advantage of the wide open spaces as Brown drives Saggers to the long-off boundary and Hollioake takes three fours off Khan - a steer to third man and two sumptuous cover drives - during his first full over at the crease. Although they are very concerned about their team's parlous position, the visiting supporters are happily enjoying this counter-blast from the exciting Surrey duo until Saggers produces a deadly yorker for Brown at the start of his next over. The batsman's stumps are left in total disarray, sadly reflecting the state of the visitors' innings, since they are now 77-6.

With just over twenty overs bowled at this point, we are witnessing some truly incredible cricket, and the loss of Brown certainly doesn't appear to inhibit Hollioake's strokeplay as he pulls Saggers high over long-on for six before the over is complete and then takes ten from the former Durham paceman's following over, courtesy of a thick-edged two and a pair of stunning drives, first back down the ground and then through extra cover.

In an attempt to put the brakes on the scoring rate, Fulton makes a double bowling change at this point, allowing Saggers and Khan to rest with three wickets apiece and introducing the medium-fast pair of Ealham and Golding. Although the new bowlers pose far fewer problems, they do indeed offer their captain greater accuracy and control, with the scoring rate dropping back accordingly. This is also partly as a result of Jon Batty playing himself in studiously and Hollioake struggling badly with a leg injury, which is clearly inhibiting his running between the wickets and causing him to turn down singles and twos that he would otherwise have taken on.

The period of relative calm, during which the visitors' hundred arrives, lasts for seven overs before a new Surrey storm blows up as Hollioake lofts Ealham over mid-off for four in the course of an over that yields twelve runs. Another surge in the scoring rate looks likely to be sustained when Batty collects the first boundary of his innings by clipping a half-volley to the rope at midwicket, but the bowler, Golding, has other ideas and gains revenge in his next over when the Surrey wicketkeeper completely mistimes a cut to provide Symonds with a simple catch at point. Having played himself in with great determination, it's a disappointing way for Batty to go, and it puts the visitors back in the mire at 126-7. Not that this fazes Hollioake, of course - he promptly hooks Ealham for six in the next over to complete a scintillating half-century from just 54 balls and carries on as if nothing had happened. Crisis? What crisis?!

With tea now beckoning, it would seem to be a good move to give the opening bowlers another short burst, especially since Saqlain Mushtaq has only just arrived at the wicket, but Fulton - heavily criticised for his captaincy in some quarters following Kent's failure to win from a dominant position in their last match, at Hove - opts to stick with his medium-pacers for a short while before turning to Patel and the part-time off-spin of Symonds for the closing overs of the session. This move certainly goes down well with his Surrey counterpart, as Hollioake instantly launches into Patel, sweeping the left-arm spinner's second ball for four, launching his third over wide long-on for six and then notching the fourth 'maximum' of his innings with a towering slog-sweep from the final ball of the over to take the visitors' total beyond 150.

After a maiden from Symonds to Saqlain, the pair enjoying a reversal of roles following their lengthy first-day battle, Patel switches to his over-the-wicket mode, conceding a leg-side wide for negative bowling in the process, as the session draws to a close. Although Surrey are still in real trouble, Hollioake has at least given his side a glimmer of hope as he leaves the field to applause from a far smaller crowd than had been in attendance on day one. Those who have stayed away today might well be regretting it, as they have already missed some terrific action.

*Lunch:- Surrey 157-7 (Hollioake 72\*, Saqlain 3\*) from 40 overs*

With Saggers and Khan restored to the attack immediately after lunch in increasingly fine weather, the first two overs are maidens, though it's not long before Hollioake is off the leash again, flashing two square drives to the boundary in the third over, bowled by Khan. On both occasions the shot is somewhat uncontrolled and the ball flies through the air within a couple of yards of Symonds at backward point, yet it is travelling at such speed that the Australian has no hope of intercepting it and the fielder at square third man is equally powerless to pull off a stop.

The Surrey skipper desperately needs support from the other end if he is to take his team past the follow-on target, so the loss of Saqlain in the next over, with fifty-six still needed, is a real blow. No blame can be laid at the Pakistani's door, though, since he is beaten by a superb late outswinger from Saggers that beats his defensive stroke and sends his off stump cartwheeling.

Despite having seen the Kent swing bowler produce a delivery that would have been good enough for far better batsmen than Saqlain, Hollioake remains calm and, after Jimmy Ormond takes a leg-bye from his first delivery, the visiting captain pulls the following ball from Saggers for six over midwicket. Incredible! Although Ormond then joins in with a lofted drive to the extra-cover boundary off Khan, his success is only fleeting, since a wild swish at the next ball, of slightly fuller length, results in his off stump going the same way as Saqlain's. At 184-9, Surrey still trail by 190 and, with only Ed Giddins for company, Hollioake will now have to produce something very special if his side is to avoid the possibility of being asked to bat again.

As Saggers starts the next over, the field for the Surrey skipper consists of two slips and seven men on the boundary! It sounds bizarre but, given the way Hollioake has been playing, the fact that he is unable to run any twos because of his leg injury, and the presence of a 'rabbit' at the other end, it is actually quite logical. Consequently, the Kent opening bowler manages to complete a maiden over, leaving Giddins to face the next over from Khan.

This is clearly bad news for the visitors, but, even though the Danish paceman manages to produce a good straight over, bar a wayward first ball that yields four leg-byes, the Surrey number eleven manages to survive, much to the relief of his skipper and the team's supporters.

It would appear that Hollioake doesn't want to put everyone through this sort of tension for the next half-hour or so, however, as he decides to get on with the job of reaching the follow-on mark as quickly as possible by launching a furious attack on Saggers in the next over. The former Durham bowler's maiden over is followed by one costing him twenty-two runs as the Surrey skipper rushes to a 95-ball century, his first in the County Championship since September 1999 (116 v Middlesex at Lord's, forty-nine innings ago), with a calculated assault that also takes the total beyond two-hundred. Having started the over with two drives for four, one either side of long-on, Hollioake is then forced to dig out a testing yorker before he squeezes a similar delivery just past his leg stump to the fine-leg boundary to reach three figures. He raises his arms aloft to celebrate his achievement, acknowledges the crowd's applause for a quite remarkable display of hitting, and then completes the over by lifting the suffering Saggers high over long-on for six and then carving him over backward point for four.

With the score having rapidly advanced to 212, thirteen runs are now required by Surrey, though Giddins has been left to face Khan. Luckily, that situation only lasts for one ball, as the former Sussex and Warwickshire bowler pushes to square cover for a single, putting his captain back on strike. With five balls remaining, who would bet against Hollioake completing his mission before the over is out? When he drives the first of those deliveries over backward point for four and then upper-cuts the second for six, the ball flying just over the head of the fielder at third man, all bets are off, though Khan responds well with two 'dot' balls, the second of which produces a bottom-edge that narrowly misses the off stump as it bounces through to Nixon. One ball left, two runs required, and the delivery is entirely predictable - it's either going to be fired well down the leg-side or it will be a high bouncer, in order to leave Giddins facing Saggers. Khan opts for the latter but overdoes it, producing a bouncer that flies so far over Hollioake's head that umpire Jesty calls it as a no-ball, thereby taking Surrey through to the magical figure of 225. The possibility of having to follow-on is therefore avoided, but the visitors get no closer to Kent's total, as Saggers has Giddins taken low at second slip by Symonds in the next over to complete a five-wicket haul and ensure that the clean sweep of wickets to spin in the first innings of the match is followed by a full-house for seam in the second.

Although swing had been favoured by conditions at the start of today's play, the sun is, however, shining brightly as Hollioake leaves the field, unbeaten on 122, to a very well-deserved ovation for a quite sensational innings that has been similar in style to his century at Hove in the C&G quarter-final. He has faced just 103 balls and hit fourteen fours and seven sixes during another knock that will be remembered for many years by those who have witnessed it.

Unsurprisingly, given his injuries, Hollioake doesn't reappear with his team ten minutes later as Kent commence their second innings with a very healthy lead of 149.

That advantage is soon dramatically increased, however, as Fulton gets away to a flyer by taking ten from an opening over by Ormond that includes two no-balls and costs a total of fifteen runs. Given the former Leicestershire man's inauspicious start, it's just as well for Surrey that Giddins is immediately on the spot, bringing the Kent skipper to book in the fifth over, courtesy of an edged drive to Batty, before almost bowling Ed Smith first ball with a fine delivery that nips back through the gate. Smith fails to profit greatly from this slice of good fortune, however, as his attempted pull at the rapidly improving Ormond, with his score on six and the total standing at thirty-three, results in a horrible miscue to Ramprakash at mid-on three overs later. With the batsmen having crossed, Ormond then completes an outstanding over by beating Key three times outside the off stump and having him missed by Batty, low to his right in front of first slip, when he finally finds the edge. The Kent opener, on eight at the time, is enjoying one of the luckiest games of his career, since he has now survived a total of four catching chances.

From a Surrey point of view, these catches simply have to be taken if they are to get back into the game. It is clear that they will also need to remove Andrew Symonds quickly, since the Aussie import immediately continues his fine form of the first innings by driving Giddins through the covers for two boundaries during his first over at the crease and takes the Kent total through to fifty in the twelfth over.

With twelve runs coming from Rikki Clarke's first over after he replaces Giddins at the Nackington Road end, and Ormond conceding two boundaries to Symonds in the last two overs of his best spell of the match to date, runs continue to flow far too freely for Surrey's liking, however, and as the fifty partnership for the third wicket comes up inside eleven overs it appears that the visitors' brief fightback is at an end. This seems to be confirmed when Saqlain's extremely disappointing first over as Ormond's replacement at the pavilion end yields twelve runs, including a drive to the rope at extra cover by Symonds and a straight-driven boundary by Key from a full-toss. Consequently, the Kent hundred arrives in just the twenty-first over, courtesy of Key's cut for four over backward point off Clarke, and all is doom and gloom in the Surrey camp as the possibility of the county suffering back-to-back Championship defeats for the first time since September 1997 grows stronger by the minute.

Learning from the lessons of the first innings, Mark Butcher then turns to his leg-spinner for the twenty-third over, a move that instantly brings forth two trademark Symonds sweeps for two, though no breakthrough seems to be forthcoming as Saqlain is milked for singles with disturbing ease. Almost unnoticed, since he has only struck half-a-dozen fours, Symonds completes his second excellent half-century of the match, from just 52 balls, as tea approaches, and the game already looks to be drifting out of Surrey's reach as Kent's lead extends well beyond 250. The visitors desperately need to split the third-wicket pair and, finally, in the penultimate over of the session, they do so, courtesy of the previously ineffective Saqlain. Since Symonds is the man dismissed, when he advances on the off-spinner and sees an inside edge onto his pad well snapped up by Ian Ward diving in from short leg, there is added delight for Surrey, and they go to tea with spirits slightly raised, despite their apparently dire position in the match.

*Tea:- Kent 135-3 (Key 45\*, Hockley 4\*) from 29 overs*

With Kent effectively 284-3 at the start of the final session, it's really a case of now or never for Surrey, since any total in excess of 350 will surely be unattainable in the final innings, even on a pitch as good as this one.

The visitors' highly experienced spin twins respond well to this pressure, however, striking three quick blows within six overs of the restart as Kent slump dramatically from 142-3 to 145-6. After clubbing Salisbury over extra cover for four, Hockley is the first to go, very well taken by Ward at short leg from a firm push off the meat of the bat, then Paul Nixon, so often a thorn in Surrey's side, departs in high dudgeon in the next over, following another controversial decision by Trevor Jesty. The Kent keeper clearly doesn't agree with the umpire's view that he has gloved the attempted sweep at Saqlain which Batty collects behind the stumps - and he might well have a case, too - but he has to go, and he is then followed back to the pavilion just six balls later by Mark Ealham. Fortunately, there is no room for doubt with this dismissal, as the former England all-rounder hits over the top of a well flighted delivery of full-length from Salisbury and loses both middle and leg stumps in sensational style.

It is just as well for Kent that Key has remained steadfast throughout this fraught period for his side and, in making his way to a highly valuable, if unspectacular, half-century from 96 balls in the midst of the middle-order capitulation, he has played the spinners with a greater degree of confidence that most.

Surrey are sensing an opportunity to retrieve a seemingly lost cause now, though, and, with their spirits revitalised, the spinners test Key and his new partner, James Golding, as the skies start to cloud over late in the day. With Saqlain and Salisbury giving nothing away, the batsmen are restricted to the occasional single for half-a-dozen overs, but the tide gradually turns and they appear to have weathered the Surrey storm with a boundary apiece when the rain that had been promised for earlier in the day arrives to drive the players from the field with the score at 172-6.

This stoppage lasts for twenty-three minutes, causing six overs to be deducted from the day's quota, before play recommences at 6.30pm with Surrey keen to pick up further wickets in the remaining ten overs. They seem to have snatched one when Golding appears to edge Salisbury to Batty in a superb second over after the restart, during which the leg-spinner beats the bat three times, but umpire Constant remains unmoved, and this turns out to be the last significant action of the day, since the rain returns with a vengeance during the next over from Saqlain.

With the players unable to return to the middle, Kent are very well placed at the halfway stage of the match and it would appear that Surrey's comeback will be a case of too little, too late, since the weather forecast for the next two days, if correct, suggests that there is no chance of any more rain coming to their rescue.

*Close:- Kent 174-6 (Key 63\*, Golding 12\*) from 45.1 overs*

## ADAM HOLLIOAKE'S 122 NOT OUT AGAINST KENT
Original run chart as compiled by Keith Seward

KENT V SURREY,      CANTERBURY      20-7-02

A. HOLLIOAKE                             NOT OUT    122
RHB

11·40 – (2·45)        145 mins       50 in 75 mins   54 balls
                      103 balls       100 in 134 mins   95 balls

4 4 4 6 2 2 4 4 1 2 111 4 2 2 2 6 111 4 6 6 1 4 1 4 11 6 1 4 4 4 6 4 4 6

## VIEWS FROM THE DRESSING ROOM

*I believe you batted throughout this game with a cracked finger. How did the injury come about and how much did it inconvenience you?*
**ADAM HOLLIOAKE** - I got hit while fielding at short leg, a pretty innocuous sort of hit on the end of the finger. I went to have an X-ray and found it was cracked through the joint - though I don't really know why I bothered going for the X-ray because it was never going to make any difference to me, I was still going to bat. It wasn't too much of an inconvenience to me anyway - a few pain-killers and I was away.

*Judging by your running between the wickets, you were also struggling with a leg injury?*
**ADAM HOLLIOAKE** - Yes, I was only in at short leg for about an over and I got a broken finger and then belted by one that just missed the pad and hit me on the side of the kneecap. My leg just stiffened up as a result of that, and it was definitely more of a hindrance than the finger.

*We only just saved the follow-on thanks to Khan's no-ball. If it hadn't been for that, do you think Kent would have invited us to bat again or not?*
**ADAM HOLLIOAKE** - I think they were quite relieved when he bowled the no-ball, actually, because it meant they didn't have to make the decision about whether or not to put us back in.

*There was a story in the papers about one of your sixes striking an elderly lady in a wheelchair. Were you aware of what had happened at the time? I gather that you 'made amends' for the accident by signing the ball and presenting it to her.*
**ADAM HOLLIOAKE** - I didn't realise straight away, but then I noticed there was a lot of commotion down there and saw that the lady had been hit, which was a bit upsetting. I was very surprised that more spectators didn't get hurt during the match, actually, because I did say before the game started that I was a bit concerned about the short boundary on that side and how close the spectators were, considering that it was a quick pitch. On slow pitches, the ball doesn't get hit as hard, but on a fast pitch like that one the ball was frequently getting flayed square of the wicket. Luckily, the lady concerned wasn't too badly hurt and it was nice to be able to sign the ball and present it to her later.

*The two first innings were rather unusual in that all their wickets fell to spinners while all ours went to seamers. Do you have any ideas as to why that happened?*
**IAN SALISBURY** - It can certainly happen the other way round, of course, but I think what happened here was that suddenly on the second day it was really overcast, which helped the seamers... so conditions had changed from favouring spin on the first day, when it was warm, to favouring seam. Kent bowled well with the new ball on the second morning and with the overcast conditions and pace and bounce in the pitch they were a handful, until the captain came in and smashed the ball everywhere. It was similar to the game against Lancashire at The Oval, where it was sunny on the first day and I got wickets but in the second innings it was really overcast and Azhar Mahmood got eight wickets because the ball swung - the weather can have a big influence on events.

*You looked particularly delighted to remove Mark Ealham in the second innings - was that joy related to a moment in the first innings when he survived an appeal for what looked a very clear catch at the wicket?!*
**IAN SALISBURY** - Yes, it was - he nicked that ball and he knew he'd nicked it, but the umpire seemingly didn't hear it. And then I also should have had Golding out when he nicked one, too. I didn't think I was very lucky with umpiring decisions in 2001, but this year seemed to be even worse.

### Third Day - Sunday 21st July
### Kent 374 and 260; Surrey 225 and 264-7

Effectively 333-6 at the start of day three, Kent are firmly in control as play gets under way with Saqlain completing his unfinished over to Golding, who drives the off-spinner's second ball through the covers for three.

Perhaps encouraged by the overcast conditions that prevail, Mark Butcher immediately opts for seam over spin, pairing Ed Giddins and Jimmy Ormond in the early stages of the morning with a fair degree of success. For the first time in the match, both Surrey opening bowlers look to be firing together and, as a result, the Kent batsmen find the going tough, with Golding edging

Giddins just wide of a diving second slip to pick up four fortunate runs and Ormond drawing first blood of the day, ending Key's vigil with a perfect outswinger that the 23-year-old edges to Batty with the score advanced to 189 and his personal contribution sixty-eight. As the Kent opener departs for the pavilion after a tenacious and disciplined effort that has again suggested he isn't England material just yet, Surrey will doubtless be ruing the four missed chances that have cost them an aggregate of 102 runs in the match, Key having been first dropped on fifteen in the first innings and eight in the second. Never has the saying 'catches win matches' looked truer than it does at this moment in time, with the visitors already facing a task of Everest proportions in the final innings.

The Surrey seamers are still striving to give their side the easiest possible route to that peak, however, by lopping off the tail as quickly as they can, and, a Patel cover drive for four off Giddins apart, the eighth-wicket pair are put under sustained pressure. Ormond, having improved throughout the match with almost every spell, has no luck at all during two successive maidens at Golding, passing the outside edge on no fewer than six occasions, though Giddins has better luck when the young Kent all-rounder hits across the line of a good delivery a few overs later and departs lbw with the total having just passed two-hundred.

Since their lead is now 352, the hosts are still holding all the aces, though, despite the efforts of the Surrey pacemen this morning, and the next few overs see their hold on the game further strengthened as Patel and Amjad Khan each pick off a boundary and a two with a series of bold strokes through the leg-side. Although Giddins is unlucky when Patel miscues a pick-up just short of Ormond at long-leg, it's clear that the seamers have given their all and that Butcher now has to turn back to his spinners.

The young Danish fast bowler immediately appears far less confident against Salisbury and Saqlain, though Patel is happy enough as he peppers the boundary boards at wide long-on - with a slog-sweep, a drive and a pull - over the course of the next few overs to send the total soaring past 250. Every run is now like a dagger to the heart for Surrey and their supporters, and when Khan drives to midwicket for a single to complete a highly valuable fifty partnership for the ninth wicket Kent look to be in an almost impregnable position. It seems almost irrelevant, in fact, when the Dane misses a sweep at Salisbury and falls leg-before in the following over, and when Nadeem Shahid, Surrey's substitute fielder for Adam Hollioake, fumbles a sharp chance offered by Martin Saggers to silly point in Saqlain's following over, with the total at 256 and the lead 405, it appears to be an insignificant miss.

Although the Pakistani spin king does finally get his man - lbw, when only half-forward to an off-break - four overs and four singles later, the visitors' target of 410 to win seems largely academic. After all, the county record fourth-innings winning total stands at 354-9 (versus Gloucestershire at Gloucester in 1994), so what chance is there of surpassing that by a massive fifty-six runs? Patel's unbeaten forty-three definitely looks to have put the game beyond the reach of the Championship leaders, despite an impressive effort by all of their bowlers this morning, and, whatever else happens, one thing is certain - with the skies clearing and a good forecast for tomorrow, we are going to get a positive result, even though it looks highly likely to be a Kent win, since there are a minimum of 170 overs still to bowled in the match.

The 'chase' starts for Surrey with four tricky overs before lunch, and the openers survive in relative comfort, with the only incident of note being an official warning from umpire Constant to Amjad Khan for running on the pitch in his follow-through when he comes round the wicket to Mark Butcher in the final over of the morning.

*Lunch:- Surrey 6-0 (Butcher 6\*, Ward 0\*) from 4 overs*

The afternoon session almost starts in the most dramatic fashion when Butcher edges the first ball, from Saggers, to Symonds at second slip and escapes as the big Queenslander spills a low, but very acceptable, chance. It is to be hoped that the England opener will take advantage of this miss in the same way that Robert Key rode his luck in both Kent innings.

At the other end, Ian Ward opens his account in the sixth over of the innings by taking successive boundaries off Khan, with a square-cut followed by a nicely timed off-drive, and it is very much to Surrey's advantage that the Kent opening bowlers appear much less threatening than in the first innings, probably because conditions are now more suited to batting than they had been yesterday morning. Consequently, any bad balls are more likely to be punished and, as the batsmen become more established at the wicket, the scoring rate duly increases, thanks largely to a purple patch by Ward, who takes three boundaries off Saggers, one through square-leg and two through the covers, in the space of two overs.

With Khan having meanwhile conceded a brace of cover-driven threes in his sixth over, Min Patel, captaining Kent in the absence of David Fulton - who, like his Surrey counterpart, is nursing a damaged finger - opts for a change... though it is an unexpected one. Rather than utilise either of his frontline medium-fast bowlers, Ealham or Golding, he throws the ball to Andrew Symonds and asks him to bowl his seamers, a move which is immediately appreciated by Surrey as a Butcher cover-drive for three and a Ward off-drive to the boundary take the opening partnership to fifty-two at the end of the fourteenth over.

Sadly for the visitors, this very promising stand goes no further, as Saggers makes a double breakthrough by taking wickets in his eighth and ninth overs, dislodging Butcher for twenty and Ramprakash for two, courtesy of catches behind the wicket. The left-handed opener's rather firm-footed slash results in a stinging throat-high catch to second slip, which Symonds holds with great aplomb, while Ramprakash is unfortunate to receive a fine outswinger that brushes the outside edge of the bat on its way through to Paul Nixon. A score of 52-0, which had permitted vague dreams of an unlikely Surrey victory, has suddenly become 54-2 and brought the visitors back to reality with a nasty bump.

Despite having taken two wickets in ten balls, Saggers is rested immediately and replaced by Mark Ealham at the pavilion end. One assumes that the bowler has requested the break after a tiring nine-over spell, though it is still a slightly surprising development. As it happens, Ealham slips straight into a decent line and length and, with Symonds having settled into a rhythm and Surrey in need of some retrenchment, the run-flow almost inevitably dries up for a few overs.

While Ward is looking nicely in control, and breaks the run-drought with a trademark on-drive for four off Symonds in the twenty-second over, Rikki Clarke has a few uncertain moments early in his innings, including a top-edged hook off Ealham that just clears the head of the fielder at long-leg to register a six. The cool-headed youngster doesn't let this bother him, however, and there can be no doubting his composure in the next over from Symonds as he adds seven to his score, with a pull for three following a good-looking off-drive to the boundary. An extra-cover drive for three by Ward later in the same over brings the Symonds experiment to a close after six largely unimpressive overs, though the left-handed opener seems to be equally at home against the more experienced Ealham, as he drives and pulls boundaries in successive overs from the Kent all-rounder to complete an excellent half-century from 80 balls. Clarke, meanwhile, feasts on some loose deliveries from the newly introduced James Golding, twice driving him to the rope at long-on to raise the visitors' hundred and then the fifty partnership for the third wicket. Regular Surrey watchers have already noted that Clarke is an especially good exponent of the on-drive, and Kent's bowlers soon begin to appreciate this, too, as the tall all-rounder reels off two more glorious examples of the stroke when Min Patel enters the attack in place of Ealham, and yet another in the following over from Golding.

By taking full toll of most of the poor balls they are receiving, Ward and Clarke are making the home attack look completely innocuous in the afternoon sunshine, forcing Patel into recalling Khan at the Nackington Road end in the hope that the Dane's slippery pace might provide him with a breakthrough. It seems a sensible idea, though the young paceman is not allowed to settle as Ward pulls his first delivery for four and then on-drives another boundary in an opening over that costs ten. When Clarke then drives Patel to the rope at wide long-on to complete a fine fifty, scored at exactly a run a ball, and Ward follows up by taking three from an extra-cover drive off Khan, Kent are looking to be desperately short of inspiration, though Surrey are quickly reminded of the huge task that still lies ahead of them when Clarke has a lucky escape in top-edging a pull at the Danish speedster over the slips for four.

It has clearly been Surrey's session, however, as Ward takes his side up to the 150 mark in the run-up to tea, before twice cutting Symonds to the rope at point when the Aussie returns in off-spin mode to bowl the last over before the break.

*Tea:- Surrey 158-2 (Ward 78\*, Clarke 55\*) from 42 overs*

Upon the resumption, Patel opts to use Saggers and Symonds, continuing in his guise as an off-spinner, as his first pair of bowlers and, with both men largely on the spot, just eleven runs come from the opening seven overs of the day's final session.

Clarke is the man who eventually breaks the shackles by advancing on Symonds and launching him high over mid-on for four but, in attempting something similar from the final ball of the over, he doesn't quite get to the pitch and pops up a catch that Hockley pouches safely as he moves round from midwicket towards wide mid-on. It's a disappointing end to a fine innings of sixty-six with the total at 177, and rising hopes of the Championship leaders pulling off something spectacular are again suppressed. Worse is to follow, too, as the grey clouds that have been gradually gathering over the ground also begin to gather metaphorically for Surrey.

After Ward glances Saggers to the fine-leg boundary in the over following Clarke's dismissal, Symonds claims his second wicket in the space of three balls when Ali Brown, pushing forward to an off-break, is adjudged by umpire Constant to be caught at slip when the balls loops gently into the air off what would appear to be nothing but his pad. Brown is clearly unhappy with the verdict, standing his ground in disbelief for what seems like an eternity - though it is probably only a few seconds in reality - before making his way from the field for what the scorebook will record as a second-ball duck. This decision is certainly not the first to leave a batsman highly disgruntled during the match, and it deals a huge blow to the visitors' admittedly very faint hopes of victory, with much now depending on Ward and the new batsman, Adam Hollioake, who makes his way out to the middle in persistent drizzle.

If the Surrey captain can reproduce his pyrotechnics of the first innings then anything is still possible, of course, and the early signs are good as a late-cut boundary at Symonds' expense is followed by a short-arm pull off Saggers that brings a second four shortly afterwards. Unfortunately for the visitors, though, a violent drive at the final ball of the former Durham bowler's over results in nothing more than a loud and clear snick to Nixon behind the wicket, ending Hollioake's run of four consecutive half-centuries in Championship cricket since his return to England and, with it, surely, his team's outside chances of winning this match. There would seem to be no way back from 190-5, especially as the feeling that luck isn't running Surrey's way is confirmed by the umpires' decision that the rain is too heavy for play to continue even before Hollioake has reached the pavilion.

The break in play lasts for nine minutes, with the loss of two overs, though it doesn't seem to disrupt Kent's surge towards victory as Jon Batty falls to the third ball after the restart, tamely poking the first ball he receives to Robert Key at short leg off Symonds. With the strapping Queenslander proving to be a surprise trump card, and Surrey reduced to a desperate 191-6 following the loss of four wickets for fourteen runs, the home side are understandably overjoyed and a three-day victory now looks a strong possibility for them.

One can only wonder what has been going through Ian Ward's mind as he has watched his team-mates come and go at the other end, but, whatever it is, it doesn't seem to affect his concentration as he moves to within three runs of a century, and takes his team's total to two-hundred, by cutting Symonds through point for four in the versatile Australian's next over.

With Saggers continuing a good spell from the pavilion end and Ian Salisbury digging in to support his team-mate, the scoreboard almost grinds to a halt over the course of the next few overs, though Ward does manage to pick off a couple of singles to deep cover as he advances his personal tally to ninety-nine.

Eventually, with his opening bowler having delivered ten successive overs since tea, broken only by the rain interruption, Patel brings Saggers' spell to a close and recalls Ealham in an attempt to split the seventh-wicket pair. And what an inspired decision it turns out to be, since the Kent all-rounder takes just five deliveries to wreak an appropriate revenge on Salisbury and push Surrey another step closer to defeat. Having had his stumps dramatically demolished by Salisbury during Kent's second innings collapse, Ealham is elated when the leg-spinner plays slightly inside the line of an outswinger that rips both off and middle stumps out of the ground. At 208-7, with a notional 202 runs still required for victory and Surrey's tail markedly weaker than usual, owing to the absence of Martin Bicknell and Alex Tudor, the game is well and truly up. There are surely only two relevant questions now - can Ian Ward, already stuck on ninety-nine for fourteen deliveries, complete his hundred, and will the match be over tonight?

For four overs we come no closer to knowing the answer to either question as the game enters a period of almost total stalemate - although Saqlain eventually gets off the mark with a steer through backward point for two, Ward plays out two successive maidens from Symonds and extends his time on ninety-nine to twenty-eight balls. A lot of the tension might have gone out of the match, following the visitors' rapid slide towards defeat, but at least the Surrey opener is managing to keep everyone on the edge of their seats! Finally, however, after thirty-two balls and thirty-four minutes on the brink, a sweep to the square leg boundary off Symonds takes Ward through to a very fine century from 208 balls, his study in concentration having contained sixteen fours and been the perfect anchoring innings for an assault on victory, if only one or two of the other batsmen, in addition to Rikki Clarke, could have stayed with him for longer.

With just four overs now remaining until the close of play, Kent's attempt to press for victory tonight, or even claim the extra half-hour, looks to be faltering somewhat, so Patel brings back Khan at the Nackington Road end in an attempt to blast out the last three wickets. The batsmen are not to be budged, though, and as Ward picks up a single from the final scheduled ball of the day to take the Surrey score to 223-7 most spectators are expecting the match to continue to its conclusion tomorrow. Umpire Constant indeed removes the bails at the bowler's end and is about to depart for the pavilion when Patel obviously indicates that he wishes to claim the extra half-an-hour (or minimum of eight overs), causing the umpires to enter into a discussion. Given that nine overs have passed since the last wicket fell, it seems rather optimistic for Patel to expect eight more to be sufficient to finish the job off, and it is highly debatable as to whether Kent should even be allowed to *ask* for the extra time, let alone be granted it.

After some debate, the umpires eventually decide to let play continue for the additional thirty-minute period, with Saggers recalled to the attack to link up with Khan after an initial maiden from Ealham. Having greeted the former Durham swing bowler's return with a crunching cover drive for four, Saqlain is then subjected to a fiery assault by Khan during a quite remarkable over. Having been struck a nasty blow on the upper arm, and then watched another wild short delivery hum past Nixon for four byes, the Pakistani sashays down the wicket and swings manically at the next ball, sending it flying to the rope at long-stop via the top edge of his bat and the tips of the leaping Kent keeper's gloves. The over extends to eight deliveries as a couple of no-balls follow, but the important thing for Surrey is that Saqlain survives with both wicket and body intact...and the twelve runs that have come their way might be useful should some sort of miracle partnership develop tomorrow.

With Khan's far from subtle approach having failed to produce the desired result, and Saggers having had no joy in his next over, Kent have now used up five of their extra overs, prompting Patel to have a go himself, though with no greater success, as Ward cuts for two and four to advance Surrey's total beyond 250.

Since just two overs now remain to be bowled, and Kent look likely to be thwarted tonight, everyone expects Saqlain to quietly play out Saggers' penultimate over of the day. How wrong can you be?! Always one for the unorthodox approach, the Pakistani off-spinner advances down the track and lifts an outswinger high over extra cover for three runs, then, when put back on strike by Ward's single to deep cover which completes a battling fifty partnership, he repeats the move and the stroke, this time middling the ball for a mighty six over the extra cover boundary. Amazing stuff.

Ward very sensibly decides not to compete with his partner and plays out a maiden over from Patel to end another magnificent day's cricket with the visitors on 264-7, thanks to the addition of forty-one runs from the eight overs bowled in the extra half-hour period. Ward has played immaculately, and the late fightback with Saqlain has been entirely admirable, yet the Surrey faithful still hold out little hope for tomorrow, especially since the Kent bowlers will be fresh, and able to claim a potentially decisive new ball after just ten overs.

*Close:- Surrey 264-7 (Ward 115\*, Saqlain 31\*) from 80 overs*

## VIEWS FROM THE DRESSING ROOM

*How did you rate our chances of making 410 to win?*
**IAN SALISBURY** - If you look at our batting line-up, we have to be confident, and it's just a Surrey mentality to believe that we will win from almost any position. To the outsider it might just seem like bravado, but we are very confident of winning, even when chasing 410. We just said to ourselves that we must see off the new ball because we knew that their bowlers would be very good early on when the ball is new and hard and swings. After that, without wanting to sound condescending, we were confident that their spinners were not going to bowl us out and their other bowlers were pretty much of a muchness, needing the ball to be moving around in order to bowl us out. When you also remembered that we'd managed to score more than 410 in a one-day game, you started to realise that if any team could do it then this team could... though I didn't expect things to work out as they did!

*Did we have any plan formulated as we set out to chase 410?*
**ADAM HOLLIOAKE** - We said we'd try and get our heads down and get off to good start and then take it from there. Not much of a plan, I know, but the plan was really not to give up hope. I remember saying that all it would take was two good partnerships, and we reminded the boys how many times we'd scored four-hundred as a team in our careers, and that this shouldn't be viewed any differently just because it was the fourth innings, especially as the wicket was pretty much at its best.

### Fourth Day - Monday 22nd July

### Kent 374 and 260; Surrey 225 and 410-8

### Surrey won by two wickets
### Surrey 16pts, Kent 7

The start of the final day of the match is blessed with sunshine, and a sprinkling of spectators have taken advantage of Kent County Cricket Club's almost inevitable decision not to charge an admission fee - after all, it is possible that the game could be over in a matter of minutes. Some of Surrey's travelling fans have, understandably, elected not to make the trip in order to preserve a day of their annual leave from work, while one or two who were staying down in Canterbury have decided to go home early to save on a night's accommodation.

There is still a reasonable Surrey representation at the ground, however, mixed in with the Kent fans who are hoping to see their team wrap up a first Championship victory over 'the old enemy' since September 1997, and there's no doubting which group of supporters are the more confident. When pressed by my fellow Surrey followers to give an assessment of our chances of victory, I find it extremely difficult to be my usual optimistic self, since it is hard to see the lads scoring another 146 runs against fresh bowlers armed with a new 'cherry', especially as we have just three wickets - or, as most people would put it, two plus Ed Giddins - in hand. Though 'Giddo' has given of his best with the bat and produced some reasonable blocking efforts during his brief spell with Surrey, there remains a strong chance that he could be blown away in just a ball or two by the likes of Saggers and Khan. With the weight of history stacked against us, too - the required total is fifty-six more than any Surrey team has ever made to win a game in the fourth innings, remember - I opt to rate our chances in percentage terms, and, with the best will in the world, I reckon them to be no greater than one percent. Given that we would need to smash, not just beat, the previous record, I feel this isn't an unreasonable assessment, and I don't find any fans ready to argue against this level of untypical pessimism.

When play gets under way, Min Patel, still in charge in the continued absence of David Fulton, employs Mark Ealham from the pavilion end and Andrew Symonds' off-spin from the Nackington Road end. Encouragingly for the visitors and rank-outsiders, Saqlain starts well with a leg-glanced boundary in Ealham's first over but, overall, there is little ventured by either side in the run-up to the new ball. Maiden overs, along with singles pushed into the gaps at point and square leg, are the staple fare, in fact, especially once Patel replaces his former England all-rounder to form an all-spin attack with Symonds from the eighty-fifth over. Consequently, just nineteen runs accrue from the day's opening ten overs, though Surrey have at least managed to keep all their remaining wickets intact as the contest starts in earnest with the taking of the new ball.

Saggers and Khan are inevitably called up to use it, and it immediately appears that Kent regard Saqlain as their only realistic target, since Ward faces a very defensive field consisting of just one slip, four single-savers and four boundary fielders as he plays out an opening maiden from Saggers. Of course they want to get the tail-ender on strike as much as possible, but surely they should be attacking ***both*** batsmen as they have a new ball in their hands?

Having expounded this view to my Surrey friends, Saqlain, on thirty-nine, at 283-7, instantly does his best to prove Patel right, running down the wicket to Khan's first ball and skying an attempted pull-slog high into the air behind the bowler. Although the ball looks sure to come down just a few yards behind the bowler's stumps, and on the off-side of the wicket, neither the bowler nor the fielder at mid-off show any immediate inclination to make a move. With his colleagues seemingly paralysed by the fear of failure, Patel, at mid-on, therefore decides to take responsibility by calling for the catch and dashing in from his fielding position. The ball seems to be in the air forever, yet it plummets to the ground just in the nick of time for Surrey and Saqlain, as Patel, plunging forward at the last moment and getting both hands to the ball, is unable to accept the chance. Cue a huge sigh of relief from everyone in the visitors' camp. It is clear from where Kent's stand-in skipper has ended up, that he had been in the third-best position to take the catch, and one can't help but wonder if this incident has betrayed a few nerves in the home team. Khan certainly seems a little low on confidence, and Saqlain dents it further - and also celebrates his lucky escape - by smashing the young quickie for a towering six over long-on later in the over.

At this stage it appears almost as if the Pakistani is trying to take the lead role, in terms of run-scoring, while Ward attempts to bat through, and three well-struck fours in the next two overs add credence to this theory. Having driven Saggers to the rope at cover and then

# CLARKE AND RAMPRAKASH MAKE THEIR MARK AT TAUNTON

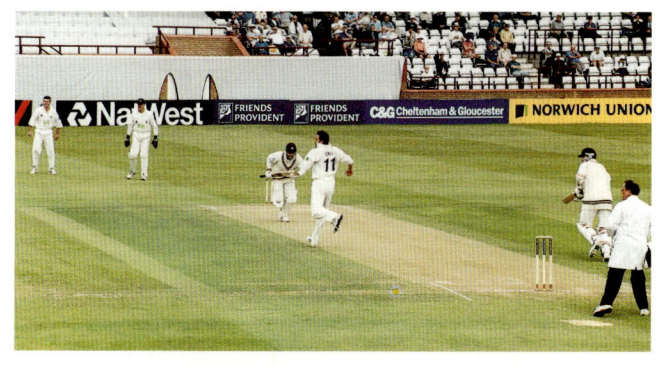

TOP - Rikki Clarke drives Keith Dutch over long-on for six
MIDDLE - Mark Ramprakash drives Steffan Jones for two runs to complete his double-century
BOTTOM - Clarke acknowledges the crowd's ovation after completing his maiden County Championship century
*(All photos by Reg Elliott)*

# RAMPRAKASH DOUBLES UP

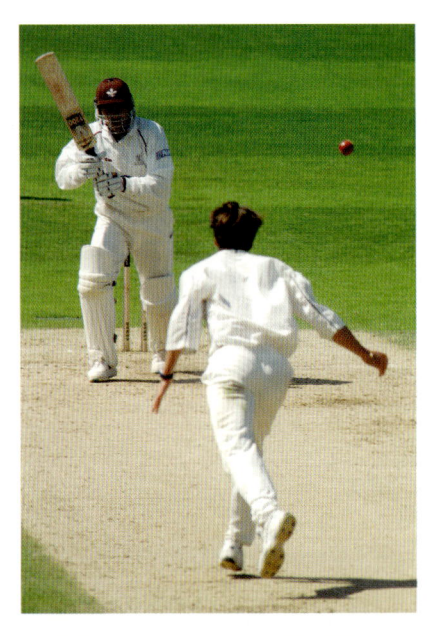

TOP - Mark Ramprakash drives Melvyn Betts down the ground on the way to his double-century against Warwickshire at The AMP Oval…
BOTTOM - …and celebrates the rare feat of completing double-tons in successive matches
*(Photos courtesy of Surrey CCC)*

# AND THEN THERE WERE TWO!

TOP - Jimmy Ormond claims his ninth victim in the Warwickshire match as Neil Smith loses a stump…
BOTTOM - …and completes a first-ever ten-wicket match haul as Melvyn Betts suffers the same fate
*(Both photos by Reg Elliott)*

# THE CANTERBURY TALE - PART ONE

TOP - Adam Hollioake pulls Martin Saggers to the boundary on the way to his stunning first-innings century
MIDDLE - Ian Salisbury makes a mess of Mark Ealham's stumps as Surrey hit back
BOTTOM - Saggers falls lbw to Saqlain Mushtaq to end Kent's second innings
*(All photos by Reg Elliott)*

# THE CANTERBURY TALE - PART TWO

TOP - Rikki Clarke lifts Andrew Symonds over mid-on for four as Surrey chase 410 to win
MIDDLE - A very determined-looking Ian Ward leaves the field at tea on the third day
BOTTOM - Ward pulls Ealham to the boundary en route to his match-winning unbeaten 168
*(All photos by Reg Elliott)*

# CHAMPIONS TOPPLED AT GUILDFORD - PART ONE

(1) - Surrey appeal in vain for lbw against Vic Craven in Yorkshire's first innings;
(2) - Adam Hollioake catches a fast-flying edge from Chris Silverwood off Rikki Clarke;
(3) - Jon Batty sweeps;  (4) - Batty goes for ninety-nine as Ryan Sidebottom penetrates the Surrey wicketkeeper's drive
*(Photo 1 - Peter Frost; 2 & 3 - Surrey CCC; 4 - Reg Elliott)*

# CHAMPIONS TOPPLED AT GUILDFORD - PART TWO

(1) - Rikki Clarke's slog-sweep off Richard Dawson earns him six runs;
(2) - Ali Brown catches Chris Silverwood at first slip off Ed Giddins in Yorkshire's second innings;
(3) - Yorkshire's second innings ends as Brown clutches a chance offered by Richard Blakey off the local boy, Rikki Clarke; (4) - Ian Ward cuts Darren Lehmann through point as Surrey close in on victory
*(Photo 1 - Peter Frost; 2, 3 & 4 - Reg Elliott)*

# NATIONAL LEAGUE SNAPSHOTS 1

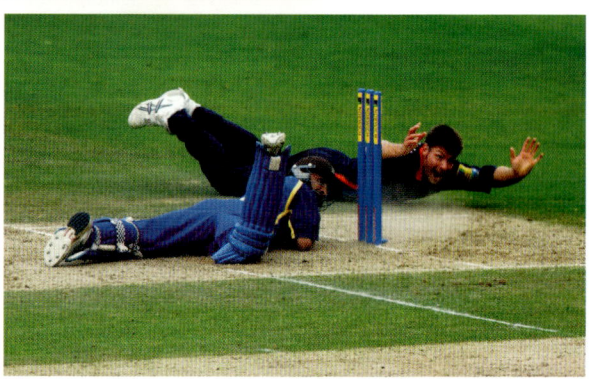

TOP - Jason Ratcliffe blasts the ball over midwicket during his explosive final innings for Surrey in the NUL match against Essex Eagles at Guildford
*(Photo by Peter Frost)*
MIDDLE - David Ward, 41, in action after being lured out of retirement for the NUL game with Northamptonshire Steelbacks at Whitgift School
BOTTOM - A batless Nadeem Shahid discovers that his dive for the crease has been in vain as Middlesex's Simon Cook wins the umpire's verdict in the NUL match at Whitgift
*(Photos courtesy of Surrey CCC)*

completed a priceless fifty from 88 balls with an off-side single, Saqlain cracks Khan through extra cover to raise the three-hundred for Surrey and then, for good measure, adds a lofted on-drive to his growing boundary collection. The eighth-wicket partnership has now added an incredible ninety-seven runs and endured for thirty-two overs, though the next over from Saggers brings a couple of slightly anxious moments - Ward, with a second slip now in place, edges airily to third man for a single, while Saqlain launches into another ambitious drive which sees the ball landing safely between two converging fielders at deep mid-off and yields the two runs that complete the century stand.

Strangely enough, despite the fact that the victory target is now almost down to double figures, it's impossible, as a Surrey fan, to get too excited. All the visiting supporters are fully aware that two good deliveries, or two batting errors, will instantly kill the game as a contest, since we can't expect too much from Giddins, one of the least resilient tail-enders on the county circuit. And, sure enough, it looks like our worst fears could be realised in the next over from Khan.

Although Ward brings Surrey's requirement down to ninety-eight with his first boundary of the day, courtesy of a typical on-drive, he loses his partner later in the over when Saqlain, seemingly caught in two minds about whether or not to go through with another hearty drive, chips a straightforward catch to Patel at wide mid-on. Looking extremely downcast, Saqlain tears himself from the crease, first rehearsing the stroke he should have played and then thrashing his bat against his pads in an act of self-admonishment as he walks slowly from the field. He receives a decent ovation from the small crowd for his bold innings of sixty, which has fallen just six short of his best score for Surrey (v Leicestershire at Oakham School in 2000), though it would seem that his dismissal has probably put the lid on the visitors' prospects of pulling off a record-breaking victory.

Unless Ward can suddenly take complete control - not really his style and, therefore, probably the wrong move - everything now depends on Jimmy Ormond playing out of his skin to produce the innings of his life. Whether the strapping fast bowler can do it under this sort of pressure is another matter, however, though he starts confidently with a classy clip to the rope at square leg off Saggers, followed by an airy, but safe, cover-driven four off Khan. Bonus runs come, too, as both Kent pacemen, presumably striving for the leg-stump yorker, concede four leg-byes with deliveries that scoot away to the rope at fine leg via Ormond's pads.

Patel clearly has some thinking to do, even though his side remain hot favourites with Surrey still more than seventy runs short of their target, and he takes responsibility on his own shoulders by returning to the attack in place of his rather inconsistent young Danish paceman. Saggers remains the major threat, though, and he reminds the visiting supporters that their team's prospects of victory are still slender by going past Ormond's outside edge three times in the course of one splendid over. The score keeps on rising, however, and boundaries in successive overs, by Ormond off Patel, and by Ward at Saggers' expense, keep the contest alive, quite miraculously, as lunch comes into view. One can only hope that the caterers have turned up to provide the players with sustenance, though it's debatable as to whether many of the participating batsmen or fielders will be feeling too hungry if the visitors are still eight wickets down at the break!

This scenario seems rather more likely when the persevering Saggers is finally rested after his ninth over of the session, though the presence of fielders around the bat for the spin pairing of Patel and Symonds represents a danger in the closing stages of the morning. Ward and Ormond both cope well, though, despite the claustrophobic pressure these close catchers exert, and the big Surrey fast bowler makes the ninth-wicket partnership worth fifty when he cuts for a single in Patel's penultimate over. The visitors' target is now down to forty-seven, and by the time the players leave the field for a wholly unexpected lunch break it has been reduced by four further carefully gathered singles and an on-driven two to Ward that has taken him through to a most worthy 150 from 336 balls. Surrey need forty-one more runs to pull off a truly incredible victory and, while no-one is yet making them favourites to win, it is clear that they are no longer facing 'mission impossible'.

*Lunch:- Surrey 369-8 (Ward 151\*, Ormond 20\*) from 113 overs*

It's a tense lunch break for everyone, though Surrey, who remain the underdogs, are probably feeling under slightly less pressure than Kent, for whom defeat would have been unthinkable at the start of the day. Of course, the closer the visitors get to their target the more the pressure will shift on to them as they become favourites.

Midway through the interval I glance across from the Woolley Stand to the Surrey dressing room balcony, where I see Ian Ward and Jimmy Ormond sat in complete silence, both staring straight ahead, preparing themselves for the final, testing period of play that lies ahead of them. It's a fascinating study in concentration, and quite an eye-opener for those uninitiated people who knock county cricket and believe that it is lacking in intensity and professionalism.

The tension and excitement of this match would certainly be very hard to beat in any sport at any level, and, as the players emerge for the final act of the drama, everyone is aware of the effect this result will have on the standings of these two teams in the Championship table. If Surrey win then they will head Kent by the very significant margin of 32.25 points, yet defeat would see the hop county close to within 8.25 points and become serious title challengers. That, in a nutshell, is how important the result is to both sides, though Kent clearly have more to lose.

So, who will Patel choose to open this vital, yet potentially short, passage of play? The general consensus is that it will be pace, in the shape of Saggers and Khan, or spin, from Symonds and the stand-in captain himself, or maybe a combination of the two, but we are proved wrong as the inexperienced Golding delivers the first over, from which each batsman picks up one run, then Ealham appears at the pavilion end and yields another four singles. It is a real shock to see the bowling entrusted to the two medium-pacers, who have so far taken just two wickets between them in thirty-two overs during the match, though no-one with Surrey leanings is going to mind, least of all the batsmen, one would assume.

Although Golding concedes just a two to square leg by Ormond in his next over, and Ealham manages to force a thick outside-edge from the same batsman in the following over, this bowling combination appears to present very little danger to the Surrey pair. To make matters worse for Kent, the odd loose delivery is easily punished, as Ormond demonstrates when he forces a short ball from Ealham through extra cover for three - thereby creating a new county record partnership for the ninth-wicket in Surrey v Kent contests (beating the 66 added by Hayward and Strudwick, way back in 1906) - and then clips a Golding half-volley to the square leg boundary. With the big fast bowler producing these high quality strokes, and the score now advanced to 385, Kentish concerns are growing.

There's still no way that Surrey can be completely confident of victory, though, and the tiny difference between success (a snick) and failure (a play-and-miss) for the fielding side is demonstrated in Ealham's next over, a maiden, when a ball beats the outside edge of the bat for the first time since the final over of Saggers' last spell.

With Kent in dire need of more such deliveries, in the hope that one will find the edge, their premier outswing bowler should be favourite to replace Golding at the Nackington Road end, but, instead of Saggers, it is Patel who returns. The first over of his new spell sees Ward clipping backward of square leg for a single, before Ormond launches into a lofted cover drive which clatters into the helmet of Key at silly mid-off, stopping the ball dead in its tracks. With the fielder, fortunately, unhurt by a truly frightening-looking blow, we are all left wondering whether or not the four, or maybe even six, runs that have been saved by the fieldsman's helmet will turn out to be significant in the final outcome. It's a real possibility, given the increasingly tense nature of the match.

As if the situation isn't nerve-wracking enough already, there's another worrying moment for the visitors in the next over when Ealham, retained in the attack after defeating Ormond with his outswinger in the previous over, again manages to pass the Surrey paceman's outside edge. With just one run, a glance to long leg by Ward, coming from the over, it is beginning to look as if the visitors are adopting the famous 'we'll get them in singles' approach until the game suddenly leaps forward during the next over from Patel.

The balance of power shifts quite dramatically in favour of Surrey as Ward produces a meaty sweep for six over backward square leg and then, having put his partner on strike with a single to midwicket, watches Ormond glance fine for two and follow up with a delightful late-cut to the rope at third man. No fewer than thirteen precious runs have come from the over, and both men have recorded personal bests in the process, with Ward, now on 163, exceeding his previous highest first-class score, made on this very ground two years ago, and his partner, on thirty-eight, registering a new highest score for Surrey. Ormond's boundary has also pushed the score up to 401, leaving his team just nine runs shy of a miraculous triumph, though there is still work to be done if the Championship leaders are to emulate Warwickshire's achievement in the previous match and come from behind to steal victory. Personally, I'm more nervous now than at any stage of the day, having stated at the start of play that the worst-case scenario would see us get to within seven or eight runs of victory and then lose the match.

With every run being counted off from here on in, a push into the leg-side by each batsman off Ealham brings the requirement down to seven at the end of the next over... though, heaven knows, I'd still be pretty happy with a tie, even at this stage!

Patel now has another decision to make, since he surely can't keep himself on after the mauling he received in his previous over. The obvious option is still Saggers, who hasn't bowled since twenty minutes before lunch, yet Kent's stand-in skipper opts to give the ball to his raw young paceman, Khan.

It's a brave move, given the Dane's inconsistency, and it almost proves instantly fatal as Ormond cracks a first-ball loosener along the ground straight to the man at square cover. Just a yard either side of the fielder and it would have been a certain four runs... will this prove to be another crucial moment or not? After this nervy start, Khan's over turns out to be a pretty respectable maiden, though Paul Nixon has to be very alert and agile to prevent any byes accruing from the fourth delivery, a vicious break-back which cuts Ormond in two and looks to be flying away at speed in the direction of fine leg until the keeper intercepts it.

Maybe it is to be Saggers now, for a last-gasp effort? No, it's still Ealham, and another tidy, but not especially threatening, over passes by with Ward gathering a single from a cover drive to take the total up to 404-8. Victory could now be achieved in one hit, though it seems unlikely that either batsman will dare to try it at this stage!

So the ball is back in Khan's court. Although his opening delivery is a slower ball, wide of the off stump, which Ward misses, drawing gasps from the small crowd, the Surrey opener remains unperturbed as he clips to deep midwicket for another run to take the score to 405. The visitors are now almost there and, when Khan's fourth ball turns out to be a wide half-volley, Ormond ensures at least a tie for his team by striking out boldly to lift a cover drive over the infield for one of the most important boundaries of his career to date. As the ball whistles to the rope, the visiting supporters begin to celebrate, and a huge cheer goes up from the Surrey balcony - probably led by Ed Giddins, who is, of course, still sat there in his pads!

Six Championship points have been secured, but there are six more to be gained if another run can be scored, so, as Khan runs in to complete his over, the visiting team and fans go quiet again. Ormond easily repels the fifth ball, before giving everyone a scare by playing the final delivery down into the ground and just over the top of his stumps.

Ward is therefore left to face Ealham, with the opportunity of striking the winning runs in a historic victory his for the taking. The first two deliveries pass without incident before the

Surrey opener forces the next ball back down the ground to the on-side of the stumps and runs through for the single that secures an astonishing and memorable triumph. Both Ward's clinching stroke and his arms-aloft celebration are carbon-copy flashbacks in time to 2nd September 1999, when he had been the man to seal Surrey's first Championship success for twenty-eight years during the thrilling climax to the match at The Oval against Nottinghamshire, and, given the lead Surrey now have in the title race, it seems likely that this win could end up being remembered as the pivotal triumph of the 2002 Championship campaign. While two of Surrey's three heroes of the day, Ward and Ormond, embrace in mid-pitch, similar celebrations are under way on the visitors' balcony and also in the Woolley Stand amongst the team's small group of stunned and delighted fans.

Even the most optimistic of Surrey supporters had expected the game to be done and dusted by lunchtime at the very latest, yet here we are at 2.35pm cheering and applauding as a grinning Ian Ward makes his way from the field, briefly glancing skywards en route. His truly outstanding eight-hour marathon innings of 168, spanning 367 balls, has been a model in terms of application and concentration, and it has guided his team through to a *"Boy's Own"* storybook success that even brings one or two of the notoriously begrudging Kent members to their feet to applaud. Saqlain Mushtaq and Jimmy Ormond are also worthy of the highest praise for their hugely impressive efforts as a truly Herculean task has ended up as something of cakewalk, with an astounding 202 runs added for the loss of just one wicket since the low point of the innings at 208-7, when the game looked over as a contest.

Even as the ground empties and I wander slowly towards the exit, taking a stream of mobile phone calls from fellow supporters who have missed all the drama for one reason or another, I can still scarcely believe what I have witnessed today.

Later, I receive a call from a journalist on one of the national broadsheets, asking me to fill him in on the day's events for tomorrow morning's report, since his newspaper hadn't felt it worth sending anyone to the game - an entirely understandable decision in the circumstances, and one that has been replicated by a great many people today.

I am, naturally, delighted that I opted to stay on in Canterbury... and I have already vowed that I will **never again** write this Surrey side off, no matter what the situation!

**Kent 374 and 260; Surrey 225 and 410-8**
**Surrey won by two wickets. Surrey 16pts, Kent 7**

Hindsight is a wonderful thing, of course, but one aspect of the game that was discussed by Surrey supporters in the Bat and Ball pub, opposite the ground, in the aftermath of the team's incredible triumph was Kent's decision to request the extra half-hour at the end of day three, and the umpires' subsequent ruling to allow it. Forty-one very valuable runs were added in that time against tired bowlers, and we wondered how much more daunting Surrey's final-day task would have been had they needed 187 to win, as opposed to 146. There is a psychological barrier for most things in life, where even those with the strongest belief start to disbelieve - for example, even the greatest sprinter in the world doesn't believe he can run 100 metres in seven seconds - and, had Min Patel opted to call it quits at the scheduled close of play, then we strongly suspected that things could have worked out differently. Would Ian Ward and his partners have felt that 187 runs were attainable in the same way that they clearly believed 146 were?

## VIEWS FROM THE DRESSING ROOM

*Without Adam's stunning 122, we could have been out of the match before the second innings even started. What can you say about that innings and the way he batted after his return?*
**IAN WARD** - He played like a man possessed, really, a man without any clutter in his mind, he just went out and struck the ball as very few people can. It was a remarkable innings and if it

hadn't been for him, and that little partnership with Ed Giddins at the end, then there was no way we would have won, no way that I would have taken all the plaudits in the second innings, and, for my money, the three big heroes of those four days were Adam, Saqlain and Jimmy. I took all the glory, but it was unjustified really... Smokey saved the follow-on single-handedly, and then Saqlain and Jimmy did the lion's share of the scoring in my partnerships with them.

*In your heart of hearts did you honestly believe we could win from the depths of 208-7?*
**IAN WARD** - Well, it was definitely odds against, wasn't it?! To be honest, though, you don't think like that when you're out in the middle - if you do, then you are going to come second. It was obviously going to be a very hard, but you've got to keep fighting. We never give up as a side and it shows what can happen if you hang on in there and keep trying to do your stuff.

*Given the weight of history against us, I gave us only a 1% chance of winning as the final day's play began. What percentage figure would you honestly have put on our chances of winning?*
**ADAM HOLLIOAKE** - I'd say about 20-25 per cent. I think with the way we've batted over the years, the confidence we've got, and the way everyone was talking after the third day, I just knew that we'd not given up hope. Then, before the start of play, I would say that figure rose to probably just under fifty per cent - I threw balls to Jimmy Ormond for about half-an-hour and I could see his confidence, and Wardy was looking so focused I could see that he just wasn't going to get out, unless it was to a freak dismissal. I can understand how it might have looked to the fans, but I stayed at Mark Ealham's place that night and I know they didn't think it was over, they were a bit concerned about it, so the pressure was very much on them, rather than us, seeing as everybody was expecting Kent to win.

*What was the plan as you and Saqi went out to bat on the final morning?*
**IAN WARD** - We both just tried to play our normal game, really. Saqi can improvise very well - he's a bit unorthodox at times, but he's effective, and he's got a Test century to his credit, which is more than I can say for myself. I was always going to go my way, picking up runs here and there, and trying to keep some of the strike, but in the end I didn't need to worry about that because Saqi played ever so well and then Jimmy came in and played as well as I've ever seen him play. All-in-all, it was just a perfect way to win from such a dreadful position, but it was all about us going out and doing our own thing, whatever that was, and just sticking to it.

*Saqi was dropped in the eleventh over of the day when he skied a drive high behind the bowler. Although the ball landed slightly to the off side of the stumps, Patel, from mid-on, was the man who attempted the catch. Did it strike you, as it did me, that the wrong man had called for, and attempted, the catch?*
**IAN WARD** - Yes, I think Khan probably should have gone for it, but it just goes to show what a bit of pressure can do to people. It didn't look as if anybody really wanted it, so poor old Min was left roaring in from twenty yards away, when there were a couple of blokes standing a lot closer. That's what happens in sport, though - pressure gets to people, it's a strange thing.

*I was amazed to see Kent start after lunch with Ealham and Golding. Were you?*
**IAN WARD** - I was surprised they didn't go with their main strike bowlers, though I wasn't bothered who I was facing, really. I was certainly surprised Saggers didn't bowl after lunch... I think he said afterwards that he didn't want to bowl down the hill, so he was going to follow Ealham at the pavilion end, something like that. It was a strange decision, but I was happy enough, as it all worked to our advantage.

*What was it like up on the dressing room balcony as the game moved towards its climax?*
**JON BATTY** - The last half-an-hour to an hour was the most nerve-wracking time of my cricketing life. I still have a mental picture of Giddo sat there for an hour or so with his helmet and pads on - normally you can't shut him up, but on this occasion he didn't say a word for all

that time! Matthew Fleming and a few other Kent guys were on that balcony and when there were about thirty runs needed Fleming said "Giddo, I think you're going to get in with about eight needed", so when we did reach the point where we needed eight we all got a bit more nervous. There was a lot of banter going on.

*The winning drive down the ground, the significance of it, and the arms-aloft celebrations instantly brought back memories of your winning stroke against Notts at The Oval in 1999. Did you notice that yourself?*
**IAN WARD** - I hadn't thought about it until you mentioned it, but I suppose, with hindsight, it must have looked very similar. I just remember a huge feeling of relief - I remember the shot, I remember hitting it and thinking 'oh, you beauty, it's beaten the fielder and we've won!'

*I guess Ben was still in everyone's thoughts, as I noted you looking skywards briefly as you walked off the field?*
**IAN WARD** - To be perfectly honest with you, I'm not a religious person, so if I looked skywards it was more out of relief than anything else, even though Ben was very much in our thoughts in everything that we did during the season. It was a grotesque tragedy for the Hollioakes and we all felt very much for them... we miss Ben dreadfully and, on special occasions, we always think of him. His name is in the song that we sing when we win and hopefully will be forever more because he was a champion and he was taken from us much too early... but, as for the look skywards, that isn't really me, so that wasn't the reason behind it.

*At the end of the third day, Kent had claimed the extra half-hour in order to try and wrap the game up. Having not taken a wicket for almost ten overs, do you think they should have been allowed to claim it and, subsequently, be granted the extra time?*
**IAN WARD** - You've got to say that the decision backfired on them because they didn't get a wicket that night and they also didn't win the match. At the time, I did say to the umpires that I thought it was wrong that they should be allowed to claim the extra overs, but it wasn't my decision, of course. Kent didn't really look like taking a wicket at that stage, and they certainly didn't look like taking ***all*** the wickets, so we were hung out there for a bit longer than we had to be really. But the umpires make the decisions and you have to live with it.

*Did claiming the extra time represent a mistake on their part, as we added a further forty-one runs, leaving us chasing an unlikely 146 on the last day rather than an almost impossible187?*
**IAN WARD** - Well, that was the danger when they asked for the last half-hour - if it wasn't to work in terms of getting a wicket, the bowlers were tired, so perhaps it would have been better for them to come back the next day all guns blazing. But, as it was, we were left with forty less runs to get, so it worked to our advantage.

*Where would Wardy's knock rate amongst all the great innings you have witnessed?*
**ADAM HOLLIOAKE** - It would be one of the toughest innings I've ever seen in first-class cricket, probably up there with Graham Thorpe's 222 against Glamorgan at The Oval in 1997, and Browny's 295 against Leicestershire at Oakham in 2000. It was a fantastic innings and definitely the best I've seen by Wardy.

*I noted a few things during the game which suggested to me that the Surrey players have about as much affection for the Canterbury/Kent crowd as we, the supporters, do!*
**IAN SALISBURY** - I couldn't believe the big billboards saying *'Kent Versus The Old Enemy'* as we drove into the town. We accept that they are a good side, but I think they built it up to be something more, and then the fans went over the top in voicing their opinions - they seemed more concerned about giving us stick than getting behind their own team. It was ridiculous that we had to put up with some very personal abuse from their fans for three days, then it was a few Surrey supporters who ended up getting kicked out of the ground for no good reason at all.

# IAN WARD'S 168 NOT OUT AGAINST KENT
### Original run chart as compiled by Keith Seward

KENT V SURREY;    CANTERBURY,    21/22-7-02

I. WARD    NOT OUT    168

LHB

1.00 – (2.35)    475 mins.    50 in 108 mins    80 balls
              367 balls    100 in 251 mins. 208 balls
                           150 in 419 mins. 336 balls

4·4·1·3·1·4·3·4·4·4·11·4·3·4·2·4·2·1·4·4·2·3·1·2·4·4·2·11·3·4·1111·4·11·4·1·2·11·2·4·11·2·1111·4·1111·2·4·1111
2·1111·6·1111

Career best score.

Shared 3rd wicket stand of 123 in 118 mins. with R. CLARKE.

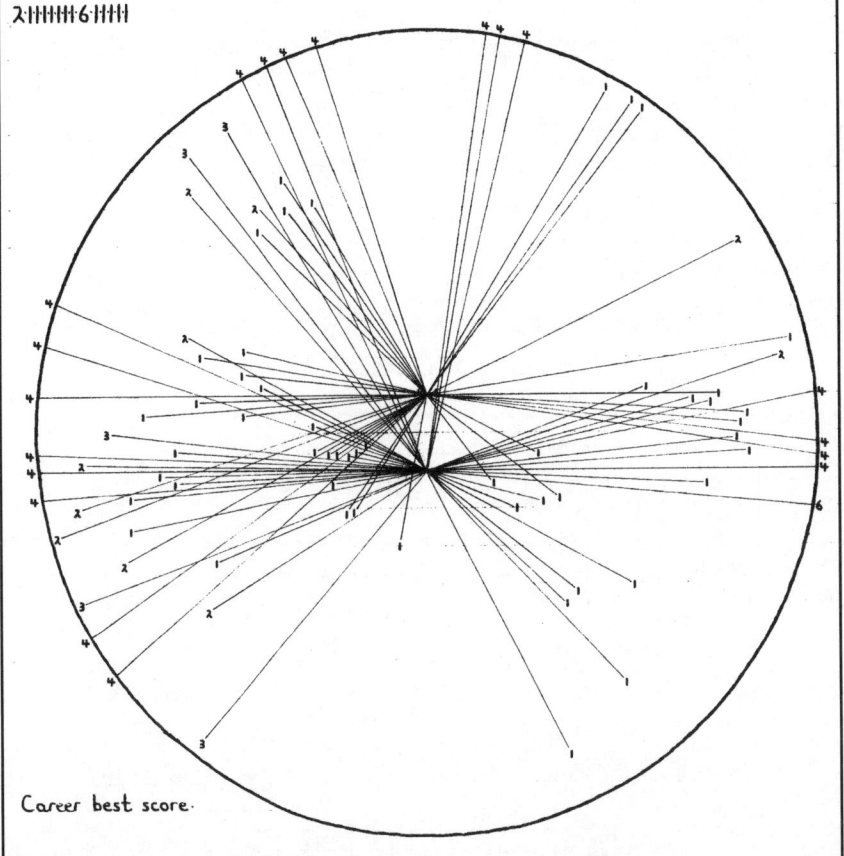

## KENT v SURREY at Canterbury    Played from 19th to 22nd July

Kent won the toss and elected to bat    Umpires:- David Constant and Trevor Jesty

### KENT - First Innings

| Fall Of Wkt | Batsman | How | | Out | Score | Balls | 4s | 6s |
|---|---|---|---|---|---|---|---|---|
| 1-121 | D.P. Fulton * | c Clarke | | b Saqlain | 62 | 84 | 8 | 0 |
| 2-122 | R.W.T. Key | | lbw | b Saqlain | 57 | 102 | 7 | 0 |
| 3-155 | E.T. Smith | | run | out | 19 | 42 | 2 | 0 |
| 6-329 | A. Symonds | | | b Saqlain | 118 | 110 | 15 | 2 |
| 4-285 | J.B. Hockley | st Batty | | b Salisbury | 46 | 79 | 3 | 3 |
| 5-321 | P.A. Nixon + | c Giddins | | b Salisbury | 8 | 16 | 1 | 0 |
| 7-371 | M.A. Ealham | c Batty | | b Salisbury | 18 | 60 | 3 | 0 |
| | J.M. Golding | | Not | Out | 24 | 47 | 3 | 1 |
| 8-373 | M.M. Patel | | | b Salisbury | 1 | 6 | 0 | 0 |
| 9-374 | A. Khan | | lbw | b Saqlain | 1 | 4 | 0 | 0 |
| 10-374 | M.J. Saggers | | | b Saqlain | 0 | 3 | 0 | 0 |
| | Extras | (6b, 4lb, 6w, 4nb) | | | 20 | | | |
| | **TOTAL** | **(91.5 overs)** | | | **374** | | | |

| Bowler | O | M | R | W | NB | Wd |
|---|---|---|---|---|---|---|
| Giddins | 17 | 5 | 39 | 0 | - | - |
| Ormond | 14 | 2 | 80 | 0 | - | 1 |
| Clarke | 8 | 0 | 56 | 0 | 1 | - |
| Saqlain Mushtaq | 33.5 | 8 | 122 | 5 | 1 | - |
| Hollioake | 2 | 0 | 8 | 0 | - | - |
| Salisbury | 17 | 3 | 59 | 4 | - | - |

### SURREY - First Innings (Needing 225 to avoid the follow-on)

| Fall Of Wkt | Batsman | How | | Out | Score | Balls | 4s | 6s |
|---|---|---|---|---|---|---|---|---|
| 5-59 | M.A. Butcher | c Fulton | | b Khan | 34 | 51 | 6 | 0 |
| 1-16 | I.J. Ward | c Nixon | | b Khan | 7 | 24 | 1 | 0 |
| 2-29 | I.D.K. Salisbury | | | b Saggers | 2 | 16 | 0 | 0 |
| 3-29 | M.R. Ramprakash | c Nixon | | b Saggers | 0 | 1 | 0 | 0 |
| 4-34 | R. Clarke | c Nixon | | b Khan | 5 | 9 | 1 | 0 |
| 6-77 | A.D. Brown | | | b Saggers | 9 | 17 | 1 | 0 |
| | A.J. Hollioake * | | Not | Out | 122 | 103 | 14 | 7 |
| 7-126 | J.N. Batty + | c Symonds | | b Golding | 8 | 35 | 1 | 0 |
| 8-169 | Saqlain Mushtaq | | | b Saggers | 4 | 38 | 0 | 0 |
| 9-184 | J. Ormond | | | b Khan | 4 | 5 | 1 | 0 |
| 10-225 | E.S.H. Giddins | c Symonds | | b Saggers | 1 | 13 | 0 | 0 |
| | Extras | (13lb, 2w, 14nb) | | | 29 | | | |
| | **TOTAL** | **(50.5 overs)** | | | **225** | | | |

| Bowler | O | M | R | W | NB | Wd |
|---|---|---|---|---|---|---|
| Saggers | 13.5 | 3 | 66 | 5 | - | - |
| Khan | 16 | 2 | 91 | 4 | 7 | - |
| Patel | 6 | 3 | 21 | 0 | - | 1 |
| Golding | 8 | 2 | 13 | 1 | - | - |
| Ealham | 6 | 2 | 21 | 0 | - | - |
| Symonds | 1 | 1 | 0 | 0 | - | - |

### KENT - Second Innings (Leading by 149 runs on first innings)

| Fall Of Wkt | Batsman | How | | Out | Score | Balls | 4s | 6s |
|---|---|---|---|---|---|---|---|---|
| 1-18 | D.P. Fulton * | c Batty | | b Giddins | 11 | 19 | 2 | 0 |
| 7-189 | R.W.T. Key | c Batty | | b Ormond | 68 | 129 | 6 | 0 |
| 2-33 | E.T. Smith | c Ramprakash | | b Ormond | 6 | 10 | 1 | 0 |
| 3-130 | A. Symonds | c Ward | | b Saqlain | 51 | 59 | 6 | 0 |
| 4-142 | J.B. Hockley | c Ward | | b Saqlain | 8 | 16 | 2 | 0 |
| 5-144 | P.A. Nixon + | c Batty | | b Saqlain | 1 | 6 | 0 | 0 |
| 6-145 | M.A. Ealham | | | b Salisbury | 0 | 5 | 0 | 0 |
| 8-203 | J.M. Golding | | lbw | b Giddins | 26 | 84 | 3 | 0 |
| | M.M. Patel | | Not | Out | 43 | 68 | 4 | 0 |
| 9-255 | A. Khan | | lbw | b Salisbury | 11 | 26 | 1 | 0 |
| 10-260 | M.J. Saggers | | lbw | b Saqlain | 2 | 26 | 0 | 0 |
| | Extras | (5b, 16lb, 2w, 10nb) | | | 33 | | | |
| | **TOTAL** | **(73.5 overs)** | | | **260** | | | |

| Bowler | O | M | R | W | NB | Wd |
|---|---|---|---|---|---|---|
| Giddins | 15 | 3 | 40 | 2 | - | - |
| Ormond | 17 | 3 | 61 | 2 | 3 | - |
| Clarke | 4 | 0 | 23 | 0 | 1 | - |
| Saqlain Mushtaq | 19.5 | 3 | 60 | 4 | 1 | - |
| Salisbury | 18 | 1 | 55 | 2 | - | 1 |

| SURREY - Second Innings (Needing 410 to win) | | | | | | | |
|---|---|---|---|---|---|---|---|
| Fall Of Wkt | Batsman | How | Out | Score | Balls | 4s | 6s |
| 1-52 | M.A. Butcher | c Symonds | b Saggers | 20 | 47 | 2 | 0 |
| | I.J. Ward | Not | Out | 168 | 367 | 19 | 1 |
| 2-54 | M.R. Ramprakash | c Nixon | b Saggers | 2 | 9 | 0 | 0 |
| 3-177 | R. Clarke | c Hockley | b Symonds | 66 | 93 | 9 | 1 |
| 4-181 | A.D. Brown | c Ealham | b Symonds | 0 | 2 | 0 | 0 |
| 5-190 | A.J. Hollioake * | c Nixon | b Saggers | 8 | 9 | 2 | 0 |
| 6-191 | J.N. Batty + | c Key | b Symonds | 0 | 1 | 0 | 0 |
| 7-208 | I.D.K. Salisbury | | b Ealham | 5 | 26 | 0 | 0 |
| 8-313 | Saqlain Mushtaq | c Patel | b Khan | 60 | 98 | 6 | 2 |
| | J. Ormond | Not | Out | 43 | 110 | 6 | 0 |
| | Extras | (17b, 13lb, 2w, 6nb) | | 38 | | | |
| | TOTAL | (126.3 overs) | (for 8 wkts) | 410 | | | |

| Bowler | O | M | R | W | NB | Wd |
|---|---|---|---|---|---|---|
| Saggers | 31 | 6 | 85 | 3 | - | - |
| Khan | 20 | 3 | 91 | 1 | 3 | - |
| Symonds | 28 | 5 | 85 | 3 | - | 1 |
| Ealham | 19.3 | 7 | 42 | 1 | - | - |
| Golding | 8 | 1 | 27 | 0 | - | - |
| Patel | 20 | 6 | 50 | 0 | - | - |

## Other Division One Results

Surrey's historic victory looked like it could prove to be very significant in the race for the title as their lead at the top of the table extended to 24.75 points. Kent's defeat represented a serious blow to their hopes, while Somerset now looked completely out of contention following their surprising annihilation at the hands of Sussex. Even though there were a lot of games still to be played, no other county was looking capable of mounting a serious charge for the Championship and a third title in four years was looking increasingly likely for the league leaders.

July 19-21
*Taunton:-* **Sussex beat Somerset by an innings and 1 run.** Somerset 270 (Bulbeck 53*) and 373 (Blackwell 114, Burns 98, Taylor 4-68, Lewry 4-112); Sussex 644 (Martin-Jenkins 205*, Cottey 120, Davis 111). **Sussex 20pts, Somerset 4**

July 19-22
*Headingley:-* **Yorkshire drew with Lancashire.** Yorkshire 515-5dec (Lehmann 187, McGrath 165) and 124-7; Lancashire 478 (Swann 128, Wood 64, Chapple 60, Keedy 57, Law 51). **Yorkshire 11pts, Lancashire 10**

## COUNTY CHAMPIONSHIP DIVISION ONE AT 22ND JULY

| Pos | Prv | | P | Points | W | D | L | Bat | Bwl | Ded |
|---|---|---|---|---|---|---|---|---|---|---|
| 1 | 1 | Surrey | 9 | 128.75 | 5 | 3 | 1 | 30 | 27 | 0.25 |
| 2 | 2 | Leicestershire | 9 | 104.00 | 3 | 4 | 2 | 28 | 25 | 1.00 |
| 3 | 6 | Sussex | 10 | 104.00 | 2 | 6 | 2 | 27 | 29 | 0.00 |
| 4 | 4 | Kent | 9 | 96.50 | 3 | 3 | 3 | 24 | 25 | 0.50 |
| 5 | 3 | Hampshire | 9 | 90.00 | 1 | 7 | 1 | 24 | 26 | 0.00 |
| 6 | 5 | Warwickshire | 8 | 85.00 | 3 | 3 | 2 | 15 | 22 | 0.00 |
| 7 | 7 | Somerset | 9 | 85.00 | 1 | 6 | 2 | 25 | 24 | 0.00 |
| 8 | 8 | Lancashire | 8 | 78.00 | 2 | 4 | 2 | 17 | 21 | 0.00 |
| 9 | 9 | Yorkshire | 9 | 61.50 | 0 | 4 | 5 | 21 | 25 | 0.50 |

# 13 Reclaiming The Crown?

The matches were coming thick and fast now, with the annual Guildford festival set to start just two days after the sensational win at Canterbury, which had been Surrey's first on that ground in the County Championship since 1989. What a way to end a barren streak!

There had, however, still been sufficient time to reflect on a fantastic game of four-day first-class cricket that had demonstrated how quickly and dramatically things can change in the course of a match, and how a positive attitude can often bring success, even when the odds are stacked against you.

With the benefit of hindsight, it was now quite amusing to look back at how everyone, including the team's hard-core supporters, had written Surrey off after the third day of the game. In the press, *The Daily Telegraph's* headline had read *"Ward A Hit But Kent On Course"*, while *The Times* had led with *"Kent Push Surrey To The Brink Of Defeat"* and *Ananova*, the Press Association's news site on the Internet, had gone with *"Kent On Verge Of Victory Despite Ward"*. I would have gone along with any of these headlines, as well as fellow fan Marcus Hook's *"Ward Century Delays The Inevitable"* which appeared on both www.surreycricket.com and the Surrey supporters' site at www.ovalworld-online.com.

It would, of course, have been easy to denigrate the supporters and journalists concerned for being short of faith or lacking in knowledge yet, in reality, these premature 'obituaries' merely underlined the brilliance of the performances we had witnessed from Messrs Ward, Saqlain and Ormond in turning the match around. Adam Hollioake had been honest enough to admit in the press that "the first three days were our worst performance for a long time", but the last day's effort had more than made up for it, leaving Ian Ward to heap praise on his team-mates, who had played so well in stands of 105 and 97 for the eighth and ninth wickets. The bottom line was, however, that none of the three Surrey heroes could have pulled it off without the efforts of the other two. They *all* had to play outstandingly well - two made their highest score for the county and Saqlain fell only six short of his - and, for this reason, as much as any other, I stood by my assessment before the start of the final day that Surrey's chance of winning was no greater than one percent. If that final day had been played a hundred times over, then I still felt Kent would have won ninety-nine times... luckily, though, this had been the other occasion!

It seemed ridiculous to say it now, with the team having moved further ahead at the top of the Championship table, but Surrey had looked to be facing a mini crisis at the end of day three at Canterbury. With Alex Tudor ruled out of the first Test against India with shin splints, Martin Bicknell still recovering from his broken wrist, Jimmy Ormond said to be carrying a knee injury, and Saqlain Mushtaq soon to miss two or three Championship matches as a result of Pakistan's involvement in a limited-overs tournament in Morocco, the bowling resources were not looking too healthy. There were also some lingering concerns about the balance of the side, and, additionally, no-one knew how the team would react to losing two successive Championship matches for the first time in some five seasons. As things turned out, though, the latter problem didn't even materialise, and the very nature of the victory at Canterbury erased any fears that the team was about to fritter away the advantage gained by those three straight wins at the start of the campaign. In fact, with no other county managing to string together a run of consistent winning form, many of us felt that eight Championship wins would now certainly be enough to seal a third title in four seasons, leaving us just three short of the mark as we went into game ten with seven matches remaining.

Our perceived problems paled into insignificance, however, against those of Yorkshire, our next opponents. Stranded at the bottom of the table, some twenty-four points adrift of safety, and without a win to their credit in the premier competition, it looked like they would need to produce some sparkling form for the rest of the campaign if the champions of 2001 were to avoid the ignominy of relegation just twelve months later. At the start of the season, Surrey versus Yorkshire at Guildford had looked as if it could be a significant match in deciding who won the 2002 title but, as the game arrived, that remained the case only for Surrey. For the struggling Tykes it was bordering on a do-or-die contest as the spectre of demotion to Division Two loomed over them.

| FRIZZELL COUNTY CHAMPIONSHIP - MATCH TEN |
|---|

### SURREY versus YORKSHIRE
### at Guildford
### First Day - Wednesday 24th July
### Yorkshire 172; Surrey 207-5

***The Teams And The Toss*** - *Surrey's team shows just one change from Canterbury, with Nadeem Shahid returning in place of Mark Butcher, who will be lining up for England in the Test match at Lord's tomorrow alongside fellow Surrey men, Graham Thorpe and Alec Stewart, and Yorkshire's Michael Vaughan, Craig White and Matthew Hoggard. Stewart will be playing in his 119th Test Match, making him England's most-capped player. Test absentees apart, Yorkshire are at full-strength, other than the injured Steve Kirby - David Wigley, a tall 20-year-old seamer, gets the nod ahead of other pace-bowling options and makes his first-class debut. Darren Lehmann wins the toss for the visitors on a very pleasant morning and elects to bat.*

As the members of a good-sized crowd settle into their seats, the Surrey faithful are probably aware that Adam Hollioake might not have been disappointed to lose the toss, since batting first at the Woodbridge Road ground has often been a hazardous affair in recent times. Matt Wood, the out-of-form England Academy batsman, is almost certainly blissfully unaware of this, though he soon learns the harsh facts about batting at Guildford on the first morning when Ed Giddins' second delivery of the match from the railway end spits to the shoulder of his bat, providing Ian Salisbury with a simple catch at gully. It's the Yorkshire opener's third successive duck against Surrey, following his pair at Headingley in April, and it gets the visitors off to the worst possible start at 0-1.

This early wicket is a great boost for Giddins, who had bowled pretty well but without much luck at Canterbury, though his bowling partner, Jimmy Ormond, starts much less impressively with two no-balls and a wide. Having bowled very well for Leicestershire on this ground in 2000, the surroundings are certainly not alien to him, however, and he quickly settles down to have Vic Craven missed by Ali Brown at first slip in the fourth over of the day, with the batsman still not off the mark and the total on fourteen.

The reprieved Craven then leads a rapid Yorkshire surge to fifty at almost five-an-over, first by driving Ormond to the rope at cover and then by capitalising on some leg-side looseness from Giddins to add three further fours to his collection. Anthony McGrath, looking equally assured at the other end, has meanwhile stroked a couple of good-looking boundaries of his own, and the bat is looking to be well on top of the ball when Giddins' tendency to stray down the leg-side to the left-handed Craven brings him the Harrogate-born youngster's wicket, courtesy of a 'strangle' to Jon Batty with the total on fifty-three.

The bat is quickly back on top again, though, with McGrath taking six from Ormond's next over, and the newly-arrived Darren Lehmann driving his second ball, the first of the following over from Giddins, through backward point for four. Before the over is out, Giddins has a third wicket, however, as McGrath departs lbw, offering no stroke and then having to wait for what seems like an eternity before being sent on his way by umpire Ken Palmer. It's 64-3 as the batsman departs for twenty-six, and the Championship leaders are really buzzing.

They know that they need to get rid of Lehmann cheaply if they are to shoot their opponents out for a low score, though, and he has been in typically excellent form since Martin Bicknell dismissed him for sixteen and one at Headingley. The left-handed Australian has been so prolific, in fact, that he becomes the second man to complete a thousand first-class runs for the season when pushing a single to cover in Giddins' next over, shortly after Michael Lumb has got his innings off to a great start with successive clipped fours through the leg-side off Ormond.

No sooner has Lehmann's achievement been announced and applauded than his innings is ended in spectacular style, however, as Rikki Clarke pulls off a truly breathtaking catch at third slip off Ormond. It's a catch that will forever remain in the memory as Lehmann, aiming to leg, gets a leading edge which flies very low, fast and wide to the left-hand side of the Surrey all-rounder. Clarke must only see the ball at the last moment, yet he dives full-length to pluck the ball out of the air just inches from the turf to complete what is surely one of the best catches ever taken at Woodbridge Road. The crowd's reaction sums this magical moment of brilliance up perfectly - there's a collective gasp, a brief stunned silence and then rapturous applause as an almost disbelieving Lehmann tears himself from the crease to start his walk back to the pavilion, while Clarke is deservedly mobbed by his Surrey team-mates.

With Yorkshire's key man gone cheaply again, for seven, Surrey are now in full control, and their position is further strengthened at the end of Ormond's next, highly eventful, over. After the new batsman, Gary Fellows, gets off the mark with a straight-driven three, Lumb drives the next ball wide of mid-on for the fourth boundary of his brief innings before Ormond out-thinks him with a slower ball next up. Hopelessly deceived, the young left-hander drives straight to mid-on, where Saqlain takes a smart low catch to reduce the visitors to a pitiful 85-5.

Fellows, having only been at the wicket for three overs, and Richard Blakey now have a serious repair job on their hands and, unsurprisingly, they approach it with caution, battening down the hatches for a few overs until Blakey unleashes an extra cover-driven boundary at Ormond's expense. He nearly comes unstuck in the next over, however, when attempting something equally aggressive off Giddins, but Salisbury is unable to cling on to a head-high gully catch from a sliced drive, with the score at ninety-two and the batsman on just five.

Shortly afterwards the hundred comes up, courtesy of Fellows' push into the covers, and this is the cue for the hard-working Surrey opening bowlers to be given a well-deserved rest at last, with Giddins through fifteen overs and Ormond thirteen.

Saqlain Mushtaq and Rikki Clarke take over the bowling duties at the pavilion and railway end, respectively, with the changes producing an initial flurry of runs, followed by the dismissal of Fellows in the penultimate over of the session. It is symptomatic of Yorkshire's batting problems this season that the 23-year-old all-rounder sells his wicket cheaply with a woeful hook off Clarke that doesn't require Nadeem Shahid, deliberately posted at deep backward square leg, to move a muscle. With Fellows, like Lumb before him, gone for sixteen, Yorkshire's innings is in tatters at 125-6 and, though only nine balls remain until lunch, they still manage to suffer two more scares - a big appeal for lbw by Clarke against Richard Dawson first ball and a miscued drive to third man by Blakey off Saqlain - before the not-out pair gratefully head off for the break.

*Lunch:- Yorkshire 127-6 (Blakey 23\*, Dawson 0\*) from 34 overs*

After Surrey's excellent morning with the ball, it's obvious that Yorkshire have plenty of work to do if they are to muster even a single batting point, and the first three overs of the afternoon offer hope, with Dawson twice glancing Clarke to the fine leg boundary. Having reached sixteen, the seventh-wicket partnership is terminated by the first ball of the next over from Saqlain, however, as Blakey, on twenty-three, pushes forward to the off-spinner and is well taken off bat and pad by Shahid diving in from short leg.

At 141-7 the visitors really are in dire straits, especially as they appear to have very little batting left in Silverwood, Sidebottom and Wigley. No-one knows much about Wigley's ability with the bat but since he is listed below Ryan Sidebottom one can safely assume that he isn't particularly talented in that department of the game!

Silverwood would seem to offer the visitors a degree of hope, since he is capable of making runs by adopting a positive approach, but he manages just a solitary on-driven two to raise the Yorkshire 150 before Clarke tempts him into a wild flash outside the off stump. The resulting edge flies like a tracer bullet to second slip, where Adam Hollioake knocks the ball upwards before completing the catch at the second attempt to leave the visitors eight down and in even deeper trouble. Clarke is clearly delighted to have captured a second wicket on the ground where he has played so much cricket for Guildford C.C., and he doesn't have to wait long for his third scalp either. Having removed Silverwood with the final ball of his fifth over, he strikes again with the opening delivery of his sixth, when he finds the outside edge of Dawson's defensive bat to provide Brown with a straightforward catch at first slip and put himself on a hat-trick. To add a little extra spice to the mix, the batsman who is coming out to face the hat-trick ball is the young Yorkshire debutant, David Wigley.

It's a big moment for both youngsters, therefore, as Clarke, encouraged by the crowd, races in from the railway end to bowl to Wigley. Much to his credit, given the excitement of the situation, the Surrey all-rounder manages to bowl a good straight delivery, but Wigley, showing an equally good temperament, meets it safely with the full blade of a defensive bat. The Bradford-born lad actually looks a better batsman than his number eleven billing suggests as he steers his fourth ball to the third man boundary to open his account in first-class cricket, though an airy slash to the rope in the same area two balls later prompts a slight rethink.

For a while, the last-wicket pair enjoy a measure of success in boosting their side's total as Ryan Sidebottom drives Saqlain to the boundary wide of mid-on and Wigley again looks competent in cutting Clarke for his third four, but the fun and games ends when the Yorkshire debutant drives Saqlain straight to Clarke at midwicket in the forty-sixth over to bring the innings to a close with the total at 172.

As the Surrey players leave the field to a well-deserved ovation, with all the bowlers having made a significant contribution, it has to be said that Yorkshire's score looks to be below par, even allowing for the fact that this hasn't, so far, looked to be the best Guildford pitch of recent times. While you wouldn't say that it looked like a 400-plus wicket, it certainly doesn't look to be a 172 track either, and we will undoubtedly get a better idea about what the par score might be once the Surrey reply gets under way.

With Mark Butcher on Test duty, Jon Batty returns to his opening role alongside Ian Ward, while Chris Silverwood and Ryan Sidebottom take the new ball for Yorkshire and attempt to regain some ground for their side.

Despite starting slowly, the early honours go to the home team, thanks to two leg-side boundaries by Ward off Sidebottom in the fourth and sixth overs of the innings, though Silverwood does eventually manage to bring Yorkshire back into contention during a fiery ninth over of the innings. Racing in from the railway end and generating good pace, he strikes twice in two balls and comes very close to a hat-trick as Surrey slip to 24-2. Although Ward becomes Silverwood's first victim in dubious circumstances, when umpire Palmer adjudges the left-handed opener to have edged a full-length delivery to Richard Blakey, there is no doubt about Mark Ramprakash's dismissal to the next ball as another near yorker-length delivery defeats the batsman's drive and removes his leg stump. While the statisticians in the crowd are busy pointing out that Ramprakash now has two double-centuries and three first-ball ducks to his name in the Championship this year, Nadeem Shahid makes his way to the middle to face the second hat-trick ball of the session.

Once the batsman has settled, Silverwood hares in and, seemingly beating Shahid for pace, the ball thuds into the batsman's pads. A very loud and confident appeal goes up from the bowler and his close fielders, leaving Surrey fans fearing the worst, but umpire Palmer remains unconvinced after a clear period of consideration. Fortunately for the home county, Shahid doesn't seem too fazed by his narrow escape, squeezing and cutting boundaries backward of point in Silverwood's next over, before driving the same bowler to the rope at cover at the end of a sparky seven-over blast that has given the reigning champions new hope.

While all the excitement has been going on at the other end, Batty has been steadfastly repelling the equally dangerous Sidebottom, gathering just two boundaries in his first fourteen overs at the crease, the first via an edge through the slips, and the second with a classy cover drive as the left-arm swing bowler's opening spell draws towards its close.

With ten overs to go until tea, Wigley takes over from Silverwood at the railway end and produces a good opening over in first-class cricket, beating Shahid's outside edge with his first ball, and then almost forcing Batty to play onto his stumps later in the over.

Alas, he finds the top level of the domestic game rather harder in his next three overs as both Surrey batsmen tuck into a number of loose balls with relish. Shahid takes his team past fifty in Wigley's second over with a rasping square-cut for four, then he hooks for six in the young paceman's third, before Batty comes to the party with three successive well-struck boundaries - a glance, an extra-cover drive and a force backward of point - during a nightmare fourth over for the debutant. With the partnership passing fifty during this sequence, and Anthony McGrath looking less than threatening as Sidebottom's replacement at the pavilion end, Surrey go to tea very well placed at 88-2.

*Tea:- Surrey 88-2 (Batty 35\*, Shahid 33\*) from 24 overs*

Since Wigley and McGrath had proved ineffective before the break, it's no surprise to see Silverwood and Sidebottom resuming hostilities after tea, though Shahid seems happy enough with this as he takes a four off each bowler in their opening over of the session.

Thereafter, the scoring rate stalls for a few overs, with Shahid picking up an occasional single to eventually see the total into three figures, while Batty's score remains anchored on thirty-five as he allows a large number of deliveries to pass by harmlessly outside the off stump. This approach is not in Shahid's nature, though, and, having made an attractive forty-five, he assays an ambitious drive at Sidebottom and miscues, at chest height, to Fellows at square cover.

At 101-3, Yorkshire sense the possibility of a fightback, but Batty and his new partner, Ali Brown, work hard to snuff out this hope, playing out three consecutive maidens before the Surrey keeper scores his first runs of the session with a cover-driven boundary at Silverwood's expense. Rather surprisingly, Sidebottom and Silverwood are then removed from the attack after just six and five overs respectively, with almost predictably dire effects for the visitors. Wigley, his promising first over just a distant memory, again finds the going tough as Brown twice pulls him for four and then drives him back down the ground for another boundary, while Batty pulls and snicks fours off McGrath. The Surrey score consequently races forward in leaps and bounds, reaching 150 in the forty-third over, following four more assorted Brown boundaries in the course of two Wigley overs, and the fifty partnership arrives with a single to square leg shortly afterwards.

With his young paceman's nine overs to date having cost sixty-one runs, and his latest spell of four having gone for thirty-three, Lehmann finally shows mercy on Wigley, pulling him out of the firing line and introducing Richard Dawson for a second spell, his first having consisted of a solitary over just before tea.

Any hopes the Yorkshire captain might have harboured of this putting the lid on the scoring rate are dashed immediately, however, as Batty whips the young off-spinner away to the rope at square leg to complete a solid half-century that has been the bedrock of his side's reply to the visitors' increasingly inadequate-looking total. Interestingly, Batty's 134-ball fifty has included no fewer than eleven fours, a very high proportion in any half-century, let alone one that has spanned so many deliveries. He soon adds a twelfth boundary, too, when driving Dawson classically through the covers in the off-spinner's next over, before drawing Surrey level with Yorkshire's score by forcing Fellows' second delivery as replacement for McGrath at the pavilion end to the rope at backward point for boundary number thirteen. With Brown clipping the same bowler for four backward of square leg and Batty dispatching Dawson to the rope on two further occasions in the next over, it's now all Surrey, with the visitors beginning to look a disillusioned outfit.

Brown then adds to their misery by reaching what is, surprisingly, only his second-ever first-class fifty against Yorkshire, courtesy of a cut for four off Fellows, his innings having consumed just fifty-nine balls and contained nine fours. The Tykes might not need reminding that his previous half-century metamorphosed into a match-winning 140-run beast at The Oval in 2000, though they are spared such punishment here when Brown carelessly cuts a rank long-hop from Fellows straight to point, where Craven clings on to a comfortable catch at chest height. It's a disappointing way for such an entertaining knock to end and it costs Surrey another wicket, too, as Ian Salisbury, coming in as nightwatchman with just under five overs left for play, lasts only three balls, one of them a no-ball, against the Yorkshire medium-pacer. At least Fellows does a little more to deserve this wicket, deceiving Salisbury in the length and bowling him, possibly via an inside-edge or a pad.

Rather than send out another nightwatchman, Adam Hollioake strides out to the middle and keeps the rock-like Batty company until the close, by which time the Surrey keeper has taken his side past two-hundred with another boundary, whipped through midwicket off Dawson. As the players leave the field at the end of day one it's very much a case of 'advantage Surrey'.

*Close:- Surrey 207-5 (Batty 78\*, Hollioake 1\*) from 56 overs*

| VIEWS FROM THE DRESSING ROOM |
|---|

*I assume you must have been very excited about playing for Surrey at your home ground in Guildford, with so many people you knew present?*
**RIKKI CLARKE** - Definitely. There were lots of people who I knew there because I've played for Guildford since I was a colt. It did seem very weird stepping out there with a big crowd around the ground, though - normally when I walk out there for Guildford there's one man and his dog… and Richard Spiller of *The Surrey Advertiser*, of course.

*Have you ever held a better catch than the one to dismiss Darren Lehmann? You must have seen the ball very late?*
**RIKKI CLARKE** - The ball was behind me and to my left-hand side and, yes, I saw it very late and it stayed low all the way, so I would have to say it is one of my best. I've taken a few good ones at youth level, but that's definitely got to be right up there with those, because of who the batsman was and the match it was in.

*Rikki Clarke's slip catch to dismiss Darren Lehmann in the first innings was something special - would it have been one of the best you've ever seen?*
**JON BATTY** - Yes, definitely - it would be in my all-time top five, just an unbelievable catch. And the fact that it got rid of Lehmann was a huge bonus.

*At the end of the innings you were on a hat-trick, with the hat-trick ball to be bowled to their number eleven, who was making his debut. How did you feel as you ran in to bowl? Confident?*
**RIKKI CLARKE** - To be perfectly honest, I felt very calm… because I didn't actually realise I was on a hat-trick!

*Apart from Silverwood and Sidebottom, the rest of the attack didn't look particularly strong - was there any plan to see them off and then make hay against the others?*
**JON BATTY** - Having bowled them out quite quickly, I knew there were three-and-a-half days left to bat, so this was one of the few innings where I went out there with the sole objective of trying to bat as long as I possibly could. With their seam attack, we will generally try to bat for long periods of time, because if they can bowl you out in forty or fifty overs then they will be fresh for the second innings. We like to make sure that they have to take the second new ball and bowl 120 or 130 overs, so that, come the second knock, they will be tired, which will make things easier for us then. So it wasn't really a case of trying to see off those two, it was just a case of making Yorkshire bowl as many overs as possible.

*You seem to enjoy opening the batting. Given the choice, would you rather open or bat at seven?*
**JON BATTY** - I much prefer opening, no contest.

## Second Day - Thursday 25th July

### Yorkshire 172 and 254-3; Surrey 382

Yorkshire, badly in need of a quick breakthrough at the start of day two, receive an early boost when Ryan Sidebottom dismisses Adam Hollioake with the tenth ball of the morning, a fine delivery that takes the edge of the Surrey skipper's defensive bat on its way through to Richard Blakey behind the wicket. Although both batsmen have already added a boundary to their overnight tallies by this stage, the early wicket, which pegs Surrey back to 215-6, is potentially priceless to the division's bottom side.

Sidebottom then almost doubles Yorkshire's joy when he manages to find a fine yorker for Rikki Clarke first up. Luckily, the excellent reflexes of the young Surrey all-rounder enable him to jab down fast on the ball, squeezing it away for a single to midwicket and preventing the disaster of a golden duck on his home ground.

With the visitors' former England left-arm seamer beating the bat from time to time and looking the pick of their attack, just as he had at Headingley in April, these early overs prove testing, though Chris Silverwood, his bowling partner, is unable to maintain a consistent line and is, consequently, picked off for a leg-side four by each batsman.

Since Sidebottom has looked the better bowler so far, it comes as something of a surprise when eleven runs flow from his fourth over as Clarke clips through square leg for four and forces straight for three, before Batty moves his score to ninety-four with a square-driven boundary. Despite the fact that he has occasionally lapsed in line and length, it is quite a surprise to see Silverwood pulled out of the attack after just four overs in favour of Richard Dawson.

The 21-year-old England off-spinner had looked well short of Test class on day one and he looks no better this morning. Even though he induces a thick edge from Batty, which enables the Surrey wicket-keeper to advance his score to ninety-nine with three runs to third man, Clarke is soon dancing down the track to drive him over mid-on for the four runs that take Surrey's total to exactly 250.

The home side look to be regaining full control at this stage, though personal disappointment is just around the corner for Batty as Sidebottom, maybe with the help of a little inswing, induces an inside edge that deflects the ball onto the stumps as the batsman aims to drive through the covers. It's rough luck for the home team's keeper to fall one short of what would have been a well-deserved century after such a dedicated and beautifully constructed innings, though the wicket does reward Sidebottom for his sterling efforts in leading a largely unimpressive Yorkshire attack. Batty receives a great reception from an appreciative crowd, however, and he will doubtless find some consolation in the fact that he has built a great platform for his side.

So good are the foundations of the innings, in fact, that Clarke, who has looked in fine form right from the start of his knock, now has the ideal launching pad for an assault on Dawson. In the space of three overs from the off-spinner, he plunders three sixes and three fours, including a couple of towering leg-side hits and two drives caressed through the covers, the second of which takes the young Surrey star through to an excellent 44-ball fifty that brings the crowd to its feet.

In this form, a quick-fire century doesn't appear to be out of the question, but Clarke and his fans are left disappointed three overs later when Anthony McGrath, Sidebottom's replacement at the pavilion end, finds a yorker that this time proves too good for the Guildford all-rounder, ending his fine knock on fifty-six, with the score advanced to 297. Another decent crowd, packed into the tiny Woodbridge Road ground, offers up enthusiastic applause to greet the 20-year-old's return to the pavilion as his fine all-round match continues.

By this stage, the Yorkshire skipper has brought himself into the attack in place of the shell-shocked Dawson, maybe in the hope of picking up some lower-order scalps, but the Surrey ninth-wicket pair of Saqlain and Ormond are in no mood to give their wickets away cheaply, especially as they are both in top form after their magnificent efforts at Canterbury. It appears that they are keen to play their shots, too, as Ormond drives McGrath to the rope at cover to raise the three-hundred for the home county and then follows up with a stunning 4-4-6 sequence in the medium-pacer's next over, with a savage cut through backward point being followed by a straight drive and a pick-up behind square on the leg side. Saqlain immediately takes this as his cue to join in the fun, deflecting and cover-driving boundaries of his own, off McGrath and Lehmann respectively, and, consequently, forcing the Yorkshire captain to recall Silverwood for another burst as lunch approaches and Surrey's lead begins to extend into the distance.

The return of his fastest bowler doesn't initially improve matters for Lehmann, however, as Ormond forces through extra-cover for four and Saqlain drives over the head of mid-on for another boundary in an over costing nine, and the Australian's demeanour is then further darkened when he personally feels the full force of another explosive sequence of strokes - this time 4-4-0-6 - from the home side's sturdy paceman in the following over. As Ormond reels off a lofted straight drive, a square cut and a mighty drive over wide long-on, Surrey race past 350 and the ninth-wicket alliance becomes worth fifty at around a run a ball, much to the frustration of the white rose county's supporters in the crowd. Their team appears to be sinking without trace, though they are cheered, momentarily, when Wood sprints towards third man from slip and completes an excellent catch following Ormond's top-edged mishook in the next over from Silverwood.

By scoring thirty-nine from just twenty-two balls, including six fours and two sixes, the former Leicestershire man may have already damaged Yorkshire's cause irreparably, though, and Saqlain shows that he hasn't finished yet, either, by reverse-sweeping Lehmann to the boundary in the penultimate over before lunch.

As if the visitors haven't suffered enough, Ed Giddins then rubs further salt into their wounds by driving the first ball of the last over from Silverwood gracefully through the covers for four. It seems rather appropriate that, given five balls in which to gain his revenge for this slight, the Yorkshire fast bowler proves incapable of bowling a single straight delivery.

*Lunch:- Surrey 364-9 (Saqlain 31\*, Giddins 4\*) from 90 overs*

After the break, Surrey's first innings extends by almost five overs and eighteen runs - including a straight-driven six by Saqlain off Wigley and a clip to the midwicket boundary by Giddins off Sidebottom - before Yorkshire's debutant fast bowler claims Saqlain as his maiden first-class victim when the Pakistani, on forty-four, miscues an on-drive to Craven. With their lead standing at 210, and a fine chance of victory thereby established, Surrey won't be too concerned about missing out on their final batting point by eighteen runs.

The Yorkshire openers face a daunting task as they take guard for the start of the second innings, though Wood will be feeling especially nervous since he is on a pair of pairs against Surrey this season.

The struggling Huddersfield-born batsman no doubt feels a huge sense of relief, therefore, when he pushes a single to mid-on in the first over bowled by Giddins, and when he takes six from the same bowler's second over, including a boundary glanced to fine leg, he must feel that his luck has really changed.

Both he and his fellow opener, Vic Craven, do need some good fortune in the early stages, as it happens, especially against the impressive Ormond, though they eventually ride out the storm and begin to expand their repertoire, with every over from the seventh to the tenth bringing a well-struck boundary to one or other of the Yorkshire pair.

Having been rather inconsistent during his opening spell, Giddins then gives way to Clarke for the eleventh over and, though the young all-rounder immediately concedes ten runs, four of these come when Wood almost falls in identical fashion to Fellows in the first innings. While his team-mate's slightly mistimed hook had gone straight down the throat of Nadeem Shahid at deep backward square leg, Wood is fortunate that the same fielder is only able to get one hand to the ball as he dives away to his right-hand side near the boundary edge.

Craven, meanwhile, looks very much in control, and the total soon passes fifty as the left-hander unfurls a succession of strokes that pierce the off-side field, largely at the expense of Clarke, whose first three overs yield twenty-five runs to the Yorkshire cause. Although the bowler regains control to concede just one run from his next two overs, it isn't long before a double bowling change sees Saqlain operating from the railway end and Giddins returning to the attack, this time from the pavilion end.

With the pitch having seemingly flattened out as the game has progressed, both Yorkshire openers post their highest Championship score of the summer, though Wood seems less comfortable with the new bowlers. Giddins certainly unsettles him and, having already lured the 25-year-old right-hander into an airy drive through square cover and a miscued pull over straight mid-on, justice is done when the former Sussex and Warwickshire bowler has him taken at the wicket by Batty to break the opening stand at eighty-three.

One wicket then almost brings a second when Giddins, looking much more impressive in this second spell, has a very confident appeal for lbw against the new batsman, Anthony McGrath, turned down in his next over, though Craven continues to find the off-side boundary, doing so twice at Saqlain's expense as the Yorkshire hundred comes up just ahead of the interval.

*Tea:- Yorkshire 101-1 (Craven 48\*, McGrath 5\*) from 31 overs*

The day's final session gets off to an explosive start with four action-packed overs from Jimmy Ormond and Ed Giddins bringing no fewer than six boundaries and, more importantly from a Surrey point of view, two wickets.

Yorkshire initially have the upper hand as McGrath drives Giddins to the rope at midwicket, Craven strikes successive deliveries from Ormond to the boundary at backward point and long-on, completing an impressive 100-ball fifty in the process, and McGrath again cracks Giddins for four, this time through the covers. Each bowler gains rapid vengeance on the batsman who has just taken boundaries off him, however, as Jon Batty claims two victims in four balls, the first courtesy of a routine defensive edge by McGrath off Giddins, and the second as a result of Craven's top-edged slash off Ormond that forces him to dive away in front of first slip to complete a fine catch.

The capture of these two wickets with the score at 117 has greatly reduced the odds of Surrey completing a third-day victory, though Michael Lumb suggests that there will be no immediate surrender by on-driving and glancing his first two balls from Ormond for four. With Darren

Lehmann also looking to dominate right from the start of his innings, the visitors quickly regain some of their lost ground, and by driving and cutting four boundaries in three overs the chunky Australian manages to bring up Yorkshire's 150 in the fortieth over.

Although it would appear that the bat is beginning to win its contest with the ball again, Ormond still proves capable of causing discomfort for the batsmen from time to time, as he demonstrates with two short deliveries that Lumb gloves away to long leg and then when he tempts Lehmann into an indiscriminate off-side slash that sends the ball flying into, and then out of, the hands of Hollioake at second slip. Though undoubtedly an awkward, head-high chance, with the ball travelling at a rate of knots, the unlucky Ormond is clearly disappointed that the catch hasn't been held, especially since the Surrey captain had taken a very similar chance to dismiss Silverwood in Yorkshire's first innings. From a Surrey point of view, one can only hope that Lehmann, on twenty-six at the time, doesn't profit too much from this let-off, as everyone is aware of how he is capable of changing the course of a match with one of his big centuries.

It seems possible that this lucky escape has actually reminded the Australian of how important he is to his side's chances of getting back into the game, since he becomes much more circumspect in his approach for a while hereafter, especially once Saqlain Mushtaq comes into the attack in place of Giddins. Fortunately for the visitors, Lumb takes over the mantle of principal aggressor in fine style, driving Ormond to the backward point boundary as the fourth-wicket partnership expands beyond fifty, and then taking advantage of two loose deliveries in the ninth over of the big fast bowler's spell to notch further fours, with a pull and a clip off his toes. This is a clear signal to the Surrey skipper that his principal strike bowler is in need of a break after pounding in whole-heartedly, but without luck, for so long and, consequently, Ian Salisbury rather belatedly joins the attack to bowl the fifty-first over of the innings.

With the Surrey spin twins now operating in tandem, there are very few loose deliveries on offer and the run rate slows, though Lehmann does eventually manage to find the boundary for the first time in eleven overs, courtesy of a sweep off Salisbury. At the other end, Lumb, looking less comfortable against spin than pace, is temporarily becalmed for almost the first time in his innings, though he helps his skipper guide Yorkshire past two-hundred, and then sees them into the lead, by tickling the former Sussex leg-spinner to fine leg for two.

Having now almost emulated his partner by going without a boundary for seven overs, the impressive Lumb then strikes twice in an over from Salisbury, forcing him to the rope at long-off to simultaneously reach a personal fifty from just 68 balls and raise the hundred partnership, and then finding the boundary at square cover with a sublime drive a few balls later.

With the spinners having, surprisingly, created no real chances during their period in harness, Hollioake opts for a couple of changes as the day draws to a close, introducing Rikki Clarke at the railway end and switching his leg-spinner to the pavilion end. Neither move proves successful, however, as Yorkshire end the day strongly, with Lumb finding the rope in each of Clarke's two overs, and Lehmann taking three fours from Salisbury's solitary over after his change of ends - a straight drive is followed by a cover drive and then a sweep to fine leg, the second of these strokes completing an 82-ball half-century for the visiting captain.

As the players leave the field, it would appear that we again have an interesting contest on our hands, since Lumb and Lehmann have really rescued the Yorkshire innings with their unbroken partnership of 137. Although the occasional ball has misbehaved slightly, the pitch looks at its best for batting now and Surrey will be pinning their hopes on picking up a couple of early wickets in the morning in order to restore their advantage.

*Close:- Yorkshire 254-3 (Lehmann 55\*, Lumb 68\*) from 63 overs*

# VIEW FROM THE DRESSING ROOM

*During your innings of fifty-six you were particularly severe on Richard Dawson, who had played for England the previous winter. I assume it must give your confidence an extra boost when you are able score so freely off someone who has so recently played at Test level?*
**RIKKI CLARKE** - I've had a lot of good advice from people like Ali Brown and Mark Ramprakash and, as they say, at the end of the day it's just a ball coming towards you - if you start worrying about who is bowling the ball then that's where you can start going wrong. So when I started playing for the first team I said to myself that no matter who bowled at me I would just see it as a ball coming down - once the bowler has let go of it then, you, as the batsman, are in control.

## Third Day - Friday 26th July

### Yorkshire 172 and 446; Surrey 382 and 110-3

Ed Giddins and Jimmy Ormond are Adam Hollioake's choices to open the bowling on the third morning of the match, perhaps in the hope that they can take advantage of a slightly grey and cloudy start to the day. The Yorkshire left-handers begin confidently, however, striking a boundary apiece off Giddins to suggest that the Championship leaders could be in for another extended period in the field.

Although it is Ormond who provides Surrey with their first ray of hope by beating Lehmann outside the off stump twice in the day's fourth over, it is actually Giddins, with an important assist from umpire Palmer, who makes the vital early breakthrough at the start of the next over. Crucially, it is the Yorkshire captain who appears to be the victim of a highly dubious lbw decision as he pushes half-forward and is given out after adding just six to his overnight tally. Suspicions that the left-handed Aussie had got an inside edge onto his pad are confirmed by Lehmann's unhappy demeanour and his pointed examination of his bat as he returns slowly to the pavilion, with his team now effectively 59-4.

Any thoughts Surrey might harbour of slicing through the rest of the batting now that they have dismissed the key batsman are quickly stymied, however, as Lumb continues to look in good form by driving Ormond to the long-on boundary, and Gary Fellows, after a very shaky start, notches a couple of square-driven fours off Giddins.

With the ball now more than seventy overs old, and the overhead conditions rapidly brightening, the Surrey pacemen do well to induce a fair amount of playing and missing, though their luck appears to be out as Fellows survives an appeal for a catch at the wicket off Giddins, and Lumb picks up four runs at Ormond's expense when an edge drops short of third slip and scurries away to the rope to take his score into the nineties. A much more impressive stroke, a flowing on-drive for four when Giddins overpitches, then moves him on to ninety-seven, and Yorkshire's score beyond three-hundred, before Fellows takes control for a while with a sequence of fine shots. Upon Saqlain's introduction, in place of Ormond at the railway end, the 23-year-old all-rounder sashays down the pitch to drive over mid-on for four, then he follows up by forcing Giddins to the rope at square cover and taking a second boundary off the Surrey off-spinner with a sweep to fine leg. This last stroke takes the fifth-wicket partnership past fifty as the visitors' lead continues to grow at a slightly disconcerting rate for the home county.

At this point, Hollioake makes a rather surprising decision by bringing himself on to bowl ahead of both Rikki Clarke and Ian Salisbury. One can only assume that the Surrey skipper has something cunning in mind, though it isn't immediately obvious as Lumb celebrates the completion of an excellent century from his 157th delivery in the previous over from Saqlain by cracking Hollioake to the cover boundary for the eighteenth four of his highly commendable innings. Whether or not poor team spirit has been a problem for Yorkshire during their troubled Championship season I wouldn't know, though it might have disappointed a jubilant Lumb to have seen just three of his team-mates - Dawson, Silverwood and Wigley - appear on the pavilion balcony to salute the arrival of his ton.

He certainly is disappointed two overs later, however, when Hollioake justifies his decision to come on and bowl by finding the outside edge of Fellows' defensive bat to provide Jon Batty with his fourth catch of the innings so far. Although the Halifax-born all-rounder's knock of thirty-three has been a rather patchy affair, it has been very valuable in helping his team to establish a lead of 127 with five wickets remaining.

This much-needed breakthrough has certainly put Surrey back in charge, though they probably won't want to chase too big a total in the fourth innings, despite having proved that anything is possible just four days ago at Canterbury. Lumb and the new batsman, Richard Blakey, are clearly not going to make things easy, though, given their side's desperate plight at the foot of the Championship table, and they go about their business in a positive fashion, with Blakey driving Hollioake through extra cover for three and Lumb forcing Saqlain to the boundary at point in consecutive overs.

Lunch is now rapidly approaching and, while Blakey sees off the Surrey captain with boundaries through square leg and cover in an over costing ten, his left-handed partner suddenly looks rather insecure against Saqlain, twice edging drives to third man in passing his previous career-best score of 122. The introduction of Salisbury in place of Hollioake for the penultimate over of the session is, therefore, an obvious move and, with fielders stationed around the bat to apply pressure, Lumb duly obliges by presenting Shahid at short leg with a bat-pad catch from the leg-spinner's second delivery. With the well-built left-hander's fine innings terminated at 124, and Yorkshire now 366-6, a fairly even session has just tilted marginally Surrey's way, since the lower-order is sure to face a stiff examination immediately after the break.

*Lunch:- Yorkshire 367-6 (Blakey 15\*, Dawson 0\*) from 97 overs*

The two Richards, Blakey and Dawson, face a predictable ordeal by spin when play restarts, though they cope surprisingly well, playing with great skill and determination as the opening seven overs of the session yield fourteen runs. With the batsmen having had only one anxious moment, an edge wide of slip by Blakey off Salisbury, their confidence grows visibly and, as a result, the sweep shot comes to the fore, bringing a flurry of boundaries. Two of these, plus a cut to the backward point boundary by Dawson, feature in a thirteen-run Salisbury over that speeds the visitors through to four-hundred in the ninth over of the session and also puts a furrow in the Surrey captain's brow. When a further series of sweeps results in the Yorkshire score advancing by another nine runs in the course of the next two overs bowled by his surprisingly ineffective spinners, Hollioake decides that the time for action has arrived, recalling his opening bowlers and immediately getting the result he requires.

Jimmy Ormond is the man who does the trick for his skipper, his second delivery luring Dawson into an edged forcing stroke that Ali Brown snaffles low down at first slip to give the big fast bowler further reward for his efforts throughout the match. Now 413-7, Yorkshire's lead has just exceeded two-hundred, though it's clear that they will need quite a few more runs yet to put pressure on the Championship leaders - and this could be a problem, considering the rather flimsy nature of their tail.

The belated taking of the new ball merely strengthens Surrey convictions that this could, in fact, be the beginning of the end for the visitors, and Chris Silverwood certainly doesn't last long, his only contribution of note, a straight-driven four off Giddins, being followed later in the same over by an edged drive that provides Brown with another catch at first slip to make the score 422-8.

Fortunately for Yorkshire, Ryan Sidebottom, unlike his recently departed colleague, is at least prepared to get his head down and, though the ninth-wicket pair are unable to make much headway in terms of run-scoring, they do manage to see off Ormond after a five-over burst. The feeling that this could be good news for the visitors is rapidly dispelled, however, when Rikki Clarke, the former Leicestershire bowler's replacement at the pavilion end, takes just two balls to exploit Sidebottom's badly flawed defensive stroke, which merely deflects the ball onto his leg stump.

Since Wigley had looked to be batting one place too low in the first innings, and Blakey remains in residence at the other end, there is still a chance that Yorkshire might extend their lead beyond the current 223, and indeed they do, as Blakey pulls Giddins for four and Wigley cuts Clarke to the rope at cover during the course of the next two overs. Blakey then completes a fighting half-century from 90 balls with a single off Giddins, before becoming Brown's third victim at first slip since lunch, and Clarke's second scalp of the innings, when he top-edges an attempted cut to bring Yorkshire's second knock to a close at 446. The young Surrey all-rounder therefore has five wickets in the match, including career-best figures of 3-41 in the first innings, plus fifty-six runs and two catches. It makes his omission from the recently announced provisional England Academy squad all the more baffling.

The reigning county champions' spirited second-innings batting performance, during which they have looked anything but a bottom-of-the-table side, has left Surrey needing to score 237 for victory, with time not a factor in the equation, since the weather is relatively settled. It is therefore safe to say that, sometime tomorrow, either Surrey will be a step closer to winning the 2002 County Championship title, or Yorkshire will have taken a step away from the relegation precipice.

Much is at stake then as the home side's openers face a tricky ten overs before tea against a fired-up new-ball attack of Silverwood and Sidebottom and, consequently, it is not surprising that the opening overs are tense, with Ward's on-driven boundary off Sidebottom in the second over proving to be an isolated moment of dominance for bat over ball. Although the bustling Silverwood manages to get a number of deliveries past the outside edge during his most consistent burst of the match to date, Ward breaks out twice to cuff Sidebottom away to the square cover boundary as the Surrey openers come through safely to the interval with their team's victory target reduced by nineteen.

*Tea:- Surrey 19-0 (Ward 15\*, Batty 2\*) from 10 overs*

Darren Lehmann has a surprise in store for us upon the resumption. His decision to persevere with his off-spinner, Richard Dawson, who had bowled a single over before tea, seems rather odd, given that the match has so far been dominated by seam, with even Surrey's celebrated spinners reduced to minor roles. Additionally, since the final innings of the match is highly unlikely to extend as far as the ninetieth over, the visitors will certainly not get another new ball, so it seems wasteful not to give both Silverwood and Sidebottom the maximum opportunity with this one.

By following his current course of action he therefore has to choose between his seamers, and his decision to employ Silverwood first clearly meets with Ward's approval as the Surrey opener clips the former England fast bowler's first delivery of the session to the midwicket boundary and then repeats the shot, this time behind square leg, later in a typically erratic over.

Although Silverwood quickly settles down, neither he nor Dawson looks especially threatening, and when Ward reels off a classy on-driven four at the pace bowler's expense, and Batty follows up by cutting the off-spinner to the cover boundary, the Yorkshire captain is forced into a change of plan, with Wigley and Sidebottom entering the fray, at the railway end and the pavilion end respectively.

This initially brings an acceleration in Batty's scoring rate as he strikes the opening delivery from each new bowler to the boundary, but, shortly after Ward raises the Surrey fifty with another of his trademark on-drives off Wigley, the Surrey wicket-keeper shoulders arms to Sidebottom and has his off stump knocked back, handing the visitors an all-important opening breakthrough.

Fortunately for the Championship leaders, Ward is unperturbed by the loss of his fellow opener, immediately driving Wigley for two boundaries in an over, though his new partner, Mark Ramprakash, makes a less than convincing start, with a rather fortunate inside edge off Sidebottom flying narrowly past his off stump on its way to the boundary. This doesn't seem to matter greatly at the moment, however, because Ward is in full flow at the other end as he completes an admirable half-century from 93 deliveries with cut and pulled fours off Sidebottom, taking the score to 79-1 in the twenty-eighth over of the innings.

With his current pair of bowlers having now contributed five overs apiece, Lehmann elects to change the bowling again, recalling Silverwood at the pavilion end and bringing his own left-arm spin into the equation at the railway end.

Since Ward looks equally at home against this new combination, picking up a boundary from each end, and Ramprakash appears to be over his edgy start as he gathers in a series of singles, Surrey seem sure to be in the driving seat come the end of the day, until a questionable umpiring decision and a good piece of bowling give Yorkshire fresh hope in the last nine overs - Silverwood, again working up a good pace, first unseats Ramprakash with the score on ninety-eight, before Dawson, having replaced Lehmann at the railway end, snares Shahid eleven runs later. Ramprakash seems a little unlucky to be adjudged lbw by umpire Palmer, since the ball looks as if it could well be passing over the top of the stumps, while Shahid is taken by Lumb at short leg when the Yorkshire off-spinner manages to get a delivery to both turn and bounce in the fourth-to-last over.

The former Essex batsman's late exit brings Ian Salisbury to the crease as nightwatchman and this produces another surprising act of captaincy from the visiting skipper. The last over of the day starts with Ward facing McGrath, Silverwood's successor at the pavilion end, and, rather than try to get the Surrey opener out, Lehmann pushes all his fielders back to allow a single in order to get the nightwatchman on strike. Predictably enough, Salisbury is happy to take the last five balls of the day, while I am left wondering what happened to the rule of captaincy that says you should usually do what the opposition *least* want you to do!

As the players leave the field at the end of yet another fine day's cricket, Surrey, requiring just 127 runs to win, look hot favourites to clinch victory tomorrow, thanks largely to Ward's excellent unbeaten sixty-seven.

*Close:- Surrey 110-3 (Ward 67\*, Salisbury 0\*) from 42 overs*

## VIEW FROM THE DRESSING ROOM

*I thought there was a rather strange piece of captaincy at the end of the day. With Ian Salisbury in as nightwatchman, Darren Lehmann spread the field for the start of the last over to give you a single and get Sals on strike. Were you as surprised as I was by that tactic?*

**IAN WARD** - Not especially. He obviously felt that, psychologically, their overnight position on the scoreboard would look far better if they could get another wicket. Also, if they were to get Sals out, they'd have a new batsman at the wicket in the morning, as opposed to Sals possibly blunting the attack for perhaps half-an-hour or more. So I suppose Lehmann paid me a bit of a complement by deciding to attack the other end, but it's all a matter of opinion - the old-fashioned way is to try and get the batsman out and then sort the nightwatchman out in the morning, whereas he went the other way, in the hope that he could remove the nightwatchman to allow his bowlers to have a roar at two specialist batsmen in the morning.

### Fourth Day - Saturday 27th July

### Yorkshire 172 and 446; Surrey 382 and 237-4

**Surrey won by six wickets**
**Surrey 19pts, Yorkshire 3**

Although the grey skies that prevail at the start of the decisive day of the match suggest the likely deployment of an all-out seam attack, Darren Lehmann again puts his faith in Richard Dawson at the railway end, pairing him with Chris Silverwood.

Needing to both contain the batsmen and grab a couple of early wickets if they are to continue the minor fightback that they started the previous evening, the reigning champions fail in both respects as Ian Salisbury makes a racing start, stealing the initiative for his side straight away. The former England leg-spinner notches a boundary in the third, fourth and fifth overs of the morning - with an off-drive and a force through square cover off Dawson and a square cut off Silverwood - and by the time Ward cuts the Yorkshire off-spinner to the rope at backward point two overs later, Surrey's target is below a hundred.

While they had shown great heart during yesterday's final session, with fielders pulling off three or four outstanding stops to prevent boundaries, the visitors' resolve seems to have been broken easily this morning by Salisbury's assault and, having competed well for large parts of the game, they suddenly look like a side bereft of confidence and fighting relegation.

Their rapidly fading hopes are then further dimmed when Salisbury drills Dawson to the rope at long-off and Ward glances a Silverwood no-ball for four, before the nightwatchman applies a twist of the knife with an edge to the boundary through an almost totally unmanned slip cordon later in the former England paceman's over. These four runs complete a fifty partnership for the fourth-wicket that looks increasingly certain to prove decisive, especially if Yorkshire continue to place just one slip when the capture of wickets represents their only hope of salvation.

Despite finding Salisbury's outside edge, Silverwood's eleven-run fifth over of the morning turns out to be his last, Ryan Sidebottom taking his place at the pavilion end, while the equally ineffective Dawson is kept going for another three overs, during which Salisbury collects his sixth four of the morning with a slog-sweep to midwicket and Ward progresses sedately through the nineties before cutting to the rope at point to move on to ninety-seven.

With just over fifty runs required now, Yorkshire's goose looks to be well and truly cooked, a feeling that is confirmed when Salisbury drives Sidebottom through extra cover for four and then greets the visiting skipper's appearance at the bowling crease with three further boundaries in quick succession. Although the Surrey leg-spinner is a little fortunate with a miscued heave over midwicket, there is no doubting the quality of the drives over, and then through, extra cover that follow, with the second of these strokes taking him through to a very impressive half-century from just sixty-six balls. Having congratulated his partner on reaching this mark, Ward then arrives at his own personal milestone later in the same over when he pushes the 190th ball of his innings backward of point for two runs to complete an outstanding century, drawing a well-deserved ovation from the understandably small final-day crowd.

With the game now over as a contest, and the Yorkshire team looking thoroughly dispirited, the debutant Wigley joins Lehmann in the attack and sees the match hurtle closer to its inevitable conclusion during the next over from his captain. After a carefree Salisbury completes a century partnership for the fourth wicket with an on-drive for six, before falling for a season's best score of fifty-nine when he edges the next delivery to Blakey behind the stumps, Ali Brown smashes his first ball, a full-toss, through the covers for four, with the crowd's applause for the nightwatchman's sparkling innings having barely died away.

The end then comes quickly as Ward feasts on some loose offerings from Wigley, picking off four varied off-side boundaries and then levelling the scores with a straight-driven three, before securing the winning single off Lehmann at 12.35pm.

As the left-handed opener leaves the field to a rousing ovation with 124 runs to his name, there can be no doubt that the Championship crown is now a step closer to being reclaimed from Yorkshire. In truth, the visitors had waved goodbye to their hopes of retaining the title some weeks ago, and all that remains to be seen now is whether any other county can challenge Surrey to become the successors to the relegation-haunted Tykes. With no-one yet emerging from the pack, a statistical bogey looks likely to be laid. On the last two occasions when Surrey completed two Championship victories over Yorkshire in the same season, the men from London SE11 failed to win the title, finishing second in 1973 and third in 1959. At this moment in time, you wouldn't bet on that being repeated in 2002.

**Yorkshire 172 and 446; Surrey 382 and 237-4**
**Surrey won by six wickets. Surrey 19pts, Yorkshire 3**

## VIEWS FROM THE DRESSING ROOM

*While you played your normal game, there appeared to be a plan for Sals to bat very positively on the final morning - was that the case or not?*
**IAN WARD** - Yes, that's what he said as we were walking out - he said he was going to be ultra-positive and would try to take the game to them. Sides have tripped over in the past when chasing small scores, and Sals felt that his best chance of success was to attack. And I was quite happy to watch him do it from the other end - it made my job a damn sight easier.

*I didn't think that Yorkshire looked like a bottom-of-the-table side for large parts of the game. Would you agree with that assessment or not?*
**JON BATTY** - They've certainly got a lot of very good players, though they did look short on confidence. After Nad and I put a little bit of a partnership together their heads soon went down in the field, which was a sign that they were struggling in the Championship.

| SURREY v YORKSHIRE at Guildford | | Played from 24th to 27th July | | | | |
|---|---|---|---|---|---|---|
| Yorkshire won the toss and elected to bat | | Umpires:- Nigel Llong and Ken Palmer | | | | |
| **YORKSHIRE - First Innings** | | | | | | |
| Fall Of Wkt | Batsman | How | Out | Score | Balls | 4s | 6s |
| 1-0 | M.J. Wood | c Salisbury | b Giddins | 0 | 2 | 0 | 0 |
| 2-53 | V.J. Craven | c Batty | b Giddins | 21 | 42 | 4 | 0 |
| 3-64 | A. McGrath | lbw | b Giddins | 26 | 45 | 4 | 0 |
| 4-74 | D.S. Lehmann * | c Clarke | b Ormond | 7 | 13 | 1 | 0 |
| 5-85 | M.J. Lumb | c Saqlain | b Ormond | 16 | 18 | 4 | 0 |
| 6-125 | G.M. Fellows | c Shahid | b Clarke | 16 | 33 | 1 | 0 |
| 7-141 | R.J. Blakey + | c Shahid | b Saqlain | 23 | 59 | 4 | 0 |
| 9-151 | R.K.J. Dawson | c Brown | b Clarke | 15 | 26 | 2 | 0 |
| 8-150 | C.E.W. Silverwood | c Hollioake | b Clarke | 2 | 7 | 0 | 0 |
| | R.J. Sidebottom | Not | Out | 6 | 18 | 1 | 0 |
| 10-172 | D.H. Wigley | c Clarke | b Saqlain | 15 | 19 | 3 | 0 |
| | Extras | (4b, 7lb, 2w, 12nb) | | 25 | | | |
| | **TOTAL** | (46 overs) | | 172 | | | |

| Bowler | O | M | R | W | NB | Wd |
|---|---|---|---|---|---|---|
| Giddins | 15 | 3 | 48 | 3 | 2 | - |
| Ormond | 13 | 3 | 51 | 2 | 2 | 1 |
| Saqlain Mushtaq | 10 | 1 | 21 | 2 | 1 | - |
| Clarke | 8 | 0 | 41 | 3 | 1 | - |

### SURREY - First Innings

| Fall Of Wkt | Batsman | How | Out | Score | Balls | 4s | 6s |
|---|---|---|---|---|---|---|---|
| 1-24 | I.J. Ward | c Blakey | b Silverwood | 12 | 26 | 2 | 0 |
| 7-250 | J.N. Batty + | | b Sidebottom | 99 | 207 | 20 | 0 |
| 2-24 | M.R. Ramprakash | | b Silverwood | 0 | 1 | 0 | 0 |
| 3-101 | N. Shahid | c Fellows | b Sidebottom | 45 | 66 | 6 | 1 |
| 4-193 | A.D. Brown | c Craven | b Fellows | 50 | 61 | 9 | 0 |
| 5-195 | I.D.K. Salisbury | | b Fellows | 0 | 3 | 0 | 0 |
| 6-215 | A.J. Hollioake * | c Blakey | b Sidebottom | 5 | 20 | 1 | 0 |
| 8-297 | R. Clarke | | b McGrath | 56 | 57 | 7 | 3 |
| 10-382 | Saqlain Mushtaq | c Craven | b Wigley | 44 | 90 | 8 | 1 |
| 9-351 | J. Ormond | c Wood | b Silverwood | 39 | 22 | 6 | 2 |
| | E.S.H. Giddins | Not | Out | 8 | 21 | 2 | 0 |
| | Extras | (5b, 7lb, 12nb) | | 24 | | | |
| | TOTAL | (94.4 overs) | | 382 | | | |

| Bowler | O | M | R | W | NB | Wd |
|---|---|---|---|---|---|---|
| Silverwood | 21 | 5 | 71 | 3 | 3 | - |
| Sidebottom | 22 | 7 | 57 | 3 | - | - |
| Wigley | 10.4 | 0 | 71 | 1 | - | - |
| McGrath | 15 | 3 | 55 | 1 | - | - |
| Dawson | 12 | 0 | 68 | 0 | - | - |
| Fellows | 5 | 1 | 21 | 2 | 3 | - |
| Lehmann | 9 | 3 | 27 | 0 | - | - |

### YORKSHIRE - Second Innings (Trailing by 210 runs on first innings)

| Fall Of Wkt | Batsman | How | Out | Score | Balls | 4s | 6s |
|---|---|---|---|---|---|---|---|
| 1-83 | M.J. Wood | c Batty | b Giddins | 43 | 71 | 6 | 0 |
| 3-117 | V.J. Craven | c Batty | b Ormond | 56 | 105 | 11 | 0 |
| 2-117 | A. McGrath | c Batty | b Giddins | 13 | 32 | 3 | 0 |
| 4-269 | D.S. Lehmann * | lbw | b Giddins | 61 | 90 | 11 | 0 |
| 6-366 | M.J. Lumb | c Shahid | b Salisbury | 124 | 196 | 20 | 0 |
| 5-337 | G.M. Fellows | c Batty | b Hollioake | 33 | 64 | 5 | 0 |
| 10-446 | R.J. Blakey + | c Brown | b Clarke | 50 | 93 | 7 | 0 |
| 7-413 | R.K.J. Dawson | c Brown | b Ormond | 20 | 48 | 3 | 0 |
| 8-422 | C.E.W. Silverwood | c Brown | b Giddins | 6 | 15 | 1 | 0 |
| 9-433 | R.J. Sidebottom | | b Clarke | 1 | 16 | 0 | 0 |
| | D.H. Wigley | Not | Out | 4 | 12 | 1 | 0 |
| | Extras | (17lb, 4w, 14nb) | | 35 | | | |
| | TOTAL | (122.3 overs) | | 446 | | | |

| Bowler | O | M | R | W | NB | Wd |
|---|---|---|---|---|---|---|
| Giddins | 35 | 6 | 113 | 4 | 2 | - |
| Ormond | 29 | 4 | 106 | 2 | 1 | 2 |
| Clarke | 9.3 | 2 | 39 | 2 | 1 | - |
| Saqlain Mushtaq | 29 | 4 | 82 | 0 | 2 | - |
| Hollioake | 7 | 1 | 27 | 1 | - | - |
| Salisbury | 13 | 2 | 62 | 1 | 1 | - |

### SURREY - Second Innings (Needing 237 to win)

| Fall Of Wkt | Batsman | How | Out | Score | Balls | 4s | 6s |
|---|---|---|---|---|---|---|---|
| | I.J. Ward | Not | Out | 124 | 217 | 21 | 0 |
| 1-52 | J.N. Batty + | | b Sidebottom | 16 | 60 | 3 | 0 |
| 2-98 | M.R. Ramprakash | lbw | b Silverwood | 16 | 33 | 2 | 0 |
| 3-109 | N. Shahid | c Lumb | b Dawson | 7 | 16 | 1 | 0 |
| 4-209 | I.D.K. Salisbury | c Blakey | b Lehmann | 59 | 70 | 10 | 1 |
| | A.D. Brown | Not | Out | 5 | 17 | 1 | 0 |
| | Extras | (6lb, 4nb) | | 10 | | | |
| | TOTAL | (68.3 overs) | (for 4 wkts) | 237 | | | |

| Bowler | O | M | R | W | NB | Wd |
|---|---|---|---|---|---|---|
| Silverwood | 17 | 7 | 45 | 1 | 1 | - |
| Sidebottom | 13 | 2 | 39 | 1 | - | - |
| Dawson | 16 | 3 | 57 | 1 | 1 | - |
| Wigley | 10 | 2 | 45 | 0 | - | - |
| Lehmann | 9.3 | 1 | 43 | 1 | - | - |
| McGrath | 3 | 1 | 2 | 0 | - | - |

| Other Division One Results |
|---|

Surrey's lead at the top of the table had now grown to 33.25 points over Kent, who had moved into second place following their victory over Leicestershire at Grace Road. Warwickshire had meanwhile advanced to fifth after thrashing Sussex at Edgbaston and, since they had a game in hand, they appeared to present a greater potential threat to Surrey's title ambitions than Kent. At the bottom of the table, Yorkshire's defeat left them with an awful lot to do if they were to avoid the drop down to division two, while Hampshire had suddenly been plunged deep into trouble by losing to Lancashire on a rogue pitch that subsequently saw them docked eight points.

July 24-27
*Leicester:-* **Kent beat Leicestershire by six wickets.** Leicestershire 131 (Saggers 5-44, Masters 4-36) and 400 (DeFreitas 114, Sutcliffe 103, Ward 70, Bevan 61, Saggers 4-68); Kent 339 (Key 127) and 193-4. **Kent 18pts, Leicestershire 3**

*Edgbaston:-* **Warwickshire beat Sussex by 208 runs.** Warwickshire 493 (Knight 245*, Powell 57, Lewry 4-151) and 284-6dec (Knight 97); Sussex 377 (Cottey 137, Montgomerie 51) and 192 (Cottey 64, Richardson 8-46). **Warwickshire 20pts, Sussex 7**

July 25-27
*The Rose Bowl:-* **Lancashire beat Hampshire by 111 runs.** Lancashire 183 (Swann 66, Tremlett 5-68, Udal 4-25) and 187 (Udal 5-59); Hampshire 132 (Kendall 54, Anderson 6-23) and 127 (Wood 4-17). **Lancashire 15pts, Hampshire 3***
\* Hampshire subsequently deducted eight points for producing a 'poor' pitch

| COUNTY CHAMPIONSHIP DIVISION ONE AT 27TH JULY |||||||||||
|---|---|---|---|---|---|---|---|---|---|---|
| Pos | Prv |  | P | Points | W | D | L | Bat | Bwl | Ded |
| 1 | 1 | Surrey | 10 | 147.75 | 6 | 3 | 1 | 34 | 30 | 0.25 |
| 2 | 4 | Kent | 10 | 114.50 | 4 | 3 | 3 | 27 | 28 | 0.50 |
| 3 | 3 | Sussex | 11 | 111.00 | 2 | 6 | 3 | 31 | 32 | 0.00 |
| 4 | 2 | Leicestershire | 10 | 107.00 | 3 | 4 | 3 | 28 | 28 | 1.00 |
| 5 | 6 | Warwickshire | 9 | 105.00 | 4 | 3 | 2 | 20 | 25 | 0.00 |
| 6 | 8 | Lancashire | 9 | 93.00 | 3 | 4 | 2 | 17 | 24 | 0.00 |
| 7 | 7 | Somerset | 9 | 85.00 | 1 | 6 | 2 | 25 | 24 | 0.00 |
| 8 | 5 | Hampshire ** | 10 | 85.00 | 1 | 7 | 2 | 24 | 29 | 8.00 |
| 9 | 9 | Yorkshire | 10 | 64.50 | 0 | 4 | 6 | 21 | 28 | 0.50 |

\*\* *Hampshire deducted 8pts for 'poor' pitch at Rose Bowl v Lancashire*

| NUL2 - Ratcliffe's Golden Goodbye Guns Down Eagles |
|---|

Ronnie Irani's highly questionable decision to insert the opposition on a blisteringly hot afternoon at Woodbridge Road was punished in style by the Surrey Lions as they romped to a 73-run victory over their promotion rivals, the Essex Eagles. On a day that was studded with impressive individual performances, Surrey's hero was Jason Ratcliffe, who contributed a magnificent quick-fire fifty and four important wickets on what turned out to be his final appearance in first-class cricket.

Supported by equally aggressive knocks from Nadeem Shahid and Ian Salisbury, 'Ratters' powered his way to fifty from just twenty-eight deliveries, hitting eight fours and a six in a high-octane innings that enabled the home side to amass ninety-two runs from the last eight overs and fully capitalise on the great start given to them earlier in the day by Ian Ward and Mark Ramprakash.

The Eagles' victory target of 311 represented a tough task, even on the fast-scoring Guildford ground, and once Tim Murtagh's excellent opening spell had reduced the visitors to 95-4 in the eighteenth over the game looked all but over. A fighting stand of ninety-nine at seven-an-over between 18-year-old Mark Pettini and Andy Flower kept Essex's hopes alive, however, and it was only when Ratcliffe returned to the attack in the thirtieth over after a disastrous first spell of 2-0-20-0 that the picture changed. With the first ball of his second comeback over, the Surrey all-rounder made the crucial breakthrough by uprooting Pettini's leg stump and, after he had followed up by claiming the wickets of Ashley Cowan and Andy Flower with successive deliveries four overs later, the Eagles declined rapidly to 237 all out as Salisbury proved too good for the tail in returning figures of 3-44.

Forced to admit defeat at the end of the season after a two-year battle with a serious knee injury, Ratcliffe had at least gone out with a bang by playing the starring role in an important victory to bring the curtain down on his eight-year Surrey career.

## SURREY LIONS v ESSEX EAGLES at Guildford
### Played on Sunday 28th July — Surrey Lions won by 73 runs
Essex Eagles won the toss and elected to field — Umpires:- Jeremy Lloyds & Ken Palmer

### SURREY LIONS

| Fall Of Wkt | Batsman | How | Out | Score | Balls | 4s | 6s |
|---|---|---|---|---|---|---|---|
| 2-120 | I.J. Ward | c Pettini | b Phillips | 62 | 57 | 10 | 0 |
| 1-43 | A.D. Brown | | b Irani | 15 | 27 | 1 | 1 |
| 4-195 | M.R. Ramprakash | c Jefferson | b Cowan | 74 | 76 | 7 | 2 |
| 3-178 | R. Clarke | c Phillips | b Cowan | 23 | 34 | 1 | 1 |
| 6-278 | N. Shahid | c Flower | b Dakin | 34 | 27 | 3 | 1 |
| 5-214 | A.J. Hollioake * | c Middlebrook | b Stephenson | 6 | 10 | 0 | 0 |
| 7-302 | J.D. Ratcliffe | c Robinson | b Cowan | 53 | 31 | 8 | 1 |
| | I.D.K. Salisbury | Not | Out | 19 | 8 | 2 | 1 |
| | A.J. Tudor | Not | Out | 1 | 2 | 0 | 0 |
| | J.N. Batty + | did not bat | | | | | |
| | T.J. Murtagh | did not bat | | | | | |
| | Extras | (7lb, 12w, 4nb) | | 23 | | | |
| | TOTAL | (45 overs) | (for 7 wkts) | 310 | | | |

| Bowler | O | M | R | W | NB | Wd |
|---|---|---|---|---|---|---|
| Irani | 9 | 0 | 49 | 1 | - | 2 |
| Cowan | 9 | 0 | 57 | 3 | - | - |
| Dakin | 3 | 0 | 32 | 1 | 2 | 3 |
| McGarry | 9 | 0 | 74 | 0 | - | 2 |
| Stephenson | 5 | 0 | 34 | 1 | - | 3 |
| Phillips | 5 | 0 | 27 | 1 | - | - |
| Middlebrook | 5 | 0 | 30 | 0 | - | 1 |

### ESSEX EAGLES

| Fall Of Wkt | Batsman | How | Out | Score | Balls | 4s | 6s |
|---|---|---|---|---|---|---|---|
| 1-42 | D.D.J. Robinson | | b Murtagh | 26 | 29 | 5 | 0 |
| 3-90 | J.M. Dakin | c & | b Clarke | 38 | 44 | 6 | 0 |
| 2-86 | W.I. Jefferson | | b Murtagh | 23 | 25 | 4 | 0 |
| 7-224 | A. Flower + | c Murtagh | b Ratcliffe | 50 | 49 | 5 | 0 |
| 4-95 | R.C. Irani * | c Ward | b Salisbury | 1 | 4 | 0 | 0 |
| 5-194 | M.L. Pettini | | b Ratcliffe | 51 | 46 | 2 | 2 |
| 6-224 | A.P. Cowan | c Hollioake | b Ratcliffe | 21 | 16 | 2 | 0 |
| 8-235 | J.D. Middlebrook | st Batty | b Salisbury | 5 | 11 | 0 | 0 |
| 9-235 | J.P. Stephenson | c Ramprakash | b Ratcliffe | 5 | 11 | 0 | 0 |
| | T.J. Phillips | Not | Out | 1 | 3 | 0 | 0 |
| 10-237 | A.C. McGarry | st Batty | b Salisbury | 1 | 3 | 0 | 0 |
| | Extras | (6b, 6lb, 3w) | | 15 | | | |
| | TOTAL | (40.1 overs) | | 237 | | | |

| Bowler | O | M | R | W | NB | Wd |
|---|---|---|---|---|---|---|
| Tudor | 7 | 1 | 43 | 0 | - | - |
| Murtagh | 9 | 0 | 41 | 2 | - | 1 |
| Clarke | 5 | 1 | 26 | 1 | - | - |
| Salisbury | 7.1 | 0 | 44 | 3 | - | - |
| Ratcliffe | 8 | 0 | 44 | 4 | - | - |
| Hollioake | 4 | 0 | 27 | 0 | - | 2 |

## Other NUL Division Two Results

Two recent wins by the Gladiators had enabled them to open up an eight-point gap at the top of the table, though they had played two more games that the Lions. Meanwhile, two consecutive defeats had greatly weakened the Essex Eagles' position, giving Surrey a little breathing space in second place.

**July 18**
*Cheltenham:-* **Gloucestershire Gladiators beat Hampshire Hawks by 71 runs.** Gloucestershire 296-9 (Spearman 107, Windows 76, Mascarenhas 4-67); Hampshire 225-9 (Udal 58, Francis 51, Smith 3-25, Harvey 3-40). **Gloucestershire Gladiators 4pts**

**July 22**
*Chelmsford:-* **Middlesex Crusaders beat Essex Eagles by 41 runs.** Middlesex 209-8 (Strauss 58, Shah 54, Middlebrook 3-40); Essex 168 (37.4ov; Cook 3-28). **Middlesex Crusaders 4pts**

**July 23**
*The Rose Bowl:-* **Lancashire Lightning beat Hampshire Hawks by 16 runs (D/L method).** Lancashire 163 (39.1ov; Law 166, Johnson 3-45); Hampshire 147 (37.4ov; Hogg 4-20). **Lancashire Lightning 4pts**

**July 24**
*Northampton:-* **Northamptonshire Steelbacks beat Derbyshire Scorpions by seven wickets.** Derbyshire 143 (43.5ov; Greenidge 3-22); Northamptonshire 146-3 (27.5ov; Hussey 72*). **Northamptonshire Steelbacks 4pts**

**July 28**
*Cheltenham:-* **Gloucestershire Gladiators beat Sussex Sharks by six wickets.** Sussex 116 (30.5ov; Ball 4-15); Gloucestershire 118-4 (17.2ov; Harvey 68*). **Gloucestershire Gladiators 4pts**

## NATIONAL LEAGUE DIVISION TWO AT 28TH JULY

| Pos | Prv | | P | Pts | W | T | L | A |
|---|---|---|---|---|---|---|---|---|
| 1 | 1 | Gloucestershire Gladiators | 10 | 30 | 7 | 0 | 2 | 1 |
| 2 | 2 | Surrey Lions | 8 | 22 | 5 | 0 | 2 | 1 |
| 3 | 4 | Northamptonshire Steelbacks | 7 | 18 | 4 | 0 | 2 | 1 |
| 4 | 3 | Essex Eagles | 7 | 16 | 4 | 0 | 3 | 0 |
| 5 | 7 | Lancashire Lightning | 10 | 16 | 3 | 0 | 5 | 2 |
| 6 | 6 | Derbyshire Scorpions | 8 | 14 | 3 | 0 | 4 | 1 |
| = | 4 | Hampshire Hawks | 8 | 14 | 3 | 0 | 4 | 1 |
| 8 | 9 | Middlesex Crusaders | 9 | 12 | 2 | 0 | 5 | 2 |
| 9 | 8 | Sussex Sharks | 9 | 10 | 2 | 0 | 6 | 1 |

## C&G Trophy Semi-Final - Yorkshire's Crushing Revenge Ends Farce

**Yorkshire v Surrey at Headingley. Played on Sunday 4th August.**
**Yorkshire won by ten wickets**

First the ground was swamped, then so were Surrey as the Cheltenham And Gloucester Trophy semi-final became a sad farce that ended with the match being played on another controversial Yorkshire pitch. Having said that, it must be recorded that the white rose county won with consummate ease, brutally brushing their opponents aside by ten wickets with almost eighteen overs to spare, to reach the final of the country's premier limited-overs cup competition for the first time since 1969 and gain swift revenge for their Championship defeat at Guildford.

With the outfield under water on the scheduled day of the match, and further rain ruling out any hope of play on either of the two reserve days, it looked at one stage as if a bowl-out might be required to decide which county went through to the final. Since both sides were desperate to avoid this scenario, other solutions were discussed with the ECB, including playing the game on a neutral venue further south, where the weather was fine. Yorkshire were, understandably, not prepared to concede home advantage, however, so the teams were allowed an extra reserve day in which to try and complete the match. Since Yorkshire and Surrey both had Norwich Union League fixtures to fulfil on the following day, Saturday 3rd August, it was decided that the Sunday, a blank date for both sides, would be the day when a final attempt would be made to play the game. Given the fact that Surrey's NUL match was at Whitgift School, the Club elected, reasonably enough, to put out a weakened team against the Northamptonshire Steelbacks, rather than ask their players to take on the return journey to Croydon and a tough game, all in the space of thirty-six hours. At this stage of the season, with plenty of NUL games left to play, a one-off semi-final simply had to be given priority. All that was needed now was a change in the weather!

Fortunately for all concerned, it relented sufficiently for Yorkshire to play their game against the Nottinghamshire Outlaws on the Saturday, though the only available pitch was the one that had been prepared for the semi-final. Considering that many one-day pitches are used for two matches, this didn't seem to present a problem but, finding that it took spin during the NUL contest, Yorkshire then made the controversial decision to cut a fresh pitch for the Surrey game the following morning. The umpires were not happy about this, firstly because they felt there was nothing wrong with the used wicket and, secondly, because the new pitch was damp, an inevitable consequence of it having been under either water or a tarpaulin for the best part of week.

Surrey were, needless to say, not greatly impressed either and it seemed almost inevitable, in the circumstances, that Adam Hollioake would then call incorrectly at the toss, committing his team to bat while conditions were at their worst against Yorkshire's battery of seamers.

The visitors' worst fears about the pitch were rapidly confirmed as Matthew Hoggard struck two early blows and, but for a masterful innings by Mark Ramprakash, Surrey could have been out of the game almost before it had started. As it was, Craig White took wickets at regular intervals to keep Surrey constantly under the cosh and when Ramprakash's skilful and patient knock was ended by a run out with the score at 152 in the forty-third over, the visitors' hopes of posting a really competitive total were finally dashed.

White then took full advantage of a lucky escape in the first over, when he was dropped on nought by Ali Brown at first slip off Alex Tudor, to punish a very disappointing bowling effort by the Surrey seamers. Even though the wicket had eased a little, there was no excuse for the lack of discipline that saw Ed Giddins mauled for sixteen runs in his third over and, following a change of ends, nineteen in his fourth. With the score on 71-0 after this lamentable eleventh over of the innings, during which White completed a 38-ball half-century, the contest was already virtually decided, and when Giddins' replacement, Rikki Clarke, then conceded eighteen runs from his first four balls to Wood, who had survived a tough caught-and-bowled chance to Tudor when on twelve, it really was game, set and match to Yorkshire.

Luckily for Surrey, White didn't allow their players or supporters to suffer for too long, completing a speedy mercy-killing when he drove the opening delivery of the twenty-fifth over to the cover boundary to complete a quite stupendous 78-ball century that had included no fewer than sixteen fours and a six.

While the whole of Headingley celebrated, Surrey slipped away to resume their quest for the Championship, with hopes of completing the double at an end for yet another season.

## YORKSHIRE v SURREY at Headingley
### Played on Sunday 4th August — Yorkshire won by ten wickets
Yorkshire won the toss and elected to field   Umpires:- Barry Dudleston & John Holder

### SURREY — Match reduced to 48 overs per side

| Fall of wkt | Batsman | How | Out | Score | Balls | 4s | 6s |
|---|---|---|---|---|---|---|---|
| 1-6 | I.J. Ward | lbw | b Hoggard | 2 | 12 | 0 | 0 |
| 2-25 | A.D. Brown | c Lumb | b Hoggard | 9 | 25 | 1 | 0 |
| 7-152 | M.R. Ramprakash | run | out | 63 | 114 | 4 | 0 |
| 3-50 | A.J. Stewart + | c Blakey | b White | 3 | 21 | 0 | 0 |
| 4-91 | Nadeem Shahid | c McGrath | b Lehmann | 21 | 39 | 2 | 0 |
| 5-124 | A.J. Hollioake * | lbw | b White | 16 | 22 | 2 | 0 |
| 6-130 | R. Clarke | c Blakey | b White | 3 | 9 | 0 | 0 |
|  | A.J. Tudor | Not | Out | 17 | 36 | 1 | 0 |
| 8-158 | Saqlain Mushtaq | c McGrath | b White | 5 | 4 | 1 | 0 |
|  | J. Ormond | Not | Out | 5 | 7 | 1 | 0 |
|  | E.S.H. Giddins | did not bat |  |  |  |  |  |
|  | Extras | (15lb, 12w, 2nb) |  | 29 |  |  |  |
|  | **TOTAL** | **(48 overs)** | **(for 8 wkts)** | **173** |  |  |  |

| Bowler | O | M | R | W | NB | Wd |
|---|---|---|---|---|---|---|
| Hoggard | 10 | 1 | 21 | 2 | 1 | 2 |
| Silverwood | 8 | 2 | 23 | 0 | - | 5 |
| Sidebottom | 10 | 0 | 35 | 0 | - | 1 |
| White | 10 | 0 | 35 | 4 | - | 3 |
| McGrath | 5 | 0 | 26 | 0 | - | 1 |
| Lehmann | 5 | 0 | 18 | 1 | - | - |

### YORKSHIRE (Requiring 167 from 42 overs after D/L adjustment)

| Fall of wkt | Batsman | How | Out | Score | Balls | 4s | 6s |
|---|---|---|---|---|---|---|---|
|  | C. White | Not | Out | 100 | 78 | 16 | 1 |
|  | M.J. Wood | Not | Out | 57 | 69 | 7 | 1 |
|  | M.P. Vaughan | did not bat |  |  |  |  |  |
|  | D.S. Lehmann * | did not bat |  |  |  |  |  |
|  | A. McGrath | did not bat |  |  |  |  |  |
|  | G.M. Fellows | did not bat |  |  |  |  |  |
|  | M.J. Lumb | did not bat |  |  |  |  |  |
|  | R.J. Blakey + | did not bat |  |  |  |  |  |
|  | C.E.W. Silverwood | did not bat |  |  |  |  |  |
|  | R.J. Sidebottom | did not bat |  |  |  |  |  |
|  | M.J. Hoggard | did not bat |  |  |  |  |  |
|  | Extras | (1lb, 5w, 4nb) |  | 10 |  |  |  |
|  | **TOTAL** | **(24.1 overs)** | **(for no wkt)** | **167** |  |  |  |

| Bowler | O | M | R | W | NB | Wd |
|---|---|---|---|---|---|---|
| Tudor | 9 | 0 | 40 | 0 | - | 1 |
| Giddins | 4 | 0 | 42 | 0 | 2 | - |
| Ormond | 4 | 0 | 20 | 0 | - | - |
| Clarke | 2.1 | 0 | 29 | 0 | - | - |
| Saqlain Mushtaq | 5 | 0 | 35 | 0 | - | - |

### NUL2 - Ward Turns Back The Clock As Steelbacks Slay Lion Cubs

The crushing C&G semi-final defeat was an especially bitter pill to swallow, since it had made an unfortunate mockery of the Club's decision to field a second-string team for the predictably doomed encounter with Northamptonshire Steelbacks in the NUL promotion battle at Whitgift School. The Lions' line-up was an interesting mix of past, present and future players, the most notable inclusion being the 41-year-old David Ward, who thereby returned to the side some six years after his retirement. Led by Ian Salisbury, the side included only Jon Batty of the eleven named in the match programme, and included three players making their first-team debuts - James Benning, Ben Scott and Danny Miller - as well as Gary Butcher, making a return appearance after being released at the end of the 2001 season. Given the Surrey team's lack of experience, it was no surprise that they ended up being comfortably trounced, especially once a couple of rain breaks had landed them with a impossible-looking Duckworth-Lewis adjusted target.

Batting first, the Steelbacks were initially well restrained by Phil Sampson and Danny Miller, but once the Carshalton-born David Sales came to the wicket in the thirteenth over, following the dismissal of his captain, the scoring rate surged ever upwards. No-one could contain him or his successor, Matt Cassar, while Mal Loye anchored the innings skilfully to reach his century, from 110 balls, in the penultimate over of Northamptonshire's reduced allocation of forty overs.

Following a heavy shower, the Lions were left to chase 265 in twenty-nine overs, which would have been a tough task with a full-strength line-up, but looked well out of reach for a skeleton team such as this one. Ward, now master in charge of cricket at Whitgift School, wasn't going to give up easily, though, and rolled back the years with a scintillating display of strokeplay that saw eighty on the board after just ten overs. He completed a stunning 37-ball half-century, including eleven fours, two overs later, but the loss of Scott Newman immediately afterwards turned out to be a watershed. Although Ward kept blasting away until his departure to a catch at long-off in the seventeenth over with the score at 125, Michael Carberry, the wrong man to be batting at number three, struggled to get the ball away, resulting in a steady loss of momentum and wickets. After Ward's 52-ball knock of seventy-eight, the Lion cubs had little else to offer against more-experienced opponents and, despite their best efforts, they slipped rapidly to defeat against Jeff Cook's variations and the off-spin of Graeme Swann. Although Surrey had lost ground to their promotion rivals, the game had at least provided some of the Club's youngsters with a valuable insight into first-team cricket.

### SURREY LIONS v NORTHAMPTONSHIRE STEELBACKS at Whitgift School
### Played on Saturday 3rd August    Northants Steelbacks won by 102 runs (D/L method)
Northamptonshire Steelbacks won the toss and elected to bat    Umpires:- Ian Gould & Jeremy Lloyds

**NORTHAMPTONSHIRE STEELBACKS**    Match reduced to 40 overs per side

| Fall Of Wkt | Batsman | How | Out | Score | Balls | 4s | 6s |
|---|---|---|---|---|---|---|---|
| 1-55 | M.E.K. Hussey * | | b Butcher | 18 | 32 | 0 | 0 |
| | M.B. Loye | Not | Out | 101 | 111 | 11 | 3 |
| 2-179 | D.J.G. Sales | c Ward | b Benning | 67 | 50 | 10 | 0 |
| 3-249 | M.E. Cassar | c Salisbury | b Sampson | 54 | 38 | 3 | 4 |
| 4-249 | J.W. Cook | | b Butcher | 0 | 1 | 0 | 0 |
| 5-267 | A.L. Penberthy | | b Benning | 12 | 6 | 1 | 1 |
| | G.P. Swann | Not | Out | 9 | 2 | 0 | 1 |
| | T.M.B. Bailey + | did not bat | | | | | |
| | C.G. Greenidge | did not bat | | | | | |
| | D.M. Cousins | did not bat | | | | | |
| | J.F. Brown | did not bat | | | | | |
| | Extras | (7lb, 9w) | | 16 | | | |
| | **TOTAL** | **(40 overs)** | **(for 5 wkts)** | **277** | | | |

| Bowler | O | M | R | W | NB | Wd |
|---|---|---|---|---|---|---|
| Sampson | 9 | 0 | 45 | 1 | - | 2 |
| Miller | 7 | 0 | 32 | 0 | - | 3 |
| Butcher | 7 | 0 | 49 | 2 | - | 4 |
| Benning | 7 | 0 | 58 | 2 | - | - |
| Amin | 3 | 0 | 33 | 0 | - | - |
| Salisbury | 7 | 0 | 53 | 0 | - | - |

**SURREY LIONS** (Requiring 265 from 29 overs after D/L adjustment)

| Fall Of Wkt | Batsman | How | Out | Score | Balls | 4s | 6s |
|---|---|---|---|---|---|---|---|
| 2-125 | D.M. Ward | c Hussey | b Brown | 78 | 52 | 14 | 1 |
| 1-89 | S.A. Newman | c Bailey | b Penberthy | 30 | 33 | 5 | 0 |
| 4-136 | M.A. Carberry | c Bailey | b Brown | 19 | 31 | 2 | 0 |
| 3-135 | J.N. Batty + | c Penberthy | b Brown | 3 | 8 | 0 | 0 |
| 6-152 | J.G.E. Benning | | b Cook | 10 | 8 | 0 | 1 |
| 5-137 | I.D.K. Salisbury * | | b Cook | 0 | 2 | 0 | 0 |
| 7-158 | G.P. Butcher | c Cousins | b Swann | 9 | 12 | 0 | 0 |
| 9-162 | B.J. M. Scott | c Loye | b Swann | 4 | 7 | 0 | 0 |
| 8-160 | P.J. Sampson | | b Cook | 1 | 2 | 0 | 0 |
| 10-162 | D.R. Miller | | b Swann | 0 | 7 | 0 | 0 |
| | R.M. Amin | Not | Out | 0 | 0 | 0 | 0 |
| | Extras | (4lb, 3w) | | 7 | | | |
| | **TOTAL** | **(27 overs)** | | **162** | | | |

| Bowler | O | M | R | W | NB | Wd |
|---|---|---|---|---|---|---|
| Cousins | 4 | 0 | 33 | 0 | - | - |
| Greenidge | 5 | 0 | 40 | 0 | - | 3 |
| Penberthy | 6 | 0 | 31 | 1 | - | - |
| Brown | 6 | 1 | 30 | 3 | - | - |
| Cook | 3 | 0 | 8 | 3 | - | - |
| Swann | 3 | 0 | 16 | 3 | - | - |

## Other NUL Division Two Results

Northamptonshire's win at Whitgift enabled them to steal second place from Surrey, though both sides were now well adrift of the Gloucestershire Gladiators, who moved twelve points clear at the top in extending their winning sequence to five matches with a straightforward win over Lancashire Lightning.

August 3
*Derby:-* **Derbyshire Scorpions beat Hampshire Hawks by two wickets.** Hampshire 143-9 (40ov; Pothas 50*); Derbyshire 137-8 (39ov). **Derbyshire Scorpions 4pts**

*Bristol:-* **Gloucestershire Gladiators beat Lancashire Lightning by five wickets.** Lancashire 183-9 (Law 55, Hegg 54, Harvey 4-41, Smith 3-36); Gloucestershire 185-5 (35ov; Harvey 56, Spearman 54). **Gloucestershire Gladiators 4pts**

## NATIONAL LEAGUE DIVISION TWO AT 3RD AUGUST

| Pos | Prv |  | P | Pts | W | T | L | A |
|---|---|---|---|---|---|---|---|---|
| 1 | 1 | Gloucestershire Gladiators | 11 | 34 | 8 | 0 | 2 | 1 |
| 2 | 3 | Northamptonshire Steelbacks | 8 | 22 | 5 | 0 | 2 | 1 |
| 3 | 2 | Surrey Lions | 9 | 22 | 5 | 0 | 3 | 1 |
| 4 | 6 | Derbyshire Scorpions | 9 | 18 | 4 | 0 | 4 | 1 |
| 5 | 4 | Essex Eagles | 7 | 16 | 4 | 0 | 3 | 0 |
| 6 | 5 | Lancashire Lightning | 11 | 16 | 3 | 0 | 6 | 2 |
| 7 | 6 | Hampshire Hawks | 9 | 14 | 3 | 0 | 5 | 1 |
| 8 | 8 | Middlesex Crusaders | 9 | 12 | 2 | 0 | 5 | 2 |
| 9 | 9 | Sussex Sharks | 9 | 10 | 2 | 0 | 6 | 1 |

## NUL2 - Centurion Shah Ensures Crusaders End Thirteen-Year Famine

All good things come to an end, so they say, and such was the case with Surrey's thirteen-year unbeaten run against Middlesex in Sunday/National League matches, home and away, when the Crusaders triumphed by 65 runs in the second of the two Whitgift School matches.

High-quality innings by Andrew Strauss and Owais Shah against some disappointingly inaccurate Lions bowling, ensured that the visitors posted a challenging total of 274-8, which Surrey only threatened while Ali Brown was at the crease. Strauss got the innings off to a vibrant start, despite another very encouraging spell of bowling from Tim Murtagh, reaching his half-century from just 49 deliveries, then Shah, completing a hat-trick of fifty-plus scores against Surrey in 2002, orchestrated a late surge to reach an excellent 89-ball century, including four sixes and six fours, in the fortieth over.

In reply, the Lions got away to a disastrous start, with both Ward (lbw) and Ramprakash (run out) appearing to receive very poor decisions from umpire Mike Harris, who then failed to notice that Middlesex had only three fielders in the 30-metre circle for the ball that followed Ramprakash's dismissal. The eagle-eyed and alert Ali Brown had spotted it, however, and, after whacking the ball for four, pointed out the error to an embarrassed Harris, who signalled a belated no-ball. With Brown in rampant form, striking two sixes and seven fours as he scorched to fifty from just 34 balls, the Surrey hundred was up in the thirteenth over, but the bizarre dismissal of Nadeem Shahid, four overs later, suggested that it wasn't going to be the Lions' day. Unable to get out of the way of a fierce Brown drive as he backed up, a startled Shahid suddenly found himself without a bat, the ball having sent it spinning from his hand before coming to rest close to the bowler, Simon Cook. In the frantic scramble that followed, Cook managed to break the stumps at the bowler's end before the batless Shahid could regain his ground with a desperate dive. Having scored ninety-four from 63 balls, Brown's hugely entertaining pyrotechnics were then ended by a catch at backward point in the next over and, thereafter, Surrey's middle- and lower-order batsmen were effectively stifled and eventually routed by the off-breaks of Weekes and Dalrymple. In recording their first Sunday/National League win on Surrey soil for sixteen years, the joyful and triumphant Crusaders had condemned the Lions to a third limited-overs defeat in the space of four days.

## SURREY LIONS v MIDDLESEX CRUSADERS at Whitgift School
### Played on Tuesday 6th August   Middlesex Crusaders won by 65 runs

Surrey Lions won the toss and elected to field     Umpires:- David Constant & Mike Harris

### MIDDLESEX CRUSADERS

| Fall Of Wkt | Batsman | How | Out | Score | Balls | 4s | 6s |
|---|---|---|---|---|---|---|---|
| 3-150 | A.J. Strauss * | run | out | 74 | 81 | 7 | 0 |
| 1-35 | A.W. Laraman | lbw | b Giddins | 7 | 14 | 0 | 0 |
| 2-60 | S.G. Koenig | c Saqlain | b Murtagh | 9 | 26 | 0 | 0 |
| 5-248 | O.A. Shah | c Brown | b Giddins | 110 | 93 | 8 | 4 |
| 4-194 | E.C. Joyce | c Hollioake | b Saqlain | 15 | 21 | 0 | 0 |
| 7-252 | P.N. Weekes | c Brown | b Hollioake | 20 | 18 | 1 | 0 |
| 6-251 | J.W.M. Dalrymple | c Brown | b Giddins | 1 | 2 | 0 | 0 |
| 8-274 | S.J. Cook | c Murtagh | b Hollioake | 11 | 11 | 1 | 0 |
|  | D.C. Nash + | Not | Out | 10 | 6 | 1 | 0 |
|  | C.B. Keegan | did not bat |  |  |  |  |  |
|  | I. Jones | did not bat |  |  |  |  |  |
|  | Extras | (4b, 3lb, 6w, 4nb) |  | 17 |  |  |  |
|  | TOTAL | (45 overs) | (for 8 wkts) | 274 |  |  |  |

| Bowler | O | M | R | W | NB | Wd |
|---|---|---|---|---|---|---|
| Giddins | 9 | 0 | 56 | 3 | 1 | 2 |
| Murtagh | 9 | 2 | 26 | 1 | - | - |
| Sampson | 4 | 0 | 37 | 0 | 1 | - |
| Clarke | 6 | 0 | 48 | 0 | - | 1 |
| Saqlain Mushtaq | 9 | 0 | 44 | 1 | - | 2 |
| Hollioake | 8 | 0 | 56 | 2 | - | 1 |

### SURREY LIONS

| Fall Of Wkt | Batsman | How | Out | Score | Balls | 4s | 6s |
|---|---|---|---|---|---|---|---|
| 1-4 | I.J. Ward | lbw | b Laraman | 4 | 5 | 1 | 0 |
| 5-135 | A.D. Brown | c Koenig | b Weekes | 94 | 63 | 15 | 2 |
| 2-27 | M.R. Ramprakash | run | out | 10 | 8 | 1 | 0 |
| 3-64 | R. Clarke | c Keegan | b Laraman | 10 | 14 | 2 | 0 |
| 4-130 | N. Shahid | run | out | 6 | 21 | 0 | 0 |
| 6-152 | A.J. Hollioake * |  | b Dalrymple | 15 | 16 | 2 | 0 |
| 7-176 | J.N. Batty + | c & | b Weekes | 19 | 41 | 2 | 0 |
| 9-187 | Saqlain Mushtaq | c Shah | b Weekes | 16 | 32 | 3 | 0 |
| 8-183 | T.J. Murtagh |  | b Dalrymple | 3 | 8 | 0 | 0 |
| 10-209 | P.J. Sampson |  | b Jones | 16 | 16 | 0 | 2 |
|  | E.S.H. Giddins | Not | Out | 4 | 6 | 0 | 0 |
|  | Extras | (2b, 3lb, 5w, 2nb) |  | 12 |  |  |  |
|  | TOTAL | (38.1 overs) |  | 209 |  |  |  |

| Bowler | O | M | R | W | NB | Wd |
|---|---|---|---|---|---|---|
| Laraman | 7 | 0 | 51 | 2 | 1 | 1 |
| Keegan | 7 | 0 | 55 | 0 | - | 1 |
| Cook | 5 | 0 | 26 | 0 | - | - |
| Jones | 2.1 | 0 | 11 | 1 | - | - |
| Weekes | 9 | 1 | 32 | 3 | - | 2 |
| Dalrymple | 8 | 1 | 29 | 2 | - | 1 |

## Other NUL Division Two Results

Although defeat at the hands of the Crusaders hadn't greatly damaged the Lions' promotion prospects, thanks largely to Middlesex having beaten Essex Eagles in their previous match, hopes of winning the second division title had all but disappeared, barring a run-in of six straight wins. Even though Gloucestershire Gladiators had been washed out by a violent thunderstorm at Hove their advantage over Surrey had extended to fourteen points.

August 4
*Lord's:-* **Middlesex Crusaders beat Essex Eagles by two wickets (D/L method).** Essex 194-8 (41.5 ov; Jefferson 111*); Middlesex 77-8 (9.5ov; Napier 3-10). **Middlesex Crusaders 4pts**

*Northampton:-* **Northamptonshire Steelbacks beat Hampshire Hawks by 16 runs (D/L method).** Hampshire 133 (41.3ov; Cousins 3-36); Northamptonshire 52-0 (14.2ov). **Northants Steelbacks 4pts**

August 5
*Hove:-* **Sussex Sharks v Gloucestershire Gladiators - No Result.** Sussex 8-0 (1.4ov). **Sussex Sharks 2pts, Gloucestershire Gladiators 2**

August 6
*Old Trafford:-* **Lancashire Lightning beat Hampshire Hawks by four wickets.** Hampshire 188-8 (Laney 71, Anderson 3-42); Lancashire 189-6 (44.4ov; Chilton 66, Law 64). **Lancashire Lightning 4pts**

### NATIONAL LEAGUE DIVISION TWO AT 6TH AUGUST

| Pos | Prv | | P | Pts | W | T | L | A |
|---|---|---|---|---|---|---|---|---|
| 1 | 1 | Gloucestershire Gladiators | 12 | 36 | 8 | 0 | 2 | 2 |
| 2 | 2 | Northamptonshire Steelbacks | 9 | 26 | 6 | 0 | 2 | 1 |
| 3 | 3 | Surrey Lions | 10 | 22 | 5 | 0 | 4 | 1 |
| 4 | 8 | Middlesex Crusaders | 11 | 20 | 4 | 0 | 5 | 2 |
| 5 | 6 | Lancashire Lightning | 12 | 20 | 4 | 0 | 6 | 2 |
| 6 | 4 | Derbyshire Scorpions | 9 | 18 | 4 | 0 | 4 | 1 |
| 7 | 5 | Essex Eagles | 8 | 16 | 4 | 0 | 4 | 0 |
| 8 | 7 | Hampshire Hawks | 11 | 14 | 3 | 0 | 7 | 1 |
| 9 | 9 | Sussex Sharks | 10 | 12 | 2 | 0 | 6 | 2 |

# 14  A Surprising Setback

Having been unceremoniously dumped out of the C&G Trophy at Headingley and then beaten twice in the NUL, it hadn't been a good few days for Surrey. Nor had it been the happiest of times for Graham Thorpe, since he had announced that he was taking a complete break from cricket, for an unspecified period, following the Lord's Test against India. It was stated that his personal problems were showing no sign of receding and he, therefore, felt unable to concentrate properly on playing cricket. Inevitably, this provoked wildly differing opinions, with some people feeling he deserved credit for giving priority to attempting to deal with his problems, while, at the other end of the spectrum, some felt that he was expecting, and receiving, more than enough support as it was, without making this latest move. Unfortunately, and inevitably, Thorpe's decision put him back in the headlines and prompted a huge debate, which was surely the last thing he needed or wanted. It seemed that maybe his best option would have been to proceed with his cricketing life as normal, in the same way that the average working man would have been forced to carry on with his daily routine, whether he wanted to or not. Being in the public eye, the Surrey and England cricketer was better off in one area and worse off in another - 'the man in the street' in Thorpe's position certainly wouldn't have had such a sympathetic reception from his employers, in being able to quit his job for an indefinite period, yet his private life wouldn't have been 'news' as Thorpe's was. The bottom line, though, was that only those who knew the *exact* nature of his marital and family problems were in a position to judge whether or not Thorpe was taking the right options.

Whether or not Yorkshire had made the correct decision in cutting a fresh pitch for the C&G semi-final was certainly up for debate. Having got to the final of the competition, it seemed like a good move, yet there were already rumours that they were going to be punished for their actions. Eventually, it was said that the county would be punished by having to concede home advantage in all C&G ties for the next two or three seasons, though this was yet to be confirmed. If the ECB's ruling stood then it looked like Yorkshire had gained in the short term but lost in the long term.

Returning to the Frizzell County Championship, things were still looking good for Surrey, despite their recent limited-overs setbacks. Although there were still one or two problem areas, with Martin Bicknell still not fully recovered from his broken wrist, and Saqlain Mushtaq set to miss the next two matches because of his involvement with Pakistan in the Morocco Cup tournament, the county's lead in the title race was already looking potentially decisive, especially since their run-in looked free of potential 'banana skins'. Home and away fixtures against Hampshire and Leicestershire, who both appeared to be in decline after promising starts to the campaign, looked sure to yield a couple of victories at least, while Warwickshire at Edgbaston looked, by a distance, the toughest game left. The next match, against Sussex at Hove, certainly represented a good opportunity for a win, given Surrey's stranglehold over the south coast county in recent years, though there was clearly no room for complacency.

Before the Championship game there was an important NUL match to play, however, with the Lions badly in need of a win to get their faltering promotion challenge back on track.

## NUL2 - Sussex's Mid-Match Rally Can't Stop Surrey

Surrey's hectic schedule of four limited-overs matches in five days finally yielded an important win, by six wickets over the Sussex Sharks, as they dominated all bar the middle twenty overs of the floodlit game at Hove.

Following up his five-wicket haul against the Sharks at The AMP Oval earlier in the season, Ed Giddins claimed another four victims in his first spell of seven overs to put Sussex in early difficulties at 49-4 after they had won the toss and elected to bat. In his first game back after a calf strain, Chris Adams then led a minor recovery with a 67-ball fifty before this comeback was snuffed out by Alex Tudor, who picked up wickets in the twenty-ninth and thirty-first overs to reduce Sussex to 110-7. From such murky depths, the Sharks were revived again, this time by Kevin Innes and Mark Davis, both of whom batted with increasing assurance to stabilise the situation and then crash forty-nine runs from the final six overs of the innings.

A victory target of 195 still looked well within the Lions' capabilities though, even under lights, until James Kirtley, another key Sussex player who was making his first appearance after a spell out injured, removed both Ali Brown and Ian Ward in the first four overs of the visitors' reply. The Sharks' mid-match surge then continued when Rikki Clarke fell to Robin Martin-Jenkins with the score on twenty-five, before Mark Ramprakash and Nadeem Shahid slowly but surely averted the threat of Surrey succumbing to a third successive NUL defeat. Ramprakash maintained his fine recent form in the competition by completing a third half-century in four innings from 69 balls - Shahid having reached the same milestone two overs earlier and from eight fewer deliveries - as the partnership gradually took the game away from Sussex. By the time the former Middlesex batsman fell to Billy Taylor in the thirty-fourth over with just thirty-nine runs needed, victory was almost guaranteed, and Adam Hollioake finished the contest by blazing the ball around in a style strongly reminiscent of his incredible C&G quarter-final innings on the same ground just a few weeks earlier.

## SUSSEX SHARKS v SURREY LIONS at Hove
### Played on Wednesday 7th August    Surrey Lions won by six wickets

Sussex Sharks won the toss and elected to bat                Umpires:- Roy Palmer & Peter Willey

### SUSSEX SHARKS

| Fall Of Wkt | Batsman | How | Out | Score | Balls | 4s | 6s |
|---|---|---|---|---|---|---|---|
| 1-3 | R.R. Montgomerie | c Ward | b Giddins | 1 | 6 | 0 | 0 |
| 7-110 | C.J. Adams * | c Hollioake | b Tudor | 60 | 74 | 7 | 1 |
| 2-13 | M.W. Goodwin | c Batty | b Giddins | 3 | 9 | 0 | 0 |
| 3-49 | P.A. Cottey | | b Giddins | 14 | 28 | 1 | 0 |
| 4-49 | M.J. Prior + | | b Giddins | 0 | 1 | 0 | 0 |
| 5-71 | R.S.C. Martin-Jenkins | c Saqlain | b Murtagh | 13 | 23 | 1 | 0 |
| 6-101 | T.R. Ambrose | c Brown | b Tudor | 9 | 38 | 0 | 0 |
| | K.J. Innes | Not | Out | 50 | 60 | 6 | 1 |
| | M.J.G. Davis | Not | Out | 27 | 31 | 2 | 0 |
| | R.J. Kirtley | did not bat | | | | | |
| | B.V. Taylor | did not bat | | | | | |
| | Extras | (9lb, 8w) | | 17 | | | |
| | TOTAL | (45 overs) | (for 7 wkts) | 194 | | | |

| Bowler | O | M | R | W | NB | Wd |
|---|---|---|---|---|---|---|
| Tudor | 9 | 0 | 32 | 2 | - | - |
| Giddins | 9 | 2 | 39 | 4 | - | 2 |
| Murtagh | 9 | 0 | 39 | 1 | - | 1 |
| Saqlain Mushtaq | 9 | 0 | 28 | 0 | - | - |
| Clarke | 4 | 0 | 14 | 0 | - | - |
| Hollioake | 5 | 0 | 33 | 0 | - | 1 |

### SURREY LIONS

| Fall Of Wkt | Batsman | How | Out | Score | Balls | 4s | 6s |
|---|---|---|---|---|---|---|---|
| 2-9 | I.J. Ward | lbw | b Kirtley | 9 | 17 | 2 | 0 |
| 1-4 | A.D. Brown | c Adams | b Kirtley | 0 | 1 | 0 | 0 |
| 4-156 | M.R. Ramprakash | c Kirtley | b Taylor | 60 | 80 | 6 | 1 |
| 3-25 | R. Clarke | lbw | b Martin-Jenkins | 12 | 26 | 2 | 0 |
| | N. Shahid | Not | Out | 74 | 95 | 7 | 1 |
| | A.J. Hollioake * | Not | Out | 26 | 17 | 3 | 0 |
| | J.N. Batty + | did not bat | | | | | |
| | A.J. Tudor | did not bat | | | | | |
| | Saqlain Mushtaq | did not bat | | | | | |
| | T.J. Murtagh | did not bat | | | | | |
| | E.S.H. Giddins | did not bat | | | | | |
| | Extras | (6b, 6lb, 2w) | | 14 | | | |
| | TOTAL | (39.2 overs) | (for 4 wkts) | 195 | | | |

| Bowler | O | M | R | W | NB | Wd |
|---|---|---|---|---|---|---|
| Martin-Jenkins | 9 | 2 | 31 | 1 | - | 1 |
| Kirtley | 8.2 | 2 | 25 | 2 | - | 1 |
| Taylor | 9 | 0 | 47 | 1 | - | - |
| Innes | 6 | 0 | 41 | 0 | - | - |
| Davis | 7 | 0 | 39 | 0 | - | - |

## NATIONAL LEAGUE DIVISION TWO AT 7TH AUGUST

| Pos | Prv | | P | Pts | W | T | L | A |
|---|---|---|---|---|---|---|---|---|
| 1 | 1 | Gloucestershire Gladiators | 12 | 36 | 8 | 0 | 2 | 2 |
| 2 | 2 | Northamptonshire Steelbacks | 9 | 26 | 6 | 0 | 2 | 1 |
| 3 | 3 | Surrey Lions | 11 | 26 | 6 | 0 | 4 | 1 |
| 4 | 4 | Middlesex Crusaders | 11 | 20 | 4 | 0 | 5 | 2 |
| 5 | 5 | Lancashire Lightning | 12 | 20 | 4 | 0 | 6 | 2 |
| 6 | 6 | Derbyshire Scorpions | 9 | 18 | 4 | 0 | 4 | 1 |
| 7 | 7 | Essex Eagles | 8 | 16 | 4 | 0 | 4 | 0 |
| 8 | 8 | Hampshire Hawks | 11 | 14 | 3 | 0 | 7 | 1 |
| 9 | 9 | Sussex Sharks | 11 | 12 | 2 | 0 | 7 | 2 |

## FRIZZELL COUNTY CHAMPIONSHIP - MATCH ELEVEN

### SUSSEX versus SURREY
### at Hove

### First Day - Thursday 8th August

### Surrey 193; Sussex 139-7

*The Teams And The Toss* - The Surrey team shows three changes from the match against Yorkshire at Guildford, all of them in the bowling department. Jimmy Ormond is out with a hand injury, Saqlain Mushtaq is away in Morocco with Pakistan, and Ian Salisbury is allowed to miss the game, as his wife is about to give birth to their first child. Their replacements are Alex Tudor, who has been released from the England squad for the second Test against India, Tim Murtagh, and, much to everyone's surprise, Mushtaq Ahmed, the 32-year-old former Pakistan leg-spinner who has been signed late in the day as temporary short-term cover for Saqlain. Sussex's team selection is much more straightforward with Chris Adams, James Kirtley and Mark Davis having all proved their recovery from injury in the previous evening's floodlit NUL match. They therefore take their places in what would seem to be a full-strength Sussex line-up, with Billy Taylor getting the nod over Jason Lewry as third seamer. The pitch is clearly damp as the captains toss up, though Sussex appear to have a reasonable excuse - the torrential rain that had fallen on Monday evening, when the floodlit match against Gloucestershire Gladiators was washed out after just ten balls, had soaked the pitch that was to be used for this fixture. It remains unclear as to whether it was, or should have been, covered with matting at the time, and there must also have been a case for playing on the Gloucestershire wicket, which was then subsequently used for the Surrey NUL game. Since the visitors appear to accept the situation with good grace and the umpires decide not to intervene, one can only assume that no-one is overly concerned, however, though the toss certainly looks to be a good one to win. When Adam Hollioake calls incorrectly, it is entirely predictable that Surrey are invited to bat.

Since Ian Ward and Jon Batty are understandably uncertain about the degree of assistance that the pitch might give the bowlers, it is scarcely a surprise that Surrey get away to a slow start against James Kirtley and Robin Martin-Jenkins, with just eleven runs coming from the first eight overs of the match. The following two overs see the scoring rate picking up a little, however, as the first boundary of the day comes via Batty's pads in the next over from Kirtley, and then Ward locates the rope at cover with a handsome drive off Martin-Jenkins to bring the first four off the bat in over number ten.

Although unspectacular, the cricket is certainly absorbing during this opening period, with accurate Sussex bowling being repelled by textbook opening batting as both Batty and Ward resist any temptation to flirt with deliveries wide of the off stump and pick up singles wherever possible. It is unfortunate, therefore, that the Surrey wicketkeeper is dismissed, with the total on twenty-nine, just as he is beginning to expand his repertoire, with boundaries backward of square on both sides of the wicket off Kirtley. Responding to his partner's call for a single following a push into the covers, Batty fails to beat Kevin Innes' direct-hit throw to the striker's end and departs for sixteen.

Mark Ramprakash is the new batsman and, seemingly relishing the challenge presented by an unreliable pitch, he plays himself in steadily and sensibly over the course of the next half-an-hour. As a result, the run-rate inevitably dips again, with Ward's extra cover drive for four off Kirtley being the only stroke of note until Sussex's opening bowlers are rested in favour of Kevin Innes, from the Cromwell Road end, and Billy Taylor, from the sea end. These changes initially accelerate the scoring, as Ward takes two boundaries off Taylor, courtesy of a back-foot force behind square on the off side and a pull through midwicket, while Ramprakash collects the first four of his innings with a forcing stroke to the rope at square cover at Innes' expense in the over that sees the arrival of the Surrey fifty.

After this rather inaccurate start, the Sussex first-change bowlers settle into a much better line and length, however, pegging the visitors back again before making the second breakthrough of the morning when Ward is caught on the crease and adjudged lbw to Taylor for twenty-eight in the twenty-sixth over.

At 60-2, honours are now just about even, though Ramprakash is starting to look well set and manages to tilt the balance slightly in the visitors' favour as lunch approaches. Having driven Innes for four through mid-off, the former England batsman takes an instant liking to the bowling of Mark Davis when the off-spinner replaces Innes three overs before the break, launching the new bowler's first delivery over long-on for six and then unfurling a sumptuous extra cover drive to dismiss his second ball to the boundary in equally impressive style.

When Nadeem Shahid then takes a third boundary off Davis, with a slog-sweep in the final over of the session, Surrey go to lunch in a very satisfactory position at 86-2. Considering the nature of the pitch, the ball has beaten the bat on surprisingly few occasions during the morning's play and, though Sussex's bowlers might be a little disappointed with their efforts, much credit for the visitors' sound start is due to the skilful and patient innings played by their top three batsmen.

*Lunch:- Surrey 86-2 (Ramprakash 31\*, Shahid 5\*) from 33 overs*

With Kirtley and Martin-Jenkins restored to the attack after lunch, the visitors' total is immediately boosted by four when Shahid cracks the latter through the covers, though they receive a serious blow three overs later when Kirtley traps Ramprakash lbw to restore equilibrium to the game at 94-3.

Fortunately for Surrey, Shahid makes light of this loss by driving and pulling successive balls to the boundary later in the same over, sending the total into three figures in the process, and, after surviving a potential run-out scare in the next over from Martin-Jenkins, he looks to be in control again as he cuts Kirtley for another four the next time the two combatants lock horns. Although Shahid follows up by driving the next ball through the covers for two, Kirtley has his revenge before the over is out, though in fortunate style, as the batsman flicks at a wayward leg-side delivery and is caught by wicketkeeper Matt Prior.

It's 111-4 as Shahid exits for twenty-eight and, with Ali Brown looking a little shaky as he sets out, Sussex appear to be gaining the upper hand. Surrey fans know that some of Brown's best innings start in unconvincing fashion, however, and there is hope that this might be true again today as he dispatches two Kirtley half-volleys to the rope in the forty-third over and then forces Martin-Jenkins through the covers for three shortly afterwards. With Adam Hollioake having made a positive start at the other end, this is a dangerous time for the home side, especially with memories of the Surrey skipper's awesome C&G Trophy century still fresh in their minds. It is not to be Hollioake's day today, however, as his innings is terminated at nine when he shuffles across his stumps and falls leg-before to Martin-Jenkins with the total on 136.

It has certainly been a different game since lunch, and the increased tempo is maintained when Rikki Clarke makes an aggressive start against Kevin Innes, Kirtley's replacement at the Cromwell Road end, twice finding the boundary at square leg in convincing style and once edging over the slips in attempting a forcing stroke on the off side.

Having scored seventeen from just twenty balls with this forthright approach, Clarke is then undone by the pitch in Innes' next over, becoming the fourth lbw victim of the innings to date when a delivery keeps a little low to punish the young batsman's movement across his crease and put Surrey on the back foot at 157-6.

Undeterred by the loss of another partner, Brown promptly greets the return of Taylor for Martin-Jenkins by blasting the 25-year-old seamer's first delivery over mid-on for four and then pulling a further boundary later in the over, before being given further food for thought by the fourth-ball departure of Alex Tudor to Innes. The Surrey paceman slices a drive low to Murray Goodwin at gully and exits without scoring to plunge his team into deeper trouble at 165-7.

Boosted by these wickets, Innes is beginning to look a genuine threat, finding the edge of Brown's bat in his next over, though the ball flies away safely to the third man boundary for four. Taylor presents Surrey's middle-order stalwart with no such problems, though, and he is forced out of the attack by a Brown blast that sees fourteen coming from his next over, including two pulled fours that take the batsman to the brink of a quick-fire fifty.

Alas for Surrey, he doesn't make it to the milestone, as James Kirtley returns to exploit the vagaries of the pitch and dismiss Brown for forty-nine with the total advanced to 189. Although Kirtley gets the wicket-taking delivery to swing away, there seems little doubt that the Surrey middle-order man is defeated more by the ball 'popping' than anything else as his attempted drive through the on side results in a gentle, lobbed catch to Mark Davis at cover.

With Brown gone, the height of the visitors' ambitions would appear to be the capture of a batting point, but they end up falling short of this objective as the tail for once folds rapidly - in the space of just fourteen deliveries, Mushtaq Ahmed falls plumb lbw to Innes when he hits across the line of a well concealed slower ball, while Ed Giddins' limp prod at a delivery outside off stump from the same bowler results in a straightforward catch to Prior behind the stumps. Surrey's all out total of 193 is their lowest of the season, Kevin Innes' figures of 4-41 are the best of his career, and the game is already well advanced as tea is taken.

*Tea:- Between Innings*

The match takes another giant leap forward after the break as Ed Giddins and Alex Tudor hit back for the visitors in the second and third overs of Sussex's reply, removing the prolific opening pair of Montgomerie and Goodwin in the space of twelve balls. Giddins strikes gold with his first delivery as Nadeem Shahid pulls off a brilliant reflex catch at short leg, miraculously latching on to Montgomerie's full-blooded clip off his toes, then the final ball of Tudor's second over brings the wicket of Goodwin when the former Zimbabwe Test batsman shoulders arms and has his off stump knocked back by a ball that seams back at him.

It's a dream start for Surrey to have removed both openers with just four runs on the board, though any hopes they have of making further inroads into the Sussex batting line-up are foiled by a feisty counter-attack from Chris Adams and Tony Cottey that takes full toll of some rather ragged bowling and fielding. Tudor, coming in off a new shorter run-up, has particular problems with Cottey as the diminutive Welshman finds the square boundaries four times in as many overs from the Surrey paceman in racing to thirty-four at better than a run a ball, and, consequently, as the first fifty of the innings rattles up in the eleventh over, Mushtaq Ahmed takes over at the Cromwell Road end.

Although the former Pakistan leg-spinner doesn't take a wicket, despite a couple of fine overs to start his Surrey career, he is very much in the thick of the action during the next fifteen minutes as the home side slide from 58-2 to 70-4 - first he is the bowler as Cottey is needlessly run out following an awful mix-up with his skipper, then he is the catcher as Adams falls to the persevering Giddins three overs later. Cottey's enterprising innings is curtailed when he fails to respond to his captain's call for a short single to square leg and sacrifices himself as the ever alert Batty chases the ball and returns it to Hollioake at the striker's stumps, while Adams top-edges a pull and sees Mushtaq take an amazing catch in dramatic circumstances. The crowd holds its collective breath as the ball spirals high into space at deep wide mid-on and, with both Ramprakash, from midwicket, and Mushtaq, from mid-on, closing in on the catch at full pelt, a nasty collision looks inevitable. As the ball plummets to earth, both fielders go to ground simultaneously in a heap, leaving everyone uncertain about the fate of all three parties involved in the incident. It seems likely that neither man has managed to take the catch until a smiling Mushtaq rises from the ground with his right arm aloft and the ball in his hand. It's a double whammy for Surrey, since Adams is out for twenty-one and both fielders are still in one piece!

Despite the fact that the visitors now appear to hold sway again, the new arrivals at the crease, Tim Ambrose and Robin Martin-Jenkins, manage to keep the score moving, even though they never look entirely at ease. Much prodding of the pitch between overs certainly suggests that the Sussex batsmen are every bit as suspicious of the surface as their Surrey counterparts had been earlier in the day.

Although Mushtaq causes some anxious moments during this passage of play, and Giddins beats the bat on occasions as his eleven-over opening spell comes to a close, the batsmen have their moments, too, with Ambrose cutting each bowler for three and Martin-Jenkins notching the first two boundaries of his innings with a square drive off the leg-spinner and a top-edged hook off the seamer that just falls out of the reach of Tudor at long leg. A more convincing pull stroke then earns the Sussex all-rounder another four runs when Tim Murtagh enters the attack in place of Giddins, and an on-driven four later in the 21-year-old seamer's opening over pushes the Sussex total close to three figures as the pendulum swings back in favour of the home side.

With Murtagh having looked ill at ease during his unimpressive first over, the Surrey captain opts to make an instant double bowling change, switching his young swing bowler to the Cromwell Road end, while recalling Alex Tudor for his first bowl of the innings from the sea end. Although Ambrose promptly cuts Tudor for four, it isn't long before the switch of ends starts to work wonders for both bowlers and brings about a rapid change in fortunes that sees three wickets falling in the space of just eleven deliveries with the score on 112 - Tudor makes the initial breakthrough when Ambrose top-edges a pull to Ramprakash at mid-off; Murtagh's outswinger produces an outside edge from Martin-Jenkins and a very good catch by Batty three balls later; and then Tudor completes Surrey's purple patch by tempting Matt Prior into a fatal 'nibble' outside off stump which results in a catch to Brown at first slip.

With both bowlers looking far happier at their new ends, Kevin Innes and Mark Davis now have a real battle on their hands to survive as the pressure mounts and the run-rate drops markedly, though they get lucky as the day draws to a close when fading light forces Hollioake to replace Tudor with Mushtaq. This allows Davis to cut loose with a slog-sweep over midwicket for six, though Murtagh remains a threat right to the last, his excellent spell from the

Cromwell Road end producing figures of 7-2-12-1, with seven of the runs conceded having come off the edge of the bat.

At the end of a day when batting has been far from straightforward, with uneven bounce proving more of a problem than lateral movement, Surrey appear to hold a slight advantage, even if only by dint of the fact that they already have their runs on the board.

*Close:- Sussex 139-7 (Innes 6\*, Davis 18\*) from 40 overs*

## VIEWS FROM THE DRESSING ROOM

*Since the pitch started damp, would I be right to assume that you would have put Sussex in to bat if you had won the toss?*
**ADAM HOLLIOAKE** - I definitely would have put them in, yes, no doubt about it - it was a pretty poor pitch throughout the match, really.

*I assume we must have been very disappointed with our first innings total of 193?*
**MARK RAMPRAKASH** - It was a slow, seamer's wicket and, although 193 is not a good total, it might just have been par for that particular day. They say the pitch got damp, but it was exactly the sort of pitch that they would have wanted to play us on - it had a lot of movement throughout the game, and gave their medium-pacers a chance to threaten our batting line-up.

*Would you like to talk me through Mushtaq Ahmed's catch to dismiss Chris Adams, when it looked, for all the world, like the two of you were going to collide in catastrophic fashion?*
**MARK RAMPRAKASH** - The ball went up and I didn't really think it was my catch, but then I looked over at Mushy and he wasn't really moving that quickly... then I think somebody shouted out 'Ramps', so I tore after it and, of course, once you are going after it you've got to go all the way, because the last thing you want is both people pulling out. When Mushy caught the ball, I had my hand exactly underneath his hand - he actually caught the ball and part of my little finger as well! It was a very important catch, so it was just as well that we didn't collide.

*You used a new shorter run-up in this game. What were the reasons behind that decision?*
**ALEX TUDOR** - I felt that I wasn't attacking the crease as I would have liked off my longer run - I knew I wasn't going to lose any pace by shortening my run-up, but I thought it might help me to stay taller at the crease, stop me jumping out as much and give me more control over the ball. Geoff Arnold saw me during the game and told me that everything looked fine off the shorter run-up, and even Peter Willey, the umpire, said that it looked as if I was attacking the crease really well and that I shouldn't change anything. I felt I bowled very well in the first innings and got the ball to go away from the right-hander, and that's a big plus for me if I can manage to do that. I was especially pleased to do well after being released from Trent Bridge by England - I'd been told that I had to play more games after having had shin splints, so I was happy to come back and get a five-for.

### Second Day - Friday 9th August

### Surrey 193 and 261-8; Sussex 203

Despite heavy overnight rain, play gets under way on time on a cloudy and humid morning that suggests the seamers will continue to dominate proceedings.

Mark Davis has no problems in the day's opening over from Ed Giddins, however, cutting and deflecting the ball backward of point for two boundaries to give his side a flying start. Although the 30-year-old off-spinner then brings up the Sussex 150 in the following over when he squeezes a Tudor yorker away behind square leg for two, the big Surrey paceman is again looking impressive coming up the slope from the sea end and it is no surprise that he is the one to make the first breakthrough of the morning, finding the outside edge of Davis' defensive bat to provide Ali Brown with a routine catch at first slip. With Sussex now 158-8 there isn't much to choose between the two sides, though it would seem that a first innings advantage of twenty or thirty runs for either team could prove extremely valuable, given that this pitch is unlikely to improve as the game goes on.

Since the home side will be batting last, they therefore need to extend their first innings as far as possible, and hopes of doing so are raised by the new batsman, James Kirtley, who makes a confident start by twice driving Giddins down the ground for three. Tudor presents the Sussex tail-ender with a more testing challenge, however, and when the England fast bowler finds some extra bounce with the final delivery of the fiftieth over he brings Kirtley to book and completes a well-deserved five-wicket haul. Fending the rising delivery away with his gloves, the Sussex number ten can only watch in horror as Adam Hollioake dives full-length to his right from second slip to hold an excellent catch just inches from the turf. At 172-9, with only Billy Taylor to come, the hosts now look likely to concede a first innings lead to their visitors, and much will clearly depend on Kevin Innes if Sussex are to get closer to Surrey's 193.

Protecting his team-mate from Tudor wherever possible, the former Northamptonshire all-rounder skilfully manages to nudge the total slowly upwards, forcing Hollioake to replace a disappointing Giddins with Mushtaq Ahmed, and records the first boundary off the bat for some fifteen overs when glancing Tudor to fine leg. By straying down the legside, the Surrey strike bowler appears to be showing early signs of fatigue and, consequently, after two further unexceptional overs, the visiting captain decides that Tudor has earned a rest after a fine ten-over spell. This boosts Sussex's hopes of extending their innings further and, following a succession of singles, Taylor takes his team ahead, against all odds, with an edge for two off Mushtaq.

With the last-wicket stand now becoming a real irritation for Surrey, Hollioake acts again, recalling Giddins in place of his leg-spinner and switching Tim Murtagh to the Cromwell Road end after a solitary over from the sea end. Although this fails to prevent Sussex reaching two-hundred, as Innes drives Giddins to the rope at extra cover, it only takes Murtagh seven balls to finish the innings from his favoured end, the left-handed Taylor edging a drive at an outswinger to provide Batty with a catch that is taken with deceptive ease in front of first slip. Sussex are all out for 203, thereby gaining a lead of ten runs, and they owe a huge debt of gratitude to the doughty Innes, who gets a good hand from the crowd as he leaves the field, having added an unbeaten forty-one to his career-best bowling figures of yesterday.

Facing an awkward seven overs before lunch, Ward and Batty come through unscathed, though the Surrey wicketkeeper has a couple of unsettling moments against Martin-Jenkins, edging him wide of, and then short of, the slips in the second and fourth overs respectively.

*Lunch:- Surrey 17-0 (Ward 7\*, Batty 8\*) from 7 overs*

When Ward square-cuts Martin-Jenkins to the boundary immediately after the restart he becomes the first Surrey batsman to complete a thousand first-class runs for the season, an achievement he celebrates by on-driving for three later in an over that ends up costing nine runs. Despite the fact that there are still occasional signs of inconsistent bounce, the left-handed opener looks confident, picking off a boundary on each side of the wicket in Kirtley's second over of the session and then driving Martin-Jenkins through mid-off and wide mid-on, for four and three runs respectively, to raise the visitors' fifty in the sixteenth over. At this point, his progress is halted, however, as a brief shower interrupts play for a little over ten minutes, causing three overs to be deducted from the day's allocation.

Fortunately, this break doesn't seem to affect the concentration of the batsmen as they are soon up and running again after the resumption, with Billy Taylor, replacing Martin-Jenkins at the sea end, immediately being clipped wide of mid-on for four, and then two, by the fluent Ward. Batty is soon joining the party, too, striking Kevin Innes for three off-side boundaries when the former Northamptonshire all-rounder relieves Kirtley at the Cromwell Road end, thereby setting alarm bells ringing for Sussex. The Championship leaders are scoring much too quickly for the south coast county's liking, and Ward underlines their need for greater control by plundering two cover-driven boundaries shortly after completing the first individual half-century of the match, from 69 balls, with a forcing stroke wide of mid-on for three off Taylor.

With forty-two runs having now haemorrhaged from just eight overs since the rain break, taking Surrey into a position of some strength, Kirtley - skippering the home side in place of Chris Adams, who is off the field with a jarred knee - is forced to introduce Mark Davis in place of Innes in an attempt to try and restore order. Much to the stand-in captain's relief, the off-spinner starts tidily, though runs continue to flow from the other end as Batty strikes Taylor for three fours in two overs to take the total, and then the visitors' advantage, into three figures. Even though he has made one or two deliveries lift wickedly from the pitch, the ex-Wiltshire bowler clearly has to be removed from the firing line at this stage, allowing Kirtley to reintroduce Innes, this time at the sea end, after his unhappy two-over spell from the Cromwell Road end earlier.

Finally, with this move, the home skipper seems to have hit upon the right combination, as a run-rate that was rising towards four is dragged back by a series of much tighter overs, during which Davis finds a fair degree of turn and eventually breaks the opening partnership with the total on 121. Batty is the man dismissed, for forty-six, thanks to an excellent one-handed reflex catch at silly point by Carl Hopkinson, the substitute fielder, and it has to be said that the wicket hasn't come a minute too soon for Sussex, who won't want to be facing a fourth-innings target much in excess of 250 on this unreliable track.

Davis now has to bowl to the newly-arrived Mark Ramprakash and, just as in the first innings, the Surrey batsman is aggressive right from the off, smashing the ball over the midwicket boundary with a slog-sweep for six in his third over at the crease in defiance of a defensive field-setting that includes a long-on and a cover sweeper. A similarly belligerent move against Innes three overs later almost brings about his downfall, however, though it would be hard to criticise Prior for fumbling a lifting delivery that seams away to beat Ramprakash as he makes a move down the track to the medium-pacer - only the harshest judge would call it a missed stumping, though it rates as a worrying moment for the Surrey faithful with the tea interval imminent. Fortunately, Ramprakash is seemingly unmoved by the incident, and when he pushes a single to square leg in Davis' next over he joins his batting partner in reaching a thousand first-class runs for the season.

*Tea:- Surrey 140-1 (Ward 75\*, Ramprakash 12\*) from 40 overs*

Kirtley pairs himself with Davis after the break, and the off-spinner provides his skipper with a breakthrough in the third over when Ward backs away to cut through the off-side but only ends up getting a top edge to Prior. It's an ideal start to the final session for the home side as they have got rid of the very determined Surrey opener - who had completed his thousand Championship runs for the season shortly before the break - with just two runs added to the total. And, with the help of a large slice of luck, things are about to get better for them.

Nadeem Shahid sweeps his first ball for a single, putting him on strike against Kirtley, drives his second ball to the cover boundary, and then departs to the pavilion one ball later with his off stump having been extracted by an evil delivery that has scudded through very low. Luckily for Ali Brown, another shooter later in the over is off line and, therefore, inconveniences Prior behind the stumps, rather than the Surrey batsman. While the sight of these two deliveries misbehaving in this manner is worrying for both sides, it is especially so for Sussex, who have to bat last.

Ramprakash does his best to add to their concerns by driving Kirtley for two off-side fours in the England one-day international's next over but, though both he and Brown look keen to attack, they are reasonably well contained for a while hereafter by a combination of accurate bowling, defensive field settings, and ground fielding that has been of a high standard throughout the game to date. Courageously, considering the batsmen he is bowling to, Davis is prepared to give the ball plenty of air and this brings him further rewards in his fourteenth over when he removes Brown and Adam Hollioake in the space of four deliveries. To be honest, he does receive a helping hand from both batsmen, since Brown is bowled middle-and-leg, possibly with an inside-edge assist, in attempting an off drive, while the Surrey captain looks to be defeated by both flight and spin as he aims a rather ambitious drive at only his third ball and loses his leg stump. Though both strokes have looked rather careless, the off-spinner deserves full marks for having the guts to toss the ball up to two such fearsome strikers of the ball.

The balance of the game has now shifted a little, with the scoreboard reading 176-5, though Surrey are fortified by the continued presence of Ramprakash, who pulls and cuts boundaries off Martin-Jenkins when the tall all-rounder replaces Kirtley at the sea end. Davis is proving rather more awkward at the other end, though, and he completes his five-for when he adds Rikki Clarke's scalp to his collection with the visitors still ten runs shy of two-hundred. While his two recently departed senior colleagues had been 'gated' on the drive, the young all-rounder disobeys the golden rule that suggests a right-handed batsman shouldn't attempt to cut an off-spinner on a turning pitch, and pays the ultimate price as he chops the ball down onto his stumps. Davis and his Sussex team-mates are understandably delighted as their comeback continues, with six wickets having now fallen for the addition of sixty-nine runs.

In an attempt to regain the initiative, Ramprakash and his new partner, Alex Tudor, attempt to take the attack to the bowlers, with a fair degree of success. While the former drives the off-spinner to the rope at long-off to reach a classy fifty from 94 balls, the latter survives a Chinese cut off Martin-Jenkins and a miscue into space off Davis, before, quite literally, sweeping Surrey into a 200-run lead with a six over backward square leg. The tall paceman then follows up with a lovely forcing shot through the covers off the returning Innes and then smites Davis for another six with a powerful slog-sweep.

With this partnership in full swing the visitors are again in the ascendancy... but not for long. No sooner has the seventh-wicket stand reached fifty than both participants depart in four balls from Innes and Davis, Ramprakash brilliantly stumped by Prior as he lunges forward to the medium-pacer and is beaten on the outside edge, and Tudor bowled leg stump as he misses another slog-sweep at the off-spinner. Since Surrey are now, effectively, 232-8, there would appear to be nothing much to choose between the two sides again, especially as the visitors have a slightly suspect tail in this match, the first innings having provided ample proof of this.

Perhaps bearing this in mind, Mushtaq Ahmed doesn't hang around. Although there are only a few overs remaining before the close of play, the Pakistani spin wizard lashes into Davis, slog-sweeping first for four and then for a rather fortunate six, when the fielder on the deep midwicket boundary steps over the rope in taking a good overhead catch, before cutting to the advertising boards at cover for another boundary. As a consequence of this calculated assault, the score rushes past 250 and, by the close of play, Surrey's overall lead stands at 251, thanks to Tim Murtagh's cover-driven four at the expense of Innes in the final over.

As the ground staff wheel the covers onto the pitch, these two counties can certainly consider themselves lucky. While we have lost just three overs here today, the rest of the day's county programme has been decimated by rain, with the other seven matches having witnessed just ninety overs of play in total.

*Close:- Surrey 261-8 (Mushtaq 17\*, Murtagh 4\*) from 72 overs*

# VIEWS FROM THE DRESSING ROOM

*We made a good start to our second innings, and I guess it would be fair to say that our steeliness at the top of the order was one of our great strengths throughout the season?*
**MARK RAMPRAKASH** - I think it's so important to see off the new ball, because most county sides don't have a world-class spinner to come on and tie things down - therefore they are relying on the new ball to make inroads. Wardy was so solid and mentally tough throughout the season, and Jon Batty must take a lot of credit, too.

*Would it be fair to say that our middle-order batted a little recklessly against Mark Davis in the second innings?*
**ADAM HOLLIOAKE** - Yes, definitely. That was probably the one time in the season where we really let ourselves down. We lost a bit of a focus for a session there and it probably cost us the match.
**MARK RAMPRAKASH** - Without a doubt, yes. It was reckless batting and I think it was due to over-confidence - the fact that Surrey's batsmen are so used to dominating off-spinners, and a lot of county bowlers in general, really. We always look to take the aggressive option, I suppose, and on this occasion it didn't work, and it certainly cost us because Sussex should have been chasing a much bigger total in the final innings. But I suppose over the course of a long campaign you're going to have your times where these things happen. Davis did bowl pretty well - he gave the ball a bit of air and turned it - but we certainly contributed towards our dismissals.

## Third Day - Saturday 10th August

### Surrey 193 and 296; Sussex 203 and 85-2

Despite overnight rain and a light shower at 10.40am, play gets under way on time, with Surrey hoping to extend their advantage beyond three-hundred, a mark which would surely make them red-hot favourites to win the match.

Hopes of achieving this goal are quickly dashed, however, when Tim Murtagh falls to the first ball of the second over bowled by James Kirtley, after Mushtaq Ahmed has scored six runs and then been dropped at short midwicket by Murray Goodwin during an eventful first over from Mark Davis. By chopping an inswinger into his stumps, Murtagh immediately increases Sussex's belief that they can finish the innings off quickly, since Ed Giddins will now be exposed to fresh bowlers.

As it turns out, though, the Surrey number eleven survives Kirtley's five remaining deliveries, giving Mushtaq licence to attack in Davis' next over. The leg-spinner clearly relishes this situation, picking up two boundaries by driving the second ball back over the bowler's head and sweeping the fourth to square leg, though he is unable to steal the strike for Kirtley's next over.

Luckily for Surrey, this doesn't prove costly, however, as Giddins manages to deflect a delivery to third man for a single and then watches from the non-striker's end as Mushtaq adds two more fours to his tally, courtesy of a pick-up over square leg and an extra-cover drive, before claiming the bowling for the next over with a steered single backward of point. Surrey's lead has now swollen to 279, and three-hundred continues to look a possibility as the visitors' stand-in overseas player cuts Robin Martin-Jenkins, a sensible replacement for Davis at the Cromwell Road end, over point for the ninth boundary of his innings and then reclaims the strike again at the end of the over.

All good things must come to an end, however, and Mushtaq's highly entertaining and valuable knock is terminated two balls later when he advances on Kirtley and miscues an attempted drive high to Goodwin at third man, thereby missing out on a debut half-century by just three runs and setting Sussex's victory target at 287. Despite receiving a late battering from Mushtaq last night and this morning, Mark Davis' figures of 6-97 remain his best for Sussex and he is therefore given the honour of leading his team from the field to a fine ovation.

The home side's hopes of recording their third Championship victory of the season will clearly be enhanced if they can make a solid start to their run chase, so there is early disappointment for them when Richard Montgomerie falls cheaply for the second time in the match. Although the former Northamptonshire opener takes ten runs from Alex Tudor's opening over, Ed Giddins produces a cracking delivery to have him taken at the wicket by Jon Batty from the twelfth ball of the innings with the score on fifteen.

After these two eventful opening overs, things inevitably quieten down a little, with Goodwin and Tony Cottey trying to stabilise the Sussex ship, and Giddins outshining Tudor until the latter comes up with an outstanding, yet desperately unlucky, fifth over, during which Goodwin, on twelve, edges at catchable height between first and second slip. Since the former Zimbabwe batsman snicks, if you are being harsh, or steers, if you are being generous, two further deliveries for four and three, Tudor's excellent over ends up costing him eleven runs without any reward, which is very rough justice for the big paceman.

Though maintaining a good line, Surrey's main strike bowler tends to bowl a little too short at times during the rest of his spell, however, allowing the Sussex duo, both good cutters and pullers of the ball, an occasional opportunity to boost the total with a boundary, and this error is initially repeated by both Rikki Clarke and Tim Murtagh when they appear in the attack shortly afterwards.

Goodwin and Cottey are looking pretty well set against this first-change pairing as their partnership passes fifty, and it is only when Hollioake introduces Mushtaq into the attack, in place of a disappointing Clarke, that Surrey start to fight back. The little leg-spinner immediately has a very confident lbw appeal against Goodwin turned down, then Murtagh makes the breakthrough for his side with a quite superb piece of bowling that even the master, Martin Bicknell, would have been proud of. Having bowled a series of outswingers at Cottey, the young swing bowler suddenly slips in an inswinger to catch the former Glamorgan batsman unawares as he shoulders arms. Umpire Roy Palmer acknowledges the most plumb lbw imaginable by slowly raising his finger and, in so doing, tilts the balance of the match slightly in Surrey's favour, since Sussex are now 77-2.

Buoyed by his excellent act of deception, Murtagh then very nearly tips the scales further against the home team when his next delivery finds the outside edge of Matt Prior's bat as the Sussex wicketkeeper - promoted to number four in the order - drives at an outswinger, only for Nadeem Shahid to grass a very difficult catch low to his right at third slip. Having looked as potent a weapon as any bowler in the match, the capture of another wicket wouldn't have flattered the youngster, and it would certainly have given the visitors a huge boost with lunch now imminent. As it is, the batsmen survive two testing final overs from the leg-spinner and the 21-year-old seamer to reach the interval at 85-2.

*Lunch:- Sussex 85-2 (Goodwin 42\*, Prior 0\*) from 26 overs*

Drizzle, which had started to fall as the players left the field for lunch, gets heavier during the break and develops into a thunderstorm that passes over the ground with devastating effects. After two hours of constant heavy rain there are puddles all over the outfield and, at around 4pm, the umpires confirm that there will be no further play today.

*Close:- Sussex 85-2 (Goodwin 42\*, Prior 0\*) from 26 overs*

## Fourth Day - Sunday 11th August

### Surrey 193 and 296; Sussex 203 and 288-6

**Sussex won by four wickets**
**Sussex 16pts, Surrey 3**

In altogether more pleasant conditions, with the ground having made a good recovery from the previous afternoon's dousing, the match enters its final day with Sussex needing 202 runs and Surrey requiring eight wickets. Since Kent have already recorded a victory over Somerset, the Championship leaders will be especially keen to triumph today in order to keep the men from Canterbury at arm's length, while Sussex need to claim victory if they are to avoid getting sucked into the relegation battle that is developing just below them in the table. There's plenty to play for, therefore, as Adam Hollioake opts to open up with Ed Giddins from the sea end and Mushtaq Ahmed from the Cromwell Road end.

Although the pitch appears to have lost a little of its venom, the overnight Sussex batsmen find both bowlers a real handful, with the ball regularly beating the outside edge, and Prior finding it almost impossible to locate the middle of his bat. Runs come only at a trickle, and it seems quite fitting that the first boundary of the day, in the seventh over, results from a Goodwin edge off Giddins that bounces short of the slips and runs away to the rope at third man. These runs take the Sussex opener through to a determined half-century from 108 balls, with the innings including eight fours, all bar one of which has come from a cut, a deflection to third man, or an outside edge.

Predictably enough, it is a push backward of point for a single that takes the total into three figures during Giddins' next over as Hollioake's chosen bowling combination continues to test the batsmen without gaining any reward. Prior is having a particularly uncomfortable time and hardly justifies his promotion up the order as a result of his skipper's knee injury. Even when he does briefly break free, at Giddins' expense, it is courtesy of a badly miscued drive, which earns him four runs through backward point, and then a Murtagh misfield, which allows him to add another two to his tally.

Having laboured hard without any luck at all during his seven overs from the sea end, Giddins finally gives way to Alex Tudor, and the big paceman keeps the pressure up with some testing opening overs. Prior, meanwhile, continues to survive by the skin of his teeth and, once again, adds to his tally thanks only to a misfield - this time by Michael Carberry, who is on the field as a substitute - and an ugly heave wide of mid-on for four. Mushtaq now knows exactly how Giddins had felt earlier in the morning.

Even though the Sussex duo have needed a generous helping of luck in the face of some superb Surrey bowling and an untrustworthy pitch, it's impossible not to admire the gutsy efforts of Goodwin and Prior as their partnership somehow manages to reach fifty in the twentieth over of the day. It might well have taken almost twenty-two overs to arrive at this milestone but its value is immense, since it has taken the home side to within 159 runs of the winning post.

At this point, however, Prior's good fortune runs out, and in some style too, as he assays a flamboyant off-drive at Tudor and only succeeds in dragging the ball onto his wicket, simultaneously sending the middle stump flying and lifting the visitors' spirits. The breakthrough has been a very long time coming, but now that the young Sussex wicketkeeper has gone for twenty, with the total on 128, the visitors will have hopes of taking another couple of wickets before lunch.

Tudor actually appears to do this in his next over, but umpire Peter Willey makes two critical decisions which look as if they could have a serious impact on the outcome of the game. The former Test umpire first rejects an extremely confident and genuine-looking appeal for a catch at the wicket against Goodwin, and then, just a few balls later, he turns down the Surrey paceman's equally impassioned plea for lbw against Chris Adams as the Sussex skipper offers no stroke to a delivery that cuts back at him and keeps wickedly low. From my vantage point behind the arm, it's hard to see why these appeals, with Goodwin on sixty-two and Adams not yet off the mark, have met with a negative response, but there is no doubting the importance of the two decisions. Had they both gone against the batsman then Surrey would have been on the way to victory; as it is, Sussex remain on top, and there is still much hard work for the bowlers to do.

Mushtaq and Tudor certainly try everything they can to dislodge one of these two key batsmen, and the ball continues to beat the bat as Goodwin and Adams are restricted to just six singles in the next nine overs.

Finally, with lunch just two overs away, Tim Murtagh replaces Tudor at the sea end and immediately induces an edge from Adams that flies at catchable height through the vacant third slip position. Like his colleagues, it seems that he is out of luck today.

As the interval arrives, two very relieved Sussex batsmen head off to the pavilion, with Goodwin having been able to score no more than twenty-five runs in the thirty-four overs bowled this morning, and the normally free-scoring Adams unbeaten on seven after fourteen overs at the crease. These figures underline the quality of the bowling we have witnessed from Messrs Giddins, Tudor and Mushtaq, with incredible accuracy and an almost complete lack of good luck the most striking features of their display. The home side's gritty batting performance has left them in the driving seat at the break, however, and much will depend on two things after the interval - whether Sussex's good fortune can hold, and whether Surrey can keep bowling so well, especially as the three experienced bowlers have put so much into the first session.

*Lunch:- Sussex 145-3 (Goodwin 67\*, Adams 7\*) from 60 overs*

Despite having bowled a good over before lunch, Murtagh is not retained in the attack after the break, as Hollioake turns back to the more experienced Giddins, while Mushtaq continues to operate from the Cromwell Road end. It seems harsh on the youngster, though it's easy to understand why the Surrey captain feels his senior bowlers might be best suited to the job.

The Sussex batsmen appear to have come out with a more positive attitude this afternoon, however, and Ian Ward, at silly point, soon has evidence of this as Adams crashes a drive off Mushtaq into the side of his neck. It looks as though the Surrey opener might have suffered a very nasty injury and, after assessing the situation on the pitch for about five minutes, Neil Walker, the Surrey physio, leads the stricken fielder gingerly from the field.

To add to their problems, further signs of growing Sussex aggression are then evident in the next two overs as Goodwin glances and on-drives fours off Giddins in the course of a very poor over that costs eleven, and then Adams starts to take on Mushtaq by twice driving him over mid-off in an over that contributes nine further runs to the home team's cause. With twenty runs having therefore come from two overs, the balance of power has shifted dramatically towards Sussex, and fears that the bowlers might not be able to maintain their amazing pre-lunch standards are being confirmed.

Despite this sudden surge, Hollioake keeps faith with his current bowling pairing and, though the next few overs bring only singles and twos, the fourth-wicket partnership passes fifty and the home team's target decreases at a steady rate. The batsmen now look to have completely broken the hold that the bowlers had over them before the break, and Surrey appear to be in real danger of defeat.

This belief is then underlined when Adams launches Mushtaq cleanly over long-on for six, and follows up by on-driving Tudor for four as soon as the tall paceman replaces Giddins at the sea end. With the Sussex batsmen firmly in control, Goodwin moves into the nineties by pulling a four of his own later in Tudor's return over, and the total passes two-hundred in the very next over, courtesy of Adams' cut to the backward point boundary off the leg-spinner.

Unusually for the Surrey skipper, he appears guilty of having allowed the game to drift with some unimaginative captaincy today, and he pays a heavy price for keeping the increasingly ineffective Mushtaq in the attack for another over, as Adams, now playing quite beautifully, plunders three successive boundaries with a brace of drives over cover and a whip through midwicket. The second of these strokes takes him to a well-played fifty from 91 balls, and his increasingly assured innings looks ever more certain to see his side to victory with only seventy runs now needed. Goodwin's cut for four off Tudor then worsens the visitors' plight and, though Hollioake finally recalls Murtagh in place of Mushtaq, it looks to be a case of too little, too late as Adams pulls the young seamer for four to raise the hundred partnership in an over costing seven precious runs.

At this point, Surrey's best chance of avoiding defeat appears to rest with the dark clouds that are gathering around the ground, though Tudor also offers a degree of hope by splitting up the Goodwin-Adams alliance in the fourth over of his spell, when the Sussex captain cuts straight to cover where Carberry, now substituting for Ward, take a routine catch. With six wickets standing and only fifty-three runs required, Adams' departure for sixty-two looks unlikely to prove hugely significant, though, especially while Goodwin continues to occupy the crease.

The former Zimbabwe international has been in situ for four minutes short of five hours in total when, later in the over of his erstwhile partner's dismissal, he finally reaches three figures with a typical deflection to third man for a single, justifiably earning fulsome applause for a gritty 223-ball innings that has contained thirteen boundaries.

Unfortunately for Sussex fans, they then have to repeat their ovation just a couple of minutes later, as Goodwin hits across the line of a Murtagh delivery that straightens from around middle-and-leg and falls lbw without addition to his hundred. With their opponents now 238-5, Surrey sniff an opportunity to turn the game on its head, though the home side are comforted by a clip to the midwicket boundary by Robin Martin-Jenkins and the very surprising replacement of Murtagh with Mushtaq at the Cromwell Road end.

It actually transpires that Hollioake has merely switched Murtagh to the sea end in place of Tudor, though this is equally puzzling, since the 21-year-old's best bowling in the match has been from the other end. Predictably enough, Murtagh looks much less comfortable after the switch and, as tea approaches, he is clipped through midwicket and driven through the covers for a brace of boundaries by the young Australian, Tim Ambrose. With Martin-Jenkins following up by lifting Mushtaq over mid-on for the third four in two overs, Sussex appear to have weathered the storm, in a metaphorical sense, though there remains a serious threat of a real-life downpour as the skies over the ground remain grey and gloomy.

To maintain any hope of pulling the game out of the fire, the visitors simply have to strike another blow before tea and, in an attempt to do so, Hollioake replaces Mushtaq with Giddins, and returns Murtagh to the Cromwell Road end. Although Giddins comes back well with a fine over at Ambrose, it is Murtagh who makes the breakthrough for his team when the 20-year-old Sussex batsman is immediately put back on strike by a Martin-Jenkins single. Trapped in front of his stumps by a very similar delivery to that which had seen off Goodwin, Ambrose is sent on his way by umpire Palmer, giving Surrey renewed hope as the players follow the dismissed batsman off the field to take tea.

*Tea:- Sussex 265-6 (Martin-Jenkins 12\*) from 87.2 overs*

Upon the resumption, with the rain still holding off, Murtagh continues to look the most dangerous bowler in the match by inducing edges from both Martin-Jenkins and Innes, the new batsman, in the remaining four balls of his unfinished over. Unfortunately for Surrey, however, Ed Giddins is unable to match his young team-mate's consistency, serving up a half-volley which Martin-Jenkins, to the delight of the home fans, dispatches to the cover boundary in the middle of an otherwise decent over.

With their team now close to what would be a very important victory in the battle to maintain first division status, it is understandable that the Hove faithful are excited enough to greet each of the five singles that accrue from the next three overs with enthusiastic applause, though it is perhaps typical of Surrey's fourth-day luck that the last of these runs comes when Innes snicks Murtagh through the vacant third slip position. When the same batsman then edges high over second slip's head for four in aiming to drive Giddins through mid-on during the next over, the visitors know that it just isn't to be their day. A firm clip to the boundary boards at square leg later in the same over puts Sussex on the brink, and when Martin-Jenkins smears Murtagh through midwicket at 4.20pm their first Championship victory over Surrey for eight years, and their first against the men from London SE11 at Hove since 1990, is confirmed.

As the home players and supporters celebrate a vital and unexpected triumph, the Surrey team troop off the field, hoping that the Club's first Championship defeat away from home since they lost at Derby in June 2000 will prove to be just a minor blip on the way to the 2002 title. Interestingly, there is a link between the last away defeat and this one, in that both matches started on damp pitches, though it seems unlikely that there will be any serious repercussions for Sussex here as there were for Derbyshire back in 2000.

**Surrey 193 and 296; Sussex 203 and 288-6**
**Sussex won by four wickets. Sussex 16pts, Surrey 3**

| VIEWS FROM THE DRESSING ROOM |
|---|

*When are you due to finish university and go full-time with your cricket?*
**TIM MURTAGH** - I'm due to finish in June 2003, so after that I'll be full-time and it will definitely be good to be able to concentrate on my cricket. As it works out, I don't tend to miss too much of the season but it will be good to be there from the start. I miss out on the best bowling conditions in the early weeks of the season and I probably miss out on a bit of match fitness as well. I've obviously been playing at university and I play my club cricket on Saturdays, but it's not the same intensity as playing and training during the week.

*I guess you must have been delighted with your dismissal of Tony Cottey, when you followed up a series of outswingers with the ball that went the other way to trap him lbw?*
**TIM MURTAGH** - Yes, I've been working hard, over the past year or so, to get my inswinger going and, although it doesn't swing that much, if I precede it with a few away swingers it can be dangerous. If the batsman is expecting the ball to go the other way then it doesn't really need to do too much in any case. But it's definitely something that got better and better as the season went on, though I probably overused it a little bit in this game, to be honest.

*Would I be right in saying that you seemed to have a strong preference for bowling from the Cromwell Road end? If so, is that normally the case for you when you bowl at Hove?*
**TIM MURTAGH** - I'd played there a couple of times before this match and I'd bowled from a different end each time, so before that game I didn't really have a preferred end. As it worked out in this match, things seemed to click from the Cromwell Road end but not so much from the sea end, though I can't really put my finger on why that was. Maybe it was because I started from the Cromwell Road end and then found it a bit difficult to switch to the other end, but I don't really know why it should have been like that.

*After some outstanding bowling in the morning, would it be fair to suggest that the game rather ran away from us in the hour after lunch?*
**ADAM HOLLIOAKE** - Yes, it did, but even though they didn't need a lot of runs when we got Adams and Goodwin out in quick succession, I still thought we would win from there... but it just didn't quite happen for us. Plus, I think I probably got a few things wrong in that game captaincy-wise. Apart from that, there was the middle-order collapse, and I think I should have caught Goodwin in the slips early on.

*I have to say that I felt you under-bowled Tim Murtagh in this game and I did make that point in my weekly column on the Club website... here is your chance to respond to that criticism!*
**ADAM HOLLIOAKE** - Basically, I just thought the other guys would do a better job, and I went with my experienced proven bowlers first. I think that game was the real coming-of-age of Tim Murtagh, though, and, in hindsight, he should bowled a bit more. As I said, I think I made a few captaincy errors in that game and that was probably one of them - I certainly remember moving him, in the middle of a good spell, down to the end from which he'd bowled quite poorly, and that was a mistake which left me chasing my tail a little bit. It was definitely a bad day at the office for the captain.

| SUSSEX v SURREY at Hove | | | | Played from 8th to 11th August | | | |
|---|---|---|---|---|---|---|---|
| Sussex won the toss and elected to field | | | | Umpires:- Roy Palmer and Peter Willey | | | |
| **SURREY - First Innings** | | | | | | | |
| Fall Of Wkt | Batsman | How | Out | Score | Balls | 4s | 6s |
| 2-60 | I.J. Ward | lbw | b Taylor | 28 | 85 | 4 | 0 |
| 1-29 | J.N. Batty + | run | out | 16 | 38 | 2 | 0 |
| 3-94 | M.R. Ramprakash | lbw | b Kirtley | 32 | 61 | 3 | 1 |
| 4-111 | N. Shahid | c Prior | b Kirtley | 28 | 41 | 5 | 0 |
| 8-189 | A.D. Brown | c Davis | b Kirtley | 49 | 52 | 7 | 0 |
| 5-136 | A.J. Hollioake * | lbw | b Martin-Jenkins | 9 | 14 | 2 | 0 |
| 6-157 | R. Clarke | lbw | b Innes | 17 | 20 | 3 | 0 |
| 7-165 | A.J. Tudor | c Goodwin | b Innes | 0 | 4 | 0 | 0 |
| 9-193 | Mushtaq Ahmed | lbw | b Innes | 7 | 21 | 1 | 0 |
| | T.J. Murtagh | Not | Out | 0 | 9 | 0 | 0 |
| 10-193 | E.S.H. Giddins | c Prior | b Innes | 0 | 7 | 0 | 0 |
| | Extras | (7lb) | | 7 | | | |
| | **TOTAL** | **(58.4 overs)** | | **193** | | | |

| Bowler | O | M | R | W | NB | Wd |
|---|---|---|---|---|---|---|
| Kirtley | 15 | 7 | 49 | 3 | - | - |
| Martin-Jenkins | 16 | 6 | 34 | 1 | - | - |
| Innes | 14.4 | 5 | 41 | 4 | - | - |
| Taylor | 11 | 1 | 44 | 1 | - | - |
| Davis | 2 | 0 | 18 | 0 | - | - |

| **SUSSEX - First Innings** | | | | | | | |
|---|---|---|---|---|---|---|---|
| Fall Of Wkt | Batsman | How | Out | Score | Balls | 4s | 6s |
| 2-4 | M.W. Goodwin | | b Tudor | 3 | 11 | 0 | 0 |
| 1-4 | R.R. Montgomerie | c Shahid | b Giddins | 1 | 2 | 0 | 0 |
| 3-58 | P.A. Cottey | run | out | 35 | 37 | 6 | 0 |
| 4-70 | C.J. Adams * | c Mushtaq | b Giddins | 21 | 39 | 3 | 0 |
| 5-112 | T.R. Ambrose | c Ramprakash | b Tudor | 25 | 45 | 2 | 0 |
| 6-112 | R.S.C. Martin-Jenkins | c Batty | b Murtagh | 23 | 49 | 4 | 0 |
| 7-112 | M.J. Prior + | c Brown | b Tudor | 0 | 5 | 0 | 0 |
| | K.J. Innes | Not | Out | 41 | 93 | 2 | 0 |
| 8-158 | M.J.G. Davis | c Brown | b Tudor | 30 | 50 | 4 | 1 |
| 9-172 | R.J. Kirtley | c Hollioake | b Tudor | 8 | 15 | 0 | 0 |
| 10-203 | B.V. Taylor | c Batty | b Murtagh | 5 | 53 | 0 | 0 |
| | Extras | (3b, 4lb, 4nb) | | 11 | | | |
| | **TOTAL** | **(66.1 overs)** | | **203** | | | |

| Bowler | O | M | R | W | NB | Wd |
|---|---|---|---|---|---|---|
| Tudor | 22 | 4 | 66 | 5 | 2 | - |
| Giddins | 21 | 4 | 68 | 2 | - | - |
| Mushtaq Ahmed | 13 | 3 | 40 | 0 | - | - |
| Murtagh | 10.1 | 2 | 22 | 2 | - | - |

| SURREY - Second Innings (Trailing by 10 runs on first innings) | | | | | | | |
|---|---|---|---|---|---|---|---|
| Fall Of Wkt | Batsman | How | Out | Score | Balls | 4s | 6s |
| 2-142 | I.J. Ward | c Prior | b Davis | 76 | 127 | 10 | 0 |
| 1-121 | J.N. Batty + | c sub (Hopkinson) | b Davis | 46 | 94 | 7 | 0 |
| 7-240 | M.R. Ramprakash | st Prior | b Innes | 64 | 111 | 5 | 1 |
| 3-147 | N. Shahid | | b Kirtley | 5 | 3 | 1 | 0 |
| 4-176 | A.D. Brown | | b Davis | 7 | 19 | 0 | 0 |
| 5-176 | A.J. Hollioake * | | b Davis | 0 | 3 | 0 | 0 |
| 6-190 | R. Clarke | | b Davis | 2 | 8 | 0 | 0 |
| 8-242 | A.J. Tudor | | b Davis | 28 | 47 | 2 | 2 |
| 10-296 | Mushtaq Ahmed | c Goodwin | b Kirtley | 47 | 31 | 8 | 1 |
| 9-267 | T.J. Murtagh | | b Kirtley | 4 | 13 | 1 | 0 |
| | E.S.H. Giddins | Not | Out | 1 | 11 | 0 | 0 |
| | Extras | (6b, 4lb, 6nb) | | 16 | | | |
| | TOTAL | (77.2 overs) | | 296 | | | |

| Bowler | O | M | R | W | NB | Wd |
|---|---|---|---|---|---|---|
| Kirtley | 17.2 | 4 | 59 | 3 | 3 | - |
| Martin-Jenkins | 15 | 2 | 53 | 0 | - | - |
| Taylor | 6 | 0 | 29 | 0 | - | - |
| Innes | 13 | 3 | 48 | 1 | - | - |
| Davis | 26 | 2 | 97 | 6 | - | - |

| SUSSEX - Second Innings (Needing 287 to win) | | | | | | | |
|---|---|---|---|---|---|---|---|
| Fall Of Wkt | Batsman | How | Out | Score | Balls | 4s | 6s |
| 1-15 | R.R. Montgomerie | c Batty | b Giddins | 10 | 9 | 2 | 0 |
| 5-238 | M.W. Goodwin | lbw | b Murtagh | 100 | 227 | 13 | 0 |
| 2-77 | P.A. Cottey | lbw | b Murtagh | 22 | 61 | 4 | 0 |
| 3-128 | M.J. Prior + | | b Tudor | 20 | 70 | 2 | 0 |
| 4-234 | C.J. Adams * | c sub (Carberry) | b Tudor | 62 | 101 | 8 | 1 |
| 6-265 | T.R. Ambrose | lbw | b Murtagh | 16 | 38 | 2 | 0 |
| | R.S.C. Martin-Jenkins | Not | Out | 23 | 41 | 4 | 0 |
| | K.J. Innes | Not | Out | 12 | 19 | 2 | 0 |
| | Extras | (9lb, 14nb) | | 23 | | | |
| | TOTAL | (93.1 overs) | (for 6 wkts) | 288 | | | |

| Bowler | O | M | R | W | NB | Wd |
|---|---|---|---|---|---|---|
| Tudor | 23 | 5 | 80 | 2 | 5 | - |
| Giddins | 25 | 7 | 64 | 1 | 2 | - |
| Clarke | 3 | 0 | 9 | 0 | - | - |
| Murtagh | 13.1 | 3 | 47 | 3 | - | - |
| Mushtaq Ahmed | 29 | 6 | 79 | 0 | - | - |

## Other Division One Results

Kent's comprehensive victory over a fading Somerset side moved them back to within 19.25 points of Surrey and made the leaders' sensational recent win at Canterbury look even more significant - had Kent won that match then their latest win would have taken them to the top of the table. Warwickshire's outside hopes of creeping up on the rails had meanwhile received a setback with a rain-affected draw at Headingley against a Yorkshire side who now needed to win at least three of their last five matches if they were to avoid relegation.

August 7-10
*Canterbury:-* **Kent beat Somerset by 153 runs.** Kent 271 (Fulton 89, Symonds 69, Caddick 5-65) and 286-7dec (Patel 71*, Ealham 60, Smith 55); Somerset 227 (Wood 55, Bowler 50, Khan 5-76) and 177 (Parsons 52, Saggers 5-42). **Kent 17pts, Somerset 4**

*Headingley:-* **Yorkshire drew with Warwickshire.** Warwickshire 233 (Knight 79) and 216-4 (Knight 109, Bell 55*); Yorkshire 313 (Lehmann 75, Taylor 50). **Yorkshire 10pts, Warwickshire 8**

August 8-11
*Old Trafford:-* **Lancashire drew with Hampshire.** Lancashire 163 (Swann 84*, Tremlett 5-57) and 52-0; Hampshire 122-8dec. **Lancashire 6pts, Hampshire 7**

| COUNTY CHAMPIONSHIP DIVISION ONE AT 11TH AUGUST |||||||||||
|---|---|---|---|---|---|---|---|---|---|---|
| Pos | Prv | | P | Points | W | D | L | Bat | Bwl | Ded |
| 1 | 1 | Surrey | 11 | 150.75 | 6 | 3 | 2 | 34 | 33 | 0.25 |
| 2 | 2 | Kent | 11 | 131.50 | 5 | 3 | 3 | 29 | 31 | 0.50 |
| 3 | 3 | Sussex | 12 | 127.00 | 3 | 6 | 3 | 32 | 35 | 0.00 |
| 4 | 5 | Warwickshire | 10 | 113.00 | 4 | 4 | 2 | 21 | 28 | 0.00 |
| 5 | 4 | Leicestershire | 10 | 107.00 | 3 | 4 | 3 | 28 | 28 | 1.00 |
| 6 | 6 | Lancashire | 10 | 99.00 | 3 | 5 | 2 | 17 | 26 | 0.00 |
| 7 | 8 | Hampshire ** | 11 | 92.00 | 1 | 8 | 2 | 24 | 32 | 8.00 |
| 8 | 7 | Somerset | 10 | 89.00 | 1 | 6 | 3 | 26 | 27 | 0.00 |
| 9 | 9 | Yorkshire | 11 | 74.50 | 0 | 5 | 6 | 24 | 31 | 0.50 |

*** Hampshire deducted 8pts for 'poor' pitch at Rose Bowl v Lancashire**

# 15 Foxes On The Run

Apart from the skipper having something of an off day, the like of which any captain is entitled to, and a period in the second innings when the batting had shown an unusual lack of discipline, it was hard to be too critical of the defeat at Hove. It hadn't been easy to admit it at the time, as the Surrey bowlers kept passing the bat without reward, but Sussex were due credit for the determined way they had stuck to their task to win the match on the last day. It proved that first division Championship cricket was gaining a tougher edge, and it was interesting to hear the comments of Chris Adams at the end of the game. The former England batsman had stated that the cricket on the final day of the match was the hardest and most intense he had experienced since his brief flirtation with the game at international level on the tour to South Africa in 1999-2000. That seemed a pretty fair and honest assessment to me, and it was also quite a compliment to Surrey. It was rather ironic, however, that the attack on which Adams had heaped so much praise was, arguably, one of the weaker line-ups, on paper anyway, that the Championship leaders had fielded all season. Additionally, it was a dramatically different attack from the one Surrey had fielded in their previous match, against Yorkshire at Guildford, where Ormond, Giddins, Saqlain and Salisbury had been the four front-line bowlers. Further changes to the bowling personnel were looking likely for the forthcoming match at Grace Road, too, with Martin Bicknell and Ormond both said to have recovered sufficiently from their injuries to play. It therefore seemed quite possible that, in the space of three matches, Surrey might have fielded eight different specialist bowlers, with none of them playing in all three games. The make-up of the attack against Leicestershire didn't matter greatly, though, so long as the team could get back on the winning trail, with Kent now pressing hard to become serious title contenders.

| FRIZZELL COUNTY CHAMPIONSHIP - MATCH TWELVE |
|---|

### LEICESTERSHIRE versus SURREY
at Grace Road, Leicester

### First Day - Wednesday 14th August

### Surrey 454-6

***The Teams And The Toss*** - *Although England request that Alec Stewart is rested, Mark Butcher is allowed to return to the Surrey line-up following the second Test against India at Trent Bridge, with Nadeem Shahid making way for him. As expected, Martin Bicknell and Jimmy Ormond make their comebacks from injury, displacing Ed Giddins and Tim Murtagh, while Ian Salisbury is allowed to miss the match in view of the fact that his wife has just presented him with a baby daughter. Leicestershire are without Vince Wells (groin) and Carl Crowe (virus), their replacements being Rob Cunliffe and Jamie Grove, while the young Indian batsman, Mohammad Kaif, makes his debut as a short-term overseas stand-in, filling the gap between Michael Bevan's return to Australia and Javagal Srinath's imminent arrival from India. The pitch looks to be an absolute beauty, so Adam Hollioake has no hesitation in deciding to bat first when he wins the toss, even though a bright and sunny morning has turned progressively grey and overcast towards the start of the game.*

By the time Ian Ward and Jon Batty take guard, the overhead conditions are looking well suited to swing bowling, so it is no surprise that the Surrey openers are forced to make a watchful start against Devon Malcolm and Phillip DeFreitas. With the ball swinging quite dramatically, as expected, the vastly experienced Leicestershire pair demand respect, and get it, with the visitors' total not reaching double figures until the ninth over, and the first boundary not arriving until the following over, when Batty cuts Malcolm to the rope at backward point.

A repeat of this stroke at the same bowler's expense two overs later precedes a double bowling change, with Darren Maddy appearing at the Bennett end and DeFreitas giving way simultaneously to Jamie Grove, the former Essex and Somerset bowler, at the pavilion end.

These changes actually change very little, however, since the bowlers continue to pose occasional problems with swing, and Batty continues to find the boundary with square cuts, twice dismissing Grove to the rope when the former England Under-19 paceman allows him too much width. Meanwhile, at the other end, Ward's first four eventually arrives in the sixteenth over when he reels off a cover drive at Maddy's expense, and he doubles his boundary tally soon afterwards with a pull through wide mid-on when Grove again fails to locate the required length.

By now the total is closing in on fifty, and Iain Sutcliffe, the Leicestershire captain, has again shuffled his pack of bowlers, switching Maddy to the pavilion end and introducing the notoriously erratic Matthew Whiley at the Bennett end in place of the equally inaccurate Grove, whose opening spell of 5-0-20-0 has been largely unimpressive. With his team on the back foot at this point, Sutcliffe is understandably delighted when his new bowling combination first drags the scoring rate back a little and then provides him with a double breakthrough, with the Surrey openers departing in successive overs to convert a score of 61-0 into 63-2.

Ward is the first to go, in controversial circumstances, and with a touch of déjà vu to boot, when umpire 'Pasty' Harris adjudges him lbw to a delivery of very full length from Whiley that the Surrey opener clearly feels he has hit. The batsman, the delivery, the umpire and the highly questionable verdict are all repeat components from the NUL match against Middlesex Crusaders at Whitgift School eight days earlier, and Ward is just as unhappy now as he was then, inspecting his bat as he leaves the field with his innings terminated at twenty-eight.

Those of us sat behind the arm are still debating the umpire's decision six balls later when Batty departs leg-before to Maddy, for the same score as his opening partner, with the total advanced by just two. This verdict, by Allan Jones, looks pretty much spot-on, however, as the Surrey keeper has missed an outswinger straightening from around middle-and-leg while aiming through midwicket.

With the home side having now evened up the contest, the Championship leaders are pleased to see Mark Butcher, batting at number three, starting positively with a square-cut boundary off Whiley, who has suddenly developed a habit of overstepping the crease once an over. The left-arm quickie has also switched to bowling round the wicket to Mark Ramprakash and, by so doing, earns himself a second wicket when the batsman edges a drive-cum-slash at head height to Maddy at second slip. The ball is travelling at a rate of knots, but the fielder makes the catch look deceptively easy and, consequently, Ramprakash is on his way for a duck and Surrey are reduced to 74-3.

On this 'shirt front' of a pitch, Leicestershire now hold a definite advantage, though Butcher and Ali Brown enhance their team's position slightly by notching three fours in the last two overs before lunch, with the left-hander driving Maddy down the ground and then in the air between extra cover and mid-off, and the right-hander deflecting a Whiley delivery to third man.

While everyone else disappears for lunch, Butcher stays on the outfield for ten to fifteen minutes, taking half-volley throw-downs in order to practise his drives.

*Lunch:- Surrey 88-3 (Butcher 13\*, Brown 4\*) from 34 overs*

With the skies having cleared again, leaving the ground bathed in warm sunshine, Butcher immediately shows the value of his pre-lunch practice by taking successive fours off the returning Devon Malcolm, courtesy of a straight drive and a clip through square leg in the first over after the restart.

Since Whiley is retained at the Bennett end, it looks like Sutcliffe is hoping to blast out another couple of batsmen with pace, though, ironically, it is a lack of this commodity that denies his side a fourth wicket in the third over of the session. With the batsman on four and the total on ninety-nine, Ali Brown pops back a simple caught-and-bowled chance to Malcolm, who is presumably deceived by the extremely low velocity of the ball as he grasses what is an absolute dolly of a catch. Although the former England paceman tries hard to make amends, beating Brown twice outside the off stump later in the same over, there is a suspicion that Leicestershire could be made to pay for Malcolm's howler if Surrey's middle-order stalwart can put this rather unnerving passage of play behind him.

It looks like he might well do so, too, since he greets DeFreitas' rapid return to the attack, in place of a very wayward Whiley, with a crunching extra-cover drive for four, and there are further signs that Surrey are turning things around when Malcolm, emulating his left-arm colleague by losing his line when he next bowls to Butcher, concedes four leg-byes and a couple of twos through midwicket as the partnership races along to fifty in the eighth over of the afternoon.

Despite receiving a clear warning that Malcolm's radar is on the blink, Sutcliffe sticks with his former Derbyshire and Northamptonshire speedster and pays a very heavy price as carnage follows and the Surrey batsmen take control. In the space of eight deliveries from Malcolm, Butcher and Brown thrash seven fours, all but the first of them, an edged drive by Butcher over the head of second slip, coming off the meat of the bat. Butcher follows his lucky snick with a glance and a drive over extra cover to take the total beyond 150, then Brown finds the rope from the first, third, fourth and fifth balls of Malcolm's next over with a sequence of on-drive, hook, cut and cover drive. In the course of this mayhem, Brown passes 10,000 career runs for Surrey, and it seems entirely fitting that he has reached the landmark during a welter of cleanly struck boundaries.

While Malcolm is being blasted out of the attack, DeFreitas is in the middle of a good spell from the Bennett end, though he is out of luck when Butcher reaches an 83-ball fifty with a Chinese cut that brings him the tenth four of his innings. The fourth-wicket partnership then reaches three figures later in the over, courtesy of a no-ball, before Maddy replaces Malcolm at the pavilion end and suffers an even worse mauling than his predecessor. Seventeen runs haemorrhage from his comeback over - Brown completes a scintillating 47-ball half-century with a one-bounce four from a drive over mid-off's head while taking thirteen from the first five balls, then Butcher drives wide of mid-on to secure four runs of his own from the final delivery.

Predictably enough, Maddy is instantly withdrawn from the attack in favour of Mohammad Kaif, bowling off-breaks, as Sutcliffe begins to run out of options, and Brown adds to the home side's misery by cutting the Indian international's second ball to the cover boundary to raise the Surrey two-hundred, the last fifty runs of which have come from just 32 deliveries.

A slight lull in the scoring now follows as deep set fields, a couple of restrictive overs from Kaif, and a continuation of DeFreitas' fine but unlucky spell - during which both batsmen edge a boundary through the vacant third slip position - give Leicestershire just a hint of control.

It doesn't last for long, though, as the batsmen quickly get the measure of Kaif, and DeFreitas' admirable ten-over spell, on what has become a very warm afternoon, comes to an end. The fourth-wicket partnership becomes worth 150 as Brown cuts the off-spinner to the rope before driving him back over his head for two sixes, one in each of his next two overs, the second of these being a monster hit which clears the pavilion by some distance and disappears out of the ground. Butcher meanwhile tucks into a few loose offerings from the recalled Grove, twice driving him through mid-on to take the total beyond 250, and, as both Surrey batsmen move into the nineties, another on-drive by the left-hander, this time off Kaif, takes the partnership past two-hundred.

With Butcher now on ninety-six, Brown on ninety-eight, and seven overs to go until tea, the beleaguered Foxes' captain elects to return to the bowling combination that served him so well at the end of the first session, namely Maddy at the pavilion end and Whiley at the Bennett end.

Although no succour is immediately forthcoming as Brown clips backward of square leg for the two runs that complete an outstanding century from 91 balls, fourteen of which have been hit for four and two for six, the run rate does eventually slow quite considerably, with Butcher almost completely becalmed. Then, with the fourth-wicket pair having added 211, the hosts finally make the breakthrough they so desperately seek when Brown forces a short-of-a-length delivery from Maddy to Trevor Ward at extra cover and departs to a well-deserved ovation for a highly entertaining 104.

Although Butcher is unable to find the runs he requires to complete his ton before tea, Surrey are now well on top after their earlier struggles.

*Tea:- Surrey 293-4 (Butcher 98\*, Hollioake 7\*) from 72 overs*

The pace of the Surrey innings is maintained after the break, especially once Butcher completes his century with a drive to the extra-cover boundary off Whiley at the start of the second over of the session. His solid and disciplined 156-ball effort, containing nineteen fours, has led his team from a tricky situation into a state of prosperity, from where they can build a mammoth score and look to press for victory.

Having been quite effective before the break, Maddy and Whiley are suddenly finding the going much tougher, with the former Nottinghamshire left-armer serving up a particularly mixed bag of wides, no-balls, long-hops and half-volleys. He had been a surprise selection in the provisional ECB Academy list that had been announced earlier in the season, and the locals tell me that this is typical of his bowling. Apart from possessing the advantages of pace and being a 'lefty', he has little to offer, they say, and I believe them as Hollioake takes him apart with four boundaries in three overs, raising the fifty partnership for the fifth wicket in the process.

Although Maddy, at the other end, has fared no better by yielding two fours to each batsman in the course of his first four overs of the afternoon, he does actually manage to enhance his figures by taking his third wicket of the innings when Butcher is well taken at the wicket by Neil Burns standing up to the stumps. As the England opener leaves the field to a healthy ovation with 116 runs to his name after a fine knock, Surrey are in a very strong position at 342-5.

The new batsman, Rikki Clarke, has only been at the wicket for a short time when the 350 comes up, courtesy of a pair of Whiley wides, and it doesn't take him long to locate the boundary for the first time as he drives Maddy down the ground at the end of the Leicestershire all-rounder's post-lunch spell.

By now, DeFreitas has replaced Whiley, in an attempt to regain some control for the home side, but even this experienced campaigner finds life difficult as his second over contains an instant replay of Clarke's stroke off Maddy, and the pace picks up again after the briefest of lulls. To be fair to the bowlers, with Clarke off to a flyer and Hollioake in the sort of form where he can rapidly dismantle an attack, their task isn't easy, and one really fears for the inconsistent Grove as he replaces Maddy at the pavilion end.

Although the former Essex and Somerset paceman gets through a relatively inexpensive first over, during which Hollioake finds the boundary just once, his second over is far less impressive. Having completed a quick-fire 51-ball fifty, including ten fours, in the previous over from DeFreitas, the Surrey skipper thrashes Grove for 4-4-6 as successive deliveries are driven wide of mid-on, driven down the ground and then pulled high over midwicket. With the over having cost fifteen runs, the 23-year-old seamer is, predictably and hastily, withdrawn from the attack.

Thanks to the significant haul of runs pillaged from Grove's over, a half-century partnership for the sixth wicket is completed barely nine overs after Clarke's arrival at the crease, and Sutcliffe's list of problems grows ever longer. Not the least of his concerns is the fact that the scoreboard shows his team to be five overs behind schedule in terms of the required over-rate at this point in time, a situation that would lead to the deduction of 1.25 points at the end of the match if it is not rectified.

Possibly with this in mind, or possibly out of sheer desperation, the Leicestershire captain turns to Trevor Ward, much to everyone's surprise, since no-one can recall having ever seen him bowl before. This seems fair enough, given that a quick check of the current *Playfair Cricket Annual* reveals his first-class career bowling record to be eight wickets at 80.87 runs apiece!

We discover that Ward purveys off-breaks that are respectable enough to bring a slight dip in the run rate, even though the total passes four-hundred at around this time, when Clarke clips Maddy, DeFreitas' replacement at the Bennett end, through midwicket for three. Operating to an understandably deep-set field, Ward is easily milked for singles, but there are no boundary hits until his third over when Hollioake lofts him wide of mid-on for four. The Surrey captain is made to pay for this before the over is out, though, as the part-time off-spinner claims his wicket with a catch by Burns behind the stumps, to end a muscular innings of eighty with the total at 419. If I am being generous, then I would say the visiting skipper has been undone by a clever arm-ball while pushing forward defensively - if I'm being less charitable, however, then I'd say the batsman has been guilty of playing for non-existent turn! Either way, Ward is delighted and Hollioake has played a terrific knock for his team, powering them towards a daunting total for the home side to chase tomorrow.

Having noted Ward's success and how quickly he is getting through his overs, Sutcliffe immediately asks DeFreitas to return to the attack in his guise as an off-spinner to form what is probably one of the least threatening spin combinations ever seen at first-class level. To give the two guys their due, however, boundaries prove hard to come by as we enter the closing stages of the day, with only three significant scoring strokes coming from the last ten overs of the session, all of them from the bat of Clarke - an on-drive off Ward that easily carries for six; a late-cut that costs DeFreitas four; and an extra-cover drive at Ward's expense in the day's penultimate over that simultaneously completes a composed 78-ball half-century and raises the Surrey 450.

Somewhat surprisingly, Ward finishes with the respectable figures of 8-0-32-1, and he should also have had Tudor's wicket in his bag, the Surrey paceman having been badly missed on five, with the total at 435, by Darren Stevens at slip from a top-edged cut.

Thanks to their middle-order batsmen, Surrey have dominated the last two sessions of the first day, scoring 366 runs for the loss of three wickets in just seventy overs to put themselves in with a fine chance of victory, especially if they can extend their total further in the morning.

*Close:- Surrey 454-6 (Clarke 52\*, Tudor 8\*) from 104 overs*

| VIEWS FROM THE DRESSING ROOM |
|---|

*When lunch arrived you stayed on the outfield taking half-volley throw-downs for about fifteen minutes. Why was that?*
**MARK BUTCHER** - Part of the reason that I played in every Surrey game I could appear in was because I felt that my form in the Test matches had gone a little bit from what it was before I had the knee operation. Thankfully, Medders was happy to have me back in the side for the Leicester game so that I could work on the things that I needed to work on, as well as score some runs to try and help the side push for the Championship. I felt that something wasn't quite right in the period up to lunch, so I thought that, while I was there with the pads on, I might as well try to sort it out.

*Although you looked in great touch while making your century, you had a couple of shaky overs early on, particularly while facing Devon Malcolm after lunch. I don't suppose you could believe your luck when he dropped that simple caught-and-bowled chance, could you?*
**ALI BROWN** - Ah well, you should remember that simple caught-and-bowled chances are never taken off me when we play Leicestershire! I think sometimes those catches are dropped because people are expecting the ball to come back harder. On the two occasions when this has happened, with Dev here, and with Jimmy at Oakham, the ball has gone back very softly, almost like underarm catches, but sometimes that lack of pace does surprise you... it's a bit like Bickers' bowling, really! The ball did actually swing a little bit after lunch and Dev bowled some good balls in that period - people talk about his pace, but they underestimate his ability to swing the ball. I think the turning point came when I hit sixteen off one over from him, with four fours. That changed the momentum a little bit and things then got easier.

## Second Day - Thursday 15th August

### Surrey 540; Leicestershire 265-6

On a glorious morning, with conditions looking perfect for batting, Surrey's hopes of building a truly huge score have been dented slightly by a back injury sustained by Rikki Clarke while playing football after the close of play yesterday. They also have to overcome the hurdle presented by the second new ball, so the first hour of play could be crucial in determining the magnitude of the visitors' final total.

Although he continues his innings, with Ian Ward as his runner, it is immediately obvious that Clarke is really struggling, even though he glances the fifth ball of the day from Devon Malcolm to the fine leg boundary to increase his score to fifty-six. Unfortunately, his partner, Alex Tudor, is unable to add to his overnight tally of eight this morning as Phil DeFreitas claims the tall paceman's wicket with his opening delivery, courtesy of an lbw decision by umpire Harris that seemingly fails to take Tudor's big forward stride into account.

This is just the start that Leicestershire require if they are to get back into the match, and they only have to wait another four overs before the deserving DeFreitas strikes a second blow by removing the potentially dangerous Mushtaq Ahmed. The Pakistani leg-spinner races to twelve in no time at all before DeFreitas tempts him into a hook that he gloves through to Burns. At 474-8, Surrey are still very well placed, though hopes of amassing six-hundred now look pretty distant.

When Malcolm is bowling, pretty much anything can happen, though, as his next few overs illustrate. While DeFreitas ties up his end, allowing no liberties, runs flow freely off his former England colleague, as Clarke picks off five boundaries in four overs, two through thick edges to third man, two with meaty leg-side blows, and the other with a sublime drive straight down the ground. The last of these five fours sees the total reaching five-hundred as the young all-rounder continues to bat beautifully, despite being very clearly inconvenienced by his injury, and, at this point, Sutcliffe opts to change both his bowlers. The end-of-spell figures paint a very accurate picture of the merits of his opening pair - while DeFreitas' burst with the second new ball reads 8-3-13-2, Malcolm's fairly dismal spell has yielded the very unflattering figures of 8-1-44-0.

The new Leicestershire bowling combination, not for the first time in the match, is Maddy and Whiley, both of whom start respectably, though the left-armer does manage to record his fifth wide of the innings in his opening over. Maddy is the first to concede a boundary, however, as Clarke takes his score up to ninety-two with a drive wide of mid-on and, by picking off singles, the lad from Guildford takes the ninth-wicket partnership beyond fifty, and his personal score to ninety-five, by the time he next faces the Leicestershire all-rounder.

With just five needed for his century, the wide outswinger that Maddy serves up probably looks like a quick route to ninety-nine but, instead, it ends up as the route back to the pavilion, as

252

an outside edge finds the safe hands of Burns behind the wicket. The youngster's flawed footwork in attempting to drive is almost certainly attributable to his back problem, though that will be little consolation to him as he makes his way gingerly back to the dressing room, accompanied by the crowd's applause and his runner, having just missed out on the third first-class century of his debut season.

From 526-9, the last pair of Bicknell and Ormond manage to add fourteen largely unconvincing runs, before the latter is comprehensively bowled by another Maddy outswinger while aiming to leg, having driven the previous ball through backward point for four. Maddy therefore ends up with 5-104, though the unfortunate DeFreitas, with 2-91 from thirty-four overs, seems more deserving of the spectators' ovation than his colleague.

Requiring a daunting 391 to avoid the follow-on, Trevor Ward and Iain Sutcliffe, the Leicestershire openers, manage to knock off twenty runs against Bicknell and Tudor in six overs before lunch, with each batsman picking up a middled and a miscued boundary in this time. Even though Surrey have done the first part of the job by posting a formidable total, it is already obvious that it is going to be no easy task to capture twenty wickets on this very good batting surface.

*Lunch:- Leicestershire 20-0 (Ward 12\*, Sutcliffe 8\*) from 6 overs*

The bowlers continue to find little joy after lunch, as the combination of flat pitch and blue sky proves very much to the taste of the batsmen. There is little or no swing, even for Bicknell, and, though the bowlers maintain a decent line and length, Ward and Sutcliffe are content to wait for the occasional half-volley that they can dispatch to the boundary. By following this simple method the total reaches fifty in the fifteenth over, with barely a false stroke in sight.

Ward does, however, start to offer the bowlers a little encouragement at this point, with a drive to the extra-cover boundary off Bicknell being sandwiched by a thick-edged four off each bowler as Tudor maintains a good off-stump line and Surrey's senior bowler at last manages to persuade the ball to swing a little. Having advanced his personal score from twenty-two to thirty-nine inside two overs, the former Kent batsman finally becomes a little too adventurous and, in attempting a flamboyant drive off Tudor, he edges to Ali Brown at first slip with the total on sixty-five. This is a very welcome breakthrough for the visitors, though the new batsman, Darren Maddy, starts confidently with two well-struck boundaries, an on-drive at Bicknell's expense and a cut off Tudor.

Unfortunately for Surrey, Bicknell, so often Maddy's nemesis, is now at the end of his spell, though Tudor almost exploits the Leicestershire batsman's recognised fallibility outside the off stump in true Bicknell style just a couple of overs after the master's retirement to the outfield. With the batsman on nine and the total on eighty-one, a cracking delivery that gains surprising height off the flat surface takes the outside edge of Maddy's bat, only to burst through the upstretched hands of Adam Hollioake at second slip, allowing the Foxes' all-rounder to pick up two runs rather than make the walk back to the pavilion. Although it is a very difficult chance - overhead and rising, at pace - that has been spurned, you get the feeling that it is the sort of chance that will need to be taken if victory is to be achieved on this fine batting pitch.

This near miss turns out to be the last act of an impressive eleven-over opening burst, either side of lunch, by Tudor, with the resultant new bowling combination seeing Jimmy Ormond operating from the Bennett end and Hollioake forcing himself into service at the pavilion end, since Rikki Clarke appears highly unlikely to play any further part in the match.

Ormond, seemingly relishing the opportunity to compete against his former colleagues, starts excellently, giving nothing away and having a confident lbw appeal against Sutcliffe turned down by umpire Harris, while Hollioake is positively Whiley-esque in the two overs he allows himself, yielding two wides, a no-ball and a couple of boundaries to Maddy through extra cover, the second of which takes the home team's total into three figures.

The Surrey captain sensibly, and predictably, gives way to Mushtaq Ahmed after conceding eighteen runs from his twelve deliveries, and, except for one Ormond over - when Maddy follows a top-edged hook that just carries over the rope at long-leg for six with an off-driven four from the next ball - the batsmen become completely becalmed by some magnificent bowling.

In the heat of the afternoon, the paceman and the leg-spinner plug away consistently, bowling scarcely a bad ball, beating the bat on a number of occasions, and conceding just six runs from ten overs at one stage. The home batsmen certainly need to demonstrate great skill and patience to repel the visitors' excellent bowling, and while the left-handed Sutcliffe shows immaculate judgement of which balls to play and which to leave alone, Maddy puts his recent poor record against Surrey to the back of his mind in looking confident and composed.

The former England international eventually forces the scoreboard back into serious action in the fortieth over by first sashaying down the track to Mushtaq and driving him wide of mid-on for four, and then, with tea fast approaching, repeating the fancy footwork in the leg-spinner's next over, though this time hitting the ball straight down the ground. This stroke takes Maddy's personal tally to forty-seven, and a push to square leg for a single in the penultimate over before the break completes a hard-earned fifty, including seven fours and a six, from his 85th delivery.

Much credit is due to the batsmen as they walk off undefeated at tea, since they have been tested to the full by exceptional spells from Ormond (12-8-17-0) and Mushtaq (9-1-21-0).

*Tea:- Leicestershire 142-1 (Sutcliffe 37\*, Maddy 50\*) from 45 overs*

While Mushtaq is switched to the Bennett end upon the resumption, Alex Tudor returns to the fray at the pavilion end, and the batsmen make a reasonably bright start, with Sutcliffe twice angling the fast bowler down to the third man boundary and Maddy driving the leg-spinner to the rope at cover.

The second-wicket partnership then reaches the hundred mark as Sutcliffe picks up rare runs in front of square with a cover-driven two off Tudor, before relief for the Surrey team, and the spectators, comes when the left-hander's painstaking innings is terminated by umpire Harris, who adjudges him to have top-edged a cut at Mushtaq to wicketkeeper Batty. The Leicestershire skipper is clearly aggrieved by the umpire's verdict as he departs the scene with forty-eight of his team's 167 runs to his name, though the Surrey 'leggie' is, by way of contrast, absolutely delighted, since he has finally taken a wicket in his fifty-fifth over for the county - and how well-deserved it is, too. The way he is bowling at the moment, it's a certainty that the next wicket won't take anywhere near as long to arrive.

Having said that, the Pakistani maybe gets a little over-excited by his hard-earned success, as his next four overs each bring a Leicestershire boundary, with the new batsman, Darren Stevens, twice cracking him through the covers, and Maddy contributing a miscued drive wide of mid-on and then a much more convincing off-drive.

Tudor has meanwhile completed another accurate spell without reward and gives way to Bicknell at the pavilion end as Hollioake looks to rotate his seamers while his leg-spinner plugs away at the Bennett end.

Although Bicknell's return doesn't start too promisingly, with Stevens pulling his second ball for four, the Surrey man's retribution follows swiftly as the Leicestershire under-achiever plays limply and indecisively at the next delivery and merely succeeds in deflecting the ball down onto his stumps. Much to the visitors' delight, the veteran swing bowler's first wicket since breaking his wrist has seen off Stevens for fifteen and pegged the home side back a little further at 196-3.

There is now a greater spring in the Surrey step as they sense the chance to make further inroads before the close, though Mohammad Kaif gets away confidently with three fours, two steered to third man and one whipped wide of mid-on, in Bicknell's next three overs. The Indian looks less assured when facing Mushtaq, however, and when he pads up to what turns out to be a googly shortly afterwards umpire Harris' index finger is once again given an airing.

From 167-1, Leicestershire have now declined to 225-4, and worse is to follow for them as the next five overs bring the loss of two further wickets, including the very valuable one of Maddy. Having snared Kaif with the first ball of his nineteenth over, Mushtaq increases his wicket-count to three with the fifth ball of his twentieth over when the former England batsman's gutsy and patient innings of eighty-one ends with him being comprehensively beaten on the back foot by another of the leg-spinner's googlies and sent on his way by the busy Harris. This is a huge blow to the hosts' hopes of avoiding the possibility of having to follow on, since they are still 157 runs short of their target at 234-5.

Their requirement has been reduced by just six runs when another Hollioake bowling change, the return of Ormond for Bicknell, again works wonders for his team. It takes the former Leicestershire fast bowler just five balls to send Rob Cunliffe's off stump rocketing out of the ground with a superb yorker that provides him with a wicket which is every bit as well-deserved as Mushtaq's earlier in the session and reduces the home team to 240-6.

Surrey are now moving in for the kill, though they meet much sterner resistance in the last seven overs of the day as the vastly experienced Burns and DeFreitas dig in to take the score past 250 and defy the best efforts of the dangerous Ormond-Mushtaq pairing.

Although they manage to make it through to the close at 265-6, they will be very well aware that their side has an extremely flimsy tail in this match, with Grove, Whiley and Malcolm highly unlikely to contribute many runs. Having seen this nine-ten-jack printed on the scorecard on the first morning of the match, I had, in fact, remarked that it looked very much a case of 'take seven wickets, get three free'. Hopefully, these words won't come back to haunt me in the morning. Assuming that they don't, Surrey are in with an excellent chance of winning the match, even though the pitch remains a belter, since the weather forecast for the rest of the game is fine. The bowlers have, by and large, performed magnificently today, with persistence very much paying off as the efforts of the middle session gained their due rewards in the final session.

*Close:- Leicestershire 265-6 (Burns 16\*, DeFreitas 8\*) from 77 overs*

## VIEW FROM THE DRESSING ROOM

*I thought Jimmy Ormond bowled a fantastic spell of twelve overs in the heat leading up to tea, without much reward. Do you recall that spell?*
**ALEX TUDOR** - Yes, I remember it well. He was beating the bat and having the batsmen in all sorts of trouble - a great spell on a very hot day. People may look at him and think he's not very fit, but he can bowl long spells, like he did that day, and we all appreciated it. Even though it wasn't rewarded with wickets, we all knew what a big spell that was for us and we all congratulated him afterwards.

### Third Day - Friday 16th August

### Surrey 540 and 42-3; Leicestershire 290 and 289

### Surrey won by seven wickets
### Surrey 20pts, Leicestershire 5

Surrey's chances of finishing off the Leicestershire first innings quickly on the third morning are greatly improved by the early dismissal of Phillip DeFreitas in the second over, with just six runs added to the overnight score. Having elected to play Mushtaq's fifth delivery of the day off the back foot, the former England paceman finds his loose defensive stroke penetrated and his middle stump extracted by an undetected googly.

With DeFreitas' innings arrested at eight, the rest of the wickets then come quietly, as anticipated. After a boundary apiece to Grove and Burns, the former loses his off stump to another sharply turning Mushtaq googly with the total advanced to 283, completing a most worthy five-wicket haul for the bowler, then Whiley surrenders his wicket in a very tame and dim-witted fashion in the leg-spinner's next over. The tall left-arm seamer loiters aimlessly outside his crease after being struck on the pads by a delivery from Mushtaq, allowing Nadeem Shahid, the substitute fielder, to throw down the stumps from short leg. This careless piece of cricket by the Leicestershire man leaves his side on the ropes at 285-9 and, after one flashing drive through the covers by Malcolm off Ormond, the innings is brought to a close at 290 when Surrey's newest recruit gains rapid revenge on his former colleague with a short ball that flicks a glove on the way through to Batty. Ormond certainly deserves this second wicket, though the equally excellent Mushtaq takes the major plaudits as he leads the visiting team from the field with figures of 30-7-71-5 to his name. The efficient cleaning up of the Leicestershire tail has left the home side trailing by a massive 250 runs, presumably making the enforcement of the follow-on almost inevitable.

This is confirmed, ten minutes later, when Ward and Sutcliffe come out to open their team's second innings against Bicknell and Tudor, who are fresh and rested. Everything is therefore perfect from a Surrey point of view, and all the visitors need now are some wickets before lunch.

This is, of course, easier said than done on what remains an excellent batting track, as the opening batsmen prove by getting away to typical starts. While Sutcliffe is as steady as ever and picks up a boundary backward of point off Tudor, Ward is much more attractive to watch, with his two early fours coming through drives down the ground off Bicknell.

Having looked rather rusty in the first innings, following his lengthy lay-off, Bicknell looks more like his normal self this time around and, in an eventful fifth over, he makes the pre-lunch breakthrough that his team had been hoping for. In the space of three balls, Surrey's senior bowler has an lbw appeal turned down by umpire Jones; sees Ormond demolish the boundary fencing at the Bennett end as the big paceman narrowly fails to stop Ward's off-drive going for four; and then wins the umpire's approval with another lbw shout as Ward is beaten on the crease by a slower ball that cuts back at him slightly. The former Kent batsman seems to feel hard done by as he departs for sixteen, with the score at twenty-six, and he might have a point, since the two appeals have looked pretty similar, and on both occasions the ball has looked to be sliding towards, or maybe past, leg stump.

The home side can't dwell on this perceived injustice, though, especially as the marginal and debatable decisions in the match have pretty much evened up by this stage of the game. Bicknell has definitely deserved this wicket, in any case, and he continues to test Sutcliffe and Maddy until both he and Tudor are rested twenty minutes before lunch with the score standing at 45-1.

The subsequent introduction of Mushtaq Ahmed at the Bennett end is no surprise, but the appearance of Mark Butcher, bowling his off-breaks at the pavilion end, most definitely is. Maddy is certainly pleased to see him as he lashes the part-time off-spinner for seventeen runs, including four successive off-side boundaries, in the final over of the session.

*Lunch:- Leicestershire 78-1 (Sutcliffe 26\*, Maddy 32\*) from 20 overs*

The runs keep on coming after lunch as Jimmy Ormond has his first bowl of the innings, with Mushtaq switching from the Bennett end to the pavilion end to accommodate him.

Ormond versus Maddy again promises to be an interesting encounter, though it's the Leicestershire all-rounder who has much the better of the battle as he accumulates twenty-five runs from his former team-mate's first four overs. Although Ormond does induce an edge to third man in his second over, Maddy has his off-side strokes in good working order and races to a 54-ball fifty by driving three deliveries to the boundary between long-off and backward point in the fourth over of his old colleague's spell.

Surprisingly, even Sutcliffe is batting with a degree of freedom at this stage, taking two fours off Mushtaq and one off Ormond to complete the second Maddy-Sutcliffe century partnership of the match, with eighty-one of these runs having come from the last twelve overs. Suddenly the Surrey bowlers seem to be under pressure and finding life every bit as tough as their Leicestershire counterparts had on this unforgiving pitch. There must, therefore, be a temptation to change the bowling, but Hollioake elects to stick with Mushtaq and Ormond, and his faith is justified as the next five overs see just nine added to the total, with three of these coming from an edged drive by Sutcliffe off the Surrey leg-spinner.

With his bowlers having now re-established control, the visiting captain decides to rest Ormond after a seven-over spell, recalling Tudor to the attack and returning his Pakistani spin wizard to the Bennett end. No immediate breakthrough is forthcoming, though, as his big paceman bowls a little too wide of the off stump to be effective against two very disciplined batsmen, and the score passes 150 when Maddy uses his feet well to advance on Mushtaq and drive him to the rope at extra cover. It's quite hard to see where the next wicket is coming from, in fact, as Sutcliffe cracks Tudor through the covers to reach a dogged half-century, containing eight fours, from his 123rd ball, and, as is so often the case, it turns out to be a bowling change that does the trick for Hollioake and his men.

While Mushtaq continues to whirl and twirl away at the Bennett end, Tudor gives way to Bicknell and, after a brief flurry of strokes from the Leicestershire skipper, Sutcliffe, on sixty-four, also gives way to Bicknell. Having enjoyed a little purple patch by pulling Surrey's swing master for four and then clipping Mushtaq to the rope at midwicket to raise the 150 partnership, Sutcliffe sees his skimming cover drive smartly plucked out of the air, to his right-hand side, by Ali Brown. Surrey's delight is clear for all to see, since the Leicestershire second-wicket pair have taken the total up to 182, leaving them just sixty-eight runs away from wiping off the first-innings deficit.

Buoyed by this breakthrough, and relieved to see the back of the gritty Sutcliffe, the visitors now hope to make further breakthroughs before tea, but, though Darren Stevens immediately looks ill at ease against Mushtaq and is beaten several times, the Leicestershire total advances steadily, if unspectacularly, towards two-hundred.

While Stevens is clearly happy against Bicknell, clipping and driving him to the leg-side boundary in successive overs, his insecurities rapidly resurface when he miscues Mushtaq over extra cover for a rather fortunate boundary that takes the total beyond two-hundred. With this false stroke having advanced his personal score to fourteen, Stevens then slices a drive at Bicknell to gully, where Tudor grasses a pretty straightforward chance to his right, though, fortunately for the crestfallen fielder, the Foxes' middle-order man fails to capitalise on this let-off as Mushtaq nails him in the very next over. Another pretty unimpressive innings by the potential England Academy batsman ends when the ball pops up into the air in front of him off bat and pad as he pushes forward, leaving Ian Ward to dive across from silly point and scoop up a good catch.

With tea imminent, Maddy finds the boundary for the first time in fourteen overs with a sweep off Mushtaq that takes his personal tally into the nineties; Bicknell completes a fine spell of 8-2-17-1; and Mohammad Kaif cracks the last two balls of the session from the Pakistani leg-spinner to the boundary with a square cut and an extra-cover drive.

*Tea:- Leicestershire 219-3 (Maddy 94\*, Kaif 10\*) from 59 overs*

Leicestershire's slim hopes of avoiding defeat receive a crushing blow immediately after the break when Jimmy Ormond nips the first ball back into Darren Maddy, striking him on the back pad and leaving umpire Harris to make one of his most straightforward lbw decisions of the season. Surrey's joy knows no bounds as the finger goes up, depriving Maddy of what would have been a well-deserved century after a fine battling effort, and exposing the home side's vulnerable lower middle-order to a potentially testing examination.

With Ormond and his co-conspirator, Mushtaq, boosted by this instant breakthrough, runs are suddenly extremely hard to come by, even for Kaif and Neil Burns, two strokeplaying batsmen, and the pressure is intense for five overs until Burns breaks loose by cutting the leg-spinner to the rope at extra cover. Kaif then manages a boundary of his own, even though it comes via an edge over the slips off Ormond, before the fifth-wicket pair combine to take the total up to 250, and thereby level the scores, with a rush of runs at Mushtaq's expense. The Pakistani's twenty-sixth over ends up costing thirteen runs as Kaif comes down the track to blast a no-ball for six over long-on, while Burns cuts for four as soon as his partner puts him on strike.

This turns out to be the storm before the surrender, however, as the Leicestershire wicketkeeper's dismissal in the leg-spinner's next over, to a fine one-handed reflex catch at silly point by Nadeem Shahid, turns out to be pretty much the beginning of the end. Although Kaif takes a couple of boundaries off Tudor as soon as the England paceman reappears in place of Ormond at the pavilion end, Rob Cunliffe, relegated to number seven in the order for reasons unknown, struggles for twenty-two balls before getting off the mark with a deflection to third man. Two balls later he is out, however, as Tudor induces a defensive snick that finds the safe hands of Ali Brown at first slip to reduce the home team to 267-6.

Phil DeFreitas then goes to the first ball of Tudor's next over, putting the Surrey speedster on a hat-trick, when he flashes loosely outside the off stump to provide Mark Butcher with a catch at fourth slip and bring the first of Leicestershire's three number elevens to the wicket. Although Tudor isn't able to complete his three-in-three, he does end up with three wickets in five balls as Grove takes a single and then watches from the other end as his team-mate, Kaif, is trapped on the crease by a ball nipping back and departs lbw with the total still only having progressed as far as 270. The last four wickets have fallen for just twenty runs, thanks to some great bowling, and from a high point of 182-1, seven men have now gone for eighty-eight.

This burst of wickets has ensured a Surrey victory, but, with Whiley joining Grove in the middle, it is even possible that the game could be wrapped up tonight. It's hard to see either of these two, or Malcolm, lasting long against the visitors' pace and leg-spin bowling combination and, though Whiley manages a couple of edgy twos off Tudor and then slogs Mushtaq for six over wide long-on, the end comes as swiftly as anticipated.

Having been missed at slip by Hollioake later in the leg-spinner's over, Whiley departs, in embarrassing fashion once again, to the next ball, as he pays no attention to where the crease is and becomes one of the easiest stumping victims of Jon Batty's career. Devon Malcolm then slogs his first ball from Mushtaq to the boundary at cow corner before Tudor tidies up the innings with the first ball of the following over, sending Grove's off stump flying with a top-class yorker to leave the hosts all out for an ultimately miserable 289 and Surrey needing just forty to win, with five overs left for play today.

It has been another superb effort by the bowlers to roll the opposition over for less than three-hundred on this flat pitch, and, though Tudor gets the lion's share of the adulation for his 4-54 demolition of the tail, much credit goes to all the bowlers, including Mushtaq Ahmed, whose return of 3-115 doesn't accurately reflect a hard-working effort that has seen him bowl unchanged, apart from a switch of ends, from the seventeenth over of the innings.

With the possibility of claiming an extra eight overs tonight, the game looks most unlikely to go into the fourth day now, especially once Sutcliffe opts to open the bowling with Whiley and Malcolm, his two rather erratic pacemen.

Predictably enough, there are twelve runs on the board after the first two overs... though also two wickets. Having cut for four and pulled for two earlier in the first over, Ward edges Whiley's fifth ball low to Maddy at second slip, while Batty follows a first-ball cut to the boundary off Malcolm with a defensive edge to the very same fielder in the very same position. The score is then rattled on by another nine runs as Butcher starts positively with a clip backward of square leg for four and a square cut for three at the beginning of Whiley's second over, though he joins his team-mates back in the pavilion at the start of the next over from Malcolm when he is taken at the wicket off an inside edge.

Anyone following progress on Ceefax would think that Surrey are swinging the bat manically in order to finish the match tonight, but it simply isn't the case, since all the wickets have fallen to passive strokes and/or decent deliveries. Additionally, runs are always likely to flow freely against these two bowlers, and they continue to do so as Whiley's next over, which includes a well-struck boundary to each batsman and a no-ball, goes for thirteen, taking the total to thirty-five at the end of the day's scheduled allocation of overs. Needless to say, play continues and within two overs, just before 7pm, Surrey pass the winning post, courtesy of Brown's flashing edged drive over the slips for four.

While Surrey's fans and players celebrate the county's first win at Grace Road, or anywhere on Leicestershire soil for that matter, since 1993 - Oakham School being in Rutland, of course - a quick look at the revised league table confirms that Keith Medlycott's squad are another significant step closer to regaining the County Championship title.

**Surrey 540 and 42-3; Leicestershire 290 and 289**
**Surrey won by seven wickets. Surrey 20pts, Leicestershire 5**

## VIEWS FROM THE DRESSING ROOM

*Did the fact that we tidied up the Leicestershire first innings very quickly on the third morning make up our minds to enforce the follow-on, or was it something that we planned to do anyway?*
**MARK BUTCHER** - We did have quite a long conversation about it because the pitch was very flat and it had been a very good effort to knock them over for as few as we did the first time round. I think we had to consider the possibility that we could run out of time if we decided to bat again, as we felt that it could take an awful lot of overs to knock them over for the second time on that wicket. So, because we didn't think there was ever going to be enough in the pitch to warrant us batting again, we stuck them back in. It was clear that the pitch was never going to deteriorate too much if we needed to bat in the fourth innings to win the game, in any case.

*Mushtaq bowled really well and turned out to be a great short-term signing for us, didn't he?*
**MARK BUTCHER** - Mushy has always been a world-class performer, so no matter what surface he was bowling on he was always confident that he would be able to take wickets for us, and it was a pleasure to watch him bowling. I hadn't played against him for a few years, not since he played for Somerset, and he was always a fantastic bowler then, and the years don't seem to have diminished that - it was a really brilliant performance. He has an awful lot of variations - he will try to bowl five or six different deliveries in an over if he can - and because of that he bamboozled Leicester on a pretty unresponsive track. He had to work really hard for his wickets and, yes, he was a fantastic little signing for us for that period of the season.

*Have you ever seen Darren Maddy bat better than he did in this match?*
**ALEX TUDOR** - No, he played very well indeed and had a very decent season. I think he's better suited to batting the middle-order. He struggled as an opener because he goes very hard at the ball.

*It clearly wasn't going to be easy to get twenty wickets on such a flat batting track, but was our task made a little easier by the fact that Leicestershire had a tail consisting of Grove, Whiley and Malcolm? At the time, I said that it looked to be a case of 'take seven wickets, get three free'.*
**ALI BROWN** - Well, Jamie Grove can hold a bat, so I wouldn't call him a rabbit, but Dev is always very exciting to bowl against, and Whiley wasn't very alert in either innings. I think our bowling is the key, though - Jimmy, Tudes and Mushy bowled really well on what was a good batting wicket and certainly found some very good balls to keep asking questions. We've got a great attack with good variation - we've got a bit of everything, with great spinners, tall pacy bowlers, big hit-the-wicket bowlers and a floaty old seamer! That's what you need because if you had three or four very similar bowlers it would be very routine.
**MARK BUTCHER** - I don't think knocking over tails has been a problem for us in the last four or five years - not like it used to be, back in the mid-Nineties, when we'd run out of steam with a team full of seam bowlers - so the focus was really on trying to remove the guys at the top of the order and then squeezing very hard on the rest of them. Most county teams have got three or four guys that you need to get out, then you can put the rest under pressure and deal with them.

*Jimmy Ormond looked especially determined to do well against his old county, yet he really didn't have any luck in the match, did he?*
**ALI BROWN** - Not only is he a very talented player, but the thing I most like about him is that, rather like Dean Headley, he gives just as much effort on a flat wicket as he does on one that is seaming about all over the place. I think there's a lot more to come from Jimmy.

*You seem to have enjoyed a lot of success at Grace Road over the years, even though it has usually been a pretty good track. Do you have any idea why that should be?*
**ALEX TUDOR** - I remember a game a few years ago when I took 7-77, even though I thought I'd only bowled about seven good balls, so maybe it's just a lucky ground for me. I felt I bowled well this year, though - I came off my shorter run and had good control on a very slow wicket. Darren Maddy said afterwards that he thought the ball went through really well when I bowled and that I was hitting his bat hard, and things went especially well for me right at the end of the game when I was feeling a little bit tired - it was very pleasing to get those last three wickets in five balls.

| LEICESTERSHIRE v SURREY at Leicester Played 14th to 16th August | | | | | | | |
|---|---|---|---|---|---|---|---|
| Surrey won the toss and elected to bat | | | Umpires:- Mike Harris and Allan Jones | | | | |
| **SURREY - First Innings** | | | | | | | |
| Fall Of Wkt | Batsman | How | Out | Score | Balls | 4s | 6s |
| 1-61 | I.J. Ward | lbw | b Whiley | 28 | 85 | 2 | 0 |
| 2-63 | J.N. Batty + | lbw | b Maddy | 28 | 78 | 4 | 0 |
| 5-342 | M.A. Butcher | c Burns | b Maddy | 116 | 170 | 21 | 0 |
| 3-74 | M.R. Ramprakash | c Maddy | b Whiley | 0 | 14 | 0 | 0 |
| 4-285 | A.D. Brown | c Ward | b Maddy | 104 | 97 | 14 | 2 |
| 6-419 | A.J. Hollioake * | c Burns | b Ward | 80 | 74 | 13 | 1 |
| 9-526 | R. Clarke | c Burns | b Maddy | 95 | 150 | 14 | 1 |
| 7-458 | A.J. Tudor | lbw | b DeFreitas | 8 | 35 | 0 | 0 |
| 8-474 | Mushtaq Ahmed | c Burns | b DeFreitas | 12 | 19 | 2 | 0 |
|  | M.P. Bicknell | Not | Out | 23 | 44 | 2 | 0 |
| 10-540 | J. Ormond |  | b Maddy | 6 | 14 | 1 | 0 |
|  | Extras | (2b, 6lb, 16w, 16nb) |  | 40 |  |  |  |
|  | **TOTAL** | **(128.4 overs)** |  | **540** |  |  |  |

| Bowler | O | M | R | W | NB | Wd |
|---|---|---|---|---|---|---|
| DeFreitas | 34 | 6 | 91 | 2 | 1 | - |
| Malcolm | 22 | 3 | 114 | 0 | - | 1 |
| Grove | 10 | 0 | 63 | 0 | - | 1 |
| Maddy | 25.4 | 4 | 104 | 5 | - | 1 |
| Whiley | 22 | 4 | 85 | 2 | 7 | 5 |
| Kaif | 7 | 0 | 43 | 0 | - | - |
| Ward | 8 | 0 | 32 | 1 | - | - |

**LEICESTERSHIRE - First Innings** (Needing 391 to avoid the follow-on)

| Fall Of Wkt | Batsman | How | Out | Score | Balls | 4s | 6s |
|---|---|---|---|---|---|---|---|
| 1-65 | T.R. Ward | c Brown | b Tudor | 39 | 55 | 7 | 0 |
| 2-167 | I.J. Sutcliffe * | c Batty | b Mushtaq | 48 | 155 | 7 | 0 |
| 5-234 | D.L. Maddy | lbw | b Mushtaq | 81 | 144 | 12 | 1 |
| 3-196 | D.I. Stevens | | b Bicknell | 15 | 24 | 2 | 0 |
| 4-225 | M. Kaif | lbw | b Mushtaq | 13 | 19 | 3 | 0 |
| 6-240 | R.J. Cunliffe | | b Ormond | 8 | 22 | 2 | 0 |
| | N.D. Burns + | Not | Out | 29 | 60 | 4 | 0 |
| 7-271 | P.A.J. DeFreitas | | b Mushtaq | 8 | 25 | 1 | 0 |
| 8-283 | J.O. Grove | | b Mushtaq | 4 | 14 | 1 | 0 |
| 9-285 | M.J.A. Whiley | run | out | 0 | 8 | 0 | 0 |
| 10-290 | D.E. Malcolm | c Batty | b Ormond | 4 | 6 | 1 | 0 |
| | Extras | (10b, 11lb, 6w, 14nb) | | 41 | | | |
| | **TOTAL** | **(87.3 overs)** | | **290** | | | |

| Bowler | O | M | R | W | NB | Wd |
|---|---|---|---|---|---|---|
| Bicknell | 15 | 1 | 76 | 1 | 2 | - |
| Tudor | 18 | 6 | 58 | 1 | 4 | - |
| Ormond | 21.3 | 9 | 46 | 2 | - | 1 |
| Hollioake | 2 | 0 | 18 | 0 | 1 | 2 |
| Mushtaq Ahmed | 30 | 7 | 71 | 5 | - | - |
| Butcher | 1 | 1 | 0 | 0 | - | - |

**LEICESTERSHIRE - Second Innings** (Following on, 250 runs in arrears)

| Fall Of Wkt | Batsman | How | Out | Score | Balls | 4s | 6s |
|---|---|---|---|---|---|---|---|
| 1-26 | T.R. Ward | lbw | b Bicknell | 16 | 32 | 3 | 0 |
| 2-182 | I.J. Sutcliffe * | c Brown | b Bicknell | 64 | 140 | 10 | 0 |
| 4-219 | D.L. Maddy | lbw | b Ormond | 94 | 141 | 16 | 0 |
| 3-203 | D.I. Stevens | c Ward | b Mushtaq | 14 | 34 | 3 | 0 |
| 8-270 | M. Kaif | lbw | b Tudor | 43 | 74 | 5 | 1 |
| 5-250 | N.D. Burns + | c sub (Shahid) | b Mushtaq | 11 | 35 | 2 | 0 |
| 6-267 | R.J. Cunliffe | c Brown | b Tudor | 4 | 24 | 1 | 0 |
| 7-269 | P.A.J. DeFreitas | c Butcher | b Tudor | 0 | 1 | 0 | 0 |
| 10-289 | J.O. Grove | | b Tudor | 3 | 10 | 0 | 0 |
| 9-285 | M.J.A. Whiley | st Batty | b Mushtaq | 13 | 11 | 0 | 1 |
| | D.E. Malcolm | Not | Out | 4 | 2 | 1 | 0 |
| | Extras | (8b, 5lb, 10nb) | | 23 | | | |
| | **TOTAL** | **(83.1 overs)** | | **289** | | | |

| Bowler | O | M | R | W | NB | Wd |
|---|---|---|---|---|---|---|
| Bicknell | 16 | 2 | 41 | 2 | - | - |
| Tudor | 17.1 | 2 | 54 | 4 | 3 | - |
| Butcher | 3 | 1 | 22 | 0 | - | - |
| Mushtaq Ahmed | 33 | 7 | 115 | 3 | 2 | - |
| Ormond | 14 | 2 | 44 | 1 | - | - |

**SURREY - Second Innings** (Needing 40 to win)

| Fall Of Wkt | Batsman | How | Out | Score | Balls | 4s | 6s |
|---|---|---|---|---|---|---|---|
| 1-8 | I.J. Ward | c Maddy | b Whiley | 6 | 5 | 1 | 0 |
| 2-12 | J.N. Batty + | c Maddy | b Malcolm | 4 | 3 | 1 | 0 |
| 3-21 | M.A. Butcher | c Burns | b Malcolm | 8 | 8 | 1 | 0 |
| | M.R. Ramprakash | Not | Out | 5 | 12 | 1 | 0 |
| | A.D. Brown | Not | Out | 14 | 10 | 2 | 0 |
| | Extras | (1lb, 2w, 2nb) | | 5 | | | |
| | **TOTAL** | **(6.1 overs)** | **(for 3 wkts)** | **42** | | | |

| Bowler | O | M | R | W | NB | Wd |
|---|---|---|---|---|---|---|
| Whiley | 3.1 | 0 | 34 | 1 | 1 | 1 |
| Malcolm | 3 | 0 | 7 | 2 | - | - |

## Other Division One Results

This was a significant round of matches, since it saw Surrey's advantage extending from 19.25 points to 36.25 points, following Warwickshire's thrashing of Kent. The Bears now looked the only side capable of stopping Surrey from winning the title, though a 37.75-point deficit looked too much to make up, even with a game in hand - and they would certainly have to win the match between the two counties at Edgbaston in a couple of weeks time. At the bottom, Yorkshire and Hampshire boosted their hopes of avoiding relegation by recording wins, while fast-fading Somerset sank further into trouble with their defeat at The Rose Bowl.

August 14-17
*The Rose Bowl:-* **Hampshire beat Somerset by four wickets.** Somerset 278 (Johnson 61, Turner 57, Parsons 51, Mullally 4-58) and 190; Hampshire 236 (Francis 53, Smith 52, Blackwell 5-49) and 233-6 (Johnson 57). **Hampshire 16pts, Somerset 5**

*Old Trafford:-* **Yorkshire beat Lancashire by 150 runs.** Yorkshire 294 (Elliott 83, Blakey 77, Anderson 5-61) and 305 (Fellows 109, McGrath 86); Lancashire 301-9dec (Swann 112) and 148 (Dawson 5-42). **Yorkshire 17pts, Lancashire 6**

*Edgbaston:-* **Warwickshire beat Kent by ten wickets.** Warwickshire 565 (Troughton 115, Wagh 109, Ostler 80, Knight 69, Giles 68, Tredwell 4-103) and 8-0; Kent 252 (Nixon 103) and 317 (Ealham 83, Masters 68, Giles 7-142). **Warwickshire 20pts, Kent 3**

## COUNTY CHAMPIONSHIP DIVISION ONE AT 17TH AUGUST

| Pos | Prv | | P | Points | W | D | L | Bat | Bwl | Ded |
|---|---|---|---|---|---|---|---|---|---|---|
| 1 | 1 | Surrey | 12 | 170.75 | 7 | 3 | 2 | 39 | 36 | 0.25 |
| 2 | 2 | Kent | 12 | 134.50 | 5 | 3 | 4 | 31 | 32 | 0.50 |
| 3 | 4 | Warwickshire | 11 | 133.00 | 5 | 4 | 2 | 26 | 31 | 0.00 |
| 4 | 3 | Sussex | 12 | 127.00 | 3 | 6 | 3 | 32 | 35 | 0.00 |
| 5 | 5 | Leicestershire | 11 | 112.00 | 3 | 4 | 4 | 30 | 31 | 1.00 |
| 6 | 7 | Hampshire ** | 12 | 108.00 | 2 | 8 | 2 | 25 | 35 | 8.00 |
| 7 | 6 | Lancashire | 11 | 105.00 | 3 | 5 | 3 | 20 | 29 | 0.00 |
| 8 | 8 | Somerset | 11 | 94.00 | 1 | 6 | 4 | 28 | 30 | 0.00 |
| 9 | 9 | Yorkshire | 12 | 91.50 | 1 | 5 | 6 | 26 | 34 | 0.50 |

**\*\* Hampshire deducted 8pts for 'poor' pitch at Rose Bowl v Lancashire**

### NUL2 - Promotion Hopes Dented By The Scorpions' Sting

Surrey's hopes of making a swift return to division one of the National League were seriously damaged by this shock defeat at The AMP Oval against the Derbyshire Scorpions, with the visitors easily reaching their target of 191 with four wickets and more than six overs to spare.

After winning the toss, it had looked so promising for the Lions as they roared away to 43-0 after four overs, led by Ian Ward, who hit Kevin Dean for five successive fours in the fourth over of the innings. Dominic Cork and Graeme Welch then launched an instant comeback, however, with the England swing bowler removing both openers, and the former Warwickshire all-rounder putting the brakes on the scoring rate with a supremely accurate spell of medium-fast seam bowling that was largely responsible for the total advancing by just forty-four runs in the next eighteen overs. Thereafter, it was pretty much a case of Mark Ramprakash versus Derbyshire's pack of seam bowlers, so little support did the former Middlesex man get from his team-mates. Despite recording his fourth half-century in his last five NUL outings before being last out, Ramprakash was unable to lift the Surrey total beyond 190, which always looked like it would be difficult to defend.

Although the Scorpions lost two early wickets in reply, they scored quickly enough in the first fifteen overs to ensure that they could cruise gently towards victory for the rest of their innings. Despite the best efforts of Tim Murtagh and Ian Salisbury in mid-innings, the Lions were never able to exert any real pressure on opponents who were always up with the required run-rate and always had sufficient wickets in hand. As Surrey's belief drained away, Steve Selwood and Jason Kerr took the Scorpions through to a comprehensive victory that really opened up the division two promotion race.

## SURREY LIONS v DERBYSHIRE SCORPIONS at The AMP Oval
### Played on Sunday 18th August    Derbyshire Scorpions won by four wickets

Surrey Lions won the toss and elected to bat                     Umpires:- Barry Dudleston & Ian Gould

### SURREY LIONS

| Fall Of Wkt | Batsman | How | Out | Score | Balls | 4s | 6s |
|---|---|---|---|---|---|---|---|
| 2-65 | I.J. Ward | c Krikken | b Cork | 31 | 35 | 6 | 0 |
| 1-45 | A.D. Brown | lbw | b Cork | 19 | 15 | 4 | 0 |
| 10-190 | M.R. Ramprakash | c Stubbings | b Lungley | 78 | 112 | 5 | 2 |
| 3-78 | S.A. Newman | c Krikken | b Lungley | 4 | 26 | 0 | 0 |
| 4-104 | A.J. Stewart + | st Krikken | b Dean | 11 | 21 | 1 | 0 |
| 5-107 | N. Shahid | | b Kerr | 1 | 4 | 0 | 0 |
| 6-148 | A.J. Hollioake * | | b Dowman | 21 | 27 | 2 | 0 |
| 7-154 | I.D.K. Salisbury | | b Dowman | 2 | 7 | 0 | 0 |
| 8-167 | M.P. Bicknell | | b Kerr | 2 | 10 | 0 | 0 |
| 9-181 | T.J. Murtagh | | b Kerr | 8 | 8 | 1 | 0 |
| | E.S.H. Giddins | Not | Out | 0 | 3 | 0 | 0 |
| | Extras | (4lb, 9w) | | 13 | | | |
| | TOTAL | (44.4 overs) | | 190 | | | |

| Bowler | O | M | R | W | NB | Wd |
|---|---|---|---|---|---|---|
| Cork | 9 | 1 | 33 | 2 | - | 3 |
| Dean | 9 | 0 | 62 | 1 | - | 1 |
| Welch | 7 | 0 | 16 | 0 | - | 2 |
| Lungley | 6.4 | 0 | 29 | 2 | - | 3 |
| Kerr | 9 | 0 | 27 | 3 | - | - |
| Dowman | 4 | 0 | 19 | 2 | - | - |

### DERBYSHIRE SCORPIONS

| Fall Of Wkt | Batsman | How | Out | Score | Balls | 4s | 6s |
|---|---|---|---|---|---|---|---|
| 1-17 | M.J. DiVenuto | c Ramprakash | b Bicknell | 5 | 6 | 1 | 0 |
| 2-38 | C.W.G. Bassano | | b Giddins | 19 | 21 | 3 | 0 |
| 3-79 | S.D. Stubbings | c Stewart | b Murtagh | 26 | 53 | 3 | 0 |
| 4-120 | D.G. Cork * | c Brown | b Murtagh | 32 | 46 | 4 | 0 |
| 6-189 | S.A. Selwood | c Salisbury | b Bicknell | 50 | 60 | 5 | 0 |
| 5-128 | M.P. Dowman | st Stewart | b Salisbury | 2 | 9 | 0 | 0 |
| | J.I.D. Kerr | Not | Out | 34 | 39 | 5 | 1 |
| | G. Welch | Not | Out | 0 | 0 | 0 | 0 |
| | K.M. Krikken + | did not bat | | | | | |
| | T. Lungley | did not bat | | | | | |
| | K.J. Dean | did not bat | | | | | |
| | Extras | (11lb, 12w, 2nb) | | 25 | | | |
| | TOTAL | (38.5 overs) | (for 6 wkts) | 193 | | | |

| Bowler | O | M | R | W | NB | Wd |
|---|---|---|---|---|---|---|
| Bicknell | 9 | 0 | 57 | 2 | 1 | 1 |
| Giddins | 7 | 0 | 34 | 1 | - | 5 |
| Murtagh | 9 | 1 | 38 | 2 | - | - |
| Salisbury | 9 | 0 | 36 | 1 | - | 4 |
| Hollioake | 4.5 | 0 | 17 | 0 | - | 2 |

## Other NUL Division Two Results

With the Gloucestershire Gladiators' promotion seemingly assured, four teams were now battling for second and third places in the table, with Northamptonshire looking favourites to clinch one of those slots. Surrey's defeat at the hands of their promotion rivals therefore represented a serious blow to their hopes of playing in the top division in 2003.

August 11
*Derby:-* **Essex Eagles beat Derbyshire Scorpions by 49 runs.** Essex 209-7 (Flower 52, Dean 4-33); Derbyshire 160 (37.3ov; Bishop 3-39). **Essex Eagles 4pts**

*Lord's:-* **Northamptonshire Steelbacks beat Middlesex Crusaders by 214 runs.** Northamptonshire 286-7 (Hussey 110, Cook 61, Loye 56, Weekes 3-44); Middlesex 72 (24ovs; Cousins 5-22). **Northamptonshire Steelbacks 4pts**

August 13
*Bristol:-* **Gloucestershire Gladiators beat Northamptonshire Steelbacks by 55 runs.** Gloucestershire 274-6 (Windows 112*, Harvey 52, Cook 4-35); Northamptonshire 219 (42ov; Penberthy 64, Sales 51). **Gloucestershire Gladiators 4pts**

August 18
*The Rose Bowl:-* **Hampshire Hawks beat Essex Eagles by five wickets.** Essex 227-4 (Flower 54, Robinson 51); Hampshire 228-5 (44ov; Francis 84*, Kendall 51). **Hampshire Hawks 4pts**

## NATIONAL LEAGUE DIVISION TWO AT 18TH AUGUST

| Pos | Prv | | P | Pts | W | T | L | A |
|---|---|---|---|---|---|---|---|---|
| 1 | 1 | Gloucestershire Gladiators | 13 | 40 | 9 | 0 | 2 | 2 |
| 2 | 2 | Northamptonshire Steelbacks | 11 | 30 | 7 | 0 | 3 | 1 |
| 3 | 3 | Surrey Lions | 12 | 26 | 6 | 0 | 5 | 1 |
| 4 | 6 | Derbyshire Scorpions | 11 | 22 | 5 | 0 | 5 | 1 |
| 5 | 7 | Essex Eagles | 10 | 20 | 5 | 0 | 5 | 0 |
| 6 | 5 | Lancashire Lightning | 12 | 20 | 4 | 0 | 6 | 2 |
| = | 4 | Middlesex Crusaders | 12 | 20 | 4 | 0 | 6 | 2 |
| 8 | 8 | Hampshire Hawks | 12 | 18 | 4 | 0 | 7 | 1 |
| 9 | 9 | Sussex Sharks | 11 | 12 | 2 | 0 | 7 | 2 |

# 16 The Spinners' Turn

With seven Championship victories in the bag now, everyone knew that a maximum of two wins from the last four games would be enough to secure the title. Since two of those matches were against a struggling Hampshire side, with an encounter at The AMP Oval being the next fixture on the list, there was every reason to feel confident. Although we all now appreciated that recent past form wasn't always an accurate indicator following the defeat at Hove, Hampshire were a unique case, since they had seemingly developed an acute inferiority complex when facing Surrey in four-day cricket. The men from London SE11 had won the last six encounters between the two sides, with the south coast county having not come out on top since 1994. Additionally, and perhaps even more significantly, Hampshire hadn't won at The Oval since a 3-run win in 1982, when Malcolm Marshall and Gordon Greenidge were the stars of the show. It would, therefore, be a major turn-up for the books if Surrey were to come out of the game without, at worst, a high-scoring draw, especially as Hampshire were probably going to be without Alan Mullally and Chris Tremlett, their leading seamers, and John Crawley, their best batsman. Since Robin Smith and his side also had a justifiable reputation for failing to perform well against Saqlain Mushtaq and Ian Salisbury, they would also have been unhappy to discover that both men were returning to the Surrey line-up for this game. Even the most dedicated and optimistic Hampshire fan must have found it hard to believe that their side could avoid defeat.

Apart from at Canterbury, the Surrey spin twins hadn't dominated any games so far this season, partly because one or other of them was often missing, but largely because the wickets around the country had often been too slow and low in the bounce. Maybe the unusual amount of rain that had fallen in mid-summer had succeeded in dampening down squares at the time when they would usually start to become drier and harder, and therefore more conducive to spin bowling? Whatever the reason, a game at The AMP Oval in August always looked likely to represent Solly and Saqi's best chance of having a major impact on a game - and the fact that it was against Hampshire made it seem all the more likely.

One player who certainly wouldn't be featuring in the match was Graham Thorpe. Having announced on 29th July, after the Lord's Test against India, that he was taking an indefinite break from all cricket, there was a further announcement on 19th August. Following a meeting between Thorpe and Paul Sheldon, Surrey's Chief Executive, a Club spokesman stated "It's extremely unlikely that Graham will play for Surrey again this season. The Club have been very supportive of him during this difficult time and have no doubt he will return from this break reinvigorated and ready for next season." Although this didn't have any serious implications for Surrey, who were hardly short of batsmen, the fact that Thorpe wasn't going to play cricket again this summer suggested that he had almost certainly ruled himself out of the winter's Ashes tour, dealing a further blow to England's already fairly gloomy prospects.

### NUL2 - Hungry Lions Devour Hapless Hawks

Needing a confidence-boosting win, following the Derbyshire debacle, Surrey's hungry Lions strolled to an emphatic victory over the Hampshire Hawks in the annual floodlit match at The AMP Oval, with the visitors never looking likely to mount a serious challenge once Neil Johnson had been dismissed in the nineteenth over after a bright innings of forty-four.

Having won the toss and elected to bat, Surrey's innings was given a fine start by Ali Brown and Ian Ward, who added seventy-six inside the first thirteen overs, before Mark Ramprakash - compiling his seventh half-century in his last eight limited-overs games - and Scott Newman joined forces for a third-wicket partnership worth eighty-two runs. Although both then fell to Johnson in the thirty-sixth over, they had established a position, at 187-4, from which the rest of the batsmen could blast away to boost the total by seventy-five in the final nine overs.

With the Hawks left to chase an unlikely 263 to win under the lights, Johnson gave his side hope until he played on to Tim Murtagh with eighty-nine on the board and, thereafter, Mushtaq Ahmed tied them up and Adam Hollioake knocked them down. The Pakistani leg-spinner, making his first, and probably last, appearance for the Lions, bowled nine immaculate overs, in two spells, to put Hampshire well behind the clock, and as soon as they tried to accelerate they found Hollioake's bag of tricks far too much to cope with as the Surrey skipper ended with 5-43.

With the Lions' promotion campaign back on track, the vast majority of a large crowd, reckoned to be in the region of six-thousand, went home happy.

## SURREY LIONS v HAMPSHIRE HAWKS at The AMP Oval
Played on Wednesday 21st August    Surrey Lions won by 70 runs

Surrey Lions won the toss and elected to bat    Umpires:- Neil Mallender & Alan Whitehead

### SURREY LIONS

| Fall Of Wkt | Batsman | How | Out | Score | Balls | 4s | 6s |
|---|---|---|---|---|---|---|---|
| 1-76 | I.J. Ward | c Johnson | b Mascarenhas | 38 | 49 | 6 | 1 |
| 2-98 | A.D. Brown | c Adams | b Hamblin | 49 | 40 | 7 | 1 |
| 4-187 | M.R. Ramprakash | c Mascarenhas | b Johnson | 50 | 69 | 3 | 0 |
| 3-180 | S.A. Newman | c Laney | b Johnson | 37 | 56 | 4 | 0 |
| 5-200 | Mushtaq Ahmed | c Mascarenhas | b Johnson | 16 | 8 | 2 | 1 |
| 6-248 | A.J. Hollioake * | c Adams | b Prittipaul | 18 | 11 | 0 | 2 |
| 7-250 | N. Shahid | c Francis | b Mascarenhas | 32 | 21 | 3 | 1 |
| 8-254 | J.N. Batty + | | b Tomlinson | 2 | 4 | 0 | 0 |
| 9-261 | M.P. Bicknell | | b Mascarenhas | 3 | 6 | 0 | 0 |
| 10-262 | T.J. Murtagh | c Johnson | b Mascarenhas | 6 | 4 | 1 | 0 |
| | E.S.H. Giddins | Not | Out | 1 | 1 | 0 | 0 |
| | Extras | (3lb, 7w) | | 10 | | | |
| | TOTAL | (44.5 overs) | | 262 | | | |

| Bowler | O | M | R | W | NB | Wd |
|---|---|---|---|---|---|---|
| Mascarenhas | 8.5 | 0 | 45 | 4 | - | 1 |
| Tomlinson | 8 | 0 | 53 | 1 | - | 2 |
| Hamblin | 5 | 0 | 34 | 1 | - | - |
| Prittipaul | 8 | 0 | 44 | 1 | - | 2 |
| Udal | 9 | 0 | 41 | 0 | - | 1 |
| Johnson | 6 | 0 | 42 | 3 | - | 1 |

### HAMPSHIRE HAWKS

| Fall Of Wkt | Batsman | How | Out | Score | Balls | 4s | 6s |
|---|---|---|---|---|---|---|---|
| 2-89 | N.C. Johnson | | b Murtagh | 44 | 52 | 5 | 0 |
| 1-64 | J.S. Laney | run | out | 25 | 46 | 4 | 0 |
| 3-92 | J.R.C. Hamblin | run | out | 13 | 21 | 1 | 0 |
| 4-109 | J.D. Francis | c & | b Hollioake | 10 | 12 | 1 | 0 |
| 5-142 | W.S. Kendall * | c Brown | b Mushtaq | 25 | 39 | 1 | 0 |
| 6-152 | J.H.K. Adams | c & | b Hollioake | 8 | 25 | 0 | 0 |
| 8-157 | S.D. Udal | | b Hollioake | 6 | 8 | 0 | 0 |
| 7-156 | A.D. Mascarenhas | | b Hollioake | 2 | 5 | 0 | 0 |
| | N. Pothas + | Not | Out | 20 | 18 | 2 | 0 |
| 9-175 | L.R. Prittipaul | | b Hollioake | 7 | 16 | 0 | 0 |
| 10-192 | J.A. Tomlinson | | b Murtagh | 6 | 7 | 1 | 0 |
| | Extras | (6b, 14lb, 6w) | | 26 | | | |
| | TOTAL | (41.3 overs) | | 192 | | | |

| Bowler | O | M | R | W | NB | Wd |
|---|---|---|---|---|---|---|
| Bicknell | 6 | 0 | 25 | 0 | - | - |
| Giddins | 7 | 0 | 32 | 0 | - | - |
| Murtagh | 8.3 | 0 | 40 | 2 | - | - |
| Mushtaq Ahmed | 9 | 2 | 19 | 1 | - | - |
| Hollioake | 9 | 0 | 43 | 5 | - | 1 |
| Ramprakash | 2 | 0 | 13 | 0 | - | 1 |

### Other NUL Division Two Result

August 20

*Hove:-* **Lancashire Lightning beat Sussex Sharks by four wickets.** Sussex 169 (45ov; Chapple 3-26); Lancashire 171-6 (44.1ov). **Lancashire Lightning 4pts**

| NATIONAL LEAGUE DIVISION TWO AT 21ST AUGUST | | | | | | | |
|---|---|---|---|---|---|---|---|
| Pos | Prv |  | P | Pts | W | T | L | A |
| 1 | 1 | Gloucestershire Gladiators | 13 | 40 | 9 | 0 | 2 | 2 |
| 2 | 2 | Northamptonshire Steelbacks | 11 | 30 | 7 | 0 | 3 | 1 |
| 3 | 3 | Surrey Lions | 13 | 30 | 7 | 0 | 5 | 1 |
| 4 | 6 | Lancashire Lightning | 13 | 24 | 5 | 0 | 6 | 2 |
| 5 | 4 | Derbyshire Scorpions | 11 | 22 | 5 | 0 | 5 | 1 |
| 6 | 5 | Essex Eagles | 10 | 20 | 5 | 0 | 5 | 0 |
| 7 | 6 | Middlesex Crusaders | 12 | 20 | 4 | 0 | 6 | 2 |
| 8 | 8 | Hampshire Hawks | 13 | 18 | 4 | 0 | 8 | 1 |
| 9 | 9 | Sussex Sharks | 12 | 12 | 2 | 0 | 8 | 2 |

FRIZZELL COUNTY CHAMPIONSHIP - MATCH THIRTEEN

SURREY versus HAMPSHIRE
at The AMP Oval

First Day - Thursday 22nd August

Hampshire 190

***The Teams And The Toss*** - *The Surrey team shows four changes from the Leicester line-up, with Mark Butcher and Alex Tudor joining Alec Stewart on England duty, Rikki Clarke ruled out by his injured back, and Mushtaq Ahmed's brief stint with the Club at an end as a result of Saqlain Mushtaq's return. Apart from Saqlain, the other players coming into the side are Nadeem Shahid, Ian Salisbury, and Scott Newman, who is making his first-class debut after a fine season in second eleven and club cricket. As a result of these changes, Surrey are now fielding a total different attack from the one that took to the field at Hove just two games ago, with Bicknell, Ormond, Saqlain and Salisbury having taken over from Tudor, Giddins, Murtagh and Mushtaq. Hampshire are, as expected, without John Crawley (England) and the injured pace duo, Alan Mullally and Chris Tremlett, with their replacements being Lawrence Prittipaul, James Hamblin, and James Tomlinson, who is making his County Championship debut. In fine conditions for batting, Robin Smith wins the toss, and first use of the wicket, for Hampshire. As a consequence of the late finish to last night's floodlit match, play starts at midday, with only 88 overs to be bowled on day one. The sixteen 'lost' overs will be made up by extending days two and three by four overs apiece, and the final day by eight overs.*

    Simon Barnes of *The Times* would have been in his element as the Hampshire openers - both, by nature, positive players - grind out just sixteen runs from fifteen overs in the first hour of the day. Although the opening spells from Martin Bicknell and Jimmy Ormond are undoubtedly accurate and testing, the batting of Neil Johnson and Jason Laney is undeniably unadventurous, especially during one sequence of thirty-eight deliveries where not a single run is scored off the bat.
    Such passive resistance, presumably brought about by a fear of what the Surrey spinners might achieve later in the match, certainly doesn't get them anywhere, since Saqlain Mushtaq, having joined the attack in place of Ormond for the fourteenth over, strikes with his seventh delivery when Laney prods a simple catch to Nadeem Shahid at short leg. A return of five runs from 42 balls suggests that the Hampshire opener would surely have done better if he had followed his natural, more aggressive, instincts.

Perhaps mindful of this, Will Kendall pulls his first ball to the midwicket boundary, while Johnson, normally such a free striker of the ball, breaks out with a sweep for three in the Pakistani off-spinner's next over, followed by a cover drive for four off Ormond soon after the big paceman replaces Bicknell at the Vauxhall end. Since Kendall then twice whips Saqlain away through square leg, it appears that the penny has finally dropped for Hampshire, but, as the short morning session draws to a close, they receive another setback when Johnson falls to a fine piece of cricket, as Ormond's high-class outswinger induces an outside edge which brings a splendid catch out of Jon Batty as he dives away low to his left-hand side.

At the end of the following over, the players leave the field for lunch with Hampshire's perceived inferiority complex having already been exposed.

*Lunch:- Hampshire 38-2 (Kendall 14\*, Smith 0\*) from 22 overs*

The visitors' more purposeful approach is initially maintained after lunch, with Kendall and Robin Smith each taking an off-side boundary off Ormond, though the Coventry-born paceman comes back well with two fine overs, during which he is unfortunate to see Kendall raising the Hampshire fifty with a thick edge to the rope at third man.

Saqlain is meanwhile spinning his web from the pavilion end, and it's no great surprise to see Smith quickly caught up in it, as Adam Hollioake snaps up a sharp bat-pad catch at silly point with the total on fifty-seven in the twenty-eighth over.

This brings the promising 21-year-old left-hander, John Francis, to the crease and, though he starts confidently with a sweep to the backward square-leg boundary, he is soon discovering how tough life can be at first team level. To be fair to the youngster, he does at least look more confident than Kendall when facing Ormond, since the Hampshire vice-captain enjoys two further strokes of luck at the big Surrey paceman's expense in quick succession, first seeing Hollioake spill a difficult chance low to his left-hand side at second slip, and then snicking through the gap in the five-man close-catching cordon to move his score on to thirty in rather fortunate fashion a couple of overs later.

There is no doubt that Ormond deserves a second wicket, and he duly gets it in his seventeenth over, though, ironically, his victim is Francis, as opposed to Kendall. It's a well-worked wicket, too, as the wicketkeeper and slips, responding to a signal from the bowler, walk forward several paces as Ormond runs in and, consequently, end up in just the right position when the batsman gets an outside edge to a slower outswinger. Batty takes the catch low down to remove Francis for six and reduce Hampshire to 72-4, amidst jubilant Surrey celebrations.

If the sturdy fast bowler thinks his luck has now changed for good, he is soon thinking again, however, since the new batsman, Nic Pothas, edges his second ball just short of the slips to get off the mark with a streaky boundary, before Kendall again employs a thick edge to earn himself another two runs at the end of the same over. Shortly afterwards, having contributed nine largely excellent overs since lunch, Ormond takes a break, allowing the Surrey spin twins to pair up and bring double trouble for the visitors with wickets in successive overs.

Saqlain makes the first of these breaches by grabbing his third wicket of the innings in his fifteenth over, bringing the curtain down on Kendall's rather charmed existence with a fine bat-pad catch by Hollioake, who dives away towards short cover from his silly point position as the ball pops up into the air. The score is 88-5 as the Hampshire vice-captain departs, and only five runs have been added when Salisbury strikes another blow for Surrey by trapping Lawrence Prittipaul plumb lbw on the back foot with a googly.

The visitors' second innings fears are now haunting them in the first innings, as the spinners turn the screw and surround the batsmen with close catchers. While Pothas does occasionally free himself from the web, whipping Salisbury wide of mid-on for the four that takes the total into three figures in the forty-seventh over and then sweeping Saqlain for a mighty 'maximum' three overs later, Mascarenhas surprisingly emulates Laney and Johnson in playing an uncharacteristically passive innings, attempting little more than an occasional sweep.

Although both batsmen survive until the interval, as Hollioake gives Saqlain a short break by allowing himself and Mark Ramprakash one over apiece, the post-tea prognosis isn't good for the struggling, relegation-threatened visitors.

*Tea:- Hampshire 124-6 (Pothas 28\*, Mascarenhas 8\*) from 56 overs*

Adam Hollioake restores Martin Bicknell and Saqlain Mushtaq to the attack after tea, though neither bowler is able to provide him with an immediate breakthrough. While Mascarenhas maintains his dogged approach, Pothas continues to keep the scoreboard ticking over with a couple of pleasant off-side boundaries off Bicknell as the seventh-wicket partnership reaches fifty. At this point, it has endured for twenty overs, and it is still going strong when Bicknell gives way to Salisbury at the Vauxhall end after a good, but unlucky, five-over spell.

With the spinners operating in tandem again, the scoring rate declines further, as the batsmen continue to hang on grimly, rather than making any attempt to disrupt the bowlers' rhythm, and it is comes as no surprise that Mascarenhas finally loses his wicket while pushing defensively at a Salisbury leg-break. Batty snaffles the resulting outside edge with ease, simultaneously putting the batsman out of his misery and pushing Hampshire deeper into trouble at 161-7. Having never seen Mascarenhas bat in such a stilted manner before, everyone is wondering if he has been batting to team orders in plodding to twenty from 95 balls. If so, then the person responsible for those orders clearly needs to think again, since the current tactics are so obviously playing straight into Surrey's hands.

Although they are in a pretty hopeless position now, Hampshire at least have the small consolation of Pothas' continued presence at the wicket, and he completes a very determined half-century from his ninety-third delivery when he whips Salisbury to square leg for a single in the next over. It's been a tenacious innings by the former South African one-day international and he has certainly been made to work hard for his runs today while sustaining his team almost single-handedly. One strongly suspects that his efforts will be in vain, however, unless the visitors' last three wickets can somehow increase the total dramatically.

This appears highly unlikely, of course, and any hopes of earning a batting point to assist their fight against relegation are soon looking forlorn as Shaun Udal and the trusty Pothas depart to consecutive deliveries after just half-a-dozen overs of desperate eighth-wicket defiance. Udal goes first, to the final ball of Salisbury's fourteenth over, when he plays back and falls lbw to a nicely concealed googly, then the first ball of the next over from Saqlain sees Pothas finally surrendering to a bat-pad catch by Shahid at short leg. With the Hampshire wicketkeeper-batsman gone for fifty-eight at 177-9, the end would appear to be nigh, as the visitors' last man, James Tomlinson, is reckoned to be a genuine number eleven batsman.

Since the day is now drawing to a close and Surrey don't want their openers to face two or three potentially awkward overs tonight, the spinners now indulge in some uncharacteristically negative tactics by bowling a series of deliveries on or outside leg stump. Although it is a far from subtle approach, the umpires fail to call a single wide - maybe they feel it is only the visiting team who deserve to be punished for negative play today?!

As soon as we reach the point where Surrey will not be required to bat tonight, Saqlain resumes normal service, and it takes him just two balls to have Hamblin taken at silly point by Hollioake to end a truly woeful Hampshire first innings at 190. Every member of the Surrey attack has perfomed excellently, with Saqlain leading way by taking 5-59, though they have been greatly assisted by the visitors' totally timid effort, which has allowed them to settle and dominate. If Hampshire require any proof that they have got their tactics wrong then they need only look at the scorecard, which reveals that no fewer than five batsmen have perished at silly point or short leg, and that just one has fallen while playing an aggressive stroke. Additionally, from an entertainment point of view, it certainly hasn't been a good day for the neutral fan. And it's been a truly dire day to be a Hampshire fan!

*Close:- End Of The Hampshire Innings*

## VIEWS FROM THE DRESSING ROOM

*Hampshire's first innings was a pretty drab and dismal affair. Was it mainly down to good bowling by Surrey or negative thinking by Hampshire?*
**IAN SALISBURY** - When some teams come to The Oval they immediately think that they've got to win the toss and get a big total on the board - no matter how they go about it - if they are to have any chance. They feel that they've got to get a total for their spinners to bowl at, so that they can make Saqi and me work hard. That's all well and good, but what people forget is that it's harder to come on as a spinner if the opposition are on top and looking to attack. They were certainly over-cautious at the start of the game, then they made a couple of errors, so they were suddenly about 40-3, which meant we were already on top when Saqi and I came on to bowl.
**ALI BROWN** - I think they got it all wrong. If you bat like that then, even if you aren't losing any wickets, you're not going anywhere, you're not hurting the opposition. I'd never seen people like Johnno and Mascarenhas just prodding it around - I couldn't believe what I was seeing. You've got to be positive, because any side that comes to The Oval in a negative frame of mind is almost beaten as soon as they turn up.

### Second Day - Friday 23rd August

### Hampshire 190; Surrey 410-5

Pitted against a far from scary new-ball attack of the debutant left-armer, James Tomlinson, and the medium-paced Dimitri Mascarenhas, the Surrey openers get their side off to a confident start in pursuit of Hampshire's inadequate-looking 190. Scott Newman scores his first runs in first-class cricket by clipping his second ball through midwicket for two in the opening over by his fellow debutant, then his first boundary comes courtesy of a well-struck off-drive, again at Tomlinson's expense, at the end of the third over. Although the Hampshire left-armer is able to swing the ball consistently in the rather overcast conditions that prevail this morning, his frequent errors in line and length are pounced upon by both Surrey openers as the ball is frequently forced and driven down the ground and, after an opening spell of four overs for twenty-one runs, he is withdrawn from the attack.

Shaun Udal is his replacement at the pavilion end for the ninth over of the innings, and the veteran off-spinner is soon forced to post an off-side sweeper after Newman forces him to the cover boundary twice in his first two overs. The 22-year-old Banstead batsman is certainly looking the part as he then follows up by cracking three back-foot fours off Mascarenhas to take the total past fifty in the fourteenth over and prompt a bowling change that sees Lawrence Prittipaul taking over at the Vauxhall end.

Ward, meanwhile, is not to be outdone by his young colleague and, as soon as Udal switches to an over-the-wicket line to the two left-handers, the senior partner promptly smacks him over the rope at deep midwicket with a perfectly executed slog-sweep.

Hampshire's total is looking smaller by the minute at this stage, and they quickly become as defensive in the field as they had with the bat, with Udal's approach and line of attack eventually persuading umpire Alan Whitehead to call a leg-side wide against the off-spinner. Having seen Surrey's spinners go unpunished while bowling in a similar style last night - albeit in a totally different context within the game - Udal reacts angrily and engages the umpire in a lengthy discussion, as does Robin Smith at the end of the over. It's an unfortunate and undesirable scenario, but it's easy to understand why the visitors are not happy.

Having played so well up to this point, and moved his score on to forty-three, Newman now gets lucky as he offers two catching chances in successive overs from Udal, and survives them both. First, Pothas juggles an opportunity off the inside edge, before the ball eventually hits the turf, then Smith grasses an absolute sitter at deepish mid-off, with the batsman's score unchanged and the total advanced by just two runs, to seventy-seven. Having spurned two fine chances to make an initial breakthrough, it is little wonder that Hampshire heads drop.

The young Surrey opener then rubs salt in the wound by completing his maiden first-class half-century from 80 balls with two fours in the next over from Prittipaul, the first edged to third man and the second driven backward of point. This brace of boundaries brings an otherwise very tight six-over spell from the Hampshire medium-pacer to a close, though he has rarely looked to be a genuine threat to the batsmen.

Prittipaul's replacement turns out to be James Hamblin, who is instantly driven through the covers for two fours by Ward as the Surrey score moves within striking distance of three figures. Newman then takes it past that mark with a beautifully struck six over long-on at Udal's expense before offering another catching chance later in the over, with his score on fifty-seven. This time, the Hampshire off-spinner has no-one to blame but himself, as Newman attempts to repeat his drive down the ground but only succeeds in hitting the ball back to the bowler at a very comfortable height. Everyone is left holding their breath for a couple of seconds as Udal juggles the ball three or fours times before he, and then the ball, finally hit the deck. This is fast becoming the morning from hell for the visitors, and there is even a suspicion that an outside edge from Ward in Udal's following over carries to Jason Laney at second slip. Whether it has carried or not, the former England left-hander certainly doesn't let it bother him as he moves closer to following his team-mate to a half-century by driving Hamblin down the ground twice - first for three runs, and then for two - in the following over.

With the 24-year-old seamer having made little impression during his four overs, Robin Smith calls upon Neil Johnson to take over at the Vauxhall end and, consequently, a period of relative calm follows in the lead-up to lunch, with the arrival of Ward's 121-ball fifty the only noteworthy incident.

*Lunch:- Surrey 132-0 (Ward 57\*, Newman 73\*) from 42 overs*

Hampshire could hardly be in a worse position as the afternoon session of the second day gets under way, and there is a definite feeling that the morning's play has already virtually decided the contest, so long as the weather doesn't intervene to any great degree over the course of the next two or three days.

Facing up to his side's desperate situation, Smith chooses Johnson and Mascarenhas as his first pair of bowlers, though he is soon forced to change tack as both men suffer serious punishment in the early overs of the session. Johnson is replaced by Tomlinson after just two overs, following a 14-run second over that sees Ward picking off three fours and taking the total past 150, while Mascarenhas is allowed five overs, despite a pretty poor third over that brings two boundaries for Newman and six runs in wides.

Having contributed three decent overs at the beginning of his second spell of the match, Tomlinson is then joined in the revamped attack by Udal, who promptly finds his first ball being cut to the boundary by Newman. This takes the Surrey's debutant's score on to ninety-five, before a single, later in the over, not only puts Newman within four runs of a place in the record books but also brings the scores level in the match.

Three further singles to deep-set fielders on the leg-side during the next two overs subsequently leave him on ninety-nine as he faces the first ball of Tomlinson's ninth over. Although most of the left-armer's deliveries have swung away from the left-handed Surrey batsmen, this ball turns out to be the one that goes straight on, and, with Newman having made the fateful decision to shoulder arms, umpire Neil Mallender is left with no choice but to raise his finger when the ball thuds into the batsman's pads and the inevitable appeal goes up. As Tomlinson celebrates his maiden first-class wicket, captured with a clever piece of bowling, Newman has to depart in disappointment to the pavilion, having come so close to record book immortality. Inevitably, he gets a great reception from his home crowd for an excellent innings that, in the short term, has put his team in complete control of the match at 198-1, and, in the longer term, has given us an exciting view into the future. His positive and aggressive approach has certainly marked Newman out as a typical Surrey player.

While plaudits are being handed out, Tomlinson mustn't be forgotten, since his spirited second spell has deserved a wicket and, though his next ball after removing Newman disappears to the midwicket fence as Mark Ramprakash makes a positive start, he has certainly justified his recall to the attack.

Udal then underlines the wisdom of his return, also, by claiming the wicket of Ward in the very next over with a sharply turning off-break that takes the outside edge of the bat on its way to Johnson at slip. The veteran spinner has certainly earned this success, and Hampshire have struck with the old one-two as Ward makes his way back to the dressing room with eighty-seven runs to his name at 202-2.

Unfortunately for the visitors they are already a dozen runs in arrears at this stage, and the fact that these breakthroughs are unlikely to change the course of the match is brutally emphasised as Ramprakash sees off Tomlinson with a couple of sweetly-struck cover drives for four, while Udal is swept for four and driven high over long-on for six, by Ramprakash and Shahid respectively, during his next two overs.

Despite suffering these two boundary blows, Udal still represents Hampshire's best hope of success, so he therefore continues to toil away at the pavilion end while Smith rotates his seamers, supported by deep set fields, at the Vauxhall end. Consequently, Johnson comes and goes with another two-over burst, before Hamblin returns and, in his second over, provides a little more succour for the visiting team by inducing a badly mistimed pull shot from Shahid that results in a catch to Mascarenhas at mid-on.

With the hosts already in a position of immense strength at 249-3, the sight of Ali Brown striding out into the middle is not a welcome one for the visitors. Their concerns are well founded, too, since he is soon on the attack, twice driving Udal to the rope at extra cover, and then bludgeoning a Hamblin full-toss in a similar direction in the next over. As tea approaches, worse is to come for Hampshire, however, as a flat hit over long-on for six at the off-spinner's expense is swiftly followed by another 'maximum', pulled over midwicket off Hamblin in the penultimate over of the session.

It's not all bad news for the persevering Udal, however, as he claims the scalp of Ramprakash in the final over, the batsman making a surprising error when he dances down the wicket and drives a catch straight to Francis at deep mid-on.

*Tea:- Surrey 295-4 (Brown 35\*) from 76.2 overs*

Tomlinson is recalled to support Udal after the break, and it isn't too long before he has a second wicket to his name. Although Brown advances his score by six with another slog-sweep off Udal in the fourth full over after the resumption, Adam Hollioake never really settles before falling to Tomlinson in the next over, skying a pull off the top edge high behind the wicket on the off-side after successfully pulling the previous ball for four. Johnson runs round towards gully to complete the catch, thereby providing Tomlinson and his team with what would appear to be little more than another consolation wicket at 316-5.

This most definitely appears to be a fair assessment as Brown completes a terrific 43-ball half-century with a single in Udal's following over, before blasting the experienced off-spinner out of the attack two overs later with a big six over wide long-on and a one-bounce four to the rope at long-off in an over that costs fourteen runs.

With Tomlinson also rested at this stage, Smith puts his trust in Prittipaul and Johnson in the run-up to the new ball, though he once again discards the former Zimbabwean international after just two overs, and turns back to Mascarenhas for the ninety-second over of the innings. The new ball is taken at this point, with the total having passed 350 and Jon Batty having managed to keep pace with Brown, thanks to a couple of square-driven fours at Prittipaul's expense.

Since the skies have gradually clouded over after a gloriously sunny afternoon, the bowlers do manage to get some swing out of the new ball and, apart from a drive to the rope at extra-cover by Brown off Mascarenhas that completes a solid fifty partnership for the sixth wicket, all is fairly quiet until Batty pierces the off-side field twice in two overs with a cover drive and a square cut.

Although they are in harness for seven overs, the medium-paced new-ball pair don't really pose any problems for the batsmen, so it is fairly predictable that the beleaguered Smith should return to his Tomlinson-Udal combination as we move into the last half-hour of the day. Brown is more than happy with this decision, however, as he moves into the nineties with a sweep to the square leg boundary off Udal, before advancing to ninety-nine with a lofted on-drive for four during the over in which the Surrey four-hundred clicks up on the scoreboard. Although Tomlinson again shows himself to be a thinking cricketer by switching to a round-the-wicket attack in an attempt to snare another batsman one short of his century, Brown is not to be denied, steering the ball to third man for the single that brings him the thirty-first first-class century of his career. As the batsman celebrates and the spectators show their appreciation with a healthy round of applause, the stats of a fine innings are announced over the Public Address system - 138 minutes, 104 balls, four sixes and eight fours - and everyone wonders if we might now be in for an explosive last four overs to top off a hugely entertaining day.

We aren't. The final overs yield no more than a handful of singles as Udal earns some end-of-day respect from batsmen looking to tomorrow, and Tomlinson completes another impressive spell by beating Brown outside the off stump twice in the final over. At the end of the second day of the game, Surrey lead by 220 runs and there can surely be no escape for Hampshire from this dire position. The Championship leaders look certain to record their eighth victory of the season sometime within the next forty-eight hours.

*Close:- Surrey 410-5 (Brown 103\*, Batty 36\*) from 108 overs*

## VIEWS FROM THE DRESSING ROOM

*You finally got a first-team opportunity here after scoring stacks of runs in the second team. I guess you have to be extra patient for an opportunity at a big and successful club like Surrey?*
**SCOTT NEWMAN** - It's not just the fact that it's a successful club, it's also about how well the guys were playing. At Surrey, there's a strong belief in giving people good runs in the first team, not to chop and change the side, and I think that's why they are so successful. But I was certainly grateful to be given this opportunity.

*I assume it must have been helpful to have an experienced guy like Ian Ward at the other end?*
**SCOTT NEWMAN** - Definitely, Wardy had an amazing season and I've got to get used to batting with him. I think it's good to have someone with a different personality at the other end - someone who can keep telling you to calm down, or to keep playing your natural game, and to just believe in yourself. That's what it's all about when you get to this standard of cricket - you don't get too many tips, you're just told to believe in yourself, and do what you are there to do, basically.

*You had quite a difficult time in the forties and gave a couple of chances. Do you think that was just down to nerves as you got close to your fifty?*
**SCOTT NEWMAN** - It was a bit of a nightmare, really, and it shouldn't have happened - things like milestones shouldn't really come into the game but, unfortunately, they do, as everybody knows. But once you've got that first fifty or hundred then the others don't really matter so much, you just play.

*You looked understandably very frustrated when you fell one run short of a debut century. Were you just disappointed with yourself, or were you unhappy with the umpire's decision?*
**SCOTT NEWMAN** - I was disappointed with myself, because I thought I was going to get not just a hundred, but a really big hundred, on debut, so I felt I'd sold myself a little bit short... but these things happen, things were meant to be that way. I spoke to the umpire, Neil Mallender, after the game and he told me that he hates giving people out on ninety-nine, but that he had no choice.

*Scott Newman's debut innings was a great effort. What can you tell me about him?*
**IAN SALISBURY** - Scott thoroughly deserved his chance as he'd been scoring runs all summer for the second team. I played in a couple of games with him and he looked the business - he's a very confident chap, but he's a very good player as well, one of the best young players I've seen in a long time, and he reminds me of a young Darren Lehmann. He's a very free spirit, who hits the ball well and, with the side we've got here, he will be able to express himself. In Scott, Rikki Clarke, Tim Murtagh, and Phil Sampson we've got four youngsters who are more than capable of stepping up to the plate in the very near future.

*And there seems to be a lot of good young talent around the other counties, too. Who has impressed you most this season?*
**IAN SALISBURY** - Jamie Troughton of Warwickshire was very impressive. He didn't perhaps show the greatest of techniques, but he had an 'Aussie' attitude - he was bullish, he was confident, he went for his shots, he didn't care who he was facing, and he was just impressive all round. And then there was Jimmy Anderson of Lancashire. He bowled very quickly - even though he was bowling on a quick wicket, he made you open your eyes and think 'yes, this is good pace, I don't want to misjudge this one.' Kyle Hogg also bowled well in the game at The Oval against Lancashire, though I think he's more the classic English seamer who will be very steady, whereas Anderson has the X factor and looks to be a very good find.

### Third Day - Saturday 24th August

### Hampshire 190 and 303-8; Surrey 576

Surrey's overnight batsmen make a great start to the day, picking up a couple of boundaries apiece during the first four overs bowled by James Hamblin and James Tomlinson. Hamblin is punished for bowling too short, initially, as the sixth-wicket partnership rapidly becomes worth a hundred, though he begins to pose a few problems as he begins to locate a better length.

With Tomlinson contributing another decent spell, the batsmen exist on a diet of singles for a while hereafter, and it isn't until the ninth over of the morning that the runs start to flow again. Batty breaks the spell by smacking a Hamblin full-toss to the rope at point to complete a 110-ball fifty, follows up with a single to raise the Surrey 450, and then watches Brown drive high over mid-on for four. The over ends up costing ten, and when the same bowler's following over yields seven further runs, including another boundary-hit by Brown, it is clear that Robin Smith needs to make a change.

Shaun Udal is his entirely predictable choice, and, though the off-spinner's third ball disappears back over his head, he soon takes vengeance on the batsman responsible for the stroke, Ali Brown, by inducing a top-edged hit to leg just two deliveries later. Although the ball spirals high into the air over the head of Jason Laney at midwicket, the fielder hares back to take a fine catch over his shoulder, terminating Brown's excellent knock at 135, with the total on 470.

With Surrey's advantage already standing at 280, the lower-order batsmen now have licence to play with total freedom, and Martin Bicknell takes full advantage, crashing twenty-four runs from just eighteen balls, including an on-driven six off Udal, before the tall off-break bowler again takes swift revenge, having his tormentor very well taken at short leg, with Laney again the fielder.

Bicknell's departure, at 495-7, brings Ian Salisbury to the crease, and the Surrey leg-spinner immediately makes it clear that he isn't going to hang about, either, by driving his first ball to the fence at cover, and then lofting his third over mid-off for another four, bringing up the home team's five-hundred in the process. This is pretty much the pattern for the rest of the innings.

While Dimitri Mascarenhas, the replacement for Tomlinson at the Vauxhall end, keeps things fairly tight for the next few overs, the batsmen tear into Udal, with fourteen coming from his next over and thirteen from the one after that. Most of these runs come from sweeps and lofted drives, with the pick of the strokes being Salisbury's massive hit over wide long-on that comes to rest on the top level of the Lock Stand.

The leg-spinner enjoys only limited success against Mascarenhas, however, before miscuing a drive over extra-cover and falling to another fine over-the-shoulder catch by that man Laney again, with the total on 542. Twenty-seven runs from only seventeen balls is a fine return for Salisbury, nevertheless, and the flow of runs dries up somewhat after his departure, despite Batty's excellent on-driven six off Mascarenhas a couple of overs later.

This blow prompts the Hampshire all-rounder's removal from the attack and also spells the end of the innings, since the new bowler, Lawrence Prittipaul, takes just nine deliveries to dispose of Saqlain and Batty. The Surrey off-spinner mistimes a drive at a full-toss to provide Francis with a catch at deepish mid-on, while his colleague is beaten by a little inswing two balls later to fall just eleven runs short of his century. Although the bulk of the applause is for Batty as the players leave the field, there is also an element of sympathy for the hard-working Udal, who has returned 4-213 from forty-seven overs, thereby becoming only the sixth bowler to concede two-hundred or more runs in an innings against Surrey.

Facing a deficit of some 386 runs, the Hampshire openers immediately demonstrate a much more positive attitude than on day one, taking thirty-seven runs from the seven overs they face before lunch, with no real alarms, as Johnson notches three boundaries and Laney two.

*Lunch:- Hampshire 37-0 (Johnson 19\*, Laney 14\*) from 7 overs*

The action immediately after lunch is centred around a contest between Neil Johnson and Saqlain Mushtaq, who has replaced Jimmy Ormond at the pavilion end. Johnson takes the early honours by driving two boundaries in the off-spinner's first over and another in his second, but the third ball of Saqlain's third over sees the left-handed opener trapped palpably lbw as he plays back and misses an off-break straightening from around middle-and-leg. The Hampshire batsman departs with thirty-two of his side's fifty-one runs to his credit as Surrey celebrate the first of the ten wickets that will put them in sight of the 2002 County Championship title.

Meanwhile, at the other end from Saqlain, Bicknell has been bowling well, though without much luck, and he is, surprisingly, proving unable to shift his long-term 'bunny', Jason Laney. The contest ends with neither man able to claim victory when the Surrey swing king rests after six good overs, allowing Ormond to return to the fray at the Vauxhall end.

While Saqlain continues to tie up the batsmen from the pavilion end, the big fast bowler starts rather loosely, conceding eleven runs in drives during his opening two overs, before changing to off-spin mode for the third over of his spell. This decision turns out to be a good one, since his second delivery, floated up wide of the off stump, tempts Laney into a cover drive and bowls him through the gate, with a possible 'assist' from the inside edge. Ormond's off-break strike sparks off jubilant celebrations from the home team, accompanied by cheers and applause from the Surrey faithful, and pegs the visitors back to 87-2 as a dejected Laney returns to the pavilion.

The fall of this wicket brings Robin Smith to the crease, and a quiet passage of play ensues as Saqlain maintains his hold over the batsmen, while Ormond demonstrates his versatility by mixing his two styles of bowling, depending on which batsman is on strike. Smith, inevitably, faces off-breaks, and Kendall is confronted by pace.

After seven overs of near stalemate, Smith finally breaks the impasse with an off-driven boundary at Saqlain's expense, thereby taking the Hampshire total into three figures, before following up with a trademark square-cut for four when Ormond reverts to pace in the last over of his spell.

Salisbury subsequently joins his spin twin in the attack, and the visiting captain continues his purple patch with a couple of pleasant cover drives that cost Saqlain four runs apiece, followed by a drive to the rope wide of mid-on in Salisbury's second over. It's a good job for Hampshire that Smith is looking more positive now, since Kendall has come to a virtual standstill at the other end, though he is, at least, still occupying the crease with his skipper as tea arrives.

*Tea:- Hampshire 134-2 (Kendall 23\*, Smith 26\*) from 42 overs*

It looks likely to be a spin-dominated final session as 'The Saqi And Solly Show' continues after the break. The Kendall and Smith partnership that had endured for so long before the interval finally becomes worth fifty runs in the second over of the day's final period when Smith glances Saqlain for two, and then promptly increases in value to fifty-five when Kendall strikes Salisbury wide of mid-on for his first boundary since the twenty-third over.

The third-wicket stand goes no further, however, as Smith becomes the first victim of a Saqlain two-in-two strike that rapidly reduces the visitors to 142-4. Having almost driven a catch to Ormond at mid-on earlier in the over, the Hampshire captain is taken by Shahid at short-leg for a battling twenty-eight, then John Francis falls, first ball, to the same combination of bowler and fielder, though this time the catch is a brilliant one-handed reflex effort, snapped up inches off the ground as Shahid dives away to his right. The fielder wheels away in delight as the batsman trudges off in despair.

Although Kendall hits back after these losses by sweeping Salisbury for four, raising the visitors' 150 in the process, the spinners now look to have a foot in the door to victory and are pressing to push it open. The new batsman, Nic Pothas, is certainly under pressure right from the start, offering two very sharp chances to the Surrey skipper at silly point in the same over from the unfortunate Salisbury, though he outlasts both Kendall and Lawrence Prittipaul, who depart in the space of thirteen balls as the Hampshire middle-order crumbles away.

Kendall becomes Saqlain's fourth victim of the innings when he presents Shahid with the most straightforward of bat-pad catches at short leg, ending a painstaking 99-ball innings at thirty-six, then Prittipaul completes the Pakistani's five-wicket innings haul and ten-wicket match haul as he goes back to a faster off-break delivered from round the wicket and is trapped plumb in front of his stumps. At this point, with the visitors on 167-6, it would appear that we might see a Surrey victory tonight, since there are still twenty-six overs left for play.

A refreshingly positive attitude by the batsmen, coupled with more bad luck for Salisbury, alters that perception slightly, however, as the total rushes on to two-hundred with a series of four powerfully driven and swept boundaries and two dropped catches. The first two boundaries come from Mascarenhas before he is missed, on fifteen, by Batty off Salisbury, a top-edged cut not quite sticking in the keeper's gloves, then Pothas, having survived those two sharp chances on two, escapes again, with his score on sixteen, when Newman just manages to get his hands to an extremely difficult chance off Saqlain as he runs back towards deep midwicket.

Although Hampshire's wicketkeeper finally runs out of luck four overs later when he falls lbw to Saqlain, in almost identical fashion to Prittipaul, for a wholly unimpressive twenty-four, Mascarenhas ups the tempo during a bright and breezy stand of thirty-nine for the eighth wicket with Shaun Udal. The Hampshire all-rounder drives Salisbury straight down the ground for two successive sixes at one point, and, predictably enough, looks a much better player when going for his shots than he had in the first innings, when his performance was totally out of character.

Having suffered without success for seventeen overs, Salisbury finally gets his just deserts for a good and unlucky spell when Udal is beaten by a leg-break, drags his foot out of his ground and falls victim to a sharp piece of glovework by Batty with the total on 247, leaving Surrey nine-and-a-half overs, plus a possible extra eight, in which to sew up the game tonight.

It looks to be a fair bet that they will do so, but Mascarenhas and Hamblin have other ideas. While the former continues to attack the bowling, taking three fours off Salisbury and reaching a feisty fifty from his 69th delivery, the latter is content to block out at the other end, except when Ormond reappears for three overs of off-spin in place of Saqlain and drops short outside the off stump on a couple of occasions.

With the Hampshire pair showing no sign of surrendering, Saqlain is forced back into the attack and, at 6.43pm, with the light fading fast, Hollioake asks for, and is granted, the extra half-hour in which to try and finish off the match.

Although this sends the batsmen into their shells, they manage to survive without too many scares, notching a half-century partnership and taking their team past the three-hundred mark in the process, despite the fact that four, and then five, lights are aglow on the scoreboard lightmeter. Almost inevitably, the umpires, who have been unhappy with the light for some while, decide to suspend play after the fifth of the eight overs, and we are all left to wait until tomorrow for confirmation of Surrey's victory.

*Close:- Hampshire 303-8 (Mascarenhas 75\*, Hamblin 13\*) from 83 overs*

## VIEW FROM THE DRESSING ROOM

*After their uninspiring first-innings effort with the bat, do you think Hampshire deliberately adopted a different approach in their second innings, with people like Johnson, Laney and Mascarenhas playing more naturally?*
**IAN SALISBURY** - I wasn't at all surprised that they batted more aggressively and scored runs second time around - it's much easier to play your natural game when the match is already lost, as opposed to when there is still something to play for.

### Fourth Day - Sunday 25th August

### Hampshire 190 and 326; Surrey 576

### Surrey won by an innings and 60 runs
### Surrey 20pts, Hampshire 3

Even before play gets under way at 10.30am, Surrey know that they are another step closer to Championship glory, since neither Kent nor Warwickshire have managed to win their match in the current round of fixtures - this game at The AMP Oval had, of course, started a day later than the others in Division One, as a result of the floodlit match being played on Wednesday night.

Today's inevitable win will, therefore, extend the leaders' advantage at the top of the table, and their spinners set about trying to rubber-stamp the result of this game in front of no more than about a hundred spectators.

The troublesome ninth-wicket partnership endures for another five overs this morning, adding a further fourteen runs, before Hamblin gets a leading edge in attempting a drive at Salisbury, providing the bowler with the simplest of return catches and a hard-earned second wicket of the innings.

Dimitri Mascarenhas is on eighty-six at this point, with only James Tomlinson left to help him to reach his century. After taking a couple of singles, the Hampshire all-rounder seemingly opts for a death-or-glory approach, advancing on Salisbury and driving him high and straight into the pavilion for six, thereby moving within another mighty hit of a well-played ton. He then betrays nerves by popping the next ball up just short of a scrambling Shahid at short leg, before gleefully identifying the following delivery as a long-hop and crashing it away on the off-side. Unfortunately for Mascarenhas, he fails to get enough elevation on the ball and, consequently, sees Jimmy Ormond, at cover, latching onto a stinging catch at head height to finish the match and leave the 24-year-old all-rounder short of his goal by six runs. While the Surrey team celebrate their expected triumph, and the spinners lead the side from the field, poor Mascarenhas must be reliving memories of Hampshire's two-run defeat at this ground in 2000 when he was, similarly, the last man out when on the verge of success, on that occasion for the team, as opposed to himself. By way of a cruel contrast, there doesn't seem to be any danger of Surrey 'blowing it' as they close in on the 2002 Championship crown.

**Hampshire 190 and 326; Surrey 576**
**Surrey won by an innings and 60 runs. Surrey 20pts, Hampshire 3**

## VIEWS FROM THE DRESSING ROOM

*This game was the exception, but you didn't seem to bowl in tandem with Saqi very often during the season. Was there any particular reason for that?*
**IAN SALISBURY** - In this game we *had* to bowl in tandem, as we only had four bowlers! I think it's partly because some of wickets haven't been as helpful to us - there was a match at The Oval this year, against Kent, where I didn't bowl a single ball, which is unheard of. We also had a couple of games where the rain stopped us from bowling together - for example, Lancashire at Old Trafford on the final day would have been a classic Saqi-Solly game, but for the rain. Then he was away for a couple of games, and I had a couple off when my wife had the baby, so the classic combination went out of the window a little bit this year. Hopefully we can rectify that in 2003, especially if the captain gives me a little bit more of a bowl and sees me as something more than a last resort!

*It did seem to me that there were very few pitches around the country that were suited to spin this season. It sounds like you would concur with that view?*
**IAN SALISBURY** - We certainly played on some excellent batting wickets this year, and our batsmen took full advantage, to their credit. The averages told the story - most of our batsmen averaged forty-plus, whereas most of our bowlers averaged in the high twenties or early thirties, even though we thought we bowled all right. A lot of the pitches were very dead, with very little seam movement, and, if they did spin, they only did so very slowly. It was remarkable, really, that we managed to win ten out of sixteen games with the pitches like that... and there were two other matches where we would have fancied winning on the last day but for rain - Somerset at home and Lancashire away. And, of course, the Warwickshire home game was one that we should have won.

## SURREY v HAMPSHIRE at The AMP Oval   Played 22nd to 25th August

Hampshire won the toss and elected to bat     Umpires:- Neil Mallender and Alan Whitehead

### HAMPSHIRE - First Innings

| Fall Of Wkt | Batsman | How | Out | Score | Balls | 4s | 6s |
|---|---|---|---|---|---|---|---|
| 2-36 | N.C. Johnson | c Batty | b Ormond | 15 | 67 | 2 | 0 |
| 1-16 | J.S. Laney | c Shahid | b Saqlain | 5 | 42 | 0 | 0 |
| 5-88 | W.S. Kendall | c Hollioake | b Saqlain | 36 | 86 | 5 | 0 |
| 3-55 | R.A. Smith * | c Hollioake | b Saqlain | 7 | 19 | 1 | 0 |
| 4-72 | J.D. Francis | c Batty | b Ormond | 6 | 24 | 1 | 0 |
| 9-177 | N. Pothas + | c Shahid | b Saqlain | 58 | 113 | 5 | 1 |
| 6-93 | L.R. Prittipaul | lbw | b Salisbury | 0 | 9 | 0 | 0 |
| 7-161 | A.D. Mascarenhas | c Batty | b Salisbury | 20 | 95 | 0 | 0 |
| 8-177 | S.D. Udal | lbw | b Salisbury | 4 | 12 | 0 | 0 |
| 10-190 | J.R.C. Hamblin | c Hollioake | b Saqlain | 10 | 25 | 1 | 0 |
|  | J.A. Tomlinson |  | Not Out | 1 | 24 | 0 | 0 |
|  | Extras | (6b, 10lb, 4w, 8nb) |  | 28 |  |  |  |
|  | **TOTAL** | **(85.2 overs)** |  | **190** |  |  |  |

| Bowler | O | M | R | W | NB | Wd |
|---|---|---|---|---|---|---|
| Bicknell | 13 | 2 | 28 | 0 | 1 | - |
| Ormond | 18 | 7 | 41 | 2 | - | 2 |
| Saqlain Mushtaq | 34.2 | 12 | 59 | 5 | 3 | - |
| Salisbury | 18 | 4 | 44 | 3 | - | - |
| Hollioake | 1 | 0 | 1 | 0 | - | - |
| Ramprakash | 1 | 0 | 1 | 0 | - | - |

### SURREY - First Innings

| Fall Of Wkt | Batsman | How | Out | Score | Balls | 4s | 6s |
|---|---|---|---|---|---|---|---|
| 2-202 | I.J. Ward | c Johnson | b Udal | 87 | 167 | 10 | 1 |
| 1-198 | S.A. Newman | lbw | b Tomlinson | 99 | 168 | 13 | 1 |
| 4-295 | M.R. Ramprakash | c Francis | b Udal | 38 | 59 | 7 | 0 |
| 3-249 | N. Shahid | c Mascarenhas | b Hamblin | 22 | 36 | 1 | 1 |
| 6-470 | A.D. Brown | c Laney | b Udal | 135 | 154 | 13 | 4 |
| 5-316 | A.J. Hollioake * | c Johnson | b Tomlinson | 9 | 21 | 1 | 0 |
| 10-576 | J.N. Batty + | lbw | b Prittipaul | 89 | 157 | 10 | 1 |
| 7-495 | M.P. Bicknell | c Laney | b Udal | 24 | 18 | 2 | 1 |
| 8-542 | I.D.K. Salisbury | c Laney | b Mascarenhas | 27 | 17 | 3 | 1 |
| 9-575 | Saqlain Mushtaq | c Francis | b Prittipaul | 18 | 19 | 2 | 0 |
|  | J. Ormond |  | Not Out | 1 | 1 | 0 | 0 |
|  | Extras | (8b, 1lb, 10w, 8nb) |  | 27 |  |  |  |
|  | **TOTAL** | **(135.3 overs)** |  | **576** |  |  |  |

| Bowler | O | M | R | W | NB | Wd |
|---|---|---|---|---|---|---|
| Tomlinson | 28 | 0 | 91 | 2 | - | 2 |
| Mascarenhas | 21 | 3 | 94 | 1 | - | 2 |
| Udal | 47 | 7 | 213 | 4 | - | - |
| Prittipaul | 13.3 | 4 | 43 | 2 | 1 | - |
| Hamblin | 16 | 2 | 81 | 1 | 3 | - |
| Johnson | 10 | 0 | 45 | 0 | - | - |

### HAMPSHIRE - Second Innings  (Needing 386 to avoid an innings defeat)

| Fall Of Wkt | Batsman | How | Out | Score | Balls | 4s | 6s |
|---|---|---|---|---|---|---|---|
| 1-51 | N.C. Johnson | lbw | b Saqlain | 32 | 40 | 6 | 0 |
| 2-87 | J.S. Laney |  | b Ormond | 39 | 72 | 4 | 0 |
| 5-157 | W.S. Kendall | c Shahid | b Saqlain | 36 | 99 | 3 | 1 |
| 3-142 | R.A. Smith * | c Shahid | b Saqlain | 28 | 77 | 5 | 0 |
| 4-142 | J.D. Francis | c Shahid | b Saqlain | 0 | 1 | 0 | 0 |
| 7-208 | N. Pothas + | lbw | b Saqlain | 24 | 43 | 2 | 0 |
| 6-167 | L.R. Prittipaul | lbw | b Saqlain | 5 | 6 | 1 | 0 |
| 10-326 | A.D. Mascarenhas | c Ormond | b Salisbury | 94 | 124 | 9 | 3 |
| 8-247 | S.D. Udal | st Batty | b Salisbury | 18 | 22 | 2 | 0 |
| 9-317 | J.R.C. Hamblin | c & | b Salisbury | 16 | 64 | 0 | 0 |
|  | J.A. Tomlinson |  | Not Out | 0 | 2 | 0 | 0 |
|  | Extras | (6b, 14lb, 2w, 12nb) |  | 34 |  |  |  |
|  | **TOTAL** | **(90.4 overs)** |  | **326** |  |  |  |

| Bowler | O | M | R | W | NB | Wd |
|---|---|---|---|---|---|---|
| Bicknell | 10 | 3 | 30 | 0 | 1 | - |
| Ormond | 14 | 1 | 51 | 1 | - | 1 |
| Saqlain Mushtaq | 39 | 9 | 121 | 6 | 2 | - |
| Salisbury | 27.4 | 5 | 104 | 3 | 3 | - |

## Other Division One Results

Surrey were close to being home and dry now, thanks to a spirited second innings fightback by Leicestershire that denied Kent victory at Canterbury, and a fine performance by struggling Somerset at Taunton that pushed Warwickshire very close to an unexpected defeat.

August 21-24

*Taunton:-* **Somerset drew with Warwickshire.** Somerset 408 (Blackwell 110, Burns 95, Wagg 4-62) and 394 (Blackwell 81, Burns 80, Wood 68, Bond 5-64, Carter 4-46); Warwickshire 304 (Knight 98, Francis 5-78) and 310-9 (Bell 77, Ostler 55, Johnson 4-60). **Somerset 12pts, Warwickshire 10**

*Canterbury:-* **Kent drew with Leicestershire.** Leicestershire 259 (Sutcliffe 125*, Saggers 4-68) and 530 (Maddy 156, DeFreitas 94, Ward 66, Patel 4-99); Kent 379 (Smith 87, Nixon 86, Patel 82, Srinath 4-70) and 58-0. **Kent 11pts, Leicestershire 9**

*Hove:-* **Lancashire beat Sussex by seven wickets.** Sussex 240 (Goodwin 87, Ambrose 60, Chapple 4-61) and 277 (Adams 61, Martin-Jenkins 55, Chapple 6-56); Lancashire 425 (Law 147, Byas 71) and 93-3. **Lancashire 20pts, Sussex 4**

## COUNTY CHAMPIONSHIP DIVISION ONE AT 25TH AUGUST

| Pos | Prv |              | P  | Points | W | D | L | Bat | Bwl | Ded  |
|-----|-----|--------------|----|--------|---|---|---|-----|-----|------|
| 1   | 1   | Surrey       | 13 | 190.75 | 8 | 3 | 2 | 44  | 39  | 0.25 |
| 2   | 2   | Kent         | 13 | 145.50 | 5 | 4 | 4 | 35  | 35  | 0.50 |
| 3   | 3   | Warwickshire | 12 | 143.00 | 5 | 5 | 2 | 29  | 34  | 0.00 |
| 4   | 4   | Sussex       | 13 | 131.00 | 3 | 6 | 4 | 33  | 38  | 0.00 |
| 5   | 7   | Lancashire   | 12 | 125.00 | 4 | 5 | 3 | 25  | 32  | 0.00 |
| 6   | 5   | Leicestershire | 12 | 121.00 | 3 | 5 | 4 | 32 | 34  | 1.00 |
| 7   | 6   | Hampshire ** | 13 | 110.00 | 2 | 8 | 3 | 25  | 37  | 8.00 |
| 8   | 8   | Somerset     | 12 | 106.00 | 1 | 7 | 4 | 33  | 33  | 0.00 |
| 9   | 9   | Yorkshire    | 12 | 91.50  | 1 | 5 | 6 | 26  | 34  | 0.50 |

**\*\* *Hampshire deducted 8pts for 'poor' pitch at Rose Bowl v Lancashire***

# 17 Almost There

The victory over Hampshire had taken Keith Medlycott's team within range of a third County Championship title in four years, with their next opponents, Warwickshire, the only realistic challengers left in the race. Trailing Surrey by a massive 47.75 points, the Bears' slim hopes of pulling off another "smash 'n' grab" act - one that would even surpass their heist at The AMP Oval - were based around the fact that they had a game in hand and the forthcoming home fixture against the leaders. This, theoretically, gave them the opportunity to close the gap by a maximum of twenty points if they won their match in hand, and another ten to seventeen if they could triumph in the Edgbaston game. Even then, Surrey would still hold a fair advantage, in addition to the comforting thought of another fixture against Hampshire, whose thrashing at The AMP Oval would still be fresh in their minds, and a final home game against Leicestershire. It was a situation that left even the most cautious of supporters feeling pretty confident.

The Championship could even be clinched in Birmingham, if Surrey were to win the match, so long as the leaders managed to come out on top by a margin of thirteen or more points. For example, an eighteen points to five triumph in this game would leave Warwickshire 60.75 points behind, with a maximum of sixty points available to them. It was certainly my personal wish that the title should be decided at Edgbaston, since Surrey were not participating in the following round of matches, leaving the strong possibility that the title could be clinched in a week when the team wasn't on the field of play to enjoy that magical 'moment' of success.

| FRIZZELL COUNTY CHAMPIONSHIP - MATCH FOURTEEN |
|---|

## WARWICKSHIRE versus SURREY
### at Edgbaston
### First Day - Tuesday 27th August
### Warwickshire 300-9

***The Teams And The Toss*** - *With Surrey resting their three England men - Alec Stewart, Mark Butcher and Alex Tudor - between the third and fourth Tests against India, their line-up shows just one change from the team that secured a comfortable victory over Hampshire in the last match, as the fit-again Rikki Clarke replaces the unfortunate Scott Newman. Warwickshire's situation is far more complicated, as their side shows no fewer than six changes of personnel following their rather lucky draw at Taunton. Unlike Surrey, they choose to include their England man, Ashley Giles, along with Jamie Troughton, Shaun Pollock, Tony Frost, Mohammad Sheikh and Melvyn Betts, all of whom missed the Somerset match. The men making way are Dominic Ostler, Neil Carter (both injured), Ian Clifford, Neil Smith (both dropped), Graham Wagg (playing for England Under-19's) and Shane Bond (temporary overseas replacement for Pollock). Despite all these changes, the Bears are fielding a side that is close to full strength, though they are missing the injured seam bowler Alan Richardson and wicketkeeper Keith Piper. When Michael Powell wins the toss he chooses to take first use of the wicket, a predictable decision in conditions that look to be set fair for batting.*

Although there is a slightly green tinge to the pitch as Martin Bicknell, from the city end, and Jimmy Ormond, from the pavilion end, square up to Michael Powell and Nick Knight, early indications are that it will play well, with the England left-hander taking three boundaries from Bicknell's third over, courtesy of two off-drives and a deflection to third man. While Knight certainly looks much the more confident of the Warwickshire openers - which is no surprise, given the outstanding season he is enjoying - Powell's early struggles encourage Adam Holloake to reinforce his close-catching cordon as the Surrey bowlers settle in to produce good opening spells. Bicknell is out of luck, however, as he induces a thick outside-edge from each batsman, at a cost of eight runs to his analysis, and, though Ormond's initial six-over burst ends with the Warwickshire captain finally locating the middle of his bat with an off-driven boundary, he can be well satisfied with his efforts as Saqlain takes over from him at the pavilion end.

Although the accuracy of the Bicknell-Saqlain combination subsequently slows the scoring, the Warwickshire fifty still arrives in reasonably good time - with a single to square leg by Powell in the sixteenth over - before the shackles loosen again as Bicknell's tenth over includes two half-volleys that the Bears' skipper drives for four through mid-on and mid-off. Despite the fact that Surrey's senior bowler manages to get a ball past the outside edge of Powell's bat before the over is out, it would appear that he has been asked to contribute one over too many at the end of a fine spell on a warm morning.

Having bowled just six overs from the pavilion end in his first spell, Ormond is the obvious replacement for Bicknell at the city end, though the switch of ends doesn't seem to suit him initially, as he consistently overpitches and is punished accordingly, with Powell finding the rope at backward point and cover, and Knight clipping to square leg for four in a comeback over that costs thirteen. Two consecutive expensive overs from the city end have enabled the score to race up to 79-0 from twenty-one overs, though relief is close at hand for Surrey.

After two consecutive maidens have restored some order for the visitors, Saqlain makes the initial breakthrough for his team, claiming Powell lbw when the Warwickshire skipper goes onto the back foot and hits across the line of an off-break. The former England 'A' batsman's innings of thirty-six has been a patchy affair, though it has enabled his team to get away to a decent start in a game they simply have to win if they are to keep their slender Championship hopes alive.

Powell's replacement in the middle, Mark Wagh, similarly fails to impress, though he proves incapable of playing his way through his difficulties, presenting a bat-pad catch to Hollioake at silly point off Saqlain after four unhappy overs at the crease. Having found just a little turn from the surface, the Pakistani spin king has brought Surrey right back into the match as Wagh departs for three at 87-2.

Fortunately for the home side, this wicket doesn't disturb Knight, as he pulls an Ormond no-ball to the midwicket boundary in the next over to complete an impressive half-century from 81 balls and then guides a Saqlain delivery towards third man for two to bring up the Warwickshire hundred shortly afterwards.

With Ormond having proved less effective during his second spell, Hollioake throws the ball to Rikki Clarke for the last over of the session from the city end, and the hosts go to lunch with their noses in front as Bell cracks a full-toss to the cover boundary.

*Lunch:- Warwickshire 110-2 (Knight 57\*, Bell 10\*) from 33 overs*

Hollioake returns to his trusty combination of Bicknell and Saqlain upon the resumption, and, with Knight kept very quiet by the off-spinner, it's Bell who is to the fore for Warwickshire, picking off three boundaries in four overs, much to the delight of a fair-sized Edgbaston crowd. These strokes aside, the young batsman is given a pretty torrid time by Bicknell, who beats him repeatedly outside the off stump and also finds the outside edge on a couple of occasions without the ball going to hand. With Saqlain twice defeating Knight at the other end, in retaliation for an on-driven boundary struck by the left-hander in his previous over, a wicket always looks possible, and when it comes, in the following over from Bicknell, it is courtesy of a quite sensational catch by Jon Batty. Groping forward once again to a fine outswinger, Bell gets a touch that results in the ball flying low towards first slip, though it looks unlikely to carry to the fielder. The Surrey keeper therefore throws himself away to his right, at full stretch, and takes the ball in the glove of his fully extended right arm, prompting exultant yelps from Bicknell and the slips to confirm that the ball has carried to Batty and that we have just witnessed a brilliant catch to dismiss Bell for thirty-four and peg Warwickshire back slightly to 146-3. As the visiting team and supporters celebrate, congratulations are not due exclusively to Batty, however, since this richly deserved wicket is Bicknell's 900th for Surrey in first-class cricket.

Unfortunately for the Championship leaders' senior bowler, he then completes the seventh over of his post-lunch spell on a rather less triumphant note, by conceding an extra-cover driven boundary to the new batsman, Jamie Troughton, and is immediately rested, perhaps a little surprisingly, in favour of Ormond.

While Troughton settles in rapidly by taking on-driven boundaries off both bowlers, and Knight whips Saqlain away through wide mid-on to notch the twelfth boundary of his innings, Ormond again takes a while to find his feet at the city end, before striking an important blow for the visitors in the third over of his new spell. Although Knight drives the first ball of the over to the rope at extra cover, the Surrey fast bowler strikes back immediately when his next delivery cuts back at the left-hander to force an inside edge that Batty pouches brilliantly after changing the direction of his dive at the very last moment. The 28-year-old wicketkeeper's second outstanding catch in the space of seven overs has seen off Knight for a nicely constructed seventy-four with the total at 179 and thereby kept the contest reasonably well balanced.

The tide turns in favour of the champions-elect during the course of the next seven overs, however, as a sustained period of high-quality bowling brings two further wickets, those of Shaun Pollock, to Ormond, and Dougie Brown, to Saqlain. Having been beaten twice in the big Surrey paceman's previous over, Pollock eventually snicks a defensive stroke at a good outswinger to Ali Brown at first slip, the fielder taking a neat catch to his left-hand side to make the score 185-5, then Warwickshire's Brown falls in a rather naïve fashion to Saqlain's wrong 'un with the total advanced by just eleven runs. The former England one-day international's attempt to disrupt the wily Pakistani's rhythm with a positive approach initially pays off as he sweeps to the backward square leg boundary but, in trying to drive down the ground later in the over, he only succeeds in getting a leading edge that spirals into the deep cover region, where Clarke takes a good catch over his shoulder.

The visitors are now holding the whip hand, though Troughton and his new partner, Tony Frost, take the home side safely past two-hundred with three boundaries in two overs from Ormond, whose two-wicket nine-over spell ends shortly afterwards, allowing Ian Salisbury to belatedly join his spin twin in the attack for the sixty-seventh over of the innings. Hereafter, the score edges forward by singles only, until Troughton pulls Salisbury for four in the penultimate over of a session that has, undoubtedly, been won by Surrey.

*Tea:- Warwickshire 223-6 (Troughton 47\*, Frost 11\*) from 72 overs*

Salisbury switches from the city end to the pavilion end after tea, as Bicknell returns to the attack and promptly concedes the three runs - from two strokes into the covers - that Troughton needs to complete a fine 67-ball fifty, which has included eight fours.

A series of cuts by the seventh-wicket pair subsequently sees the partnership extend to the half-century mark, before Troughton steers a Bicknell delivery to the third man boundary to raise the Warwickshire 250 in the seventy-ninth over. The emerging left-hander fails to make it through to the end of the over, however, as the experienced Surrey swing bowler defeats him with a slower inswinger of yorker length that wins an affirmative lbw verdict from umpire Mervyn Kitchen, thus ending Troughton's second impressive innings of the season against the Championship leaders and putting them back in the box seats.

As Troughton departs the scene, with sixty-one runs against his name, so Ashley Giles arrives at the crease and Saqlain reappears in the attack, taking over from Salisbury at the pavilion end. Although Frost sweeps fine for four in the off-spinner's first over, Saqlain is right on the mark thereafter, and the batsmen are extremely grateful for the nine-run over with which Bicknell ends another decent stint of six overs.

Predictably enough, Ormond is his replacement at the city end, and this new bowling combination quickly strangles the scoring rate before bringing two further Surrey success stories as the total crawls up to 279. Frost is the first to go, at 271, when he hits across the line of a ball delivered from round the wicket by Saqlain and is bowled for thirty-five - his sensible knock seemingly ended by a lapse of concentration and patience - then Giles, after a miserable fourteen-over occupation of the crease that has brought just one scoring stroke, has his bails trimmed by Ormond when prodding forward indeterminately.

These scalps put the visitors in an excellent position, though the last-wicket pair of Mo Sheikh and Melvyn Betts, both competent tail-enders, manage to resist long enough for Ormond to be replaced by Salisbury with six overs remaining for play.

Surrey are clearly not keen to start their reply tonight, though, since their spin twins concentrate on a negative leg-stump line for a few overs until the possibility of Ward and Batty having to bat has passed. The last few overs of the day see them back in attacking mode, however, as Betts edges Salisbury all along the ground for four to third man, before a single to Sheikh in the final over allows Warwickshire to reach three-hundred.

Although they haven't quite managed to bowl the opposition out, the visitors must be delighted with their first-day performance on what looks to be a very good pitch. The figures of Bicknell and Ormond don't truly reflect how well they have bowled, while Saqlain's immense value to the side has been shown by his ability to hold an end for most of the day in returning 43-13-88-4. The only area of concern is the workload these three have had to carry, while Salisbury has been a virtually unemployed spectator - it is to be hoped that all three will be well rested by the time the second innings comes around. The icing on the cake for the champions-in-waiting has been their very good fielding effort, led by Jon Batty, who has been faultless behind the stumps, in addition to holding those two excellent catches.

Close:- *Warwickshire 300-9 (Sheikh 9\*, Betts 14\*) from 104 overs*

## VIEWS FROM THE DRESSING ROOM

*I didn't think Jon Batty got the credit he deserved, in all the press reports, for two excellent catches (Bell and Knight) on the first day. Would you agree?*
**ALI BROWN** - He's a very good keeper and he gets a lot of praise from within the side, even if not from outside. He's getting better all the time, with both his batting and keeping, and his confidence is growing, too. I think Rikki's slip catch at Guildford was probably the best catch of the season, but the Bell catch was probably a close second.
**NADEEM SHAHID** - Yes, certainly. JB does a great job for us - not only is he a brilliant keeper, but he fills many batting roles for us. I am surprised that his name is never mentioned when it comes to the England squad, even though there are some good keepers about.

### Second Day - Wednesday 28th August
### Warwickshire 345; Surrey 319-3

Ian Salisbury and Saqlain Mushtaq are paired by Adam Hollioake at the start of day two in the hope of finishing off the Warwickshire first innings quickly. They meet stubborn resistance, however, and, with the off-spinner completely tying up Sheikh at the pavilion end, all the action takes place at the city end, where Salisbury versus Betts proves to be a particularly riveting confrontation. In the course of the first four overs from the Surrey leg-spinner, the former Durham seamer sweeps twice for four and forces through the off-side for a third boundary, while Salisbury almost bowls the Bears' number eleven with a googly, before inducing edged and miscued strokes which each earn Betts two very fortunate runs. Although Sheikh then edges a boundary of his own off the leg-spinner, it is Salisbury, rather than Saqlain, who is withdrawn from the attack in favour of Ormond for the eleventh over of the morning, a move that Betts welcomes as he forces the new bowler away to the rope at cover to take the last-wicket partnership up to fifty, much to the home supporters' delight. The stand has endured for 133 balls at this point and Betts has contributed thirty-six of the runs.

With his spinners having failed to polish off the innings, Hollioake then decides to take the new ball and recall Martin Bicknell in place of Saqlain. Since the Bears are closing in on 350, and therefore a fourth batting point, there is a serious need to strike quickly if Surrey wish to sew up the title during this match, as every extra point that Warwickshire gain is one more that the champions-elect will need to get.

The hosts move seven runs nearer to their bonus point target in the first over with the new ball, four of these runs coming when Betts miscues a pull off Ormond over mid-on, though the sturdy Surrey pace bowler gains rapid revenge in the next over. Although the Warwickshire swing bowler takes his score to within three runs of a very valuable half-century by clipping Ormond's first ball over backward square leg for four, he falls to the next delivery, with Warwickshire still five short of the 350 mark, when Saqlain takes a beautifully-judged catch from a top-edged hook after making good ground around the long-leg boundary. Ormond therefore joins his off-spinning team-mate in having taken four wickets in the innings and, as the visitors leave the field, they now know what they have to do if they are to secure the Championship title with a win here at Edgbaston.

Since Warwickshire have gained three batting points, their maximum possible haul of points from a defeat is now six, leaving Surrey to get nineteen from their win to leave them mathematically certain of becoming champions. With three bowling points in the bag and the win worth twelve, the champions-elect therefore have to earn four batting points by scoring over 350 in their forthcoming first innings. On such a good pitch, that looks a fair bet, but can they secure a large enough lead to be able to force the victory?

Shaun Pollock and Melvyn Betts open the bowling at the start of Surrey's reply, and it is soon obvious that little has changed since the recent encounter at The AMP Oval... except the colour of Betts' hair. While the South African is right on the spot from ball one, the former England 'A' man, sporting a shocking ginger rinse that had been hidden under his helmet while he was batting, is all over the place. As well as conceding a square-driven boundary to Batty during his opening over, Betts also oversteps the crease twice, which doesn't surprise anyone, since he had the same problem at The AMP Oval and is just fresh from a second team game during which he bowled fourteen no-balls in seventeen overs.

It would seem that things can't get much worse for Betts, but they do, as Ward twice finds the rope at midwicket during a second over of deliveries fired exclusively down the leg-side, despite the placement of a six-three off-side field. With his new red hair, the 27-year-old seamer may now look a little more like Pollock, but he definitely isn't bowling anything like him, and there is little improvement in his third over as another no-ball combines with a Batty square cut for four to further damage bowling figures that read 3-0-22-0 as Surrey maintain their positive start.

Poor Michael Powell must already be wondering what he can do about the situation when Pollock then adds to his problems by suddenly leaking on-driven and cover-driven boundaries to Ward in his fourth over, though the South African skipper does also induce an edge that drops short of third slip, to his credit.

After much head-scratching, Powell decides to persevere with Betts and, remarkably enough, the former Durham man breaks the opening partnership with the third ball of his fourth over, surprising everyone, including Batty, with a fine delivery that lifts and leaves the bat to produce a defensive edge to Pollock at first slip with the score on thirty-two. Since this is just about the first time that Betts has located anything like a good line and length, the Surrey keeper can consider himself very unlucky as he departs with eight runs to his name.

As Mark Ramprakash appears at the crease, so Pollock is rested, with Mo Sheikh the new bowler at the pavilion end. The Surrey number three is quickly away, though in unconvincing style, with a top-edged hook over the slips, but since it comes from another Betts' no-ball it's possible that the batsman has heard the umpire's call.

This turns out to be the 'bottle red' bowler's last over of a typically erratic spell, with Pollock switching ends to form an accurate attack with the steady Sheikh. Consequently, four of the next five overs are maidens, though the home side's genuine redhead is guilty of not making the batsmen play at very many deliveries. After rather unimpressive overs, he retires from the attack again and takes his place at slip as Ramprakash pulls successive balls from Sheikh to the midwicket boundary, thereby taking the Surrey total to fifty in the seventeenth over.

Although Ashley Giles takes Pollock's place at the city end for an exploratory pre-lunch over, he fails to make any immediate impact, being milked for a few easy singles as the score advances to sixty by the break.

*Lunch:- Surrey 60-1 (Ward 22\*, Ramprakash 19\*) from 19 overs*

The introduction of Dougie Brown after the break allows Giles to switch to the pavilion end, though nothing disturbs the progress of Messrs Ramprakash and Ward in the opening overs as the former cuts Brown over backward point for four, and the latter increases his score by eight, with an on-driven boundary, a leg-glance and a clip through square leg at Giles' expense. By finding the rope at extra cover and fine leg in Brown's third over, Ward subsequently increases the value of the second-wicket partnership to fifty, before Ramprakash reaches a personal milestone in the following over, when his forcing stroke for two runs to deep point off Giles completes his thousand runs in the 2002 Championship campaign. Warwickshire are certainly becoming sick of the sight of him this season and he looks capable of adding another big score to the double-century he had scored at The AMP Oval as he takes consecutive fours from the England left-arm spinner's next over with a paddle sweep and a well-timed back-foot forcing stroke through backward point.

As the ineffective Giles gives way to Sheikh, and the Surrey total slips into three figures on a very warm afternoon, Warwickshire are becoming desperate for a breakthrough, but, with the pitch offering nothing to the bowlers except for a degree of inconsistent bounce, the visiting batsmen plough on relentlessly towards their half-centuries. Ward gets there first, from 95 balls, when he is opened up by a good Brown delivery that he edges to the third man boundary, then Ramprakash emulates his partner's feat in the Scotsman's next over by crashing his eighty-ninth delivery to the rope at backward point with a square drive. By steering Brown's next ball to the third man boundary and then dispatching Sheikh for the tenth and eleventh fours of his innings to raise the hundred partnership an over later, Ramprakash then prompts a double bowling change, forcing Powell to pair his two current Test men, Pollock and Giles.

Although Ward instantly drives both bowlers to the rope at long-on, they come back well to cause a few flutters in the Surrey camp - the South African achieves the rare feat of getting a ball past Ramprakash's bat, before inducing an edgy steer to third man from Ward, while the England spinner finds the former Middlesex batsman's edge, only to see the ball run away to the third man boundary for the four that raises the visitors' 150.

These prove to be isolated moments of hope for Warwickshire, however, and it isn't long before the Bears have sore heads again as Ward clips Pollock to the midwicket boundary and then sweeps Giles fine for four in the following over. Having switched to an over-the-wicket approach when bowling to the right-handed Ramprakash, the left-arm spinner is also called for a leg-side wide as the home team's frustration grows, and his personal anguish shows no sign of abating when the Surrey number three drives him for a glorious straight six an over later.

At this point, since Pollock has come to the end of another five-over spell, Powell turns back to Betts in a move that looks to be fraught with danger for the hosts. To no-one's great surprise, the former England 'A' seamer is immediately driven for three by Ward to complete the second-wicket pair's 150 partnership, but, thereafter, supported by tidy ground fielding and defensive fields, he actually manages to keep a tight grip on the batsmen, conceding just eight runs in five overs up to tea. Unfortunately for Warwickshire, Betts' good work is quickly undone, as Mark Wagh, replacing Giles at the pavilion end, finds Ramprakash in punishing mood - the occasional off-spinner concedes two mighty sixes and a four to strokes over and through wide long-on in the course of three overs just before the break.

*Tea:- Surrey 208-1 (Ward 86\*, Ramprakash 90\*) from 55 overs*

The Surrey batsmen continue to prosper as Dougie Brown and Mo Sheikh take up the attack for Warwickshire at the start of the day's final session. With Ramprakash driving Brown to the rope at extra cover in the first over and Ward picking up four runs from a lovely straight drive off Sheikh in the second, it continues to look like men against boys rather than men against Bears out in the middle.

While Sheikh is again steady without looking threatening, Brown's post-tea tactics are clear and complementary, as he continually tests out the middle of the pitch in an attempt to unsettle two players who are within sight of a century. The scoring rate drops back a little, as a result, with the familiar pattern of progression by singles looking to be the chosen route to three figures for the Surrey pair.

Although Ramprakash has looked likely to beat his partner to the mark since his pre-tea assault on Wagh, the ninth over of the session, bowled by Brown, proves decisive for both men, in very different ways. The first ball of the former England one-day international's over sees Ward pulling another short delivery to deep midwicket for his sixteenth boundary, thereby taking him through to an excellent century from 198 balls, then, after the left-handed opener takes a single from the next ball, Ramprakash misses an attempted push to leg with his score on ninety-nine and sees the dreaded finger of umpire Kitchen being raised in response to a confident Warwickshire appeal for lbw. Incredibly, it's the fourth time in the Championship campaign that a Surrey batsman has fallen short of a ton by just a single run - Stewart, Batty and Newman being the others - and one has to feel desperately sorry for Ramprakash as he leaves the field to a well-deserved ovation for a top-class innings with the score now 236-2. His 204-run partnership with Ward has put his team well on top, however, and greatly improved the chances of the Championship title being sewn up within the next couple of days.

Having made one breakthrough, the Bears then almost make another when Ward has an amazing escape as he pops a checked drive off Sheikh just over the head of short midwicket yet just short of mid-on with miraculous precision. Fortunately for the hosts, the Surrey opener doesn't profit too much from this lucky break, adding a pulled four off Brown to his score before the Stirling-born all-rounder's replacement, Shaun Pollock, strikes another blow for Warwickshire.

The South African's return starts promisingly for the Championship leaders as Ward drives the opening delivery to the extra-cover boundary, taking the total beyond 250, but it only takes Pollock two balls to hit back with a delivery that bounces a little more than the Surrey opener expects and results in a top-edged cut to Nick Knight at slip. Ward's superb 114 has contained eighteen fours and is rightly acknowledged by the Edgbaston crowd as he returns to the pavilion.

Looking at the bigger picture, the champions-elect have now secured two batting points, with the other two they are seeking likely to be pocketed sometime tomorrow, barring a collapse of dramatic proportions. Then it will be all about trying to complete the necessary victory.

Warwickshire certainly appear to have given up all hope of winning the game to close the gap on the league leaders, even at this relatively early stage, since Pollock operates with just one slip, despite the fact that there are two new batsmen at the wicket. The latest arrival, Ali Brown, gets away well with an on-drive for three before the over is out, though this is nothing compared to the punishment meted out by Nadeem Shahid to Pollock in the Proteas' skipper's next over. Although there might be a shade of good fortune about an edge-cum-steer to the third man boundary at the start of the over, there is no doubting the quality of the clip through midwicket or the cover drive that add further fours to Shahid's score. Buoyed by these successes against one of the world's finest bowlers, the former Essex batsman continues to prosper, while Brown goes through something of a shaky patch as both Sheikh's determined and restrictive spell of eleven overs and Pollock's four-over burst come to an end.

The return of Betts and Giles certainly seems to be appreciated by both batsmen, especially since the seamer looks set to contribute another of his less impressive spells as he concedes fifteen runs from his second over, including the inevitable no-ball, two fours to Shahid and one to Brown. The three-hundred - and, with it, a third batting point - consequently arrives at speed in the following over, and a square-cut boundary by Brown off Giles two overs later completes a fifty partnership that has ensured the magnificent Ward-Ramprakash partnership will not be wasted. Although there are only four overs left for play at this point, that is still time enough for the hapless Betts to surrender a square-cut four to Shahid and a cover-driven three to Brown before stumps are drawn.

As the batsmen take their leave, Surrey are in a powerful position, with the Championship title now almost secured, even if Warwickshire can somehow manage to find a way of fighting back to win this match. The most likely result is looking to be a Surrey win, though, since the pitch has shown increasing signs of wear and variable bounce during the day, Shahid having been struck a nasty blow on the hand by a 'popping' delivery from Sheikh during this final session and several balls having kept rather low.

*Close:- Surrey 319-3 (Shahid 43\*, Brown 25\*) from 87 overs*

### Third Day - Thursday 29th August

### Warwickshire 345 and 154-3; Surrey 544

With a sprinkling of rain having fallen during the night, and the weather cool and cloudy at the start of day three of the match, the Surrey faithful wonder whether Warwickshire might have the conditions to help them launch a fightback in some shape or form, especially since there is a new ball available to them after just three overs.

Melvyn Betts and Mo Sheikh get proceedings under way and, apart from when Ali Brown edges the latter for two in the second over, there are no real early alarms, with Nadeem Shahid driving Betts wide of mid-on for the first boundary of the day, and the ninth of his innings, in the next over, before completing a fine 82-ball half-century a couple of balls later with a single to the cover sweeper that is already in place.

Predictably, the new ball is taken straight away, with Sheikh being allowed to use it for one over before Shaun Pollock takes over at the city end to join forces with Betts. The former Durham paceman is, sad to say, way off target again and concedes three boundaries to Shahid and one to Brown in three unimpressive overs before giving way to the much more reliable Sheikh. This flurry of fours off Betts brings a number of significant landmarks, as Surrey take the lead; the hundred partnership for the fourth wicket arrives; and, most importantly, the champions-elect pass 350, thereby claiming the all-important bonus point that will seal Championship success here at Edgbaston if the visitors can now go on to win the match. The sight of several balls misbehaving this morning has increased hopes that this might well be possible - indeed, the Shahid boundary that has clinched the fourth batting point has resulted from the batsman having to jab down late on a shooter, sending the ball flying off to the rope at fine leg.

The Surrey duo don't let these inconsistencies of bounce worry them too much, however, as they average a boundary an over in seeing off a below-par Pollock and a less frugal than usual Sheikh, the final four conceded by the Birmingham-born seamer taking Brown through to a thousand Championship runs for the season at the same time as moving him to within one run of a half-century in this innings.

His fifty - rather a slow one by his very high standards, having taken 103 balls - arrives in Dougie Brown's opening over of the day, though he only lasts a few more overs before he advances on the other new bowler, Ashley Giles, and is beaten on the outside edge to be comfortably stumped by Tony Frost for fifty-seven, with the total on 397.

Any sense of relief that Warwickshire might be feeling at having rid themselves of the potentially explosive Brown soon evaporates, however, as Adam Hollioake joins Shahid to launch a ferocious attack on the bowling.

The Surrey captain makes his intentions known right from the start as he takes three fours off Brown during his first full over at the crease, courtesy of two thumping extra-cover drives and a rather less impressive Chinese cut, before he and his partner-in-crime plunder sixteen runs from the next over bowled by Giles, during which two reverse-swept boundaries by Shahid sandwich a big six over extra cover by Hollioake.

Despite the fact that twenty-eight runs have come from the last two overs, Powell retains the services of Brown and Giles, but, despite their best efforts, the experienced Warwickshire pair are unable to stop the batsmen picking off a boundary in each of the next six overs, with three of these hits being sixes - Hollioake twice drives Giles over long-on, while Shahid completes an excellent 144-ball century in the grand manner, with a mighty pull over the midwicket boundary off Betts, who has only just returned to the attack at the pavilion end. The two batsmen embrace in mid-pitch, not only to celebrate Shahid's top knock, which has included nineteen fours and that century-clinching six, but also a fifty partnership that has arrived in just 37 balls. There is nothing for Warwickshire to celebrate, however, since Surrey have just steamed past 450, and both Betts and Giles have completed their personal bowling centuries in consecutive overs.

With the Bears' attack having been laid bare during this onslaught, they are grateful for succour on two fronts at this point, firstly when Betts manages to produce a rare boundary-free over, and then when Giles breaks the partnership with the total at 474. Although the left-arm spinner has been driven and cut for fours earlier in the over, he enjoys a small degree of vengeance when Shahid is taken at slip by Pollock from a delivery that, encouragingly for Surrey, turns, albeit out of the rough from an over-the-wicket line of 'attack'.

As Shahid soaks up a well-deserved round of applause on his return to the pavilion, lunch is not too far away, though there is still time for more thrills and spills at the end of what has certainly been an action-packed session. While the new batsman, Rikki Clarke, is instantly away with two fours, the first being a pull off Betts and the second a sweep at Giles' expense, his captain launches the England spinner high over long-off for the fourth six of his innings to complete a wondrous 39-ball fifty, which has also included five fours. It has been a quite stunning effort, and it has provided valuable impetus to Surrey as they strive to build a huge lead, while also leaving themselves sufficient time to bowl Warwickshire out and, consequently, clinch the Championship crown.

With lunch imminent, Betts' misery continues as he oversteps the crease on three occasions to take Surrey's first innings total beyond five-hundred for the third successive Championship match, following totals of 540 against Leicestershire and 576 versus Hampshire, while Giles enjoys further success as Clarke is stumped, in identical fashion to Brown before him, from the second ball of the session's final over.

*Lunch:- Surrey 502-6 (Hollioake 57\*) from 121.2 overs*

Surrey's lunchtime total is unchanged when Giles strikes again with the final delivery of his incomplete over, though Martin Bicknell looks unlucky to have been given out for a fourth-ball duck - caught off bat and pad by Dougie Brown at silly point - by umpire Kitchen.

Spurred on by this success, Brown and Giles, Powell's post-lunch picks, maintain commendable control, with Hollioake managing just a couple of boundaries - a glance off Brown and a cut at Giles' expense - before he loses another partner when Warwickshire's Scottish all-rounder wins his second lbw decision of the innings as Ian Salisbury aims across the line of a delivery of full length.

At 525-8, Surrey's prospects of scoring 600-plus have receded quite dramatically, and the Bears' bowlers continue to do a good job as they restrict Hollioake to singles, thanks largely to deep-set fields. Although the Surrey skipper does eventually manage to get going again, with a hook off Brown that sails over the head of the fielder posted on the deep midwicket boundary, the end of his team's innings comes shortly afterwards when Warwickshire's former England one-day international captures the last two wickets in two balls - Saqlain runs down the wicket to the final ball of the 32-year-old all-rounder's twenty-eighth over and skies a miscued slog to extra cover, where Betts takes a good catch after running round from mid-off, then Ormond checks a drive at the first ball of Brown's following over and sees the bowler pull off a fine one-handed return catch leaping high to his left.

This rare, though pretty disappointing, disintegration of the Surrey tail leaves the unfortunate Hollioake stranded on eighty-two and cuts short the innings at 544, giving the Championship leaders a 199-run advantage with 148 overs left to play in the match. These figures sound vaguely familiar, and a check of the details of the home fixture between these counties reveals why. At The AMP Oval, the Warwickshire second innings started at 3pm on the third day - as it will do here - with 148 overs left for play and the Bears facing a first-innings deficit of 182. Although Surrey batted first in that match, as opposed to second here, the parallels between the two games are quite amazing. The champions-elect will, however, be hoping that we get a different result this time, though the discovery we have just made serves notice to the Surrey faithful at the ground that the visitors certainly don't yet have this game sewn up.

A further reminder of this comes as the Warwickshire openers set off at a blistering pace, with Powell glancing and off-driving fours in Bicknell's opening over, and Wagh locating the rope no fewer than three times as soon as Ormond steps up to the crease, with a glance, a square cut and a back-foot force through wide mid-on. Twenty runs from two overs - maybe the hosts still think they can amass a big total, declare and then bowl Surrey out in the remainder of the game?

Almost inevitably, the visiting bowlers regain control immediately, though they rarely threaten, and both appear to be suffering from their first-day exertions as another burst of three fours brings Ormond's opening spell to a halt in favour of Saqlain. With the ball having rarely beaten the bat in the first eleven overs, the only encouragement for Surrey has come from a Bicknell delivery to Powell that has shot through low in the seventh over.

The Bicknell-Saqlain combination does at least continue to slow the run-rate for the visitors, though the Warwickshire opening pair cruise comfortably enough to a fifty partnership before Adam Hollioake returns Ormond to the attack in place of Bicknell as tea approaches.

Hopes that this change might bring a wicket are quickly dashed, though, as a sudden four-boundary blast sees Powell finding the rope twice at the off-spinner's expense and Wagh taking two sweetly-driven fours off Ormond as the hosts reach the break in a surprisingly comfortable position, with both batsmen looking in fine touch.

*Tea:- Warwickshire 83-0 (Powell 36\*, Wagh 36\*) from 20 overs*

As far as the bowling is concerned, there's no change in personnel after tea, though Saqlain and Ormond come up with much-improved spells that produce both pressure and wickets.

The first breakthrough comes quickly, too, with Wagh departing to the third ball of the second over, when he plays back to Saqlain and is beaten by an off-break that traps him right in front of his stumps. Umpire Barrie Leadbeater has no trouble in ruling the Warwickshire opener out for thirty-nine, much to Surrey's delight.

This early wicket, with the total having advanced by just three runs, is exactly what the Championship leaders had needed and it certainly seems to lift Ormond as he suddenly begins to beat the bat again, and almost defeats the new batsman, Ian Bell, with a fine yorker. Although the Warwickshire hundred eventually arrives in the twenty-eighth over, the whole tempo of the game has changed and, in sharp contrast to the pre-tea session, there isn't a single boundary stroke in sight.

Surrey need to capitalise on this period of supremacy, however, and they do so in style by making two further breakthroughs in the space of four deliveries during the thirty-first and thirty-second overs. The wicket that Ormond's fine post-tea spell demands comes when Bell edges a good delivery to Jon Batty with the total having crept up to 105, then Saqlain strikes with the second ball of the following over when Powell nicks an off-break onto his pad in attempting to drive and sees the ball dolly up to Nadeem Shahid at short leg.

This third success, with the total unchanged and Warwickshire still ninety-four runs in arrears, brings Nick Knight to the crease with Mark Wagh as his runner. Knight apparently has a hip injury, which explains why he had not been on the field for a fair part of the Surrey innings, and why the man now running for him had taken his place at the top of the order.

With the England left-hander clearly inconvenienced by his injury - even though he does manage to dispatch a rare Saqlain full-toss to the boundary wide of mid-on soon after his arrival - and his team in desperate trouble, everyone appreciates that the capture of another couple of wickets now could leave Surrey on the brink of claiming the title by the end of the day. The bowlers therefore step up their efforts, with Saqlain forcing the normally very aggressive Troughton to play out four successive maidens, while Ormond finishes a good stint of nine overs before handing over to Bicknell at the pavilion end. Surrey's senior bowler looks rather tired and surprisingly innocuous during a short three-over spell, however, with Knight twice forcing deliveries away to the rope at extra cover, and it is no great surprise when Ian Salisbury receives a rather belated call-up to bowl the forty-fifth over.

Although the pitch has played fewer tricks than expected since tea, there is a little slow turn available to the spinners and, with fielders around the bat, they certainly appear to represent Surrey's most potent bowling combination as we enter the last eight overs of the day. Consequently, Knight retreats almost completely into his shell and ventures next to nothing, though Troughton drives each bowler for an off-side four and then, in the third-to-last over, boldly launches Saqlain over mid-on for a boundary that takes the total up to 150.

For reasons unknown, possibly a minor injury, the Pakistani spin king departs from the scene at the end of the over, leaving Ormond to bowl the last over of the day from the city end in his secondary role as an off-spinner. Although his first delivery, from round the wicket to the left-handed Troughton, comes perilously close to hitting the off stump as the batsman shoulders arms, the rising Warwickshire star sweeps the next ball to the fine leg boundary and sees out the rest of the over in comfort to keep his team very much alive and kicking at the end of day three. Having held the Surrey bowlers at bay for the last twenty overs of the session, and looked largely untroubled during that time, Troughton and Knight leave the field to a well-deserved ovation, though the Championship leaders still look well placed to complete a hugely significant victory tomorrow.

Close:- Warwickshire 154-3 (Troughton 30*, Knight 14*) from 52 overs

| VIEW FROM THE DRESSING ROOM |
|---|

*How did this century rate, compared to your ton against Sussex?*
**NADEEM SHAHID** - The Sussex ton will always be special to me, due to the emotions involved. I did play well here, though, and I was quite pleased with this hundred as my position in the team was perhaps under threat.

### Fourth Day - Friday 30th August
### Warwickshire 345 and 404-9dec; Surrey 544
### Match Drawn
### Warwickshire 9pts, Surrey 12

As the last day commences, the similarities between this game and the match at The AMP Oval are still striking, with Warwickshire, three wickets down in both cases, starting forty-five runs in arrears here, as against seventeen runs in debit in last month's contest. If this turns out to be anything like as exciting as the last day of the Oval match then we are in for a great day, though it will be interesting to see how Surrey play it if they do end up having to chase a total against the clock later this afternoon. On one hand, the visitors will be desperate to complete the victory to tie up the Championship title, yet, on the other hand, a victory for Warwickshire would keep the Bears in contention as outsiders to snatch the crown away from the long-time leaders in the closing days of the campaign.

Play gets under way on time, despite overnight rain and a sprinkling of drizzle at around 10.15am, though conditions are cool and very grey as Warwickshire start brightly in Martin Bicknell's first over. Nick Knight's clip through midwicket instantly completes a fifty partnership for the fourth wicket, before his partner, Jamie Troughton, unleashes a cover-driven boundary later in the over.

And then... nothing. The next six overs from Bicknell and Saqlain Mushtaq yield just one run - a bye - as the Bears suggest that they harbour no ambitions of trying to get far enough ahead to set a target and try to win the match. It appears that a draw, and the enhancement of their prospects of claiming runners-up spot, will suit the home side, though Surrey's ambitions are loftier, given their desire to tie up the title today.

Even though a few runs start to flow after this barren spell, the ball continues to dominate the bat, and it is only when Jimmy Ormond replaces Bicknell at the pavilion end for the eleventh over of the morning that we see the second boundary of the day when Troughton pulls a short delivery away wide of mid-on. Since the game is still in a state of stalemate, Ormond attempts to liven up proceedings with a few fiery overs, liberally sprinkled with bouncers, with the field set accordingly for any mishooks or fend-offs. This certainly has an effect, as Troughton hooks for six to complete his second impressive half-century of the match, from 110 balls, and then the bowler gets no-balled for having three men behind square on the leg-side to bring the scores level in the match.

With the two Warwickshire left-handers still in control after nineteen overs, and the pitch behaving surprisingly well, Adam Hollioake finally turns to Ian Salisbury, giving him an opportunity at the city end in place of Saqlain, while Ormond turns off-spinner for a couple of fairly mediocre overs that see Troughton twice driving to the rope at extra cover and raising the century partnership in the process.

At this point it is beginning to look as if the game is going to start drifting into dreariness but, with half-an-hour to go until lunch, Salisbury finally makes the breakthrough for his side, with the total on 214 and the Warwickshire lead still only fifteen. His victim is Troughton, who, having miscued a pull into space at deep midwicket earlier in the over, plays back to a big leg-break and falls lbw, much to the relief and pleasure of the whole Surrey team. As the highly promising young batsman returns to the pavilion having scored sixty-three, the public address announcer reveals that Troughton has completed a thousand first-class runs for the season during his innings - a fine effort in his first full campaign - and the champions-in-waiting know that another wicket before lunch will put them back in business.

With Saqlain inevitably returning to the attack in place of Ormond, the visitors pile on the pressure again and, though Salisbury looks the man more likely to strike again for Surrey, it's his spin twin who delights the visiting fans by snaring Shaun Pollock - well taken by Shahid plunging forward from short leg - with the second ball of the session's final over. The South African doesn't look too convinced that the ball has hit anything apart from his pad, but umpire Kitchen is, and the champions-elect therefore head off to lunch in high spirits with Warwickshire effectively 26-5, and sixty-five overs still to play today. Knight's brave effort has seen him advance his score from fourteen to forty-one by the interval, and he is clearly going to be an important figure this afternoon if Surrey are to clinch their third Championship title in four years.

*Lunch:- Warwickshire 225-5 (Knight 41\*) from 82.2 overs*

The Surrey spin twins continue in tandem upon the resumption, and neither Knight, nor his new partner, Dougie Brown, attempt very much in the early stages of the session, with just nine runs accruing from the opening five overs.

Brown seems to reassess his tactics, however, following two consecutive traumatic overs, during which he gloves Saqlain over the head of slip for two, edges Salisbury wide of the same fielder for another two, and then almost plays on a few balls later. Perhaps deciding that attack is the best form of defence in the circumstances, he suddenly takes successive boundaries off the Surrey leg-spinner with a forcing stroke through extra cover and a pull wide of mid-on, thereby taking the total past 250, and then driving the first ball of the next over from Saqlain over wide mid-on for a third four. This bold approach fails to shake the Pakistani spinner, however, as the very next ball, a perfectly pitched wrong 'un, takes the outside edge of Brown's defensive bat to provide Jon Batty with a catch, Saqlain with his fiftieth first-class wicket of the season, and the visitors with renewed hopes of forcing a much-desired victory.

A Warwickshire score of 257-6 then very nearly becomes 257-7 when the new batsman, Tony Frost, edges just short of slip later in Saqlain's successful over as a host of predatory fielders cluster around the bat. Knight looks increasingly likely to hold the key to the match, and the feeling that the England man is probably playing the most dogged innings of his career is soon borne out by the stats on the main Edgbaston scoreboard when he completes his half-century by forcing Saqlain away to deep cover for a single - 194 balls, 236 minutes, 4 fours. This is a hugely valuable innings for his team, however, and he receives equally determined support from Frost as the overs tick by.

Although Knight accelerates after passing fifty, courtesy of a few back-foot boundaries off Salisbury, his partner remains stuck on nought after a dozen overs at the crease, and his determined defiance is slowly eroding the Championship leaders' prospects of victory.

Frost's chance to get off the mark appears to arrive shortly afterwards, however, when Saqlain leaves the field after his forty-third over of the innings, with his place in the attack taken by Nadeem Shahid. The former Essex man's efforts with the ball prove highly respectable, however - he has an lbw appeal against Frost turned down at one point - prompting Hollioake to retain the part-time leg-spinner's services even though Saqlain's absence turns out to be only temporary.

Nothing seems to break the batsmen's resolve, however, and the visitors' victory hopes are already starting to fade when Frost finally scores his first runs, from his fifty-third ball, by edging Shahid, on the bounce, past slip for two runs.

Although Salisbury comes desperately close to making the all-important breakthrough shortly afterwards, when Knight glances the ball into and out of the hands of Hollioake at leg slip, with the batsman's score on eighty-three and the Warwickshire lead standing at ninety-eight, the weather on a blustery day is now starting to close in. Could this miss prove to be crucial to the outcome of this match? It's possible, though the visitors are already tight for time.

The Surrey skipper immediately attempts to atone for his error, in any case, by bringing himself on to bowl, though he only succeeds in yielding a boundary to Frost with a full-toss, and an early tea is taken as soon as the over is complete, at 3.30pm, since rain is now falling.

Given an improvement in the weather, there will be thirty-five overs to bowl in the final session, though the visitors will need to pick up wickets pretty quickly, with the Bears already 102 runs ahead. As the mightily determined seventh-wicket pair head off for a hard-earned tea, their partnership has managed to keep Surrey at bay for twenty precious overs, even though it has only brought the addition of forty-four runs.

*Tea:- Warwickshire 301-6 (Knight 83\*, Frost 7\*) from 113 overs*

Fortunately, the rain relents rapidly, allowing a prompt restart, with Surrey immediately taking the new ball that has been due to them for some twenty-three overs.

The feeling that this really is a last throw of the dice, and not an especially optimistic one at that, is confirmed by the fact that Jimmy Ormond, who has already bowled fifty-four overs in the match, isn't given the ball. In his place, Rikki Clarke, who has bowled just one, delivers the first over and gets away to a terrible start, conceding a no-ball; a batch of six wides that completes the Knight-Frost fifty partnership; and a six, slashed away over backward point by the Warwickshire keeper. Surrey's young all-rounder isn't alone in being on the receiving end of some rough treatment, though, as Knight takes three fours from Bicknell's second post-tea over, with and on-drive, a cut and a lofted off-drive, as the visitors' dream of clinching the title here at Edgbaston fades more rapidly than anyone could have imagined.

Frustratingly, Frost falls to the third ball of the next over from Clarke, when he gloves a short delivery through to Batty, but with Warwickshire 131 ahead, at 330-7, and only thirty overs left to play, everyone knows that only a phenomenal tail-end collapse can now revive Surrey's hopes of glory today. Frost has certainly played a very important role in defying the champions-in-waiting, and the true value of his 86-ball innings of thirteen to Warwickshire will surely go unappreciated in years to come when people glance at the scorecard.

The man whose efforts will stand out on the card is, of course, Nick Knight, especially once he completes a brave and brilliant hundred in the over following his partner's dismissal when he pushes the ball back past Bicknell - in the air, but safely so - to pick up the two runs he requires. As the small crowd rises to acknowledge the former Essex left-hander's achievement, the statistics of his innings flash up on the hugely impressive scoreboard, revealing that he has batted for 325 minutes, and in that time he has faced 260 balls and hit eleven fours.

With the game looking increasingly doomed to a draw by the minute, Frost's replacement, Ashley Giles, enjoys himself at Clarke's expense with four boundaries in two overs as the score hurtles past the 350 mark, before the Surrey all-rounder takes revenge by having the England spinner caught by Ormond at mid-on. It's all purely academic now, anyway, with the main bowlers having been on and off the field throughout the early stages of the session - no doubt all suffering from exhaustion! - and Neil Walker, the physio, spending plenty of time in the field.

Everyone seems pretty relaxed, though, in the knowledge that the Championship has been all but mathematically secured, and the inevitable high jinks soon begin with Nadeem Shahid bowling a couple of overs of medium pace - and having Mo Sheikh missed at square leg by Ian Ward along the way - and Ali Brown sending down a few overs of his off-breaks.

The amusement factor is increased when, amidst all the comings and goings, Surrey try to fool the umpires by having twelve players on the field at one stage, but a seemingly unimpressed Merv Kitchen makes a point of counting the fielders very deliberately and sends Ed Giddins off. Then, to cap it all, Ward is called up to bowl and, having conceded an off-driven four to Knight straight away, claims his maiden County Championship wicket when he induces the rock on whom Surrey have faltered to drag his fourth ball onto his stumps. If only someone could have got Knight to do that about a two hours ago!

The England one-day international opener receives a well-deserved ovation as he departs with his runner at the end of an outstanding innings for his team and then, just two overs later, at 5.20pm, Michael Powell declares, thus putting everyone out of their misery. It's the first draw in a fixture between these two counties since 1992, so I suppose we shouldn't complain! Especially as it has all but ensured that Surrey are the 2002 county champions.

**Warwickshire 345 and 404-9dec; Surrey 544**
**Match Drawn. Warwickshire 9pts, Surrey 12**

## VIEWS FROM THE DRESSING ROOM

*At lunch on the final day, Warwickshire were effectively 26-5, so I guess we still had high hopes at that point of clinching the victory and the Championship here at Edgbaston?*
**ALI BROWN** - We knew that if we could grab another two or three quick wickets we were in with a chance, but it was a very good batting wicket and it was never going to be a cakewalk to take those final five wickets.
**NADEEM SHAHID** - Definitely, we all thought it was just a matter of time.

*At what stage did we realise that the champagne would be staying on ice?*
**IAN SALISBURY** - I had Nick Knight dropped at leg slip just before tea, and if that had been caught then I would have backed us to bowl them out. We battled so hard, though, and I've never been so tired at the end of the game as I was there. It was intense cricket and a lot of effort went into those four days because we badly wanted to win that game so we could clinch the Championship there and then.
**ALI BROWN** - When I started bowling!

*Were the bowlers ultimately too tired to complete the job, following their excellent efforts in the first innings?*
**NADEEM SHAHID** - Yes, perhaps that was the case. It was the kind of wicket where you couldn't blast people out and it wasn't taking much spin either... until I came on to bowl!

*I don't think I'd ever seen Nick Knight bat so well. What was your view, and do you think he has been unfairly labelled as a limited-overs specialist at international level?*
**ALI BROWN** - He looked in very good form, yes, and his stats for the year certainly indicate that he would have been very happy with his technique. His technique seems to change from time to time, but I think he probably opens the face a little bit too much for Test cricket. But he's a very good player, especially in the one-day game, and he could do a job in Test cricket. He was certainly wrongly ruled out of the World Cup in 1999.
**NADEEM SHAHID** - I know Nick's game very well, as I grew up with him at Essex. Both he and Browny are class players in both the one-day and the first-class format. Sometimes in Test cricket you need initial success to make yourself believe that you belong and maybe that's been the case with Nick.

*I was impressed by Jamie Troughton in both matches against Warwickshire - how about you? What are his strengths, do you think?*
**NADEEM SHAHID** - I think he's a very good cricketer and a definite name for the future. I see his main strengths as being his temperament and his determination to stick to his game plan, whatever the situation. He seems cool under pressure, too.

### WARWICKSHIRE v SURREY at Edgbaston — Played 27th to 30th August
Warwickshire won the toss and elected to bat    Umpires:- Mervyn Kitchen and Barrie Leadbeater

**WARWICKSHIRE - First Innings**

| Fall Of Wkt | Batsman | How | Out | Score | Balls | 4s | 6s |
|---|---|---|---|---|---|---|---|
| 1-79 | M.J. Powell * | lbw | b Saqlain | 36 | 73 | 7 | 0 |
| 4-179 | N.V. Knight | c Batty | b Ormond | 74 | 156 | 13 | 0 |
| 2-87 | M.A. Wagh | c Hollioake | b Saqlain | 3 | 16 | 0 | 0 |
| 3-146 | I.R. Bell | c Batty | b Bicknell | 34 | 49 | 5 | 0 |
| 7-251 | J.O. Troughton | lbw | b Bicknell | 61 | 80 | 10 | 0 |
| 5-185 | S.M. Pollock | c Brown | b Ormond | 2 | 21 | 0 | 0 |
| 6-196 | D.R. Brown | c Clarke | b Saqlain | 6 | 12 | 1 | 0 |
| 8-271 | T. Frost + | | b Saqlain | 35 | 100 | 7 | 0 |
| 9-279 | A.F. Giles | | b Ormond | 3 | 38 | 0 | 0 |
| | M.A. Sheikh | Not | Out | 19 | 107 | 2 | 0 |
| 10-345 | M.M. Betts | c Saqlain | b Ormond | 47 | 67 | 8 | 0 |
| | Extras | (3lb, 4w, 18nb) | | 25 | | | |
| | **TOTAL** | **(118.2 overs)** | | **345** | | | |

| Bowler | O | M | R | W | NB | Wd |
|---|---|---|---|---|---|---|
| Bicknell | 24 | 6 | 87 | 2 | 3 | - |
| Ormond | 30.2 | 5 | 108 | 4 | 2 | 1 |
| Saqlain Mushtaq | 49 | 16 | 94 | 4 | 4 | - |
| Clarke | 1 | 0 | 5 | 0 | - | - |
| Salisbury | 14 | 2 | 48 | 0 | - | 1 |

**SURREY - First Innings** (Needing 196 to avoid the follow-on)

| Fall Of Wkt | Batsman | How | Out | Score | Balls | 4s | 6s |
|---|---|---|---|---|---|---|---|
| 3-251 | I.J. Ward | c Knight | b Pollock | 114 | 215 | 18 | 0 |
| 1-32 | J.N. Batty + | c Pollock | b Betts | 8 | 22 | 2 | 0 |
| 2-236 | M.R. Ramprakash | lbw | b Brown | 99 | 169 | 14 | 3 |
| 5-474 | N. Shahid | c Pollock | b Giles | 116 | 157 | 21 | 1 |
| 4-397 | A.D. Brown | st Frost | b Giles | 57 | 121 | 8 | 0 |
| | A.J. Hollioake * | Not | Out | 82 | 77 | 7 | 5 |
| 6-502 | R. Clarke | st Frost | b Giles | 10 | 13 | 2 | 0 |
| 7-502 | M.P. Bicknell | c Brown | b Giles | 0 | 4 | 0 | 0 |
| 8-525 | I.D.K. Salisbury | lbw | b Brown | 8 | 29 | 1 | 0 |
| 9-543 | Saqlain Mushtaq | c Betts | b Brown | 6 | 20 | 1 | 0 |
| 10-544 | J. Ormond | c & | b Brown | 0 | 6 | 0 | 0 |
| | Extras | (1b, 4lb, 7w, 32nb) | | 44 | | | |
| | **TOTAL** | **(136.1 overs)** | | **544** | | | |

| Bowler | O | M | R | W | NB | Wd |
|---|---|---|---|---|---|---|
| Pollock | 21 | 7 | 64 | 1 | 2 | - |
| Betts | 24 | 2 | 122 | 1 | 12 | - |
| Sheikh | 26 | 7 | 79 | 0 | - | - |
| Giles | 34 | 4 | 134 | 4 | - | 3 |
| Brown | 28.1 | 1 | 124 | 4 | 2 | - |
| Wagh | 3 | 1 | 16 | 0 | - | - |

**WARWICKSHIRE - Second Innings** (Needing 199 to avoid an innings defeat)

| Fall Of Wkt | Batsman | How | Out | Score | Balls | 4s | 6s |
|---|---|---|---|---|---|---|---|
| 3-105 | M.J. Powell * | c Shahid | b Saqlain | 48 | 102 | 5 | 0 |
| 1-86 | M.A. Wagh | lbw | b Saqlain | 39 | 62 | 8 | 0 |
| 2-105 | I.R. Bell | c Batty | b Ormond | 4 | 27 | 0 | 0 |
| 4-214 | J.O. Troughton | lbw | b Salisbury | 63 | 133 | 9 | 1 |
| 9-403 | N.V. Knight | | b Ward | 133 | 302 | 15 | 0 |
| 5-225 | S.M. Pollock | c Shahid | b Saqlain | 3 | 17 | 0 | 0 |
| 6-257 | D.R. Brown | c Batty | b Saqlain | 20 | 31 | 3 | 0 |
| 7-330 | T. Frost + | c Batty | b Clarke | 13 | 86 | 1 | 1 |
| 8-376 | A.F. Giles | c Ormond | b Clarke | 25 | 25 | 5 | 0 |
| | M.A. Sheikh | Not | Out | 7 | 26 | 0 | 0 |
| | M.M. Betts | Not | Out | 0 | 5 | 0 | 0 |
| | Extras | (2b, 14lb, 8w, 25nb) | | 49 | | | |
| | **TOTAL** | **(134 overs)** | **(for 9 dec)** | **404** | | | |

| Bowler | O | M | R | W | NB | Wd |
|---|---|---|---|---|---|---|
| Bicknell | 20 | 5 | 71 | 0 | 3 | - |
| Ormond | 24 | 2 | 95 | 1 | 3 | 1 |
| Saqlain Mushtaq | 43 | 15 | 80 | 4 | 4 | - |
| Salisbury | 25 | 4 | 53 | 1 | - | - |
| Shahid | 6 | 0 | 17 | 0 | - | - |
| Hollioake | 4 | 0 | 12 | 0 | - | - |
| Clarke | 7 | 1 | 49 | 2 | 2 | 1 |
| Brown | 3 | 0 | 7 | 0 | - | - |
| Ward | 2 | 1 | 4 | 1 | - | - |

## Other Division One Results

Ten points would now be sufficient to claim the title at The Rose Bowl, though it was quite possible that Surrey could be crowned champions before then, if Warwickshire and Kent dropped points in the fixtures they were playing while the leaders sat out next round of matches. At the other end of the table, Yorkshire's victory over Hampshire looked to have come too late to preserve their first division status, though it seemed very likely to condemn the men from The Rose Bowl to second division cricket in 2003. Somerset appeared pretty sure to go the same way after capitulating feebly to Lancashire at Blackpool.

August 27-29
*The Rose Bowl:-* **Yorkshire beat Hampshire by seven wickets.** Hampshire 269 (Smith 58, McGrath 4-49) and 161 (Dawson 5-49); Yorkshire 280 (Elliott 92, Udal 5-69) and 152-3 (Craven 72, Elliott 52*). **Yorkshire 17pts, Hampshire 5**

*Blackpool:-* **Lancashire beat Somerset by 336 runs.** Lancashire 251 (Law 77, Johnson 6-47) and 296 (Byas 81, Schofield 77, Caddick 6-84); Somerset 140 (Anderson 6-41) and 71 (Chapple 6-30). **Lancashire 17pts, Somerset 3**

*Leicester:-* **Leicestershire beat Sussex by eight wickets.** Sussex 215 (Martin-Jenkins 62, Adams 60, Malcolm 5-38) and 142 (DeFreitas 4-42); Leicestershire 247 (Sutcliffe 75, Kirtley 4-89) and 111-2. **Leicestershire 16pts, Sussex 4**

## COUNTY CHAMPIONSHIP DIVISION ONE AT 30TH AUGUST

| Pos | Prv | | P | Points | W | D | L | Bat | Bwl | Ded |
|---|---|---|---|---|---|---|---|---|---|---|
| 1 | 1 | Surrey | 14 | 202.75 | 8 | 4 | 2 | 49 | 42 | 0.25 |
| 2 | 3 | Warwickshire | 13 | 152.00 | 5 | 6 | 2 | 32 | 36 | 0.00 |
| 3 | 2 | Kent | 13 | 145.50 | 5 | 4 | 4 | 35 | 35 | 0.50 |
| 4 | 5 | Lancashire | 13 | 142.00 | 5 | 5 | 3 | 27 | 35 | 0.00 |
| 5 | 6 | Leicestershire | 13 | 137.00 | 4 | 5 | 4 | 33 | 37 | 1.00 |
| 6 | 4 | Sussex | 14 | 135.00 | 3 | 6 | 5 | 34 | 41 | 0.00 |
| 7 | 7 | Hampshire ** | 14 | 115.00 | 2 | 8 | 4 | 27 | 40 | 8.00 |
| 8 | 8 | Somerset | 13 | 109.00 | 1 | 7 | 5 | 33 | 36 | 0.00 |
| 9 | 9 | Yorkshire | 13 | 108.50 | 2 | 5 | 6 | 28 | 37 | 0.50 |

*\*\* Hampshire deducted 8pts for 'poor' pitch at Rose Bowl v Lancashire*

### NUL2 - Clarke Makes Light Of Injury To Foil Scorpions At The Last

In a gripping finish to a crucial match that was shown live on Sky Sports, a limping Rikki Clarke saw Surrey home to a one-wicket victory with two balls to spare, with the 20-year-old coming desperately close to notching his first limited-overs century for the county in so doing. Unfortunately for Clarke, the single that his side required for victory was completed before his square cut off Dominic Cork crossed the boundary rope at deep cover, meaning that the young Lions' all-rounder had to settle for an unbeaten ninety-eight rather than 101, though victory under the floodlights at The County Ground was clearly the most important thing at the end of a fluctuating contest.

Although Surrey had started the match well, with Ed Giddins reducing the Scorpions to 6-2 after the first four overs, the home side hit back strongly through a steady knock by Cork and a more belligerent effort from 21-year-old Nathan Dumelow, who added 111 runs for the third wicket in just nineteen overs. Fine spells in mid-innings by Clarke and Ian Salisbury then helped to regain some control for the Lions before Adam Hollioake entered the fray in the thirty-fourth over to sweep the Derbyshire middle-order away in dramatic fashion, leaving the hosts indebted to a last-wicket stand of twenty-three to push the total beyond two-hundred and up to a challenging score of 213.

With Surrey's openers faring no better than their opponents, and Cork producing an excellent first spell of 7-3-12-1, the Scorpions took the early honours when the visitors replied, though Clarke then shared stands of forty-eight with Mark Ramprakash - who completed five-hundred NUL runs for the season during his innings - and fifty-eight with Nadeem Shahid to put the Lions firmly back on track by the halfway stage of their innings.

Although he was already struggling with an injury sustained when edging a ball onto the inside of his knee, Clarke battled on without a runner as Graeme Welch and Matt Dowman rapidly routed the visitors' middle-order to turn the game around and leave Surrey in real trouble at 172-7 after thirty-nine overs. The Scorpions' wicketkeeper, Luke Sutton, then missed an awkward chance offered by Salisbury from the third ball he faced, allowing the Surrey leg-spinner to go on and play a crucial knock of twenty-one from only 15 balls, just as Clarke began to struggle to get the ball away and was, himself, dropped twice in the deep, on ninety-three and ninety-four.

The forty-third over looked to be decisive as Salisbury drove the returning Cork for three boundaries to take the score to 209-7 with twelve balls remaining, but the Lions' 'leggie' and Tim Murtagh then fell in the space of three balls in the penultimate over of the match, bowled by Mohammad Ali, to set up a finale that became increasingly tense when Giddins inexplicably took a leg-bye from the final ball, thereby retaining the strike for the start of the last over. Having somehow survived a big lbw appeal from Cork's first delivery - television replays showed the umpire to have been very generous in ruling in the batsman's favour - a wide, and then a single to Giddins, when the Surrey number eleven did well to dig out a yorker, left the excellent Clarke to finish the job and boost the Lions' promotion prospects.

## DERBYSHIRE SCORPIONS v SURREY LIONS at Derby
### Played on Monday 2nd September     Surrey Lions won by one wicket

Derbyshire Scorpions won the toss and elected to bat     Umpires:- Graham Burgess & George Sharp

### DERBYSHIRE SCORPIONS

| Fall Of Wkt | Batsman | How | Out | Score | Balls | 4s | 6s |
|---|---|---|---|---|---|---|---|
| 1-3 | M.J. DiVenuto | c Batty | b Giddins | 1 | 7 | 0 | 0 |
| 2-6 | C.W.G. Bassano | | b Giddins | 3 | 14 | 0 | 0 |
| 3-117 | N.R.C. Dumelow | c Bicknell | b Salisbury | 52 | 57 | 7 | 0 |
| 4-162 | D.G. Cork * | c Batty | b Hollioake | 51 | 84 | 6 | 0 |
| 7-188 | S.A. Selwood | c Batty | b Hollioake | 38 | 59 | 5 | 0 |
| 5-173 | M.P. Dowman | c Batty | b Hollioake | 7 | 9 | 1 | 0 |
| 6-187 | J.I.D. Kerr | | b Hollioake | 3 | 11 | 0 | 0 |
| 8-188 | G. Welch | | b Murtagh | 1 | 3 | 0 | 0 |
| 9-190 | L.D. Sutton + | run | out | 0 | 1 | 0 | 0 |
| | Mohammad Ali | Not | Out | 10 | 12 | 0 | 0 |
| 10-213 | K.J. Dean | run | out | 12 | 15 | 1 | 0 |
| | Extras | (17lb, 14w, 4nb) | | 35 | | | |
| | **TOTAL** | (45 overs) | | 213 | | | |

| Bowler | O | M | R | W | NB | Wd |
|---|---|---|---|---|---|---|
| Bicknell | 5 | 1 | 29 | 0 | 1 | 1 |
| Giddins | 7 | 0 | 37 | 2 | 1 | 2 |
| Murtagh | 9 | 0 | 46 | 1 | - | 2 |
| Clarke | 9 | 0 | 36 | 0 | - | 2 |
| Salisbury | 9 | 0 | 25 | 1 | - | 1 |
| Hollioake | 6 | 0 | 23 | 4 | - | 2 |

## SURREY LIONS

| Fall Of Wkt | Batsman | How | Out | Score | Balls | 4s | 6s |
|---|---|---|---|---|---|---|---|
| 2-17 | I.J. Ward | lbw | b Cork | 2 | 16 | 0 | 0 |
| 1-17 | A.D. Brown | | b Dean | 9 | 13 | 2 | 0 |
| 3-65 | M.R. Ramprakash | c Sutton | b Mohammad Ali | 28 | 31 | 5 | 0 |
| | R.Clarke | Not | Out | 98 | 121 | 14 | 0 |
| 4-123 | N. Shahid | c Kerr | b Dowman | 20 | 34 | 2 | 0 |
| 5-151 | A.J. Hollioake * | | b Welch | 6 | 22 | 0 | 0 |
| 6-153 | J.N. Batty + | lbw | b Welch | 0 | 6 | 0 | 0 |
| 7-154 | M.P. Bicknell | | b Dowman | 2 | 6 | 0 | 0 |
| 8-210 | I.D.K. Salisbury | c Dean | b Mohammad Ali | 21 | 15 | 4 | 0 |
| 9-210 | T.J. Murtagh | c Kerr | b Mohammad Ali | 0 | 2 | 0 | 0 |
| | E.S.H. Giddins | Not | Out | 1 | 4 | 0 | 0 |
| | Extras | (8lb, 15w, 4nb) | | 27 | | | |
| | **TOTAL** | (44.4 overs) | (for 9 wkts) | 214 | | | |

| Bowler | O | M | R | W | NB | Wd |
|---|---|---|---|---|---|---|
| Cork | 8.4 | 3 | 30 | 1 | - | 3 |
| Dean | 7 | 0 | 39 | 1 | - | 4 |
| Welch | 7 | 0 | 42 | 2 | - | 1 |
| Mohammad Ali | 9 | 0 | 42 | 3 | 2 | 3 |
| Kerr | 4 | 0 | 17 | 0 | - | - |
| Dowman | 9 | 0 | 36 | 2 | - | - |

## Other NUL Division Two Results

This was indeed a vital victory for the Lions as it enabled them to take advantage of the Northamptonshire Steelbacks' fast-fading challenge and move into second place in the table. Essex were on a hot streak, though, recording three victories in the space of a week, including a triumph over the Gladiators that kept alive their own hopes, and Surrey's, of overhauling the long-time leaders to claim the second division title.

August 25
*Colchester:-* **Essex Eagles beat Northamptonshire Steelbacks by four wickets.** Northamptonshire 167-8 (Stephenson 3-21); Essex 168-6 (41.5ov; Flower 57*, Penberthy 3-31). **Essex Eagles 4pts**

*Lord's:-* **Derbyshire Scorpions beat Middlesex Crusaders by 32 runs.** Derbyshire 243-8 (DiVenuto 94); Middlesex 211-6 (Strauss 70). **Derbyshire Scorpions 4pts**

August 27
*Colchester:-* **Essex Eagles beat Gloucestershire Gladiators by five wickets.** Gloucestershire 97 (33.4ov; Grant 3-13, Stephenson 3-14); Essex Eagles 98-5 (36.1ov). **Essex Eagles 4pts**

September 1
*The Rose Bowl:-* **Hampshire Hawks beat Middlesex Crusaders by 24 runs.** Hampshire 241-7 (Kendall 110*, Udal 58); Middlesex 217-8 (44ov; Hutton 63). **Hampshire Hawks 4pts**

*Old Trafford:-* **Essex Eagles beat Lancashire Lightning by seven wickets.** Lancashire 153-9 (Middlebrook 3-14); Essex 154-3 (34.1ov; Robinson 54). **Essex Eagles 4pts**

*Northampton:-* **Sussex Sharks beat Northamptonshire Steelbacks by six wickets.** Northamptonshire 195-8; Sussex 197-4 (43.4ov; Adams 64*). **Sussex Sharks 4pts**

## NATIONAL LEAGUE DIVISION TWO AT 2ND SEPTEMBER

| Pos | Prv | | P | Pts | W | T | L | A |
|---|---|---|---|---|---|---|---|---|
| 1 | 1 | Gloucestershire Gladiators | 14 | 40 | 9 | 0 | 3 | 2 |
| 2 | 3 | Surrey Lions | 14 | 34 | 8 | 0 | 5 | 1 |
| 3 | 6 | Essex Eagles | 13 | 32 | 8 | 0 | 5 | 0 |
| 4 | 2 | Northamptonshire Steelbacks | 13 | 30 | 7 | 0 | 5 | 1 |
| 5 | 5 | Derbyshire Scorpions | 13 | 26 | 6 | 0 | 6 | 1 |
| 6 | 4 | Lancashire Lightning | 14 | 24 | 5 | 0 | 7 | 2 |
| 7 | 8 | Hampshire Hawks | 14 | 22 | 5 | 0 | 8 | 1 |
| 8 | 7 | Middlesex Crusaders | 14 | 20 | 4 | 0 | 8 | 2 |
| 9 | 9 | Sussex Sharks | 13 | 16 | 3 | 0 | 8 | 2 |

# 18 Triumph

Apart from the NUL game at Derby, people might have expected the period between the conclusion of the Warwickshire match and the round of Championship matches that would decide whether or not Surrey could be crowned champions before their next fixture, to have been pretty quiet. That was far from being the case, however, as there was news on several other fronts.

On 30th August, Rikki Clarke was announced as the winner of the Cricket Writers' Club's Young Cricketer Of The Year award, with the 20-year-old Guildford all-rounder beating Kent's Robert Key by just one vote. Having enjoyed an outstanding debut season, it was a very well deserved accolade for Clarke, who had also beaten off competition from Graham Wagg and Ian Bell (both Warwickshire), Kabir Ali (Worcestershire), Richard Dawson (Yorkshire), Kyle Hogg (Lancashire), Tim Ambrose and Matt Prior (both Sussex). This honour was then followed, just a matter of days later, by an even greater reward for his efforts, as he was called into the England squad for the ICC Champions Trophy, to be held in Sri Lanka from September 12th-29th, after Paul Collingwood, Michael Vaughan and Craig White all withdrew with injuries.

At about the same time as Clarke was receiving his international call-up, Surrey announced that their only other player in the ICC Trophy squad, Alec Stewart, was being awarded a Testimonial Season in 2003. On the Club website, Chief Executive, Paul Sheldon, stated, "Alec has shown tremendous loyalty and service to both England and Surrey County Cricket Club over the past two decades. The Club is delighted to mark Alec's career and achievements by making this well deserved award." The player responded by saying, "Playing for Surrey throughout my career has been a fantastic privilege. I have been lucky enough to play with some great players and particularly to be a part of the huge success the Club has achieved over the last six years. I hope that I can continue to contribute both on and off the pitch in years to come."

Graham Thorpe, Stewart's troubled England colleague, had meanwhile suggested that he could yet take part in the winter's Ashes trip by announcing that he shouldn't yet be ruled out of contention. According to media reports he had said, "I want a bit longer. I've not really spoken to anyone on a regular basis since Lord's, so I want to see what kind of vibes I'm getting from the selectors. I'm well aware that I haven't played for a month, so I'm not looking for assurances. But I don't want to muck them around either and would like to know where I stand." Then, within a couple of days, he was sounding even more positive, telling a Sunday newspaper that he wanted to go to Australia and would make himself available for Surrey for last three weeks of the season in order to press his case. According to the story, Thorpe had stated, "I spoke to Duncan (Fletcher) and told him I want to be considered for Australia. Duncan took on board the reasons for my decision and, although he made no commitment to me, it was important for me to let him know where I stand. I know Duncan and Nasser (Hussain) will be concerned that the risk in taking me might be too great. But all I can do is try to assure them of my focus and commitment. There would be no point in making myself available if I wasn't utterly convinced that I would be able to cope with the situation. I will also make myself available for Surrey for the final three weeks of the season. It's important for me to demonstrate that my commitment is real. I'm ready." Unfortunately, when questioned about Thorpe's situation during a stint in the commentary box on Sky Sports during Surrey's NUL match at Derby, Keith Medlycott said that he knew nothing about his player's decision to make himself available for the county for the rest of the season. This was rather disconcerting. Since Medlycott had no reason to be lying, it appeared that Thorpe had informed the press - who had raked over his private life - before telling the Club who had stood by him, and it didn't go down too well with most of the supporters I spoke to. Was it just another case of a man in turmoil not thinking clearly? One hoped that this was the simple reason for an apparent slap in the face for the Club and everyone connected with it.

The fact that the Championship was as good as clinched at least meant that Thorpe could be included in the side, if necessary, without causing any disruption or resentment among the players who had played so brilliantly to take Surrey to the brink of success. It certainly would have given Keith Medlycott and Adam Hollioake a serious headache had they been requested to drop someone who had been an integral member of the side in order for Thorpe to 'prove he was ready' for the Ashes campaign. There was time to consider everything carefully in any case, since the match at The Rose Bowl was still a week away.

In the meantime, the days of reckoning for Warwickshire and Kent had arrived as they began their matches against Lancashire and Somerset respectively. Everyone knew that it was just a case of *when* Surrey were crowned champions, rather than *if*, as this round of games got under way, and I was actually hoping that one or other of our 'rivals' would get the required number of points to keep the pot simmering until the Hampshire match. Apart from my preference for Surrey's triumph to be confirmed while the side was on the field of play, rather than resting, I always felt it would be rather nice, from a historical point of view, to be the first county to win the County Championship at the new Rose Bowl stadium.

It soon became clear that Warwickshire and Kent were going to struggle to keep the Championship 'race' alive, however, as both sides conceded big first innings totals to their opponents, with Warwickshire even dropping a bowling point along the way. Although Kent managed to gain a full set of bonus points, they were always going to struggle to get the win they required at Taunton, and the loss of time to rain on the final afternoon as they chased 377 completely scuppered their very slim chances. Meanwhile, at Old Trafford, with the game having long since died as a meaningful contest, Warwickshire needed to gain maximum batting points before the close of play to leave Surrey needing a point at The Rose Bowl. Having collapsed badly, they rallied late in the day before eventually falling seventy-two runs short of their target, thereby handing the title to the men from The AMP Oval. An eighteenth Championship triumph was thoroughly deserved after a dominant campaign, especially considering the pre-season traumas, which might have knocked the stuffing out of lesser teams.

Predictably enough, within minutes of being confirmed as the new champions, Surrey announced that the win would be dedicated to Ben Hollioake, and brother Adam later spoke about what had been a season of truly mixed emotions. Talking about the dedication of the title to his late brother, the Surrey captain said, "For me, personally, that was never a factor - to me it doesn't bring Ben back. The other guys would be likely to treat it more that way, because they probably thought it was a way of paying their respects to him. I just found it a nice gesture from the club to say that." Continuing his tribute to his team-mates, Hollioake then went on to say, "What they have done for the Club, and for me and my family, has been more than a tale of winning the Championship. I feel honoured to know them, they are a special bunch. People within cricket talk about us as being a hated side, but if you get to know these people you could never say that."

Turning his attention then to the way the Championship had been won, and comparing it to the other recent triumphs, he stated, "In the other two years when we won it, we went through huge periods, we won something like eight games on the spin the first year with some of them by an innings. This year it's been a bit more disjointed, perhaps more of a sustained effort. We lost a couple but made sure we came back from that immediately." He also took time out to underline the fact that the side had contained unsung heroes as well as the better-known stars, saying, "Having great players doesn't guarantee you are going to win the Championship, and this year, more than any other season, it's been the year of the non-stars. People like Nadeem Shahid and Jon Batty have been exceptional. The spirit Nadeem has shown is incredible, he stands at short leg, watches the ball whistle past his face all day and then scores runs when it's tough. He got left out after scoring 150 and there wasn't the slightest hint of a moan. Other sides don't have players like that, guys elsewhere are not in the side and they want to go and play for another county." Hollioake's own performances and captaincy has also been crucial, of course, and he revealed that, during the winter, he had tried to re-evaluate the way he captained the side. "I have always been positive, but I just encouraged the guys to attack at all times and play their own way," he said. "At times we have come unstuck but in the long run we have played some good cricket." And this attitude had certainly met with the approval of his team, with Martin Bicknell paying tribute to his captain by saying, "We wanted him to come back with us sitting at the top of the table, so he could jump straight back in. He came back and was a breath of fresh air, coming in and playing a very positive game and adding another dimension to our cricket. I wouldn't want to play under anyone else. He's a great leader of men. He's very instinctive and he knows what to do at the right time. He's the best captain I've played under."

### Division One Results

Hampshire's draw with Sussex confirmed their relegation to the second division, with Yorkshire and Somerset looking more than likely to join them after both teams failed to win their match.
September 4-7
*Old Trafford:-* **Lancashire drew with Warwickshire.** Lancashire 598 (Martin 117*, Byas 101, Schofield 91, Chapple 65, Swann 62); Warwickshire 328 (Carter 70, Brown 68*, Ostler 63). **Lancashire 12pts, Warwickshire 9**
*Taunton:-* **Somerset drew with Kent.** Somerset 460 (Wood 196, Parsons 68, Cox 62, Saggers 4-87, Khan 4-88) and 316-9dec (Bowler 81, Cox 79); Kent 400-6dec (Smith 154, Nixon 88, Tredwell 58) and 171-4 (Nixon 51). **Somerset 11pts, Kent 12**
*Scarborough:-* **Yorkshire drew with Leicestershire.** Yorkshire 276 (White 161, Malcolm 4-95) and 347-8dec (Dawson 74*, Blakey 63*, Wells 5-39); Leicestershire 279 (Burns 59, Srinath 52, Sidebottom 5-60) and 231-5 (Maddy 86, Stevens 80). **Yorkshire 8pts*, Leicestershire 9**
\* deducted 1pt for slow over rate
September 5-8
*Hove:-* **Sussex drew with Hampshire.** Sussex 631-6dec (Montgomerie 196, Goodwin 119, Prior 102, Martin-Jenkins 64); Hampshire 401 (Laney 89, Smith 60, Johnson 51, Kirtley 6-107) and 67-1 (Johnson 51*). **Sussex 12pts, Hampshire 10**

### COUNTY CHAMPIONSHIP DIVISION ONE AT 8TH SEPTEMBER

| Pos | Prv |  | P | Points | W | D | L | Bat | Bwl | Ded |
|---|---|---|---|---|---|---|---|---|---|---|
| 1 | 1 | Surrey | 14 | 202.75 | 8 | 4 | 2 | 49 | 42 | 0.25 |
| 2 | 2 | Warwickshire | 14 | 161.00 | 5 | 7 | 2 | 35 | 38 | 0.00 |
| 3 | 3 | Kent | 14 | 157.50 | 5 | 5 | 4 | 40 | 38 | 0.50 |
| 4 | 4 | Lancashire | 14 | 154.00 | 5 | 6 | 3 | 32 | 38 | 0.00 |
| 5 | 6 | Sussex | 15 | 147.00 | 3 | 7 | 5 | 39 | 44 | 0.00 |
| 6 | 5 | Leicestershire | 14 | 146.00 | 4 | 6 | 4 | 35 | 40 | 1.00 |
| 7 | 7 | Hampshire ** | 15 | 125.00 | 2 | 9 | 4 | 32 | 41 | 8.00 |
| 8 | 8 | Somerset | 14 | 120.00 | 1 | 8 | 5 | 38 | 38 | 0.00 |
| 9 | 9 | Yorkshire | 14 | 116.50 | 2 | 6 | 6 | 30 | 40 | 1.50 |

\*\* *Hampshire deducted 8pts for 'poor' pitch at Rose Bowl v Lancashire*

### VIEWS FROM THE DRESSING ROOM

*Was it a major disappointment to clinch the title during the week when we weren't playing?*
**JON BATTY** - No, it wasn't a disappointment. Obviously you'd rather do it on the field during a game, but winning the Championship at any time cannot be considered a disappointment.

**MARTIN BICKNELL** - It was, yes. I would have loved to have done it at The Oval on a Saturday afternoon in glorious sunshine, but it just doesn't happen like that... you can't pick and choose where and when you win trophies. I was a little disappointed, though - it took a little piece of the gloss off, but not a huge amount.

**ALI BROWN** - I must admit I was hoping that we'd just a need a point or two at Hampshire, but I don't think it makes a major difference... it's not the moment so much as what you've put in beforehand that has won it for you. It would have been nice, but it wasn't to be.

**RIKKI CLARKE** - It was a bit disappointing, it would have been nice to win it at Warwickshire. I think it's always better to win a game and know you are all together at the time, but we won the title and that's all that counts, really.

**ADAM HOLLIOAKE** - No, not at all. I'll take the title at any time and any way it comes along. A major disappointment would be getting relegated, not winning the title when you're not playing.

**TIM MURTAGH** - I think it was for a few of the guys. I think they wanted to get it finished at Warwickshire, but winning a Championship is winning a Championship, and you'll take it however it comes about.

**MARK RAMPRAKASH** - Yes, it was a bit of an anticlimax, but when you win the Championship you take it any way it comes.

**IAN SALISBURY** - Yes, we went all out to win at Warwickshire, and put in a lot of effort because we really wanted to win it up there, so it was disappointing.

**NADEEM SHAHID** - Yes, it was a disappointment and it did seem a bit of an anticlimax.

**IAN WARD** - The best way to do it was how we did it against Notts in 1999, but that was a bit of a fairy-tale, really. So, yes, it would have been great to go out needing three wickets or 200 runs and doing it one evening and then being able to have a beer with your colleagues afterwards, but a Championship is a Championship and three out of four is pretty good, so we'll take it anyway we can.

*At what point on Saturday 7th September did you become aware that we had just secured the title and how did you find out?*

**ALEC STEWART** - I was playing in the Oval Test Match, alongside Tudes and Butch, of course. The members who sit in front of the sight screen at the pavilion end shouted out to me and Butch that we'd clinched it, so we told Tudes, and then it was announced over the Tannoy about an over later. I took great pleasure in running around in between overs, shaking all our team's hands and saying 'thanks very much for congratulating Surrey'. Then I went to the committee room at the end of the day for a small glass of champagne with the committee members.

**ALEX TUDOR** - I was down at third man, and there were Surrey members in the crowd, of course. Alec and myself were always keeping tabs on what was going on, and then a couple of guys in the crowd punched a hand up in the air - Stewie and me looked at each other and we both had a big smile on our face, even though we were chasing leather all day... it helped to get us through the two days, basically, although it annoyed Nasser massively, of course - which was pleasing for the Surrey boys!

**JON BATTY** - I was acting as twelfth man at the Test Match, so I was actually in the dressing room with Tudes, Butch and Stewie around the time we clinched it. We had a little jump around in the dressing room and then it was straight on the phone to everyone else, and then up to the committee room at the end of the day.

**ALI BROWN** - I was at the Test Match, sitting in the executive restaurant with Barry Kitcherside, who was very much involved with my benefit year, when someone came up and told me that we had clinched it.

**MARTIN BICKNELL** - I was in the car, as we were driving to Chelmsford for the Sunday League game, and I heard it on the radio. But we knew before then that we were going to win anyway, of course.

**RIKKI CLARKE** - I actually found out through Neil Walker, our physio, who sent me a text message saying 'Congratulations on the Championship win', and then I spoke to Nad. It didn't really sink in at first, it was a bit of an anticlimax, but it's great to know that I've been part of a Championship-winning side. I think it meant most to the senior players, because a lot of them remember the times when we were struggling down at the bottom of the table, and they have worked hard to change things. I'm lucky, really, to have just walked straight into a Championship-winning side.

**ADAM HOLLIOAKE** - I can't remember exactly, but I know I was at home. I think maybe my Dad rang up, as he'd been following the games on the internet. Someone rang anyway, closely followed by several other phone calls of congratulations. The team travelled to Essex that evening for the National League match, so we all just sat round in the hotel and had a few glasses of champagne. As we had a game the next day, we couldn't do too much.

**TIM MURTAGH** - We were travelling up to Essex for the Sunday League game, and Medders rang us up while we were en route and told us we were the champions.

**MARK RAMPRAKASH** - I didn't know the exact moment, but I knew we'd won it anyway. Once we'd drawn at Warwickshire that was it, really.

**IAN SALISBURY** - I was travelling up to Essex with Nad, and my Dad rang me up to offer his congratulations - he'd been following the games on Ceefax. Then I had some text messages and everybody was ringing one other.

**NADEEM SHAHID** - Sals and I were driving up to Essex to play in the Sunday League game the next day, and we heard it on the radio as soon as it was mathematically certain that we were the champions. We beeped our horn a few times and then rang as many of the other players as we could. Then we had a few celebrations that evening at the hotel.

**IAN WARD** - I think Bickers rang me and said 'congratulations', and I didn't have a clue what he was on about because I was in the middle of doing something... it took me about twenty seconds to realise what he was talking about! Then a few other phone calls came in and a few phone calls went out... the boys were just generally ringing round and congratulating one another. Yes, thinking about it, it was definitely Martin Bicknell, which is par for the course because he's pretty clued up at any stage of the season about how many points we need or whatever. I dread to think how many hours he must spend in front of his TV watching Ceefax!

## NUL2 - Lions Roar Back In Dramatic Style To Clinch Promotion

Those defeats in close-run limited-overs matches at the start of the season were just a distant memory as a one-wicket triumph over Derbyshire at the start of the week was followed by an even more dramatic win by two runs over Essex Eagles six days later, after an astonishing eleventh-hour fightback by the Lions. There seemed to be no way that the home side could lose when they stood twenty-six runs short of victory at 137-4 in the thirtieth over, and certainly not when they were 155-6, with eleven overs left in which to score just eight runs, yet Martin Bicknell bowled Ronnie Irani through an ugly slog at the first of these Essex high points, while Adam Hollioake and Ed Giddins sliced through the tail to take four wickets for five runs in twenty-four balls at the second, to leave Surrey victorious in incredible circumstances - and their players dancing a joyous jig on the outfield. With Northamptonshire losing to Lancashire at Old Trafford, this win also confirmed promotion for the Lions, since their only remaining rivals, the Eagles and the Steelbacks, were due to clash next week at Northampton.

The game had started very inauspiciously for the newly crowned county champions, with both openers gone by the end of the fourth over, and no-one escaped the grip of the Eagles' tidy attack until the Surrey skipper came in to thrash two sixes and three fours during a belligerent

16-ball innings of twenty-seven. After Hollioake's departure to a miscued hook at 82-5, Essex regained full control, and it was only thanks to a stand of thirty-two for the ninth wicket between Saqlain Mushtaq and Tim Murtagh that the Lions managed to make it as far as the forty-fourth over and a score of 162.

This didn't look likely to be enough, even when Bicknell and Giddins claimed the early scalps of Robinson and Stephenson - the latter brilliantly caught one-handed diving yards to his right at slip by, who else, Hollioake - to peg the Eagles back to 27-2.

Will Jefferson and Andy Flower soon got their side back on track at 61-2 in the fifteenth over, though Surrey's ninth-wicket batting heroes then managed to cause a few flutters again by taking a wicket apiece to make it 63-4, before Paul Grayson and Irani joined forces for a stand of seventy-four in fourteen overs that looked to have decided the contest. Then came Irani's unnecessary slog.

**ESSEX EAGLES v SURREY LIONS at Chelmsford**
**Played on Sunday 8th September — Surrey Lions won by 2 runs**

Essex Eagles won the toss and elected to field. Umpires:- Jeff Evans & Jeremy Lloyds

### SURREY LIONS

| Fall Of Wkt | Batsman | How | Out | Score | Balls | 4s | 6s |
|---|---|---|---|---|---|---|---|
| 2-7 | I.J. Ward | | b Cowan | 5 | 11 | 1 | 0 |
| 1-7 | A.D. Brown | c Napier | b Irani | 2 | 6 | 0 | 0 |
| 4-42 | M.R. Ramprakash | | b Napier | 13 | 42 | 1 | 0 |
| 3-30 | R. Clarke | c Grant | b Irani | 17 | 29 | 2 | 0 |
| 6-92 | N. Shahid | c Flower | b Grant | 18 | 35 | 2 | 0 |
| 5-82 | A.J. Hollioake * | c Grant | b Cowan | 27 | 16 | 3 | 2 |
| 8-124 | J.N. Batty + | c Jefferson | b Grant | 19 | 32 | 2 | 0 |
| 7-111 | M.P. Bicknell | | b Grant | 9 | 13 | 1 | 0 |
| 9-156 | Saqlain Mushtaq | | b Cowan | 28 | 40 | 3 | 0 |
| | T.J. Murtagh | Not | Out | 14 | 30 | 0 | 0 |
| 10-162 | E.S.H. Giddins | c Flower | b Cowan | 2 | 7 | 0 | 0 |
| | Extras | (2lb, 6w) | | 8 | | | |
| | **TOTAL** | **(43.3 overs)** | | **162** | | | |

| Bowler | O | M | R | W | NB | Wd |
|---|---|---|---|---|---|---|
| Irani | 7 | 2 | 19 | 2 | - | 2 |
| Cowan | 8.3 | 1 | 16 | 4 | - | - |
| Napier | 6 | 1 | 32 | 1 | - | - |
| Dakin | 5 | 0 | 27 | 0 | - | 1 |
| Stephenson | 2 | 0 | 11 | 0 | - | - |
| Grant | 7 | 0 | 28 | 3 | - | 1 |
| Grayson | 8 | 1 | 27 | 0 | - | 1 |

### ESSEX EAGLES

| Fall Of Wkt | Batsman | How | Out | Score | Balls | 4s | 6s |
|---|---|---|---|---|---|---|---|
| 1-3 | D.D.J. Robinson | | b Bicknell | 2 | 14 | 0 | 0 |
| 4-63 | W.I. Jefferson | c Batty | b Murtagh | 29 | 40 | 4 | 0 |
| 2-27 | J.P. Stephenson | c Hollioake | b Giddins | 5 | 15 | 1 | 0 |
| 3-61 | A. Flower + | c Brown | b Saqlain | 13 | 21 | 2 | 0 |
| 5-137 | R.C. Irani * | | b Bicknell | 41 | 49 | 4 | 0 |
| 6-145 | A.P. Grayson | c Batty | b Hollioake | 29 | 48 | 3 | 0 |
| 8-159 | M.L. Pettini | | b Giddins | 6 | 11 | 1 | 0 |
| 7-155 | J.M. Dakin | c Batty | b Hollioake | 8 | 14 | 1 | 0 |
| | G.R. Napier | Not | Out | 5 | 10 | 1 | 0 |
| 9-159 | A.P. Cowan | | b Giddins | 0 | 9 | 0 | 0 |
| 10-160 | J.B. Grant | lbw | b Hollioake | 0 | 1 | 0 | 0 |
| | Extras | (6lb, 12w, 4nb) | | 22 | | | |
| | **TOTAL** | **(38.2 overs)** | | **160** | | | |

| Bowler | O | M | R | W | NB | Wd |
|---|---|---|---|---|---|---|
| Bicknell | 9 | 3 | 28 | 2 | - | 4 |
| Giddins | 9 | 2 | 43 | 3 | 1 | 5 |
| Murtagh | 6 | 0 | 28 | 1 | - | - |
| Saqlain Mushtaq | 9 | 0 | 35 | 1 | 1 | 1 |
| Clarke | 2 | 0 | 9 | 0 | - | - |
| Hollioake | 3.2 | 1 | 11 | 3 | - | 1 |

## Other NUL Division Two Results

With Gloucestershire's victory over the Derbyshire Scorpions clinching the Division Two title, and Surrey definitely promoted, the only significant remaining issue was who would claim the other promotion slot. Since Northamptonshire Steelbacks' losing run had just extended to four matches following a sound thrashing at Old Trafford by Lancashire Lightning, Essex were clear favourites going into next week's big showdown at Northampton.

September 3
*Hove:-* **Sussex Sharks beat Hampshire Hawks by seven wickets.** Hampshire 126 (33ov; Innes 4-26); Sussex 127-3 (25.1ov; Goodwin 76*, Mascarenhas 3-24). **Sussex Sharks 4pts**

September 8
*Bristol:-* **Gloucestershire Gladiators beat Derbyshire Scorpions by 52 runs.** Gloucestershire 292-8 (Spearman 81, Alleyne 54, Kerr 3-34, Dowman 3-38); Derbyshire 240 (41.4ov; Selwood 93, Bassano 61, Smith 3-33). **Gloucestershire Gladiators 4pts**

*Old Trafford:-* **Lancashire Lightning beat Northamptonshire Steelbacks by 97 runs.** Lancashire 270-5 (Law 133, Chilton 61); Northamptonshire 173 (41.2ov; Martin 3-18, Law 3-41). **Lancs Lightning 4pts**

### NATIONAL LEAGUE DIVISION TWO AT 8TH SEPTEMBER

| Pos | Prv | | P | Pts | W | T | L | A |
|---|---|---|---|---|---|---|---|---|
| 1 | 1 | Gloucestershire Gladiators | 15 | 44 | 10 | 0 | 3 | 2 |
| 2 | 2 | Surrey Lions | 15 | 38 | 9 | 0 | 5 | 1 |
| 3 | 3 | Essex Eagles | 14 | 32 | 8 | 0 | 6 | 0 |
| 4 | 4 | Northamptonshire Steelbacks | 14 | 30 | 7 | 0 | 6 | 1 |
| 5 | 6 | Lancashire Lightning | 15 | 28 | 6 | 0 | 7 | 2 |
| 6 | 5 | Derbyshire Scorpions | 14 | 26 | 6 | 0 | 7 | 1 |
| 7 | 7 | Hampshire Hawks | 15 | 22 | 5 | 0 | 9 | 1 |
| 8 | 8 | Middlesex Crusaders | 14 | 20 | 4 | 0 | 8 | 2 |
| = | 9 | Sussex Sharks | 14 | 20 | 4 | 0 | 8 | 2 |

# 19 Ward's West End Premier Performance

The announcement of England's winter touring squads on 10th September revealed that the selectors had decided to show faith in Graham Thorpe but not in Alex Tudor. Despite his problems and lack of cricket, the 33-year-old left-hander was included in the 16-man squad, alongside his Surrey colleagues, Alec Stewart and Mark Butcher, while the 24-year-old paceman was omitted because of "concerns about his strength and stamina", according to the chairman of selectors, David Graveney. While Tudor confessed to being "surprised and disappointed" by the decision, Keith Medlycott was rather more forthright in his comments, justifiably leaping to the defence of his player. "He is a very fine cricketer, and it hurts Surrey, hurts me and, most of all, hurts him to be left out," said the Surrey manager. "He has worked hard and bowled longer spells than ever this season, so, of course, it will be a kick in the teeth," he added, concluding that Tudor had "spearheaded attacks and put his hand up when others have been injured, and got through." The selectors had at least awarded Tudor the consolation prize of a place in the Academy squad, along with Rikki Clarke, who thoroughly deserved his call-up after a magnificent first season. One had to feel sorry for Ian Ward, whose equally excellent season had proved insufficient to earn him another opportunity with England on the Ashes trip, while Mark Ramprakash, who had been touted as a possible selection, was also omitted, though this wasn't a huge surprise, since the feeling that Duncan Fletcher and Nasser Hussain had lost faith in him had continued to grow throughout the summer.

They had decided to take a chance on Thorpe, however, as well as the injured Darren Gough and Andy Flintoff. Following the announcement of his selection, the Surrey man claimed that the tour would be "as big a challenge as there's been at this stage of my career" and said that it was "a great opportunity for me to start up again and work with the other players in the England cricket team again." It seemed reasonable that the man rated by many as the best batsman in the country should be given another chance on such a difficult tour, though he confessed that "I've been lucky the selectors have been so understanding because I'm sure they'll see it as a bit of a gamble." Thorpe was saying all the right things in order to put people's minds at rest, however, telling the press: "I am committed to working hard for my team and on my own game, which is something that slipped a bit during the summer. I know the scale of the task, but I'm looking forward to working hard with the team again. If I didn't believe I could play cricket for three months, knowing what could happen during that time, I wouldn't have put my name in the hat." It was obvious that England would certainly benefit from a fully focused Thorpe, and everyone hoped that he had now put the worst of his problems behind him as he prepared to return to the Surrey fold for the remainder of the season.

For the match at The Rose Bowl, Thorpe would be taking the place of Adam Hollioake, who was missing the game in order to take part in the memorial match that Sussex had arranged in memory of Umer and Burhan Rashid, which was to take place under lights at the County Ground, Hove on Friday 13th September. Adam, who would be playing for the Angus Fraser XI against the Chris Adams XI, had said, "When I heard about the Rashid memorial match I knew I wanted to play. It's been a terrible year and these tragedies have brought our two families together. I know how crucial support is at times like this and I'm glad to be representing the Hollioake family at this match."

There had been two other significant items of news in the lead-up to the Hampshire match. While everyone was delighted to hear that the Championship trophy would be presented to the Club at the close of play on the first day of the final match of the season at The AMP Oval against Leicestershire, there was also the sad, though not unexpected, news that Jason Ratcliffe had lost his battle with a persistent knee injury, and was retiring after eight years on the Surrey staff.

| FRIZZELL COUNTY CHAMPIONSHIP - MATCH FIFTEEN |
|---|

## HAMPSHIRE versus SURREY
at The Rose Bowl
First Day - Wednesday 11th September
Surrey 348-7

***The Teams And The Toss*** - *The Surrey team shows three changes from the Warwickshire match, with Adam Hollioake, Rikki Clarke (away at the ICC Trophy) and Mark Ramprakash (rested) making way for Graham Thorpe, Tim Murtagh and Scott Newman. Hampshire, meanwhile, rest Robin Smith, while welcoming John Crawley back from Test duty. Alan Mullally misses out with 'flu, so James Schofield deputises. With Hampshire relegated and Surrey already assured of the title, neither side has much to play for, which explains the presence of a number of youngsters in the two sides. Although several pitches at The Rose Bowl have been of poor quality this season, this one looks good, so Ian Ward, Surrey's stand-in captain, has no hesitation in electing to bat when he wins the toss on a beautiful late-summer morning.*

After a terrible opening over from James Tomlinson, during which he fires four balls way down the legside and is then square-cut to the boundary by Ian Ward, we witness a quite amazing second over of the match, bowled by James Schofield, which includes two boundaries, a wicket and a dropped catch. The 23-year-old seamer's first ball is pulled through midwicket for four by Scott Newman; the second sees Jimmy Adams, at short leg, taking a brilliant catch as the young opener fends a short ball down almost vertically; the fourth is cracked to the rope at cover by Nadeem Shahid; and the next has the Surrey number three edging at shin height to Dimitri Mascarenhas at first slip and surviving as the fielder fumbles the chance.

Inevitably, things calm down a little after such a frenetic start, though Ward still manages to find the off-side boundary three times as Tomlinson fails to locate any sort of line or length and is pulled from the attack after just four overs. Unfortunately for Hampshire, Schofield then loses his way after a decent start and, after twice being cut for four in his sixth over by the in-form Ward, he, too, is withdrawn by his captain, Will Kendall, with the Surrey total already past fifty.

Although the first-change bowlers, Neil Johnson and Mascarenhas, manage to impose a little restraint on the batsmen, neither of the medium-pacers looks especially dangerous on what appears to be a very good pitch, prompting the Hampshire captain to turn back to Tomlinson at the pavilion end for the nineteenth over of the morning in an attempt to conjure up another breakthrough.

The left-arm swing bowler's second spell, in place of Johnson, certainly turns out to be an improvement on his first, though he is unable to stop Ward advancing to a 73-ball fifty, containing eight fours, or to prevent Surrey's total moving into three figures in the twenty-seventh over. With Shahid having opened up after a slow start by pulling and hooking Mascarenhas for two fours, Kendall is eventually forced into calling up Shaun Udal to replace the medium-pacer some forty-five minutes before lunch.

The tall off-spinner is fairly tidy from the Northern end until the break, though Schofield's second spell in place of Tomlinson yields square-cut and cover-driven boundaries to Shahid as the former Essex batsman completes his half-century from his eighty-ninth delivery in the penultimate over of the session.

*Lunch:- Surrey 131-1 (Ward 67\*, Shahid 52\*) from 36 overs*

The Surrey duo continue to hold the whip hand after lunch, with the recalled Mascarenhas and Johnson making little impression as the total and the partnership both pass 150 in the forty-third over.

Ward is then pretty severe on Tomlinson when the left-armer rejoins the attack at the northern end in place of Johnson, with cut, glanced and cover-driven boundaries in the space of three rather inaccurate overs taking his personal tally into the nineties. An impressive 156-ball century, containing sixteen fours, subsequently arrives when the stand-in captain drives the returning Schofield to the fence at extra cover three overs later. This stroke has also taken the Surrey score through to two-hundred and thereby earned the 2002 county champions their fiftieth batting point of the summer.

At this stage of proceedings it seems that nothing can disturb the visitors' progress, but Schofield, the pick of the attack so far, has other ideas as he unseats Shahid with the batsman on eighty-two and the second-wicket partnership three shy of two-hundred. By mistiming a pull shot and providing Udal at mid-on with a simple catch, the Surrey number three offers Hampshire just a glimmer of hope that they can find a way back into the game, even though their opponents are already strongly placed at 205-2.

Shahid's dismissal - coincidentally a carbon copy of the way he had been dismissed by these same opponents in the recent game at The AMP Oval - finally brings Graham Thorpe into the game, with a polite smattering of welcoming applause greeting his entrance. He doesn't enjoy a very happy return to competitive action, however, as he starts slowly, understandably looks rather rusty, and then brings about the run-out of his partner with a call for a very tight single to cover. Ward is perhaps unlucky that the 21-year-old Jimmy Adams pulls off a brilliant direct hit on the striker's stumps, but he has always looked to be struggling to make his ground in any case. It's a sad way for the Surrey skipper's fine innings of 112 to end, and it puts a little extra pressure on Thorpe as he battles to find some form.

After a few overs of reconnaissance against Udal, who has replaced Tomlinson at the northern end, the England middle-order man finally appears to be finding his feet when he drives and cuts the off-spinner for two boundaries in an over, though it turns out to be a false dawn as the experienced Hampshire man takes vengeance in his next over. Sneaking a delivery through Thorpe's ineffective defensive stroke to hit the leg stump, Udal ends the left-hander's comeback innings on nineteen and pegs Surrey back to 239-4.

And two balls later it's 239-5 when the Hampshire veteran extracts a little extra bounce to have Jon Batty edging to Johnson at slip. We have a contest on our hands at last, thanks to the off-spinner's fine efforts, and there are a few more nervy moments for the new batting combination of Alistair Brown and Martin Bicknell in the lead-up to tea as Udal and a recalled Mascarenhas manage to keep the pressure on.

*Tea:- Surrey 253-5 (Brown 7\*, Bicknell 9\*) from 72 overs*

Kendall perseveres with the same bowlers after tea, and the Surrey batsmen continue to show restraint and respect, with just two boundaries - from a top-edged cut and a cover drive by Brown off Udal - coming from the first ten overs of the session. Batting certainly looks a lot more difficult now than it has done all day, though the reintroduction of Tomlinson for Mascarenhas looks like it might change things, since the left-armer's opening over costs ten runs, including a pulled four by Brown.

Tomlinson quickly settles down to produce what is by far his best spell of the day, however, and, apart from a slog-swept six by Brown off Udal that takes the total past three-hundred, the batsmen are kept relatively quiet, even though the sixth-wicket pair have been together long enough to have completed a half-century partnership.

Having laboured long and hard to score twenty-five from sixty-five balls, Bicknell then appears to lose patience as he drives Udal straight to Crawley at mid-on with a shot born of frustration, before Ian Salisbury, seemingly determined not to get bogged down like his predecessor, comes and goes within the space of six balls. After pulling Tomlinson to the midwicket boundary and then enjoying a stroke of luck with a Chinese cut for two, the Surrey leg-spinner scythes recklessly at a near-wide from the left-armer and edges to Pothas behind the stumps. As Salisbury makes his way back to the dressing room with the score now 312-7, the feeling that he has done well to actually reach the delivery is confirmed as the bowler's end umpire, John Holder, turns to his colleague, John Steele, and signals a wide.

Although the loss of these two wickets initially prompts a sudden boundary glut - Brown sees off Tomlinson with an extra-cover drive and then greets the new bowler, Schofield, with a lofted off-drive, followed by a pull high over square leg for six that completes the Surrey beneficiary's 108-ball half-century - the bowlers quickly regain control as the day draws to a close.

Having taken full advantage of a pitch that has allowed him just a degree of turn and slightly unpredictable bounce, Udal has certainly been Hampshire's best bowler, while the new county champions will probably feel satisfied with their score at the close of play.

*Close:- Surrey 348-7 (Brown 59\*, Saqlain 11\*) from 104 overs*

## Second Day - Thursday 12th September

### Surrey 418; Hampshire 327

Having decided against taking the new ball yesterday evening, Hampshire elect to claim it at the start of the second day's play and soon make the breakthrough that dashes any lingering Surrey hopes of building a huge total. Only two runs have come from the first four overs of the day, bowled by Dimitri Mascarenhas and James Schofield, when Ali Brown shuffles across his stumps, is beaten by a ball nipping back at him, and is adjudged lbw by umpire Holder. Mascarenhas' early strike immediately lifts Hampshire spirits, and, with the pitch misbehaving a little as both Saqlain Mushtaq and the new batsman, Jimmy Ormond, get hit by balls that appear to 'pop' slightly, the ninth-wicket pair are put to the test by some well controlled bowling.

Although the Pakistani manages an off-driven boundary at Schofield's expense in the day's eighth over, Ormond never looks comfortable, and, after a terrible struggle, it is something of a relief when he edges a drive to Johnson at second slip.

With Schofield having been the man to claim Ormond's scalp, both bowlers now have some reward for their impressive performances this morning, though, much to Will Kendall's disappointment, they prove unable to polish the innings off. Mascarenhas is driven nicely through extra cover for four by Tim Murtagh before giving way to Shaun Udal, while Schofield receives a fearful hammering from Saqlain in the last two overs of his spell - three off-drives and a slog-pull over midwicket all go for four - prompting the return of James Tomlinson.

Although this new bowling combination proves effective in staunching the flow of runs for four overs, Saqlain makes up for this period of famine with a mighty feast in the next over, delivered by Tomlinson. Having turned down an easy single at the start of the over, he takes 4, 6, 4, 4 from the next four deliveries, courtesy of a top-edged pull, a solidly middled pull, a drive over mid-on, and an edge to third man. The second of these boundary hits has raised the Surrey four-hundred, while the third has completed a valuable fifty from 110 balls, with eight fours and that pulled six.

Murtagh then joins in the fun as he drives Udal down the ground for a one-bounce four in the following over, but when Saqlain next faces Tomlinson he perishes to the first ball he receives, as he charges down the pitch and loses his off stump in attempting a big hit over extra cover.

With Surrey's last-wicket pair having added fifty-seven runs and advanced the total to 418, Hampshire require 269 to avoid the follow-on as they face a tricky nine-over period before lunch, and disaster nearly befalls them immediately as Laney cuts Ormond straight to Salisbury in the gully in the second over of the innings, without a run on the board. Fortunately for the 29-year-old opener, the Surrey leg-spinner is unable to cling on to the head-high chance that would have given his side the perfect start, and, thereafter, the batsmen quickly take charge. While

Laney picks off three boundaries during Bicknell's fourth over - two of them cracked through the off-side and one sailing away to third man via the outside edge - Johnson twice cuts to the rope in Ormond's following over to boost the score by twenty runs in two overs, and send the openers to lunch in high spirits.

*Lunch:- Hampshire 34-0 (Johnson 12\*, Laney 22\*) from 9 overs*

Tim Murtagh joins Bicknell in the attack after the break, but neither bowler is able to contain the same Hampshire openers who had batted so negatively in the game at The AMP Oval just a few short weeks ago. Bicknell receives surprisingly rough treatment from Laney, who cuts and drives three fours in the space of two overs to take the total past fifty, while Murtagh starts steadily before being driven to the boundary on three occasions in his fourth over by Johnson.

Predictably enough, both bowlers are replaced at this stage, with Saqlain taking over at the pavilion end and Ormond doing likewise at the northern end. Things don't start too promisingly for them, though, as Johnson's full-blooded drive at the off-spinner crashes into the throat of Nadeem Shahid at silly point, requiring the badly shaken fielder to retire from the action, then Laney drives Ormond down the ground for four in the next over.

Despite these unsettling incidents, both bowlers hit back with a wicket in their second over, Saqlain removing Johnson for thirty-two in the twentieth over with the total on seventy-nine, and Ormond dismissing Laney for forty-eight an over later with the score advanced by just a single. The former Zimbabwean international falls to a good catch by Murtagh at deep extra-cover after getting a leading edge to an attempted drive, while his opening partner finds his defensive stroke comprehensively defeated by a fine outswinger that clips the outside edge of the off stump.

As Surrey push for further breakthroughs, Ormond's pace and swing continue to cause problems, with John Crawley surviving a very confident appeal for a catch at the wicket with only three runs to his name, and only a couple of pleasant, but isolated, off-side boundaries by the left-handed Jimmy Adams keep the score moving forward. The third four of his innings, courtesy of a square cut in the sixth over of Ormond's impressive spell, turns out to be his last, however, as the big paceman gains retribution with his next delivery when Scott Newman, at short leg, takes a fine one-handed reflex catch off bat and pad. With Hampshire now 109-3, the county champions are suddenly threatening to take control of the match.

It is fortunate for the home side, therefore, that Ormond is coming towards the end of his stint and appears to be tiring slightly, while, simultaneously, Crawley is becoming increasingly fluent after his slightly sticky start. Consequently, the England batsman and his new partner, Will Kendall, plunder three confident boundaries from as many overs by the former Leicestershire fast bowler as they begin to establish a significant partnership for their side.

With Saqlain having had no joy from his opening ten-over spell, Ian Ward decides to make a double bowling change at this point, introducing Ian Salisbury at the pavilion end and recalling Murtagh at the northern end. Neither man looks to be at his best, however, as Crawley immediately pulls the young Surrey seamer for two fours on the way to an impressive half-century from 69 balls, while Salisbury is easily milked for three or four singles an over. The fourth-wicket partnership subsequently passes fifty when Crawley again takes two fours from a Murtagh over - this time with a glance and a cut - and the game's almost inevitable 'end of term' feeling grows as Hampshire continue to rattle along at four-an-over up until the break.

*Tea:- Hampshire 184-3 (Crawley 63\*, Kendall 22\*) from 46 overs*

Ian Ward pairs Bicknell and Saqlain after tea in an attempt to break the Crawley-Kendall alliance, though this doesn't initially look to be a good move as Crawley hands out more punishment to Bicknell, pulling and glancing to the rope on three occasions as the total hurries past two-hundred in the forty-ninth over. With Saqlain conceding a string of singles and twos at the other end and the century partnership arriving during the fourth over of the session,

Hampshire are looking to be the team on top, and, as a result, Surrey are mightily relieved when their Pakistani spin king suddenly gets a ball to pop at Crawley, producing a gloved catch to Newman at short leg. As the England batsman departs for an excellent eighty-two at 209-4, equilibrium appears to have been restored to the contest.

The pendulum almost swings back towards the visitors in the next over from Bicknell, though, when edges from both Kendall and the newly arrived John Francis fly to the boundary rather than into the hands of fielders behind the wicket. The Surrey swing maestro is probably thinking that it isn't his day by now, though his fortunes change just a couple of overs later when the Hampshire skipper suddenly drives loosely to his opposite number at cover, with the total advanced to 231.

Unperturbed by the loss of his partner to the final delivery of Bicknell's over, the left-handed Francis, seemingly bristling with aggression, dances down the track to the second ball of the next over from Saqlain and plants the ball into the crowd at long-off. It's good to see the relegated county playing so much more positively in this game... especially when Nic Pothas' attempt to emulate his colleague's positive strokeplay fails dismally, as an on-drive at the off-spinner's 'dousra', or wrong 'un, results in a leading edge and a dolly catch to Murtagh at cover. A score of 246-6 now spells danger for Hampshire - even though they look certain to pass the follow-on mark of 269 - since the champions will be strong favourites to win if they can establish a decent first-innings lead.

The outside possibility of having to follow-on is virtually wiped away in the space of four balls in Bicknell's next over, as a sequence of 4, 3, 4, 4 by Francis and the new batsman, Dimitri Mascarenhas, takes the total up to 263. Surrey's senior bowler leaves the field at the end of a chastening over that has seen three off-side drives and a clip through square leg make rather a mess of his already expensive figures, and Ormond replaces him at the northern end.

With Saqlain having been lofted down the ground for four in the over following the assault on Bicknell, the new bowler quickly feels the force of some rather manic batting himself when Francis drives him just over the head of Ward at wide mid-on and then slices him away over gully for the second four of the paceman's comeback over. At the other end, Mascarenhas is more than happy to join in with this free-spirited batting display, reeling off three well-timed drives at Ormond's expense, and, with Saqlain sufficiently frustrated following a lofted straight drive from Francis to deliver a bouncer that the 21-year-old left-hander hooks for four, things are getting out of control. By way of contrast, the young Hampshire batsman remains composed enough to push the single that completes a stunning 38-ball fifty, including eight fours and a six, later in the over, and with the fifty partnership and the Hampshire three-hundred arriving shortly afterwards the game has regained an even balance.

Since his Pakistani off-spinner is clearly at the end of his tether, Ward recalls Salisbury to partner Ormond, and this new pairing quickly tilts the match back towards Surrey, coincidentally just moments after Adam Hollioake has come out to act as a substitute fielder in place of Keith Medlycott, who has been filling the role since Bicknell's departure earlier in the session.

With both partners in the exhilarating seventh-wicket stand departing in successive overs, Hampshire's position of prosperity quickly crumbles away, as 314-6 becomes 316-8. The visitors' comeback starts when Francis becomes Ormond's fiftieth first-class victim of the season, gloving a hook at the Surrey fast bowler and being well taken away to his right-hand side by Batty, and continues when Mascarenhas carelessly puts up a towering skier off Salisbury that Ed Giddins, the substitute for Shahid, pouches safely some fifteen yards in from the rope at long-off.

Now that they have removed Francis for a splendid fifty-nine and Mascarenhas for a lively thirty, Surrey storm through the tail, as James Schofield falls to his first ball, an ideal leg-stump yorker from Ormond, and the innings ends nine runs later, at 327, when James Tomlinson is lbw when barely half forward to a Salisbury leg-break.

Since the visitors have worked things out to perfection, there is no time left for them to bat tonight, so the players leave the field at the end of another beautiful day with the new county champions having established a 91-run lead on first innings, thanks to some decent bowling by Ormond, Saqlain and the under-used Salisbury in the face of Hampshire's feisty and entertaining batting effort.

*Close:- End of the Hampshire innings*

### Third Day - Friday 13th September
### Surrey 418 and 422-8; Hampshire 327

Both Surrey openers get off the mark with an edgy four this morning, with Ian Ward's snick off James Schofield looking like a potential catch had there been a third slip in place. Neither batsmen is duly perturbed, though, and Scott Newman cracks James Tomlinson for a couple of pleasing off-side boundaries before a very poor umpiring decision ends his innings in the seventh over, with the total on twenty-seven. The big left-hander's inside edge onto his pad can be clearly heard from the top of the magnificent Rose Bowl pavilion, yet umpire Holder adjudges him lbw to Schofield. It's no wonder that Newman looks extremely frustrated as he leaves the field.

Despite taking that nasty blow at short leg yesterday, Nadeem Shahid comes out at number three, and, while he shows no ill effects, he is very subdued in the early stages of his innings, apart from one well-struck cover drive off Tomlinson, who is looking much more impressive than on day one. Shahid's slow start isn't a problem for the visitors, however, since Ward is now moving through the gears, and greets Dimitri Mascarenhas with cut, glanced and straight-driven boundaries in the medium-pacer's first over after replacing Tomlinson at the pavilion end.

Although the Hampshire all-rounder then comes back well with a maiden to Shahid, Will Kendall opts for a double bowling change, replacing Schofield with Tomlinson, and giving Shaun Udal an early taste of the action.

The left-arm swing bowler soon induces an edge from Ward that brings the left-hander four runs, though Shahid seems to be settling down nicely as he locates the off-side boundary twice in four overs, once off each bowler, raising the fifty partnership in the process. Ward's personal fifty isn't too long coming, either, though the square-cut four off Udal that takes him to the milestone is a rather more convincing shot than the miscued drive just over the head of the fielder at cover that has preceded it. The in-form opener's half-century has come in quick time, from 55 balls, and contained nine fours.

Up until now, it has all been plain sailing for the Surrey batsmen, but the reappearance of Mascarenhas, this time at the northern end, in place of Tomlinson, changes the pace of the game completely. Not only does the all-rounder's pairing with Udal produce four successive maidens, it also brings the wicket of Shahid, who sashays down the wicket to Mascarenhas and top-edges a cut through to Nic Pothas after making twenty out of a total of ninety-three.

Although, Graham Thorpe is away much more positively and confidently than in the first innings by cutting three boundaries in quick succession, two off the recently successful bowler and then one at the expense of the returning Schofield, the rest of the morning session turns out to be very uneventful with just six runs coming from the last seven overs. There is a noteworthy statistic to record, however, since Ian Ward becomes the leading run-scorer in Division One of the Championship by passing Nick Knight's tally of 1,520. Since the Warwickshire opener's season is already complete, it looks likely that the Surrey left-hander will retain that honour.

*Lunch:- Surrey 117-2 (Ward 59\*, Thorpe 17\*) from 36 overs*

With Jimmy Adams purveying left-arm medium-pace in tandem with Tomlinson, we have the unusual scenario of two left-arm bowlers up against two left-handed batsmen in the opening stages of the session. After a couple of promising overs from Tomlinson, it's the batsmen who come out on top, however, as a cluster of four boundaries in the eighth and ninth overs after the break bring the fifty partnership for the third wicket, the Surrey 150, and the removal of both bowlers from the attack.

The Hampshire skipper hopes he might see a reduction in the scoring rate, as well as a breakthrough, by recalling his most experienced bowlers, Udal and Mascarenhas, but, though Thorpe does offer a very sharp one-handed caught-and-bowled chance to the off-spinner with his score on forty-two, the Surrey pair continue to have much the better of things, with Ward moving towards a possible third successive County Championship century and Thorpe completing an increasingly assured fifty from exactly a hundred balls.

Since the pitch appears to have flattened out again after some unpredictable moments earlier in the match, there is now nothing to trouble Ward, and when he cuts Udal to the point boundary in the fifty-sixth over he advances his score to ninety-five and makes the third-wicket stand worth a hundred. Thorpe, meanwhile, has a couple of edgy moments during an over from Udal as the total passes two-hundred, before clipping Schofield for two boundaries as soon as the opening bowler returns to the attack in place of Mascarenhas.

As his partner nudges ever closer to three figures, the England left-hander now takes over the more dominant role by pulling Udal wide of mid-on for another four and then punishing Schofield twice in an over again when the 23-year-old overpitches. Later in the same over, a Thorpe single puts Ward back on strike and, after thirty balls in the nineties, the Surrey captain takes full advantage of a short delivery to hook high over square leg for a six that takes him through to a 175-ball century and earns him a place in the record books as the first Surrey batsman to score three successive first-class centuries since John Edrich in 1965. As the crowd offers up their congratulatory applause, the announcement over the public address system reveals that Ward's hundred has come up in 234 minutes and has contained seventeen fours in addition to that crowning six.

Although the run flow slows just a fraction in the run-up to tea as Adams returns to the fray in support of Udal, there are still a number of milestones that the Surrey duo pass, with the Ward-Thorpe partnership exceeding 150 as the latter moves into the nineties with successive cuts to the boundary off Adams, and the Surrey 250 arriving shortly afterwards.

Having inched up from ninety-six to ninety-nine with a run of singles, the England left-hander then completes a fine comeback century three overs before the interval by means of a push to square leg from his 161st delivery. Thorpe's innings has been studded with fifteen fours and will clearly have pleased the England selectors, since it appears to have instantly justified their faith in the Surrey batsman.

Two cover-driven fours by Ward off Adams then take us to tea with Surrey leading by 363 runs, making a declaration during the last session extremely likely.

*Tea:- Surrey 272-2 (Ward 123\*, Thorpe 102\*) from 75 overs*

Tomlinson and Adams are back in harness after the break, reviving the left-versus-left confrontation, and, while Thorpe goes through a quiet period, Ward grabs the initiative with a couple of boundaries off each bowler, taking the partnership past two-hundred, the total beyond three-hundred, and completing an excellent personal 150 from the 228th delivery he receives. Twenty-four fours and a six have adorned his excellent five-hour innings.

Although Thorpe suddenly cuts loose again by taking three fours from the first over delivered by the Hampshire captain, who has brought himself into the attack in place of Tomlinson, Ward rather stalls after passing his latest landmark and then departs a few overs later when he overbalances in attempting to drive Adams and is stumped by Pothas for 156.

The crowd's applause for his fine knock has barely died away when his replacement, Ali Brown, falls lbw to the same bowler two balls later. Since Surrey already lead by 423 at this stage, the visitors' total and personal performances are pretty much irrelevant, though Brown won't have been happy to have recorded a duck, especially as the ball that has dismissed him must have pitched perilously close to leg stump.

After some attractive strokes from both Thorpe and the new batsman, Jon Batty, push the total beyond 350, Hampshire take the new ball, put it in the hands of Tomlinson and Schofield, and quickly dispose of both Surrey batsmen, as the left-hander slices a drive at the former straight to point, and the right-hander edges the latter to Johnson at second slip.

With the champions advantage having now extended to 451 and no declaration forthcoming, Martin Bicknell and Ian Salisbury enjoy themselves at the bowlers' expense, picking off seven boundaries in four overs before the leg-spinner is beaten on the back foot and has his stumps rearranged by Schofield. Thereafter, as the day draws to a close and the Surrey four-hundred arrives, there is little to get excited about until Saqlain hits successive balls from Schofield back over the bowler's head for four, and Bicknell edges a flailing drive at Tomlinson in the final over to be well caught in front of first slip by the flying Pothas.

*Close:- Surrey 422-8 (Saqlain 15\*) from 103.2 overs*

## Fourth Day - Saturday 14th September

### Surrey 418 and 422-8dec; Hampshire 327 and 390

### Surrey won by 123 runs
### Surrey 20pts, Hampshire 6

Surrey's expected overnight declaration leaves Hampshire to score a theoretical 514 to win, and the home team gets away to a disastrous start as Martin Bicknell claims three wickets in his first four overs to reduce them to 27-3.

Jason Laney is his first victim, in the third over of the morning - just as the words 'Bickers appears to have lost the knack of getting Laney out' have passed my lips - edging an attempted steer to third man into Jon Batty's gloves just a couple of balls after profiting by four runs from the very same shot. Then, with the ball swinging in slightly cloudy and hazy conditions, Bicknell adds two further victims to his bag in the space of three balls in his fourth over. Jimmy Adams is the first of these as he is beaten on the front foot by inswing and falls to a leg-before verdict, then the crucial wicket of John Crawley follows as the England batsman pops back a simple catch off the leading edge. As a delighted Bicknell and his team-mates celebrate, it looks like we might be heading home early this afternoon.

Neil Johnson and Will Kendall get their heads down to repair the damage, however, and, though they have occasional moments of good fortune and uncertainty, they take the score beyond fifty, seeing off Jimmy Ormond at the pavilion end in the process. His replacement, Tim Murtagh, doesn't settle too well, even though the conditions look tailor-made for him, but this isn't a major concern for the county champions, since Bicknell soon picks up a fourth wicket at the other end when Kendall, on twenty-three, erroneously shoulders arms to an inswinger that clips his off stump with the total on sixty-five.

Given his side's current predicament, the new batsman, John Francis, is unable to play in the same free-flowing style as in the first innings, though he and Johnson play out the last two overs of Bicknell's excellent ten-over opening stint and also see off a rather disappointing Murtagh at the pavilion end.

The resulting double bowling change brings the introduction of Saqlain Mushtaq and the return of Ormond, this time at the northern end, though the off-spinner starts dismally, with Johnson instantly driving and pulling him for three boundaries. With the skies clearing and the sun breaking through strongly, Ormond fares little better, and the batsmen steadily take control, as the total races into three figures and the former Zimbabwe international completes an impressive 81-ball half-century with a forcing stroke backward of point off Saqlain in the penultimate over before lunch. It looks like we won't be going home early after all!

*Lunch:- Hampshire 137-4 (Johnson 59\*, Francis 27\*) from 29 overs*

While Ian Salisbury makes his first appearance of the innings immediately after lunch, Martin Bicknell returns in style at the northern end, immediately completing a five-wicket haul with his second ball when Francis, only half-forward, is defeated by an inswinger and sent on his way by umpire Holder's upraised digit.

Unfortunately for the bowler and for Surrey, Bicknell is soon out of action for the rest of the day, though, as he contributes just three more overs - during which Nic Pothas twice drives him to the cover boundary - before being forced to retire with what appears to be an ankle injury.

Tim Murtagh consequently takes over from his senior colleague and finds Johnson edging the first ball of his new spell to third man for four, before the Hampshire opener falls to Salisbury in the next over. Having twice been driven through extra cover for four, the leg-spinner evens the score with Johnson, thanks to a leg-break that creeps through low to clip the off stump with the left-hander's score on eighty-three and the total on 189.

Since the chances of his side securing a draw are now paper-thin, it seems quite likely that Dimitri Mascarenhas will bat to enjoy himself and entertain, and so it proves. Although Murtagh goes past the outside edge a number of times during his best spell of the match and Salisbury's variations cause occasional miscues, the runs start to flow as the Hampshire all-rounder, ably assisted by Pothas, pulls, sweeps and drives four early boundaries, before raising a rapid fifty partnership for the seventh wicket with a towering on-drive for six off Salisbury.

The following over then brings greater mayhem with Mascarenhas taking 6, 6, 2, 4 from the Surrey leg-spinner, as a pull, a slog-sweep, a late cut and an off-drive complete a highly entertaining 44-ball fifty. It is doubtful whether Salisbury enjoys this no-pressure strokeplay quite as much as the Hampshire public, however, and his spin twin finds the going just as tough when he replaces Murtagh at the northern end for the next over. Mascarenhas adds four more boundaries to his growing collection in the next two overs of spin, in fact, prompting Ian Ward to make a surprising, but effective, move... he brings himself on to bowl in place of his leg-spinner and snares the Hampshire all-rounder lbw with the final ball of his over, a delivery of full-length that clearly takes the batsman by surprise.

Having secured the breakthrough, the acting skipper retires gracefully from the attack, handing the ball back to Salisbury and watching Pothas register an 86-ball half-century just before the break.

*Tea:- Hampshire 294-7 (Pothas 53\*, Udal 1\*) from 59 overs*

With three wickets required in order to complete their victory, Surrey's tactics appear fairly obvious as the spinners continue in tandem after tea - they have clearly been given licence to make even greater attempts to lead the batsmen into temptation.

Shaun Udal seems happy enough with this as he sweeps Salisbury for three fours in an over, while Saqlain seemingly takes the idea of 'tossing the ball up' a little too literally as he concedes a no-ball for bowling a full-toss over waist height. Surprisingly, Udal's sweeps are isolated boundaries as runs accrue almost exclusively through singles until he drives the leg-spinner through extra cover for four in the ninth over of the session. Salisbury wreaks revenge for this stroke before the over is out, however, taking his side within two wickets of victory when Udal attempts to cut and is bowled by a googly.

Hopes that Surrey are now almost home and dry at this point are, however, dashed by an increasingly eccentric display from Saqlain. Operating off an ever shortening run-up, the off-spinner concedes four boundaries to Pothas during a completely shambolic fifteenth over, and, when he ends his next over by bowling from a standing start, Ian Ward takes the hint that it's time for a bowling change!

The end-of-term atmosphere continues with Ormond returning to purvey his off-spin, which is much to the liking of the Hampshire wicketkeeper, who slog-sweeps and cuts boundaries to move his score on to ninety-six, and when Salisbury is twice driven to the rope by James Schofield in the following over, it is all starting to get rather irritating.

Fortunately, the Surrey 'leggie' puts everyone out of their misery with two wickets in five balls shortly afterwards. First Pothas falls one short of his century when his defensive edge to a leg-break is caught, after three juggles, by Ali Brown at slip, then James Tomlinson provides Scott Newman with a simple bat-pad catch at short leg in Salisbury's next over.

Surrey 418 and 422-8dec; Hampshire 327 and 390
Surrey won by 123 runs. Surrey 20pts, Hampshire 6

## VIEWS FROM THE DRESSING ROOM

*Would it be fair to say that the team was a little demob happy, with the title already sewn up?*
**MARTIN BICKNELL** - Yes, without a doubt. It's very difficult to maintain that intensity once you've won the Championship. I know we get criticised for not declaring and whatever, but it's tough when there's no intensity or desire to go and win the game because you've already done the hard work. You strive so hard to get there and once you've achieved your goal it's such a massive relief that it's very difficult to start forcing the issue to get people really switched on again to win games. Saying that, at that stage of the season we were still playing well and it was important for me to try and bowl well because I'd struggled a bit after my wrist injury.
**IAN SALISBURY** - Yes, I won't deny that we did enjoy ourselves down there. We obviously got a bit of stick, but when you've won the Championship and bodies are very sore there is nothing in the world worse than fielding, believe me. We wanted to be batting, and the batters were awesome - Wardy was just a machine at this stage, we could have blindfolded him and he still would have made a hundred. People were getting on at us because we set them such a big score, but we still left them a day to get the runs and managed to bowl them out on a very good pitch. I think things were better in the last game of the season because we played a couple of young seamers with something to prove.

*After some of the horror stories we'd heard about pitches at The Rose Bowl, were you surprised at how well this one played?*
**MARTIN BICKNELL** - Yes, I was absolutely devastated, I expected to turn up and find a green, nightmare wicket, but the Hampshire lads said it was the best pitch they played on all year there. Seriously, though, I don't like playing on poor pitches - if I take wickets then I like to take them on good pitches because it means so much more. Fortunately, I bowled well in the second innings and picked up a few.

*Your first and second innings bowling performances were pretty much like chalk and cheese. Do you have any idea why that might have been?*
**MARTIN BICKNELL** - I was going through a patch there in the first innings where nothing was really going right for me - I had a few edges over the slips and things like that, and in a couple of spells I didn't get it right. To be fair, I wasn't fully fit when I came back from the injury, and I found it really difficult, after being out for eight weeks, to come back and resume from where I'd been before. If you come back into the side, like I did, and then don't bowl so well, all of a sudden your confidence goes a bit.

*I assume you were pleased to see Solly get some wickets here, too, since it had been a pretty frustrating season for spinners?*
**MARTIN BICKNELL** - Yes, it was difficult for spinners, because we did play on some very flat pitches this year, but the thing about Ian Salisbury is that every other side in the country would like to have him in their team because he is the X-factor in our attack. With his wicket-taking ability he can get the best players out, and he gives us that bit of variety that other sides don't have.

*Wardy notched his third successive Championship century in the second innings. He was in unbelievable form at this particular time, wasn't he?*
**MARTIN BICKNELL** - Yes, he got on a roll and he batted incredibly well. The thing about Wardy is that he's very hungry for success and once he's got himself in he's never going to give it away. That's the sign of a very good player - he's like Mark Ramprakash in that respect.

*I guess it must have been nice to have Thorpey back in the side and to see him play so well in the second innings?*
**IAN WARD** - It's always nice to see Thorpey playing - I always enjoy watching him bat, and I think he's one of the finest players I've seen, and certainly one of the finest I've played with. I've learnt a lot from him, watching the way he goes about things and talking things over with him - he's very open with his advice. He was having a pretty tough time at that stage, so it was nice to get him back playing a bit of cricket, and he played really well... until he ran me out!

### HAMPSHIRE v SURREY at The Rose Bowl   Played 11th to 14th September
Surrey won the toss and elected to bat                              Umpires:- John Holder and John Steele

#### SURREY - First Innings

| Fall Of Wkt | Batsman | How | Out | Score | Balls | 4s | 6s |
|---|---|---|---|---|---|---|---|
| 3-225 | I.J. Ward * | run | out | 112 | 188 | 17 | 0 |
| 1-8 | S.A. Newman | c Adams | b Schofield | 4 | 2 | 1 | 0 |
| 2-205 | N. Shahid | c Udal | b Schofield | 82 | 153 | 13 | 0 |
| 4-239 | G.P. Thorpe | | b Udal | 19 | 45 | 4 | 0 |
| 8-350 | A.D. Brown | lbw | b Mascarenhas | 60 | 136 | 5 | 2 |
| 5-239 | J.N. Batty + | c Johnson | b Udal | 0 | 2 | 0 | 0 |
| 6-305 | M.P. Bicknell | c Crawley | b Udal | 25 | 65 | 2 | 0 |
| 7-312 | I.D.K. Salisbury | c Pothas | b Tomlinson | 7 | 6 | 1 | 0 |
| 10-418 | Saqlain Mushtaq | | b Tomlinson | 55 | 112 | 9 | 1 |
| 9-361 | J. Ormond | c Johnson | b Schofield | 4 | 28 | 0 | 0 |
| | T.J. Murtagh | Not | Out | 15 | 28 | 2 | 0 |
| | Extras | (12b, 13lb, 8w, 2nb) | | 35 | | | |
| | **TOTAL** | **(127.2 overs)** | | **418** | | | |

| Bowler | O | M | R | W | NB | Wd |
|---|---|---|---|---|---|---|
| Tomlinson | 26.2 | 3 | 118 | 2 | - | 2 |
| Schofield | 30 | 7 | 98 | 3 | 1 | - |
| Johnson | 8 | 2 | 16 | 0 | - | - |
| Mascarenhas | 29 | 9 | 79 | 1 | - | 2 |
| Udal | 34 | 6 | 82 | 3 | - | - |

#### HAMPSHIRE - First Innings  (Needing 269 to avoid the follow-on)

| Fall Of Wkt | Batsman | How | Out | Score | Balls | 4s | 6s |
|---|---|---|---|---|---|---|---|
| 1-79 | N.C. Johnson | c Murtagh | b Saqlain | 32 | 57 | 5 | 0 |
| 2-80 | J.S. Laney | | b Ormond | 48 | 61 | 9 | 0 |
| 3-109 | J.H.K. Adams | c Newman | b Ormond | 17 | 34 | 3 | 0 |
| 4-209 | J.P. Crawley | c Newman | b Saqlain | 82 | 100 | 12 | 0 |
| 5-231 | W.S. Kendall * | c Ward | b Bicknell | 38 | 81 | 4 | 0 |
| 7-314 | J.D. Francis | c Batty | b Ormond | 59 | 50 | 9 | 1 |
| 6-246 | N. Pothas + | c Murtagh | b Saqlain | 4 | 7 | 1 | 0 |
| 8-316 | A.D. Mascarenhas | c sub (Giddins) | b Salisbury | 30 | 37 | 4 | 0 |
| | S.D. Udal | Not | Out | 8 | 14 | 1 | 0 |
| 9-318 | J.E.K. Schofield | | b Ormond | 0 | 1 | 0 | 0 |
| 10-327 | J.A. Tomlinson | lbw | b Salisbury | 1 | 16 | 0 | 0 |
| | Extras | (4lb, 4nb) | | 8 | | | |
| | **TOTAL** | **(76 overs)** | | **327** | | | |

| Bowler | O | M | R | W | NB | Wd |
|---|---|---|---|---|---|---|
| Bicknell | 17 | 2 | 92 | 1 | 1 | - |
| Ormond | 20 | 1 | 87 | 4 | 1 | - |
| Murtagh | 9 | 1 | 52 | 0 | - | - |
| Saqlain Mushtaq | 20 | 1 | 68 | 3 | - | - |
| Salisbury | 10 | 2 | 24 | 2 | - | - |

**SURREY - Second Innings** (Leading by 91 runs on first innings)

| Fall Of Wkt | Batsman | How | Out | Score | Balls | 4s | 6s |
|---|---|---|---|---|---|---|---|
| 3-332 | I.J. Ward * | st Pothas | b Adams | 156 | 240 | 24 | 1 |
| 1-27 | S.A. Newman | lbw | b Schofield | 15 | 18 | 3 | 0 |
| 2-93 | N. Shahid | c Pothas | b Mascarenhas | 20 | 59 | 4 | 0 |
| 5-360 | G.P. Thorpe | c Adams | b Tomlinson | 143 | 222 | 21 | 0 |
| 4-332 | A.D. Brown | lbw | b Adams | 0 | 2 | 0 | 0 |
| 6-360 | J.N. Batty + | c Johnson | b Schofield | 13 | 29 | 1 | 0 |
| 8-422 | M.P. Bicknell | c Pothas | b Tomlinson | 28 | 30 | 4 | 0 |
| 7-396 | I.D.K. Salisbury | | b Schofield | 16 | 12 | 3 | 0 |
| | Saqlain Mushtaq | Not | Out | 15 | 9 | 2 | 0 |
| | Extras | (8b, 4lb, 2w, 2nb) | | 16 | | | |
| | **TOTAL** | **(103.2 overs)** | **(for 8 dec)** | **422** | | | |

| Bowler | O | M | R | W | NB | Wd |
|---|---|---|---|---|---|---|
| Schofield | 23 | 7 | 94 | 3 | - | - |
| Tomlinson | 23.2 | 3 | 112 | 2 | - | - |
| Mascarenhas | 12 | 5 | 39 | 1 | 1 | 1 |
| Udal | 25 | 6 | 69 | 0 | - | - |
| Adams | 18 | 3 | 81 | 2 | - | - |
| Kendall | 2 | 0 | 15 | 0 | - | - |

**HAMPSHIRE - Second Innings** (Needing 514 to win from a minimum of 96 overs)

| Fall Of Wkt | Batsman | How | Out | Score | Balls | 4s | 6s |
|---|---|---|---|---|---|---|---|
| 6-189 | N.C. Johnson | | b Salisbury | 86 | 116 | 13 | 0 |
| 1-13 | J.S. Laney | c Batty | b Bicknell | 8 | 6 | 2 | 0 |
| 2-27 | J.H.K. Adams | lbw | b Bicknell | 8 | 12 | 1 | 0 |
| 3-27 | J.P. Crawley | c & | b Bicknell | 0 | 2 | 0 | 0 |
| 4-65 | W.S. Kendall * | | b Bicknell | 23 | 31 | 4 | 0 |
| 5-141 | J.D. Francis | lbw | b Bicknell | 28 | 43 | 4 | 0 |
| 9-384 | N. Pothas + | c Brown | b Salisbury | 99 | 142 | 12 | 0 |
| 7-287 | A.D. Mascarenhas | lbw | b Ward | 67 | 62 | 9 | 3 |
| 8-335 | S.D. Udal | | b Salisbury | 28 | 32 | 5 | 0 |
| | J.E.K. Schofield | Not | Out | 18 | 42 | 4 | 0 |
| 10-390 | J.A. Tomlinson | c Newman | b Salisbury | 2 | 4 | 0 | 0 |
| | Extras | (4b, 7lb, 4w, 8nb) | | 23 | | | |
| | **TOTAL** | **(81.2 overs)** | | **390** | | | |

| Bowler | O | M | R | W | NB | Wd |
|---|---|---|---|---|---|---|
| Bicknell | 14 | 3 | 56 | 5 | 2 | - |
| Ormond | 14 | 2 | 52 | 0 | - | 2 |
| Murtagh | 11 | 1 | 54 | 0 | 1 | - |
| Saqlain Mushtaq | 16 | 0 | 100 | 0 | 1 | - |
| Salisbury | 25.2 | 1 | 116 | 4 | - | - |
| Ward | 1 | 0 | 1 | 1 | - | - |

## Other Division One Results

Kent and Warwickshire both won to keep the race for the runners-up spot very much on the boil, while Somerset and Yorkshire suffered defeats that relegated them to the second division.

September 11-14
*Canterbury:-* **Kent beat Lancashire by six wickets.** Kent 405 (Fulton 177, Key 75, Smith 68) and 144-4 (Smith 68); Lancashire 197 (Saggers 4-34) and 351 (Chilton 90, Law 90, Saggers 4-64). **Kent 19pts, Lancashire 2**

September 12-13
*Leicester:-* **Leicestershire beat Somerset by an innings and 18 runs.** Somerset 191 (Burns 97*, Srinath 4-60) and 101 (Srinath 5-25); Leicestershire 310 (Ward 84). **Leicestershire 18pts, Somerset 2.75***
* deducted 0.25pt for slow over rate

September 12-15
*Edgbaston:-* **Warwickshire beat Yorkshire by six wickets.** Warwickshire 601-9dec (Ostler 225, Frost 103, Piper 64*, Powell 58) and 232-4 (Powell 92*, Wagh 90); Yorkshire 351 (Elliott 74, Blakey 70, White 53, Dawson 50, Wagh 5-137, Spires 4-99) and 481 (Elliott 127, Blakey 103, Fellows 88, McGrath 66, Spires 5-165). **Warwickshire 20pts, Yorkshire 6**

| COUNTY CHAMPIONSHIP DIVISION ONE AT 15TH SEPTEMBER | | | | | | | | | | |
|---|---|---|---|---|---|---|---|---|---|---|
| Pos | Prv | | P | Points | W | D | L | Bat | Bwl | Ded |
| 1 | 1 | Surrey | 15 | 222.75 | 9 | 4 | 2 | 54 | 45 | 0.25 |
| 2 | 2 | Warwickshire | 15 | 181.00 | 6 | 7 | 2 | 40 | 41 | 0.00 |
| 3 | 3 | Kent | 15 | 176.50 | 6 | 5 | 4 | 44 | 41 | 0.50 |
| 4 | 6 | Leicestershire | 15 | 164.00 | 5 | 6 | 4 | 38 | 43 | 1.00 |
| 5 | 4 | Lancashire | 15 | 156.00 | 5 | 6 | 4 | 32 | 40 | 0.00 |
| 6 | 5 | Sussex | 15 | 147.00 | 3 | 7 | 5 | 39 | 44 | 0.00 |
| 7 | 7 | Hampshire ** | 16 | 131.00 | 2 | 9 | 5 | 35 | 44 | 8.00 |
| 8 | 8 | Somerset | 15 | 122.75 | 1 | 8 | 6 | 38 | 41 | 0.25 |
| 9 | 9 | Yorkshire | 15 | 122.50 | 2 | 6 | 7 | 34 | 42 | 1.50 |

*\*\* Hampshire deducted 8pts for 'poor' pitch at Rose Bowl v Lancashire*

**NUL Division Two Results**

Essex Eagles clinched the third promotion slot with a comfortable victory over the Northamptonshire Steelbacks, whose dismal run of five straight defeats had seen them slip from title contenders to fifth place in a matter of weeks.

September 15
*Shenley:-* **Lancashire Lightning beat Middlesex Crusaders by six wickets.** Middlesex 198 (Compton 86*, Hutton 71*); Lancashire 199-4 (40.4ov; Chilton 84*, Schofield 52). **Lancashire Lightning 4pts**

*Northampton:-* **Essex Eagles beat Northamptonshire Steelbacks by 42 runs.** Essex 258-9 (Jefferson 102); Northamptonshire 216 (43.1ov; Penberthy 54, Brophy 54). **Essex Eagles 4pts**

*Hove:-* **Derbyshire Scorpions beat Sussex Sharks by 74 runs.** Derbyshire 240-8 (Bassano 55, Taylor 4-39); Sussex 166 (41.4ov; Dumelow 3-24). **Derbyshire Scorpions 4pts**

| NATIONAL LEAGUE DIVISION TWO AT 15TH SEPTEMBER | | | | | | | | |
|---|---|---|---|---|---|---|---|---|
| Pos | Prv | | P | Pts | W | T | L | A |
| 1 | 1 | Gloucestershire Gladiators | 15 | 44 | 10 | 0 | 3 | 2 |
| 2 | 2 | Surrey Lions | 15 | 38 | 9 | 0 | 5 | 1 |
| 3 | 3 | Essex Eagles | 15 | 36 | 9 | 0 | 6 | 0 |
| 4 | 5 | Lancashire Lightning | 16 | 32 | 7 | 0 | 7 | 2 |
| 5 | 6 | Derbyshire Scorpions | 15 | 30 | 7 | 0 | 7 | 1 |
| = | 4 | Northamptonshire Steelbacks | 15 | 30 | 7 | 0 | 7 | 1 |
| 7 | 7 | Hampshire Hawks | 15 | 22 | 5 | 0 | 9 | 1 |
| 8 | 8 | Middlesex Crusaders | 15 | 20 | 4 | 0 | 9 | 2 |
| = | 8 | Sussex Sharks | 15 | 20 | 4 | 0 | 9 | 2 |

# NATIONAL LEAGUE SNAPSHOTS 2

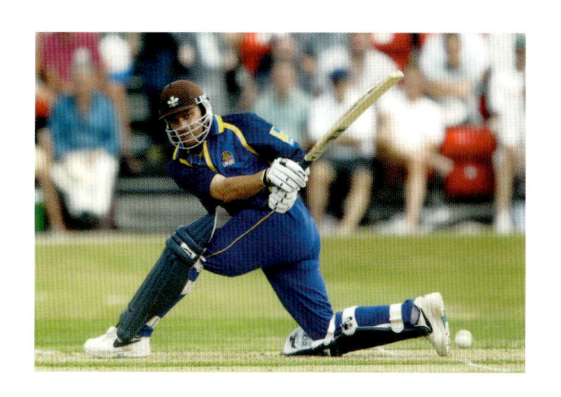

TOP - Mark Ramprakash, Surrey Lions' leading run-scorer in the promotion-winning campaign, sweeps
MIDDLE - Ed Giddins, Surrey Lions' leading wicket-taker during the NUL season
BOTTOM - The pavilion at The AMP Oval during the floodlit match versus the Hampshire Hawks
*(All photos courtesy of Surrey CCC)*

# POSTCARDS FROM HOVE

(1) - Adam Hollioake takes a brilliant catch to dismiss James Kirtley at the end of Sussex's first innings;
(2) - Joy for Jon Batty and Ed Giddins as they combine to remove Richard Montgomerie at the start of Sussex's second knock; (3) - The one that got away? The bowler and fielders are convinced that Murray Goodwin has edged to Batty... but umpire Peter Willey disagrees;
(4) - Tim Murtagh rekindles Surrey's hopes late in the game by claiming Goodwin lbw
*(All photos by Reg Elliott)*

# HAMPSHIRE HUMBLED AT THE OVAL

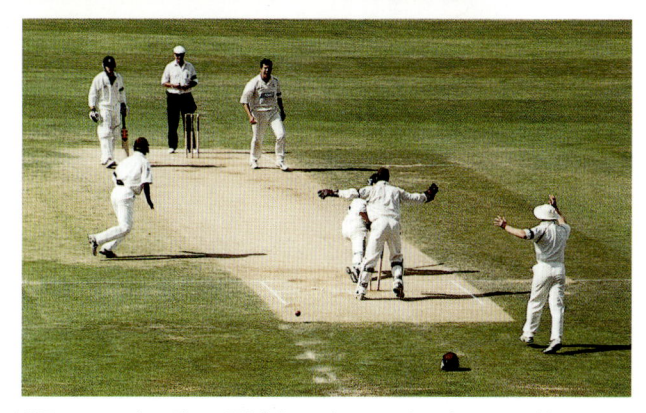

TOP - Take cover everyone! Ali Brown crashes Shaun Udal down the ground on the way to his century
MIDDLE - Nic Pothas falls lbw to Saqlain, one of eleven victims for the Surrey off-spinner in the match
BOTTOM - Anything you can do… Jimmy Ormond turns off-spinner to bowl Jason Laney
*(All photos by Reg Elliott)*

# WARD MAKES IT THREE-IN-THREE AT THE ROSE BOWL

TOP - Ian Ward cuts to the boundary during his first-innings century…
MIDDLE - … and clips through square leg as he makes his way to a third successive first-class hundred
BOTTOM - Nadeem Shahid cuts for four during his first-innings partnership with Ward
*(All photos by Reg Elliott)*

# CELEBRATIONS

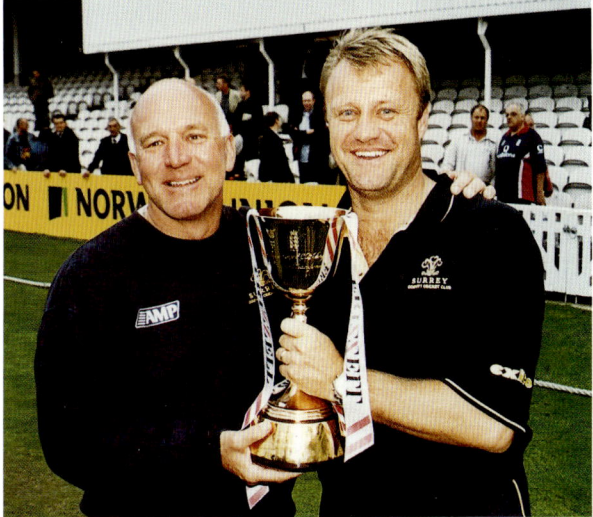

TOP - Bowlers united. Jimmy Ormond, Ian Salisbury, Martin Bicknell,
Alex Tudor and Saqlain Mushtaq with the coveted Championship trophy
MIDDLE - Alan Butcher and Keith Medlycott take their well-deserved turn in the limelight
BOTTOM - We are the champions…. again!
*(All photos by Richard Spiller)*

# LEICESTERSHIRE LANDMARKS

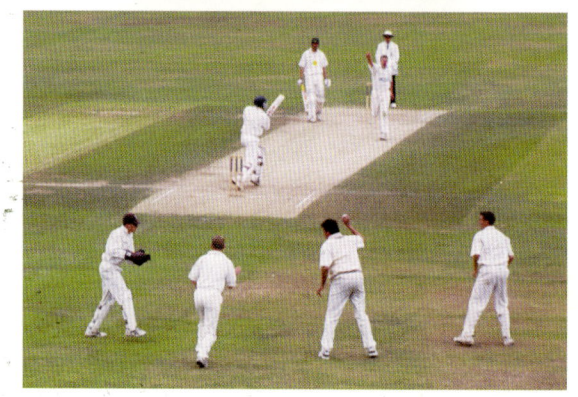

TOP - Ian Ward celebrates the completion of his fourth successive first-class century, thereby equalling the Surrey record
MIDDLE - With his maiden first-class century safely under his belt, Scott Newman returns to the pavilion after being dismissed for 183
BOTTOM - Phil Sampson secures his maiden County Championship wicket by having Ashley Wright caught behind the wicket by Jon Batty
*(Top and Bottom photos by Reg Elliott; Middle photo by John Banfield)*

# NEW CHAMPIONS BATTER FOXES INTO SUBMISSION

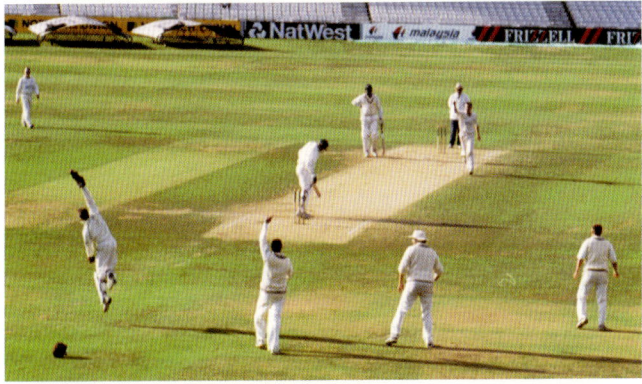

TOP - Adam Hollioake is embraced by Ian Salisbury after completing
his maiden first-class double-century
MIDDLE - Phil DeFreitas is bowled by Tim Murtagh as Leicestershire subside in their second innings
BOTTOM - Ian Salisbury has Javagal Srinath taken by Nadeem Shahid at short leg to complete
a record-breaking victory by 483 runs
*(All photos by Reg Elliott)*

# SURREY C.C.C. SQUAD - 2002 SEASON

Back row (L to R) - Tim Murtagh, Scott Newman, Rikki Clarke, Philip Sampson, Ben Scott
Middle row (L to R) - Keith Booth (Scorer), Neil Walker (Physio), Dale Naylor (Physio), Rupesh Amin,
James Ormond, Ed Giddins, Michael Carberry, Keith Medlycott (Cricket Manager), Alan Butcher (Coach)
Front row (L to R) - Ian Ward, Alex Tudor, Jason Ratcliffe, Alistair Brown, Martin Bicknell, Alec Stewart,
Mark Butcher, Graham Thorpe, Ian Salisbury, Nadeem Shahid, Mark Ramprakash, Jonathan Batty

# 20  Young Guns Fire Champions

Michael Soper, the Surrey chairman, must have had slightly mixed feelings as the season drew to a close with the final Championship match against Leicestershire. Although he would have been delighted by his side's success in the premier county competition, he discovered on 13th September that his attempt to win the nomination to take over from Lord MacLaurin as chairman of the England and Wales Cricket Board had failed, with David Morgan, the former Glamorgan chairman and current deputy chairman of the ECB, winning the election by eleven votes to eight. It was a real disappointment for Soper, who had campaigned hard on a number of issues but he had no regrets about standing for the position, as he made clear in the following statement that appeared on the Club website:-

*"Although I am naturally disappointed not to have won the election, I wish David Morgan every success in this most challenging role. If there are any ways in which I can help in the future, then I will always be pleased to do so. I have absolutely no regrets in standing and was never afraid of putting my head on the block. I believe that I have been able to highlight some of the real concerns and challenges facing cricket in the coming years. If I have been able to bring forward the immense passion I have for the game, then I have achieved what I wanted to. Cricket must remain at the very top of the agenda and I want to devote the rest of my life to ensuring it is. We need to act quickly and decisively if we are to preserve and build on all the things, which are good in the game. Nothing will give me more pleasure than being at my Club and with its members on Wednesday when we are presented with the Frizzell County Championship trophy."*

On the playing side of the game, Sussex announced that they had signed Mushtaq Ahmed as their second overseas player for 2003. 'Mushy' had certainly impressed Surrey fans with his performances during his brief spell with the Club, and he had clearly done enough to convince Sussex of his enduring skills with his efforts at Hove.

| FRIZZELL COUNTY CHAMPIONSHIP - MATCH SIXTEEN |
|---|

### SURREY versus LEICESTERSHIRE
### at The AMP Oval
### First Day - Wednesday 18th September
### Surrey 397-3

***The Teams And The Toss*** - *The Surrey team shows two changes from the eleven that took the field at The Rose Bowl, with Adam Hollioake returning to captain the side and 22-year-old Philip Sampson being given his Championship debut. Saqlain Mushtaq and Martin Bicknell join the list of Surrey players who are being rested in order to give the Club's youngsters further first-team experience. Leicestershire, who could, mathematically, still finish second, also include a couple of young players in Ashley Wright and Damian Brandy, since captain Vince Wells is out with a broken finger and Trevor Ward is sidelined by a groin strain. With a typically good-looking Oval pitch having been prepared, Hollioake makes the predictable decision to bat upon winning the toss.*

Ian Ward and Scott Newman are quickly out of their blocks on a cool, overcast morning, with both men notching an early boundary at the expense of Javagal Srinath and Devon Malcolm, respectively. Ward, looking for his fourth consecutive first-class century, shows how confident he is by driving the Indian over extra cover for four in only the fifth over of the day and then dismissing Malcolm to the rope at cover twice in the eighth over, while Newman peppers the boundary either side of point as the Surrey fifty comes up at the very respectable rate of four an over.

Apart from a few fiery Malcolm deliveries and the occasional 'jaffa' from Srinath, Leicestershire's weary-looking veterans don't really make full use of a pitch that seems to offer decent pace and good carry, prompting Iain Sutcliffe to turn to Carl Crowe's off-spin from the fourteenth over and Phillip DeFreitas' swing from the fifteenth. Crowe makes a poor start, however, sending down a couple of full-tosses in his first two overs and paying the price as Ward smashes them to the midwicket fence. Although DeFreitas is a little steadier and manages to complete the first maiden of the innings midway through the session, Ward takes two fours from his fifth over, reaching his fifty from 65 balls with the second of these boundaries, a glorious straight drive. It is looking almost too easy for the Surrey openers, really, and though Newman has a slightly nervy period in the forties, with the home county's hundred already on the board, he soon recovers to record his second first-class half-century, from 88 balls, by cutting DeFreitas backward of point for the ninth boundary of his innings.

While Newman is, hereafter, well contained by Crowe and Darren Maddy, DeFreitas' replacement at the pavilion end, Ward continues on his merry way and, as lunch approaches, adds three further boundaries to the ten that were included in his fifty.

Although DeFreitas probably rates as the pick of an unimpressive Leicestershire attack during the morning period, it is Crowe who almost makes their first breakthrough when he has Newman missed at slip by Maddy in the penultimate over of the session, with the batsman on fifty-six and the total at 132-0. It's a sharp chance from an edged drive but it already seems clear that the visitors can't afford to spurn any opportunities offered by the champions if they are to stand a chance of being competitive in this match.

*Lunch:- Surrey 133-0 (Ward 72\*, Newman 56\*) from 37 overs*

The start of the day's second session mirrors the start of the first, with the same bowlers bowling to the same batsmen and the bat continuing to dominate the ball. Newman certainly takes a liking to Srinath's bowling early on, twice driving him to the off-side boundary, while Ward takes a couple of back-foot fours off Malcolm before offering a difficult chance, on eighty-four, to Rob Cunliffe at point from a well-struck square-cut off the former England fast bowler. With the ball having arrived at a good height for him as he dives away to his right, Cunliffe would probably have been expected to do better than merely deflect the ball away to the boundary.

While Ward takes advantage of his good fortune to move to ninety-two with a top-edged hook for four off Malcolm, Newman is fast catching him up with glanced, cut, slashed and driven boundaries in the space of three fairly wretched overs from the visitors' opening bowlers. Having reached ninety with the last of these four well-timed strokes, Newman is breathing down his partner's neck in the race to three figures until Ward picks up three from Srinath's next over and then greets DeFreitas' return in place of the battered Malcolm with a textbook extra-cover drive to the rope that earns him a place in the history books. By completing his fourth successive first-class century, from 134 balls with eighteen fours, the left-handed opener becomes only the fourth Surrey batsman to achieve the feat, and the first since Sir Jack Hobbs in 1925. Hobbs also turned the trick in 1920, while the other player to achieve four-in-four was Tom Hayward in 1906. Ward's record-equalling feat is announced over the Public Address system and warmly applauded both out on the pitch and all around the ground. It has been a marvellous effort by the Surrey opener at the end of a fantastic summer that now looks certain to see him ending as the season's leading run-scorer in the County Championship - this, incredibly, will be the first time a Surrey batsman has earned this accolade since Laurie Fishlock notched 2,077 runs from 49 innings in 1950.

While Ward can relax a little now that he has completed his ton, Newman becomes becalmed in the nineties by Crowe and DeFreitas, taking six overs to move from ninety to ninety-two and then being dropped overhead by Cunliffe at cover off a no-ball from the former England seam bowler. Unfazed by this temporary blip in his progress, the 22-year-old left-hander nudges ever closer to the magical three-figure mark, and when the opening partnership reaches 209 it beats the 96-year-old record for either side in Surrey versus Leicestershire matches, set, strangely enough, by the men Ward has just joined in the record books, Hayward and Hobbs.

Having reached ninety-five with a run of five singles, Newman suddenly surges closer to his target with a square drive off DeFreitas that takes him to the familiar territory of ninety-nine, then, banishing any concerns about what had happened in his debut match, he advances on Crowe in the next over and drives him to mid-on for the single that enables him to celebrate a 129-ball maiden first-class century. A well-deserved ovation greets his arrival at this special milestone in the middle of a session that has become a tale of two centuries.

The crowd are then on their feet again shortly afterwards as Ward returns to the pavilion with 118 runs to his name after being smartly taken at second slip by Darren Maddy off DeFreitas, with the opening stand having realised 227 runs.

This hard-earned wicket for DeFreitas is then almost followed by another straight away when Jon Batty survives a confident shout for lbw as he pads up to his first ball, but, thereafter, Surrey dominate the rest of the session as Newman cuts loose to advance his score by forty-one runs in fifteen overs, the pick of his strokes being an off-driven six off Crowe, and Batty settles in to find the leg-side boundary on four occasions. As if Leicestershire don't have enough problems already, there are further negatives for them either side of the second-wicket partnership reaching fifty in the sixty-eighth over, with Neil Burns missing a tough top-edged chance offered by Newman on 127 off Crowe, then, more seriously, Maddy limping off the field with some kind of leg injury after bowling his fifth over. With two part-time bowlers, Darren Stevens and Damian Brandy, pressed into action just before the interval, things are not looking at all good for the visitors.

*Tea:- Surrey 291-1 (Newman 141\*, Batty 21\*) from 72 overs*

While Srinath contributes a couple of tight overs after rejoining the attack at the start of the final session, Brandy is positively butchered, with Batty's brace of drives to the boundary taking Surrey to three-hundred immediately after the resumption and Newman's three fours in the occasional medium-pacer's next over seeing him past 150 from the 235th delivery of his innings. The big left-hander has so far struck twenty-four fours and a six, with six of the fours and the six having come since he reached his hundred.

Stevens then replaces Brandy but soon feels the force of Newman's blade, disappearing through extra cover for four and over midwicket for six in an over costing fourteen as the partnership streaks past a hundred in just twenty overs. Even Srinath isn't immune to punishment, conceding three fours in two overs, though he does bring an end to Newman's magnificent, punishing innings shortly after the total has passed 350 when the Surrey opener snicks an attempted steer to third man into the gloves of wicketkeeper Burns with his score on 183. It has been a wonderful knock by any standards and the crowd rises to show their appreciation for the entertainment provided by the Epsom-born youngster as he makes his way from the field.

With Batty seeing the ball really well by now there would seem to be no chance of the run-rate dropping, and so it proves as the Surrey keeper lofts Crowe over mid-on and then cuts him to third man for the two boundaries that complete an impressive 80-ball half-century before following up with a mighty six over extra cover in the beleaguered off-spinner's following over.

By this stage, the light is starting to close in, however, and though the Surrey batsmen turn down one offer to retreat to the pavilion as they continue to make hay, the taking of the new ball makes life a little more difficult since it brings the reintroduction of Devon Malcolm. Despite this, Graham Thorpe does manage to notch his first boundary with a pleasing cover drive, but Batty perishes for an attractive seventy-four two overs later when he upper-cuts high to Srinath at third man. Before Nadeem Shahid can reach the middle to take guard play is suspended for the day.

The fact that play has finished some eleven overs early is not a great hardship, however, since the photographers who are here for the presentation of the County Championship trophy will want some natural light to do a proper job of recording the celebrations for posterity.

Everything is hurriedly organised out on the pitch - since it seems that is where the trophy is to be handed over this season, as opposed to on the Committee Room balcony - and before too long the vast majority of the Surrey squad are welcomed back out on to the field. The usual brief speeches are made, before the Lord's Taverners' Trophy is presented to a smiling Adam Hollioake, who very deliberately looks to the heavens before raising county cricket's premier cup above his head. Scores of photos are then taken as the trophy is passed around from one Surrey hero to the next and the champagne corks start to pop. Once most of the group photos have been taken, the players are free to make their way around the roped-off area behind which the fans are gathered, shaking hands and receiving words of congratulations as they go. We are getting quite used to this routine now, after three titles in four years... but I'm sure we won't get tired of these scenes of celebration for a good few seasons yet!

*Close:- Surrey 397-3 (Thorpe 9\*) from 93.1 overs*

## VIEWS FROM THE DRESSING ROOM

*How did it feel to record your fourth successive century and put yourself up there with the famous names from Surrey history, like Hobbs and Hayward?*
**IAN WARD** - Well, it was a bit humbling, really. I'm not sure I should be spoken of in the same breath as those sort of people - it seems a bit strange and unjustified, but it's a nice achievement and I was certainly in very good form at the time. It was just a shame that I couldn't go on and get the fifth century, though getting four in four innings was still very pleasing.

*What was it like to be facing three guys with so many Test caps in only your third Championship match?*
**SCOTT NEWMAN** - I'm not actually very good on who plays for which team around the county circuit, because I'm just concentrating on what I'm doing myself with my cricket. So, on the morning of the game, I looked through the paper - first of all to see who we were playing because I didn't even know that - and I saw it was Leicestershire, with Malcolm, Srinath and DeFreitas in their team. So I thought it should be pretty interesting. Having Dev run in at me was good fun, Daffy was swinging it both ways, and Srinath was hitting a length every other ball, so I enjoyed it.

*Which of them did you find the most testing?*
**SCOTT NEWMAN** - DeFreitas. Although I didn't give any chances, I did get some inside-edges, and he put me through my paces with a few little tricks he tries - it was quite funny, but it was good fun.

*Ian Salisbury says you remind him of a young Darren Lehmann. Can you see that for yourself?*
**SCOTT NEWMAN** - I can understand what he's saying because Lehmann hits the ball in all areas and is an attacking player. I've seen him batting over the last three years and he's now matured and really knows his game, so that's a real compliment for Sals to put me in that kind of bracket, with players of that class. I'd certainly like to think I can get as many first-class runs as Lehmann has got.

## Second Day - Thursday 19th September
## Surrey 494; Leicestershire 303-5

After Devon Malcolm completes the over he started last night he retires to the outfield, with the bowling duties transferring to Javagal Srinath and Phil DeFreitas, both of whom make unimpressive starts against an aggressive Graham Thorpe. The England left-hander looks in great touch, reeling off four off-side boundaries in the first three overs before he loses his partner, Nadeem Shahid, to the fifth ball of the ninety-sixth over of the innings when DeFreitas wins an lbw verdict from umpire Mark Benson. The next ball is then promptly lashed through the covers for four by Alistair Brown, giving the former England seamer figures of 1-19 from his two overs this morning.

With DeFreitas unusually erratic and Srinath also coming under fire, the score rattles along nicely, with Thorpe and Brown matching one another stroke for stroke as the Surrey 450 flashes up in the hundredth over. This hugely entertaining batting looks set to power the champions to a massive match-winning total until Thorpe top-edges a pull at DeFreitas and is well caught by Srinath in what had seemed to be a ludicrously square long-leg position. Credit then to Iain Sutcliffe and his bowler for what was, presumably, a well-planned dismissal that sees the back of Thorpe for forty-four with the total on 456.

With Adam Hollioake now joining Brown out in the middle, further fireworks are forecast and, sure enough, it isn't long before the latter is pulling Srinath over midwicket for six and his skipper is upper-cutting and pulling DeFreitas for fours. The former England seamer is rested shortly afterwards, having had a very mixed morning, though the wickets he has picked up today have been just reward for his efforts in the innings as a whole.

DeFreitas' replacement at the pavilion end is Carl Crowe and, though the off-spinner has a chastening start when Brown cuts him to the boundary at backward point, he manages to split the dangerous sixth-wicket pair later in his opening over by tempting Surrey's master-blaster into holing out to Malcolm at long-off. As Brown leaves the field, having made a rapid thirty-four from just 28 balls, an amusing incident out in the middle confirms the feeling that there is something of an end-of-term atmosphere to this match. With Leicestershire in their usual post-wicket huddle, Adam Hollioake sidles up and pretends to listen in on what is being said. The visiting players consequently 'absorb' him into their circle, only to then manoeuvre him into the middle of the huddle where they pretend to give him a really good kicking! It's always great to see the game being played in such a friendly spirit and it's especially heart-warming to see Adam enjoying his cricket so much after the dark days of the spring.

The fact that Surrey are enjoying the game is hardly surprising, though, because they are still well placed for a very big total at 490-6. Well, in theory they are, but, as they say, cricket's a funny game. Just sixteen balls later they are all out for 494, thanks largely to a hat-trick that goes almost completely unnoticed.

An incredible sequence of events starts when Salisbury is comprehensively beaten and bowled by the fourth delivery he faces, a fantastic break-back from Srinath, then continues when Jimmy Ormond edges the last ball of the Indian paceman's over to Stevens at second slip, thus becoming the second man in the over to go for a fourth-ball duck. An over from Crowe follows, during which Hollioake takes a single, then Srinath commences a new over bowling at the Surrey captain. The first ball is straight and of good length, Hollioake swings wildly across the line and his middle stump goes flying out of the ground, making the score 494-9.

We are witnessing a shocking tail-end collapse and it's possibly the buzz around the ground that this creates, linked to the fact that his two-in-two feat has been spread over two overs, that draws almost everyone's attention away from the fact that a hat-trick ball is coming up. Phil Sampson, on his Championship debut, is the man to face it and, though he is more than competent with the bat, he is completely unable to cope with another stunning delivery that cuts back some way to remove his off stump. Five wickets have fallen for four runs in seventeen deliveries and Srinath has claimed a hat-trick. Amazing! The Indian Test star's bowling figures have been transformed from 25.1-1-114-1 to 26.2-1-114-5 and, suddenly, a pretty unimpressive performance has been transformed into a display worthy of him leading his side off the pitch!

Facing a tricky period before lunch in their quest to score 345 to avoid the follow-on, the visitors get away well through Ashley Wright and Iain Sutcliffe as Jimmy Ormond and Tim Murtagh struggle to make any impression on this good pitch. The Leicestershire captain completes his thousand first-class runs for the season with the first of three off-side boundaries off Murtagh, while Wright's three fours all come at the expense of Ormond, as forty-two runs are knocked off the follow-on target by the interval.

*Lunch:- Leicestershire 42-0 (Wright 16\*, Sutcliffe 21\*) from 11 overs*

Tim Murtagh has a new bowling partner after lunch as Phil Sampson steps up for his first overs in Championship cricket. With Sutcliffe driving and deflecting two boundaries in his opening over, the Manchester-born fast bowler doesn't have the happiest of starts, though he soon settles down to bowl a maiden before capturing his first wicket in his third over in the premier county competition. He is denied an opening scalp with his thirteenth ball when Murtagh misses a fairly easy catch off Wright at third slip, but only has to wait three more deliveries before the same batsman edges a drive to Jon Batty and departs, amid Surrey celebrations, for twenty-two with the score at sixty.

Thereafter, the home county's two young seamers are given a very stiff examination by the experienced pair of Sutcliffe and Darren Maddy, as a glut of boundaries sees both the Leicestershire hundred and the visiting captain's fifty, from 67 balls, coming up in the twenty-fourth over. Murtagh and Sampson are far from disgraced during this period, however, with the former managing to find the edge of the bat on a couple of occasions and the latter generating decent pace to force a miscued hook from Sutcliffe and a gloved fend-off from Maddy.

Having given their all for eighteen overs, the two young pacemen are finally replaced by Ian Salisbury and an off-spinning Ormond. Although each new bowler concedes a four in his first over, this move soon calms the run-rate and eventually provides Surrey with a welcome breakthrough when Sutcliffe, on seventy-two, attempts a bizarre stroke of his own invention off the leg-spinner and top-edges a catch to Ward at deepish mid-on. Leicestershire are now 140-2 and enjoying batting on this track just as much as their Surrey counterparts had earlier.

The pitch looks ideally suited, in fact, to the new batsman, Darren Stevens, a talented strokeplayer who has yet to fulfil his potential, and he certainly starts impressively, taking eighteen from three Ormond overs to bring up the 150 and force the introduction of Nadeem Shahid, thereby creating an all leg-spin attack. Stevens' response is to drive Salisbury over mid-on and then smash a full-toss to deep midwicket before Shahid lures him into a low, skimming drive that Hollioake fails to cling on to at extra cover, with the batsman on forty-five and the total one short of two-hundred.

Maddy has meanwhile been going steadily about his business to reach a measured half-century from 93 balls, despite having to use a runner because of the leg injury he had sustained on day one, and he is joined on the fifty mark just two overs later when his partner whips his forty-fifth ball, from Shahid, to deep midwicket for a single. With no real pressure on him, and the bowling, from one end at least, not exactly out of the top drawer, the 26-year-old Stevens looks an impressive strokemaker, though his tendency to lose concentration is demonstrated again in the final over of the session when the Surrey skipper misses an almost identical chance off Salisbury to the one offered off Shahid earlier in the afternoon.

*Tea:- Leicestershire 216-2 (Maddy 54\*, Stevens 53\*) from 52 overs*

Having flirted with danger twice before tea, it's no great surprise to see Stevens surrender his wicket tamely immediately after the break as he clubs Shahid's third delivery, a full-toss, straight down the throat of Ian Ward at deep midwicket.

At 217-3, Leicestershire are still well placed, however, as Hollioake continues with his all legspin attack and, even though the pitch isn't offering them a great deal, both Salisbury and Shahid bowl tidily enough, with the only strokes of note in the next half-hour coming when the London-born Damian Brandy smashes Shahid over midwicket for six and Maddy cuts Salisbury through extra cover for four.

The fourth-wicket pair do, eventually, start to cut loose, however, taking the score beyond 250 with four boundaries in three overs, prompting the Surrey captain to bring himself into the attack... though only to perform a rather unconvincing impression of a leg-spinner! With the best will in the world, the most apt description of the skipper's attempted leggies would have to be 'garbage', not that Maddy minds as he cuts a long-hop to the cover fence and then sweeps a full-toss to the rope at backward square leg in taking the partnership with Brandy past fifty.

Despite this rough treatment, Hollioake allows himself another over, though sensibly reverting to his normal medium-pace when bowling to Maddy. He clearly feels that Brandy might still be a sucker for his wrist-spin, though, and he proves right, too, as the 21-year-old top-edges a sweep high to midwicket, where Ormond takes a routine catch to peg the visitors back slightly to 277-4.

Seeing his captain pick up a wicket with his leg-breaks must almost make Ian Salisbury want to weep, especially as his genuine offerings have only brought him 1-77 from twenty overs to date... and when Shahid is then chosen to replace him at the pavilion end it must seem like the end of the world! Although he probably can't believe his luck, Maddy maintains his concentration to move his score on to ninety-eight with an on-driven four off Shahid and then ninety-nine with a swept single later in the over. He is then kept waiting for several minutes before progressing to his century, though not by the quality of the bowling, but by what seems to be a fire alarm which goes off somewhere in the ground and takes some while to silence before play can continue. It all seems quite appropriate, given the rather farcical nature of much of the action today!

Unfazed by this delay, Maddy soon hooks the Surrey captain for four to reach what is not only probably one of the easier centuries of his career, from 154 balls with fourteen fours, but also one of the most unusual, in that it has been compiled with help from his runner throughout.

With the light now fading fast and the total having just hit three-hundred, Hollioake picks up another wicket shortly afterwards when Neil Burns drags a drive into his stumps, then as soon as Tim Murtagh is returned to the fray at the pavilion end the umpires offer the light to the batsmen, who are happy to accept the chance to call it a day with 10.3 overs left to play.

*Close:- Leicestershire 303-5 (Maddy 109\*, Cunliffe 0\*) from 73.3 overs*

### Third Day - Friday 20th September

### Surrey 494 and 335-4; Leicestershire 361

After short and relatively uneventful bursts from Tim Murtagh and Adam Hollioake at the start of the day, the Surrey skipper soon turns back to his leg-spin duo, largely in order to fill in time until the new ball becomes due.

Surprisingly, Maddy is very subdued this morning, failing to register a single scoring stroke worth more than one run in the first eighteen overs, while Rob Cunliffe finds the boundary three times in the arc between extra cover and wide mid-on with well-timed drives off the spinners.

The former Gloucestershire batsman departs as soon as Phil Sampson appears in place of Shahid, however, getting a thin edge to an airy drive at the young paceman's first delivery and being taken behind the wicket by Jon Batty for thirty with the total at 348. Cunliffe doesn't seem totally convinced about his dismissal, which is rather unfortunate, since umpire Nigel Llong's decision turns out to be a very significant one as the visitors' tail subsequently folds in the same dramatic way that Surrey's had on the second day, with Murtagh and Sampson picking up four further wickets inside four overs.

Following Cunliffe's controversial dismissal, Phil DeFreitas drives the third ball of Sampson's over to the cover boundary, prompting the bowler to take the new ball and then remove the batsman with the first delivery he bowls with it. DeFreitas' strange scooped drive almost defies description but the most important thing is that the ball ends up in the safe hands of Salisbury at mid-off to reduce the visitors to 352-7.

Murtagh then gets into the act with his third ball back in the attack when his outswinger provides him with a well-deserved first wicket of the innings, courtesy of an edged forcing stroke from Javagal Srinath to Batty, and, by the end of the 21-year-old swing bowler's next over, he has trebled his haul. After Maddy finally comes alive to hook Sampson for four, Carl Crowe mirrors the stroke, and the result, from the second ball of Murtagh's following over before he and his replacement, Devon Malcolm, fall to successive balls later in the same over. Although both men turn out to be further victims for Batty, who therefore ends the innings with five catches, the mode of their departures are vastly different, since Crowe is offering a defensive bat when defeated by a perfectly pitched outswinger while Malcolm is attempting something altogether more aggressive and agricultural. With the end result being the same in both cases, though, the young Surrey seamers have picked up five wickets for thirteen runs in just twenty-three deliveries to send Leicestershire sliding from 348-5 to 361 all out, handing the champions an unexpected but useful first innings lead of 133.

As the hosts start their second innings, the focus is very much on Ian Ward, who has an opportunity to rewrite the Surrey record book if he can notch a fifth successive century. With the pitch playing extremely well, and no time pressure on him, the chance is there for him to grasp and he starts brilliantly, too, taking fours from the second, fourth and fifth balls of DeFreitas's opening over, courtesy of a cover drive, an on-drive and a pull.

Although it is inevitable that he is unable to maintain such a dominant start against the former England seamer and the equally experienced and talented Srinath, the Surrey opener underlines how confident he is feeling by hooking DeFreitas for four in the seventh over, even though the bowler has, quite bizarrely, posted three men close together in a row on the leg-side boundary.

It's all looking pretty easy for both Ward and his partner, Scott Newman, in fact, until the former's hopes of record-breaking glory are dashed in very controversial circumstances at the start of Srinath's fifth over. Receiving a short delivery outside off stump, Ward forces the ball away off the back foot, at pace, towards backward point, where Darren Stevens appears to take the ball on the half-volley. The fielder instantly claims a catch, however, much to the delight of his team-mates, and, though Ward stands his ground, umpire Mark Benson eventually gives him out. As the clearly unconvinced batsman leaves the ground with twenty-two runs to his name and the total on thirty-five, words are exchanged with the fielder and, having had a clear view of the 'catch' from my vantage point on the pavilion balcony, I can understand Ward's frustration, even if the verbal exchange is perhaps uncalled for. It's an unfortunate end to a great run by the County Championship's leading run-scorer of 2002 but at least he still has a share of the record at the end of a magnificent season.

Although there are just five balls to go until lunch when he arrives at the crease, Nadeem Shahid still manages to fit in a slash over gulley for four and a loose cut that provides the cover point fieldsman, DeFreitas, with a routine catch… which he puts down.

*Lunch:- Surrey 39-1 (Newman 11\*, Shahid 4\*) from 10 overs*

After a couple of decent overs to start the session, the bowling of Srinath and DeFreitas quickly degenerates to a farcical level, as the Indian oversteps the crease four times in two overs and the Englishman bowls four wides in the same period. Needless to say, Newman, at Srinath's expense, and Shahid, tucking into DeFreitas, are quick to capitalise on such tired and shoddy bowling with a couple of boundaries apiece, prompting Sutcliffe to make a double change that sees Devon Malcolm and Carl Crowe taking up the attack, with instant results.

Although Shahid takes fourteen from Malcolm's opening over, with an edged four, a second boundary whipped through midwicket and a hooked six, he is on his way back to the pavilion soon afterwards when he edges a drive at the first ball of the big former England paceman's next over and is caught behind for twenty-eight with the score on eighty-nine.

Graham Thorpe then comes and goes within five balls, losing his middle stump to the final delivery of the same Malcolm over, before Newman gets an outside edge to a big off-break from Crowe and sees Maddy pull off a great catch diving low to his right at slip. Having batted with a runner, it is rather a surprise to see Maddy on the field, though his off-spinning team-mate will have no complaints and nor will the rest of the Leicestershire side, since this inspired bit of fielding has transformed the Surrey score from 89-1 to 89-4 in the space of just eight deliveries.

Although he has probably had quite a rush to get his pads on and get to the wicket, Adam Hollioake certainly appears unconcerned by the situation that faces him as he late-cuts his first ball to the boundary and quickly sets the tone for the rest of the afternoon, which develops into an exhibition of attacking strokeplay by Hollioake and Brown.

Within five overs of their arrivals at the wicket, both men have hit a six, the Surrey captain's 'maximum' hooked off Malcolm and Brown's driven over long-off at the expense of Crowe, and by the time they've been together for seven overs their partnership is already worth fifty. Malcolm consequently retires mauled, while Crowe appears to pick up an injury after seven respectable overs and also disappears from the scene, leaving the bowling in the hands of Darren Stevens' medium-pace and Iain Sutcliffe's very occasional leg-breaks, making the Leicestershire captain the fourth 'exponent' of wrist-spin in the match thus far. Although both bowlers do their best and only really suffer at the hands of Hollioake, who races to a 44-ball fifty with a sudden glut of three boundaries in two overs, they never really look like splitting a fifth-wicket partnership that progresses beyond the hundred mark at six runs per over.

With the scales now heavily tilted in the champions' favour, Sutcliffe eventually becomes another who is forced to concede that the leg-spinner's art is beyond him after a gruesome over that includes two drives to the rope at extra cover by his opposite number and a delivery that costs him six wides as the ball sails away over the head of wicketkeeper Burns. His replacement, DeFreitas, purveying his own particular variety of off-spin, does at least start tidily and both he and Brandy, taking over from Stevens at the Vauxhall end, manage to find the outer-half of Brown's bat as he goes through to a relatively subdued half-century from 80 balls.

The tea break is almost upon us as Hollioake cuts the medium-paced Brandy to the boundary, thereby taking his own score into the nineties and the partnership to 150, and, timing his advance to perfection, the Surrey skipper completes a very bold century from 100 balls in ninety-nine minutes with pulled and on-driven fours in the final over of the session from the Leicestershire youngster. It's been an excellent knock, containing a dozen fours and two sixes, and as Hollioake acknowledges the crowd's applause it seems entirely appropriate that he should end the season with his first County Championship century at The AMP Oval since September 1996.

*Tea:- Surrey 257-4 (Brown 57\*, Hollioake 103\*) from 50 overs*

With his bowling resources stretched to the limit, the Leicestershire captain hands the ball to DeFreitas and Brandy upon the resumption, though he soon takes it off the latter after the London-born 21-year-old gets hammered for twenty runs, including three boundaries, in just two overs. Bowling to these two Surrey batsmen when they are well set is a thankless task even for an experienced bowler, let alone a young lad like Brandy, as DeFreitas finds to his cost in his next over when Hollioake cuts him for three fours to take the partnership beyond two-hundred and establish it as a new fifth-wicket record for Surrey against Leicestershire. The previous mark of 196 had been set in 1953 by Raman Subba Row and Eric Bedser at Loughborough.

Despite his mauling at the hands of the home county's captain, DeFreitas is given one more over before being replaced by Srinath, while Stevens battles on at the other end after relieving Brandy. This combination manages to restrict the scoring to some degree, though Hollioake does break out at one point to lift Stevens over long-on for six as the light again begins to close in late in the day.

Two bouncers in Srinath's next over leave the Surrey skipper taking hasty evasive action, so it is therefore no surprise that as soon as Sutcliffe beckons Malcolm to return to the attack the umpires offer the light to the batsmen and they gratefully accept an early closure with nineteen overs left to bowl. Since Surrey already lead by 468 runs and there is still a whole day left to play, it is entirely understandable that the safety of the batsmen is given top priority.

*Close:- Surrey 335-4 (Brown 89\*, Hollioake 146\*) from 63 overs*

## VIEW FROM THE DRESSING ROOM

*It was a great pity that your attempt to secure a fifth successive century ended on such a controversial note. From my position on the balcony, I could have sworn that the ball bounced just in front of the fielder and I assume that was your view too?*

**IAN WARD** - Yes, I must admit that I was convinced it had bounced. He said he'd caught it, and expressed the fact very clearly as I walked off, but you have to take the rough with the smooth. I didn't think it was out and I stood my ground, as I'm entitled to, but the umpire is paid to make a decision and gave it out, so you just walk off and accept it.

### Fourth Day - Saturday 21st September

### Surrey 494 and 492-9dec; Leicestershire 361 and 142

### Surrey won by 483 runs
### Surrey 20pts, Leicestershire 7

Much to everyone's surprise, Adam Hollioake decides against declaring at the overnight total, leaving spectators to face the prospect of an extremely dull final day of the Championship season. On this good pitch, with nothing to play for, there seems little doubt that Leicestershire will be able to bat out the game as and when Surrey are bowled out or declare.

Initial impressions suggest that we might be heading down the declaration route, in fact, since the visitors open the bowling with Darren Stevens' medium-pace and Javagal Srinath bowling off-breaks, amidst rumours that most of their bowlers in this match are now injured. With deep-set fields and neither batsman showing any sign of urgency, the first ten-over period of the day features just one boundary, a pull to midwicket by Brown off Srinath, yet five milestones or records - the 250 partnership; Hollioake's 150 from 156 balls, including eighteen fours and three sixes; Surrey's 350; the setting of a new record for any wicket in Surrey versus Leicestershire matches as the stand reaches 262 to beat the 261 posted by Ducat and Shepherd for the third wicket at The Oval in 1926; and, finally, Ali Brown's century, from 121 balls with twelve fours and one six, completed with a clip to square leg for two off Srinath.

Brown doesn't last long after reaching his fifth Championship ton of the season, however, as he edges a drive at a Stevens outswinger to be caught at the wicket by Burns, then poor Jon Batty, having waited so long to bat, goes back to his third ball from Srinath and is trapped lbw for nought.

Despite the loss of these wickets at 371 and 374, with the lead stretched out beyond five-hundred, Hollioake still clearly has no intention of declaring, much to the disappointment of the spectators and the Leicestershire fielders. One has to be philosophical about it, though. This Surrey team has provided the fans with any number of incredibly entertaining matches, most of them resulting in wins, during the course of the season, so I suppose we have to accept a dull draw on occasions. We have probably been spoilt in recent times, if we are honest enough to admit it. The only thing that disappoints me, personally, is that a declaration would give our two young opening bowlers time to shine and show everyone what they can do. Surely they will be hungry to impress, even if those who have been through a long hard season in the first team aren't?

The rest of the morning session drifts by fairly pointlessly, with the only bowling change seeing Damian Brandy being given four overs and the boundary drought broken just once, by a burst of three in three overs, during which Hollioake posts a new career-best score.

The high point of the morning's 'entertainment' arrives with lunch almost upon us when the visitors take the new ball and the Surrey captain edges Brandy to the third man boundary to record the first double-century of his first-class career from his 241st delivery. He has hit twenty-one fours and three sixes and, though much of it has been against less than demanding bowling, it has been chanceless and, for the most part, highly entertaining.

Having celebrated reaching this new career milestone and acknowledged the crowd's applause, Hollioake then departs in the last over before the break when he drives Brandy straight to DeFreitas on the deep extra-cover boundary in front of the Bedser Stand. Lunch is taken immediately, with the Surrey skipper's dismissal quite likely to bring a declaration during the interval.

*Lunch:- Surrey 445-7 (Salisbury 21\*) from 95 overs*

Wrong! Ian Salisbury emerges from the pavilion with a new partner, Jimmy Ormond, after the break as the Surrey innings grinds on.

To be perfectly honest, I don't witness any of the next forty-five minutes play as I have taken the chance to interview Ali Brown for a commemorative booklet about his 268 against Glamorgan in the sensational C&G Trophy match back in June. Well, it seemed sensible to use my time as productively as possible and Browny had nothing better to do!

When I return to my seat on the pavilion balcony I am told that I haven't missed much... no surprise there then. Apparently, Jimmy Ormond has had a jolly slog for a few balls before being bowled through the gate in attempting another big heave at Brandy, and Tim Murtagh has batted impressively and attractively in making twenty-two before miscuing a drive to deep mid-on. The declaration has then followed a few balls later, leaving Leicestershire the highly theoretical target of 625 from a minimum of fifty-one overs.

I'm not entirely surprised to see Rob Cunliffe opening the batting with Ashley Wright as the Leicestershire second innings gets under way, since the extremely affable former Gloucestershire batsman had been speaking to me while I was waiting to see Ali Brown and had told me that at least five of the visiting team were carrying injuries and every one of them was absolutely exhausted.

This soon shows, too, as Tim Murtagh and Phil Sampson tear in and cause havoc, removing four batsmen in the first thirty-seven balls of the innings. Cunliffe goes first, gloving the fifth ball of the second over from Sampson to Hollioake in the gully with the score on four, then wickets in the fifth, sixth and seventh overs reduce the visitors to a sorry 11-4. Brandy is the second man to be dismissed when Murtagh skilfully follows a series of outswingers with an inswinger that rearranges the youngster's stumps as he shoulders arms; Ashley Wright cuts Sampson at head height to the substitute fielder, Ian Sykes, (a writer from *'Direct Hit'*, who is acting as twelfth man for an article in the Surrey CCC magazine); then Darren Stevens departs lbw to Murtagh as he shuffles into line and misses a push to leg.

As so often happens, a reshuffled batting order has proved disastrous and, suddenly, with forty-four overs left for play, Surrey have a sniff of a quite remarkable triumph. On this fine pitch, there is still much to be done, however, and those experienced campaigners, Neil Burns and Iain Sutcliffe, batting at five and six, block the home side's path to victory in the remaining overs up until tea. Taking advantage of predictably attacking field-settings, Burns plunders three fours from Sampson's sixth over and two from his seventh with a variety of well-executed drives and pulls to advance the total to forty-nine without further loss at the break.

*Tea:- Leicestershire 49-4 (Burns 31\*, Sutcliffe 11\*) from 14 overs*

Ian Salisbury replaces Tim Murtagh in the attack immediately after tea but there's no change in Neil Burns' approach as he drives the leg-spinner straight down the ground for four and then twice pulls Sampson to the boundary as the young quickie puts in another lively spell.

With Sutcliffe playing a fairly dogged role, it is no surprise that the Leicestershire wicketkeeper continues to dominate the scoring, adding further fours to his tally with a sweep off Salisbury and a square drive at Sampson's expense to reach a breathtaking half-century, out of a total of 75-4, from just 49 balls in the twentieth over of the innings.

Although Sampson follows up with a couple of good short deliveries that induce gloved and miscued hooks from the batsmen, Adam Hollioake decides to take a turn from the Vauxhall end after his young paceman's third post-tea over. He, too, finds Burns in belligerent mood, however, as the sturdy left-hander collects the thirteenth four of his innings with a crunching off-drive in the Surrey skipper's opening over and then finds the rope on two further occasions two overs later, with a steer to third man and an extra-cover drive.

It doesn't take Hollioake long to get even, though, as he clings on to a violent head-high return catch at the start of his third over to terminate Burns' innings for the second time in the match and, consequently, put Leicestershire back in trouble at 99-5.

Surrey know that the hardest part of their task is yet to come if they are to pull off an amazing victory, however, since the limpet-like Sutcliffe is now joined in the middle by Darren Maddy and his runner. With their two best batsmen together at the crease, the visitors' hopes of holding out for the draw still look reasonably good, and Maddy emphasises this point by opening his account instantly with a crisp square-cut to the boundary off Hollioake.

Fortunately for the hosts, Ian Salisbury is up to the task, though, and when Sutcliffe goes back to the third ball of the former Sussex bowler's next over and is beaten by a leg-break, the raising of umpire Llong's finger again pushes the door of opportunity open for the 2002 county champions.

Even though he is faced by a scoreboard reading 105-6 with twenty-four overs still left to play, no-one expects the new batsman, Phillip DeFreitas, to play anything other than his natural game and, sure enough, he is soon cutting Hollioake to the fence at cover and prompting a change of tactics.

Resisting the undoubted temptation to allow himself another over, the Surrey captain recalls Tim Murtagh at the Vauxhall end in the hope that the 21-year-old swing bowler can make another breakthrough for him, and his faith is repaid in duplicate as the Lambeth-born youngster claims two very important scalps in the space of three balls. Crucially, the first of his victims is Maddy, palpably lbw to the fourth ball of the over when caught on the crease by a ball cutting back and keeping low, then DeFreitas has his bails trimmed by another break-back two balls later, Srinath having picked up a rather fortunate inside-edged single from his first ball.

At 124-8, the scent of a tense finish is growing stronger, though there are clouds on the horizon for Surrey, both metaphorically and in reality. Although the scoreboard says that there are twenty-one overs left for play, bad light seems certain to intervene as it has done on the first three days of the game, especially since the skies are cloudy. Consequently, everyone has one eye on the action and one eye on the light meter on the scoreboard as, over the course of the next half-a-dozen overs, the batsmen batten down the hatches and the first of the five indicator bulbs begins to glow, followed shortly afterwards by the second and the third.

Then, almost miraculously, the sun begins to pierce through the clouds and the light actually begins to improve, dramatically reducing the visitors' chances of securing a suspension of play and the draw that their second innings batting display would not warrant.

Spurred on by the promise of extra time in which to complete the job, almost eight overs of resistance from the ninth-wicket pair is finally ended by Murtagh, whose career-best Championship figures become a maiden five-for when Carl Crowe falls leg-before in almost identical fashion to Maddy to reduce Leicestershire to 142-9 and put Surrey on the verge of success.

Since the sun is now shining quite brightly, it looks like we could get through all of the thirteen remaining overs, if necessary, but Salisbury only requires five balls to finish the match at 5.15pm, deceiving Srinath with his googly and inducing a bat-pad nudge to short leg, where Nadeem Shahid takes the match-winning catch to spark off Surrey celebrations. With Leicestershire bowled out for 142 in 38.5 overs, the home county thereby record their biggest-ever victory in terms of runs, having triumphed by the enormous margin of 483, a figure that beats the previous record, set in 1939, by ninety-five runs.

As Tim Murtagh leads his team from the field with figures of 5-39 to his credit, the stunned but happy home fans can reflect on another amazing day's cricket, where the unbelievably dull first two-thirds of the day has been balanced by a pulsating last third that has seen Murtagh and Sampson capitalise on the earlier efforts of Scott Newman to make it a game to remember for Surrey's young guns.

The dark days of March and April seem almost a world away as the small crowd disperses at the end of an incredible County Championship campaign with the ground bathed in warm sunlight. It is almost as if a lost friend is smiling down on us.

**Surrey 494 and 492-9dec; Leicestershire 361 and 142**
**Surrey won by 483 runs. Surrey 20pts, Leicestershire 7**

## VIEWS FROM THE DRESSING ROOM

*Did it rate as a special moment when you completed your maiden first-class double-century?*
**ADAM HOLLIOAKE** - Not really, no. Statistically, it was a first, but I don't particularly pride myself in getting runs in easy situations - it's something I'm not usually good at, so probably the most satisfying thing about it was that I did manage to cash in for once. But, overall, it's not an innings I will particularly remember

*Did you honestly feel we had enough time to win the match when Adam finally declared?*
**TIM MURTAGH** - To be totally honest, you would have to say 'no', because the pitch was still playing pretty well and there wasn't much time left, but you can never tell what's going to happen in cricket. Phil Sampson and I hadn't bowled that much, so we were still fresh and we thought we'd give it a crack for the first ten overs to see what happened. We were pleasantly surprised by the results!
**SCOTT NEWMAN** - Yes, I always believe that whatever side I am playing for, whether it's first-team cricket or second-team cricket or my club side, is going to win the match - that's how I keep interested in the game. Having the bowlers that we do in our side, and grabbing a few early wickets, there was always that feeling that we were going to run through them.

*Surely, hand on heart, you didn't expect us to win the match when you finally declared?*
**ADAM HOLLIOAKE** - I probably thought it was about fifty-fifty. I couldn't have said we were definitely going to win the match, no, but I said to the guys that I'd rather we went out there and put in sixty overs of hard work, rather than have ninety-six overs of going through the motions. I didn't want us to go out there and let ourselves down by settling in for a comfortable day in the field. I was also thinking ahead to the National League game the next day against Gloucestershire, as I didn't want us spending the whole day in the field ahead of that.

*You got some stick from the crowd for the delayed declaration... if they read my book they will now know what the plan was and what you were up to!*
**ADAM HOLLIOAKE** - We don't worry about criticism. We know what we're doing, and sometimes we are right and sometimes we are wrong. When we are wrong we put our hands up, and, hopefully, when we are right other people can do the same thing.

*All the young lads were fantastic in this match, so I suppose you can already see yourself having a few team selection problems over the course of the next few seasons?*
**ADAM HOLLIOAKE** - Yes, but there's nothing different there, because I've had selection problems ever since I became captain. It was just fantastic to see them all coming on... there's so much talent there, and they are all progressing well. I don't think other sides realise just how good our young players are.

*It was a great game for the 'young guns' - why do you think you are all able to come into the team and perform straight away?*
**TIM MURTAGH** - As a young player, I think it helps when you can come into a dressing room that is obviously very confident, where the team is winning, and where you have a lot of experienced players around you. In the seconds, Alan Butcher has been excellent - I've worked with him for about four or five years now, and he's helped my game immensely. Even though he is known as a batting coach, he has helped my bowling no end by studying it and going through video after video. I think a lot of my improvement is down to him.

*What are the principal strengths of Phil Sampson and Tim Murtagh as bowlers?*
**SCOTT NEWMAN** - Murts is a very good swing bowler, an excellent prospect - he just puts the ball in good areas very regularly. Sammo can do that as well when he's on form, but he's got a bit more pace than 'Murts' - he hits the deck hard and when he hits the seam he does cause problems for the batsmen. They are good aggressive bowlers, and they are both looking good for Surrey's future.

*What are Phil Sampson's strengths as a bowler and Scott Newman's strengths as a batsman?*
**TIM MURTAGH** - Sammo is a hit-the-deck bowler, who hits the seam regularly - not your typical kind of English bowler, who will pitch the ball up and swing it - so he's very useful on flat wickets, where he can make things happen from nowhere. He's got a bit of pace about him as well. As for Scotty, well, he goes out there and plays his shots from the start, he's a very aggressive cricketer, who takes the attack to the opposition - he's not one who's going to sit around and push for singles. He's had a couple of pretty amazing seasons in the second team, and he's had to wait a while for his chance as well, but when he got it he took it well.

*As someone who has played regularly for the second eleven and knows the up-and-coming young players well, who are the guys we should be looking out for over the next year or two?*
**TIM MURTAGH** - James Benning impresses me. A few of the guys have remarked how similar he is to Ali Brown in the way he plays - he loves to play his shots, which is a common trait amongst many of our batsmen - so he's one to look out for. I've also been impressed by the seam bowlers, Neil Saker and Danny Miller. It's hard to say who's the better of the two at the moment, but they've both got a lot of potential and pace, and they can swing the ball, too.

## SURREY v LEICESTERSHIRE at The AMP Oval   Played 18th to 21st September

Surrey won the toss and elected to bat    Umpires:- Mark Benson and Nigel Llong

### SURREY - First Innings

| Fall Of Wkt | Batsman | How | Out | Score | Balls | 4s | 6s |
|---|---|---|---|---|---|---|---|
| 1-227 | I.J. Ward | c Maddy | b DeFreitas | 118 | 168 | 20 | 0 |
| 2-352 | S.A. Newman | c Burns | b Srinath | 183 | 257 | 28 | 2 |
| 3-397 | J.N. Batty + | c Srinath | b Malcolm | 74 | 107 | 12 | 1 |
| 5-456 | G.P. Thorpe | c Srinath | b DeFreitas | 44 | 65 | 8 | 0 |
| 4-419 | N. Shahid | lbw | b DeFreitas | 2 | 9 | 0 | 0 |
| 6-490 | A.D. Brown | c Malcolm | b Crowe | 34 | 28 | 4 | 1 |
| 9-494 | A.J. Hollioake * | | b Srinath | 20 | 29 | 3 | 0 |
| 7-493 | I.D.K. Salisbury | | b Srinath | 0 | 4 | 0 | 0 |
| 8-493 | J. Ormond | c Stevens | b Srinath | 0 | 4 | 0 | 0 |
| | T.J. Murtagh | Not | Out | 0 | 3 | 0 | 0 |
| 10-494 | P.J. Sampson | | b Srinath | 0 | 1 | 0 | 0 |
| | Extras | (5lb, 14nb) | | 19 | | | |
| | TOTAL | (111.2 overs) | | 494 | | | |

| Bowler | O | M | R | W | NB | Wd |
|---|---|---|---|---|---|---|
| Srinath | 26.2 | 1 | 114 | 5 | 5 | - |
| Malcolm | 13 | 0 | 70 | 1 | - | - |
| Crowe | 28 | 4 | 100 | 1 | - | - |
| DeFreitas | 28 | 3 | 121 | 3 | 1 | - |
| Maddy | 5 | 0 | 16 | 0 | - | - |
| Brandy | 4 | 0 | 28 | 0 | - | - |
| Stevens | 7 | 0 | 40 | 0 | 1 | - |

### LEICESTERSHIRE - First Innings (Needing 345 to avoid the follow-on)

| Fall Of Wkt | Batsman | How | Out | Score | Balls | 4s | 6s |
|---|---|---|---|---|---|---|---|
| 1-60 | A.S. Wright | c Batty | b Sampson | 22 | 49 | 4 | 0 |
| 2-140 | I.J. Sutcliffe * | c Ward | b Salisbury | 72 | 110 | 12 | 0 |
| | D.L. Maddy | Not | Out | 127 | 204 | 15 | 0 |
| 3-217 | D.I. Stevens | c Ward | b Shahid | 53 | 50 | 7 | 1 |
| 4-277 | D.G. Brandy | c Ormond | b Hollioake | 23 | 50 | 2 | 1 |
| 5-300 | N.D. Burns + | | b Hollioake | 7 | 17 | 0 | 0 |
| 6-348 | R.J. Cunliffe | c Batty | b Sampson | 30 | 70 | 4 | 0 |
| 7-352 | P.A.J. DeFreitas | c Salisbury | b Sampson | 4 | 3 | 1 | 0 |
| 8-353 | J. Srinath | c Batty | b Murtagh | 1 | 4 | 0 | 0 |
| 9-361 | C.D. Crowe | c Batty | b Murtagh | 4 | 7 | 1 | 0 |
| 10-361 | D.E. Malcolm | c Batty | b Murtagh | 0 | 1 | 0 | 0 |
| | Extras | (6b, 4lb, 4w, 4nb) | | 18 | | | |
| | TOTAL | (93.5 overs) | | 361 | | | |

| Bowler | O | M | R | W | NB | Wd |
|---|---|---|---|---|---|---|
| Ormond | 13 | 2 | 49 | 0 | - | 2 |
| Murtagh | 18.5 | 2 | 62 | 3 | - | - |
| Sampson | 11 | 1 | 52 | 3 | 1 | - |
| Salisbury | 26 | 4 | 94 | 1 | - | - |
| Shahid | 16 | 1 | 55 | 1 | 1 | - |
| Hollioake | 9 | 0 | 39 | 2 | - | - |

### SURREY - Second Innings (Leading by 133 runs on first innings)

| Fall Of Wkt | Batsman | How | Out | Score | Balls | 4s | 6s |
|---|---|---|---|---|---|---|---|
| 1-35 | I.J. Ward | c Stevens | b Srinath | 22 | 24 | 4 | 0 |
| 4-89 | S.A. Newman | c Maddy | b Crowe | 21 | 68 | 2 | 0 |
| 2-89 | N. Shahid | c Burns | b Malcolm | 28 | 30 | 5 | 1 |
| 3-89 | G.P. Thorpe | | b Malcolm | 0 | 5 | 0 | 0 |
| 5-371 | A.D. Brown | c Burns | b Stevens | 107 | 134 | 13 | 1 |
| 7-445 | A.J. Hollioake * | c DeFreitas | b Brandy | 208 | 252 | 21 | 3 |
| 6-374 | J.N. Batty + | lbw | b Srinath | 0 | 3 | 0 | 0 |
| | I.D.K. Salisbury | Not | Out | 36 | 87 | 4 | 2 |
| 8-455 | J. Ormond | | b Brandy | 9 | 4 | 2 | 0 |
| 9-491 | T.J. Murtagh | c Stevens | b Srinath | 22 | 28 | 5 | 0 |
| | P.J. Sampson | Not | Out | 1 | 2 | 0 | 0 |
| | Extras | (6lb, 20w, 12nb) | | 38 | | | |
| | TOTAL | (105.1 overs) | (for 9 dec) | 492 | | | |

335

| Bowler | O | M | R | W | NB | Wd |
|---|---|---|---|---|---|---|
| DeFreitas | 17 | 1 | 74 | 0 | - | 4 |
| Srinath | 26 | 1 | 89 | 3 | 5 | - |
| Malcolm | 6 | 1 | 41 | 2 | - | - |
| Crowe | 7 | 2 | 33 | 1 | - | - |
| Stevens | 30 | 1 | 125 | 1 | - | 1 |
| Sutcliffe | 5 | 0 | 35 | 0 | 1 | 1 |
| Brandy | 13 | 0 | 86 | 2 | - | 2 |
| Cunliffe | 1.1 | 0 | 3 | 0 | - | - |

**LEICESTERSHIRE - Second Innings** (Needing 626 to win)

| Fall Of Wkt | Batsman | How | Out | Score | Balls | 4s | 6s |
|---|---|---|---|---|---|---|---|
| 3-7 | A.S. Wright | c sub (Sykes) | b Sampson | 7 | 20 | 1 | 0 |
| 1-4 | R.J. Cunliffe | c Hollioake | b Sampson | 0 | 5 | 0 | 0 |
| 2-5 | D.G. Brandy | | b Murtagh | 0 | 8 | 0 | 0 |
| 4-11 | D.I. Stevens | lbw | b Murtagh | 0 | 2 | 0 | 0 |
| 5-99 | N.D. Burns + | c & | b Hollioake | 68 | 61 | 15 | 0 |
| 6-105 | I.J. Sutcliffe * | lbw | b Salisbury | 24 | 58 | 2 | 0 |
| 7-123 | D.L. Maddy | lbw | b Murtagh | 12 | 13 | 2 | 0 |
| 8-124 | P.A.J. DeFreitas | | b Murtagh | 9 | 12 | 2 | 0 |
| 10-142 | J. Srinath | c Shahid | b Salisbury | 9 | 31 | 1 | 0 |
| 9-142 | C.D. Crowe | lbw | b Murtagh | 8 | 23 | 2 | 0 |
| | D.E. Malcolm | Not | Out | 0 | 1 | 0 | 0 |
| | Extras | (3lb, 2nb) | | 5 | | | |
| | **TOTAL** | **(38.5 overs)** | | **142** | | | |

| Bowler | O | M | R | W | NB | Wd |
|---|---|---|---|---|---|---|
| Murtagh | 12 | 2 | 39 | 5 | - | - |
| Sampson | 10 | 3 | 49 | 2 | - | - |
| Salisbury | 12.5 | 4 | 28 | 2 | 1 | - |
| Hollioake | 4 | 0 | 23 | 1 | - | - |

## Other Division One Results

Surrey's maximum-point victory left them with a final winning margin of 44.75 points at the top of the table, with Warwickshire matching Kent's last-game triumph to hold on to the runners-up spot. Yorkshire and Somerset, considered genuine title contenders at the start of the campaign, both lost their final match as they slipped into Division Two.

September 18-19
*Taunton:-* **Lancashire beat Somerset by eight wickets.** Somerset 221 (Martin 4-52) and 129 (Martin 4-29, Schofield 4-35); Lancashire 228 (Hogg 50, Bulbeck 6-93, Johnson 4-68) and 124-2 (Byas 63*, Law 57*). **Lancashire 16pts, Somerset 4**

September 18-20
*Headingley:-* **Kent beat Yorkshire by eight wickets.** Kent 399 (Waugh 146, Smith 67, Tredwell 61, Patel 52, Sidebottom 4-61) and 103-2; Yorkshire 218 (White 62, Saggers 4-44) and 283 (Blakey 94). **Kent 19pts, Yorkshire 2.25***
* deducted 1.75pts for slow over rate

September 18-21
*Hove:-* **Warwickshire beat Sussex by three wickets.** Sussex 352 (Goodwin 93, Innes 60*, Brown 5-103, Richardson 4-76) and 341 (Goodwin 111, Davis 66, Sheikh 4-78); Warwickshire 293 (Carter 103, Frost 73, Taylor 5-90) and 405-7 (Powell 103, Ostler 90, Brown 79). **Warwickshire 17pts, Sussex 7**

## FINAL COUNTY CHAMPIONSHIP DIVISION ONE TABLE 2002

| Pos | Prv | | P | Points | W | D | L | Bat | Bwl | Ded |
|---|---|---|---|---|---|---|---|---|---|---|
| 1 | 1 | Surrey | 16 | 242.75 | 10 | 4 | 2 | 59 | 48 | 0.25 |
| 2 | 2 | Warwickshire | 16 | 198.00 | 7 | 7 | 2 | 42 | 44 | 0.00 |
| 3 | 3 | Kent | 16 | 195.50 | 7 | 5 | 4 | 48 | 44 | 0.50 |
| 4 | 5 | Lancashire | 16 | 172.00 | 6 | 6 | 4 | 33 | 43 | 0.00 |
| 5 | 4 | Leicestershire | 16 | 171.00 | 5 | 6 | 5 | 42 | 46 | 1.00 |
| 6 | 6 | Sussex | 16 | 154.00 | 3 | 7 | 6 | 43 | 47 | 0.00 |
| 7 | 7 | Hampshire ** | 16 | 131.00 | 2 | 9 | 5 | 35 | 44 | 8.00 |
| 8 | 8 | Somerset | 16 | 126.75 | 1 | 8 | 7 | 39 | 44 | 0.25 |
| 9 | 9 | Yorkshire | 16 | 124.75 | 2 | 6 | 8 | 35 | 45 | 3.25 |

**\*\* Hampshire deducted 8pts for 'poor' pitch at Rose Bowl v Lancashire**

### NUL2 - Thorpe Puts Gladiators To The Sword To Earn Runners-Up Spot

The season ended on a winning, if rather low-key, note with a straightforward Graham Thorpe-inspired victory over the Division Two champions, Gloucestershire Gladiators. Surrey clinched the runners-up spot with their victory, but things could have been very different had the Lions won in Bristol at the start of the campaign, rather than going down by one wicket. A result that looked important at the time, ended up being the difference between winning the division and coming second.

After electing to bat and getting into early difficulties against Mike Smith, the Lions bounced back well from 58-4 as Thorpe received good support from Adam Hollioake and Jon Batty while compiling an excellent century that led an impressive Surrey recovery to 263-8.

In reply, the Gladiators were going well at 68-0 in the thirteenth over, before Ed Giddins and Hollioake made crucial breakthroughs to reduce them to 78-3 in the space of two overs. Thereafter, wickets fell at regular intervals as the Gloucestershire challenge fizzled out rapidly, and Giddins, playing his last game for the Club before his move to Hampshire, had the honour of taking the match-winning boundary catch to reward him for a fine season of white-ball cricket.

### SURREY LIONS v GLOUCESTERSHIRE GLADIATORS at The AMP Oval
### Played on Sunday 22nd September    Surrey Lions won by 79 runs

Surrey Lions won the toss and elected to bat    Umpires:- Mark Benson & Nigel Llong

**SURREY LIONS**

| Fall Of Wkt | Batsman | How | Out | Score | Balls | 4s | 6s |
|---|---|---|---|---|---|---|---|
| 3-31 | I.J. Ward | | b Smith | 17 | 25 | 3 | 0 |
| 1-5 | A.D. Brown | lbw | b Smith | 0 | 1 | 0 | 0 |
| 2-28 | M.R. Ramprakash | c Spearman | b Smith | 11 | 22 | 0 | 0 |
| 8-262 | G.P. Thorpe | c & | b Smith | 114 | 105 | 14 | 0 |
| 4-58 | N. Shahid | lbw | b Lewis | 17 | 21 | 3 | 0 |
| 5-140 | A.J. Hollioake * | c Windows | b Angel | 38 | 34 | 4 | 1 |
| 6-221 | J.N. Batty + | st Russell | b Fisher | 30 | 41 | 1 | 0 |
| 7-252 | I.D.K. Salisbury | c Hancock | b Smith | 17 | 13 | 2 | 0 |
| | Saqlain Mushtaq | Not | Out | 4 | 8 | 0 | 0 |
| | T.J. Murtagh | Not | Out | 1 | 1 | 0 | 0 |
| | E.S.H. Giddins | did not bat | | | | | |
| | Extras | (8lb, 4w, 2nb) | | 14 | | | |
| | **TOTAL** | (45 overs) | (for 8 wkts) | 263 | | | |

| Bowler | O | M | R | W | NB | Wd |
|---|---|---|---|---|---|---|
| Smith | 9 | 0 | 30 | 5 | - | 1 |
| Angel | 9 | 0 | 47 | 1 | - | 1 |
| Lewis | 9 | 0 | 65 | 1 | - | 1 |
| Alleyne | 7 | 0 | 41 | 0 | - | - |
| Fisher | 9 | 0 | 50 | 1 | - | - |
| Bressington | 2 | 0 | 22 | 0 | 1 | 1 |

## GLOUCESTERSHIRE GLADIATORS

| Fall Of Wkt | Batsman | How | Out | Score | Balls | 4s | 6s |
|---|---|---|---|---|---|---|---|
| 1-68 | C.M. Spearman | c Shahid | b Giddins | 37 | 35 | 6 | 0 |
| 2-78 | R.C. Russell + | c Shahid | b Hollioake | 31 | 49 | 3 | 1 |
| 3-78 | T.H.C. Hancock | c Batty | b Hollioake | 5 | 5 | 1 | 0 |
| 6-145 | M.G.N. Windows | c Giddins | b Saqlain | 37 | 54 | 3 | 0 |
| 4-105 | R.J. Sillence | run | out | 11 | 13 | 2 | 0 |
| 5-108 | M.W. Alleyne * | c Salisbury | b Hollioake | 1 | 9 | 0 | 0 |
| 10-184 | A.N. Bressington | c Giddins | b Ramprakash | 22 | 50 | 2 | 0 |
| 7-146 | I.D. Fisher | c Giddins | b Ramprakash | 1 | 7 | 0 | 0 |
| 8-151 | J. Angel | | b Giddins | 2 | 4 | 0 | 0 |
| 9-182 | J. Lewis | c & | b Hollioake | 24 | 10 | 3 | 1 |
| | A.M. Smith | Not | Out | 1 | 1 | 0 | 0 |
| | Extras | (2b, 2lb, 6w, 2nb) | | 12 | | | |
| | TOTAL | (39.2 overs) | | 184 | | | |

| Bowler | O | M | R | W | NB | Wd |
|---|---|---|---|---|---|---|
| Giddins | 9 | 0 | 44 | 2 | 1 | 1 |
| Murtagh | 9 | 0 | 57 | 0 | - | 1 |
| Hollioake | 6 | 1 | 24 | 4 | - | 1 |
| Saqlain Mushtaq | 7 | 1 | 17 | 1 | - | 1 |
| Salisbury | 5 | 0 | 19 | 0 | - | - |
| Ramprakash | 3.2 | 0 | 19 | 2 | - | 2 |

## Other NUL Division Two Results

The bookies had got it right by making Surrey and Gloucestershire their clear ante-post favourites to bounce straight back into Division One. Essex took the third promotion slot and, having beaten Sussex in their final match, were only denied the runners-up position by the Lions' victory over the Gladiators.

September 22
*Derby:-* **Derbyshire Scorpions beat Middlesex Crusaders by 22 runs.** Derbyshire 210-8 (Selwood 81*, Bloomfield 3-28); Middlesex 188 (43.3ov; Joyce 58, Dalrymple 52, Welch 6-31). **Derbys Scorpions 4pts**

*Chelmsford:-* **Essex Eagles beat Sussex Sharks by 29 runs (D/L method).** Essex 189 (38ov; Habib 53, Hutchison 3-38); Sussex 158 (38.3ov; Goodwin 55, Waugh 3-14, Grayson 3-27). **Essex Eagles 4pts**

*The Rose Bowl:-* **Hampshire Hawks beat Northamptonshire Steelbacks by six wickets.** Northamptonshire 285-6 (Sales 93, Powell 64); Hampshire 289-4 (44.3ov; Francis 103*, Johnson 73, Crawley 52). **Hampshire Hawks 4pts**

## FINAL NATIONAL LEAGUE DIVISION TWO TABLE 2002

| Pos | Prv | | P | Pts | W | T | L | A | NRR |
|---|---|---|---|---|---|---|---|---|---|
| 1 | 1 | Gloucestershire Gladiators | 16 | 44 | 10 | 0 | 4 | 2 | 12.75 |
| 2 | 2 | Surrey Lions | 16 | 42 | 10 | 0 | 5 | 1 | 6.53 |
| 3 | 3 | Essex Eagles | 16 | 40 | 10 | 0 | 6 | 0 | 3.94 |
| 4 | 5 | Derbyshire Scorpions | 16 | 34 | 8 | 0 | 7 | 1 | -0.98 |
| 5 | 4 | Lancashire Lightning | 16 | 32 | 7 | 0 | 7 | 2 | -6.99 |
| 6 | 5 | Northamptonshire Steelbacks | 16 | 30 | 7 | 0 | 8 | 1 | 7.63 |
| 7 | 7 | Hampshire Hawks | 16 | 26 | 6 | 0 | 9 | 1 | -2.81 |
| 8 | 8 | Sussex Sharks | 16 | 20 | 4 | 0 | 10 | 2 | -7.42 |
| 9 | 8 | Middlesex Crusaders | 16 | 20 | 4 | 0 | 10 | 2 | -12.51 |

# 21 Summing Up

It was a season that had just about everything - stunning cricket, incredible matches, moments to treasure and, sad to say, far more than our fair share of tears. Since the Ben Hollioake tragedy had cast a huge, dark shadow over the pre-season period, it represented an amazing achievement for the Surrey team to go on and win the County Championship title by a huge margin. Additionally, though the limited-overs performances weren't always convincing, promotion back to Division One of the National League had been secured, and the side had also made it through to the semi-finals of the C&G Trophy. We had witnessed some superb individual and team performances, and, as a result, the rest of the sides in the first division of the Frizzell Championship had been unable to get close enough to mount a serious challenge, especially after the pivotal triumph against Kent at Canterbury, which effectively ensured that the county champions pennant would be flying atop the Oval pavilion in 2003.

There were so many individual feats that stood out for me, including Ali Brown's record-shattering 268; Adam Hollioake's breathtaking hundreds in the Championship at Canterbury and in the C&G Trophy quarter-final at Hove; Ian Ward's record-equalling run of centuries, plus his match-winning unbeaten 168 at Canterbury; Mark Ramprakash's double-centuries in consecutive matches, and his consistency in limited-overs matches, where he scored close on a thousand runs; the emotionally-charged tons by Ali Brown and Nadeem Shahid in the opening match of the season; Rikki Clarke's amazing debut season; Jon Batty's emergence as a top-class wicketkeeper-batsman after showing incredible improvement with the bat; Azhar Mahmood's sensational match-winning 8-61 against Lancashire; Martin Bicknell's completion of a full set of five-wicket hauls against all the other counties; ten-wicket match returns from Saqlain Mushtaq (v Hampshire) and Jimmy Ormond (v Warwickshire), along with the performances with the bat by those two men in the aforementioned Canterbury triumph; and the encouraging early appearances of Tim Murtagh, Scott Newman and Philip Sampson. The obvious conclusion to be drawn from this lengthy list is that it was very much a season for the batsmen, as pitches around the country continued to improve. Those who knock the domestic game and say that the counties are not making sufficient efforts to improve the standards of play and the players they produce please take note... if you can be bothered to watch or follow the scores, that is! It is my firm belief that the quality of both the cricket and the pitches - the two are, of course, inextricably linked - continues to improve and, with a number of talented young players emerging around the country, I predict that things will continue on an upward curve, so long as we leave the current two-division system in place. It is working, even if it has, as you would expect, taken a little time to bed in, and I was horrified to hear the new chairman of the ECB saying that he favoured a return to one division. Please, Mr Morgan, no more of this talk, at least not until you have some evidence that the two-tier set-up is not improving the standard and competitiveness of the domestic game. The fact that pitches were so good - Paul Brind's team at The AMP Oval shared the groundsman's award for producing the best surfaces with the Canterbury ground staff - meant that the side with the best bowling attack was always likely to come out on top, and so it proved. Although some of their averages didn't look that special come the end of the summer, the Surrey bowlers most certainly earned their corn and did fantastically well to bowl the opposition out twice in all ten of the matches that were won. The excellence of their performance was magnified by the fact that the bowling line-up was very unsettled at times during the summer, and, though they may not have made the list above, there were many vital three- and four-wicket hauls along the road to success.

As far as team performances were concerned you would have to say that the stunning victory at Canterbury tops a list which also includes the completion of a rare double over the previous champions, Yorkshire, and a quite amazing victory-from-the-jaws-of-defeat triumph in the National League at Chelmsford that clinched promotion. Indeed, it was a good season for one-day matches, with the two phenomenal games in the C&G Trophy against Glamorgan and Sussex, and a number of close and exciting finishes in the other two limited-overs competitions.

The team's greatest achievement, however, was to produce a string of performances throughout the summer that did their lost colleague proud. It was quite a remarkable effort, especially for those who were experiencing the pain of the devastating loss of a team-mate for the second time, and I feel sure that the players' desire to lift the trophy for Ben at the end of the season inspired them on any number of occasions when the going got tough. Adam Hollioake was even quoted as saying after his astonishing C&G innings at Hove that "it wasn't me batting out there, it was Ben", and I have to say that, at times, it was hard to believe that there wasn't a higher power at work as the sun shone on Surrey while rain fell elsewhere. Although the team was almost certainly denied victory by bad weather at Old Trafford, we were extremely fortunate to play almost without interruption at both Taunton and Hove while rain was ruining all the other games around the country, and it was easy to read something into the way the clouds parted to allow the sun to shine through at the end of the final match of the season at The AMP Oval. Were these just mere coincidences or not? Everyone has to draw their own conclusions according to their own beliefs, of course. One thing that was obvious, however, was that the tragedy had bonded a close-knit group of players even more closely together. Perhaps the most telling comment on this matter came from an opponent, Matthew Fleming of Kent. Writing in his 'Diary Of The Season' in *The Cricketer International* magazine about the now legendary Canterbury contest he said, "Ben's death, and Adam's resulting perspective on life, have affected the Surrey team deeply. In the army it is often said that the truest team spirit is forged in times of adversity. I believe and understand it even more now than I did then. Most players at most counties like each other and get on with each other. Surrey love each other, accept each other's weaknesses and embrace their strengths." It sounded like an accurate assessment, as did his later assertion that "They are the best team by some way and deserve everything they get in this turbulent season. They are well managed, well supported by their county, very professional and excellently captained. Surrey continue to set the standards in domestic cricket."

And it is hard to believe that success will not continue, at the very least in the short term, since the current squad is awesomely strong. The biggest challenge facing the likes of Keith Medlycott and the cricket committee in the next four or five years is to ensure that the dynasty continues, with intelligent succession planning taking place. No-one wants to see great players cast aside, but there are lessons to be learned from previous winning teams in all sports, including the great Surrey side of the fifties - if a side is allowed to grow old together without selective 'pruning' then it can take an age to recover after the era of success ends. Surrey undoubtedly have talented youngsters, as we saw on a number of occasions in 2002, and they need to be sensibly and skilfully integrated into the team, which will be no easy task - it's going to be tough to tell members of this squad when their time is up, especially given the way they are so closely bonded. I would even venture to suggest that the limited-overs side already needs a bit of an overhaul, so maybe a gentle 'revolution' could start there? It was obvious from the games in the C&G Trophy that the side lacks energy and intensity in the field in the shortened version of the game, a fact that was brought home to me during the match at Hove when I looked at the four fielders who were stationed in the 30-metre circle. Essentially, we were 'hiding' people in that area of the field where sharpness was vital. With Adam Hollioake, Azhar Mahmood and Rikki Clarke likely to provide the team with a terrific core of all-rounders in the one-day format of the game in 2003, it might be sensible to save some of the senior bowlers for the Championship and bring in a young bowler and/or batsman on a regular basis - especially if this move adds vim to the fielding. Without wishing to sound greedy or ungrateful, I strongly believe that Surrey should be capable of winning a one-day trophy as well as the Championship with this current squad and this is perhaps one way in which it could be achieved.

One skilled and experienced bowler from the 2002 limited-overs side, Ed Giddins, left for pastures new at the end of the season, signing on for Hampshire, while Rupesh Amin and Michael Carberry, who, understandably enough, didn't really get the opportunities to prove whether or not they could build on their early promise, joined Leicestershire and Kent respectively. I always felt that Giddins had been signed as something of a stop-gap until the likes of Tim Murtagh and Philip Sampson came through, and the signing of Jimmy Ormond further dented his prospects of being offered a new contract. 'Giddo' almost always performed well in the one-day game for Surrey, being a key member of both the Benson & Hedges Cup-winning side of 2001 and the National League team that secured promotion in 2002, but more had been expected of him, if we are to be brutally honest. I wish all three departing players every success as they make a fresh start with their new counties.

Graham Thorpe is another who will have something to prove in 2003 after a pretty miserable time last year. Having pulled out of the Ashes squad on 24th September following another change of heart, it remains to be seen how much sympathy he will receive from the England captain and coach. It was disappointing to see him withdraw from the tour and it appeared to confirm that he still hadn't really got his head together properly. Hopefully, his situation will have improved during the winter, enabling him to make the sort of contributions to the Surrey and England causes in 2003 that he is obviously capable of.

On the field, the people facing the hardest task in 2003 would appear to be Keith Medlycott and Adam Hollioake as they try to keep their squad of hugely talented players happy, since we are, regrettably, not allowed to field fifteen players in the team! Even allowing for a few England call-ups, there is sufficient strength in depth to ensure that Surrey will be firm favourites to win the Championship again, even though the introduction of a second overseas player should further sharpen standards and level the playing field to a degree.

Off the field, meanwhile, Adam Hollioake will be facing an even stiffer task at the end of the 2003 season, since he has elected to take on an incredible triathlon-type feat to raise money for The Ben Hollioake Fund. At the time of going to press, his journey will take him from Edinburgh to Tangiers and will take around two months. Further details will be revealed throughout the summer and I'm sure Adam's efforts will be very well supported.

Things remain tough for the Hollioake family in the light of their loss, but I am at least able to conclude this book with good news on the condition of Ben's girlfriend, Janaya Scholten. Many people at The AMP Oval were asking how she was recovering from her injuries during the season, but no-one seemed to know the answer. I therefore got the latest position from John Hollioake shortly before this book went to the printers and this is what he told me:-
"Janaya is improving all the time, although a little more slowly now than she was. The last bit is the hard bit. She is managing pretty well and calls her life a bittersweet life now. A big step forward will be when she goes back to University, I think in June this year, to complete her degree in journalism. She is also doing another part-time course to complement the degree, and she hopes to complete everything in two years time. She has the bit between the teeth and is saying that she is going to do Ben proud. He helped her more than anyone could ever know. She struggles a bit with some of her movements, but is working on them with a physio every two days. She has learned how to use her left arm and left leg again, as the part of her brain that controls them was damaged. She is getting there through sheer willpower and is a very determined lass. When she gets full movement back she can then work on her strength - both her leg and arm/shoulder have been out of action for so long they have wasted a little, but she will almost certainly get that back. She is pretty sharp mentally, as she always was, and she continues to improve. She is very sad, as she has had a very good life basically taken away from her. She seems to be going on with life because she believes Ben wants her to - it is quite sad and we find it hard to cope with that. We hope she changes with time, but in the meantime she is concentrating on making sure she gets her degree and starts working."

# 22 Leading Questions, Leading Answers

*Even though we won the title by quite a distance, I felt the standard of play in the Championship was very good this year. Was it as competitive as you have ever known it to be?*

**IAN WARD** - I think that having two divisions has worked - at the end of the season we saw that when there is nothing on the game it can degenerate a little bit and standards do drop. That used to happen a lot more often when all eighteen counties were together in one division, with some sides having no chance of winning the title after about a month and a half. The competitiveness now goes right the way through until the end of the season, which is good, though I still think it should be two up and two down, rather than three. There are some quality sides around and some good cricket being played, but I still believe we play too much - we still have to push forward the restructuring and play less cricket, in order to have more time to prepare and practise.

**MARK BUTCHER** - Yes, I think so. A lot of the wins that we had while I was playing were very hard-fought ones and, with the exception of the Yorkshire game, there were very few walkovers - the win at Canterbury was just one of the most phenomenal victories of all time; the game at Leicester was very tough; the Sussex game at Hove was hard as well - their performance was very creditable, seeing as it was their first game back up in the first division against, arguably, the best side, and at The Oval. Ignoring the games at the end of the season when we'd won the Championship, the games in the heart of the season, when it really mattered, were very competitive. With the exception of there being a lack of out-and-out quick bowlers in the division, the cricket has been very good.

**MARTIN BICKNELL** - I think the standard was good, but we were better than we had been before, we have improved. I honestly feel that we are now much better than anybody else in the division, and there is a bit of a gulf there. How long that gulf remains is questionable but, where this year was concerned, once Yorkshire had fallen by the wayside there was no-one else who could come at us - Warwickshire had a poor start, and Kent were there or thereabouts without being a really good side. But I was a little bit surprised at how easily we won it in the end.

*Pitches seem to have improved greatly - have they reached a new high too?*

**ALI BROWN** - I think the system of having five batting points and three bowling points has certainly helped - in the past, with four batting and four bowling, people were too happy to just play for sixteen points by producing a green top. Counties are now producing better wickets, better cricket and better cricketers. By having five batting points, you encourage people to get big scores and play positive cricket.

**IAN WARD** - Yes, we played on some good pitches this year. We are spoilt at The Oval because we get to play on good wickets all the time, but the pitch at Old Trafford was a magnificent cricket wicket, Taunton is a very fine pitch, Canterbury is a very good wicket... there are a few shockers still around in county cricket, though that seems to be mainly in the second division, where people are still searching for result pitches.

**MARK RAMPRAKASH** - Without a doubt, the pitches now are very different to when I started playing in 1987. Most are now very good, and to bowl people out twice is a big achievement.

*Would you say this was the most satisfying of our three recent Championship wins?*

**ALI BROWN** - No, I'd say the most satisfying would definitely have to be the first one, because it feels so much better to achieve something for the first time. We played exceptionally well this year, though, and we had a little bit of luck on our side... and perhaps a guiding light to take us through when things didn't quite go our way.

**ADAM HOLLIOAKE** - They are all special in their own way. The first one is very hard to beat as it was our first time Championship for 28 years, but I think everyone wanted to win this year for very obvious reasons - so it was nice that we were able to do that and achieve what we set out to do.

**IAN WARD** - I don't think you will ever beat the first one, because it ended that long run without a win - it was great to grab the Championship back, especially considering the way it was constructed and the way it was won at The Oval in the sunshine after claiming the extra half-hour. This one was obviously special for a different reason - in the year that Ben passed away it was nice to have a big trophy in the cabinet for him.

**MARTIN BICKNELL** - Looking at all three Championship wins, I think this was the best we've played as a team. The batting was as good as I've seen from a team over a period of time - it was a pleasure to play in a side where you walk out knowing you will get 450 or 500 every time. It was harder for the bowlers, though, trying to get twenty wickets on flat pitches.

**MARK BUTCHER** - They all have a lot of good memories about them, though the way that everything started for us this year made the triumph extra special. Whether we had come out and said it publicly or just

said it in the dressing room, we knew it was something we would love to do in Ben's memory, and we ended up doing it in quite magnificent style. So, from where everybody started, and considering the emotions that were around at the beginning of the season, it was fantastic to finish up winning it so well.
**IAN SALISBURY** - Each one has been special for a different reason. The first one was satisfying because we hadn't won the Championship for so long; the second one was good because it proved we could defend it; and this one was special for two reasons - one, because it proved we could come back after the disappointment of 2001 when we loaned the title to Yorkshire, and, two, because of the terrible events of the pre-season - a very difficult and very emotional time, even though it gave everybody a focus.
*And those dark pre-season days affected the way the team played the game, I guess?*
**IAN SALISBURY** - Yes, we played a lot of carefree cricket throughout the season. It made us realise that life is too short to worry about menial things, and one of those things can, at times, be chasing a cricket ball around the field. Also, several of us had children born this summer, so life became a bit different for a lot of people, when it came to our perspective on life and cricket... at times it helped us to play a more free-spirited brand of cricket. And it definitely brought us together as a side even more, unbelievably so - I don't think there can be a team as close-knit as this team is, no way. You can't manufacture the sort of togetherness that we have developed as a result of the tragedy - and even more so for those who have been through it twice, with the Graham Kersey tragedy. It's what pulls you through in games like the one at Canterbury.
*How does the current squad compare with other recent Surrey squads - is it the strongest you have been involved with?*
**ADAM HOLLIOAKE** - Yes, definitely. Personally, I think it's the strongest squad ever assembled in county cricket. I'm not saying we've got the best eleven ever, but the strength in depth is incredible. I'm sure we've still got some way to go to match the Fifties *team*, but as a *squad* this one is remarkable.
**ALEC STEWART** - This current Surrey squad is as good as any, if not the best ever in terms of overall strength and balance. There's no reason why we can't dominate domestic cricket for the foreseeable future.
**IAN SALISBURY** - It's a very strong squad when everybody is fit, though I still think that there were a few people who didn't hit top form this year. Our batsmen were very good, but there is more to come from Ormond, Bicknell, Salisbury, Saqlain - as bowlers, we got through, got wickets at the right time and did alright, but none of us really got on a roll and hit top form.
**MARTIN BICKNELL** - Yes, without a doubt. We've had people like Scott Newman and Rikki Clarke coming through this year, which is very important to the future of the club. It would be nice to see a couple more come through at some stage but, saying that, the guys who are playing at the moment are not yet on their last legs. There's still plenty of cricket left in the guys that are in the team, so while we do have to look to the future we mustn't disregard what we've got at the moment. And because what we've got at the moment is exceptional - second only, probably, to what they had in the Fifties - we've got to be a little bit careful about throwing out players to replace them with young players for the future just for the sake of it. If the youngsters are there and they are good enough then they will play in the side - I'd like to see a natural progression rather than a forced one.
*There must be concerns, though, that some of our younger players might leave if they don't get given sufficient opportunities?*
**MARTIN BICKNELL** - Well, you've got to have players who are hungry to play for Surrey. They are with the best club in the country, so if they want to go off and play for a bit more money somewhere else then their desire is not with Surrey and we should let them go. There are exceptions to that, of course, like Gareth Batty - we didn't want to lose him but then he wouldn't have played much again this year, so we were just holding his career back. Young players at Surrey have got to be looking to come into the side to replace international cricketers, which is very difficult to do. In Rikki and Scott's cases, they have the potential to do that, they have the potential to play for England. That's the sort of player you want to have playing for Surrey.
*How does this Surrey squad compare with some of the very strong Middlesex squads that you were a part of?*
**MARK RAMPRAKASH** - The Middlesex side I played with in 1993 was very strong - a very good squad - but the thing with this Surrey team is that we are never bowled out... we've got people coming in at seven, eight, nine, ten who can all bat, and if the side is in trouble they can all play a big innings - so I think, without doubt, this is the strongest side I've been involved with.
*I suppose there is still room for improvement though?*
**MARK RAMPRAKASH** - It's a very exciting time to play for Surrey at the moment because not only are there many very good experienced players but the youngsters are coming in and doing well, too. I can't see any weak

link at all, and with Azhar Mahmood coming as our second overseas player it's a very strong squad of players. There is certainly room for improvement in our one-day cricket, though.

*Might there possibly be a case for completely reviewing our approach to one-day cricket?*
**ALEC STEWART** - In one-day cricket you need to plan as much as you do for four-day cricket - in fact probably more so, because in four-day cricket the game evolves whereas in one-day cricket it all happens so much quicker - so if you haven't planned well you get caught short. I believe the thoroughness that we show in the Championship must be shown in one-day cricket as well.
**IAN WARD** - Yes, I think so - I don't think our approach has been particularly special for a while. We've got to sit down and work out a bit more of a plan because with the quality of players we have in the side we should be winning more one-day tournaments than we have done. Having said that, one-day cricket, by its nature, levels the playing field - whereas our skill levels per man are easily shining in the longer form of the game, the one-day game, being at shorter and more frenetic, does bring sides closer together. We've got to counter that with greater intensity, more preparation, and by being a bit more clever. It's a challenge that we will meet head on, I'm sure, as we always tend to do, and we'll put it right. I think it's right that the Club always puts the emphasis on Championship cricket, but the realities of life are that the marketing guys and the sponsorship guys want one-day trophies and one-day success because that's where the TV revenues are and where the bigger attendances come from - so it's a balancing act, one-day cricket is important, but the blue riband will always be County Championship cricket. Having said that, every time you go across the rope to play for Surrey you've got to give it your all, and we certainly do that.
**MARK RAMPRAKASH** - We've got the personnel, so I think it's our approach that we need to change. You can tinker around with the line-up, but I think we need greater intensity, the fielding has to be really aggressive, and the bowlers have to adjust from bowling just outside off stump in Championship cricket to bowling a little bit straighter in one-day cricket.
**MARTIN BICKNELL** - Yes, quite possibly. There is a fine line between success and failure, and we haven't been consistent enough in one-day cricket. I'm not sure where it stems from - you look around the side and you think these players are good enough, but we often don't do ourselves justice - we don't score enough runs, we probably aren't disciplined enough in the bowling, and our fielding is never going to be exceptional because of the people we have in the side. The squad we have at the moment is very orientated towards Championship cricket, and that is the competition the guys want to win. It's very difficult to have a multi-dimensional side that plays well in every type of competition.

*Surrey keep producing and, perhaps most importantly, developing very good young players who seem to fit in instantly at first team level. What do you think is/are the reasons for this? Is Alan Butcher perhaps the most unsung hero the Club has in its ranks?*
**ADAM HOLLIOAKE** - He certainly isn't unsung amongst us - we fully appreciate what he does. He's a very quiet unassuming man, he just goes about his business, and he's a fantastic batting technician. But the Club also has a great youth system, we mustn't forget that.
**MARTIN BICKNELL** - I think it reflects the strength of the squad - if they are good enough to be in the Surrey squad in the first place then they are good enough to be playing first-team cricket. It also helps that they are also encouraged to be positive when they come into the side and we have a pretty relaxed set-up. Alan Butcher is an excellent coach - the main man as far as the coaching side goes - and he does a great job with the youngsters.
**RIKKI CLARKE** - Alan Butcher isn't just brilliant with the seconds - he also goes to a lot of under-14 to under-19 cricket, where he looks for good young talent and gets them playing at the highest level they can play at, which is brilliant for the future of Surrey cricket. We do well straight away because we just don't have fear of failure at Surrey. The senior players just welcome us in and give us great advice on how to play - things like what the opposition players can and can't do - so we can just come in and play our own game.

*Is there any special memory of the season that stands out for you?*
**IAN SALISBURY** - From my point of view, it would be how the players responded to what happened in March, and how everybody pulled together. I got a lot of pleasure out of watching Adam come back and play some amazing innings... it really made the hair on the back of my neck stand up.
**IAN WARD** - Canterbury was good, of course, but I just think the whole season was fantastic - the atmosphere in the dressing room was just brilliant, the guys genuinely like one another and play for one another. And, although it's not something to look back on and remember with any enjoyment, what does stand out is all the boys standing up at Ben's funeral out in Perth. We looked around and everybody to a man was there, and it summed up the way we played all year.. with everyone very much together.

# Appendix - Statistical Compendium
## (Compiled by Richard Arnold)

### FRIZZELL COUNTY CHAMPIONSHIP AVERAGES 2002 - BATTING

| Player | M | I | NO | R | HS | Ave | 100 | 50 | R/100b | Ct/St |
|---|---|---|---|---|---|---|---|---|---|---|
| A.J. Hollioake | 9 | 13 | 2 | 738 | 208 | 67.09 | 2 | 5 | 90.89 | 10 |
| I.J. Ward | 16 | 29 | 3 | 1708 | 168* | 65.69 | 7 | 7 | 52.93 | 9 |
| S.A. Newman | 3 | 5 | 0 | 322 | 183 | 64.40 | 1 | 1 | 62.77 | 3 |
| M.R. Ramprakash | 14 | 24 | 4 | 1073 | 218 | 53.65 | 3 | 6 | 59.31 | 6 |
| A.D. Brown | 16 | 26 | 2 | 1211 | 188 | 50.46 | 5 | 3 | 74.16 | 18 |
| A.J. Stewart | 4 | 6 | 0 | 301 | 99 | 50.17 | 0 | 3 | 60.44 | 18/2 |
| R. Clarke | 9 | 14 | 1 | 580 | 153* | 44.62 | 1 | 4 | 68.40 | 7 |
| M.A. Butcher | 6 | 11 | 1 | 385 | 116 | 38.50 | 1 | 2 | 65.25 | 3 |
| J.N. Batty | 12 | 22 | 2 | 740 | 151 | 37.00 | 2 | 3 | 51.35 | 41/5 |
| N. Shahid | 12 | 19 | 1 | 647 | 150 | 35.94 | 2 | 2 | 67.19 | 25 |
| G.P. Thorpe | 4 | 8 | 0 | 274 | 143 | 34.25 | 1 | 0 | 60.62 | 1 |
| Azhar Mahmood | 3 | 4 | 1 | 96 | 64* | 32.00 | 0 | 1 | 60.00 | 3 |
| M.P. Bicknell | 10 | 14 | 5 | 258 | 35* | 28.67 | 0 | 0 | 60.71 | 6 |
| Saqlain Mushtaq | 10 | 13 | 2 | 278 | 60 | 25.27 | 0 | 2 | 46.80 | 4 |
| T.J. Murtagh | 3 | 5 | 3 | 41 | 22 | 20.50 | 0 | 0 | 50.62 | 4 |
| A.J. Tudor | 6 | 9 | 0 | 176 | 61 | 19.56 | 0 | 1 | 49.30 | 1 |
| I.D.K. Salisbury | 14 | 20 | 2 | 340 | 59 | 18.89 | 0 | 1 | 53.97 | 11 |
| J. Ormond | 15 | 17 | 4 | 208 | 43* | 16.00 | 0 | 0 | 59.94 | 6 |
| E.S.H. Giddins | 6 | 7 | 4 | 23 | 9 | 7.67 | 0 | 0 | 25.56 | 2 |
| Also Batted:- | | | | | | | | | | |
| Mushtaq Ahmed | 2 | 3 | 0 | 66 | 47 | 22.00 | 0 | 0 | 92.96 | 1 |
| M.A. Carberry | 1 | 2 | 0 | 34 | 24 | 17.00 | 0 | 0 | 22.67 | 1 |
| P.J. Sampson | 1 | 2 | 1 | 1 | 1 | 1.00 | 0 | 0 | 33.33 | 0 |

### FRIZZELL COUNTY CHAMPIONSHIP AVERAGES 2002 - BOWLING

| Player | O | M | R | W | Ave | Best Blg | Runs/Over | Balls/Wkt | 10 Wm | 5 Wi |
|---|---|---|---|---|---|---|---|---|---|---|
| Azhar Mahmood | 109.2 | 27 | 345 | 20 | 17.25 | 8-61 | 3.16 | 32.80 | 0 | 1 |
| T.J. Murtagh | 74.1 | 11 | 276 | 13 | 21.23 | 5-39 | 3.72 | 34.23 | 0 | 1 |
| A.J. Tudor | 202.1 | 44 | 739 | 31 | 23.84 | 5-66 | 3.66 | 39.13 | 0 | 1 |
| Saqlain Mushtaq | 488.4 | 112 | 1359 | 53 | 25.64 | 6-121 | 2.78 | 55.32 | 1 | 3 |
| M.P. Bicknell | 326.0 | 78 | 1067 | 34 | 31.38 | 6-42 | 3.27 | 57.53 | 0 | 2 |
| I.D.K. Salisbury | 341.3 | 50 | 1192 | 37 | 32.22 | 4-59 | 3.49 | 55.38 | 0 | 0 |
| J. Ormond | 485.1 | 87 | 1780 | 51 | 34.90 | 5-62 | 3.67 | 57.08 | 1 | 2 |
| E.S.H. Giddins | 208.5 | 41 | 696 | 19 | 36.63 | 4-113 | 3.33 | 65.95 | 0 | 0 |
| Mushtaq Ahmed | 105.0 | 23 | 305 | 8 | 38.13 | 5-71 | 2.90 | 78.75 | 0 | 1 |
| R. Clarke | 76.3 | 7 | 398 | 10 | 39.80 | 3-41 | 5.20 | 45.90 | 0 | 0 |
| Also bowled:- | | | | | | | | | | |
| I.J. Ward | 3.0 | 1 | 5 | 2 | 2.50 | 1-1 | 1.67 | 9.00 | 0 | 0 |
| P.J. Sampson | 21.0 | 4 | 101 | 5 | 20.20 | 3-52 | 4.81 | 25.20 | 0 | 0 |
| A.J. Hollioake | 37.0 | 1 | 178 | 5 | 35.60 | 2-39 | 4.81 | 44.40 | 0 | 0 |
| N. Shahid | 22.0 | 1 | 72 | 1 | 72.00 | 1-55 | 3.27 | 132.00 | 0 | 0 |
| A.D. Brown | 3.0 | 0 | 7 | 0 | 0.00 | - | 2.33 | 0.00 | 0 | 0 |
| M.A. Butcher | 8.0 | 2 | 43 | 0 | 0.00 | - | 5.38 | 0.00 | 0 | 0 |
| M.R. Ramprakash | 2.0 | 0 | 2 | 0 | 0.00 | - | 1.00 | 0.00 | 0 | 0 |

## LIMITED-OVERS AVERAGES 2002 - BATTING

| Player | M | I | NO | Runs | HS | Ave | 100 | 50 | R/100b | C/St |
|---|---|---|---|---|---|---|---|---|---|---|
| M.R. Ramprakash | 23 | 23 | 6 | 952 | 107* | 56.00 | 2 | 7 | 73.74 | 5 |
| A.D. Brown | 24 | 24 | 0 | 899 | 268 | 37.45 | 1 | 6 | 123.15 | 9 |
| A.J. Hollioake | 15 | 13 | 3 | 351 | 117* | 35.10 | 1 | 0 | 116.61 | 9 |
| R. Clarke | 15 | 14 | 2 | 379 | 98* | 31.58 | 0 | 4 | 69.66 | 8 |
| N. Shahid | 22 | 21 | 4 | 432 | 74* | 25.41 | 0 | 3 | 73.34 | 6 |
| I.J. Ward | 24 | 24 | 0 | 596 | 97 | 24.83 | 0 | 4 | 67.34 | 6 |
| Azhar Mahmood | 6 | 5 | 0 | 111 | 50 | 22.20 | 0 | 1 | 98.23 | 2 |
| S.A. Newman | 4 | 4 | 0 | 85 | 37 | 21.25 | 0 | 0 | 64.39 | 1 |
| J.N. Batty | 15 | 9 | 2 | 122 | 30 | 17.42 | 0 | 0 | 52.81 | 20/2 |
| I.D.K. Salisbury | 13 | 10 | 3 | 118 | 21 | 16.85 | 0 | 0 | 90.76 | 6 |
| A.J. Tudor | 10 | 8 | 3 | 79 | 28* | 15.80 | 0 | 0 | 56.83 | 2 |
| A.J. Stewart | 11 | 10 | 1 | 126 | 52 | 14.00 | 0 | 1 | 41.72 | 16/1 |
| Saqlain Mushtaq | 13 | 6 | 1 | 56 | 28 | 11.20 | 0 | 0 | 60.86 | 2 |
| M.P. Bicknell | 14 | 10 | 2 | 74 | 19* | 9.25 | 0 | 0 | 43.27 | 2 |
| T.J. Murtagh | 9 | 6 | 2 | 32 | 14* | 8.00 | 0 | 0 | 60.37 | 3 |
| Also Batted:- | | | | | | | | | | |
| G.P. Thorpe | 2 | 2 | 0 | 175 | 114 | 87.50 | 1 | 1 | 96.68 | 0 |
| M.A. Butcher | 3 | 3 | 0 | 114 | 62 | 38.00 | 0 | 2 | 77.55 | 1 |
| J. Ormond | 10 | 4 | 2 | 24 | 14* | 12.00 | 0 | 0 | 75.00 | 3 |
| M.A. Carberry | 5 | 4 | 1 | 35 | 19 | 11.66 | 0 | 0 | 49.29 | 5 |
| E.S.H. Giddins | 22 | 10 | 7 | 31 | 13* | 10.33 | 0 | 0 | 38.75 | 5 |
| P.J. Sampson | 5 | 4 | 1 | 20 | 16 | 6.66 | 0 | 0 | 90.90 | 2 |

One innings:- (3 matches) J.D. Ratcliffe 53 (r/100b - 170.96); (1 match) R.M. Amin 0*; J.G.E. Benning 10 (125.00, 1ct); G.P. Butcher 9 (75.00); D.J. Miller 1 (14.28); Mushtaq Ahmed 16 (200.00); B.J.M. Scott 4 (57.14); D.M. Ward 78 (150.00, 1ct)

## LIMITED-OVERS AVERAGES 2002 - BOWLING

| Player | O | M | R | W | Ave | Best Blg | Runs/Over | 4Wi |
|---|---|---|---|---|---|---|---|---|
| A.J. Hollioake | 80.1 | 2 | 446 | 30 | 14.86 | 5-43 | 5.56 | 4 |
| J.D. Ratcliffe | 21.0 | 0 | 118 | 7 | 16.85 | 4-44 | 5.61 | 1 |
| M.P. Bicknell | 112.1 | 18 | 444 | 22 | 20.18 | 5-26 | 3.95 | 1 |
| Azhar Mahmood | 44.4 | 1 | 181 | 8 | 22.62 | 4-34 | 4.05 | 1 |
| E.S.H. Giddins | 170.0 | 15 | 771 | 34 | 22.67 | 5-20 | 4.53 | 2 |
| T.J. Murtagh | 77.3 | 3 | 353 | 13 | 27.15 | 3-38 | 4.55 | 0 |
| P.J. Sampson | 36.0 | 0 | 192 | 7 | 27.42 | 3-42 | 5.33 | 0 |
| I.D.K. Salisbury | 67.1 | 1 | 329 | 9 | 36.55 | 3-44 | 4.89 | 0 |
| A.J. Tudor | 77.5 | 3 | 388 | 9 | 43.11 | 3-28 | 4.98 | 0 |
| J.Ormond | 65.3 | 2 | 349 | 8 | 43.62 | 3-52 | 5.32 | 0 |
| R. Clarke | 75.3 | 3 | 421 | 9 | 46.77 | 2-32 | 5.57 | 0 |
| Saqlain Mushtaq | 98 | 4 | 422 | 8 | 52.75 | 1-14 | 4.30 | 0 |
| Also bowled:- | | | | | | | | |
| M.R. Ramprakash | 11.2 | 0 | 63 | 3 | 21.00 | 2-19 | 5.56 | 0 |
| I.J. Ward | 6.0 | 0 | 48 | 2 | 24.00 | 2-27 | 8.00 | 0 |

One innings:- R.M. Amin 3-0-33-0; J.G.E. Benning 7-0-58-2; G.P. Butcher 7-0-49-2; M.A. Butcher 2-0-12-0; D.J. Miller 7-0-32-0; Mushtaq Ahmed 9-2-19-1

| COUNTY CHAMPIONSHIP CENTURIES (25) | | | |
|---|---|---|---|
| | Batsman | Opponents | Venue |
| 218 | M.R. Ramprakash | Somerset (1st) | Taunton |
| 210* | M.R. Ramprakash | Warwickshire (1st) | The AMP Oval |
| 208 | A.J. Hollioake | Leicestershire (2nd) | The AMP Oval |
| 188 | A.D. Brown | Kent (1st) | The AMP Oval |
| 183 | S.A. Newman | Leicestershire (1st) | The AMP Oval |
| 177 | A.D. Brown | Sussex (1st) | The AMP Oval |
| 168* | I.J. Ward | Kent (2nd) | Canterbury |
| 156 | I.J. Ward | Hampshire (2nd) | The Rose Bowl |
| 153* | R. Clarke | Somerset (1st) | Taunton |
| 151 | J.N. Batty | Somerset (2nd) | Taunton |
| 150 | N. Shahid | Sussex (1st) | The AMP Oval |
| 143 | G.P. Thorpe | Hampshire (2nd) | The Rose Bowl |
| 135 | A.D. Brown | Hampshire (1st) | The AMP Oval |
| 124* | I.J. Ward | Yorkshire (2nd) | Guildford |
| 122* | A.J. Hollioake | Kent (1st) | Canterbury |
| 119* | M.R. Ramprakash | Lancashire (2nd) | The AMP Oval |
| 118 | I.J. Ward | Leicestershire (1st) | The AMP Oval |
| 116 | M.A. Butcher | Leicestershire (1st) | Leicester |
| 116 | N. Shahid | Warwickshire (1st) | Edgbaston |
| 114 | I.J. Ward | Warwickshire (1st) | Edgbaston |
| 112 | I.J. Ward | Hampshire (1st) | The Rose Bowl |
| 107 | A.D. Brown | Leicestershire (2nd) | The AMP Oval |
| 106 | I.J. Ward | Lancashire (2nd) | Old Trafford |
| 104* | J.N. Batty | Lancashire (1st) | Old Trafford |
| 104 | A.D. Brown | Leicestershire (1st) | Leicester |

| COUNTY CHAMPIONSHIP FIVE-WICKET HAULS (11) | | | |
|---|---|---|---|
| | Bowler | Opponents | Venue |
| 8-61 | Azhar Mahmood | Lancashire (2nd) | The AMP Oval |
| 6-42 | M.P. Bicknell | Kent (1st) | The AMP Oval |
| 6-121 | Saqlain Mushtaq | Hampshire (2nd) | The AMP Oval |
| 5-39 | T.J. Murtagh | Leicestershire (2nd) | The AMP Oval |
| 5-56 | M.P. Bicknell | Hampshire (2nd) | The Rose Bowl |
| 5-59 | Saqlain Mushtaq | Hampshire (1st) | The AMP Oval |
| 5-62 | J. Ormond | Warwickshire (2nd) | The AMP Oval |
| 5-66 | A.J. Tudor | Sussex (1st) | Hove |
| 5-71 | Mushtaq Ahmed | Leicestershire (1st) | Leicester |
| 5-116 | J. Ormond | Warwickshire (1st) | The AMP Oval |
| 5-122 | Saqlain Mushtaq | Kent (1st) | Canterbury |

| HIGHEST TOTALS (400-plus) BY SURREY | | |
|---|---|---|
| 608-6dec | Somerset (1st) | Taunton |
| 576 | Hampshire (1st) | The AMP Oval |
| 575-8dec | Sussex (1st) | The AMP Oval |
| 544 | Warwickshire (1st) | Edgbaston |
| 540 | Leicestershire (1st) | Leicester |
| 510 | Yorkshire (1st) | Headingley |
| 494 | Leicestershire (1st) | The AMP Oval |
| 492-9dec | Leicestershire (2nd) | The AMP Oval |
| 475 | Warwickshire (1st) | The AMP Oval |
| 422-8dec | Hampshire (2nd) | The Rose Bowl |
| 418 | Hampshire (1st) | The Rose Bowl |
| 410-8 | Kent (2nd) | Canterbury |

| HIGHEST TOTALS (400-plus) AGAINST SURREY | | |
|---|---|---|
| 554 | Somerset (1st) | Taunton |
| 446 | Yorkshire (2nd) | Guildford |
| 404-9dec | Warwickshire (2nd) | Edgbaston |

| LOWEST TOTALS (Under 200) BY SURREY | | |
|---|---|---|
| 137 | Warwickshire (2nd) | The AMP Oval |
| 193 | Sussex (1st) | Hove |

| LOWEST TOTALS (Under 200) AGAINST SURREY | | |
|---|---|---|
| 140 | Yorkshire (1st) | Headingley |
| 142 | Leicestershire (2nd) | The Oval |
| 153 | Kent (1st) | The Oval |
| 172 | Yorkshire (1st) | Guildford |
| 190 | Hampshire (1st) | The Oval |
| 194 | Lancashire (1st) | Old Trafford |

| HIGHEST PARTNERSHIPS FOR EACH WICKET - FOR SURREY | | | | |
|---|---|---|---|---|
| 1st | 227 | Newman (183) and Ward (118) | Leicestershire (1st) | The Oval |
| 2nd | 204 | Ward (114) and Ramprakash (99) | Warwickshire (1st) | Edgbaston |
| 3rd | 239 | Ward (156) and Thorpe (143) | Hampshire (2nd) | Rose Bowl |
| 4th | 211 | Butcher (116) and Brown (104) | Leicestershire (1st) | Leicester |
| 5th | 282 | Brown (107) and Hollioake (208) | Leicestershire (2nd) | The Oval |
| 6th | 210 | Ramprakash (218) and Clarke (153*) | Somerset (1st) | Taunton |
| 7th | 87 | Tudor (45) and Bicknell (35*) | Somerset (2nd) | The Oval |
| 8th | 105 | Ward (168*) and Saqlain (60) | Kent (2nd) | Canterbury |
| 9th | 97* | Ward (168*) and Ormond (43*) | Kent (2nd) | Canterbury |
| 10th | 57 | Saqlain (55) and Murtagh (15*) | Hampshire (1st) | Rose Bowl |

| HIGHEST PARTNERSHIPS FOR EACH WICKET - AGAINST SURREY | | | | |
|---|---|---|---|---|
| 1st | 202 | Holloway (79) and Wood (106) | Somerset (1st) | Taunton |
| 2nd | 156 | Sutcliffe (64) and Maddy (94) | Leicestershire (2nd) | Leicester |
| 3rd | 97 | Key (68) and Symonds (51) | Kent (2nd) | Canterbury |
| 4th | 152 | Lehmann (61) and Lumb (124) | Yorkshire (2nd) | Guildford |
| 5th | 88 | Burns (68) and Sutcliffe (24) | Leicestershire (2nd) | The Oval |
| 6th | 106 | Blackwell (98) and Turner (34) | Somerset (1st) | The Oval |
| 7th | 98 | Pothas (99) and Mascarenhas (67) | Hampshire (2nd) | Rose Bowl |
| 8th | 63 | Turner (56*) and Bulbeck (27) | Somerset (1st) | Taunton |
| 9th | 70 | Mascarenhas (94) and Hamblin (16) | Hampshire (2nd) | The Oval |
| 10th | 66 | Sheikh (19*) and Betts (47) | Warwickshire (1st) | Edgbaston |

| BATSMEN - MODE OF DISMISSAL | | | | | | | | |
|---|---|---|---|---|---|---|---|---|
| Player | B | CTwk | C&B | CT | LBW | RO | ST | NO | Total |
| Ward | 2 | 7 | 0 | 11 | 3 | 2 | 1 | 3 | 29 |
| Brown | 4 | 3 | 0 | 11 | 4 | 1 | 1 | 2 | 26 |
| Ramprakash | 3 | 6 | 0 | 3 | 5 | 2 | 1 | 4 | 24 |
| Batty | 3 | 0 | 0 | 10 | 6 | 1 | 0 | 2 | 22 |
| Salisbury | 6 | 4 | 0 | 7 | 1 | 0 | 0 | 2 | 20 |
| Shahid | 1 | 5 | 0 | 9 | 3 | 0 | 0 | 1 | 19 |
| Ormond | 5 | 0 | 1 | 6 | 1 | 0 | 0 | 4 | 17 |
| Clarke | 2 | 2 | 0 | 5 | 3 | 0 | 1 | 1 | 14 |
| Bicknell | 2 | 2 | 0 | 4 | 1 | 0 | 0 | 5 | 14 |
| Hollioake | 3 | 3 | 0 | 4 | 1 | 0 | 0 | 2 | 13 |
| Saqlain | 2 | 1 | 1 | 5 | 2 | 0 | 0 | 2 | 13 |
| Butcher | 2 | 2 | 0 | 4 | 2 | 0 | 0 | 1 | 11 |
| Tudor | 3 | 0 | 0 | 2 | 4 | 0 | 0 | 0 | 9 |
| Thorpe | 2 | 0 | 0 | 5 | 1 | 0 | 0 | 0 | 8 |
| Giddins | 0 | 1 | 1 | 1 | 0 | 0 | 0 | 4 | 7 |
| Stewart | 0 | 2 | 0 | 3 | 1 | 0 | 0 | 0 | 6 |
| Newman | 0 | 1 | 0 | 2 | 2 | 0 | 0 | 0 | 5 |
| Murtagh | 1 | 0 | 0 | 1 | 0 | 0 | 0 | 3 | 5 |
| Azhar | 0 | 1 | 0 | 1 | 1 | 0 | 0 | 1 | 4 |
| Mushtaq | 0 | 1 | 0 | 1 | 1 | 0 | 0 | 0 | 3 |
| Sampson | 1 | 0 | 0 | 0 | 0 | 0 | 0 | 1 | 2 |
| Carberry | 0 | 1 | 0 | 1 | 0 | 0 | 0 | 0 | 2 |
| Grand Total | 42 | 42 | 3 | 96 | 42 | 6 | 4 | 38 | 273 |

## BOWLERS - HOW WICKETS TAKEN

| Player | B | CTwk | C&B | CT | LBW | ST | Tot. |
|---|---|---|---|---|---|---|---|
| Saqlain | 5 | 4 | 0 | 32 | 9 | 3 | 53 |
| Ormond | 11 | 13 | 0 | 20 | 7 | 0 | 51 |
| Salisbury | 4 | 6 | 2 | 12 | 10 | 3 | 37 |
| Bicknell | 4 | 7 | 3 | 12 | 8 | 0 | 34 |
| Tudor | 9 | 4 | 0 | 15 | 3 | 0 | 31 |
| Azhar | 2 | 8 | 0 | 6 | 4 | 0 | 20 |
| Giddins | 0 | 7 | 0 | 5 | 7 | 0 | 19 |
| Murtagh | 2 | 5 | 0 | 0 | 6 | 0 | 13 |
| Clarke | 1 | 1 | 0 | 6 | 2 | 0 | 10 |
| Mushtaq | 2 | 1 | 0 | 2 | 2 | 1 | 8 |
| Sampson | 0 | 2 | 0 | 3 | 0 | 0 | 5 |
| Hollioake | 2 | 1 | 1 | 1 | 0 | 0 | 5 |
| Ward | 1 | 0 | 0 | 0 | 1 | 0 | 2 |
| Shahid | 0 | 0 | 0 | 1 | 0 | 0 | 1 |
| Grand Total | 43 | 59 | 6 | 115 | 59 | 7 | 289 |

## BREAKDOWN OF WICKETS LOST

| MODE | SURREY | | OPPOSITION | |
|---|---|---|---|---|
| Bowled | 42 | 17.9% | 43 | 14.5% |
| LBW | 42 | 17.9% | 59 | 19.9% |
| Caught | 141 | 60.0% | 180 | 60.8% |
| Stumped | 4 | 1.7% | 7 | 2.4% |
| Run Out | 6 | 3.6% | 7 | 2.4% |
| Hit Wkt | 0 | 0.0% | 0 | 0.0% |
| TOTAL | 235 | 100.0% | 296 | 100.0% |

## FRIZZELL COUNTY CHAMPIONSHIP DIVISION TWO 2002

| | P | Pts | W | D | L | Bt | Bw | Ded |
|---|---|---|---|---|---|---|---|---|
| Essex | 16 | 219.00 | 10 | 3 | 3 | 42 | 46 | 1.00 |
| Middlesex | 16 | 211.75 | 7 | 6 | 3 | 61 | 43 | 0.25 |
| Nottinghamshire | 16 | 201.75 | 8 | 3 | 5 | 47 | 48 | 1.25 |
| Worcestershire | 16 | 200.00 | 7 | 5 | 4 | 53 | 43 | 0.00 |
| Glamorgan | 16 | 169.00 | 5 | 6 | 5 | 41 | 44 | 0.00 |
| Derbyshire | 16 | 167.75 | 7 | 2 | 7 | 37 | 48 | 9.25 |
| Northamptonshire | 16 | 162.50 | 5 | 4 | 7 | 46 | 41 | 0.50 |
| Gloucestershire | 16 | 136.50 | 2 | 7 | 7 | 42 | 44 | 1.50 |
| Durham | 16 | 90.75 | 1 | 4 | 11 | 21 | 42 | 0.25 |

## NORWICH UNION LEAGUE DIVISION ONE 2002

| | P | Pts | W | L | T | A | NRR |
|---|---|---|---|---|---|---|---|
| Glamorgan Dragons | 16 | 50 | 12 | 3 | 1 | 0 | 8.36 |
| Worcestershire Royals | 16 | 48 | 11 | 3 | 0 | 2 | 10.68 |
| Warwickshire Bears | 16 | 38 | 9 | 6 | 0 | 1 | 8.41 |
| Yorkshire Phoenix | 16 | 34 | 8 | 7 | 0 | 1 | 1.47 |
| Kent Spitfires | 16 | 30 | 7 | 8 | 1 | 0 | 5.85 |
| Leicestershire Foxes | 16 | 30 | 7 | 8 | 0 | 1 | 3.53 |
| Somerset Sabres | 16 | 22 | 5 | 10 | 0 | 1 | -3.53 |
| Durham Dynamos | 16 | 20 | 5 | 11 | 0 | 0 | -21.17 |
| Nottinghamshire Outlaws | 16 | 16 | 3 | 11 | 0 | 2 | -11.28 |

# Acknowledgements

As ever, I couldn't do it all myself. Many thanks to all of the following people who have assisted me, in ways both large and small, with the production of this book. Every contribution is very much appreciated.

Thanks, first of all, to Keith Medlycott and the players, who provided all of us with some special memories and another County Championship triumph. As I've said before, if you keep winning it then I'll do my best to keep writing about it. Special thanks to those who freely subjected themselves to my end-of-season cross-examination. I hope my books will provide you with a tangible reminder of your success in years to come.

PHOTOGRAPHS
Reg Elliott
Surrey CCC
Richard Spiller
Peter Frost
John Banfield
Phil Booker

STATISTICS
Richard Arnold
Mark Newson

RUN CHARTS
Keith Seward

PROOFREADING
Sue Leach

OTHER
Johnny Grave, Surrey CCC
Jacinta Hassett-Brown
John Hollioake
Marcus Hook

All the staff at Surrey County Cricket Club who I have contact with throughout the year

## Surrey C.C.C. Supporters' Club

Should you wish to become a member of the Surrey C.C.C. Supporters' Club please write to:-
Sarah Atkins, 236 Ashbourne Road, Mitcham, Surrey, CR4 2DR
Membership rates for 2003 are:- Full Members £5, Junior and Senior Members £3
(Junior members - under 18 on 01/01/2003; Senior members - over 60 on 01/01/2003)

# Sponsor-Subscribers

*'From Tragedy To Triumph'* would not have been possible without the support and financial backing of the following sponsor-subscribers. Many thanks to all of you.

| | | | |
|---|---|---|---|
| Robin Acock | Dave Gardner, MBE | Sue Leach | Alec Sidebotham |
| Les Allen | Phil Garrard | Charles Lehec | Brian Simmons |
| Stuart Allen | Andrew Gasson | Chris Levitt | Cliff Simpson |
| J.A. Allison | Brian Gee | Stephen Lilley | Gordon Smith |
| Paul Ames | Neil Gelder | Jerry Lodge | Mark Smith |
| Derek Annetts | Peter Gent | Chris Luff | Stuart Solomons |
| Richard Arnold | Doug Ginn | Hugh Massingberd | Richard Spiller |
| Sarah Atkins | R.D. Gooby | Iain McConachie | Chris Stoneman |
| Keith Bain | John Gough-Cooper | Don McKay | Rev Arthur Stubbs |
| John Banfield | Michael Greensmith | Steve Mills | Surrey CCC |
| John Barrett | Chris Gudgeon | Doug Minde | Gary Sutton |
| Andrew Bartlett | John Hall | Peter Molyneux | John Taverner |
| Ian Barton | Roger Hancock | Paul Monaghan | Colin Taylor |
| Derek Beard | Edward Handley | R.S. Mountford | Iain Taylor |
| Derek Biscoe | Andy Harris | Leslie J.A. Murrell | Jim Taylor |
| Philip Booker | Raymond Hart | David North | Mike Thorn |
| Peter Bourne | Jacinta Hassett-Brown | R.A. O'Leary | Richard Thorp |
| Lester Brown | Barry Hatcher | Michael O'Malley | Steve Tyler |
| Andrew Bruton | Kevin Henriques | Michael Organ | David Waghorn |
| Justin Clark | Matthew Hewitt | Tony Packwood | Eric Waldron |
| Robin Cooper | N.C. Hewitt | Chris Payne | Brian Walton |
| Ron Cronin | Marcus Hook | Wayne Pearce | Mary Ward |
| Michael Culham | Roger Hudson | John Per | David Watts |
| Michael Cunnew | Elliott Hurst | Gary Phillips | David Webber |
| Alan Curtis | Mike Hyde | Nigel Pocock | Peter Withey |
| Tony Dey | Blaise Jenner | Keith Porter | Edwin Woodcock |
| Paul Edwards | Alan B. Jones | William A. Powell | Steve Wooding |
| Reg Elliott | Alan & Joyce Jones | Alison Prater | Andy Wotton |
| Keith Evemy | Graham Jordan | Lorna Price | David Murray |
| Chris Finch | Chris Keene | David Ratcliffe | James Murray |
| David Flin | Gillian Kempster | Brian Sanders | Jim Murray |
| Evelyn Fowler | Victor Klarfeld | David Sawyer | David Rankin |
| Peter Franks | David Lane | Don Scott | Tony Legall |
| Jean Galsworthy | Dominic Lang | David Seymour | (Perth, Australia) |

---

*Congratulations to Surrey on their 2002 County Championship success*
*from **Nigel Wood** of*
### SAUNDERS, WOOD & CO.
Chartered Accountants
The White House, 140A Tachbrook Street, London SW1V 2NE
Tel: (020) 7821 0455    Fax: (020) 7821 6196
Email: s-wood@dircon.co.uk    Website: www.saunders-wood.co.uk

---

If you would be keen to become a sponsor-subscriber for any future books about Surrey County Cricket Club that might be produced by Trevor Jones then please write to the author at **P.O. Box 882, Sutton, Surrey, SM2 5AW** or email him at **tj@sportingdeclarations.co.uk**

# Other Books By Trevor Jones

The following books by Trevor Jones about Surrey County Cricket Club are still available and may be purchased directly from the publisher at the discounted prices detailed below.

Order from **Sporting Declarations Books, P.O. Box 882, SUTTON, SM2 5AW**.
Cheques/postal orders payable to *Sporting Declarations Books*, please.

## Pursuing The Dream - My Season With Surrey C.C.C.

The ultimately doomed Championship challenge of 1998 forms the central plank of Trevor Jones' first book, a fan's diary of a season following his team around the country. The author's personal day-by-day account of the summer balances sharp observations and opinions on both the county and international game with tales of the lighter moments of his season with Surrey. Received impressive critical acclaim, including a three-ball review in Wisden Cricket Monthly.

 256 pages    Published April 1999
 Hardback edition  0 9535307 0 1    Price - £8.99 (inc UK p&p)
 Softback edition  0 9535307 1 X    Price - £4.99 (inc UK p&p)

## The Dream Fulfilled - Surrey's 1999 County Championship Triumph

The most detailed account of a Championship-winning season ever written, *'The Dream Fulfilled'* records Surrey's first County Championship triumph for twenty-eight years. Features full descriptions of every session of play, along with exclusive in-depth interviews with the players, twenty-four pages of full-colour photos, run charts and official Surrey CCC scorebook extracts of significant innings/events, press quotes and views from the other counties. Highly acclaimed everywhere it was reviewed, this book will be treasured by Surrey fans for years to come.

 376 pages, including 24 pages of full-colour photographs    Published April 2000
 Hardback only    0 9535307 2 8    Price - £13.99 (inc UK p&p)

## Doubling Up With Delight - Surrey's Twin Triumphs 2000

The in-depth story of Surrey's first-ever double-winning season when they added the National League Division Two title to a second successive County Championship victory. The author's presence at every day's play ensures that each session is again covered in detail and embellished with fascinating dressing room insights from the players. Run charts, scorebook extracts and twenty-four pages of colour photos are again included in another essential volume for followers of Surrey County Cricket Club.

 312 pages, including 24 pages of full-colour photographs    Published April 2001
 Softback only    0 9535307 3 6    Price - £12.99 (inc UK p&p)

## 268 - The Blow-By-Blow Account Of Ali's Amazing Onslaught

The definitive record of Ali Brown's world record-breaking innings of 268 in the remarkable C&G Trophy match at The AMP Oval in 2002 when six other world records and countless other UK, competition, club and personal records fell as plucky Glamorgan came within ten runs of trumping Surrey's 438-5.

 80 pages, including 8 pages of full-colour photographs    Published November 2002
 Softback only    0 9535307 4 4    Price - £7.99 (inc UK p&p)

Further information and a special multiple-purchase book deal can be found at
**www.sportingdeclarations.co.uk**

Comments can be directed to the author at **tj@sportingdeclarations.co.uk**